Formed From This Soil

Formed From This Soil
An Introduction to the Diverse History of Religion in America

Thomas S. Bremer

WILEY Blackwell

This edition first published 2015
© 2015 Thomas S. Bremer

Registered Office
John Wiley & Sons, Ltd, The Atrium, Southern Gate, Chichester, West Sussex, PO19 8SQ, UK

Editorial Offices
350 Main Street, Malden, MA 02148-5020, USA
9600 Garsington Road, Oxford, OX4 2DQ, UK
The Atrium, Southern Gate, Chichester, West Sussex, PO19 8SQ, UK

For details of our global editorial offices, for customer services, and for information about
how to apply for permission to reuse the copyright material in this book please see our website
at www.wiley.com/wiley-blackwell.

The right of Thomas S. Bremer to be identified as the author of this work has been asserted
in accordance with the UK Copyright, Designs and Patents Act 1988.

Library of Congress Cataloging-in-Publication Data is available for this title

Bremer, Thomas S., 1957–
Formed from this soil : an introduction to the diverse history of religion in America /
Thomas S. Bremer.
     pages   cm
  Includes bibliographical references and index.
  ISBN 978-1-4051-8927-9 (cloth) – ISBN 978-1-4051-8926-2 (pbk.)   1. United States–Religion.
I. Title.
  BL2525.B74 2014
  200.973–dc23

                                                2014030507

A catalogue record for this book is available from the British Library.

Cover image: Moira Gil, *Arbol de la Vida*, acrylic. www.sincronizarte.com
Cover design by Design Deluxe

Set in 11/13pt Dante by SPi Publisher Services, Pondicherry, India

Printed in Singapore by C.O.S. Printers Pte Ltd

1   2015

To the teachers who introduced me to the pleasures of learning,
and to the students who inspire me to continue learning,
this book is affectionately dedicated.

About the Website

Additional materials are available at www.wiley.com/go/bremer/formed fromthissoil.

Contents

Acknowledgments

Like many professors who teach courses in American religious history, I had long been dissatisfied with the offering of textbooks in this field, and consequently I had taught courses cobbled together using a variety of primary- and second-source readings. So when Andrew Humphries, at that time a commissioning editor for Wiley Blackwell, first approached me with the idea of producing a new textbook in American religious history that would present a different narrative, one that focuses on diversity, I was enthusiastic about undertaking the challenge. Of course, without Andy's encouragement it would never have become more than an idea; he was instrumental in helping me think through the scope of the book and shepherding me through the proposal process at Wiley Blackwell. When he left for other opportunities in publishing, Rebecca Harkin took over editing responsibilities as I struggled through too many years of false starts and thinking through how to structure the book. Rebecca's patience and support allowed me to work through the myriad issues in producing a narrative that tells a different story of American religious history but is also teachable for a new generation of students. As I neared completion of the manuscript, Georgina Coleby took over the editing responsibilities. I am especially grateful for her help throughout the production process, answering my many questions and concerns with cheerful promptness and keeping me on track to finish this undertaking. As well, Hazel Harris's expert copy-editing has made the text far more readable. In short, this book has benefited tremendously from the many talented people at Wiley Blackwell.

A number of friends, colleagues, and students have made helpful contributions to the production of this work. Tisa Wenger of Yale University commented on an early draft of the proposal for the book. Gregory Johnson at the University of Colorado provided helpful guidance on the religious history of Hawaii, and iconographer Anna Edelman commented on the history of Russian Orthodoxy in Alaska. Several of my colleagues in Religious Studies at Rhodes College read parts of the manuscript and made useful suggestions that I have incorporated in the text. In particular, Luther Ivory offered helpful comments on discussions of African

American religions; Kendra Hotz as well as former colleagues Michelle Voss Roberts and Ellie Gebarowski-Shafer read and commented on an early version of the second chapter, greatly helping me to summarize the Christian theological debates of the sixteenth century; and Rhiannon Graybill saved me from settling for inadequate discussions on voice, gender, and sexuality in Box 6.1, Box 6.2, and Box 9.2.

My attempt to construct a narrative that is accessible to students while incorporating additional elements to aid student learning has benefited from feedback from my students at Rhodes College. Student remarks in the "Religion in Colonial America" class that I taught during the fall semester of 2010 and in the "Religion in Nineteenth-Century America" class offered during the fall semester of 2012 helped me to reconceptualize key parts of the book. In the fall of 2013 I used a draft of the complete manuscript for my "Religion in America" class, and student comments on virtually every chapter have been incorporated into the final version of the text. In addition to those enrolled in my classes, three students in particular served key roles in producing this book. Bailey Romano read all of the chapters and commented specifically on the history of Judaism in America, a topic she has pursued in graduate school at Hebrew Union College. Both Leanne Naramore and Lauren Hales helped to identify images for the various chapters; in addition they each read early drafts of the manuscript and provided invaluable feedback.

Without question, the most important help came from Melanie, my partner in this endeavor. Besides putting up with my impatience and frustration working through this project, she read every chapter carefully more than once, making innumerable comments and suggestions about the content, organization, and grammar. She ably managed the complicated and often frustrating process of acquiring images for each chapter, a task I certainly would not have completed without her help. More helpful than all else, though, have been her constant inspiration and encouragement; without them, this work would not have been possible.

The comments and help of all of these people and others have improved this book immensely; its faults and shortcomings, however, are mine alone.

Prelude for Instructors
A Decentered Narrative of American Religious History

Scholars of American religious history have long called for a retelling of the story of religions in America.[1] This book responds to such calls for new narratives by repositioning American religious developments in larger global contexts with an emphasis on diversity. The story here highlights the diverse origins of religious orientations, communities, and phenomena found in America, with attention to the influences of peoples originating in the Americas as well as those coming from Europe, from Africa, from Asia, and elsewhere. It presents the historical dynamics of how these diverse peoples have encountered and interacted with each other, and how their religious lives and experiences have contributed to the various meanings of America. This history is laid out in three parts arranged chronologically. The first part covers the initial periods of contact between peoples of the Americas, Europe, and Africa and the subsequent centuries of colonization. The second part encompasses the nineteenth century, while the final part covers the twentieth century and the beginning of the twenty-first century.

One primary goal in writing this book has been to make it teachable and flexible. As a pedagogical tool, it does not pretend to be comprehensive in telling a story of religion in American history. Some readers certainly will be disappointed by particular omissions: there is nothing, for instance, on Freemasonry, the Amish, or Scientology, and only scant mention of the Bahá'í Faith. On the other hand, several groups rarely mentioned in typical survey courses on religion in America get attention here, such as indigenous Hawaiian traditions, Sikhs, and Santeríans. In constructing a teachable and flexible textbook that will be useful in many different classroom situations, I have aimed more for the evocative and provocative rather than for comprehensive knowledge.[2] Students will find much here to engage with, both in the historical narrative and in the various critical terms and interpretive concepts introduced throughout the book; the goal has been to evoke various interpretations of the historical record and to provoke students to become aware of, to engage critically with, and to synthesize their own understandings of the many perspectives and experiences that make up American religious history.

Individual instructors certainly will bring their own interests and areas of specialized knowledge to the teaching of this material, supplementing and enriching the narratives presented here; every teacher, I trust, will use this book in a way that reflects their own interests, strengths, and areas of expertise. In my own experience of teaching the complete draft version of the book, I was happily surprised by students' engagement with the interpretive concepts that are introduced throughout the chapters. These concepts, highlighted in boxes, give brief introductions to theoretical and methodological terms and concepts for analyzing and interpreting the historical materials; they include contact zones, animism, millenarianism, authority, sacred space, pluralism, syncretism, voice, gender, nativism, race, orientalism, fundamentalism, sexuality, civil religion, class, spirituality, and globalization. Not only do these concepts offer transferable knowledge and skills for student learning but they also provide structure for organizing class lectures and discussions and may serve as the basis for exam questions and paper assignments.

As a historical narrative, this book preserves the chronological integrity found in many renderings of religion in American history, but it departs from its predecessors in two important ways. First, regarding the narrative itself, the emphasis here is on diversity, not only regarding the variety of religious traditions found in America but also concerning the many and creative ways of being religious, as well as how religious orientations, practices, and communities have contended with other sorts of differences, specifically regarding race, gender, sexual orientation, ethnicity, national origin, and socioeconomic class. The story here lacks an obvious center or dominant teleological narrative of religion in America; instead, it leaves American religious history more open to various interpretations. In contrast to narratives of Protestant Christians triumphantly bringing Christianity to the New World, this book regards America as a place of interaction between groups from four areas of origin, each with peculiar religious orientations formed in their own complex histories of contact, conflict, and exchange; these four geographically oriented groups are the indigenous peoples of the Americas, Europeans and their descendants, Africans and their descendants, and Asians and their descendants;[3] each of these populations remains part of the story throughout the book (with the exception of Asians, who do not enter the narrative until the nineteenth century). Certainly, Christian orientations are prominent among all of these groups, and Christianity receives much attention, but other religious orientations are kept in view in addition to the remarkable variations among Christians in America.

The second way that this book departs from earlier texts on American religious history is in how it encourages students to think of religion in broader terms. Besides the emphasis on the differences that underlie religious diversity, attention is given to the concept of religion itself as an analytic category. To help students think of religion as something more than church, synagogue, mosque, temple, or shrine, or even in more generic terms as beliefs and worldviews, the critical terms and interpretive concepts introduced throughout the book provide learning opportunities that go far beyond a mere historical survey of religions in the American context.

To supplement the historical narrative and the interpretive concepts offered throughout the text, other pedagogical features also aim to enhance student learning. Images add a visual-learning component to the chapters, and maps give geographical orientation to the historical materials. Each chapter includes questions for discussion that can be used for paper assignments, to initiate classroom discussions, and for exam reviews. All but the introductory chapter have a short list of relevant suggested primary-source readings for supplementing the topics covered. In addition, citations in the notes include numerous secondary sources; instructors can refer to these for additional background information, and teachers will find many of them useful as additional readings for students. Finally, the glossary includes some of the terms that students may not be familiar with; these glossary terms are emboldened in their initial appearance in each of the chapters.

In sum, the goals of this book are twofold. First, it is a chronological survey of American religious history; it introduces students to the diverse complexities of religious orientations, communities, and practices that have been crucial factors in American society over the centuries. Second, the materials found in each chapter equip students with critical tools for understanding and interpreting religious diversity in America. Together the chapters aim to prepare students for understanding and interpreting the ongoing tale of American religiosity.

Notes

1   See for instance Thomas A. Tweed, "Expanding the Study of US Religion: Reflections on the State of a Subfield," *Religion* 40, no. 4 (2010), 250–258.

2   I am in agreement with Philip Deloria on this emphasis of the evocative and provocative; see Philip J. Deloria, *Indians in Unexpected Places* (Lawrence: University Press of Kansas, 2004), 12.

3   Of course, these are not the only populations in the Americas; other groups, such as those from the Arabian Peninsula and from Oceania, also make appearances in the historical narrative.

Beginnings

The Diversity of Religion in America

On Memorial Day weekend in 1996, visitors to the San Antonio Missions National Historical Park found Native American tipis set up in the compound yard at the San Juan Capistrano mission, a quaintly charming Spanish colonial site preserved as part of the national park in San Antonio, Texas. A small group of native dancers, described as "Aztec performers," had chosen the busy holiday weekend to hold religious observances inside the national park. Even though they lacked the proper permits from the National Park Service to perform their ceremonies, the dancers occupied the large grassy area at the center of the historic mission complex with the consent of the parish priest at the San Juan church. Because of the special arrangement between the federal government, local officials, and the Roman Catholic Church, park rangers were prevented from removing the group, despite the extreme danger posed by their ceremonial fires amid the dry grasses of the mission compound.[1]

There was more at stake, however, than public safety in the appearance of Indians in the churchyard at the national park. In particular, they were making a claim to the history of the mission itself, and, by extension, to the long and conflicted history of religious traditions in America. The Indian group at Mission San Juan insisted on their right to have sweat lodges, perform dances, and hold vigils there based on their descent from the native Coahuiltecan people who originally built and occupied the mission under the tutelage of eighteenth-century Franciscan missionaries. Moreover, they claimed that their native ceremonies properly belonged within the religious traditions of the Roman Catholic Church, and therefore they needed only the cooperation of the parish priest to perform their ceremonies unimpeded by the National Park Service.

In fact, the parish priest had invited them to the mission in the first place. He had come to Texas just a few years earlier from his native Mexico, where his

Formed From This Soil: An Introduction to the Diverse History of Religion in America, First Edition. Thomas S. Bremer.
© 2015 Thomas S. Bremer. Published 2015 by John Wiley & Sons, Ltd.

ministry had been involved with the native peoples of Mexico. Soon after arriving in San Antonio, the priest met the Indian dancers performing for tourists in a downtown plaza, and he invited them to participate in worship services in the church at Mission San Juan. Although the dancers claimed an ancestral heritage to Coahuiltecan people who were among the earliest inhabitants of San Antonio's colonial missions, their costumes, musical and dance styles, **ritual** practices, and other trappings of indigenous culture exhibited a broad, eclectic mix of native traditions from North and Central America, with no distinctly Coahuiltecan cultural emphasis. Nevertheless, they asserted their right to perform their religious rituals in what they claimed was their ancestral home, and with the support of the parish priest they regularly danced at the Mission San Juan church.

But the introduction of a native element in the religious life of the San Juan parish did not go without notice. Longtime parishioners of the church, some of whom also claimed Coahuiltecan ancestry, resented the imposition of what many regarded as pagan practices in their Christian worship; as one parishioner exclaimed, they come to church for worship, "not to see a show." Their priest, however, sided with the dancers, whom he encouraged to practice their native traditions at the church and on the mission grounds.[2]

This incident involving Catholics, Native Americans, the National Park Service, and others in San Antonio suggests a number of dilemmas for narrating a coherent tale of American religious history. Throughout its history, America has been marked by religious difference. The presence of multiple religious orientations and traditions has been a pervasive feature of American cultural landscapes from long before the arrival of Europeans right up until the present day. Moreover, adherents of the many religions found in America have constantly crossed the borders of nation, of language, of ethnicity, of religion, sometimes in creative cooperation but many times in bitter conflict. Consequently, there are many histories to be told of religions in America, and the stories are dynamic beyond comprehension. For instance, the conflicts over native dancers at Mission San Juan suggest complex histories involving contemporary struggles over sacred places, painful memories of colonial conflicts, church authority at odds with local parishioners, religious adherents at odds with civil authorities, and religious imaginations that meld disparate traditions into novel systems of spiritual practice. In all of its complexity and messiness, this brief episode in San Antonio exemplifies the histories of religious life in America.

In whatever manner we choose to characterize its religious narratives, we cannot ignore the historical reality that America has been from the beginning a place of religious encounter, contention, and struggle. In the words of historian Perry Miller, America is and has always been "a congeries of inner tensions,"[3] and one goal of this book is to consider the role of religion in producing and sustaining these tensions. Indeed, people with diverse religious orientations and cultural traditions have met and confronted each other throughout history, sometimes with hopeful outcomes but often with tragic consequences. Yet, despite the dominance of Protestant perspectives in the most popular renderings of the nation's history, America remains not a single, unified "universe" of American religion with

Protestant Christianity providing its gravitational center; instead the American religious landscape is more like a "multiverse" of very different religious universes, each with their own assumptions, commitments, and priorities, as well as their own systems of religious ideas, practices, traditions, and institutions. This book seeks to explore the historical contours of this American religious multiverse.

In exploring this multiverse of religious orientations in America, it would be a mistake to assume that everyone agrees on what is meant by "American religions." In fact, there is a surprising range of views on what the term "America" means and who or what exactly can claim to be American. Likewise, coming to an agreement on what constitutes a "religion" and what sorts of practices, cultural traditions, communities, places, and material objects we should regard as religious remains an elusive task. Before tackling significant themes of American religious history, we must first contemplate how we think of both America and religion.

Defining America

An exploration of American religious history must begin by considering what we regard as America. In fact, pinpointing precisely what is meant by "America" can quickly turn into a complicated exercise in fluid definitions. Consider, for instance, a few of the many ways of thinking about America. One obvious approach is to define America geographically, a nation delineated by its physical boundaries. It is simple enough to see America by the colors on a map, the multicolored array of states wedged between the red of Mexico to the south and the blue of Canada to the north. But, depending on what historical era the map depicts, America looks very different from century to century. Its borders have shifted radically over time as the United States of America expanded from a thin sliver of former English colonies along the Atlantic coast of North America to a country encompassing the breadth of the continent and even beyond as it incorporated the territories of other nations. Moreover, as folks both north and south of the United States will point out, America is much more than the United States. Just as individual states constitute the nation, the United States is one of many nations that constitute the Americas.

But, one might argue, the nation's borders reflect more than geographical boundaries. Another approach to defining America is according to the political and legal structures that make up the nation. Certainly, the idea of America as a single, unified nation is essentially a political one. The relationship of the United States to other nations in the Americas is fundamentally different from the political relationships between the various states within the United States. Moreover, implicit in this political perspective is the idea of America as a nation defined by its laws, beginning with the US Constitution and supplemented by hundreds of thousands of pages of legal codes, regulatory policies, and judicial opinions, with even more layers at the state and local levels. Taken together, this complex web of legal structures and political institutions constitutes the American nation.

On the other hand, as important as the law may be to the collective life of the nation's citizens, America is much more than the technical intricacies of its legal apparatus. Alternatively, we could regard America according to moral or ideological dimensions. A tradition of national civic culture has long promulgated ideals of a nation defined by its democratic principles. After all, America is, according to the national anthem of the United States, "the land of the free and home of the brave." But the ideological approach to defining America loses its traction in the complicated histories of actual practice. From the beginning, disenfranchised populations have been legion in America: women; people of color; non-English-speakers; those who do not own property – the list of populations left out of the story of American democracy is quite long. Even today, the prevalence of poverty, the inadequacy of such basic amenities as healthcare and education, and an overburdened criminal justice system with the largest prison population in the world all point to the contingent and compromised nature of the United States from an ideological perspective.

However we choose to configure the nation – geographically, politically, ideologically, or otherwise – the questions "What is America?" and "Who is American?" are never easy to answer. As we consider the diversity of religious life in American history, we must consider a variety of ways to address these and other questions regarding the nation and national identities.

Defining Religion

Just as different people have different understandings of America, there are many ways of being religious, making religion equally difficult to define. For centuries students of religion have struggled to find a satisfying definition of the term, one that encompasses the diversity of the world's traditions and enjoys wide acceptance among scholars. Their efforts thus far have not yielded agreement. It seems that, no matter how we define it, all notions of religion fail in some way to account for all instances of religious behavior, all **worldviews**, and all traditions. For example, an early attempt by the nineteenth-century anthropologist Edward B. Tylor (1832–1917) famously defined religion as "belief in Spiritual Beings." But, as numerous critics have insisted, many religions do not concentrate on "beliefs" as their defining characteristic, in contrast to the predominantly Christian culture of nineteenth-century Europe where Tylor developed his ideas about religion. Countless religious people around the world value practical goals in their devotional lives over abstract beliefs. Thus, for the adherents of many religious traditions, the correct performance of appropriate rites at the proper time carries more importance than professing orthodox beliefs.

A number of scholars have tried to go beyond the emphasis on beliefs as the defining characteristic of religion. Some, like French sociologist Émile Durkheim (1858–1917), focus more on the collective, communal aspects of religious life.

Durkheim went so far as to claim that religion is inextricably linked to all societies and that, just as all religious traditions, practices, and beliefs are essentially social, no society can exist without religion. Phenomenologists of religion, on the other hand, turn their attention to the human experience of religion, in particular what is often called "the experience of the sacred." Rudolf Otto (1869–1937), a German Protestant theologian working in the early part of the twentieth century, set out to describe these religious experiences as "mysterium tremendum et fascinans," emphasizing both the frightening awesomeness and compelling fascination involved when humans come into direct contact with divinity. Taking a cue from Otto's insights, the Romanian phenomenologist of religions Mircea Eliade (1907–1986) regarded all humans as *Homo religiosus*, insisting that at some level the desire for interactions with sacred forces and beings is fundamental to human nature.

Other scholars have concentrated on the ethical aspects of religious systems. A particularly influential approach introduced later in the twentieth century by the American cultural anthropologist Clifford Geertz (1926–2006) links the ethical system of a culture to its assumptions about the nature of reality. This is done, according to Geertz, through systems of religious symbols, including symbolic actions performed in religious rituals. His five-part definition of religion reveals how religious symbols and traditions serve to synthesize a people's worldview with how they behave and act ethically in their lives.[4]

As this brief review of a few approaches to understanding religions suggests, the list of ways that scholars, theologians, religious communities, civic governments, and others have defined "religion" quickly grows to unwieldy proportions. This prolific attention to marking out the boundaries of religion is not merely a frivolous exercise in erudition; on the contrary, how we regard what is and is not religious can have very real and often significant consequences for particular groups of people. For instance, many American Christians have long viewed non-Christian religious traditions with suspicion. This has had disastrous consequences for many groups; Native American peoples, for example, have suffered religious persecution since their earliest contacts with European Christians. By deeming Native American religions as illegitimate and therefore not subject to the guarantees of religious freedom in the US Constitution, the dominant Christian population in the nineteenth and early twentieth centuries effectively suppressed the religiosity of indigenous peoples.

The history of religious oppression reveals a dominant way of thinking about religion for many Americans. The prevailing model for "religious" has been Christianity, especially Protestant Christianity, which has served as the standard by which to measure the beliefs, practices, and traditions of other people. In this regard, those who do not meet the "religious" standards of a Christian-informed view of religion are often depicted as savage, barbaric, a cult, and therefore a dangerous threat that must be contained and eliminated; or, on the other hand, some people have found it easy to dismiss unfamiliar, non-Christian traditions or practices as superficial, trivial, and not serious enough to be regarded as religion.

Hence, alternative ways of religious understanding, of devotional practice, of social organization that remain alien to Christian conventions are beyond the purview of "religious" in the minds of many Americans.

The historical prevalence of a Christian, and specifically Protestant, model of religion has encouraged another common distinction in American society: the difference between "religious" and "spiritual." It is not uncommon for people to deny being religious while claiming to be spiritual. Most often this amounts to a rejection of the formal institutions of organized religion in favor of personal spiritual growth, a stance that has a long history in Protestant critiques of other religions, especially Catholicism. For those making this claim, the distinction is usually between the public and communal aspects of religion versus the private and personal dimensions of spirituality. Such claims are generally critical, sometimes overtly and sometimes merely implicitly, of organized religion or the public institutions of religiosity. In effect, they serve as a way to claim religiosity while not affiliating with any particular religious community, tradition, or institution.[5]

In our studies of American religious history, however, it is not useful for us to exclude any manner of being religious, whether religiosity takes the form of affiliation with an organized religious institution such as a church, synagogue, mosque, or temple or whether it involves merely the private contemplations of one's personal sense of spirituality. Consequently, instead of seeking an adequately comprehensive definition of religion, the approach in this book will be to use various perspectives for investigating the diverse ways of being religious in America; throughout the book we will learn of interpretive concepts for considering the claims, practices, traditions, institutions, and communities characterized as "religious." Notions such as "contact zones," "syncretism," "pluralism," "sacred space," "animism," "fundamentalism," and "civil religion," as well as other theoretical models that appear in the chapters, can serve as intellectual tools for better understanding the diversity of religions and religious people in American history. These interpretive concepts, however, are not intended to lead us toward conclusions that define either "America" or "religion." The meanings of these terms throughout history have never been stable in the experiences of people who regard themselves as American. Americans have continuously found new ways of being religious even as they have reinvented their self-understandings of being American.

The Diversity of American Religious History

One particular interpretive concept informs this entire book. This overarching rubric for interpreting the history of religions in America is the notion of "diversity," a concept reinforced in every chapter as we learn of the complex interactions between religious people originating in the Americas and those coming from Europe, Africa, and Asia. Diversity in its simplest meaning indicates differences. To make a claim of diversity is to state the rather obvious fact that people are different, both at the individual level (i.e., no two people are alike) and at the collective level (i.e., no two groups of people, communities, societies, etc. are alike). Applying this idea of diversity to religions, however, highlights far more than the different beliefs or even ritual practices and traditions of different groups of religious people. In other words, religious diversity has to do with more than differences in religions. Certainly, different religious groups vary in their histories as distinct communities; in their professed beliefs and commitments as religious people; in their religious rituals and practices; and in their accepted theologies. But religious communities also display a range of social, economic, and cultural diversities. Indeed, differences in race, ethnicity, national origin, geographic region, language, socioeconomic class, educational level, gender, sexual orientation, and many other characteristics distinguish the great number of groups characterized as religious. Moreover, these various points of difference are not separate from religious identity; they interact in complex ways that encompass religious differences and in many cases are definitive of particular religious orientations. Thus, a suburban Protestant congregation in twenty-first-century America may be identified by their beliefs in Jesus Christ as a source of salvation, their reliance on the Christian Bible as a source of wisdom and guidance in their everyday lives, and by the formal structure of their worship services. But they also can be characterized by the degree of socioeconomic difference between their members, the racial makeup of the congregation, the relative proportions of genders, or their acceptance (or rejection) of members with nonheterosexual orientations. In contrast, urban practitioners of Haitian Vodou might be described according to their devotion to the Vodou spirits, their performance of traditional Vodou ceremonies, and their observance of feast days in honor of the saints. But their common national origin and ethnic heritage, the racial and gender makeup of the group, linguistic distinctiveness, and other characteristics all also contribute to their self-understandings as well as to the way that outsiders view them as a unique religious community. In both examples, social and cultural differences are intimately linked to their distinctiveness as a religious community. In fact, diversity, or the differences between individuals and groups, is at the very core of identities, both personal and collective; understandings of one's self and others depend to a large extent on perceptions of differences. In this regard, diversity is constantly present, from the most intimate private moments to the most public collective institutions and events. In addition, these differences are not at all static but rather constantly change in dynamic processes of interaction, affiliation, and conflict.

Attention to the diversity of religious people, practices, and traditions in America, as well as to how the differences between groups have played out over time, has many advantages for understanding the multiverse of American religious history. At the same time, however, it poses many difficulties for narrating a coherent tale of religion in the Americas. Not least is the problem of where to begin telling the story. Do we begin with Asian people more than ten thousand years ago crossing the Bering Land Bridge into what is now Alaska? Or do we give priority to Native American versions of the first people emerging directly into American landscapes in some ancient time? Is it more appropriate to start the story with the first Europeans to come to America, the Norse explorers who settled tentatively along the northern Atlantic coast in the eleventh century of the **Common Era** (CE)? Or should the famous first voyage of Christopher Columbus in the last decade of the fifteenth century mark the beginning of religious history in America? Perhaps the story should start with the Pilgrims arriving from England on their ship the *Mayflower* in the early seventeenth century. Whichever of these starting points we choose to begin with, we certainly can think of many others that would be equally plausible. Moreover, each of these various beginnings of America's story are important to different religious groups. Thus, where we choose to start has distinct implications for the diverse peoples who inhabit American religious history. Equally important for how we regard religion in America, the choice of where to begin has a strong impact on the sort of narrative one tells. For instance, the story of American religious history that begins with English Puritans settling in New England has a tendency to follow the course of Protestant Christian history while diminishing, and in many cases eliminating altogether, the stories of Native Americans, African Americans, Hispanic Catholics, Russian Orthodox, Asian Buddhists, and a host of others. In a narrative that starts with a Puritan orientation there may not appear the sort of conflict discussed at the beginning of this chapter between local Catholic parishioners and groups identifying with ancestral Coahuiltecan people in Texas; on the other hand, beginning with Spanish colonization in the Americas may make this sort of example more relevant.

Compounding the problem of narrating this history is the sheer complexity of religious phenomena practiced and expressed by the many religious people who have populated the Americas throughout the centuries. The people who make up American society today are truly global in origin, and to tell their story in its entirety would entail tracing the origins of virtually all of humanity and the numberless religious traditions that have found their way onto American soil. This, of course, is an impossible task. The aim of this book is far more modest. The story here concentrates on the United States, although it pushes the beginnings of the nation's tale back to the time before Columbus. Moreover, since the United States throughout its history has been a dynamic entity with uncertain boundaries, the story in this book includes other areas of the Americas that would eventually become, or possibly could have become, incorporated into the United States. Thus, the early chapters include discussions of what are now Mexico and Canada, places that have significance for what eventually would become the United States. Likewise, other chapters take religion in the United States beyond the nation's current borders, as Americans have extended their cultural influence, including religiosity, throughout the world.

The story of American religious history, at least as it is told in these pages, reflects the dynamic uncertainties that have characterized the origins, growth, and continued viability of the nation itself. It tells especially how the American context transformed religious people and their traditions, how these became something new, as the narrator proclaims in Walt Whitman's poem *Song of Myself*, "Formed from this soil, this air." This is a tale, however, that continues. Indeed, where to end the story remains as perplexing as where to begin. The final chapter takes us into the early years of the twenty-first century, but this remains an open story that cannot be confined to these pages. Indeed, it continues all around us.

Questions for Discussion

(1) How do the terms "America" and "religion" influence the ways we study religious history?
(2) In what ways is the notion of "a 'multiverse' of very different religious universes" helpful in studying the history of religions in America?
(3) How are religious differences related to other types of social difference?

Notes

1 This book uses the terms "Indians," "Native Americans," "native peoples," and "indigenous peoples" interchangeably for people who claim ancestral origins in the Americas. All of these terms are problematic, with long histories of dispute and conflict. Many scholars and indigenous peoples themselves prefer to use self-designated tribal and/or clan names, a preference followed here where appropriate. Many of these terms, however, are equally problematic; for instance, the name "Mohawk" is a derogatory Narrangansett term meaning "flesh eaters." Whatever terms we use, it is always important to cultivate a critical awareness of the history and culture of names that we apply to the different people we are discussing, as scholar Peter d'Errico emphasizes. For a concise discussion of the issues involved in the terminology for indigenous peoples of the Americas, see Peter d'Errico, "Native American Indian Studies: A Note on Names" (self-published, 2005), http://people. umass.edu/derrico/name.html (accessed June 21, 2014).
2 The controversy over Indian dancers at Mission San Juan Capistrano in San Antonio is discussed in Thomas S. Bremer, *Blessed with Tourists: The Borderlands of Religion and Tourism in San Antonio* (Chapel Hill: University of North Carolina Press, 2004), 132–134.
3 Perry Miller, "Errand into the Wilderness," in *Religion in American History: A Reader*, ed. Jon Butler and Harry S. Stout (New York: Oxford University Press, 1998 [1956]), 28.
4 For an introduction to the religious theorists mentioned here, see Daniel L. Pals, *Eight Theories of Religion*, 2nd edn (New York: Oxford University Press, 2006). Pals' book includes chapters on Tylor, Durkheim, Eliade, and Geertz; Otto's ideas are briefly summarized in the chapter on Eliade.
5 For a brief discussion of the distinctions between spirituality and religion, see the section "Spirituality as an Alternative to Religion" in Mary N. MacDonald, "Spirituality," in *Encyclopedia of Religion*, ed. Lindsay Jones, vol. 13 (Detroit, MI: Macmillan Reference USA, 2005), 8720–8721.

Part I

New Worlds

1

Encounters

In this chapter, we learn about religious encounters between peoples of the Americas, Africa, and Europe as they established new relationships in an increasingly complex world of social, political, economic, and cultural connections and interdependence. In this emerging **Atlantic world**, people relied on religious orientations and understandings to guide their encounter of, and often violent conflict with, people, cultures, landscapes, and traditions very different from their own. The new worlds that the indigenous Americans, Africans, and Europeans made in their first encounters served as the foundation for the religious history of America.

America astonished Christopher Columbus (1451–1506). The legendary Admiral of the Ocean Sea, whose voyages initiated permanent European settlement in the Americas, encountered wonders beyond his imagination. He reported seeing mermaids with "something masculine in the countenance," armored with copper plates and brandishing bows and arrows.[1] He reveled in the astounding variety of plant life as well as an abundant array of strangely unfamiliar animals. Resorting to the imagery of his Christian faith, Columbus described one place he explored as the Garden of Eden, stating, "I believe the earthly paradise lies here, which no one can enter except by God's leave."[2]

Although few details are known concerning his personal life, the surviving record of his voyages reveals that Christopher Columbus stood at the crossroads of the medieval and Renaissance periods of European cultural history.[3] Historians recognize his capabilities as a superb seaman, a skillful navigator, and a sensitive observer of the places he encountered. His observations reveal an educated curiosity typical of the European Renaissance, reflecting a mind well informed of the

Formed From This Soil: An Introduction to the Diverse History of Religion in America, First Edition. Thomas S. Bremer.
© 2015 Thomas S. Bremer. Published 2015 by John Wiley & Sons, Ltd.

Figure 1.1   The European entry into the contact zones of America was later imagined as a pious act of bringing Christianity to the "pagan" peoples of America, as illustrated in this nineteenth-century engraving of Columbus' first landing in the New World. (Courtesy of the Library of Congress, LC-DIG-pga-01974.)

scientific understandings of his era. On the other hand, Columbus retained a deep Christian piety that reflected centuries of medieval concern for the human place in the cosmos. His scientific observations were tempered by a pious struggle to fit new findings into a medieval Christian view of divine order.

This struggle becomes apparent in Columbus' ambivalence toward native peoples who inhabited the islands and other lands that he explored in the western hemisphere. His widely divergent views of indigenous Americans reflect his circumstance in a changing European world; in particular, they draw attention to a dramatic tension between the medieval world of the old and a newly emerging modern perspective. On the one hand, Columbus often expresses genuine admiration of the indigenous people he encountered in the Americas. "They are affectionate people," he wrote of the natives who came to his aid in December 1492, when his ship had run aground, "free from avarice and agreeable to everything." In fact, he concludes, "in all the world I do not believe there is a better people or a better country. They love their neighbors as themselves, and they have the softest and gentlest voices in the world and are always smiling." He commends their propensity for Christian values; indeed, calling them people who "love their neighbors as themselves." But elsewhere, he condemns people who violate his deepest human convictions. For instance, Columbus learned of a people called Caribes, who, he surmised, "must be a very daring people since they go to all the islands and eat the people they are able to capture." When one of his exploring parties came under attack, he concluded that "the people here are evil, and I believe they are from the island of Caribe, and that they eat men."[4]

Box 1.1   Zones of contact

As he landed on the island beaches of the Americas, Christopher Columbus entered an ambiguous space between worlds. His Atlantic crossing had removed him from the familiar places of Europe, and as he stepped from his boat onto the sand the captain passed into a borderland of worlds altogether unknown to him. Columbus carried with him into this borderland his own universe of European tradition, **worldview**, and especially his Christian **ethos**, and he found there indigenous people with their own sense of tradition, worldview, and ethos.

The ambiguous space where very different people first encounter each other has been described by literary historian Mary Louise Pratt as a "contact zone." Pratt uses this term "to refer to the space of colonial encounters, the space in which peoples geographically and historically separated come into contact with each other and establish ongoing relations, usually involving conditions of coercion, radical inequality, and intractable conflict."[5] This idea of a contact zone draws attention to the momentous encounters between individuals and groups of people who had no previous familiarity or even knowledge of each other. These encounters most often resulted in the establishment of colonial relationships where one group dominated and controlled the other group, usually for economic advantage. But, in nearly all cases, subjugated peoples did not accept colonial domination with passive submissiveness. Even when they found themselves in traumatic circumstances of forced submission that involved relinquishment of lands, separation from families and communities, and prohibitions against religious traditions that had sustained their communities for centuries, colonized people found creative ways to engage the dominant cultures that kept them in submission. Pratt emphasizes a process of "transculturation" to describe "how subordinated or marginal groups select and invent from materials transmitted to them by a dominant or metropolitan culture."[6] In this way, dominated and colonized people continuously engaged with the dominant culture and made it their own through incorporating the ideas, practices, and material objects of the foreign culture into their own worldviews and ways of living, sometimes creating altogether new cultural forms that in turn found their way back into the dominant culture.

Contact zones, then, are the circumstances in which unfamiliar people encounter each other and initiate colonial relationships. But the term can have more broad applications; in particular, we can think of a contact zone as the space and time of encounter with otherness and difference. In other words, contact zones are historical moments and places where people are confronted by new and unanticipated modes of living and manners of social interaction, by moral codes that contradict their own moral understandings and commitments, and by religious traditions that involve alien conceptions of reality and peculiar devotional practices. Many times the encounters of difference that occur in these contact zones devolve into violent conflict as each side perceives threats to its own ways of living and understandings of the world. But the circumstances of encounter can also generate opportunities for creative and productive engagements with otherness. Throughout human history people have forged altogether new and unforeseen modes of social organization and ways of living from their mutual engagement with others who were complete strangers before their initial encounter. The results have nearly always involved one group benefiting at the expense of others, but at the same time dominated groups have shown remarkable resourcefulness in finding ways to resist and subvert domination, and to adapt and survive by creatively using the resources of the dominating people for their own gain.

The profound strangeness of peoples and places that he encountered in the Americas amazed Columbus, yet he never relented in his commitment to the triumph of the Christian gospel in ushering in a new world order. In fact, he reveals in the log of his first voyage that his true purpose for sailing to the Indies was to gain the wealth necessary to launch an assault to recapture Jerusalem from the Muslims who controlled the holy city; he relates, "I have already petitioned Your Highness to see that all the profits of this, my enterprise, should be spent on the conquest of Jerusalem."[7] In other words, Columbus sailed the ocean sea not to prove that the world was round or even to expand Spanish claims in new lands, but to reclaim the Holy Land for Christian pilgrims.

The importance of pilgrimage in the piety of Christopher Columbus became evident on the return trip across the Atlantic from his initial voyage to the Indies. Columbus appealed to his Christian faith when faced with disaster on the high seas. On the morning of February 14, 1493, with fierce winds driving huge waves that broke over the sides of his ship, Columbus "ordered that a pilgrimage to Santa María de Guadalupe be pledged." He himself drew the lot, and he thereby "considered [himself] obliged to fulfill the vow and make the pilgrimage." In the same storm, he ordered that two more pilgrimages be pledged.[8] Upon his safe return to

Spain, Columbus endeavored to fulfill these vows; his Christian faith brought him to the Spanish shrine of the Virgin of Guadalupe following his first voyage to the Americas.

As both Christian pilgrim and accomplished mariner, Columbus straddled a world suffused with the scientific and philosophical thinking of the Renaissance period while remaining deeply implicated in the medieval world of Christian religiosity. His superb skill as a navigator and his excellent seamanship enabled his bold crossing of the Atlantic Ocean into lands previously unknown to Europeans, but in his mind it was only by God's **providence** that the strange and marvelous lands of what he thought were the far eastern reaches of Asia were delivered to him and the Spanish sovereigns Isabella (1451–1504) and Ferdinand (1452–1516). The riches encountered there, he thought, were God's provision to return Jerusalem to faithful Christians, and the people he met in these new lands were potential converts to the Christian faith who also would serve as laborers to harvest the riches of the land. What Columbus discovered was not so much a new world but an expanded vision of what he regarded as God's providence for bringing Christian redemption to a fallen world. He set out as a devout Christian who, like other European Christians seeking routes to India, understood his voyage as a means to defeat the Muslim enemy. The strangely unfamiliar lands and people he found, however, shook the very foundations of the medieval world of Christian Europe; at the same time, his arrival in America changed forever the lives of people who encountered these Christians entering their homelands.

As we consider the many ways that people encountered others who seemed to them altogether strange and unfamiliar, it becomes apparent that such encounters lie at the center of the historical processes that gave rise to what scholars have called the Atlantic world, the early modern colonial world of Africa, Europe, and the Americas. Our studies of religions in America, beginning with Christopher Columbus, highlight the enormity of these encounters, some would say collisions, of people and their cultures, heritages, institutions, and cosmological perspectives in a rapidly expanding Atlantic world that would come to define America. However, the historical Columbus, who represents the initiation of these global encounters, is not the heroic Admiral of the Ocean Sea celebrated in the spellbinding tales often repeated as a staple of primary education in the United States; instead, he represents the late medieval Christian obsession with recapturing Jerusalem from Muslims and the conquistador ethos of conquest, both material and cultural. Christopher Columbus marks a starting point for us to contemplate the complex and diverse histories of religious encounters in America.

We must keep in mind too that, far from representing an anomalous figure in the European confrontation of new territories, the enigmatic character of Christopher Columbus represents just one moment in this complex story of first contacts, exchanges, and conflicts that changed familiar worlds and ushered in new relationships based on an increasingly global perspective. This rapidly changing world not only involved Columbus and the Europeans who followed him to the

Map 1.1   The Leardo Map of the World, produced by the Italian mapmaker Giovanni Leardo in the 1450s, shows how Europeans understood the world in the middle of the fifteenth century. The map is oriented with east at the top and has Jerusalem at the center, marked by the large edifice at the top of (i.e., east of) the Mediterranean Sea. (From the American Geographical Society Library, University of Wisconsin-Milwaukee Libraries.)

western hemisphere; it also included the diverse peoples of Africa, the islands of the Caribbean Sea, North America, Mesoamerica, and South America, and eventually the many cultures of the Pacific Ocean regions as well as Asia. In virtually every case, the religious orientations of the people involved in these encounters were key determining factors in how they responded to the dynamics of contact and made sense of their changing world. Nearly everyone who experienced sudden disruptions of familiar ways turned to their gods and other supernatural powers,

Box 1.2 Abrahamic religions

The two largest religious traditions in the world today both emerged from a common monotheistic orientation originating in the Middle East. Both Christianity, the largest worldwide religion in numbers of adherents, and Islam, with the second-largest number of followers, share a common beginning in the monotheism of the Judaic religion; all three religions trace their roots to the patriarch Abraham, and this triumvirate of monotheistic orientations are thus known as the Abrahamic religions.

According to the Torah, the sacred text of Judaism, Abraham worshiped the god Yahweh (although this name for the god was not revealed until later), and Abraham received a covenant from Yahweh giving him children in his old age. First, a son was born to Hagar, the servant of Abraham's wife Sarah; the son was named Ishmael. Then the elderly Sarah herself bore a son, named Isaac. The Torah traces the ancestry of the Jewish people to Isaac. Moses, a descendant of Isaac, was born under Egyptian enslavement of the Jews; auspicious circumstances saved the child from orders to kill all male Hebrew infants. Subsequently, the Jewish god Yahweh called on Moses to lead his people out of captivity in Egypt to a promised land in Palestine; the Torah tells of Moses' death just before the Hebrews' arrival in their promised land. The Tanakh, or Jewish Bible, consists of the Torah together with the prophetic works of the Nevi'im and the other collected canonical writings of the Ketuvim. Together they tell the story of the Jewish people and document the wisdom, poetry, and ethical requirements of Judaism.

In the first century CE in the region of Palestine, a Jewish prophet by the name of Jesus of Nazareth sought to renew and transform Jewish traditions. His followers regarded him as the Messiah (or *Christ* in Greek), from the Jewish tradition of an "anointed one," originally referring to Jewish kings as anointed to lead Yahweh's people but later referring to the hope that Yahweh would send a new king to restore the greatness of the Jewish kingdom. According to the Christian sacred narrative, Jesus suffered martyrdom at the hands of the ruling Romans around 30 CE. In subsequent centuries the various Jewish sects devoted to Jesus Christ established separate identities and were eventually recognized as a non-Jewish religion in the Roman empire; by the fourth century a dominant Christian establishment had supplanted the Roman state religion as the official religion of the empire.

In the seventh century CE, a religious community emerged on the Arabian Peninsula that also traced its roots to the Jewish patriarch Abraham. According to Islamic tradition, Abraham took his first son Ishmael and Ishmael's mother Hagar to the city of Mecca, where they established the Ka'bah, the house of Al-Lah (the God), as a refuge and place of pilgrimage. This holy site, however, had become a desecrated shelter for various religious cults of the region over the centuries, until Al-Lah called on the last of the prophets, Muhammad (570–632 CE), who subsequently reclaimed the Ka'bah as the shrine of Al-Lah in 629 CE. Muhammad's career as holy prophet began when the angel Gabriel appeared to him in a vision as he meditated alone in a cave in the nearby mountains. After this first vision, when the angel commanded Muhammad "Recite!," Muhammad received numerous divine communications that were subsequently collected in the Muslim holy book of the Qur'an. News of the prophet's visions quickly spread, and Muhammad and his followers were eventually banned from Mecca. Their migration to the city of Medina, known as the Hijra, marks the beginning of the Ummah, or worldwide community of Muslims; it also denotes the start of the Islamic calendar. After several years in Medina, Muhammad returned to Mecca, capturing it without bloodshed and resanctifying the Ka'bah. By the time of Muhammad's death, much of the Arabian world had submitted to the religion of Islam (the term in Arabic means "submission"), and within a century it had spread throughout the Middle East and into parts of Asia, Africa, and Europe.

engaged in **rituals** of purification or propitiation, consulted their **mythic** traditions, and otherwise relied on religious resources for understanding, solace, and assistance.

African Encounters

Christopher Columbus was not the first European to attempt to reach Asia by sea. In fact, the history of explorations that brought him to American shores had begun decades earlier, when Europeans started seeking sea routes that would allow them to dominate European–Asian trade, which had been going on for centuries. European desire for silks, spices, metal and ceramic products, medicinal herbs, and a variety of technologies from Asia, along with Asian demand for European goods, generated trade networks that spanned differences of culture, religion, and ethnicity on a global scale. What became known as the Silk Road, a series of trade routes connecting Europe and Asia, had been in use since before the time of Jesus of Nazareth in the first century of the **Common Era** (CE). By the late medieval period, Europeans sought alternative routes to Asia in order to gain control of this lucrative trade from the Muslims who oversaw much of it. Nearly a century before Columbus first sailed west across the Atlantic Ocean, other explorers had begun exploring sea routes to the east with incursions into Africa that would have profound consequences for Europeans, Africans, and Asians and would eventually bring the Americas into a new global order.

Early in the fifteenth century, the European nation of Portugal sought to expand the kingdom's wealth with a plan to control trade with Asia by circumventing Muslim-dominated routes. It devised a scheme to invade northern Africa with the goal of reaching the legendary Christian kingdom of Prester John in the heart of the African continent. According to the proposed strategy of the Portuguese, the two Christian nations then could establish a new trade route from the Red Sea directly across Africa to Portugal. But, after capturing the Mediterranean port of Ceuta on the African side of the Strait of Gibraltar in 1415, the plan proved impossible; the Portuguese quickly discovered that there was no easy way across the formidable African continent. They turned their attention instead to finding a sea route around Africa.[9]

Box 1.3   Prester John

The legendary figure of Prester John, a mysterious Christian king and priest who, according to tales circulated in Europe, ruled over a vast empire of the Orient, entered the Christian imagination of medieval Europe in the twelfth century. In 1145 stories first reached Europe of a great Christian king of the Orient, Prester John, who had come to the aid of the Christian Crusaders. He was said to be a descendant of the Magi of the Christian Gospels and to rule over a large and prosperous kingdom in India. For the next five centuries, European Christians sought this kingdom of the mysterious Prester John; his legend grew while the purported location of his kingdom shifted from southern Asia to the Steppes of central Asia and finally to Africa, where the Portuguese in the fifteenth century hoped for his aid in defeating the Muslims and establishing dominance over trade with Asia. Although predominantly fictional, the stories of Prester John that circulated in medieval Europe may have contained bits of historical fact. But their historicity became lost in fanciful tales that expressed a European desire to find a Christian ally in the threatening lands beyond the known borders of Christendom.[10]

Figure 1.2 Medieval and early modern Europeans imagined Prester John as a powerful Christian monarch in Africa who would join with European Christians to conquer Muslims in Africa and the Christian Holy Land. (Image © Mary Evans Picture Library / Alamy.)

Indigenous Africa

Finding a sea route around Africa involved establishing contact with coastal Africans and exploring the interior of the continent. As Europeans entered Africa, they found diverse religious traditions that paralleled an equally diverse range of cultural groups, although many of these groups, which inhabited broad regions of the continent, shared a number of common characteristic traits in their religious lives.[11] For many African tribal groups, especially in central and western sub-Saharan Africa, powerful spiritual forces, whether gods or other supernatural powers, were largely localized; each tribe revered its own gods and ancestor spirits, which were located in specific sacred places and vested in particular objects that displayed magical powers. Familial and tribal affiliations joined with religious sentiment and tradition in rites honoring the ancestors, spiritual beings who watched over the living with powers that could bring either rewards or harm to individuals or to the tribe as a whole. Many of these tribal groups, including the Akan, Ewe, Yoruba, and Ibo, turned to their particular local spirits for help with the practical concerns of human life, especially regarding health, fertility, prosperity, and conflict with others. At the same time, above these local deities was a distant, inaccessible supreme god who ruled over a highly structured cosmos for many of the tribal peoples of western and central Africa.[12]

Living in a universe suffused with the powers of spiritual beings, whose presence was felt at every level of human life, including the individual, tribal, environmental, and cosmic levels, local people interacted with tribal deities in a variety of ways. These supernatural beings had powers that could bring either harm or reward, not only at the personal level of the individual but also between individuals and even groups of people in social relationships. Consequently, humans were careful to please their ancestors and the gods with regular ritual offerings. Common throughout western and central Africa were propitiatory rituals of sacrifice to appease gods and ancestral spirits.[13]

Humans relied on their relationship with supernatural powers for protection, healing, and divining the future. In many areas, Africans carried amulets on their bodies or displayed them conspicuously nearby to guard against misfortune and evil. Many of these magical objects contained spiritual beings that interacted with and often assisted humans. These powerful spirits could be found in fabricated materials, such as bags or sculpted containers or figurines, or in unusual natural objects of sacred significance, such as twisted, misshapen roots or stones.[14]

Among the most direct interaction between humans and their tutelary deities was spirit possession. A specially selected and trained class of priests served as mediators in many African tribal societies. Among the Yoruba, for instance, certain devotees would undergo rigorous training that included the novice's "death," a lengthy period of training in the rites of the gods and the secret language of sacred communication, and then the novice's "resurrection" as a cultic initiate. These ritual specialists were then capable of being possessed by the spirits of supernatural beings. During ritual ceremonies involving prolonged periods of rhythmic music and dance, they would enter ecstatic trances and become the character and voice of the god, who became present to the tribe through possession of the priest in the ceremonial dance.[15]

In addition to direct possession by spirits, various forms of divination were common throughout western and central Africa.[16] Ritual specialists who communicated with spirits played key roles in determining courses of action in times of conflict, in dealing with illness or misfortune, or in deciding one's prospects for marriage, even in the naming of children. Believing that ancestors commonly returned to earthly life through rebirth in descendants, parents often relied on the divination specialists to determine which ancestor had returned in their child, and would name the child accordingly.

Along with their practices of spirit possession, divination, and propitiatory sacrifices to the gods, the ritual life of tribal peoples of western and central Africa was characterized by vibrant musical traditions. Sacred drumming, ritual dancing, and stylized singing accompanied nearly every facet of religious life. Ceremonies of spirit possession, as an example, required specific drumming and dancing to the particular songs of the gods being called. When devotees were "mounted," or possessed, in such ceremonies, the identity of the god could be determined by the distinctive dance steps of the possessed priest. In fact, rhythmic music was so essential to these religious traditions that they are sometimes referred to as "danced religions."[17]

In addition to the vast diversity of local tribal religions throughout western and central Africa, the people of these areas were not immune to outside influences, especially monotheistic religions that found their way into the region from the north. Principally Islam, and to a lesser extent Christianity, had penetrated into sub-Saharan Africa by the time that Europeans began entering the African continent. Indeed, Muslims had controlled most of northern Africa since the eighth century CE, and they had traded extensively throughout the continent, bringing not only material goods but also the teachings of Muhammad's revelations.

Religious conflicts in Africa

As they first encountered the cultural, linguistic, and religious diversity of Africa, Europeans harbored more than economic ambitions for controlling trade with Asia. They also sought religious conquest, especially in northern Africa, which was predominantly Muslim; European Christians had long sought to defeat and eventually eradicate what they understood to be the heretical followers of Muhammad. In addition, they also intended to **proselytize** among non-Muslim Africans. Indeed, the Portuguese entered the contact zones of Africa as zealous Christian evangelists and soldiers of the faith.

Besides their religious intentions to bring the European variety of Christianity to Africa, the Portuguese also carried less noble causes into the zones of contact. Specifically, they hoped to conquer and enslave the Africans. However, their early expectations of easy victory faltered when they met effective resistance from African forces well equipped to protect the coast. The Portuguese soon realized that diplomacy and peacefully regulated trade based on treaties with powerful African nations was a more reliable and profitable approach.[18] These arrangements brought great wealth for Portuguese merchants trading in African agricultural products such as pepper and sugar; traders also became rich by acquiring African gold, and many built their fortunes in the slave trade.

Economic wealth, however, did not displace religion entirely as an important objective of the Portuguese's encounter with the peoples of Africa, an encounter that supported the needs of traders as well as those of the Portuguese monarchy. The intertwining of religious, political, and economic goals in the contact zones of Africa is clearly evident, for instance, in Portugal's colonization of the Congo, beginning in 1483. Portuguese officials realized that friendly relations with the

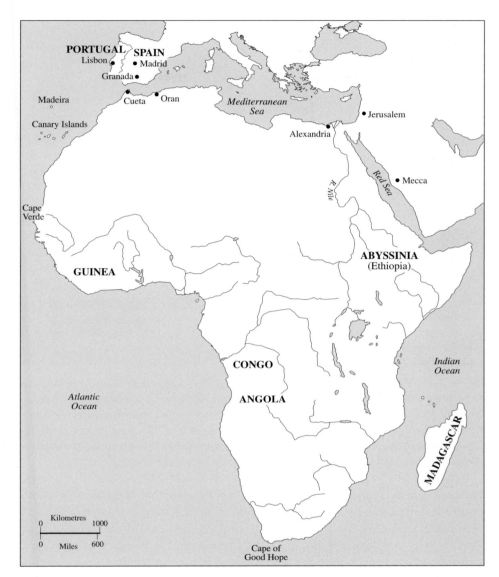

Map 1.2   The African continent with a few of the major areas of Portuguese exploration listed. Portuguese emissaries eventually found the Christian ruler King Eskender in Abyssinia (Ethiopia); Europeans regarded him as the legendary Prester John.

Manicongo, ruler of the Congo people, whose vast kingdom covered much of the continent's interior, would allow not only the benefits of trade but also the possibility of establishing contact with the legendary Christian king Prester John, whom the Portuguese believed was in Ethiopia. Key to securing this alliance was gaining the Manicongo's spiritual allegiance, for he was not only a political ruler but also embodied devotion to the tutelary deities of the region. Consequently, the

Figure 1.3   This illustration from the middle of the seventeenth century shows the Manicongo receiving Portuguese soldiers while three missionaries stand beside the African king. As both political and religious leader of the Congo region, the Manicongo's alliance with the Portuguese was strengthened by his acceptance of Christianity. But powerful economic interests in the slave trade eventually undermined the missionaries' religious efforts in central Africa. (Image © Everett Collection Historical / Alamy.)

Portuguese sent colonists to the Congo in 1490 to strengthen their alliance and to evangelize among the people of the region. The Manicongo, his eldest son and eventual successor Afonso, and other high-ranking members of the ruling class all were baptized as Christians. But efforts to Christianize the Congo met resistance, most powerfully from adversaries who had benefited from the slave trade. Despite their success among the native ruling class, Christian missionaries were no match for the powerful economic and political forces involved in the capture and sale of slaves that came to dominate the Congo.[19]

As the Portuguese continued to explore and colonize Africa, they eventually succeeded in rounding the southern tip of the continent, allowing them to dominate European trade with Asia by controlling sea routes around Africa and across the Indian Ocean. Moreover, they also found Prester John. In 1493 an emissary representing the king of Portugal presented himself at the court of the Ethiopian Christian ruler King Eskender (1471–1494), whom the Portuguese regarded as the legendary Prester John.[20] Indeed, finding the elusive Christian king in Africa had remained a key goal in Portugal's plans not only to dominate trade with Asia but also to defeat the

Muslims and regain Christian control of the Holy Land. But finding Prester John did not yield a strategic advantage as the Portuguese had hoped it would. Ultimately the isolated kingdom in Ethiopia proved of little use in Portugal's colonial ambitions.

Portuguese ambitions did, however, initiate an era of European expansion and colonization that encompassed not only the African continent but also Asia, the Americas, and much of the Pacific region. The Portuguese eventually came to America and established the colony of Brazil in South America. And, although Portugal itself had no significant direct involvement in colonizing North America, we can see that its early exploits on the African continent continue to have an impact on the peoples and cultures of North American society. In particular, their engagement with the indigenous peoples of Africa initiated European involvement in the trading of slaves, which would transport Africans across the Atlantic Ocean to American shores, bringing with them religious traditions and practices that would alter the religious landscapes of the Americas. The long and troubled history between European and African nations that began with Portuguese attempts to dominate trade with Asia would have profound consequences for all of the Americas, drawing the people of all three continents into the complex Atlantic world that emerged from their mutual encounters. Indeed, the many zones of contact where European Christians met indigenous African religions, Arabian Muslim traditions, Indian Hindu civilizations, and even the unfamiliar Christian world of Ethiopia precipitated changes on all sides of these encounters that would become the foundations of an enduring world order built on European colonial domination.

European Conquests in America

Christopher Columbus certainly was not the first outsider to enter the Americas. Evidence of Asian artifacts in present-day Ecuador suggests some sort of transpacific contact in the early centuries of the Christian Era, and Norse explorers attempted unsuccessfully to establish settlements along the northern Atlantic coast of North America in the eleventh century.[21] Columbus' significance is not as "discoverer" of America but as colonizer. His voyages to the Americas in the late fifteenth century initiated permanent European settlement in the western hemisphere. Consequently, Columbus' ambitions as a zealous crusader for the Christian cause also opened the way for Christianity to enter the cultural worlds of the Americas.

The Spanish come to America

While Portuguese explorers, traders, and missionaries were establishing themselves in Africa during the fifteenth century, their Spanish neighbors were engaged in a religious war at home to recapture areas under Muslim rule. Arab and Berber Muslims had entered the Iberian Peninsula, the area of present-day Spain and

Portugal, early in the eighth century from northern Africa and remained until nearly the end of the fifteenth century. Under the rule of Islamic law, Muslims had devised a social order in the Iberian Peninsula that on the one hand allowed Jews and Christians to flourish as subordinated groups but on the other limited their social mobility and economic opportunities. Some of the Christian leaders, however, were not content to remain under Muslim rule. They engaged in *reconquista*, a series of holy wars to reconquer formerly Christian regions and oust their Muslim overlords. Joining a tradition of medieval crusades that began in the last decade of the eleventh century with Pope Urban II's call to defend Christian lands against Muslim invaders, Iberian Christians took up arms against their Muslim rulers and pursued a military conquest that eventuated in one of the few successful Christian crusades. They recaptured the city of Toledo in the eleventh century, and other major cities in the thirteenth century. But the Muslims held on in the southern areas of the Iberian Peninsula until 1492, when the Christian monarchs Isabella of the Spanish province of Castile and Ferdinand of Aragon finally recaptured Granada and drove out the Muslim rulers for good.[22]

Box 1.4   *Convivencia*

For nearly eight centuries, Muslims ruled significant parts of the Iberian Peninsula with a social system that historians have described as *convivencia*, a term literally meaning "living together" but usually translated as "coexistence," connoting a mutual acceptance and creative influence between different social groups. Under this system of governance, Christian and Jewish people enjoyed official status as *dhimmis*, a special designation that recognized their close relatedness to Islam as people who shared significant religious narratives, scriptures, and histories with Muslims as descendants of the patriarch Abraham. This approach to governing subordinated groups by giving them special privileges allowed for centuries of peaceful coexistence between Muslims, Christians, and Jews, although there remained a degree of mutual friction, rivalry, and suspicion between groups. Yet, despite occasional tensions that sometimes erupted in violence, the Muslim rulers in the Iberian Peninsula managed to encourage a vibrant intellectual culture where the greatest of Muslim, Jewish, and Christian thinkers of the era came together in a fertile context of intellectual, philosophical, and artistic accomplishment. Great universities in the Iberian Peninsula became not only centers of study and learning but also sites of cultural transmission. For instance, the classical heritage of such monumental thinkers as Plato and Aristotle had been lost for the most part to Europeans for centuries, but their philosophical and literary works had been preserved and studied by Muslim scholars, who reintroduced them to western Europe through universities that were among the great achievements of the Muslim rulers in the Iberian Peninsula.[23]

The end of Muslim rule in the Iberian Peninsula in 1492 had monumental consequences for the future of the world, and especially for the Americas. The newly triumphant Christian monarchs immediately ordered the expulsion of all Jews from lands they now controlled, bringing to an end centuries of *convivencia* and the legacies of peaceful coexistence among religious people of different traditions. Tens of thousands of Iberian Jews either left or became *conversos*, Jewish converts to Christianity. At the same time that shiploads of Jews were departing from Iberian ports, a small fleet of three ships under the command of Christopher Columbus was leaving in hopes of finding a new route to the Indies.

Columbus carried with him the confidence of a Christian nation triumphant in its crusades to conquer the non-Christian infidels and spread the gospel of Christianity to all lands. He initiated centuries of conflict emboldened by a con-quistador vision of God's providence. Success in driving the Muslims out of the Iberian Peninsula and back into Africa fueled the expansionist ambitions of the Spanish Christians and motivated them to extend their culture of conquest to the Americas. After centuries of battling Muslims, the Spanish Christians were accustomed to a society organized around military conflict with the heroic conquistador assuming a role of saintly proportions. But, with the final defeat of Muslim rule in Granada, the conquistadors needed a new adversary to conquer. The Spaniards were ripe for "discovering" new lands for conquest. They entered the contact zones of the Americas confident in their providential mission.

Their enthusiasm for conquest was based upon a profoundly religious hope of a Christian millennial age. As they recaptured areas that had been under Muslim control, the Spaniards set about to convert non-Christians to Christianity. This was accomplished less by force than by adaptation. Former mosques became Christian churches with remarkably little architectural renovation.[24] When Fernando de Talavera (1428–1507) became the first archbishop of Granada after its return to Christian control in 1492, he studied Arabic language, music, and dance and he used these in his efforts to convert local Muslims to Christianity.[25] His evangelizing enjoyed the support of a powerful and influential group of Franciscan friars, the Order of Friars Minor. They preached a millennial view of world history that rec-ognized divine providence in Christian successes of conquering Muslims. According to their prognostications, the successful conversion of all peoples in the world to the Christian faith would herald the end days foretold in the Christian sacred texts. It was the divine duty of the Christian monarchs, the Friars Minor believed, to precipitate this promised age by conquering and converting non-Christian peoples.[26]

These efforts to convert the infidel, in particular the Muslim residents of Granada after it fell back into Christian hands, bolstered millennial hopes of converting the newly "discovered" (by Europeans) peoples of the Americas in order to bring about the Christian **apocalypse**. From the beginning of the colonial enterprise in the Americas, religious conquest motivated and justified European activities. But bringing Christianity to America was no simple task. Christians met native inhabitants in contact zones where both sides vied to incorporate the other into their own understanding of the world.

Conquistadors in Mexico

A particularly dramatic and consequential example of the Spanish encounter of native peoples occurred in Mexico. The Spanish conquistador Hernán Cortés (1485–1547) arrived with his small band of soldiers in November 1519 at the outskirts of the magnificent city of Tenochtitlan, the seat of the ruling Mexicas (or Aztecs). The imposing splendor and overwhelming size of the Mexica capital astounded the Spaniards; Bernal Díaz del Castillo (1492–1585), who accompanied Cortés that day, recalled,

> [W]e were amazed and said that it was like the enchantments they tell of in the legend of Amadis, on account of the great towers and cues and buildings rising from the water, and built of masonry. And some of our soldiers even asked whether the things that we saw were not a dream ... I do not know how to describe it, seeing things as we did that had never been heard of or seen before, not even dreamed about.[27]

With a population over two hundred thousand in the city and more than a million in the valley, Tenochtitlan was larger and more sophisticated than any city in Europe, nearly five times as large as London at the time. An advanced system of aqueducts brought water and sanitation to the city, and the complex network of *chinampas*, or floating gardens, produced food for the population. All males attended public schools, where they learned the history of the Mexicas and the intricate details of religious life, as well as their civic duties as citizens of the empire; some also became adept in their oral traditions and the system of writing that supported it, in the highly developed poetic tradition, in art and architecture, and other facets of Mexica culture. The Spaniards found in the grand city of Tenochtitlan extravagance rarely known in Europe; Díaz del Castillo was especially impressed by the royal aviary and its magnificent collection of native birds; at the zoo, however, he decried "the infernal noise when the lions and tigers roared and the jackals and foxes howled and the serpents hissed."[28]

As much as the dazzling city of Tenochtitlan amazed Cortés and his companions, they were horrified by the religious practices of the Mexica people. At the center of the city was a sacred precinct of religious structures dominated by the Templo Mayor, the great pyramidic temple that the Mexica knew as Coatepec, or Serpent Mountain, with shrines to Tlaloc, god of rain and agriculture, and to Huitzilopochtli, the deity of war and tribute.[29] Upon these shrines the Mexica performed human heart sacrifices on an unimaginable scale; during special festivals that marked auspicious times in their calendar system, thousands of sacrificial victims were offered in large public rituals that encompassed virtually the entire city of Tenochtitlan. Moreover, this temple stood at the very center of the Mexica cosmos as well as at the heart of the extensive empire of the Mexica rulers. Causeways leading in the four cardinal directions connected the island city of Tenochtitlan to the shores of the expansive lake in which it stood and with the outlying areas under Mexica rule and influence. The temple of the built mountain of Coatepec also united the terrestrial world with the celestial realm where divine events took place, as well as with the underworld of the dead. At the very center of the city, of the empire, and of the cosmos, the Mexica performed their religious spectacles that nourished the divine powers of their universe and thereby sustained their civilization.

Figure 1.4 The Spaniards were horrified by Mexica rituals of human sacrifice. This drawing shows a ritual heart sacrifice atop one of the Mexica temple structures. (Courtesy of Richard Erdoes Papers, Yale Collection of Western Americana, Beinecke Rare Book and Manuscript Library.)

Cortés entered into the contact zone of this Mexica world with brash confidence. In a scene that would be repeated innumerable times in various ways during the coming centuries, the Christian conquistador marched toward Tenochtitlan to confront the supreme ruler, Motecuçomo II (ca. 1466–1520; the Aztec king's name is sometimes rendered as Motecuhzoma, Moctezuma, Mutezuma, or Montezuma). It was by all accounts a momentous occasion.[30] Cortés' report of their first meeting relates how the Mexica sovereign told of an ancient tradition regarding a great ancestor-god who had long ago departed across the sea who would someday return and, according to Motecuçomo, "conquer this land and take us as their vassals."[31]

We cannot know for certain exactly how Motecuçomo and other native peoples of central Mexico interpreted the sudden arrival of Spaniards on their shores; the eyewitness accounts are only from the Spanish perspective or from native accounts filtered through Spanish conventions and genres. But, despite the compromised nature of the sources, evidence suggests that at least initially Motecuçomo regarded Cortés as the Mexica hero-ancestor Quetzalcoatl, whose tradition was long established in their sacred texts and articulated in sacred architecture and ritual performances across central Mexico. Native writers working in the latter half of the sixteenth century tell of Motecuçomo's consultations with "the elders and wise men of his kingdom," who all agreed that "the one who had arrived was Quetzalcoatl. A long time ago he had gone by sea to join the Sun God, who had summoned him to the kingdom of Tlapalla, leaving word he would return, and that all their predecessors had expected him. It was impossible that he would be anyone else."[32] It seems that the Mexicas made sense of the impending cataclysm that would crumble their empire and the world as they knew it by appealing to their sacred traditions.

On the other side of that first meeting between Motecuçomo and Cortés in the outskirts of the city that the Spaniards would rename Mexico City, we know with greater certainty how the Christian conquerors understood their mission in the land they would colonize as New Spain. Cortés arrived on the Mexican mainland with the authority to act in "the service of God and their highnesses," the royal monarchs of Spain. God, as confirmed by the Pope in Rome, had entrusted the Spanish king with bringing the native peoples of the Indies (the region first claimed by Columbus, which would later be known as the Americas) into the Christian realm, making them faithful servants of God and loyal subjects of the monarch in Spain as God's earthly representative.[33] Cortés arrived in Mexico with the crusader's zeal for Christian conquest. Indeed, both Motecuçomo and Cortés understood their initial encounter as a religious event of epic proportions.

The great Mexica dynasty, however, could not withstand the invasion of Europeans. Already overextended politically, economically, and militarily, the Mexicas were vulnerable to a sudden shift in the balance of power. Like indigenous groups throughout the Americas, the Mexicas were in perpetual conflict and war with rival groups. Consequently, with a small band of Spanish soldiers supported by a vast army of native allies, and aided by diseases that the Spaniards unwittingly

---

Box 1.5   The divine arrival of Europeans

The notion that European explorers came as gods into the indigenous worlds of the Americas is a surprisingly common theme in accounts of their first encounters. Motecuçomo's initial assumption that Cortés was Quetzalcoatl echoes similar stories of native reactions to Europeans throughout the Americas. The Delaware people of the mid-Atlantic coast, for instance, regarded their first sighting of a Dutch ship in the early seventeenth century as the coming of "Mannitto," their Supreme Being. They prepared for meeting this great deity with meat for sacrifices, by arranging their religious effigies in proper order, and by staging a dance for his benefit.[34]

The frequency of these stories, however, about native peoples regarding European newcomers as deities raises doubts concerning their trustworthiness. Virtually all such reports come through the filter of European interpretations of Indian reactions, sometimes decades after the purported incidents. Since there is no contemporary native documentation of their first encounters, we will never know for certain how natives regarded the first Europeans to come into their world. Certainly many of them must have resorted to their religious worldviews to interpret the sudden appearance of strangers. But native religions display great diversity, invoking skepticism about the similarity of such stories, and often their religious understandings include far greater complexity about supernatural beings than the European terms "gods" or "demons" encompass. Very likely, the notion of Indians regarding the Europeans as "gods" has more to do with how Europeans interpreted native responses and behaviors than it does with actual indigenous interpretations of their first encounters. Indeed, such stories actually may have more to say about the Europeans' self-regard, bestowing divine status upon themselves, than about the Indians' understandings of otherness.

---

introduced to vulnerable native populations, Cortés prevailed over Motecuçomo in a protracted war that ended with the fall of Tenochtitlan in 1521. After defeating the Mexicas and taking control of their empire, the conquistadors began to dismantle the splendid Native American city and to build upon its ruins the colonial capital of Mexico City. As they did with hundreds of other native shrines throughout the Americas, the Spanish conquerors razed the great Templo Mayor; leveled the revered mountain, Coatepec, that marked the sacred center of the Mexica world; and erected on the site their own holy place, a Christian church, where they could perform the rituals of the European religion. The sacred precinct of indigenous ritual sacrifices became the place of the Christian Mass, another sort of sacrificial performance, heralding the dominance of Christianity at the heart of the Spanish colonial empire.

Africans in New Spain

Into this colonial world of Europeans and Native Americans the Spaniards also introduced Africans. Shortly following their conquest of central Mexico, they began importing slaves from Africa to provide labor for the colony of New Spain. As diseases, famine, wars, and displacement killed millions of native peoples of Mexico, the Europeans relied on Africans to fill their need for additional laborers in the mines and on the ranches of their newly conquered territories.[35] Stripped of their native religious traditions and separated from the sacred places and intimate communities of their African homelands, many of the newly arrived slaves underwent a process of acculturation to European ways in New Spain. Spanish colonial policy encouraged evangelization among slaves and facilitated their religious conversion to Catholicism. Colonial administrators regarded the integration of African slaves into Christian society as a useful strategy for stabilizing and developing the colony through shared culture and religion between Europeans and Africans. This approach enjoyed some degree of success as the rituals of Catholic worship and the many festivals celebrating the Catholic saints and other religious holidays helped relieve the inherent tensions of the slave system while offering momentary respite from the hardships of bondage. Moreover, the ethical logic underlying the Christian narrative urged slaves to remain obedient in deferring to the demands of their masters in order to achieve spiritual equality in the paradise of the afterlife.[36]

Official policy in New Spain promoted the humane treatment of slaves as citizens and Christians, with opportunities for liberation through purchase of their freedom or through policies that encouraged manumission. Few slaves, however, actually gained their liberty through these policies; more successful means to freedom were through intermarriage and miscegenation. The Catholic Church urged slaveowners involved in illicit sexual unions with their slaves to consecrate those relationships through marriage, and a number of slave women gained freedom this way. Other slaves found freedom by marrying free native peoples and integrating into the native population; even when Spain later decreed that such marriages would not liberate enslaved spouses, such unions with free Indians continued so that their children would not be born into slavery. In addition, many of the children born of illicit unions between slaves and non-slaves were freed, contributing to a substantial free mulatto population in the colony of New Spain.[37]

Yet, despite the efforts of the Church and the colonial government to enforce humane circumstances for enslaved peoples, pervasive mistreatment and systematic cruelty characterized much of slave life in Spain's American colonies. Slave rebellions became common, even where efforts to Christianize the slaves had enjoyed success. In fact, the first uprising in the colonies in 1523 involved Christian slaves who celebrated their freedom by erecting crosses to demonstrate their gratitude to God for their liberty.[38]

A significant number of African slaves fled bondage and took up life among native peoples of Mexico. These fugitive communities, known as "maroons," with their mixing of racial groups and commingling of cultural traditions, including religion, became sites of resistance to the colonial policies of conquest, subjugation, and enslavement. They were also fertile ground for the processes of transculturation as Native American and African traditions, influenced by the introduction of European Christianity, developed distinctive cultural forms, including novel religious beliefs and practices. In fact, by the seventeenth century the commingling of African and indigenous American populations had become so pervasive that the Inquisition in New Spain devised a complex system of racial categories to distinguish between the various mixtures of Native Americans, Africans, and Europeans; the most numerous of the mulatto groups was *mulato pardo*, the "dark mulatto" of Native American and African parentage.[39] As sources of innovative religious practices, the mulatto populations often came to the attention of the Inquisitors.

Box 1.6   The Inquisition

Christian concerns regarding the sincerity of recent converts to Christianity in the Iberian Peninsula led the monarchs Ferdinand and Isabella in 1480 to authorize the establishment of the Tribunal of the Holy Office of the Inquisition, commonly known as the Spanish Inquisition, for the investigation and punishment of religious heresies and other deviations from Christian orthodoxy. The Inquisition's immediate concern had to do with former Jews, known as *conversos*, who had converted to Christianity, in many instances under coercive conditions. The Inquisition sought to ensure orthodoxy among the *converso* Spaniards, who were often accused of maintaining only a pretense of Christian faith while continuing to practice their Jewish traditions.[40] The Inquisition's role shifted, however, with new challenges posed by the Protestant **reformations** of the sixteenth century; in addition, Spanish colonization of peoples practicing unfamiliar Native American and African religions introduced a wide range of heretical unorthodoxies to the Inquisitorial tribunal. With the Spanish conquest of Mexico, the Holy Office established itself in New Spain, where it undertook investigations of Native Americans, Africans imported as slaves, free mulattos, errant Spanish colonists, and former Jewish *conversos*. In its earliest years in the new colony, the Inquisition contributed to the persecution of native peoples; in fact, the first Inquisition trial in Mexico, in 1522, was of an Indian accused of concubinage. But, by the middle of the sixteenth century, Indian populations were for the most part exempt from the Inquisition in colonial Mexico as Church and colonial officials shifted from a strategy of persecution and punishment to one that concentrated on securing a sincere and lasting conversion to the Catholic faith.[41] African slaves, however, continued to suffer under the Inquisition; their most common crime was blasphemy, often committed by denouncing God and his saints while enduring severe punishments for running away or other misdeeds.[42]

Reluctant conquerors

As records of the Inquisition clearly indicate, encounters between indigenous Americans and European invaders brought significant conflicts, more commonly away from the field of battle than in actual armed confrontation. In places where Europeans prevailed, their subsequent treatment of native peoples raised difficult moral questions for at least a few of the more reflective Christian thinkers. The precipitous decline of native populations in the first decades of European presence in the Americas caused great alarm for a number of Spanish theologians and others, including the Dominican missionary Bartolomé de las Casas (ca. 1484–1566), who spent most of his life working among Indians in the Americas and who articulated the profound moral issues for Christian efforts there. Las Casas came to the Americas as one of the earliest priests serving in the Spanish colonies, gaining prominence among his fellow colonists and even himself acquiring Indian slaves. But he experienced a profound conversion in 1514 that brought painful awareness of the Indians' plight, of their extreme suffering and cruel treatment at the hands of the Spanish colonizers.[43] For the rest of his long life, he remained an indefatigable defender of Indians' rights and a formidable opponent to colonial administrators, jurists, and theologians who justified enslavement and maltreatment of native peoples according to long-established Christian principles. Las Casas engaged in a famous debate in 1550–1551 with Juan Ginés de Sepúlveda (1489–1573), an articulate defender of the colonists' right to wage war on Indians and enslave them based on the presumed inferior status of indigenous peoples as barbarians. In their exchange, las Casas laid out legal and theological arguments demonstrating native peoples' humanity and innocence. For him, wholesale slaughter and enslavement of Indians was not only unjustified but also anathema to the Christian principles that were the foundation of the European presence in the Americas.

At the same time that las Casas was debating the appropriate Christian treatment of native peoples based on his many years of experience as a missionary working in the contact zones of the American colonies, another Spaniard's experience likewise brought him to a more profound sympathy for the humane treatment of Indians. The account of Álvar Núñez Cabeza de Vaca (ca. 1490–1559) chronicles his experience on an ill-fated expedition that left him and three comrades, including an African slave by the name of Estebanico (ca. 1500–1539), as the first foreigners from across the Atlantic Ocean to spend significant time in the interior of North America. During their ordeal, the four survivors of the expedition not only relied on their own religious traditions but also incorporated elements of the indigenous religions that they encountered. Their willingness to conform to native practices allowed them not merely to survive but also to flourish as venerated religious healers among the tribes of what would become the southwestern United States.

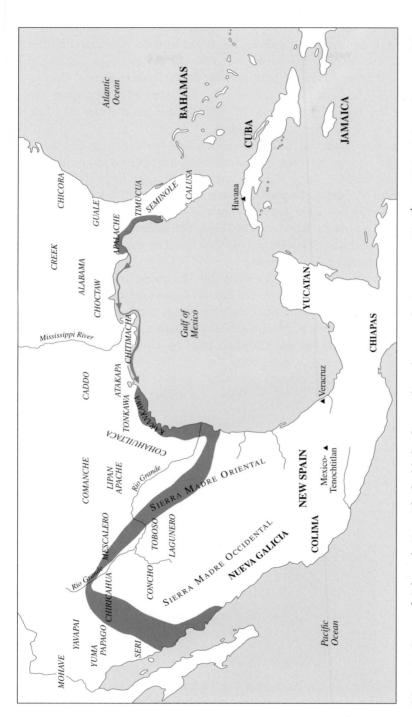

Map 1.3 Route of Cabeza de Vaca. The highlighted areas show the general route traversed by Álvar Núñez Cabeza de Vaca and his companions between 1528 and 1536 from the Florida peninsula by raft to what is today the Gulf Coast area of Texas, and eventually to the Pacific Ocean in what is now Mexico. Some of the major Native American groups are listed. The triangles show the locations of Spanish colonial settlements.

Cabeza de Vaca served as royal treasurer on an expedition led by the Spanish conquistador Pánfilo de Narváez (1478–1528). Narváez had been among the earliest Europeans in the Americas, gaining fame and fortune as a conquistador of Cuba. He was also a vocal opponent of Bartolomé de las Casas, arguing that enslavement of Indians was in the best interests of the Spanish crown. Hoping to extend his influence and add to his fortunes, Narváez received in December 1526 a grant to settle the region along the Gulf of Mexico from the central coast of Mexico all the way to the Florida peninsula.

After a series of setbacks and misfortunes, including severe storms that blew the expedition far off course, Narváez landed on the Florida peninsula in April 1528. But his quest for fortune there soon encountered disaster from illness, Indian attacks, shortages of food and water, and desertion by a number of the expeditionary force. Having lost their boats, the survivors built rafts that carried them westward to what is now the Gulf coast of Texas. The native peoples they encountered there captured the hapless explorers as slaves, and eventually only four members of the original expedition remained.

During his captivity, Cabeza de Vaca learned the languages and cultural ways of the indigenous peoples of the region. He eventually was reunited with the other three remaining members of the Narváez expedition, and together they moved from village to village attempting to find their way back to the Spanish-held territories of New Spain. Along the way, they earned a reputation as powerful healers.

Figure 1.5   Cabeza de Vaca and his companions spent eight years among the indigenous people of North America, where they earned reputations as healers with supernatural powers. (Courtesy of New York Public Library, #814629.)

According to Cabeza de Vaca's account, they enjoyed great success in making the ill and crippled healthy again, and he even claims to have brought back to life a man who had died. In his report, Cabeza de Vaca is careful to attribute their healing powers to the Christian god, but his descriptions of their healing practices also include native medicinal traditions he learned while living with various tribes. His successful combination of Christian faith and native healing brought him and his companions great fame among the indigenous tribes they encountered.

Cabeza de Vaca came to North America as a conquistador, an officer of an expedition to conquer new lands and extract wealth from the people there. His years among native peoples, first as a slave and later as a religious healer, changed him profoundly, especially in regard to his attitudes about the indigenous groups he encountered. For the rest of his life, Cabeza de Vaca remained a defender of the Indians, which put him in conflict with European conquerors and settlers. Unlike those who sought only wealth and personal glory, Cabeza de Vaca emerged from the contact zone with an enlarged understanding of the human community.[44]

We must keep in mind, however, that the noble efforts and sympathetic attitudes of Europeans such as Bartolomé de las Casas and Álvar Núñez Cabeza de Vaca were rare exceptions, and even the most compassionate Europeans never regarded non-Christian societies as being as equally advanced as their own. The Spanish experience of *reconquista*, their successful crusade against Muslims in the Iberian Peninsula, strengthened their confidence that a Christian triumph was imminent and would encompass all peoples of the world in a millennial age. As the Spanish conquistadors successfully subjugated the native peoples of the Caribbean islands, Mexico and Central America, and Peru and eventually extended their empire into North America, they were certain that they were fulfilling God's plan. We now know that, although religion, technology, and culture all contributed to their success, the single most important element was biological. New diseases that the Europeans introduced to vulnerable indigenous populations in America gave the conquistadors a crucial advantage that Native Americans could not overcome. A new Christian culture of European colonial domination arose on the ruins of traditional native cultures.

Native Encounters

As European conquerors and colonists entered into the diverse regions of the Americas, they found many different native peoples with distinct cultures, languages, and religious practices, many of which seemed bizarre and even frightening to Christian sensibilities. In central Mexico the conquistadors marveled at grand urban centers but they were horrified to witness (and in some cases to become victims of) the elaborate spectacles of human sacrifice. Further north, Europeans met sedentary peoples who inhabited permanent villages sustained by agriculture, and elsewhere they confronted a range of native cultures that relied on the natural environment for sustenance through various combinations of hunting animals, harvesting wild plant foods, and growing crops. Just as the Europeans discovered them, all of these indigenous groups likewise discovered the European newcomers who entered their homelands, often accompanied by slaves from Africa and many of them with other Native Americans brought from elsewhere to serve the Christian conquerors. Time and again Europeans and Native Americans met directly in contact zones throughout the Americas, but often their first contacts were indirect, through rumor, trade, and the spread of diseases that often preceded the arrival of the invaders. In virtually every case, the delicate balances of native societies suffered extraordinary disruptions with the arrival of foreigners into their sacred geographies.

Places of emergence

Across a broad region that today encompasses New Mexico, Arizona, and parts of Texas, Colorado, and Utah, the Pueblo peoples built permanent villages that include the oldest continuously inhabited communities in North America. Perhaps the oldest of these is Oraibi (now called Old Oraibi), which dates from around 900 CE and continues today as a Hopi village in northeast Arizona.[45] According to Hopi traditions, their forebears emerged into this world from an underworld realm and then wandered the earth before settling on three adjacent mesas in the harsh desert country. They settled as sedentary agriculturists to grow blue corn on the mesas, where they built villages that included, besides domestic living spaces, the sacred spaces of their Kachina religion. In fact, the villages themselves reflect Hopi religious sensibilities. As a contemporary Hopi scholar relates,

> During the time of our migrations and when we were building our first Hopi communities, we settled on the mesas as Cloud People. One group migrating from the south was designated as the Water People, my people. We were blessed as Cloud Children by the great Water Serpent, our Father. And so, like clouds, we settled on the high mesas, and as Cloud People we designed our buildings after the cumulus clouds. Our homes are multi-storied structures, made of native sandstone and plastered with mud. Our multi-storied Hopi architecture is a reflection of the high-climbing cumulus clouds.[46]

With rain as the sacred gift that allows their crops to grow and their villages to thrive, Hopi architecture displays their devotion to the powers that bring life-giving waters.

At the center of the traditional Hopi village is a plaza where religious dances are performed, and in the plaza are *kivas*, the underground chambers of sacred activities. Much of what goes on inside the *kivas* has remained a closely guarded secret over the centuries, available only to properly initiated members of the Hopi community. What is apparent, however, is the religious significance of the *kiva*

Box 1.7   The Anasazi, or Ancient Pueblo peoples

Archaeologists have identified thousands of ancient village sites of people commonly known as the Anasazi, or Ancient Pueblo peoples. Covering a large area in what is now Arizona, New Mexico, Texas, Utah, and Colorado, these earliest Pueblo communities probably began around 1200 BCE. The earliest groups lived in partially subterranean dwellings known as pit houses, but by the eighth century CE they were building stone or adobe dwellings in above-ground clusters.[47] At the height of their civilization, from roughly the eleventh through the thirteenth centuries CE, they inhabited very complex and sophisticated villages that also included numerous *kivas*, large ceremonial chambers of circular or rectangular shape that lay entirely, or sometimes only partially, below the surface. The inhabitants of these sites, however, suddenly abandoned their villages sometime around the end of the thirteenth century. Their disappearance remains a mystery, although archaeological evidence suggests that internal or intertribal conflicts precipitated by climate change and possible environmental degradation may have contributed to their migrations to the south.

No one knows for certain what the inhabitants of these ancient settlements called themselves. The name "Anasazi" has become popular among many archaeologists as well as the general public, but it is a term with derogatory overtones from the Navajo language, traditional enemies of the Pueblo peoples. Many of the Hopi and other Pueblo peoples, who regard the ancient inhabitants of these sites as their ancestors, find the term "Anasazi" offensive. As an alternative, some scholars prefer the terms "Ancient Pueblo" or "Ancestral Pueblo." Others have suggested using native Pueblo terms, such as the Hopi word "Hisatsinom" or the Zuni word "Enote."[48]

structures themselves. Most have an opening in the roof with a ladder descending into the interior of the chamber; inside, a small hole in the floor of the *kiva* is the *sipapu*, representing the mythical place where the ancestors first emerged from the three previous worlds into the present "fourth world."[49] In the Hopi vision of life, all beings and forms on the terrestrial Earth came forth from the original *sipapu*, and deceased beings return to the nonmaterial world through the *sipapu*. The six directions of the Hopi world (the four cardinal directions, plus up into the celestial realm and down into the underworld) all emanate from this sacred place of emergence, represented in the ritual architecture of the *kiva*.[50] Moreover, ceremonial exiting from the *kiva* into the village plaza ritually reenacts the original emergence of the first ancestors into the fourth world. The sacred precinct at the center of the village is the nexus of the Hopi universe.

Figure 1.6   These ruins of an ancient *kiva* in present-day New Mexico reveal the structure of the underground ritual spaces that serve as ceremonial centers of Pueblo communities, from ancient times to the present. (Courtesy of the Library of Congress, HAVS NM, 23-CHACA, 1–2.)

Europeans first entered this Hopi universe in 1540 when members of a Spanish expedition led by Francisco Vásquez de Coronado (1510–1554), which included a Franciscan missionary, invaded the Hopi mesas. They forced the Hopis to surrender, but their search for riches soon led them elsewhere. It was not until the next century, in 1629, that the Spanish left a more permanent mark by establishing the first Christian mission among the Hopi. Their efforts to Christianize Pueblo peoples, however, met with little success in the furthest outlying areas where the Hopi resided. Consequently, the Hopi have been able to continue their ancient ways of life and to practice their native religious traditions with only minimal interference from Christian outsiders.[51]

The harvest of sacred animals

The relative freedom from colonial interference that the Hopis experienced was an exceptionally unusual circumstance among the indigenous peoples of the Americas. More often than not, Native American societies experienced severe disruptions of their familiar worlds and traditions, with many native groups becoming entirely extinct. The European newcomers devastated indigenous people with newly introduced diseases; with military conquest and subservience under colonial rule, often involving enslavement of native peoples; and with forced conversions to European cultural ways, including the eradication of indigenous religious traditions in favor of Christianity. One major point of contention between Native Americans and the Europeans who arrived to colonize the Americas was their respective views of the land and the natural world. Europeans tended to view the land as a wilderness adversary to be tamed and made economically productive, usually through extractive activities such as mining and trapping, or through agricultural improvements. In contrast, many Native American societies understood the natural world as an integrated whole that included humans as a part of the natural balance. Consequently, European goods and ways of life, including Christianity, threw the native worlds out of balance and in many cases plunged them into a tragic downward spiral from which they were unable to recover; those groups that survived often did so by adapting their native ways to the

---

Box 1.8   Animism

A common form of religion among relatively small hunter and gatherer societies has been identified as "animism." The animistic worldview regards non-human animals and plants, a variety of nonliving objects, and other natural phenomena as being animated by an invisible force or power that transcends its material being; put more simply, it regards these things as having spirits. Among Native Americans, the Algonquian people called this power *manitou*, and in the Iroquois language it was *orenda*. For many animistic orientations, this possession of a spiritual essence is true not only for living beings, such as plants and animals, but also for features of the land such as mountains, rivers, streams, and lakes; for unusual climatological phenomena such as thunder, lightning, and tornadoes; and even for such inanimate objects as rocks, soil, and minerals. Most of these animistic religious systems rely on **shamans**, specially designated individuals who are able to "travel" to spiritual realms, usually in a trance induced by special rituals and practices. These shamans, who are common in many indigenous cultures throughout the Americas and around the world, lead communal rituals and celebrations as they communicate with spirits of the natural world for powers in healing, fertility, food-gathering and hunting, war, and other vital concerns of human well-being.

Animistic religious orientations were common among Native American groups of North America before the arrival of Europeans, and many continue even to the present day in some form or another. In virtually all cases, the animistic religious orientation mediates the relationship between humans and the natural environment, as well as the social relationships among individuals and between tribal groups. Thus, animism provided much of the logic and structure of indigenous life for many groups throughout the Americas, including their social systems, economics, aesthetics, food acquisition and preparation, migration, and virtually every other aspect of their native ways of life.[52]

demands of European culture, sometimes abandoning their indigenous traditions and assimilating themselves entirely to European traditions.

One of the earliest North American groups to encounter Europeans was the Mi'kmaqs (or Micmacs), the easternmost tribe of the Algonquian federation, situated along the far northern Atlantic coast, occupying what are now the maritime provinces of Canada and northern portions of New England. They had first encountered Europeans as early as the eleventh century CE when Vikings first landed on the island of Newfoundland, and may have met Basque fisherman from Europe who occasionally fished the Grand Banks off Newfoundland in the late fifteenth century. Prior to significant influence from Europeans, the Mi'kmaqs understood the relationship between their society and the natural, nonhuman world in religious terms. A spiritual link formed a sacred bond between humans and the natural world, including the land and all that it contained (animals, plants, minerals, rivers and lakes, even the ocean and coastline), and shamans served as intermediaries in a complex web of relationships between human society and the environment. These relationships made such life-sustaining pursuits as hunting into religious activities. The killing of animals was an important economic resource for indigenous Mi'kmaq people, for food, clothing, and a variety of everyday needs, but they did not take the abundance of wildlife for granted. They regarded their prey as sacred, and they killed only to fulfill their basic needs. For the Mi'kmaqs, the entire hunting process was regulated by spiritual concerns, with shamans communicating between humans and the spirits of animals. The "holy occupation" of hunting, as one historian has characterized it, involved a set of religious guidelines and ritual practices that limited the killing of sacred animals and maintained the intimate spiritual link between human hunters and animal prey.[53]

The Mi'kmaqs' reverence for the entirety of the natural environment began to change with regular exposure to Europeans, starting early in the sixteenth century when fishing fleets from Europe made annual voyages to the Grand Banks fishery and the Gulf of St. Lawrence. These fishermen initiated trade with the native peoples of the region, exchanging such European goods as beads, kettles, and knives for animal furs. They also introduced diseases that would decimate the native population and weaken or destroy much of traditional Mi'kmaq culture, including religion. As thousands of native people fell ill to ailments previously unknown in the region, with entire communities dying, the ineffectiveness of the shamans and their healing practices undermined confidence in their spiritual capabilities. Without an effective response to disease, the authority of the shamans eroded quickly as competing claims entered into Mi'kmaq society, including both economic and spiritual alternatives to their traditional ways. The usefulness and desirability of European material goods created demand to supply more animal furs for trading purposes, and the deterioration of the shamans' spiritual authority removed the limitations on killing animals. At the same time, an alternative spiritual system arrived from Europe to displace the Mi'kmaqs' traditional religion. Jesuit missionaries from France, beginning in the first decade of the seventeenth century, brought a different religious outlook; the European religion of Jesus provided an explanation for the misfortune that the Mi'kmaqs suffered by painting their native religion as the work of the devil. At the same time, Christianity offered a justification for abandoning the Mi'kmaqs' traditional ways in favor of accepting the material benefits of European goods and technology. The Jesuits came, as one of the early missionaries reported, "to domesticate and civilize them" and "to make them susceptible of receiving the doctrines of the faith and of the Christian and Catholic religion, and later, to penetrate further into the regions beyond."[54] Intent on spreading the Christian message and "civilizing" the native peoples, these missionaries sought to conquer the land by converting its people; in the process they displaced the indigenous understanding of an intimate and holy relationship to the natural world. The sacred geography of the Mi'kmaq world was little more than an untamed "region" to be "penetrated" in the eyes of the European people carrying their Christian message.

It is evident from our twenty-first-century vantage that, despite their best intentions, European missionaries introduced more than Christianity to native peoples

Figure 1.7 French Jesuits brought Christianity and European civilization to Native Americans. This nineteenth-century drawing titled "The Jesuit Teacher" depicts the missionary as benevolent teacher instructing a rapt Indian in the powers of literacy. (Courtesy of New York Public Library, #807998.)

Box 1.9   French Jesuit missionaries in North America

Missionaries of the Society of Jesus (widely known as the Jesuits) began their work among the Mi'kmaq people in the first decade of the seventeenth century; eventually, they expanded their missionary activities in North America along the St. Lawrence River in what is now Canada, as well as in the Great Lakes region and the upper Mississippi River valley. They also served French possessions in Louisiana.

The primary goal of the Jesuits in New France was the conversion of indigenous peoples to Christianity. Their unrelenting dedication to this effort relied to a large extent on the teachings of Ignatius of Loyola (1491–1556), the founder of the Society of Jesus. His book of *Spiritual Exercises*, a collection of meditations, prayers, and mental exercises for Christian life, teaches his followers to subordinate their own will to the will of Christ. According to Ignatius, Christ's will includes conquest of "all the lands of the infidel." This conquest, at least as the Jesuit missionaries understood it, involved the eradication of indigenous religions and the introduction of Christianity to the conquered people. Nevertheless, Ignatius advocated a tolerant strategy of accommodating native beliefs and customs that did not contradict the Christian teachings of the Catholic Church. He instructed missionaries to learn from the ways of Satan, who, he noted, "goes in by the other's door to come out by his own." Tolerance, according to Ignatius, would help the Jesuits to gain "sympathy and further our good purpose."[55] In New France this meant learning indigenous languages and seeking the trust of native peoples by living among them for extended periods. In many cases, they introduced Christianity by relating it to the Indians' more familiar religious understandings, attempting to demonstrate parallels between the beliefs and practices of Catholicism and native religious systems. On the other hand, the early Jesuit missionaries in New France also needed the support and cooperation of French traders, and they helped facilitate native transitions from an indigenous subsistence economy to an economy intimately tied to Europe through fur trading and an increasing dependence on European goods and technologies. Moreover, Jesuit schools were built in New France for educating Indian youth according to western traditions. Despite their appreciation for native cultures, the Jesuits were powerful colonial agents who sought to instill the values of European culture among the indigenous peoples of New France.[56]

of the Americas. Their inability to comprehend indigenous views of the land, their ignorance of native relationships between natural and human worlds, and their refusal to acknowledge the role of local religious figures in maintaining social and economic balances brought disaster to many native societies. Intent on imposing European civilization, and especially its religious understandings and practices, upon the native peoples inhabiting the wild regions that they were penetrating, Christian missionaries successfully disrupted and in most cases eventually displaced indigenous ways of life throughout the Americas.

New Worlds of Contact

Although Europeans would eventually dominate virtually all of North America, it was a group of Africans who likely were the first non-native peoples to settle in what is now the United States, beginning with an abortive Spanish colony along the coast of present-day South Carolina in 1526. Following an uprising by slaves, who burned much of the settlement and then fled to join the local Guale people, the Spaniards withdrew from the area, leaving behind the rebellious Africans.[57] These first newcomers to North America began a long tradition of outsiders joining forces with sympathetic others and adapting to unfamiliar ways of life in the contact zones of America. This process of adaptation and integration includes innovative mergings of religious practices, beliefs, and perspectives. Those first Africans who fled the Spaniards certainly brought something of their own religious traditions to the Guale people even as they entered a native world built upon Guale religious traditions.

The tale of Europeans bringing to North America Africans who then joined local native peoples illustrates for us the dynamic complexities of the Atlantic world, which generated new relationships among the diverse groups who constituted Europe, Africa, and America. We can see how Portuguese efforts to gain control of Asian trade, motivated in part by their Christian imperative to defeat Muslims, initiated an age of exploration, conquest, and new trading relationships in Africa that in turn established deep interdependencies between Europeans and Africans. Consequently, when the Spanish succeeded in ending Muslim rule on the Iberian Peninsula and then took their millennial vision of conquest to America, they also brought Africans with them as slaves. The conquistadors, along with the missionaries and colonial settlers who followed them, imposed European cultural standards and a Christian worldview, including its moral precepts and system of religious practices, on the indigenous people they conquered. To a lesser degree, the slaves they brought with them across the Atlantic Ocean introduced the traditional perspectives and religious practices of Africa into the transcultural milieu of colonial America. As we sort through the complex relationships between cultures, religious orientations, environments, economic concerns, and political arrangements and take into account the sheer drama of encounter and conflict, we can see how quickly the world changed for a great number of people.

By the end of the sixteenth century, Europeans for the most part had forgotten the initial religious impulse that had brought Columbus to America and that had figured in Portuguese interests in Africa. No longer consumed by the medieval Christian imperative to liberate the Palestinian Holy Land from the Muslims, Europeans in the century following Columbus' voyages took their Christian faith to American shores as justification for extracting wealth from and extending their influence over the people and resources of colonized territories. The Spaniards in the Caribbean and on the American continents, as well as the Portuguese in Brazil, would be followed by other European nations: the Dutch, the French, the English, the Germans, the Russians, and others all would establish colonies in the Americas that brought varying degrees of wealth and power to their nations.

These European colonizing efforts exacted a heavy toll on the indigenous peoples of the Americas. Diseases, the disruption of social and economic networks, and the introduction of foreign cultural practices, including religion, radically transformed native societies. Moreover, the European settlement of the Americas became a global enterprise involving a cross-Atlantic slave trade and increased commerce with Asian peoples. In time, colonial ambitions transformed virtually every corner of the globe as Europeans left the confines of familiar lands and took their Christian orientations to Africa, Asia, and America. Their encounters in these foreign places transformed them and irrevocably changed the worlds of the people they met.

Questions for Discussion

(1)   How was the religious rivalry between Muslims and Christians relevant to the European discovery and conquest of America?
(2)   In what ways did indigenous African religions and Native American religions differ from western European Christianity? In what ways were they similar?
(3)   How did diseases that Europeans introduced to Native American populations affect the colonization of the Americas, specifically in regard to the Europeans' efforts to displace native religions?
(4)   In what ways do the concepts of "contact zone" and "transculturation" help us to make sense of religions in the Atlantic world?

Suggested Primary-Source Readings

William H. Worger, Nancy L. Clark, and Edward A. Alpers, *Africa and the West: A Documentary History*, 2nd edn, 2 vols. (New York: Oxford University Press, 2010): The documents in the first chapter of volume one cover the period of Portuguese conquest and the beginnings of the slave trade between Africans and Europeans.

Kenneth Mills and William B. Taylor, eds., *Colonial Spanish America: A Documentary History* (Wilmington, DE: Scholarly Resources, 1998): This collection of documents and images from Spain's colonies in America includes primary sources on the indigenous peoples prior to contact with Europeans in addition to numerous sources on the first contacts between Europeans and Native Americans as well as the colonial aftermath, with much emphasis on religion. It also includes several documents from the period of *convivencia* in Spain.

Miguel León Portilla, ed., *The Broken Spears: The Aztec Account of the Conquest of Mexico*, expanded and updated edn (Boston, MA: Beacon Press, 1992): Taken from a variety of sources, this volume presents native perspectives on the Spanish conquest of Mexico.

Alvar Núñez Cabeza de Vaca, *The Narrative of Cabeza de Vaca* (Lincoln: University of Nebraska Press, 2003): The dramatic narrative of the first Europeans to enter the interior of the North American continent, Cabeza de Vaca's account tells of his experience as a failed conquistador, his time as a slave of his Indian captors followed by a period as an itinerant merchant among the native tribes of the Texas region, and finally a period as a revered healer and religious figure among the Native Americans. It includes detailed descriptions of native cultures, including references to indigenous religious practices.

Notes

1 Tzvetan Todorov, *The Conquest of America: The Question of the Other*, trans. Richard Howard (New York: HarperPerennial, 1992), 15.

2 Quoted in Martin Dugard, *The Last Voyage of Columbus: Being the Epic Tale of the Great Captain's Fourth Expedition, Including Accounts of Swordfight, Mutiny, Shipwreck, Gold, War, Hurricane, and Discovery* (New York: Little, Brown and Co., 2005), 56.

3 Robert Fuson's introduction to the log of Columbus' first voyage makes this point; see Christopher Columbus, *The Log of Christopher Columbus*, trans. Robert Henderson Fuson (Camden, ME: International Marine Pub. Co., 1987), 1.

4 Ibid., 153, 72, and 73.

5 Mary Louise Pratt, *Imperial Eyes: Travel Writing and Transculturation* (New York: Routledge, 1992), 6.

6 Ibid., 7.

7 Columbus, *The Log of Christopher Columbus*, 157.

8 Ibid., 185.

9 Robert Silverberg, *The Realm of Prester John* (Athens: Ohio University Press, 1996), 194–195.

10 Ibid.

11 Yvonne Patricia Chireau, *Black Magic: Religion and the African American Conjuring Tradition* (Berkeley: University of California Press, 2003), 37.

12 Albert J. Raboteau, *Slave Religion: The "Invisible Institution" in the Antebellum South*, updated edn (New York: Oxford University Press, 2004), 8–10.

13 Ibid., 10–11.

14 Chireau, *Black Magic*, 46 and William D. Piersen, *From Africa to America: African American History from the Colonial Era to the Early Republic, 1526–1790* (New York: Twayne Publishers, Prentice Hall International, 1996), 97.

15 Raboteau, *Slave Religion*, 10–11.

16 Chireau, *Black Magic*, 50.

17 Raboteau, *Slave Religion*, 15.

18 John Thornton, *Africa and Africans in the Making of the Atlantic World, 1400–1680* (New York: Cambridge University Press, 1992), 38.

19 James Duffy, *Portugal in Africa* (Cambridge: Harvard University Press, 1962), 38–43.

20   Silverberg, *The Realm of Prester John*, 204.

21   Emilio Estrada and Betty J. Meggers, "A Complex of Traits of Probable Transpacific Origin on the Coast of Ecuador," *American Anthropologist* 63, no. 5 (1961); Samuel Eliot Morison, *The European Discovery of America* (New York: Oxford University Press, 1971).

22   Joseph F. O'Callaghan, *Reconquest and Crusade in Medieval Spain* (Philadelphia: University of Pennsylvania Press, 2003).

23   This discussion of *convivencia* relies on Thomas F. Glick, *Islamic and Christian Spain in the Early Middle Ages* (Princeton, NJ: Princeton University Press, 1979); María Rosa Menocal, *The Ornament of the World: How Muslims, Jews, and Christians Created a Culture of Tolerance in Medieval Spain* (Boston, MA: Little, Brown and Co., 2002); and David Nirenberg, *Communities of Violence: Persecution of Minorities in the Middle Ages* (Princeton, NJ: Princeton University Press, 1996).

24   Amy G. Remensnyder, "The Colonization of Sacred Architecture: The Virgin Mary, Mosques, and Temples in Medieval Spain and Early Sixteenth-Century Mexico," in *Monks and Nuns, Saints and Outcasts: Religion in Medieval Society: Essays in Honor of Lester K. Little*, ed. Sharon A. Farmer and Barbara H. Rosenwein (Ithaca, NY: Cornell University Press, 2000).

25   Roger Highfield, "Christians, Jews, and Muslims in the Same Society: The Fall of *Convivencia* in Medieval Spain," in *Religious Motivation: Biographical and Sociological Problems for the Church Historian*, ed. Derek Baker (Oxford: Basil Blackwell, 1978), 135.

26   John Leddy Phelan, *The Millennial Kingdom of the Franciscans in the New World: A Study of the Writings of Gerónomino De Mendieta (1525–1604)* (Berkeley: University of California Press, 1956), 17–24.

27   Bernal Díaz del Castillo, *The History of the Conquest of New Spain*, ed. Davíd Carrasco (Albuquerque: University of New Mexico Press, 2008), 156.

28   Ibid., 171.

29   Davíd Carrasco, *Religions of Mesoamerica*, 2nd edn (Long Grove, IL: Waveland Press, 2013), 90.

30   For instance, see Díaz del Castillo, *The History of the Conquest of New Spain*, 159.

31   Hernán Cortés, *Letters from Mexico*, trans. Anthony Pagden (New Haven, CT: Yale University Press, 1986), 86.

32   Bernardino de Sahagún, *Conquest of New Spain: 1585 Revision*, trans. Howard F. Cline (Salt Lake City: University of Utah Press, 1989), 39.

33   Cortés, *Letters from Mexico*.

34   James Axtell, *Beyond 1492: Encounters in Colonial North America* (New York: Oxford University Press, 1992), 37.

35   David M. Davidson, "Negro Slave Control and Resistance in Colonial Mexico, 1519–1650," *Hispanic American Historical Review* 46, no. 3 (1966), 236.

36   Ibid., 241–242.

37   Ibid., 239.

38   Ibid., 242.

39   Jack D. Forbes, *Africans and Native Americans: The Language of Race and the Evolution of Red-Black Peoples*, 2nd edn (Urbana: University of Illinois Press, 1993), 175.

40   Henry Kamen, *The Spanish Inquisition: A Historical Revision* (New Haven, CT: Yale University Press, 1998), 28–65.

41 J. Jorge Klor de Alva, "Colonizing Souls: The Failure of the Indian Inquisition and the Rise of Penitential Discipline," in *Cultural Encounters: The Impact of the Inquisition in Spain and the New World*, ed. Mary Elizabeth Perry and Anne J. Cruz (Berkeley: University of California Press, 1991), 3–22.

42 Kathryn Joy McKnight, "Blasphemy as Resistance: An African Slave Woman before the Mexican Inquisition," in *Women in the Inquisition: Spain and the New World*, ed. Mary E. Giles (Baltimore, MD: Johns Hopkins University Press, 1999), 229–230.

43 Anthony Pagden, *European Encounters with the New World: From Renaissance to Romanticism* (New Haven, CT: Yale University Press, 1993), 72.

44 Details about Cabeza de Vaca and the Narváez expedition can be found in Rolena Adorno and Patrick Charles Pautz, *Alvar Núñez Cabeza de Vaca: His Account, His Life, and the Expedition of Pánfilo De Narváez*, 3 vols. (Lincoln: University of Nebraska Press, 1999).

45 Lomawywesa (Michael Kabotie), "Hopi Mesas and Migrations: Land and People," in *Hopi Nation: Essays on Indigenous Art, Culture, History, and Law*, ed. Edna Glenn, John R. Wunder, Willard Hughes Rollings, and C. L. Martin (Lincoln: University of Nebraska Press, 2008), 48.

46 Ibid., 46.

47 Helga Teiwes, *Kachina Dolls: The Art of Hopi Carvers* (Tucson: University of Arizona Press, 1991), 21.

48 Kendrick Frazier, *People of Chaco: A Canyon and Its Culture* (New York: W. W. Norton, 1986), 13.

49 Ingrid Mendoza, "Kivas of the Southwest," *Lamda Alpha Journal* 33 (2003), 18.

50 Frazier, *People of Chaco*, 19.

51 Peter Iverson, "The Enduring Hopi," in *Hopi Nation: Essays on Indigenous Art, Culture, History, and Law*, ed. Edna Glenn, John R. Wunder, Willard Hughes Rollings, and C. L. Martin (Lincoln: University of Nebraska, 2008), 144.

52 For animistic religious orientations among native peoples of northeastern North America, see James Axtell, *The Invasion Within: The Contest of Cultures in Colonial North America* (New York: Oxford University Press, 1985), 15–19.

53 Frank G. Speck, quoted in Calvin Martin, "The European Impact on the Culture of a Northeastern Algonquian Tribe: An Ecological Interpretation," in *Religion in American History: A Reader*, ed. Jon Butler and Harry S. Stout (New York: Oxford University Press, 1998 [1974]), 13.

54 From the *Jesuit Relations*, quoted in ibid., 18.

55 Quoted in Peter A. Dorsey, "Going to School with Savages: Authorship and Authority among the Jesuits of New France," *William and Mary Quarterly* 55, no. 3 (1998), 399.

56 For details on Jesuits in New France, see Carole Blackburn, *Harvest of Souls: The Jesuit Missions and Colonialism in North America, 1632–1650* (Montreal: McGill-Queen's University Press, 2000).

57 Herbert Aptheker, *American Negro Slave Revolts* (New York: International Publishers, 1963), 163.

2

Reformations

In this chapter we consider how religious **reformations** among European Christians in the sixteenth century influenced colonizing efforts in America. Religious conflicts between Protestants and Catholics led to intense rivalries between European nations in establishing colonies on the American continents. We focus on the beginnings of England's colonies in North America and the diversity of religious groups who populated the new English settlements. This chapter also notes how European colonists in North America had profound consequences for native peoples. At the same time, the importation of slaves brought the religions of Africa to American soil. As we will learn, America became a place of extraordinarily diverse religions in the course of seventeenth-century colonization.

In 1497 a contemporary of Christopher Columbus (1451–1506), the Italian explorer Giovanni Caboto (known in English as John Cabot, ca. 1450–ca. 1499), sailed under the royal flag of England in search of a northwest passage to the Indies. He never found the hoped-for passage across North America to Asia, but he did make landfall somewhere in the far northeastern portion of the American continent. As it turned out, this first tentative foray to America under English sponsorship never took hold; Cabot's fleet was assumed lost at sea when he failed to return from a later expedition. In fact, it would be more than a century before English colonization would take root in the Americas.

Among the various European nations that established colonies in the Americas, the English settled there rather late in comparison to the Spanish and the Portuguese. Their activities in the Americas began in earnest with their entry in the sixteenth century into transatlantic commerce, including the slave trade. It was a time of great

Formed From This Soil: An Introduction to the Diverse History of Religion in America, First Edition. Thomas S. Bremer.
© 2015 Thomas S. Bremer. Published 2015 by John Wiley & Sons, Ltd.

upheaval and change in England and across the European continent, which put the English sovereigns in conflict with rival nations, especially the Spanish. Foremost among their differences was religion, as England settled in the latter half of the 1500s into an ardent Protestantism bitterly opposed to the papacy of the Roman Catholic Church, which commanded the faith and loyalty of the Spanish monarchy. The divisiveness of these religious conflicts is evident in the career of England's earliest great sea warrior, Francis Drake (ca. 1540–1595). Born into a world divided by religious reformations that pitted Catholics against Protestants in brutal confrontations and protracted wars, Drake encountered both Catholic rivals and native peoples from unfamiliar lands with his often overly dramatized Protestant faith.

In fact, Drake learned early in life the value of flexibility and strategic accommodation in matters of religion. His father, Edmund Drake (1514–1567), had negotiated the shifting tides of religious sentiment in sixteenth-century England with varying success. The elder Drake served for a while as a Catholic priest when the English monarchy attempted to return England to the Catholic Church in the 1550s, but he was eventually forced to leave the post, most likely when Church officials learned that he was a married man. By 1559, however, Edmund Drake had demonstrated sufficient Protestant loyalties to secure a position in the Church of England.[1] Yet his father's changing loyalties in matters of faith were not the only influence on the religious attitudes of the young Francis. As a child he went to live in the household of his kinsmen, the Hawkins family of Plymouth, England. In their household the impressionable Francis encountered yet again the shifting religious loyalties that characterized much of England in the sixteenth century. The Hawkins family harbored a pragmatic approach to religious commitment, remaining "flexible in religion," according to one historian, who characterizes them as pursuing a course that was neither "'rigid Catholic' nor … 'ardent Protestant,' but something in between."[2]

The Hawkins family were seafarers growing wealthy on the slave trade, and Francis Drake's first experiences at sea were on their ships. He first crossed the Atlantic at around the age of twenty-two on a slaving voyage in 1562–1563. On these early voyages, Drake learned not only the intricacies of sailing and navigation but also the lessons of leadership and the importance of maintaining discipline among crew members. He soon realized that flexibility in matters of religion could serve him well. Once, when faced with a possible mutiny, Drake turned to Christian sacraments to quell the unrest among his crew members. He ordered all on board to receive communion and profess their sins to the priest in hopes of imposing obedience to divine authority and perhaps revealing the rebellious culprits among his crew. Drake himself held no special devotion to such practices, regarding the priestly intercessor as unnecessary for religious salvation, but, when faced with mutinous hostility, a sacramental intervention seemed prudent.[3]

Drake's reputation, for better or worse, rested most conspicuously on his feats as a privateer, conducting lucrative raids on Spanish vessels and ports. The Spaniards considered him a formidable military threat to their outposts and shipping operations, but they also characterized him as a threat to their Catholic faith. Spanish Catholics branded Drake as a *gran luterano*, their term for Protestants, whom they regarded as bitter enemies whose blasphemous religious beliefs threatened the very foundations of the Christian tradition. For his part, Drake relished and encouraged his persona as a Protestant crusader whom the Spanish Catholics feared.

Today Drake is best remembered as the first Englishman to circumnavigate the globe. This feat, however, came as a bold strike against Spanish shipping interests in the Americas, particularly along the Pacific coast of Spain's American colonies. Drake left England in late 1577 and did not return until the fall of 1580, crossing the Atlantic and passing through the Strait of Magellan at the southern end of the South American continent. After successful plundering along the Pacific coast of the Americas, Drake crossed the Pacific and Indian oceans before returning to England around the Cape of Good Hope at the southern tip of the African continent. Along the way, Drake encountered Catholic rivals and indigenous peoples from many unfamiliar lands. His dealings with various peoples often involved a pragmatic and flexible approach to religious sentiment, but he also relied on his own religious understandings to make sense of tragic circumstances and bewildering differences. For instance, a week before Christmas in 1578 along the Pacific coast of South America, Drake and his crew learned the cruel truth of their differences with their Catholic rivals. A band of his sailors had gone ashore in search of water and food, only to find vengeful Spaniards lying in wait with their Native American allies; their confrontation brought to martyrdom one of the more devout Protestants among Drake's men. Drake describes the fate of his crew member, whose dead body was "manfully by the Spaniards beheaded, the right hand cut off, the heart pluct out, all which they carried away in our sight, and for the rest of his carcase, they caused the Indians to shoot it full of arrows." Drake attributed such atrocities solely to the Catholics, refusing to blame their Indian allies, whom he described as "innocent and harmelesse."[4]

Drake's experiences with the diverse groups of native peoples along the Pacific coast of the Americas ranged from the harmless to the dangerous. Religious concerns often accompanied Drake and his band of seafaring adventurers into the contact zones where they met the indigenous groups they happened upon. As an example, Drake landed for a period in 1579 somewhere in what is now California (either Upper California in the United States or Baja California in Mexico – the exact location remains a mystery). While there, he appears to have interpreted the behaviors of native peoples who greeted his party as signs of adoration. Some years after their return to England, Drake's younger cousin (who accompanied him on the famous voyage) recounted their time in California: "During their stay the Indians came many times. When they saw the Englishmen, they wept and bloodied their faces with their fingernails. Since they did this as a sign of adoration, Captain Francis told them in signs that they should not do that, because they [the Englishmen] were not gods."[5] Another unidentified witness reported that "drake set up a great post and nayled thereon a vi^d [sixpence coin], which the countreye people woorshipped as if it had bin god[;] also hee nayled uppon this post a plate of lead, and scratched therein the Queenes name."[6] The Indians, at least in this Englishman's recollection, were pious by nature, although their devotions remained naïve and easily manipulated; still, Drake revealed something of his own faith in the artifacts he left for the Indians in California. An English coin and the queen's name were the symbolic centers of his ambitions to gain wealth and status in his European Christian world. He presumed that Indian reactions to his arrival in their world were nothing more than the innocent and naïve responses of primitive people unaware of the true faith. He took their weeping and bloody faces as signs of their adoration of the Englishmen as gods. Such pretensions left Drake oblivious to native understandings of their encounter, understandings that may well have incorporated prescient glimpses of the sorrows and sufferings that would come with European incursions onto American shores. Perhaps, we might surmise, the Indians wept and bloodied their faces as **ritualized** responses to a new reality that would engulf the entire continent in the coming centuries.

Figure 2.1   This romanticized depiction shows native people greeting Francis Drake in the contact zone of California. In actuality, the Indians of California "wept and bloodied their faces with their fingernails," according to an eyewitness account. Drake interpreted their behavior as adoration, for which he rebuked them, declaring that the Englishmen were not gods. (Image © Bettmann / Corbis.)

The career and exploits of Francis Drake were closely tied to relationships of the colonial **Atlantic world** of the sixteenth century. His early involvement in the cross-Atlantic slave trade that brought Africans to the Americas, the deadly rivalries between Protestant and Catholic Christians of western Europe, and the mutually incomprehensible perceptions, beliefs, and actions of Europeans and Native Americans in contact zones throughout the western hemisphere all contributed to the emerging structure of European colonizing efforts on the American continents and the islands of the Atlantic, Caribbean, and Pacific oceans. As we will see in this chapter, religious turmoil in Europe was crucial to the new realities in the Americas. Europeans such as Francis Drake carried the religious conflicts of their homelands to distant places, where they transformed native cultures and planted European traditions in new soils but also introduced new sources of dispute, conflict, and loss.

Religious Upheavals

Francis Drake inhabited a European world shaken to its foundations with religious conflict. A tectonic shift in religious authority subsequently known as the Reformation ruptured the sixteenth-century world of Christianity in western Europe with profound consequences for the subsequent settlement of Christians in North America. Although the controversy erupted in full force during the early decades of the sixteenth century, it had been building up throughout the late medieval period, when most of western Europe was religiously unified under the traditional authority of the Catholic Church, the western branch of Christianity headed by the Pope in Rome. In the latter centuries of the medieval period in Europe, major social and cultural institutions, especially the institutional authority of the Catholic Church, experienced a gradual erosion. A number of developments in particular hastened this shift in the medieval world, including biological agents that devastated much of Europe, institutional conflicts within the Catholic Church, new cultural interests among European elites, and the introduction of technologies that facilitated new modes of communication and debate.

First, regarding biological factors that contributed to changes in European religious authority, a plague epidemic in the fourteenth century known as the Black Death decimated Christian populations throughout western Europe and significantly weakened the very structures of society, including the power of the Catholic Church. On the heels of this biological catastrophe came a second factor affecting religious authority in the form of internal disputes within the Catholic Church between popes and bishops in the fifteenth century; these controversies added to older tensions between papal authority and the secular authority of European monarchs, further eroding the legitimacy of the

Box 2.1   Authority

Religious conflicts among European Christians in the sixteenth century draw our attention to questions of how religious people assert various types of authority. In order to be effective, authority needs legitimacy; in turn, legitimized authority enables the wielding of power. In social terms, power involves the ability to enforce, or at least assert, one's own will, or the collective will of one's group or community, over the will of others. One can attain this sort of power by gaining legitimized authority through a variety of strategic means. But such legitimacy is never an entirely settled affair. Maintaining one's authority, whether it be religious, political, or personal, is an ongoing process, subject to challenges and the ability to adjust and respond to constant change and new circumstances. In this sense, authority is not so much a goal that an individual or group can achieve, nor is it an object or characteristic that one can possess, but rather a continuous process that engages rhetorical strategies of legitimacy and power.

Individual claims to authority rarely operate entirely independent of collective or institutional sources of authority at the level of social groups. Among the various kinds of collective authority, especially in regard to religious groups, the German social philosopher Max Weber (1864–1920) identified three modes of what he called "ideal types" of religious authority: traditional, **charismatic**, and legal-rational. The first type rests on the claim of an accepted tradition, especially religious traditions and their sacred texts, practices, holy places, and related institutions. The mere fact of its survival over time can serve as evidence of a tradition's legitimacy; its ability to withstand the vagaries of changing historical, political, cultural, and social circumstances demonstrates the validity of its claim to authority. Charismatic authority, in contrast, emanates from the personality of a particular leader. Charisma, according to Weber, indicates "a certain quality of an individual personality by virtue of which he is set apart from ordinary men and treated as endowed with supernatural, superhuman, or at least specifically exceptional powers or qualities. These … are not accessible to the ordinary person, but are regarded as of divine origin or as exemplary, and on the basis of them the individual concerned is treated as a leader."[7] These charismatic individuals wield great power, oftentimes both religious and political, based on the authoritative weight of their inherent characteristics. Weber's third mode of authority, legal-rational, generates legitimacy from abstract rules, laws, and sociopolitical powers; legal-rational authority resides in the impersonal powers of an office or position rather than the personal characteristics of the individual who holds that office or position. In regard to religion, legal-rational power derives from the institutional structure of formal, bureaucratic religious organizations.

Weber acknowledges that these three ideal types of authority are not always distinct in actual historical circumstances. Traditional authority often relies on charismatic leaders to establish the tradition and to sustain it through the ages. Likewise, nearly all charismatic leaders establish their authority to some extent on appeals to tradition; this can be easily seen in such powerful religious figures as Jesus, Muhammad, and Gandhi, all of whom understood themselves to be rehabilitating older traditions. Moreover, rational claims and legal principles are rarely absent in assertions of authority, even though they are sometimes spurious. Recognition of one's legitimacy and power always requires a degree of rational justification. No leader can maintain power indefinitely through force and coercion alone.

Long-term legitimacy requires a constant appeal to multiple sources of authority. This in turn draws attention to the rhetorical aspect of religious legitimacy. The American philosopher and social critic Kenneth Burke (1897–1993) argues that religion itself is essentially and fundamentally about rhetoric, what he describes simply as the art of persuasion.[8] Religious authority rests on the ability to persuade others of one's own legitimacy to wield power, and surviving and flourishing in an environment of diversity requires compromise, tolerance, and even acceptance of differences, religious and otherwise. In these circumstances, the rhetorical contexts of authority are naturally unstable; authoritative claims must constantly contend with counterclaims, differences of perspective and opinion, and resistance of many sorts. Indeed, authority and legitimacy are never settled matters; they are processes asserting themselves in dynamic and sometimes volatile circumstances.

Church's power and setting the stage for the dramatic developments of the sixteenth century.[9]

A third consequential development was the growing influence of humanist thinking among Europe's elites in what is commonly known as the Renaissance. Using ancient classical texts that were reintroduced to western European society during the medieval period, a humanist curriculum developed in the fourteenth century that included thorough studies of the classical works of Cicero, Plato, and Aristotle. In the context of this new interest in the ancient world of classical Greece and Rome, historical authority gained much importance. Humanist scholars adopted a rigorous adherence to the notion of *ad fontes* ("back to the sources") in assessing whether particular interpretations were convincing.

The humanist concern with the authority of historical texts coincided with a fourth momentous development that contributed to changing European society: the introduction of printing technologies. German inventor Johannes Gutenberg (ca. 1398–1468) built a printing press with movable type, using technology first developed much earlier in China; it initiated a new era in European culture.[10] As printing technology became more widespread, literacy became a valuable skill for people other than the educated **clergy**. Increased availability of religious texts, sermons, and commentaries, coupled with greater literacy among the **lay** populations, facilitated debate among European Christians and posed challenges to Church power and authority. Moreover, the experience of reading placed more emphasis and authority on individualized, inward-oriented personal devotion for religious people in contrast to the collective orientation of public ritual life.[11] As reading spread through European society, individuals began confronting the sacred texts of the Christian tradition on their own terms.

Reforming Christianity

The changing circumstances of western and northern Europe came together early in the sixteenth century in the form of direct challenges to the institutional authority of the Christian Church and even rebellion from certain segments of the Church. One of the most consequential of these challenges came from an Augustinian monk in the German city of Wittenberg. Martin Luther (1483–1546) was an extraordinarily devout German Catholic living on the tumultuous cusp of the medieval and modern worlds. On the one hand, he lived a cloistered life in an Augustinian monastery that adhered to the traditional authority of medieval religious life. As a devout monk, Luther did not intend to overthrow or even abandon the Church, at least in the early years of his dispute with Church authorities in Rome; his goal was to reform Christian practice and life, to bring it more in line with accepted traditions based on the word of God as he understood it. On the other hand, however, Luther's outlook was steeped in the intellectual influences of early modern humanism. His father had planned a career in secular law for the young Martin Luther and prepared him with a strong humanist education.[12] Some years after taking vows as an Augustinian monk, Luther was assigned to teach at the University of Wittenberg, which offered a humanist education; the university also benefited from a new printing enterprise that operated in the city of Wittenberg.[13]

Martin Luther flourished at Wittenberg, and soon his criticisms of Church practices, and especially his attacks on the authority of the Pope as God's representative, put him in direct conflict with the Catholic Church, which eventually excommunicated him as a heretic. Yet despite its attempts to silence him, Luther continued a relentless attack on the traditional theological underpinnings of the Church's authority among Catholics in western and northern Europe. His voluminous writings cover many issues in Christian theology, but three broad ideas have come to characterize Luther's Reformation theology. *Sola fide*, or faith alone, expresses the idea of "justification by faith," which insists on salvation given through God's grace and not earned through righteous works, penances, or other

Box 2.2   Luther's ninety-five theses

Sometime late on the night of October 31, 1517, the evening before All Saints Day, Martin Luther dramatically nailed onto the doors of Castle Church in Wittenberg, Germany, his intention to hold an academic disputation on the topic of indulgences. His posting on the church door, as the story goes, included a list of ninety-five statements, or theses, to be disputed regarding the Catholic Church's practice of selling indulgences, or promises to lessen suffering in the afterlife, as a means of raising funds; Church officials had found a lucrative source of capital in allowing Christians to purchase the excess merit accumulated by Christ's sacrifice and the virtues of past saints in order to reduce the consequences of their own sinful lives. By Luther's time, the Church's need for funds had led to abuses in the sale of indulgences, and he joined other critics in condemning the practice. More importantly, his arguments posed a direct challenge to the traditional religious authority of the Pope as God's sole representative on earth; Luther's criticisms of the Church's practices and of the very foundations of its authority in the religious lives of European Christians became the basis of the Protestant Reformation.

Historians remain unsure whether or not Luther actually posted his ninety-five theses on the church doors in Wittenberg. But, despite the uncertainty of stories about this dramatic moment, it is clear that Luther gathered together his concerns about the whole system of indulgences in a list of theological arguments that concludes, "Christians should be exhorted to seek earnestly to follow Christ, their Head, through penalties, deaths, hells. And let them thus be more confident of entering heaven through many tribulations rather than through a false assurance of peace."[14] In other words, Luther opposed the traditional authority of the Roman Catholic Church by appealing to the charismatic authority of Christ.

Luther enclosed his list of arguments in a letter of protest to the local Church representative, Archbishop Albrecht von Brandenburg (1490–1545), who dutifully forwarded it to Rome. More importantly, printed copies of Luther's protest were published and circulated in Germany, precipitating a war of pamphlets over the Catholic Church's traditional authority by German theologians. The scholastic disputation that Luther proposed became a public debate in print that had a lasting impact far beyond Wittenberg.

efforts of the Christian. *Sola scriptura*, or scripture alone, places final authority on the biblical texts and not on Church tradition; Christians must consult scripture for proper behaviors and practices. Finally, the "priesthood of all believers" reiterates the personal nature of faith and salvation without mediation of priests or other Church officials; if the Christian's salvation relies on faith alone, the authority of

Figure 2.2 Reformation leader Martin Luther sought to make Christianity more accessible to common parishioners; he is shown here preaching to villagers. His Protestant revolt against the Catholic Church in Rome plunged Europe into a series of bloody religious conflicts. (Courtesy of New York Public Library, #1644762.)

the Church as mediator and its administration of sacraments are not necessary for redemption of the sinful life.

The confrontational nature of Luther's theology and his revolt against the authority of the Catholic Church precipitated an explosive period of religious and political unrest across Europe, accompanied by much violence and even war, as multiple Christian groups broke from the Church in Rome and established autonomous denominations, some of them widespread, such as Luther's followers, whose Lutheran Church covered much of Germany and Scandinavia, and others more local in their reach. Together, these many revolts against the Church, each with their own particular circumstances and outcomes, have become known collectively as the Protestant Reformation, although they are more accurately regarded in the plural, as *Reformations*.

The spread of reformation

One of the more influential of these reformations occurred in the Swiss city of Geneva. Under the leadership of the French reformer John Calvin (1509–1564), a later contemporary of Martin Luther, the citizens of Geneva in the sixteenth century transformed their city into a model of Reformed tradition that attracted

Protestants from all over Europe; many of these reformers subsequently returned to their homelands and instituted Calvin's theology across the Protestant world.

John Calvin initially studied theology in hope of securing a position in the Catholic Church, but later at his father's insistence he studied law. Eventually he returned to theological studies as he came under the influence of Protestant scholars who exposed him to the ideas of Martin Luther and the humanist biblical scholar Desiderius Erasmus (1466–1536), as well as others who opposed the Catholic Church's traditional authority. Calvin, however, experienced a religious conversion that finalized his break from the Catholic Church but also led him to a renunciation of religious humanism. He became acutely aware of what he regarded as God's word that in turn revealed to him the direct force of God's **providence**; he felt that God controlled his path toward a vocation of religious reformation.

In the mid-1530s, leaders from the French-speaking Swiss city of Geneva invited Calvin to institute Protestant reforms in their municipality. Initially, his reforms were not well received by the Genevans, and in 1538 he and the other Protestant reformers in the city were forced into exile. Calvin settled in the city of Strasbourg, where he wrote commentaries on the Bible and finished his theological treatise, *The Institutes of the Christian Religion* (1536). After returning to Geneva in 1540, Calvin began instituting his model of reformed Christianity. This involved not only changes in church governance but also reforming both the church and the city itself. Among the many changes he initiated, Calvin organized a school system and a hospital, started a system of charity for the poor, and designed a public sewage system. Calvin modeled his vision of the political and social organization of both religious and civic institutions on his interpretation of biblical principles. Eventually he gained greater control over both church and civic affairs in Geneva, and he remained uncompromising with those who opposed his reforms. Anyone who questioned Calvin's theological principles or who proposed ideas at odds with his interpretations of scripture was either banished from the city or, in the case of Michael Servetus (1511–1553), who denied the Christian Trinity in an attempt to make Christianity acceptable to Muslims and Jews, condemned to death for heresy. Calvin allowed no tolerance for diverse views of Christian traditions.

Calvin's emphasis on the absolute authority of God's majesty entailed a theology of predestination similar to theological ideas of Martin Luther and derived from the work of the early medieval Christian theologian Augustine of Hippo (354–430). An individual's fate, according to Calvin, is previously decided, or predestinated, by God, and human actions and choices have no bearing on whether one will enjoy salvation. Those whom God has "elected" for salvation are the "saints," who constitute the invisible church known only to God. All others God has predestined for eternal condemnation. Consequently, unlike the Catholic Church of medieval times, which admitted all who lived within the boundaries of its jurisdiction, Calvin's version of the Reformed Church allowed into its congregations only the elect who publicly professed their faith. These saints were identified by their willingness to adhere to the rather strict standards of religious belief and behavior imposed by Calvin's Reformed Church.

By the mid-1550s, Calvin's success in Geneva had made it Europe's most important Protestant center, and Protestant exiles from all over Europe found it to be a hospitable place of refuge. Calvin himself oversaw the Academy, a new civic institution of higher education for training ministers of the Reformed Church, and many of the students there were religious exiles from places such as England, France, the Netherlands, and Scotland. Calvin staffed the school with loyal followers and molded its curriculum according to his theological principles, and soon students were carrying Calvinist theology and reforms back to their homelands, spreading the Calvinist model for organizing both church and state throughout much of Europe. Calvinism soon reigned as the leading Protestant theology in many parts of Europe.

Box 2.3 Calvinism, Arminianism, and the Synod of Dordt, 1618–1619

Among the difficult challenges that Calvin's theology posed for Christians, not least was the issue of human free will in the face of an unwavering divine providence. In response to the inflexibility of the Calvinist doctrine of predestination, which leaves no possibility of human choice or effort in attaining salvation, the Dutch theologian Jacob Arminius (1560–1609) disputed a number of Calvin's most fundamental theological principles, emphasizing the role of human free will rather than the complete and thorough sovereignty of God's majesty. Following his death, Arminius' followers proclaimed in the *Remonstrance of 1610* five theological points that summarized what they understood as the essential principles of his theology. Their theological treatise conflicted directly with central tenets of orthodox Calvinism and has come to define the early seventeenth-century Protestant movement known as Arminianism. Arminians contend that God's election of those Christians who are to be saved is based on their faith, which God is able to foresee; that the atonement of sin is universally available to everyone, not just the elect; that humans are only partially depraved and are able to participate in the process of redemption; that humans can choose to resist the offer of God's grace; and that humans who have accepted God's grace are capable of subsequently falling from grace and losing the promise of salvation.

As these Arminian principles gained popularity, a crisis developed within the national Dutch Reformed Church over its strictly Calvinist orthodoxy, and in the fall of 1618 the Church convened a meeting, or synod, in the Dutch city of Dordt, with delegates representing the reformed churches of the Netherlands but also including representatives from eight other countries. Their deliberations produced responses to the five points of the Arminians' *Remonstrance* in a theological consensus regarding orthodox Calvinism. In the Canons of the Synod of Dordt, the Reformed Church delegates insisted that

God's election of Christian saints is unconditional and is not warranted in any way upon the merits of those elected; that the atonement of one's sins through the sacrificial death of Christ is limited only to the elect; that humans in their very nature are totally depraved and thoroughly sinful because of the original sin of Adam and Eve, and therefore are entirely incapable of redemption except through the grace of God; that God's grace given to the elect cannot be resisted or rejected, but all elected saints will accept this unmerited gift from God; and that the saints elected by God and given the gift of grace will persevere through temptations and sinfulness with the help of God's mercy and grace, which will lead them to repentance and an abiding assurance of their ultimate redemption and salvation.

The Canons decided upon at Dordt articulated the orthodox principles of Calvinism and declared as heresy the Arminian theological principles, but the dispute over theological authority did not end in the seventeenth century. The principles of both the Calvinists and the Arminians, including variations of both, continue to appear in the religious lives of Protestants right up to the present, and the inherent theological tension between an all-powerful sovereign God and the human experience of autonomy and choice can be seen in many religious disputes among Protestants, especially in America.

Religious reforms, though, did not hinge only on doctrinal issues; indeed, theological arguments by reformers such as Luther and Calvin did not persuade all Christians in Europe. In England, for instance, the Reformation took hold for more strictly political reasons rather than theological principles. In fact, early attempts at reform in England during the first decades of the sixteenth century had little success as the monarchy remained aligned with the Catholic Church in Rome, with the English ruler King Henry VIII (1491–1547) even earning the title Defender of the Faith (*Defensor Fidei*) from the Roman pontiff for the former's defense of the Catholic sacraments against Protestant claims. However, in a dispute of epic proportions between Henry VIII and Pope Clement VII (1478–1534), the king claimed for himself authority over the Church within his kingdom. The dispute centered upon his marriage to Catherine of Aragon (1485–1536), whom he had married in 1509. Nearly two decades of matrimony had failed to produce a male heir for the king, and for this, as well as for reasons of romance and political expediency, Henry VIII sought to end his marriage. But the Pope refused the king's request. Henry responded by breaking from the Catholic Church. In 1534 the English Parliament passed the Act of Supremacy, effectively transferring religious authority from the Pope in Rome to Henry VIII, establishing the king as Supreme Head of the Church of England. Thus began England's tumultuous conversion to Protestantism as the people of England joined other Europeans in the revolt against the authority of the Catholic Church in Rome.

   The Church of England under King Henry VIII retained its Roman Catholic character in practice and theology. After the death of Henry in 1547, however, his young son acceded to the throne as King Edward VI (1537–1553). The new king, persuaded by Protestant reformer Thomas Cranmer (1489–1556), enacted reforms to move the Church of England unequivocally toward Protestantism. The reign of the sickly Edward, however, lasted only six years, and in 1553 his half-sister, a devout Catholic, acceded to the throne as Queen Mary I (1516–1558) and began a bloody campaign to restore Catholicism to England. Her reign was also short lived, and in 1558 she was succeeded by Queen Elizabeth I (1533–1603), whose long and stable rule returned England to Protestantism. The turbulent religious convulsions of sixteenth-century England, however, produced an environment where dissent flourished, even in the face of persecution. The Church of England remained the official church of the nation, but a diversity of other Christian communities also

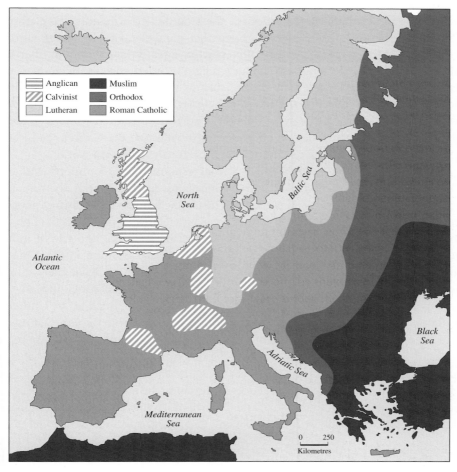

Map 2.1   Areas of religious dominance in western Europe following the reformations of the sixteenth century.

thrived in the shifting contours of England's religious landscape, eventually spawn-ing such groups as the Puritans, Baptists, Society of Friends (commonly known as Quakers), Methodists, and others.

The Catholic Reformation

Martin Luther was not the only reformer situated within the Roman Catholic Church. Others connected to the Church also called for changes, with at least some of these calls coming before Luther's revolt. In fact, an aggressive campaign for reli-gious reform was well underway in Spain under the leadership of Francisco Ximénes de Cisneros (1436–1517) long before Martin Luther began his efforts in northern Europe. But the Protestant rebellion against papal authority brought new urgency for change, and Catholic officials accelerated their program of reforms during the middle decades of the sixteenth century. In a series of developments known alter-natively as the Catholic Reformation or the Counter-Reformation, the Catholic Church undertook a program of change that paralleled developments among Protestants in the sixteenth century, often reacting against the accusations of critics of the Church. Along with these changes, religious orders such as the Franciscans experienced a revival, while new orders, such as the Society of Jesus (or Jesuits), flourished in their opposition to Protestant heresies. Ignatius of Loyola (1491–1556), founder of the Jesuits, advocated a militant obedience to Church authority, but he also placed great importance on education for revitalizing the Church, and Jesuit schools and colleges sprang up throughout much of the Christian world.

The Roman Catholic Church made a formal response to calls for reform with the Council of Trent, a meeting of Church officials to discuss Church doctrine and changes to Church policies and practices. The Council met in three distinct periods between 1545 and 1563 and dealt with far-reaching issues of the Church. High on the agenda was the elimination of abuses, especially regarding the sale of indul-gences and the ability of individuals to gain an official position in the Church through influence or purchase. On the other hand, much of what the Council accomplished involved repudiation of Protestant theological doctrines. Indeed, the canons and decrees of the Council defended and reaffirmed much of the Church's traditional doctrines. Hence, the Church in Rome emerged from the conciliar meet-ings strengthened in its commitment to the authority of tradition. It also inspired a revitalization of Catholic piety among religious orders and other clergy, who in turn implemented many of the reforms among the laity with a new catechism, the official manual of doctrines and practices for teaching the faithful. Among the prac-tices that proliferated in the wake of the Council of Trent were increased emphasis on sacraments, especially regular confession to a priest, and such devotional prac-tices as reciting the prayers of the rosary. There was tension, however, in many regions where the attempt to centralize Church authority and standardize worship and doctrine met with resistance. Most often parishioners objected to changes in popular forms of local worship, especially devotion to locally important saints.[15]

Box 2.4   Cardinal Ximénes of Spain

Following their success in routing Muslim rulers from the Iberian Peninsula, the Spanish monarchs pursued an aggressive campaign to Christianize their lands. Leading their efforts was Francisco Ximénes de Cisneros (1436–1517), who became the most powerful religious leader in the land when Isabella I (1451–1504), Queen of Castile and León, named him the Archbishop of Toledo in 1495. As a member of the Franciscan order of monks, the new archbishop made reform of the Franciscans among his earliest projects. With the powerful backing of the queen, Archbishop Ximénes was able to enforce strict rules of ascetic piety on the monks, despite opposition from many of them, and he then turned to reforming the other religious orders in Spain. Eventually, Ximénes oversaw sweeping reforms among Spain's Catholics, and he enforced harsh means to ensure conformity among all Spanish subjects. As Grand Inquisitor, a position he attained in 1507, Ximénes oversaw the machinations of religious obedience. Recognizing his prominence in the most powerful and loyal of the Roman Catholic nations, the pope made Ximénes a cardinal in 1507.

The career of Cardinal Ximénes, however, involved far more than enforcement of religious conformity and obedience among Spain's Catholics. He supported institutions of higher learning, and he opened the prestigious Complutense University of Madrid in 1508. He began work in 1502 on publishing the first printed Bible, which included different versions of the Christian sacred texts in parallel columns alongside the original languages; the project continued for fifteen years until the end of his life, and the entire work was not published until after his death. Ximénes also involved himself in **liturgical** reforms, reinstituting the Latin rite for Catholic worship. In 1500 he published a missal, the liturgical guide for celebrating the Catholic mass, and in 1507 he produced a new breviary, a collection of prayers, hymns, and other texts to guide daily worship. At the same time, his public influence continued to grow. Closely involved with the Spanish monarchs, Cardinal Ximénes served as a powerful political ally and mediator in matters of state. He also sought to extend the Spanish empire into Africa with a crusade against Moors along the Mediterranean coast of what is now Algeria. The effort resulted in the capture of the city of Oran in 1509, but King Ferdinand (1452–1516) lost interest in the crusade and did not support Cardinal Ximénes' further plans for conquest in Africa.[16]

The religious upheavals of Christian reforms in western Europe in the sixteenth century eventually erupted in widespread violence. A series of armed conflicts in the late sixteenth and early seventeenth centuries known collectively as the Wars of Religion pitted Catholics against Protestants. Beginning with civil war in France that witnessed the slaughter of thousands of Huguenots, or French Protestants,

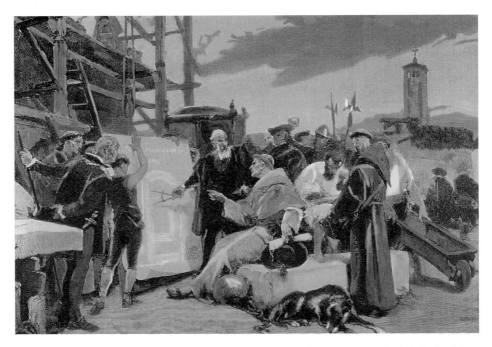

Figure 2.3   The efforts of Cardinal Francisco Ximénes de Cisneros included the building of public projects in addition to his religious reforms and political concerns. Here he is shown in a nineteenth-century Spanish painting directing the construction of a hospital. (Courtesy of Album / Prisma / Album Superstock, #4409–157766-N-X999.)

including many unarmed civilians, and culminating with the Thirty Years' War, which involved nearly every European nation and ended with the Treaty of Westphalia in 1648, Europe suffered unprecedented carnage in the name of religious faith. In these savage conflicts, political struggles over religious beliefs among various Christians unleashed extraordinarily ferocious violence that covered Europe with bloodshed. Religious authority had become justification for aggression and cruelty.

As we reflect on the early history of Europeans coming to the Americas, we cannot overlook the prodigious religious transformations that racked Europe at precisely the same time that colonists were establishing new settlements on the other side of the Atlantic Ocean. Even before Martin Luther's bold challenge to the authority of the Catholic Church, leaders of the Church such as Cardinal Ximénes in Spain were linking ecclesiastical reforms to colonial expansion; conquests of native peoples in the American colonies brought both the opportunities of evangelism and the challenges of maintaining the Church's authority. As Luther's initial rebellion grew, the divisions between Catholics and Protestants in Europe followed the colonists to their new settlements. America became an outpost of Reformation rivalries.

Colonizing America

Amid the conflicts between European powers in the sixteenth and seventeenth centuries, some Protestants saw opportunity in America. In particular, English colonists established a Protestant presence in North America in the seventeenth century, in part to stem the advance of the Catholic nations of France and Spain in the Americas. An early attempt during the reign of Queen Elizabeth I to settle on Roanoke Island off the coast of Virginia ended with the mysterious disappearance of the entire colony, but not before it celebrated the first recorded Protestant worship service in North America in August 1587 and witnessed that same month the birth of the first English baby born in America, Virginia Dare (born 1587, death date unknown).

England's first American colonies

The failure of the Roanoke colony did not deter advocates back in England, who envisioned a vast English colonial empire. King James I (1566–1625), successor to Queen Elizabeth I, granted two charters in 1606 to companies wishing to establish English colonies in North America. Both companies were commercial enterprises, concerned primarily with profiting from trade, although the original charters included an acknowledgment of religious purposes in colonizing America. Indeed, for English Protestants engaged in violent rivalries with European Catholics, even the pursuit of financial profit had religious overtones. When the first settlers arrived in Virginia in 1607 to start England's first permanent colony in America, they carried a letter with instructions that stated their religious purposes, "to serve and fear God, the giver of all goodness, for every plantation which our Heavenly Father hath not planted shall be rooted out."[17] Among their ranks was a chaplain from the Church of England to remind them of their religious duty and to serve their religious needs, but also to evangelize the Indians.

The first Virginia colonists established the village of Jamestown, named in honor of the monarch who granted them the colony. Its success, however, was extremely precarious as half the settlers died in the first year and the survivors were ravaged by Indian attacks, fire, sickness, and famine. One of the original colonists, John Rolfe (ca. 1585–1622), famous for his marriage in 1614 to Pocahontas (ca. 1595–1617), the daughter of a local Algonquian ruler, later framed the colony's survival in biblical terms as he urged evangelizing among his wife's people: "What need we then to fear but to go up at once as a peculiar people marked and chosen by the finger of God to possess it? For undoubtedly He is with us."[18] Yet, even Rolfe's zeal for bringing native peoples into the Christian fold became an occasion for furthering the profitability of the colonial enterprise; back in England with his wife Rebecca (formerly Pocahontas), Rolfe received money from colonial investors to establish a mission for Indian children in Virginia in an attempt to strengthen English investments through religious conversions.

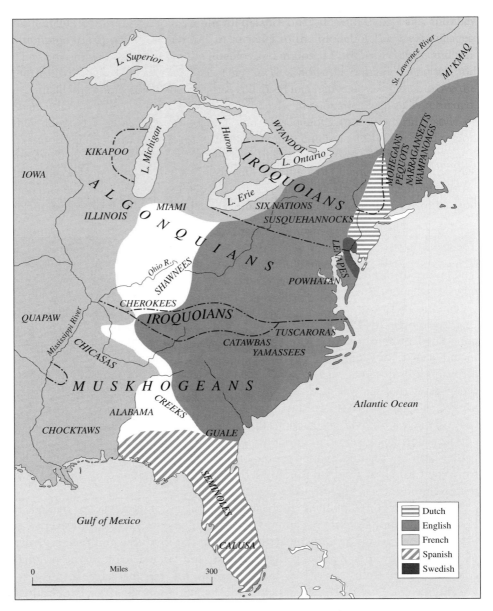

Map 2.2   Europeans and Native Americans in eastern North America during the colonial period. The map shows approximate locations of major Native American groups during the early decades of the colonial period. The areas of the five European nations with claims in eastern North America are shown at their greatest extent. The Dutch and Swedish colonies ended in the seventeenth century; the English, French, and Spanish claims are shown for the 1770s.

Figure 2.4 The baptism of Pocahontas, daughter of a local chieftain in Virginia. During hostilities between her father's people and the Jamestown colonists, she was taken hostage and held for ransom. While in captivity she converted to Christianity and chose to stay with the English, taking the name Rebecca and eventually marrying colonist John Rolfe. (Reproduced by permission of HistoryPicks.com.)

The plan, however, came to an end with the young Rebecca's sudden death just before she and her husband were to return to Virginia.[19]

As the colony continued to grow, religion never amounted to more than a peripheral concern for most colonists in Virginia. When the English government made it a royal colony in 1624, the Church of England became the established church of Virginia, but religious involvement continued to remain low. Historians have offered two explanations for the relatively low level of religious involvement among colonial Virginians: geography and slavery. Virginia's exceptionally large and thinly populated area put a strain on the parish system prevalent in England. Much of the population was geographically disbursed on isolated farms and estates, with churches that were very few in number and often far from where settlers actually resided. Many of the churches were not served by permanent clergy, and the priests who served the colony were often apathetic or incompetent, and sometimes actually criminal. More than a century after the founding of Jamestown, Virginia's twenty-nine counties had only forty-four parishes with about seventy places of worship, but only about half of these had ministers, with lay readers performing services in the vacant parishes.

Compounding the geographic challenges of providing religious services to the colonists was the early introduction of slavery. The colony's early and profitable success growing tobacco soon turned to slave labor as cultivation expanded. A Dutch slave ship sold twenty African slaves to the Virginia colonists in 1619, initiating the long and brutal history of race-based slavery in North America. By the turn of the eighteenth century, the slave population in Virginia was close to ten thousand. As the number of slaves grew, fear of rebellion and the attempt to maximize productivity through constant and increasingly violent disciplinary measures made slaveholders less inclined to concern themselves with the religious well-being of their slaves. As a result, the Christian religion became a marker of social and economic class; the Church of England in Virginia almost exclusively served the colonial elites.

Puritan New England

In contrast to the marginal role of religion in Virginia, the colonies of New England to the north made religion central to colonial society. Reform-minded separatists, derisively known as "Puritans" for their insistence on "purifying" the Church of Catholic influences, felt the Church of England had not gone far enough in its reforms and advocated more radical changes in its theology and religious practices. Emerging during the reign of Queen Elizabeth I, the separatists began establishing their own congregations independent of the Church of England; the royal government, however, aggressively repressed them. The persecutions continued under Elizabeth's successor, King James I, who pledged to "make [the Puritans] conform themselves or I will harry them out of the land."[20] A small group of the more radical of the separatists fled first to Amsterdam in the Netherlands, and, after thirteen years of exile in Holland, decided to try settling in America. After a brief return to England, they sailed on the ship *Mayflower* from the English port city of Plymouth in the fall of 1620. Landing in Massachusetts, far north of their intended destination of Virginia, and arriving in November with the cruel New England winter bearing down upon them, the newly arrived settlers suffered under harsh conditions without adequate shelter or food; nearly half of the company died in the first winter. The survivors persevered, however, and the small Plymouth Colony gained a foothold for religious separatists in America.

A decade after the arrival of the *Mayflower* with the first group of separatists in New England, a much larger group of more moderate Puritans came to settle in Boston and establish the Massachusetts Bay Colony as a society focused exclusively on devotion to God.[21] These later arrivals did not advocate separation from the Church of England but instead sought to transform the Church. They were led by John Winthrop (1588–1649), whom they elected as the first governor of the new colony before they left England. He characterized the new colony as "a city upon a hill," a model of the ideal Christian society for other Europeans to emulate. The objective of the Puritan colonists was to fulfill the Christian covenant with God and each other; they were not to serve themselves or seek individual freedoms but to dedicate themselves to fulfilling God's will. The Puritans had no tolerance for dissent or deviance from their hallowed mission. Winthrop insisted on preordained distinctions between social classes; he proclaimed that "in all times some must be rich, some poor, some highe and eminent in power and dignitie; others mean and in subjeccion." Enforcing obedience to the covenant of Puritan society would be, according to Winthrop, "a due forme of Government both civill and ecclesiasticall."[22] Yet, despite its strictness and intolerance, the Puritan commitment to self-governance made the Massachusetts Bay Colony more democratic than what the colonists had experienced in England; the Puritan form of colonial self-rule allowed all "freemen" (meaning adult males in good standing in a local church) to choose their leaders at annual elections. Moreover, despite the common goal to establish and maintain a covenantal community of God's people, Puritan governance separated civil and ecclesiastical roles, granting each religious congregation full autonomy and barring ministers from holding public office. The civil officials could punish ministers, including imprisonment or banishment, for violating civil

---

Box 2.5   Protestant church polity

The Puritans arranged their churches according to a congregational model of polity, or institutional organization, with authority vested in the local congregation. This nonhierarchal approach to church governance became popular among some Protestant groups that wished to emphasize the Reformation principle of a priesthood of all believers. In particular, critiques of the Catholic papacy and the role of priests led some Protestants to free themselves entirely from hierarchical structures of church polity. Today, this congregational model remains active among such Protestants as Congregationalists and Baptists.

In contrast to the congregational form of church polity is an episcopal model, which was used by the Roman Catholic Church and had been continued with the Church of England. The Latin term *episcopalis* refers to the office of bishop, and this form of church governance involves a hierarchical structure of bishops, with ultimate authority concentrated in a single person or small group of bishops at the highest level of the church structure.

A third common approach to church polity among Protestant Christians is the Presbyterian model, a representative form of governance where authority begins at the local level and then follows a system of ascending representative bodies. In churches that use a presbyterian model, the local congregation vests authority in a "session" made up of representatives from the congregation; congregations then send representatives to an area "presbytery"; presbyteries are represented in regional "synods"; and the entire denomination sends representatives to a "general assembly."

laws or committing heresy, but the government had no jurisdiction over their church office. A minister found guilty in civil court could still remain the leader of a church if the congregation wished him to continue.

The intolerance of Puritan society in the Massachusetts Bay Colony met challenges nearly from the beginning. The most threatening controversy in the early years of the colony was what became known as the Antinomian Crisis, which centered around Anne Hutchinson (1591–1643), who had immigrated to New England in 1634. Antinomianism (from the Latin for "against law or rule") had been a source of theological tension within Christianity from ancient times, but it saw revived interest in the Reformation. Martin Luther's emphasis on justification by faith alone undermined the need for faithful Christians to abide by laws, both the civil laws of the state and the more general moral laws of society. Luther himself had argued that Christians were free from the law, but he also insisted that Christians must abide by the law in order to discipline their carnal bodies and to serve others. For New England's Puritan community in the 1630s, a Calvinist "covenant of grace" brought salvation to the elect who were predestinated for redemption. Although it was impossible to know for certain who had received God's grace, sanctification through good works and living an outwardly righteous life served as evidence of one's election. But this idea of sanctification brought controversy to Boston when Anne Hutchinson accused church leaders of preaching a "covenant of works" rather than relying solely on a covenant of grace. Her accusations, however, were more than a theological debate over the role of good works in Christian life. She posed a direct challenge to the theological authority of church ministers and to the social and political order of the colony, which did not allow women's voices in public discourse. Although women were more likely than men to be members of New England churches, they were denied positions of leadership and excluded from participation in church governance.[23]

Anne Hutchinson's willingness to challenge the male authority of the Massachusetts Bay Colony resulted in formal charges against her in civil court; she faced trial in November 1637 for having "troubled the peace of the commonwealth and the churches here" by holding meetings that, according to the accusations in court, "hath been condemned by the general assembly as a thing not tolerable nor comely in the sight of God nor fitting for your sex."[24] Although she demonstrated skill and intelligence before the court, and even claimed "an immediate revelation" from God, the political forces aligned against her made the proceedings a foregone conclusion. The episode concluded with her excommunication and banishment from the Massachusetts colony. Her departure brought an end to the antinomians in Boston, but not to the tensions of an intolerant authoritarianism that felt threatened by dissent of any kind.[25]

Puritan intolerance continued to assert itself in sometimes violent ways, but over time the isolation and exclusiveness of John Winthrop's ideal "city upon a hill" could not be sustained. Regarding the new religious movement of the Society of Friends, derogatively known as Quakers, as heretical agents of Satan, in 1658 Massachusetts enacted a provision that specified death for any Quaker returning to

Figure 2.5 The Puritan teacher Anne Hutchinson stood trial in 1637 for challenging the religious and civil authorities of the Massachusetts Bay Colony. Although her charismatic authority gained many supporters, her trial ended with her excommunication and banishment from the colony. She resettled in Rhode Island, where she joined another Puritan dissenter, Roger Williams. (Courtesy New York Public Library, #808160.)

the colony after banishment, and in the next few years four Quakers met their fates under the law. Not all Puritans in Massachusetts, however, supported the persecution of Quakers, and eventually the violence ended with a royal order from England. Likewise, Baptists were initially prohibited in Massachusetts, but by the 1680s they were allowed their own meetinghouse in Boston. With a rapidly growing and increasingly diverse population, intolerance became less acceptable.

Dissent and diversity

Between the strict intolerance of Puritans in Massachusetts and the relative laxity of religious life in Virginia were a diverse group of "middle colonies" that were more ethnically diverse and more religiously tolerant than colonies to the north or south.

As more immigrants arrived in America to escape oppressive conditions at home and to pursue promises of economic opportunity in the colonies, strict conformity in religious orientation and practice became less tenable. A bewildering mix of ethnic and religious enclaves soon populated England's American holdings.

The colony of Rhode Island originated as a haven for dissenters from Massachusetts. The separatist minister Roger Williams (ca. 1603–1683) came to Massachusetts in 1631 and quickly came into conflict with the colonial leadership there. Initially he refused to serve the church in Boston because of its affiliation with the Church of England. He later clashed with officials in Plymouth and Salem over such issues as the civil government's authority to enforce matters of personal religious conscience and the taking of Indian lands without consent or proper payment. Eventually his controversial opinions resulted in his expulsion from the colony. Williams fled Massachusetts in January 1636 and established a new settlement on Narragansett Bay to the south. He bought land from the native peoples there and founded the city of Providence. In 1638 Williams helped the group of exiles who accompanied Anne Hutchinson when she was banished from Massachusetts to purchase from the native peoples an island in Narragansett Bay, where they set up the village of Portsmouth. The new colony of Providence Plantations became a refuge for dissenters from Massachusetts and elsewhere, and welcomed diverse religious views. In fact, the colonists included religious liberty in their founding documents, stating in 1647 that "all men may walk as their consciences persuade them, every one in the name of his God."[26] Williams himself became a Baptist for a brief period, forming America's first Baptist church in Providence, but eventually he rejected all organized churches as lacking authority. The Baptists, however, continued to flourish in Rhode Island, as did the Society of Friends, or Quakers, and other groups that found religious tolerance there and used the colony as a base for their forays into less tolerant areas. Even a small group of Dutch Jews settled in Newport in 1658.

Further south, other colonies also welcomed a degree of religious diversity. The mid-Atlantic colonies of New Jersey, Delaware, and especially Pennsylvania adhered to principles of religious tolerance that allowed a variety of Protestant groups to settle and flourish. In particular, the idealistic "holy experiment" of William Penn (1644–1718) in Pennsylvania and Delaware, founded upon Quaker principles of egalitarianism, quickly became a haven for all sorts of Protestant groups. Penn was an early follower of the Society of Friends, which had begun in England in the 1650s as a radical form of Puritanism preached by George Fox (1624–1691). Disavowing formal churches, the Quakers sought instead a personal communion with God in communal meetings where anyone could participate and speak as the spirit led them. They claimed an "inner light," which amounted to a direct revelation from God, and they mistrusted the Bible as an imperfect human record of past revelations. In a direct denial of the Calvinist understanding of predestination, the Friends insisted that everyone was capable of salvation by following their own inner light. They rejected the notion of original sin as well as sacramental rituals, ministers, and sermons. Instead, they embraced an egalitarian social view; in contrast to the

Calvinism of the Puritans, who restricted church membership to predestined visible saints, the Quakers welcomed everyone regardless of their social status, stressing the inherent spiritual worthiness of each individual. They advocated toleration and religious pluralism, and, as strict pacifists, they opposed all wars and capital punishment. Strongly nonconformist, Quakers seemed to invite confrontations with authorities, deliberately ignoring the conventions of polite society and refusing deference to social superiors. The Society of Friends also maintained strong commitments to missionary outreach, and its members traveled widely to establish new Friends' meetings in England and abroad.

William Penn envisioned a new colony in America where the Society of Friends could find refuge from the severe persecutions they suffered at home. An aristocrat with considerable influence in England, he had acquired land in America in 1681 to settle a debt that Charles II (1630–1685), King of England, owed his father. He named the place Pennsylvania at the king's insistence in honor of his father, and proceeded to implement his plans for "a blessed government, and a vertuous ingenious and industrious society, so as people may Live well and have more time to serve the Lord, then [sic] in this Crowded land."[27] With the protections of a

Figure 2.6 William Penn's Quaker principles included fair treatment of local native groups. This painting, commissioned by Penn's son, shows the founder of the Pennsylvania colony making a treaty with members of the Lennie Lenape tribe at Shackamaxon on the Delaware River. (Benjamin West (1738–1820), *Penn's Treaty with the Indians*, 1771–1772, oil on canvas; 75 ½ × 107 ¾ in., Pennsylvania Academy of the Fine Arts, Philadelphia, Gift of Mrs. Sarah Harrison (The Joseph Harrison, Jr. Collection), 1878.1.10.)

tolerant colonial government, Quakers flourished in Pennsylvania, New Jersey, and Delaware, and also gained influence throughout the other colonies. They became especially despised in the south, however, for their strong criticisms of slavery and their willingness to include enslaved worshipers in their meetings; and they met opposition among the Congregationalists in New England for their inclusive views, which challenged the religious and political authority of clergy.

William Penn's idealized vision for his "holy experiment" in Pennsylvania quickly ran into obstacles, and soon there emerged a contest between Penn and his settlers, who were faced with more pragmatic problems of colonial life. Financial difficulties eventually overwhelmed Penn as the colonists steered control of the colony away from him; the turn of events forced him back to England, where he was sent to debtor's prison. But, even as he languished, Pennsylvania became William Penn's legacy, a place of religious toleration and pluralism, and, not coincidently, one of England's most prosperous colonies. Not just Quakers but a variety of religious groups flourished there, including German Pietists who settled the village of Germantown near Philadelphia in 1683. In the eighteenth century, Scotch-Irish Presbyterians also would find a welcome climate for settlement in Pennsylvania.

Another colony founded explicitly on principles of religious freedom was Maryland, although the tolerance allowed there was more confined than in other colonies. King Charles I (1600–1649), a Protestant, chartered Maryland in 1632 as a grant to George Calvert (1579–1632), the first Lord Baltimore, a convert to Roman Catholicism who had served in the king's court and remained in favor with the monarch. Calvert died before receiving the charter for the new colony where Catholics could live freely, but it went to his son Cecilius Calvert (1605–1675), the second Lord Baltimore, who governed through the proxy of his brother, Leonard Calvert (1606–1647). They made clear that, although ostensibly a place for Catholics, all Christians were welcome. As the colony grew, however, Protestants were soon in the majority, including a growing number of Puritans. In the 1650s, Puritans seized power in the colony and outlawed Roman Catholicism. All Catholic priests were forced into exile, and at least four Catholics were executed. Eventually a compromise was reached between the Protestants and Catholics in the colony, but by the end of the seventeenth century Maryland was a royal colony with the Church of England as the officially established church; by then the colony's capital had moved to Annapolis, a predominantly Protestant town.

Far to the south, the Carolinas posed an unattractive and formidable land for settlement. In an effort to encourage colonists to settle there, the proprietors of the original Carolina colonies granted religious liberty, although religion remained largely peripheral to the primary interests of trade and commercial development. Later attempts to establish the Church of England as the official religious body were largely ineffectual, and dissenters, especially Quakers, made up a sizable portion of the settlers. In fact, their founder George Fox visited North Carolina in 1672. Also in the Carolinas were Baptists, Presbyterians, New England Puritans, and French Huguenots, among others.

Even as the English established themselves along the Atlantic coast of North America, other European nations made colonial claims in the region. The English navigator Henry Hudson (ca. 1565–ca. 1611) sailed for the Dutch East India Company in 1609 when he explored the river that today bears his name, claiming the area for the Netherlands. The Dutch soon set up trading posts along the Hudson and Connecticut Rivers, as well as on Long Island Sound. The first permanent settlers on Manhattan Island arrived in 1624, and the town of New Amsterdam on the island became the capital of New Netherland in 1626. Primarily a commercial enterprise under the control of the Dutch West India Company, the colony never attracted many permanent settlers, but those who came made up a very diverse population. By 1630, New Amsterdam had about 270 residents, of whom only about half were Dutch. The others included French-speaking Walloons from Belgium, French Huguenots, and a variety of English Protestants. A report from 1644 states that eighteen different languages could be heard in New Amsterdam.[28] Later, Swedish could be heard in the colony after Peter Stuyvesant (ca. 1612–1672), the Director-General of New Netherland, conquered and annexed a small settlement of Swedish Lutherans on the Delaware River in 1655. Dutch Jews also arrived in New Amsterdam in the 1650s, fleeing persecution in Brazil, thus beginning the long history of Jewish presence in North America. The Dutch proprietors were rather intolerant of diverse religious practices, expecting membership in the Dutch Reformed Church for all settlers; but enforcing religious conformity was not a high priority. After the English took possession of the Dutch colony in 1664 and renamed it New York, it grew much more rapidly under less harsh policies and a more tolerant religious climate.

In fact, all of England's colonies in America experienced rapid growth after their precarious beginnings. The opportunities were many for a variety of people with diverse interests in the offerings of the American settlements. Many came for purely economic reasons, including investors seeking to expand their fortunes as well as the nearly destitute looking to find a better life. Some came for religious opportunities, escaping persecutions in their homelands to establish new communities based on shared religious faith. But, as we see especially in Massachusetts, religious freedom was not an ideal held in high esteem by most who came to America. Originally seeking their own freedom, once they were established in America, few of the colonists wished to extend religious liberty to others who held dissenting views. Rhode Island and Pennsylvania remain as notable exceptions, but even in those areas, where the ideals of religious diversity gained some traction, there were limitations on their acceptance of unfamiliar traditions. In particular, nearly all of the colonists regarded the religious traditions of Native Americans and African slaves as having demonic undertones and harbored no reservations concerning their eradication. Moreover, most Protestants in the English colonies had no sympathy for Catholics; animosities bred by the Christian reformations in Europe only hardened on American soil.

Reforming Native Religions of America and Africa

As Europeans established settlements in America, their presence had profound consequences for the native peoples who inhabited lands that came under colonial domination. The colonists claimed native territories, occasionally arranging formal purchases
but usually simply taking land by force. Trade relations with the newcomers introduced new material products into native cultures, and religious missionaries sought to
convert indigenous people not only to the European religion but also to the cultural
habits of European civilization. Coinciding with the precipitous rise in the colonial
population, diseases devastated native communities; soon the Indians were greatly
outnumbered and vulnerable to the overtures of the European settlers.

At the same time, another population of non-Christian peoples was taking hold
in the Americas. The early cultivation of tobacco farming in Virginia required
intense labor, and the colonists were soon bringing Africans to work the land. Less
willing to acculturate their slaves to European civilization, the colonists made little
effort to Christianize their imported Africans. Although separated from their traditional lives and with few resources for maintaining the religions of Africa, enslaved
people persisted in their religious practices, which they adapted to the harsh conditions they endured in their lives of bondage.

Native conversions

Converting the native peoples of the lands where they settled was an important
element of the colonial enterprise, at least in theory. In New England, for instance,
the original charter in 1629 for the Massachusetts Bay Colony included **proselytizing** Indians as one justification for Puritan migration to America. It stipulated,

> whereby our said People, Inhabitants there, may be soe religiously, peaceablie, and
> civilly governed, as their good Life and orderlie Conversacon, maie wynn and incite
> the Natives of the Country, to the Knowledg and Obedience of the onlie true God
> and Savior of Mankinde, and the Christian Fayth, which in our Royall Intencon, and
> the Adventurers free Profession, is the principall Ende of this Plantacion.[29]

Fulfilling this mandate, however, was not a priority for the first colonists in New
England. In 1641, ministers back in England complained that the Puritans did not
exert themselves "in pitty to mens soules, but in hope to possesse the land of those
Infidels, or of gaine by Commerce."[30] In fact, deliberate efforts to Christianize Indians
in New England did not begin in earnest until 1643, when Thomas Mayhew, Jr. (1621–
1657) embarked on a mission of preaching to the Wampanoag people on Martha's
Vineyard just a year after Puritans first settled on the island. The following year, five
Indian leaders voluntarily submitted themselves to the authority of the English colonists; their agreement included, at least as stipulated in the document they assented
to, a desire "to be instructed in the knowledge and worship of God." News of the

Indians' submission to the European religion brought renewed enthusiasm for proselytization among the native peoples, although, without adequate infrastructure to
provide missionaries, the effort was frustratingly slow to begin.[31]

In the fall of 1646, colonial officials selected the minister of the church in
Roxbury, Massachusetts, John Eliot (1604–1690), to deliver a missionary sermon to
the Massachusett Indians near their village of Nonantum on the Charles River.
Widely known in his time as "Apostle to the Indians," Eliot dedicated himself to
bringing Christianity to the Massachusett people and other tribes of New England.
He had learned the Algonquian language from a Montauk Indian by the name of
Cockenoe (birth date unknown, died 1699) who had been taken captive in the
Pequot War and worked as a house servant for one of the colonists. Eliot preached
his first sermon to the Indians with the help of an interpreter, but the Massachusett
people did not receive his words with any sort of enthusiasm. His second effort a
short time later, however, met with a warm reception; he spoke to the people of
Nonantum for three hours and left gifts of tobacco and apples. Eliot continued his
preaching with them in the coming months, and soon he was able to claim a

Figure 2.7   Puritan missionary John Eliot became known as the "Apostle to the Indians"
for his evangelizing efforts among the Native Americans of New England. He eventually
established fourteen "praying towns" for native converts to Christianity, and he oversaw
the translation of the Christian Bible into the Algonquian language. (Courtesy of the
Library of Congress, LC, USZ62-3025.)

number of native converts to Christianity. When Nonantum needed to relocate because of pressure from colonial expansion, Eliot helped the Indians establish the new village of Natick, where they were joined by members of other tribes in the first "praying town" settlement of Native American Christians.[32]

Eventually, John Eliot oversaw the establishment of fourteen praying towns in New England. His efforts both inspired and benefited from the first formally organized missionary enterprise of Protestant Christians, the Society for the Propagation of the Gospel in New England. Established by the British Parliament in 1649 to raise funds for missionary efforts among native peoples in the colonies, it supported Eliot's praying towns and his other missionary efforts, especially his translation of the entire Christian Bible as well as other Christian works into the Algonquian language. Schools for native children were taught in both Algonquian and English, and eventually at least four Indians attended Harvard College, with one graduating.[33]

John Eliot's success among the Massachusett and other tribes of New England cannot be attributed solely to the persuasiveness of the Christian religion and the Indians' eagerness to hear the Christian gospel, as many of the colonists claimed. As one historian notes, the Indians' subjugation to English authority was prompted by complex motives that included "a hope for sheer survival of groups that were devastated by disease, that had lost most of their land, and were surrounded by enemies on all sides."[34] The traditional culture of the native peoples who inhabited the praying towns was sustained to varying degrees by a mix of hunting, fishing, and agriculture. Although they maintained their traditional way of life in their villages, the number of residents would fluctuate widely in the course of a year as the rather mobile groups pursued various food sources, returning to the villages to harvest crops. Their fluid social arrangements included sachems, or chiefs, who governed less on formal political structures and more on their personal traits. Likewise, the authority of **shamans**, who communicated with their animistic spirits, had no formal social structure; like the sachems, their power was constantly challenged by other shamans who made competing claims on the loyalty of tribal members.[35] When Christian missionaries such as John Eliot brought new sources of religious authority and political influence, especially to groups made vulnerable by the failure of traditional leaders to protect them from disease and the incursions of enemies, the Indians were already inclined to accept the Europeans' religion.

The Indians' acceptance of Christianity, however, did not involve complete abandonment of their indigenous religions and cultures. Certainly, life in the praying towns represented a significant departure from their former ways; as Eliot reports in his *Indian Dialogues* (1671), one native resident exclaimed, "I am another man than I was." Their new life involved permanent residence in the praying towns rather than their previous seminomadic lifestyle; European forms of agriculture; new social expectations with unfamiliar gender and generational roles; English names, clothing, and hair styles; and a variety of European products suited to a "civilized" life. But many of their old ways continued: traditional wigwams continued to house many of the Indians, and some of the praying towns were

Box 2.6   Eliot's Indian Bible

John Eliot's efforts to bring literacy to the native peoples of New England was meant primarily for instruction to prepare them for conversion to Christianity. As a number of Indian students became proficient in English, however, several of them assisted Eliot in translating the Christian Bible into their native Algonquian language. In 1653, the Society for the Propagation of the Gospel in New England published a primer and catechism in the Algonquian language for instructing Indians in Christian doctrine, printed on the only operating press in New England, at Harvard College. By 1661, Eliot was able to publish a translation of the entire New Testament, and in 1663 a complete volume of both the Old and New Testaments in Algonquian appeared, plus an Algonquian Psalter, or collection of the Psalms.

Eliot's scriptural translations were adequate for his missionary purposes, although they bore few literary qualities and included numerous inaccuracies as he struggled to render Christian concepts in a Native American language that assumed a very different **worldview**. In fact, some colonial leaders wondered whether a better tactic would be to teach the Indians English rather than try to have them understand the Christian texts and doctrines in their own language. Yet, despite its shortcomings, the Society for the Propagation of the Gospel in New England sponsored a second edition of the Indian Bible in 1685. A proposal in the early eighteenth century to publish yet another edition, however, faced the earlier debate of whether it was better to teach Indians Christianity in their own language or teach them English before introducing them to the intricacies of the colonists' religion. As one critic of the Indian Bible exclaimed, "It is very sure, the best thing we can do for our Indians is to Anglicize them in all agreeable Instances; and in that of Language, as well as other. They can scarce retain their Language, without a Tincture of other Savage Inclinations, which do but ill suit, either with the Honor, or with the design of Christianity." This emphasis on acculturating Indians more thoroughly to English ways prevailed, and a new printing of the Algonquian-language Indian Bible was never undertaken.[36]

protected by the indigenous architecture of palisaded forts. Native drumming called them to worship, not the bells familiar in the English towns. Above all, Algonquian remained their primary language.[37] The forces of transculturation created hybrid communities of native peoples living quasi-English lives in a land overrun by colonial settlers.

The optimism of the Puritan missionaries' success with the praying towns, however, came to an ignoble end with the outbreak of armed conflict in the 1670s known as King Philip's War. At the end of this particularly bloody period of warfare between the New England colonists and the local native tribal groups, Eliot's missionary enterprise was nearly ruined. No longer harboring an innocent regard toward native peoples, most colonists viewed Indians as cruel enemies of Christian civilization, and many considered the praying town converts as a hostile threat.[38] The elderly John Eliot was never able to reestablish his mission to the same level of success it had enjoyed before the outbreak of war, and, although many of the converts remained faithful to their Christian commitments, the Puritan missions eventually disappeared from the New England landscape.

Passages to America

In contrast to the European colonists' commitment, tenuous as it was, to converting Indians in America to Christianity, their attitudes toward Africans were far more conflicted. Certainly, there were calls to introduce the Christian religion to African slaves in the colonies, but the moral dilemmas of slavery and fears that religious teachings would incite rebellions made evangelism among the enslaved populations nearly nonexistent in the early years of colonization. Indeed, for the most part Africans in the English colonies were left to their own devices regarding their religious lives. But, for those who managed to survive the passage across the Atlantic Ocean, there were few resources to support their traditional ways. They arrived on American soil stripped of all cultural and material assets that had sustained their lives in Africa; under slavery, these Africans lost the very touchstones of their humanity. Family units were torn apart; individuals suffered unspeakable physical cruelties, including all manner of forms of sexual violence; and familiar cultural patterns, such as religious rituals honoring the ancestors, sacred song and dance traditions, even their native languages, all disappeared in a life of forced labor and unremitting hardship. Yet, despite such harsh conditions, they carried the gods and the traditional ways of Africa in their memories.[39]

The gods of Africa that crossed the deadly Middle Passage with the slaves were a diverse array of deified characters, including the monotheistic Al-Lah of Islam and the Christian god in the person of Jesus Christ, along with the many tribal deities found throughout the African continent. Most of the African slaves who came to North America were taken from the western and central areas of sub-Saharan Africa, and they brought with them an array of indigenous African religious orientations, although stripped of the hallmarks of their traditional religions, especially the communities that upheld their spiritual traditions and the sacred places inhabited by the ancestors.[40] In addition, besides the local tribal religions that were familiar to most slaves, some were Muslim. In fact, by the eighteenth century at least a few towns in western and central Africa had mosques and even schools of Qur'anic studies. The Fulbe people, for instance, a prominent ethnic group of West African Muslims, were proud of their tradition of literacy made possible by their Qur'anic schools.[41] Moreover, Christianity also had found its way onto the African continent. In the eastern part of Africa, a powerful Christian king (known to Europeans as Prester John; see Chapter 1) dominated much of the Ethiopian region. Further west, European missionaries had enjoyed some success spreading the Christian gospel among indigenous Africans, especially in the Congo, although Christianity never gained widespread acceptance among most African tribal groups. Indeed, despite the limited success of Christianity and Islam in some regions, the vast majority of African slaves came to the Americas bearing the magical, musical tribal religions of western and central Africa.

With the Africans torn from their familiar worlds of gods, spirits, and ancestors, separated from the ties of family and tribal society, stripped of all their worldly possessions, brought into a land of unfamiliar topography with strange languages and alien customs, and suffering unimaginable physical and emotional abuses, their religious traditions could not remain intact under the conditions of slavery. But Africans built new religious traditions in the Americas that drew on the one hand from the memory of their diverse religious heritages in Africa and on the other from their experiences of enslavement and their contact with other religious traditions. Especially in the British colonies, the African religious heritage had little opportunity to flourish or even survive. Yet, while they were unable to replicate their old-world religious institutions, Africans in America created new, often clandestine, traditions. They transformed their older African religions into traditions that could be sustained under slave conditions, while also attempting to maintain a semblance of their ancient spiritual moorings. Distinctive musical forms and traditional uses of magical charms are just two examples of African influences that survived in the cultures of slavery.

The indigenous religions of both Africa and America underwent rapid transformations as they encountered the colonizing forces of European Christianity. Faced with new realities that the colonists brought to the American religious landscape, the native peoples of both America and Africa adapted their religious orientations, sometimes incorporating elements of Christianity into indigenous traditions, other times holding on to traditional elements in resistance to the colonizers' religion. Either way, European colonization in America reformed the religious traditions of everyone.

New Worlds of Reformed Authorities

European settlements in North America in the seventeenth century reflected their historical status as products of Christian reformations in western Europe. The diverse Christian sects that proliferated in the wake of Martin Luther's revolt against what he regarded as a corrupt Catholic Church in Rome came to settle uneasily on American shores, bringing with them their different theologies and worship practices as well as their various models of authority, in regard to both

political governance and church organization. The two earliest of the English colonies, Virginia and Massachusetts, mark sharp contrasts in English religious life of
the seventeenth century. On the one hand, Virginia was primarily a commercial
enterprise with little emphasis on religion; the Church of England served as the
officially established religious body of the colony, but it remained largely ineffectual and was limited for the most part to social elites. On the other hand, the
Puritans who founded the Massachusetts Bay Colony imagined themselves as a
religious model to shine an exemplary light on the rest of the world, or at least on
the Christian world of western Europe. In their Puritan zeal, these reformers dili-
gently policed their community boundaries to exclude the dissenting opinions of
those who deviated from the singular Puritan vision. Ultimately, their exclusivist
model could not withstand the forces of progress and the diverse interests that
came with the colony's growth. By the end of the seventeenth century, the pluralistic mixture of groups that characterized the other English colonies in North
America had begun to make inroads into New England.

As the seventeenth century progressed, the European colonists along the
Atlantic seaboard of North America included far more than Anglicans of the
Church of England and Puritan separatists; their numbers also included radical
dissenters such as the Quakers and Baptists, as well as Lutherans and Presbyterians,
Dutch Reformed and French Huguenots, and even some Catholics and a few
Jewish congregations. Martin Luther's challenge to the authority of the Catholic
Church had irrevocably fractured the religious unity of Christians in Europe into
a baffling array of sects, each with their own forms of authority and governance,
most of whom landed in the Americas.

Yet, even as the number of Protestants grew in the Americas, they remained a
minority, confined largely to the English colonies along the east coast of North
America. Roman Catholics in territories held by the Spanish, French, and
Portuguese remained the most populous Christians in the western hemisphere.
Moreover, millions of Native Americans continued practicing their indigenous
religions, although their numbers declined precipitously in the wake of genocidal
contact with Europeans. In addition, growing numbers of Africans imported as
slaves throughout the Americas brought their own indigenous religions, which
they continued to practice in various ways, and a few of the Muslim Africans who
arrived on the slave ships were able to practice their Islamic faith, even under conditions of slavery. Indeed, Protestant Christians constituted a small, though
significant, sector of the diverse religious landscape in the complex colonial multiverse of the Americas in the seventeenth century.

Questions for Discussion

(1) How did religious reformations in sixteenth-century Europe affect the colonization
of the Americas?

(2) In what ways did the various English colonies in America differ in their religious makeup?

(3)   Compare and contrast how colonists used various types of religious authority in the American colonies; specifically, how did traditional, charismatic, and legal-rational forms of authority operate among the religious communities in the English colonies?

(4)   What limitations did European colonists face in their goal of Christianizing Native Americans and African Americans?

Suggested Primary-Source Readings

John Rolfe, "Letter to Governor regarding Marriage to Pocahontas," in *A Documentary History of Religion in America*, vol. 1, 3rd edn, ed. Edwin S. Gaustad and Mark A. Noll (Grand Rapids, MI: W. B. Eerdmans, 2003): The Jamestown colonist justifies his marriage to the daughter of Powhatan, the leader of local native tribes.

John Winthrop, "A Model of Christian Charity," available online at the Internet Archive at https://archive.org/details/AModelOfChristianCharity: The sermon that the leader of the Massachusetts Bay Colony purportedly delivered during the voyage of the Puritan colonists to America; the "city on a hill" imagery has often been quoted throughout American history.

"The Examination of Mrs. Anne Hutchinson at the Court at Newton," in *The Antinomian Controversy, 1636–1638: A Documentary History*, 2nd edn, ed. David D. Hall (Durham, NC: Duke University Press, 1990), 311–348: This is the long version of the transcript of Anne Hutchison's civic trial in November 1637.

Roger Williams, "Letter to the Town of Providence on the Limits of Religious Liberty," in *American Religions: A Documentary History*, ed. R. Marie Griffith (New York: Oxford University Press, 2008): This represents Williams' attempt to clarify the relationship between religious liberty and civic responsibility, as he understood it.

Michael Clark, ed., *The Eliot Tracts: With Letters from John Eliot to Thomas Thorowgood and Richard Baxter* (Westport, CT: Praeger, 2003): The tracts and letters related to John Eliot's proselytization of native peoples in New England represent the most detailed record of English missionary work in seventeenth-century America.

Samuel Sewall, "The Selling of Joseph: A Memorial," in *A Documentary History of Religion in America*, vol. 1, 3rd edn, ed. Edwin S. Gaustad and Mark A. Noll (Grand Rapids, MI: W. B. Eerdmans, 2003): The prominent Puritan merchant and judge argues in 1700 that slavery is immoral and wrong.

Notes

1   Harry Kelsey, *Sir Francis Drake: The Queen's Pirate* (New Haven, CT: Yale University Press, 1998), 9–10.

2   Ibid., 10.

3   Ibid., 111.

4   Francis Drake and Francis Fletcher, *The World Encompassed* (Ann Arbor, MI: University Microfilms, 1966), 52–53.

5   Quoted in Kelsey, *Sir Francis Drake*, 175–176.

6   Quoted in ibid., 176.

 7 Max Weber, *The Theory of Social and Economic Organization* (Glencoe, IL: Free Press, 1957), 358–359.

 8 Kenneth Burke, *The Rhetoric of Religion: Studies in Logology* (Berkeley: University of California Press, 1970), v.

 9 Mark A. Noll, *The Work We Have to Do: A History of Protestants in America* (New York: Oxford University Press, 2002), 16.

10 Diarmaid MacCulloch, *The Reformation* (New York: Viking, 2004), 71.

11 Ibid., 74–75.

12 Martin E. Marty, *Martin Luther* (New York: Viking, 2004), 2–3.

13 MacCulloch, *The Reformation*, 116–117.

14 Quoted in Michael A. Mullett, *Martin Luther* (New York: Routledge, 2004), 75.

15 Michael A. Mullett, *The Catholic Reformation* (New York: Routledge, 1999), 142.

16 Erika Rummel, *Jiménez De Cisneros: On the Threshold of Spain's Golden Age* (Tempe: Arizona Center for Medieval and Renaissance Studies, 1999).

17 Quoted in Richard Samuel Thomas, *The Old Brick Church, near Smithfield, Virginia* (Richmond: Virginia Historical Society, 1892), 7.

18 Quoted in Keely Susan Kuhlman, " Transatlantic Travel and Cultural Exchange in the Early Colonial Era: The Hybrid American Female and Her New World Colony" (Ph.D. dissertation in the Department of English, Washington State University, May 2006), 92.

19 Ibid., 93–94.

20 Quoted in Henrietta Elizabeth Marshall, *This Country of Ours: The Story of the United States* (New York: George H. Doran Co., 1917), first paragraph of chapter 23.

21 Noll, *The Work We Have to Do*, 32.

22 Perry Miller, "Errand into the Wilderness," in *Religion in American History: A Reader*, ed. Jon Butler and Harry S. Stout (New York: Oxford University Press, 1998 [1956]), 31–32.

23 David D. Hall, *Worlds of Wonder, Days of Judgment: Popular Religious Belief in Early New England* (Cambridge, MA: Harvard University Press, 1990), 14.

24 "The Examination of Mrs. Anne Hutchinson at the Court at Newton," in *The Antinomian Controversy, 1636–1638: A Documentary History*, ed. David D. Hall, 2nd edn (Durham, NC: Duke University Press, 1990), 311–348.

25 For a more complete discussion of Anne Hutchinson and the Antinomian Crisis, see Michael P. Winship, *Making Heretics: Militant Protestantism and Free Grace in Massachusetts, 1636–1641* (Princeton, NJ: Princeton University Press, 2002) and Michael P. Winship, *The Times and Trials of Anne Hutchinson: Puritans Divided* (Lawrence: University Press of Kansas, 2005).

26 Quoted in Sydney E. Ahlstrom, *A Religious History of the American People* (Garden City, NY: Image Books, 1975), 168.

27 Quoted in Edmund S. Morgan, "The World and William Penn," in *Religion in American History: A Reader*, ed. Jon Butler and Harry S. Stout (New York: Oxford University Press, 1998 [1983]), 65.

28 "Novum Belgium by Father Isaac Jogues, 1646," in *Narratives of New Netherland, 1609–1664*, ed. J. Franklin Jameson (New York: Charles Scribner's Sons, 1909), 259.

29 Quoted in Michael Clark, ed., *The Eliot Tracts: With Letters from John Eliot to Thomas Thorowgood and Richard Baxter* (Westport, CT: Praeger, 2003), 1.

30 Quoted in ibid.

31 Ibid., 9–10.

32   Ibid., 9–11.
33   Ibid., 12.
34   Ibid., 9.
35   Ibid., 6–17.
36   Ibid., 13–14.
37   Ibid., 18–19.
38   Ibid., 22–23.
39   Albert J. Raboteau, *Slave Religion: The "Invisible Institution" in the Antebellum South*, updated edn (New York: Oxford University Press, 2004), 16.
40   Ibid., 7.
41   Allan D. Austin, *African Muslims in Antebellum America: Transatlantic Stories and Spiritual Struggles*, rev. and updated edn (New York: Routledge, 1997), 23.

3

Conflicts and Persecutions

Our attention in this chapter will be on the struggles, conflicts, and persecutions between the diverse groups involved in the colonization of North America in the seventeenth century. The chapter begins with the Spaniards among Pueblo peoples in the southwestern part of the continent and ends with witch trials in New England; in these and other cases we will learn how religion played a key role in numerous conflicts of the colonial period. In particular, our focus on the assorted religious orientations of the people involved in the various conflicts will demonstrate an array of ways in which the perspectives, attitudes, beliefs, practices, and traditions of a religion determine the manner in which religious people engage in contentious battles with others and how they attribute meaning to such struggles.

From the earliest years of European exploration and settlement, the diversity of religious orientations made America a place of religious contact, exchange, tensions, and conflicts. Even before the famous voyages of Columbus that initiated European incursions onto the American continents, the indigenous peoples of the Americas displayed a wide range of cultural and religious modes whose differences often conflicted. The coming of Europeans, and the Africans they brought with them, introduced even more diversity into the religious geography of the Americas, and along with these differences came clashes that in many instances resulted in violent measures. Often the violence was overt and obvious, resulting in physical harm and even death for individuals and sometimes entire groups; far more common, however, were less obvious strategies of domination that displaced and often destroyed cultural traditions; in nearly every circumstance, the processes of

Formed From This Soil: An Introduction to the Diverse History of Religion in America, First Edition. Thomas S. Bremer.
© 2015 Thomas S. Bremer. Published 2015 by John Wiley & Sons, Ltd.

colonization tore apart social bonds and enforced new ways of living and working that utterly transformed the familiar worlds of long-established native groups.

Religion played a crucial role in conflicts between groups of people in the early years of contact. These conflicts most often were between European newcomers and the indigenous inhabitants of a region; the introduction of colonial relations, though, also exacerbated conflicts between various Native American groups as well as intensified national rivalries between groups of Europeans. As they encountered each other in the contact zones of the Americas, these various groups relied on their respective religious orientations to make sense of their differences and to interpret the circumstances of their encounters. Many of the indigenous Americans appealed to sacred traditions, stories, and texts for understanding the strangeness of other peoples' traditions and actions; they relied on their religious leaders to perform necessary **rituals** in response to the arrival of newcomers on their horizons; and, perhaps most importantly, they turned to the moral teachings of their religious outlook to judge the actions of the strangers and to justify their own course of action in response to them. As bewildering and sometimes incomprehensible as their reactions may seem to outsiders, in virtually every case a group's response to unanticipated circumstances made sense in the logic and expectations of their own cultural and religious understandings. For instance, as horrified and baffled as Hernán Cortés (1485–1547) and his compatriots were when the Aztecs marched their captives to the top of the Templo Mayor as sacrificial victims, it made perfect sense as an unquestioned necessity to the Aztecs. From the perspective of their religious understandings, the world itself could not survive without the sacrifice of their war captives on their sacred temple.

Besides the resources that religions provide for responding to the circumstances of encounters with unfamiliar peoples, religious traditions and practices also serve as powerful tools in subjugating dominated groups. In particular, converting others to one's own religion also entails converting them to one's culture and way of living. To the extent that religions involve a cultural logic for the way that people organize their lives and determine the moral basis for their actions, the acceptance of another's religious orientation also includes the acceptance of their cultural logic. As an example, when native peoples in what is now the American southwest fell under the protection of Franciscan missionaries, not only did they accept the precepts of the Franciscans' form of Christianity but they also accepted European notions of time that required an orderly schedule regulated by the mission bells, in addition to a sedentary mission life organized around agriculture and the needs of the mission community. Thus, the spread of Christianity among groups that European Christians colonized also entailed the spread of European cultural ideas and ways of living.

Of course, accepting the religions of others, along with the cultural, social, political, and economic changes that accompanied religious conversions, was never a simple or easy process. Indeed, we cannot separate a group's religious orientations, the beliefs and practices that they regard as essential and sacred to their understandings of themselves and the world, from other aspects of their cultural, social, political, and economic lives. In this chapter we consider the complexities of religious encounters by examining a few instances of conflict between people with different religious orientations during the seventeenth century. In the examples discussed here, we begin to understand not only the complex circumstances of religious conflict but also how dominated groups resisted the persecutions of those who dominated them, as well as how different people relied on their own religious orientations to interpret and respond to adverse circumstances and disastrous events.

Native Revolutions

European settlements in the Americas had much to do with national rivalries back in Europe. Mistrust, animosity, and outright violent conflict between different European nations accompanied the settlers as they explored, established colonies, and settled in the various regions of the Americas. Hence, the Spanish remained wary of French ambitions to encroach on Spanish claims in North America, and both Spanish and French Catholics held deep hatred for English Protestants settling along the Atlantic coast of North America. Caught between the extension of Old World conflicts to New World contexts, native peoples encountered the newly arrived Europeans in a variety of contact zones. Different Native American groups, however, responded differently to the invading strangers and to their gradual settlement and colonization of the native territories. By briefly considering a few examples of the many different circumstances of colonial relations between Europeans and native peoples, we can glimpse how very different historical contexts and religious orientations resulted in different outcomes, both for the success of European colonizing efforts and for the ability of Native American groups to adapt and survive when faced with severe upheaval in their traditional ways of living.

The Pueblo Revolt

Before the arrival of Europeans, Pueblo peoples had long subsisted as sedentary agriculturists in the arid regions of the American southwest, most of them devoted to local variations of the Kachina religion (described in the discussion of the Hopis in Chapter 1). Beginning in the sixteenth century, a new force entered the sacred worlds of the Pueblos. Based on reports from the Spaniard Álvar Núñez Cabeza de Vaca (ca. 1490–1559) and his companions who had survived the disastrous Narváez expedition and had lived among native groups of the American southwest for a number of years in the 1530s, Spanish expeditions came north from central Mexico in search of great riches to be found in fabled Indian cities. Estebanico (ca. 1500–1539), the Moorish slave who had survived with Cabeza de Vaca, guided a preliminary reconnaissance in 1539 into Pueblo territory, only to meet his end at the hands of the people of the Zuni Pueblo of Hawikuh, what the Spaniards regarded as the legendary city of Cíbola and where they expected to find immense riches. According to others with him who fled the Pueblo, the leaders of Hawikuh killed Estebanico as a witch. The leader of the expedition, Fray Marcos de Niza (ca. 1495–1558), insisted on seeing Cíbola for himself, and he viewed it from a distance. Upon his return, Fray Marcos spread stories of great wealth in the north, enticing yet another expedition, led by Francisco de Coronado (1510–1554) in 1540. Returning to Hawikuh with Fray Marcos and a substantial military force, Coronado discovered nothing resembling the wealth he expected to find there, expressing profound disappointment in Fray Marcos' previous reports, writing that the Franciscan had "not told the truth in a single thing."[1]

It was not until the following century that Spanish missionaries began in earnest to establish themselves in the Pueblo region as they played a key role in the Spanish transformation of what they called New Mexico. By the 1630s, there were nearly fifty Franciscan missionaries working in thirty-five of the Pueblo settlements; they were part of the roughly 750 non-native people living in New Mexico, including Spaniards, a number of Indians they brought up with them from central Mexico, and African slaves.[2] In addition, because so few Spanish women came to New Mexico, Spaniards took native Pueblo women, African slave women, and Apache captives for concubines, mistresses, and occasionally legal wives.[3]

Over the course of the seventeenth century, the Pueblo peoples were caught in the middle of conflicts between the missionaries on the one hand and the colonial civil government on the other. Many of the disputes between the colonists revolved around economic issues, with both sides vying for the labor of the native peoples. For their part, the civil authorities exploited Indians held in *encomienda*, a system of forced labor that the Spaniards instituted throughout the colonies to benefit from the toil of conquered peoples. As the Spaniards established ranches throughout New Mexico for raising cattle and sheep, they benefited from Indian labor to operate the ranches. In exchange for receiving the rights to Indian labor, the *encomenderos*, or owners of the *encomiendos*, were obligated to provide military service and Indian labor to the colonial government. In addition, the government enlisted native Puebloans to help with slaving raids among Plains Indians to the north.[4] As a key form of capital for the colonists, Indian slaves in *encomienda* became highly regarded commodities. In 1633, a Franciscan missionary in Santa Fe complained of Indian children being stolen from their parents at an early age "as if they were yearling calfs or colts … and placed in permanent slavery." By 1680 half of the Spanish households in New Mexico had at least one Indian, and some had as many as thirty.[5]

Franciscan missionaries publicly opposed the exploitation of Pueblo peoples by the civil authorities, and they sought to keep the Indians under their control in the missions. Nonetheless, they also exploited Indian labor as the missions themselves developed significant sheep-ranching operations. Despite the

Franciscans' protestations of exploitation and abuse of Indians by the civil authorities in the *encomienda* system, the Pueblo people suffered instances of severe cruelty at the hands of the missionaries themselves. Their relative autonomy allowed the missionaries in New Mexico considerable latitude in disciplining their native subjects. Whipping was widely used for purported transgressions of missionary rules, and a few of the missionaries applied this punishment zealously. Indians were flogged for such things as missing religious services, sexual offenses, and a variety of minor offenses. In one particularly brutal case, a missionary working among the Hopi people beat one man to death and often whipped even children for relatively minor offenses; reportedly he followed the beatings with an application of hot turpentine poured onto his victims' wounds. There were also reports of missionaries perpetrating sexual abuse of Indians in the Pueblos.[6]

Despite reports of abuse and brutality, it remains clear that the overriding goal of the missionaries, and the justification of their work in New Mexico, was to bring Christianity to the Pueblo peoples. This meant, foremost, eradicating native religions. They especially attacked Pueblo religious ceremonies and celebrations, and they regarded the public Kachina dances, the central communal religious celebration in the Pueblos, as satanic events that must be forbidden.[7] In many cases, enforcement required martial force, and missionaries acknowledged that their **proselytizing** efforts had little chance of success without the military support of the colonists. Religious conversions occurred, according to one Franciscan missionary, when their religious efforts were "reinforced by the fear and respect which the Indians have for the Spaniards," which came from the military force that the soldiers provided in subjugating native populations.[8] The missionaries soon realized, however, that Pueblo religions were closely tied to native social and political systems, and successful conversion to Christianity would also entail adoption of European culture and values. They focused their evangelization and enculturation efforts on the children, who were required to attend Christian church services every week, even daily, where they learned the rituals and doctrines of Christianity and were constantly told that the native celebrations of Pueblo traditions were evil. Pueblo leaders, however, resisted the eradication of their culture and religious traditions, and in some cases they enjoyed the support of civil authorities in their efforts to resist the missionaries. Although the Spanish governors sought to exploit the native peoples, they also wished to limit the power of the missionaries. Thus, they sometimes refused to enforce restrictions on Indian dances, and in at least one case a governor actually encouraged the dances over the objections of the Franciscan missionaries.[9]

The Pueblos also suffered the devastating effects of newly introduced diseases; populations declined precipitously as epidemics of such illnesses as smallpox and typhus swept through the region. Exacerbating the suffering wrought upon the Pueblos by the Spaniards and their introduction of deadly microbes, a series of droughts in the 1660s and early 1670s intensified the harsh conditions in New Mexico, and these in turn encouraged raids by more nomadic groups such as the Apache. By the 1670s, a number of Pueblo settlements had been abandoned altogether.[10]

As conditions became unbearable, rebellions broke out among the Pueblo natives, beginning in 1640 when the natives of Taos Pueblo killed their resident priest. In 1649, a rebellion at Jemez Pueblo resulted in the execution of twenty-nine Indians, plus the flogging and imprisonment of others. The Spaniards were able to subdue a general rebellion of several Pueblos in 1653; nine of the purported leaders were hanged.[11] In 1672, residents of Abó Pueblo burned the Christian church there and brutally killed the priest. They placed his naked body on a cross hugging an image of the Virgin Mary, and at its feet were three lambs, representing the Christian Trinity, with their throats slashed.[12]

Tensions in the region continued to build. A new Spanish governor arrived in New Mexico in 1675 and commenced a campaign to eradicate Indian idolatry. He executed several native "sorcerers" and took into custody another forty-seven Pueblo religious leaders accused of practicing witchcraft. In response, an armed force of Tewa people laid siege to Santa Fe and demanded the release of their leaders, who had suffered floggings and were to be sold into slavery. Faced with an overpowering show of native military might, the governor gave in and released the Pueblo religious leaders.[13] Among them was Popé (often spelled Po'pay, ca. 1630–ca. 1688), a Tewa religious leader from the Pueblo of San Juan, who afterward sought refuge in the Taos Pueblo and began planning a retaliation against the Spaniards. By 1680, he had organized an alliance among the diverse and sometimes rival Pueblo peoples, along with others who opposed Spanish rule, such as native peoples from central Mexico brought north as slaves and a number of people of African descent also enslaved by the Spaniards. In addition, some Navajo and Apache people, long enemies of the Pueblos, joined in the Pueblo alliance against the Spaniards in hopes of capturing the large herds of cattle and horses from the colonists.[14]

Popé set out to organize a rebellion with a strong religious millenarian character. He envisioned a coming time when the peoples of the region would be freed from the oppressive and brutal regime of Spanish rule, with the promise that good health and prosperity would return to the Pueblos.[15] Killing the Christians and their god, Popé told his followers, would allow the native gods to return and restore the harmony that the ancestors had enjoyed following their first emergence from the underworld.[16]

What historians have called the Great Pueblo Revolt began at dawn on August 10, 1680 and it primarily targeted the Franciscan missionaries located in the Pueblos; twenty-one of the thirty-three missionaries died at the hands of the rebels. An Indian military force laid siege to the colonial capital of Santa Fe, and, by the time the surviving Spaniards fled to Texas, over four hundred had been

---

Box 3.1   Millenarianism

In conditions of extreme hardship and suffering at the hands of others, people often turn to religious traditions and resources for relief. In many cases, religious leaders will instigate a rebellion by appealing to religious understandings of justice, by stipulating ritual practices designed to invoke religious powers to transform social conditions, and by offering religious hope for a renewal of peace, prosperity, and the end of suffering. Scholars of religions have called these sorts of religious movements that precipitate an expectation of an imminent social transformation "millenarianism," referring to the specifically Christian notion of a millennial age of peace and paradise on earth marked by the thousand-year reign of Christ prior to God's final judgment of the world, according to the Christian sacred Book of Revelation. Although the term retains its Christian origin in reference to a thousand-year period of prosperity, "millenarianism" has been used to describe a diverse range of religiously grounded social movements aimed at transforming current conditions, often with rebellious intentions that include violent displacement of oppressive rulers.[17] Historians have noted the millenarian rhetoric in Popé's organization of the Pueblo Revolt of 1680, and millenarianism has undergirded many other instances of Native American resistance to Euro-American conquest and oppression, and sometimes eradication, of Indian cultural traditions; these include the early nineteenth-century Red Sticks War of Muskogee people in what are now the states of Alabama and Georgia, and the Ghost Dance among various native peoples of the American west late in the nineteenth century. Numerous rebellions among African American slaves in the antebellum period also included strong millenarian elements, such as the famous insurrection led by Nat Turner (1800–1831) in 1831.

---

killed.[18] The Spaniards regarded the fallen friars as martyrs of the faith, whose deaths were to be celebrated; their Franciscan colleagues declared, "We do not mourn the blood shed by twenty-one of our brothers, for from them comes to our sacred religion such an access of faith and such honor and glory to God and His church." Another added that "what the world calls losses, [are] really the richest treasure of the church."[19]

For a time, the Pueblos were free from Spanish influence. They proceeded to rid their settlements of most traces of European culture, especially the churches and ritual paraphernalia of Christianity. But the Pueblos' freedom from Spanish interference would be short lived. The promised period of peace and prosperity in the rebels' millenarian vision did not materialize, and the unity they experienced in their uprising against the Spaniards could not be maintained. The coalition

Figure 3.1   Popé, leader of the Pueblo Revolt of 1680, was commemorated with the dedication of his statue in the Rotunda of the US Capitol building, September 2005. (Photograph by Chris Maddaloni, CQ-Roll Call, Inc., from Getty Images.)

between the various Pueblo peoples and their non-Pueblo allies soon deteriorated in the face of competing interests and cultural diversity spread over great distances.[20] Disappointed that Popé's promises did not materialize, and by his own subsequent demands for women, grain, and livestock, the Pueblo people deposed their rebel leader. Eventually, disputes and power struggles at the various Pueblos, exacerbated by continuing drought, hunger, and disease as well as frequent raids from Apaches and others, led to a complete collapse of the coalition that had ousted the Spanish colonial regime from New Mexico.[21] In 1692, the Spaniards returned to reconquer the New Mexico Pueblos, and by the turn of the eighteenth century all of the Pueblos except the Hopi were under the colonial reign of the Christian conquerors.

Being furthest from the colonial capital of Santa Fe, the Hopi people did not succumb to the reassertion of Spanish sovereignty in New Mexico, and many residents from other Pueblos fled there for safety from the Spanish conquerors. In fact, the animosity among Hopi people toward Spanish Christians extended even to their own people who cooperated with Spaniards in their attempt to reestablish Christianity in the Hopi Pueblos. In one particularly brutal instance, the people of the Hopi village of Awatobi submitted to the overtures of a Franciscan missionary in 1700, but their hospitality turned tragic when neighboring Hopis descended upon the village during the night and killed all the Awatobi men; they carried off the surviving women and children to other Hopi villages and then burned Awatobi to the ground. Thereafter, the Hopi had very limited contact with the Spanish, and were able to continue their ancient ways of life and to practice their native religious traditions with only minimal interference from Christian outsiders.[22]

The Hopis' preservation of their ancient cultural ways is a rare exception to the deleterious consequences of colonization. In fact, one historian has characterized the Pueblo Revolt as resistance to "cultural genocide." Christianizing native peoples, according to how the missionaries understood their role, required the complete extirpation of Pueblo religious beliefs and practices, but this also brought severe disruptions to the very fabric of Pueblo lifeways at virtually every level. Learning from their previous experience, the Spanish missionaries who returned to New Mexico were less adamant about regarding every aspect of native culture as the work of Satan, and consequently they were more tolerant of what they regarded as the Indians' "superstitions."[23] Their success is evident in a continuous Christian presence in many Pueblo villages that has lasted even to the present.

Jesuit penetrations

In contrast to the early efforts of Spanish Franciscans in New Mexico, French Jesuit missionaries working in what is now eastern Canada were more willing to accommodate indigenous customs and ways of living from the outset, even as they sought to eradicate the native religious traditions. By 1632, Jesuits were the sole missionaries working in New France, and their efforts among native peoples, especially the Wyandots (whom the French called Hurons[24]), played a key role in the success of Europeans in exploiting the rich resources of the woodlands and their inhabitants in the northernmost portions of the continent.

Unlike indigenous peoples of the region, who saw every element of the land and nature as suffused with religious significance, the Jesuits viewed lands in America as hostile, barren, and dangerous. It was an untamed wilderness where Satan dwelled, reflecting what they understood to be the spiritual condition of its native inhabitants.[25] To tame and civilize both the land and its people, the Jesuits engaged in a strategy of what they called "flying missions," which involved living among indigenous peoples, learning their native languages, and allowing them to preserve much of their traditional ways of life, thereby building trust by pursuing missionary goals largely on native terms. In fact, the Jesuit missionaries' resistance to converting Wyandot and other native peoples to French culture and European standards of living frustrated French civil authorities in the colony, who even attempted to discipline the Jesuits in the 1660s and 1670s for refusing to cooperate with the authorities' efforts to bring Indians more in line with European expectations and standards.[26]

The Wyandot were actually a confederation of four tribal groups that dominated the region of Georgian Bay, a large and prominent cove along the north shore of Lake Ontario in the southern region of what is now the Canadian province of Ontario. They lived in a series of villages supported by agriculture, fishing, and

Box 3.2   *The Jesuit Relations*

For more than four decades, from 1632 through 1673, the Jesuits published an annual report from the missionary field, *The Relations des Jesuites de la Nouvelle-France*, commonly known in English as *The Jesuit Relations*. This collection of field reports has been a rich source of ethnographic information about the native peoples of the Great Lakes region during the early period of European colonization.[27] They included reports on the efforts and successes of Jesuit missionaries in the field working among the indigenous tribes and also transmitted substantial information about the native peoples themselves, including their ways of life, customs, and beliefs. Living among the Indians for long periods gave the missionaries an intimate view into their societies, their traditions, their relations with others, and even their personal lives, all of which has been a valuable trove of insight for historians, anthropologists, and other scholars into the indigenous worlds of America at the time of first contact with Europeans.

Contemporary scholars, however, must read the Jesuits' accounts of native cultures with caution; the *Relations* were not written as careful historical accounts or accurate ethnographic portraits of native society. They served as justifications of Jesuit efforts in New France and as promotional materials for gaining economic and political support for their missions. In this regard, scholars have long recognized the distorting effect of the Jesuit agenda of presenting their accomplishments among the Indians in the best possible light. Nearly all readers, including many in the seventeenth century, have viewed the enthusiastic accounts of zealous Indians embracing Christianity with considerable skepticism. Likewise, more recent scholarship has demonstrated the need for skeptical readings of the Jesuits' descriptions of native cultures and customs. Produced as an artifact of the colonial enterprise, the *Relations* are careful to present Native Americans as inferior humans in need of European guidance and protection. They are, as one historian notes, an "integral component of the politics of colonialism, because they expressed the themes, ideas, and ideologies that served domination and justified the colonial endeavor."[28] This does not mean that they do not reveal important information about native understandings and practices, but that such information comes through a very particular filter that tends to distort our vision of how native peoples lived and how they understood themselves, others, and their relations to their environment. In other words, far from trusting the *Relations* at face value, we must read them carefully, skillfully, and with considerable skepticism.

hunting. Although they remained sedentary for the most part, excellent skill in canoeing and an intricate system of trails contributed to considerable mobility.[29] Their religious proclivities were thoroughly integrated into every facet of Wyandot life, and thus remained largely invisible to the European Christians who wished to convert them to their own religion. In the absence of an obvious group of **clergy** or particular places designated as sacred, Christians had difficulty identifying the religious dimensions of Wyandot society and culture. Their animist orientation regarded all things as being suffused with animating spirits; the spirits they called *oki* were able to influence human activities for either good or bad, including such important undertakings as war, travel, and procreation. Consequently, Wyandot people were careful to perform the proper rituals to ensure a felicitous outcome whenever they engaged in vital activities.[30]

Jesuit missionaries sought to penetrate the unfamiliar world of the Wyandot by residing among them in their native villages. When the French returned to the area in the 1630s, after having lost the territory for a time to the English, they demanded that the Wyandot accommodate Jesuit missionaries to live among them as a condition for reestablishing trade relations with the French. This strategy of pursuing their missionary activities within native society derived from the Jesuits' long experience in Asia, where they had enjoyed success by seeking to alter indigenous customs as little as possible as they introduced Christianity in terms that the native peoples could understand and easily adopt.[31]

Among the Wyandot, Jesuit missionaries concentrated on a threefold strategy of evangelism that involved supporting local political leaders, discrediting and eventually displacing religious leaders, and gaining the general trust and support of new converts to Christianity, thus building acceptance among the native populace.[32] Much of their efforts went toward undermining the authority of **shamans**, whom the Christian missionaries regarded as satanic practitioners. The Jesuits used a coordinated strategy for weakening the shamans' position in native society that included attacking the religious beliefs that supported shamanic authority, assailing their practices as nothing more than charlatanry designed to gain wealth and power for the shamans, and insisting that Christianity was a better, more efficacious and reliable religious orientation.[33] Moreover, the Jesuit missionaries' sincerity contrasted with that of other French colonists, which aided their efforts to Christianize the Wyandot people; unlike the fur traders and other Europeans in New France, the missionaries showed little interest in acquiring Indian lands, in undertaking sexual liaisons with Indian women, or in making war on native peoples, which bolstered their trust among the Wyandot.[34] Their exclusive devotion to religious purposes kept them focused on bringing Christianity to the people in the wild lands of the far north.

Yet, despite the sincere devotion with which the Jesuits pursued their quest to convert Wyandot peoples, many of the native converts adopted Christianity less out of religious motives and more for economic, political, and social reasons. Indeed, Christian Wyandot enjoyed the benefits of a closer and stronger relationship to the French colonists, including not only the material benefits of European products but also social ties and political support against non-Christian rivals.[35] On the other hand, the introduction of Christianity into Wyandot society weakened the social bonds between individuals as competing factions formed around the division between Christian converts and those who remained faithful to their native religious traditions. In fact, the Jesuits' narrow focus on the religious salvation of individuals made the Wyandot people as a whole more vulnerable to traditional foes such as the Iroquois; deep divisions that the missionaries introduced into Wyandot society made it more difficult to agree collectively on key political, economic, and military strategies. Indeed, the Jesuit missionary effort had the unfortunate result of putting the salvation of individual souls ahead of the collective safety and well-being of the Wyandot people.[36]

The Jesuits also realized that religious conversion was not the end of their work among native peoples; enticing converts to remain faithful to their new religious orientation proved more difficult than securing their conversion in the first place. Regardless of their desire to conform to the missionaries' insistence on disavowing their former religious beliefs and practices, Wyandot converts could not avoid continuing with much of their native religion, which pervaded every aspect of their way of life.[37] The Jesuits came to believe that a genuine conversion to Christianity must involve a thorough eradication of native religious practices in every aspect of Wyandot life. They began to insist on a complete renouncement of native religious beliefs and practices as a condition for baptism, and they lent powerful support to native Christian leaders who opposed traditionalist anti-Jesuit factions in Wyandot society.

Eventually, the Jesuits prevailed over the Wyandot; by 1648, the anti-Jesuit Wyandot sector had been defeated, and the missionaries began to relax many of the more stringent regulations they had imposed on native traditional practices. Their success in Christianizing Wyandot society, however, ended the following year when a large Iroquois force attacked the Wyandot. Within a few years, the Wyandot had fallen to the Iroquois, and the Jesuits turned their attention to evangelizing the new dominant group.[38]

Like the Spanish missionaries in New Mexico, the Jesuits in New France garnered considerable zeal for evangelizing Native American people and bringing them into the religious and cultural orbit of Europe. In both cases, the religious goals of the missionaries came into direct conflict with the economic and administrative goals of other colonists. The Jesuits' resistance to pressures by colonial administrators to instill European standards and culture among the Wyandot caused tensions between the religious and civic elements of French colonial efforts. For the Franciscans in New Mexico, however, their own economic ambitions to build prosperous missions conflicted with the economic opportunities of other colonists. Moreover, the very different geographies and native cultures of the Wyandot and Pueblos involved varying approaches to the missionary enterprise, with assorted outcomes. In arid and sparsely vegetated New Mexico, the Franciscans encountered sedentary agricultural settlements subsisting without significant reliance on trade with Europeans, and they attempted to convert these semiurban societies to the model of European villages. They built mission churches in the Pueblos and imposed European culture and religion onto the native peoples by force. Their success, however, remained tenuous, and eventually the entire colonial enterprise collapsed in a native uprising that drove the Spaniards out of New Mexico for a time. When the missionaries eventually returned, they adopted a more accommodating, and subsequently more enduring, style of missionizing. In contrast, the Jesuits in New France entered a lushly forested region inhabited by semisedentary people who benefited greatly from trade with Europeans. Insisting on living among the Wyandot with a strategy of "flying missions," the missionaries enjoyed success over the course of several decades by building more trustful relationships through accommodating much of indigenous culture, customs, and

Figure 3.2   This 1869 painting shows the Jesuit missionary Jacques Marquette (1637–1675) in New France. Marquette joined the 1673 expedition of French fur trader Louis Joliet (1645–1700) to explore and map the Mississippi River. They went as far south as the mouth of the Arkansas River, claiming much of the Mississippi River Valley and the Great Lakes region for France. (Wilhelm Lamprecht, German, 1838–1901, *Pere Marquette and the Indians*, 1869, oil on canvas, 43 ½ × 53 in, 110.5 × 134.6 cm, 00.3, Gift of Rev. Stanislaus L. Lalumiere, S. J., Collection of the Haggerty Museum of Art, Marquette University; courtesy of the Haggerty Museum of Art, Marquette University.)

society. Though both the Franciscans and the Jesuits came to America out of zeal to evangelize native peoples, they brought very different strategies to very different cultural settings and garnered very distinct results from their efforts.

Improvements upon the Land

Unlike the French and the Spanish, England's colonial enterprise involved less engagement with Native American populations and more attention to the American landscape. From the beginning, English colonizing efforts focused more on making improvements to what the settlers regarded as a barren and harsh wilderness; in particular, they tended to claim lands by demarcating boundaries, building houses with gardens, clearing fields, and planting crops. In fact, the metaphor of "planting" defined much of how the English understood their settlement of American lands. For instance, the original charter for Virginia, the first successful English colony in North America, employed the planting metaphor in allowing the prospective colonists "to begin their Plantation and Habitation" in the newly claimed country. This "plantation" of Virginia, moreover, had biblical import for the colonists; the official directive to the first settlers of the colony instructed them "to serve and fear God, the Giver of all goodness, for every plantation which our heavenly Father hath not planted shall be rooted out."[39] Indeed, the eventual success of the first settlement of Jamestown seemed like a carefully cultivated plant sprouting vigorously in a wild land, at least to the assessment of one colonist, who declared in 1641 that Jamestown "hath taken better root; and as a spreading herbe, whose top hath been often cropped off, renewes her growth, and spreads herselfe more gloriously."[40] By the middle of the seventeenth century, the English settlers had planted themselves successfully in

---

Box 3.3   Sacred space

Distinctive attitudes toward land by different groups of religious people reveal spatial aspects of religious orientations, which often involve religious conflicts. According to phenomenologist of religions Mircea Eliade (1907–1986), humans understand space according to two heterogeneous categories: sacred and profane. Particularly powerful places of religious significance are set apart as sacred in contrast to all other space, regarded as profane. "The sacred," according to Eliade's phenomenological view, is an autonomous and transcendent force or reality not subject to human needs, desires, or manipulations, which on occasion expresses itself, or becomes manifest in, human experience. The places of these powerful and memorable experiences of supernatural appearances become sacred sites to which humans are drawn to practice their devotion and to experience sacred power.[41]

In contrast to Eliade's phenomenological interpretation of space, sociological interpretations, built largely on the pioneering work of the French sociologist Émile Durkheim (1858–1917), regard sacred space in terms of social functions.[42] A Durkheimian view agrees with the phenomenological distinction between sacred and profane, but it does not regard the sacred as an autonomous being or force outside the empirical human realm. Instead, a sociological approach regards the sacred as an expression of social relations; as Durkheim himself famously wrote, "religion is something eminently social."[43] In this sense, sacred space is a constructed location of social solidarity; it is a place where the religious community finds its ultimate meaning in practices of devotion, propitiation, contemplation, or other religious activities that express and reinforce their sense of human relatedness. Rather than experiencing an autonomous sacred site that reveals itself to humans, a sociological interpretation in the Durkheimian mode suggests that the transcendence that humans experience in sacred places is a social awareness of something greater than the individual.

The Durkheimian notion that societies construct sacred spaces as a means of expressing social solidarity does not exclude the possibility of disagreements and conflicts. Inevitably, different factions within a social group will contest the control, use, and meanings of the community's sacred sites; this is in addition to claims of outsiders who wish to seize control of a particular space. Indeed, people with different interests in a place and who pursue different purposes in the use of the sacred space, as well as in the interpretation of its significance, will struggle with each other over its control.[44]

Defining sacred space only according to how it functions in purely religious contexts or as an important social catalyst has been challenged by more recent studies in a variety of fields. Human geographers, cultural anthropologists, and qualitative sociologists have contributed to expanded notions of space that provide for more robust understandings of the relationships between people and spaces. For instance, the notion of "affective spaces" draws attention to how people actually experience particular spaces under specific circumstances. For instance, the manner in which bodily responses such as hair standing on the back of one's neck in a terrifying encounter or the warm sensations of comfort gained in holiday festivities indicate how spatial experiences are literally felt in the body. But, as one scholar has pointed out, these bodily responses to space are themselves inseparable from social processes that establish the relationships that people have to particular spaces and to each other.[45] Thus, sacred space remains a thoroughly human phenomenon.

America as they brought civilized cultivation to a land they regarded as wild, savage, and uncultivated.

The importance of "improving" the wild land through planting and cultivation had great symbolic importance for English claims to occupy and "own" lands in America. The English terms "wild" and "cultivated" carried significance beyond distinguishing between plants growing unrestrained in natural habitats versus those under the management and care of diligent human gardeners. These terms also distinguished between the savage and the civilized, a crucial difference in the English colonial sensibility. Improving land in England traditionally meant establishing a definite border, usually with some sort of fence or hedge. When they came to America, the English brought this notion of claiming lands by fixing boundaries, often with nothing more than a hedge around a field. Sometimes enclosing all of the land they claimed with a fence or hedge was impractical, so on occasion the colonists took possession of land with a symbolic gesture of enclosure. This involved planting a garden on the land and enclosing only the garden to demonstrate their intentions to "improve" the larger area that they claimed for themselves. Thus, actual cultivation of plants signaled possession of lands they understood to be unclaimed, since in their eyes the indigenous uses of the land lacked the formal and civilized signs of enclosed gardens and fields. The English assumed that the Indians, because they had not established proper boundaries between the wild and the cultivated, made no claim to their lands.[46]

Over the course of their first hundred years in America, the English planted prosperous colonies that transformed the sacred landscapes of the areas they possessed. Perhaps the most prominent indication of their claim of divine right in occupying and transforming the landscape was the building of churches. As the colonies became more established and settled, more and more churches appeared. These houses of worship crowned the colonists' struggle to improve what they regarded as a wild and savage land.

On the backs of slaves

English improvements, however, were not accomplished by the colonists alone. From the time that a Dutch ship arrived in Virginia in 1619 with the first enslaved Africans in the English colonies, the improvement of colonial lands relied on the forced labor of slavery. Eventually, all thirteen of the English colonies allowed slaveholding in some form or another, each with its own distinct understanding of race relations and its own system of slavery.

Slaves in England's colonies included captured Native Americans, but most living in bondage were imported Africans. These captured people came with a diversity of religious orientations, including a few practicing Muslims and Christians, although the circumstances of slavery estranged most of them from their native traditions. At least some of the English colonists, though, showed concern for the spiritual salvation of enslaved peoples, and a few tentative efforts at Christian evangelism among slaves began early in the colonial period. In fact, a directive from King Charles II in 1660 instructed the colonists to consider how individuals living in bondage "may best be invited to the Christian Faith, and be made capable of being baptized thereunder."[47] But English common law prohibited Christians from owning other Christians as slaves; thus, most slaveowners denied Christian sacraments to their slaves. This, however, violated a principal justification for the institution of slavery, that "heathen" slaves could find salvation through conversion to Christianity. Consequently, colonial governments sought to rectify the conundrum of holding Christians under slavery with laws stipulating that slaves would continue in bondage after religious conversion. Virginia, for instance, adopted a provision in 1667 that declared, "baptism doth not alter the condition of the person as to his bondage or freedom in order that diverse masters freed from this doubt may more carefully endeavor the propagation of Christianity." South Carolina's constitution included a similar provision, and Maryland followed suit in 1692. In 1705, Virginia repealed a law granting freedom to children born of Christian parents. New York encouraged evangelizing among Indians and blacks with a 1706 provision that conversion would not result in freedom.[48]

Box 3.4 Maroons

A few Africans living in bondage in the English colonies escaped slavery and established their own isolated communities, known as "maroons" (derived from the Spanish word *cimarrones*, which meant "outlaws" or "runaways"). These communities often inhabited swamps, mountains, caves, or other hidden locations, and sustained themselves as self-sufficient societies. One of the largest, with roughly two thousand inhabitants, was in the Dismal Swamp between Virginia and North Carolina.[49] Sometimes these maroon communities included other escapees from servitude, including whites and Native Americans, resulting in multiracial cooperation that was rare in the English colonies.[50]

These maroon groups of fugitive slaves posed a threat to the colonies and remained dangerous adversaries throughout the colonial period, often forming alliances with Native Americans, Spaniards, and other enemies of the English colonists. As early as 1672, the colonial government in Virginia offered rewards to destroy these communities, and the governors of Virginia, Maryland, North and South Carolina, Georgia, and New York all made treaties with native peoples that rewarded them for capturing and returning slaves. Such incentives, however, were often not effective; the Creek people, for instance, mostly ignored their agreements with the southern colonies, preferring instead to benefit from the superior agricultural skills of the escaped Africans, skills that proved more valuable than the rewards that the colonists offered.[51] Moreover, a shared experience of conflict with English colonists as well as the mutual influences of sacred traditions encouraged closer alliances between African maroons and Native American groups.

Figure 3.3   This illustration of a maroon community in the Louisiana swamps appeared in the *Harper's Weekly* periodical in 1873. It offered to nineteenth-century American readers a somewhat romanticized view of maroon life. (Courtesy of the Library of Congress, LC-USZ62-111153.)

Despite official encouragement to propagate Christianity among enslaved people, most slaveowners continued to resist efforts at evangelism. The moral implications threatened to complicate relationships between masters and slaves, and many colonists who owned slaves continued to fear, despite laws to the contrary, that baptism would mean emancipation for those living under bondage. Moreover, most slaveowners worked their slaves relentlessly, and allowing them time for religious activities interfered with work schedules. Plus, many feared that religious instruction would incite rebellion. Consequently, very few people living in slavery had any regular exposure to Christianity in the colonial period; not until the nineteenth century would any widespread and persistent **evangelical** activity reach significant portions of the enslaved population.[52]

Although enslaved Africans in the English colonies of North America had little exposure to Christianity, they were not without religious influences. Most worked in areas where Native Americans made up a majority of the population, and Africans and Native Americans often found themselves together owned by the same slaveowner. Also, since African slaves were predominantly male and many Indian populations suffering from the effects of contact with Europeans ended up predominantly female, there was considerable sexual activity and marriage between the two groups, resulting in significant social and racial intermixture. In fact alliances between Africans and Native Americans generated much concern for the English colonists, who implemented policies of pitting the two groups against each other, such as using black troops to fight Indians and hiring Indians to hunt escaped African slaves. These attempts, however, of fostering animosity between Africans and native peoples were largely ineffective, with blacks and Indians remaining in close contact in many areas, often sharing cultural ties, participating in each other's religious traditions, and joining forces against the English.[53]

The conflicts between native peoples, Africans, and Europeans in colonial America often centered on claims to land, usually with religious justifications. The religions of indigenous tribes that occupied lands before colonization were profoundly connected to the land. Christian colonists arrived with their own religious understandings of the land, commonly regarding it as wilderness to be tamed by the divine right of their god's **providential** mandate. For the English, this meant planting and cultivating, or civilizing the land by clearing it of the "heathen" other. It also required the forced labor of non-Christian peoples, especially slaves imported from Africa. For these Africans brought in bondage, however, American lands had little meaning and offered no solace for their suffering. Estranged from ancestral homelands with few resources to perpetuate their ancient traditions, for the Africans these new lands in America were primarily places of severe toil for the benefit of their captors. Nevertheless, a few Africans were able to build new connections to land through their alliances with Native Americans. The American landscape indeed became a place of many gods and spirits.

Captivities

As we have seen, conflicts abounded throughout the period of European colonization of the Americas. Europeans clashed with native peoples, European nations fought each other over colonial claims, and African slaves resisted bondage in a variety of ways; in addition, the diverse native tribes engaged in shifting alliances with other tribes, with European nations, and with escaped African slaves, and all undertook armed conflict with each other. A significant number of individuals involved in the contact zones of these many hostilities wound up as captives being held by people with strangely unfamiliar cultures, religions, and ways of living. In order to survive captivity, prisoners had to rely on their own cultural resources, including their own religious orientations and understandings, as well as their ability to adapt to the unfamiliar circumstances of their captors' culture and demands. Yet, despite the trauma that captives suffered, their experiences represent key instances of transculturation, in which both sides of conflict encounter the cultural resources and opportunities of the other. The circumstances of being held by others in many cases gave captives an intimate view of the cultures, attitudes, perspectives, practices, and ways of life of their enemies. In most cases, however, especially those involving European hostages, close contact with unfamiliar cultures and religions had little effect in encouraging empathy or influencing changes in one's own traditions or values.

The history of captivity in the Americas is as old as the human presence in the western hemisphere. Ancient native peoples commonly captured members of other tribes under a variety of circumstances and for various purposes. Among the people of the eastern woodlands where the English established their colonies, long traditions of captivity and hostage exchange were in place prior to colonization. These practices relied on religious understandings of powerful spirits residing in captured enemies, spirits that would benefit the captors. In fact, the capture of enemy hostages sometimes resulted in human sacrifices and cannibalism. Iroquoian people, for instance, sometimes sought to incorporate the spiritual power of enemy prisoners through the ritual killing and ingestion of their bodies; in other instances, Iroquois matriarchs gained the spiritual benefits of captured enemies by adopting them into their clans. The practice of taking enemies' scalps or beheading them was another way to capture the power of spirits residing in their bodies.[54]

Europeans brought their own practices of captivity to the Americas, beginning with their earliest encounters with native peoples. In fact, one of Columbus' first accomplishments in the New World was to capture by force several indigenous residents of the island where he first landed. Europeans often justified these practices of taking others as hostages with religious rationalizations; but, despite the profession of religious reasons, capturing others usually related to narrower concerns, such as economic gain, especially with the proliferation of slavery. In many cases military or political considerations were foremost, as in the kidnapping of Pocahontas (later Rebecca Rolfe, ca. 1595–1617) in order to secure concessions from the local native people.[55] Rarely, if ever, did European Christians capture others purely for religious merit.

This does not mean that colonists refrained from understanding their captivity practices in the larger context of religious conflicts. English Protestants in America, for instance, often resorted to a Christian **mythology** of Satan's presence to interpret the dynamics of conflict and captivity in the colonies. In short, it was Satan whom they understood to be the underlying force that they must contend with. Consequently, their efforts to eradicate these diabolical forces sometimes led the colonists to extreme measures that included the slaughter of Indian people, whom the Christian colonists regarded as Satan's proxies, and even to executing a few of their own citizens who, as they understood it, had fallen under the Devil's spell.

The white woman in the wilderness

The English Puritans' and native Algonquian people's very different understand-ings of captivity contended with each other in New England. In a final effort of Algonquian resistance to the Puritan colonies of southern New England, a native leader by the name of Metacom (ca. 1638–1676), dubbed "King Philip" by the colonists, organized an alliance of several tribal groups who rose up in rebellion in 1675. This so-called King Philip's War proved deadly to both sides. At the end of hostilities, numerous colonial settlements on the frontier were destroyed and some 2500 colonists had died, roughly five percent of the population in the Puritan colonies. Things were even worse for the Indians, with about five thousand killed, representing about forty percent of their people; many of those who survived lived under some form of captivity, either as slaves, indentured servants, or closely watched residents of "praying towns," while others fled as refugees. The period of coexistence and cooperation between the Puritan colonists and the Algonquian people of southern New England effectively ended.

In the midst of hostilities, the wife of a Puritan preacher and mother of three children, Mary White Rowlandson (ca. 1637–1711), became a victim of the war. While her husband was away securing additional defenses for their small frontier town of Lancaster, Mrs. Rowlandson waited in her fortified house with other villagers who sought refuge there. As she would write some years afterward, "On the tenth of February 1675,[56] Came the Indians with great numbers upon Lancaster: Their first coming was about Sun-rising; hearing the noise of some Guns, we looked out; several Houses were burning, and the Smoke ascending to Heaven."[57] In the raid, the native warriors killed twelve residents and took twenty others as captives, some of whom died while in captivity, including Mary Rowlandson's youngest daughter, who eventually succumbed to a gunshot wound sustained during the attack. Rowlandson and her other two children became captives among the native people, although they rarely saw each other during their ordeal as they belonged to different captors and moved frequently. Rowlandson spent nearly twelve weeks in captivity among the Indians before being ransomed and returned to her husband. Her two children were held even longer before being returned to Puritan society.

An account of Mary Rowlandson's captivity appeared in 1682 as a spiritual autobiography under the title "The Sovereignty and Goodness of God, Together with the Faithfulness of His Promises Displayed: Being a Narrative of the Captivity and Restauration of Mrs. Mary Rowlandson"; her book not only became one of the most widely read works of American literature but also served as a prototype for the mythical figure of the white woman captured by Indians that has reappeared time and again in stories, novels, poems, art, films, and other forms through the centuries since its first appearance in Puritan New England of the seventeenth century.[58] The enduring power of Rowlandson's dramatic account of her captivity, however, relies on a very particular framing of the story. Her tale takes the form of a Puritan conversion narrative that removes it from the complexities of the historical and cultural contexts of the New England contact zone and places it instead in a religious context of spiritual trial. The Indians in her story are not the complicated actors caught in the conflicts of competing societies, each with their own traditions, values, and interests; instead, she characterizes them as devotees of Satan who carry her and her children into a wilderness where she undergoes a trial of her spiritual worthiness.[59] These devilish fiends serve God's greater purpose, not for their own salvation, according to Rowlandson's Puritan perspective, but "that God strengthned them to be a scourge to His people."[60] Her faithfulness and devotion were being tried in a wilderness of suffering, according to her interpretation, and this indicated a reliable sign in the Calvinist Puritan **worldview** of her election as one of God's chosen saints.

The image of the vulnerable Christian undergoing a spiritual trial while in captivity to other people who are regarded as dangerous and threatening has been a remarkably useful figure for enforcing boundaries of racial differences and for

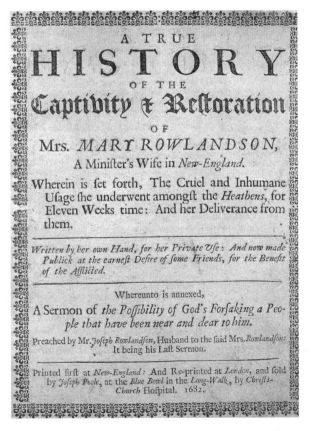

Figure 3.4 Cover of the 1682 London edition of Mary Rowlandson's account of her captivity among "King Philip's" people. Her book was one of the first American bestsellers, both in Europe and the colonies, and became the standard for subsequent captivity narratives. (Courtesy of Robert Dechert Collection, Kislak Center for Special Collections, Rare Books & Manuscripts, University of Pennsylvania Libraries.)

Box 3.5   Captivity narratives

Mary Rowlandson's tale was the first narrative of a captive to receive widespread attention in New England, but she certainly was not the first captive in the colonization of the Americas. The history of Spanish conquest and colonization included many tales of captivity by both Europeans and native peoples. Among the more widely circulated of these is the story of La Malinche (ca. 1496 or ca. 1505–ca. 1529), known to the Spaniards as Doña Maria, a young enslaved multilingual native woman who was acquired by Hernán Cortés early in his campaign against the Aztecs. Over the course of a long and intimate relationship of profound consequence, the Indian captive served the famous conquistador as translator and adviser and even bore him a son whom he recognized and had baptized into the Christian faith. As for Spanish captives living among native peoples, Cabeza de Vaca's story about the ordeal that he and his companions suffered as the first Europeans to enter the interior of North America has been an influential narrative of captivity (a discussion of their experience appears in Chapter 1).

Among the English colonists in Virginia, Captain John Smith relates his captivity by the Indian leader Chief Powhatan in the third volume of his book *The Generall Historie of Virginia, New England & the Summer Isles* (published in London, 1624). In his version, the native leader's daughter saves the Englishman from execution, introducing the Indian princess Pocahontas to the American historical imagination. What is often overlooked in the retelling of Pocahontas' story is that she was herself a captive of the English colonists, taken prisoner to protect the Jamestown colony from attack by her father. It was during her imprisonment that she converted to Christianity and married John Rolfe (ca. 1585–1622). Without her own account of the events leading up to her marriage, it is a matter of speculation as to what extent coercion was involved in her acceptance of the Christian religion, her receiving a new Christian name, and her marriage to the English colonist.

Another group of captives virtually never mentioned in the tradition of heroic captivity tales are the thousands, then tens of thousands, and eventually millions of Africans captured and brought to America as slaves. The long, complex, and difficult story of Africans in America is at its most elemental level a captivity narrative, one that originated in the capture of individuals who were subsequently transported to the Americas where they participated in the cultural transformations that have largely defined American society.[61]

reiterating dominant views of proper gender roles. In Mary Rowlandson's seminal story of her ordeal in captivity, the racial difference of the Indian other is accentuated by images that rarely regard her captors as human but instead paint them as treacherous animals. Surveying the aftermath of the raid on Lancaster, Rowlandson remarks, "It is a solemn sight to see so many Christians lying in their blood, some here, and some there, like a company of Sheep torn by Wolves, All of them stript naked by a company of hell-hounds, roaring, singing, ranting and insulting, as if they would have torn our very hearts out." Forced to leave her home with "those Barbarous Creatures," she recalls, "Oh the roaring, and singing and danceing, and yelling of those black creatures in the night, which made the place a lively resemblance of hell."[62] Indeed, her dark and vicious tormenters provide an apt contrast to the whiteness of her Puritan soul.

Rowlandson's narrative expresses special disdain for one of the wives of the Narragansett leader Quanopin (birth and death dates unknown) who was her "master" during most of her captivity. In building an alliance among the various tribes, Quanopin had married Wetamo (birth and death dates unknown), whom Rowlandson calls Wettimore, herself a powerful female leader who reportedly commanded three hundred warriors and whom the English colonists greatly feared, a fact that Rowlandson surely would have known by the time she wrote her account if she did not know it at the time of her captivity. Nevertheless, the powerful influence that Wetamo exerted over her people is not at all evident in Rowlandson's account; instead, she portrays the Indian leader as a vain, proud, and insolent servant of Satan whose purpose is merely to torment Rowlandson during her spiritual trial.[63] Rather than presenting Wetamo in defiance of Puritan understandings of proper gender roles, Rowlandson again directs the story toward her own soul, her own salvation.

On the other hand, the publication of Rowlandson's story in 1682 itself defies the gender conventions of her time. Ever since Anne Hutchinson's banishment some half-century earlier, women's voices were rarely heard in Puritan New England. In fact, Rowlandson's story was the first publication by a living female in English North America (the earlier publication of poetry by Anne Bradstreet (ca. 1612–1672), usually credited as the first book by a female author to be published in America, appeared posthumously). Yet its publication relied on the authority of males: it begins with a preface, likely composed by the Puritan cleric Increase Mather (1639–1723), that introduces Mary Rowlandson not as herself but through her relationship as wife of "that reverend servant of God, Mr. Joseph Rowlandson." And, as if to punctuate her status as obedient wife, early editions of her narrative included an outline of her late husband's final sermon, which invokes the image of the proper role of a wife in relation to her husband as an exemplary model of the relationship between the elect saint and God. Thus, her story reinforced the place of women in Puritan society on at least three levels, by excluding any reference to the powerful autonomy of the Indian woman Wetamo, by defining her own status as wife to a prominent male, and by sanctifying the subordinate status of the wife as analogous to the Christian's subordination to God. The female voice becomes, in Mary Rowlandson's tale of captivity and redemption, the firm voice of conformity to the racial and gender limits of Puritan society.

Witches

The Puritans' understanding of the proper place of women in colonial society once again contended with their pervasive fear of Satan's efforts to capture vulnerable Christians when they uncovered witchcraft in Salem Village, Massachusetts, in 1692. This time, the dangerous and menacing enemy lurked within Puritan society, an internal threat rather than remaining external among the Devil's savage devotees who roamed outside the civilized boundaries of colonial settlements. Early in 1692, two young girls in the household of the Reverend Samuel Parris (1653–1720), the Salem Village minister, fell ill, "sadly afflicted of they knew not what Distempers," according to the Reverend John Hale (1636–1700) from nearby Beverly, who witnessed the girls' illness and described how they "were bitten and pinched by invisible agents; their arms, necks, and backs turned this way and that way, and returned again, so as it was impossible for them to do of themselves, and beyond the power of any Epileptick Fits, or natural Disease to Effect."[64] The local physician determined that the girls had fallen "under an Evil Hand," that they were bewitched. Soon two other young females succumbed to similar fits, and the four girls together named an Indian slave woman by the name of Tituba (birth and death dates unknown), plus two other women in the community, as the cause of their afflictions, "that they or Specters in their Shapes did grievously torment them," according to the account of Rev. Hale. Significantly, one of the newly afflicted, Elizabeth (Betty) Hubbard (born ca. 1675, death date unknown), an indentured maidservant, was seventeen years old, of legal age to serve as a credible witness and to give binding testimony in court. With four afflicted girls and three women accused of witchcraft, the ordeal moved from a strictly religious conflict to a criminal action in the civil court. Villagers filed formal complaints against the three women with the Salem magistrates, and a public examination of the accused began on March 1, 1692.[65]

Further allegations of witchcraft seized the Massachusetts colony in and around Salem Village through the spring and summer of 1692. Included among the earliest accused witches was a girl of only four or five years, plus two members of the local congregation, whose church membership made them unlikely suspects. One of the latter, Martha Corey (late 1620s–1692), answered the charges by insisting on her innocence, since, as her interrogators recounted, "shee had made a profession of christ and rejoyced to go and hear the word of god and the like."[66] But, with the weight of public opinion and the evidence of witchery configured against her, Corey's insistence on her innocence came to no avail: "What can I do [when] many rise up against me?" she asked in exasperation. Eventually she and nineteen others

Figure 3.5 The testimony of young women and girls, some of them seized with hysteria and even collapsing in the courtroom, led to the convictions of accused witches in Salem, Massachusetts, in 1692. (Time & Life Pictures / Getty Images.)

met ignoble deaths as convicted witches and were hanged (or, in one case, pressed to death under a pile of stones); in total the witchcraft crisis of 1692–1693 in Essex County, Massachusetts, involved legal actions against at least 144 people, mostly female. Many of them were jailed for long periods of time. A total of fifty-four confessed of practicing witchcraft. Fourteen women and six men were executed; another four adults and several infants died in custody.[67]

The collective panic generated in the witchcraft episode in Salem Village eventually subsided as skeptical voices began to assert themselves. In particular, questions arose about the reliability of testimony and evidence, especially from young women and girls. In August 1692, Robert Pike (1616–1706), a local court official and outspoken critic of the proceedings, surmised that "diabolical visions, apparitions, or representations" were "more commonly false and delusive than real, and cannot be known when they are real and when feigned, but by the Devil's report; and then [can]not be believed, because he is the father of lies."[68] That fall, the court that heard the cases of witches was terminated and new judicial procedures, including revised rules of evidence, were instituted. Following these changes, only three additional suspects were found guilty, but all three subsequently received reprieves from the governor. By the spring of 1693, the witchcraft crisis of Essex County, Massachusetts, had come to an end.

Of course, accusations of witchcraft did not originate with the crisis in Salem, Massachusetts, in the 1690s. The notion of witches and other beings with super-natural powers, usually of a sinister nature, had long been part of European culture as an explanation for mysterious events and conditions, including illnesses, accidents, and an assortment of misfortunes that might befall individuals, families, or entire communities. Not unlike the animism of indigenous peoples of Africa and the Americas, most European Christians of the seventeenth century recognized an animated world of invisible spirits that surrounded and often overlapped with the visible mundane world that they inhabited. Certain people in collusion with Satan, according to folk understandings of European Christians, could direct malevolent spirits to bring harm to others. Throughout the medieval period and into the early modern era of Europe and its colonies, numerous natural disasters, outbreaks of disease, and political or economic reversals were blamed on the designs of witches.

The indictments in Salem, however, were different in several key regards. First, the mere scale of allegations far exceeded any other outbreak of witchcraft in New England. The next largest incident occurred some three decades earlier in Connecticut and involved only eleven accused witches. Second, the geographic reach of the accusations in Salem is remarkable, covering twenty-two different places, unlike other witchcraft episodes in New England, where the accused came from no more than two adjacent towns. Third, whereas in other instances the accusers were predominantly adult males, in Salem the crucial complaints came from girls and young women. Moreover, unlike elsewhere, these accusers often did not previously know those whom they accused of tormenting them, and a few of the accused did not fit the common pattern of marginalized citizens; some were church members, and a few held prominent positions in local society. Finally, unlike most incidents of such charges, the judges in Salem were disposed to believe the accounts of the accusers and quite willing to convict and even exe-cute accused witches; the skepticism and reluctance of judges elsewhere to believe such accusations and administer severe punishments was nearly absent in Salem, at least in the early months of the crisis.[69]

Underlying the anomalous circumstances and outcomes of the witch accusations in colonial Salem were the upheavals of disastrous Indian wars that had plagued the Puritans of New England. Accustomed to viewing all events as signs of God's favor or displeasure, the people of Salem and surrounding villages understood the losses they had suffered in northern New England to native tribes and their Catholic allies as indications that God did not favor the Puritans' efforts to build an exemplary Christian society in America. Much like Mary Rowlandson, the citizens of Essex County, themselves closely tied to the hostilities, attributed their failures against the Indians not to the political, cultural, or even military con-texts of the particular conflicts but to God's need to teach them a lesson, to sub-ject the Puritans to a spiritual trial. Notably, several of the judges in the witch trials had themselves been key political and military leaders in the Indian wars; the notion that Satan had a hand in their defeats deflected blame away from these leaders' personal failings in defending the colony.[70]

Also paralleling Mary Rowlandson's account of her captivity is the prominence of female voices in the Salem witch trials. The seriousness with which prominent citizens regarded the claims of young woman and girls, many of them, like the indentured servant Betty Hubbard, of marginal status beyond their gender, may seem remarkable. Yet, similarly to Rowlandson's case, the female voices in Salem served male prerogatives. Far from liberating women from their highly constrained status, the accusations fit well with the aspirations of powerful men who needed an explanation for their own failures in defending the colony. That powerful men took seriously the testimony of women and girls whose place in New England society was mostly invisible reflects their desire to place blame on God's providence and the efforts of the Devil working against them. In fact, critics of the trials focused on the disrepute of the young women's testimony. Once the female voices were properly discredited, the prosecution of witches soon halted. The young women and girls once again returned to their subservient, predominantly invisible status in male-dominated Puritan society.

The Diversity of Religious Conflicts

As the examples of Mary Rowlandson and the Salem witch trials demonstrate, European Christians often harbored doubts about their god's plan for them in America. Especially in the case of the Puritan Protestants who settled New England in hopes of shining an exemplary light for all the world, or at least the Christian world, to emulate, their failures and reversals were a shock to their confidence in God's providence. Their abiding presumption, however, of cultural, racial, and religious superiority prevented them from accepting their losses as the natural outcome of complex and contentious relations between peoples with very different perspectives, values, traditions, and interests. As religious people do everywhere, these Christians on the far outposts of European civilization resorted to a religious framework to provide meaningful explanations for their plight.

Likewise, the indigenous peoples of the Americas also resorted to their own religious structures to interpret contentious relations with Europeans and others, and they often based their responses to conflict on religious considerations. The capture of European hostages such as Mary Rowlandson and her children was not merely a bloodthirsty cruelty perpetrated by savage brutes, nor can it be explained simply as an economic ploy to extract ransom from the colonists, as Rowlandson herself suggests. A long native tradition of hostage taking involved a religious orientation that recognized the spiritual power such captives brought to their captors. In contrast, the Pueblo peoples of the arid west could not abide the deliberate eradication of religious traditions that undergirded their entire way of life; without the proper ritual celebrations, the Kachinas would cease to deliver the rain necessary to feed the people. Suffering from famines, diseases, and the perpetual cruelties inflicted by missionaries intent on converting their entire society to European values, the Pueblo people embraced a millenarian vision and engaged in armed rebellion that drove the Spaniards from their ancestral lands, at least for a time. Guarding their religion against the onslaught of Christian evangelism was in fact a desperate defense of their entire culture and way of life.

The conflicts and persecutions of colonial America spanned multiple lines of difference, including cultural, racial, gender, and especially religious differences. Religion figured into these conflicts in a variety of ways: as a resource for understanding and interpreting differences; for asserting the will, often by force, to conquer and rule others; and for organizing and maintaining social relations between disparate peoples. In conflicts between groups and even within communities, religion often serves as a framework for determining a course of action and for interpreting the consequences. For the diverse people contending for lands and prosperity in seventeenth-century America, their respective religions lent meaning and purpose to otherwise unthinkable events.

Questions for Discussion

(1)   How did religion contribute to conflicts between different groups of people in colonial America, either negatively as the source of strife or productively in resolving differences or in helping religious adherents to cope with contentious circumstances? Give specific examples to support your answer.

(2)   In what ways did Spanish Franciscans in New Mexico differ from French Jesuits in New France regarding their respective missionary efforts? Which of these missionary enterprises were more successful in your opinion? Support your answer with evidence from the text.

(3)   How did the differing religious perspectives of European Christians, indigenous Africans brought to America as slaves, and native peoples of the Americas affect their respective relationships to the natural environment and their understandings of sacred space? Include examples of each.

(4)   To what extent did Puritan standards concerning proper gender roles affect their interpretations of both the captivity of Mary Rowlandson and the accusations of witchcraft in Salem, Massachusetts?

Suggested Primary-Source Readings

"Declaration of Pedro Naranjo of the Queres Nation [1681]," in *Revolt of the Pueblo Indians of New Mexico and Otermín's Attempted Reconquest, 1680–1682*, 2 vols., vol. 2, ed. Charles W. Hackett (Albuquerque: University of New Mexico Press, 1942), 245–249: An account of the Pueblo Revolt by a captured Native American who presented his testimony to Spanish authorities in December 1681.

Black Robes and Buckskin: A Selection from the Jesuit Relations, ed. and trans. Catharine Randall (New York: Fordham University Press, 2011): A modern translation of selections from the *Jesuit Relations* that offer insight into missionary enterprises in New France in the seventeenth century.

Mary White Rowlandson, "The Sovereignty and Goodness of God, Together with the Faithfulness of His Promises Displayed: Being a Narrative of the Captivity and Restauration of Mrs. Mary Rowlandson," in *Held Captive by Indians: Selected Narratives, 1642–1836*, ed. Richard VanDerBeets (Knoxville: University of Tennessee Press, 1973), 41–90: Rowlandson's account of her captivity during King Philip's War.

Cotton Mather, *The Wonders of the Invisible World: Being an Account of the Tryals of Several Witches Lately Executed in New-England* (1693): This defense of Mather's role in the prosecution of witches in Salem, Massachusetts, proclaiming the demonic threat that the witches represented to Puritan society, was subsequently refuted in *More Wonders of the Invisible World* by Robert Calef, published in 1700.

Notes

1   Ramón A. Gutiérrez, *When Jesus Came, the Corn Mothers Went Away: Marriage, Sexuality, and Power in New Mexico, 1500–1846* (Stanford, CA: Stanford University Press, 1991), 42–43.

2   Carroll L. Riley, *Rio Del Norte: People of the Upper Rio Grande from Earliest Times to the Pueblo Revolt* (Salt Lake City: University of Utah Press, 1995), 55–56.

3   Gutiérrez, *When Jesus Came*, 103.

4   Gutiérrez, *When Jesus Came*, 105 and Riley, *Rio Del Norte*, 258–259.

5   Gutiérrez, *When Jesus Came*, 104.

6   Riley, *Rio Del Norte*, 262–263.

7   Ibid., 261.

8   Quoted in Gutiérrez, *When Jesus Came*, 107.

9   Riley, *Rio Del Norte*, 262.

10 Ibid., 266.

11 Ibid.

12 Gutiérrez, *When Jesus Came*, 130.

13 Ibid., 131.

14 Riley, *Rio Del Norte*, 266–267.

15 Ibid., 267.

16 Gutiérrez, *When Jesus Came*, 131.

17 Regarding the scholarly concept of "millenarianism," see Hillel Schwartz, "Millenarianism," in *Encyclopedia of Religion*, ed. Lindsay Jones, vol. 8 (Detroit, MI: Macmillan Reference USA, 2005), 8718–8721.

18 Gutiérrez, *When Jesus Came*, 130–135 and Riley, *Rio Del Norte*, 267–268.

19 Quoted in Gutiérrez, *When Jesus Came*, 137.

20 Riley, *Rio Del Norte*, 268.

21 Gutiérrez, *When Jesus Came*, 139.

22 Peter Iverson, "The Enduring Hopi," in *Hopi Nation: Essays on Indigenous Art, Culture, History, and Law*, ed. Edna Glenn, John R. Wunder, Willard Hughes Rollings, and C. L. Martin (Lincoln: University of Nebraska, 2008), 144.

23   Riley, *Rio Del Norte*, 269–270.

24   For explanation of the term "Huron," see Virgil J. Vogel, *Indian Names on Wisconsin's Map* (Madison: University of Wisconsin Press, 1991), 31–32.

25   Carole Blackburn, *Harvest of Souls: The Jesuit Missions and Colonialism in North America, 1632–1650* (Montreal: McGill-Queen's University Press, 2000), 42, 45.

26   James Axtell, *The Invasion Within: The Contest of Cultures in Colonial North America* (New York: Oxford University Press, 1985), 68 and Bruce G. Trigger, *Natives and Newcomers: Canada's "Heroic Age" Reconsidered* (Kingston: McGill-Queen's University Press, 1985), 227.

27   Peter A. Dorsey, "Going to School with Savages: Authorship and Authority among the Jesuits of New France," *William and Mary Quarterly* 55, no. 3 (1998), 401.

28   Blackburn, *Harvest of Souls*, 9.

29   Bruce G. Trigger, *The Children of Aataentsic: A History of the Huron People to 1660*, 2 vols. (Montreal: McGill-Queen's University Press, 1976), 27–45. Trigger's book includes a rather thorough description of Wyandot (i.e., Huron) society and culture.

30   Ibid., 75–77.

31   Trigger, *Natives and Newcomers*, 227.

32   Axtell, *The Invasion Within*, 77–78.

33   Ibid., 93.

34   Ibid., 85.

35   Trigger, *Natives and Newcomers*, 254, 257.

36   Ibid., 259.

37   Ibid., 256.

38   Ibid., 267, 273, 279.

39   Quoted in Richard Samuel Thomas, *The Old Brick Church, near Smithfield, Virginia* (Richmond: Virginia Historical Society, 1892), 7.

40   From Reverend Alexander Whitaker's book *Good Newes from Virginia*, quoted in Patricia Seed, *Ceremonies of Possession in Europe's Conquest of the New World, 1492–1640* (New York: Cambridge University Press, 1995), 29.

41   Eliade details his ideas about sacred space in Mircea Eliade, *The Sacred and the Profane: The Nature of Religion*, trans. Willard R. Trask (New York: Harvest/HBJ, 1959). For a concise overview of Eliade's approach, see Daniel L. Pals, *Eight Theories of Religion*, 2nd edn (New York: Oxford University Press, 2006), 193–228.

42   For an overview of Durkheim's sociological interpretation of religion, see Pals, *Eight Theories of Religion*, 85–117.

43   Emile Durkheim, *The Elementary Forms of Religious Life*, trans. Carol Cosman (New York: Oxford University Press, 2001), 11.

44   In the introduction to their collection of essays on sacred space in America, David Chidester and Edward T. Linenthal emphasize contestations over places regarded as sacred. See David Chidester and Edward Tabor Linenthal, eds., *American Sacred Space* (Bloomington: Indiana University Press, 1995).

45   Kevin Lewis O'Neill, "Beyond Broken: Affective Spaces and the Study of American Religion," *Journal of the American Academy of Religion* 81, no. 4 (2013), 1093–1116.

46   Seed, *Ceremonies of Possession*, 16–40.

47   Albert J. Raboteau, *Slave Religion: The "Invisible Institution" in the Antebellum South*, updated edn (New York: Oxford University Press, 2004), 97.

48 Oscar Reiss, *Blacks in Colonial America* (Jefferson, NC: McFarland & Co., 1997), 217–218.

49 Reiss, *Blacks in Colonial America*, 190.

50 William D. Piersen, *From Africa to America: African American History from the Colonial Era to the Early Republic, 1526–1790* (New York: Twayne, Prentice Hall, 1996), 82.

51 Reiss, *Blacks in Colonial America*, 190–194.

52 Yvonne Patricia Chireau, *Black Magic: Religion and the African American Conjuring Tradition* (Berkeley: University of California Press, 2003), 41–42.

53 Piersen, *From Africa to America*, 79–81.

54 For a discussion of indigenous practices of captivity and hostage taking, see Pauline Turner Strong, *Captive Selves, Captivating Others: The Politics and Poetics of Colonial American Captivity Narratives* (Boulder, CO: Westview Press, 1999), 77–80.

55 For a description and analysis of the kidnapping of Pocahontas, see ibid., 63–70.

56 Actually, the year would be 1676 according to the calendar we use today, what is known as the Gregorian calendar. Prior to 1752, most Protestant countries, including England and its colonies, adhered to the Julian calendar and its convention of beginning the new year with the vernal equinox in March. Thus, during Rowlandson's time, what is now February 1676 under the Gregorian calendar would still be 1675 until the equinox in the following month according to the Julian calendar.

57 Mary White Rowlandson, "The Sovereignty and Goodness of God, Together with the Faithfulness of His Promises Displayed: Being a Narrative of the Captivity and Restauration of Mrs. Mary Rowlandson," in *Held Captive by Indians: Selected Narratives, 1642–1836*, ed. Richard VanDerBeets (Knoxville: University of Tennessee Press, 1973 [1682]), 42.

58 Rebecca Blevins Faery, *Cartographies of Desire: Captivity, Race, and Sex in the Shaping of an American Nation* (Norman: University of Oklahoma Press, 1999), 24–25.

59 Strong, *Captive Selves, Captivating Others*, 86.

60 Rowlandson, "Captivity and Restauration of Mrs. Mary Rowlandson," 82.

61 For an excellent overview of captivity narratives, see the introductory chapter of Strong, *Captive Selves, Captivating Others*.

62 Rowlandson, "Captivity and Restauration of Mrs. Mary Rowlandson," 45.

63 Strong, *Captive Selves, Captivating Others*, 99–101.

64 Quoted in Mary Beth Norton, *In the Devil's Snare: The Salem Witchcraft Crisis of 1692* (New York: Alfred A. Knopf, 2002), 18–19.

65 Ibid., 24–29.

66 Ibid., 44–46.

67 Ibid., 3–4.

68 Quoted in ibid., 266.

69 Ibid., 8–10.

70 Ibid., 296–300.

4

Resistance, Revival, and Revolution

In this chapter we focus on changes in the colonial world that led to the establishment of the United States of America. A growing slave population, especially in the southern colonies, generated both challenges and opportunities for Christians concerned about the spiritual well-being of people living under slavery. As Christianity became more widespread among enslaved people, however, it provided resources for resisting bondage. More importantly, religious revivals in the middle decades of the eighteenth century were occasions for African Americans to participate alongside white Protestants in Christian worship. These revivals, in particular the widely publicized tours of itinerant preacher George Whitefield (1715–1770), marked a momentous shift in the religious culture of England's American colonies. The more egalitarian nature of the revivals gave impetus to more tolerant attitudes that eventually translated into religious pluralism as an official doctrine of the new nation that emerged from the American Revolution.

Taken into slavery as a child from her African homeland, sold at age seven to a prominent Boston merchant and given a new name, young Phillis Wheatley (ca. 1753–1784) quickly learned English and was soon reading both English and Latin while studying the Christian Bible, classical literature, and a range of other topics. Enthralled with the poets, especially Alexander Pope (1688–1744), she began writing verse that revealed a prodigious poetic talent. At age seventeen, she penned a tribute on the death of the renowned Anglican evangelist George Whitefield; her praise begins,

> Hail, happy saint! on thine immortal throne,
> Possest of glory, life, and bliss unknown:

Formed From This Soil: An Introduction to the Diverse History of Religion in America, First Edition. Thomas S. Bremer.
© 2015 Thomas S. Bremer. Published 2015 by John Wiley & Sons, Ltd.

> We hear no more the music of thy tongue,
> Thy wonted auditories cease to throng.

The young Wheatley goes on to extol the revivalist preacher's devotion to Christians in America:

> He prayed that grace in ev'ry heart might dwell;
> He longed to see America excel;
> He charged its youth that ev'ry grace divine
> Should with full lustre in their conduct shine.

The poem ends with the assurance of seeing the great preacher once more in the hereafter:

> But, though arrested by the hand of death,
> Whitefield no more exerts his lab'ring breath,
> Yet let us view him in the eternal skies,
> Let ev'ry heart to this bright vision rise;
> While the tomb, safe, retains its sacred trust,
> Till life divine reanimates his dust.[1]

This poetic elegy to George Whitefield is notable not so much for the profundity of its sentiment as for the circumstances of its composition. A young woman in colonial Boston, captured into slavery as a young girl just a decade earlier, penning elegant verses for a recently deceased Anglican preacher who himself owned slaves, seems remarkably ironic to our retrospective sensibilities. Her status as an African, as a slave, as a female, as a child, made Phillis Wheatley about as socially distant from the famed **evangelical** preacher as one could get. Moreover, Whitefield's ambivalence on the issue of slavery makes this affectionate poem written in 1770 by a young slave a testimony to the complexities of colonial society in England's American holdings on the eve of revolution. We can find in the tribute of the young poet to the aged evangelist a confluence of two particular currents in the revolutionary atmosphere that erupted in the colonies in the 1770s: the growing presence of enslaved peoples and the establishment of evangelical Protestantism as a challenging addition to the American religious landscape.

In many ways, both Whitefield and Wheatley defied typical expectations for people of their respective circumstances. The vast majority of people living in bondage in the colonial society of Wheatley's time had no opportunity for literacy, and extraordinary literary talents such as hers were seldom recognized, let alone cultivated in any meaningful way. A few slaveowners, though, took an interest in their slaves' intellectual, cultural, and religious development. The Boston merchant John Wheatley (birth and death dates unknown) purchased the young slave girl as a servant for his wife and named her Phillis after the ship that had brought her from Africa. Tutored by the Wheatleys' older daughter, her prodigious

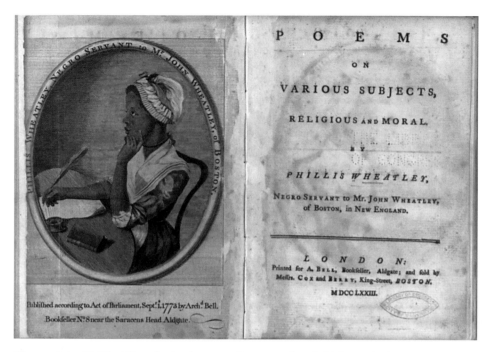

Figure 4.1   Phillis Wheatley's elegy to George Whitefield brought her international acclaim when her collection of poems was published in London in 1773. (Courtesy of the Library of Congress, LC-USZ62-56850.)

intellectual capacity soon freed young Phillis from the constant drudgery of a household servant; she quickly became proficient in English, Latin, literature, history, and the sciences and she began composing poems of her own. Her homage to George Whitefield upon his death brought her international acclaim, and she became a celebrity in her own right among Boston's elite society while still in her teens. Her enhanced social standing, however, did not erase her awareness of bondage; for example, she declined to dine as a guest at the tables of the scholars, **clergy**, and merchants who invited her into their homes, as she remained mindful of the distance between the enslaved and the free. Nevertheless, her fame continued to grow, and a collection of her works, *Poems on Various Subjects, Religious and Moral*, appeared in 1773, one of the earliest books by an African American ever published.[2] Included in this collection is a short poem, *On Being Brought from Africa to America*, that portrays her own life story as a religious allegory. Although the poem does not condemn the slave trade, and in fact reads more as an apologetic justification of slavery, it resists the racist assumptions of most colonists and other Europeans; it ends,

> Some view our sable race with scornful eye –
> "Their color is a diabolic dye."

> Remember, Christians, Negroes black as Cain
> May be refined, and join the angelic train.[3]

Maligned by latter-day critics as failing to be more forthright in her criticisms of slavery, Phillis Wheatley's poems demonstrate considerable ambivalence about slavery as, on the one hand, an institution of inhumane practices and, on the other, an opportunity to allow pagan Africans to "join the angelic train." In this regard, the famed itinerant evangelist George Whitefield shared her ambivalence. In 1740, Whitefield warned the colonists of Maryland, Virginia, and North and South Carolina "that God has a quarrel with you for your cruelty to the poor negroes." Sidestepping the larger question about the moral justification of slavery itself, being an owner of slaves himself, he assured the colonists "that it is sinful … to use them worse than brutes." His letter mentions atrocities perpetrated upon slaves by their owners and warns that such inhumane and seemingly un-Christian treatment will bring God's wrath in the form of slave rebellions; if such eventualities should come to pass, he concludes, "all good men must acknowledge, the judgment would be just."[4] Though unwilling to attack the entire institution of slavery itself, Whitefield nonetheless advocated humane treatment of slaves. In fact, much like Wheatley, he regarded the enslaving of Africans as an opportunity for fulfilling a religious duty to enlighten pagan sensibilities with the Christian gospel.

The threat of rebellion, which Whitefield and others understood in **providential** terms as God's judgment, simmered throughout much of the eighteenth century and into the nineteenth, occasionally erupting in violent conflicts. Many of these incidents sprang directly and overtly from religious interpretations. Likewise, the English colonists themselves eventually took arms against the colonial government in a prolonged war of independence that relied to a large extent on the moral justifications of religious precepts. But, although the revolution that the English colonists fomented against their king certainly had distinctly religious currents running through it, the self-evident truths they enumerated in their Declaration of Independence were not the grounds of a capacious liberty for all people, or even for all of those devoted to the Creator who endowed the unalienable rights that were the basis of their revolution. As we will see in this and other chapters, numerous marginalized groups remained beyond the reach of the political liberties that constituted the new nation, and their longing for such freedoms would languish long after the American Revolution.

Resisting Slavery

As we learned in Chapter 3, very few enslaved persons were exposed to Christianity during the early part of the colonial period in British North America; for many colonists, anxieties about the moral, economic, and political implications of converted slaves usually took precedence over the Christian imperative to evangelize among the captive Africans living in bondage. Besides resistance and outright hostility on the part of slaveowners, missionaries also had to overcome differences in language and unfamiliar cultural assumptions on the part of the slaves themselves. Compounded by a persistent shortage of financial resources, efforts at Christian evangelization faced daunting obstacles.[5] Still, with their native African traditions and practices weakened, a number of slaves recognized the power of the Christian god in America. For many people living under bondage, the message of the Christian gospel allayed the suffering they endured; in addition, the authority of the Christian message offered political and moral resources for resisting and under-mining the institutions of slavery itself.

In most cases, enslaved people who converted to Christianity reinterpreted the reli-gion in ways that better corresponded to their indigenous African beliefs. For instance, they often put little or no emphasis on the Christian concept of sin, and many slaves tended to regard the Christian Devil more as a trickster figure who demonstrated pro-found wisdom through confounding and often contradictory ideas and behaviors rather than as an absolute embodiment of evil. An experiential orientation to other-worldliness gave less authority to knowledge of scripture or carefully reasoned profes-sions of faith for Africans than they had among Euro-American Christians; consequently, enslaved Africans tended to regard being filled with the Holy Spirit as the sign of the religious initiate, and many of them emphasized the importance of music and dancing to invoke the spirit.[6] In short, Africans brought to America as slaves remade the authority of Christianity to suit more familiar orientations and practices.

Evangelizing among the slaves

The remaking of Christianity among Africans in America began in the contact zones where European Christians first introduced their religion to enslaved peo-ple. One of the better organized missionary efforts in the eighteenth century involved the Society for the Propagation of the Gospel in Foreign Parts (SPG), chartered in 1701 "for the better Support and Maintenance of an Orthodox Clergy in Foreign Parts," particularly in England's colonies.[7] The SPG began in earnest to evangelize among Indians and blacks in the first decade of the century, supplying priests, teachers, and missionaries throughout the American colonies. An early historian of the organization wrote in 1730, "The Society looked upon the Instruction and Conversion of the *Negroes*, as a principal Branch of their Care; esteeming it a great Reproach to the Christian Name, that so many Thousands of Persons should continue in the same State of *Pagan* Darkness … as they lay before under, in their own Heathen Countries."[8] Significantly, the SPG opened a number of so-called "Negro schools" in both New England and the southern colonies; by focusing on a Christian education for enslaved children, it hoped to instill Christian values in a new generation of slaves.[9]

Teachers of the SPG occasionally benefited from the cooperation and active efforts of the slaveowners themselves. For instance, a preacher in South Carolina related in 1711 that two local women, concerned about the spiritual well-being of their slaves, had "taken extraordinary pains to instruct a considerable number of Negroes in the principles of the Christian Religion, and to reclaim and reform them."[10] More often, however, the teachers and missionaries of the SPG met resistance from slaveowners, and sometimes they encountered outright hostility. Nevertheless, their continued efforts throughout the colonies bore some fruit. In one notable enterprise, Elias Neau (1662–1722), a French Huguenot working for the SPG in New York, established a school there that enjoyed considerable success in teaching Christianity to black slaves; others continued to operate Neau's school long after his death.[11] In South Carolina, the SPG was able to open the Charleston Negro School in 1742 with thirty pupils and two young African American slaves serving as teachers. The SPG subsequently sent one of the teachers to Barbados, while the other remained as the school's sole teacher. But the school was forced to close after twenty-two years when the slave teacher died and no successor could be found to continue training slave children in the basics of Christianity.[12]

The SPG sustained its efforts in the American colonies up until the time of the Revolutionary War, when Anglicans were forced to end their presence in the newly independent nation. But they were not the only group concerned with evangelizing among enslaved people. In fact, most Christian groups in America made some effort at exposing non-Christians to their religion. Among the more active were Baptists, Methodists, Moravians, Presbyterians, and Quakers, all of whom ministered to the spiritual lives of slaves with mixed success. Quakers in particular took a strong stance on the need to educate people living in bondage and make them Christians, and a number of them even called for the elimination of slavery altogether. Most Quaker meetings were open to Africans, and Quakers who owned slaves were encouraged to bring them to the religious meetings; in fact, Pennsylvania Quakers established special meetings for Africans.[13]

Despite the various efforts to introduce Christianity to the African slaves, progress was slow and gradual and met with setbacks and resistance all along the way; most people living under slavery were unwilling to accept the authority of the masters' religion. Over the course of the eighteenth century, however, more and more African Americans learned about and accepted Christian understandings and practices, but in most cases according to the moral authority of their own interpretations. Most significant in this trend were religious revivals that proliferated in the colonies beginning in the 1730s. Enslaved people often joined in the fervent celebrations of Protestant renewal. Still, the majority of slaves in the American colonies had no exposure to the Christian message; for many, their salvation lay in other means, including resistance and rebellion against slavery itself. Those who embraced Christianity, though, found additional religious resources for enduring hardships under bondage but also for opposing the entire slave system.

Figure 4.2   A few schools for African American children appeared in the eighteenth century, though they rarely lasted. One of the more successful efforts was in Philadelphia, started by the Quaker teacher and antislavery activist Anthony Benezet (1713–1784), shown here in a nineteenth-century illustration. Benezet began teaching African American children in his home in 1754, and in 1770 he opened the Negro School at Philadelphia with the support of the local Quaker community. (Reproduced by permission of Haverford College Special Collections.)

Resistance and rebellion among the slaves

Revolution in England's American colonies did not begin with the Declaration of Independence in 1776; indeed, resistance to authoritarian rule and outright rebellion had precedents much earlier in the eighteenth century, as is evident among the growing numbers of people held in bondage. As the colonists' economic success came to rely increasingly on slave labor, the slave population continued to grow. Many of the enslaved people, though, sought ways to resist their captivity, including religious means. Slave resistance took many forms, including such strategies as theft; sabotaging the owner's property, tools, and crops; feigned illnesses; running away; self-mutilation; and even such drastic measures as suicide. On occasion, slaves would also resort to armed insurrection.[14]

The fear of slave revolts in the English colonies led to increasingly repressive controls on Africans, including restrictions on religious practices. South Carolina's slave code of 1712 served as a model for other colonies. Among other provisions, it prohibited masters from giving slaves a pass to leave their plantation on a Sunday or other holy day, except to perform some specific duty.[15] After numerous violent uprisings in 1739 and 1740 in South Carolina, additional laws were passed to control the slave population. Included were prohibitions on learning to read or write, except under the supervision of the SPG.[16]

Blame for deadly slave uprisings often coincided with the Protestant colonists' hatred of Catholicism, exacerbated by tensions with rival French Catholics to the north and the threat of Spanish Catholics in Florida. The Maryland Assembly in 1740 accused Catholic clergy in the colony of colluding with Spanish Catholics to encourage rebellions among slaves against their Protestant owners.[17] In New York, colonial officials accused a Latin teacher by the name of John Ury (birth date unknown, died 1741) of conspiring to organize slaves in revolt; the accusations stated that he was actually a Catholic priest working undercover to overthrow the English colony.[18] Gripped by fear, Protestant colonists enacted ever more repressive controls over slaves, Catholics, Indians, and others who posed threats, real or imagined.

Reviving Religious Fervor

Despite threats of violent slave rebellions, the presence of Catholic enemies to both the north and the south, continuing tensions with displaced native peoples, and a growing dissatisfaction with religious institutions, English's Protestant colonies continued to grow and flourish. By the middle of the eighteenth century, however, the religious climate had noticeably shifted. The change was best reflected in the preaching tours of the English itinerant minister George Whitefield, who brought an excitement of piety that would forever alter the religious landscape of the colonies. Whitefield first arrived in America from England in 1738; there he worked to convert souls and established an orphanage near Savannah, Georgia. His return to America the following year caught the attention of northern colonists, who flocked to hear him in Philadelphia and New York. A news account of his first appearance in New York, where he "preached in the Fields to many Hundreds of People," indicates the intensity and appeal of his religious gatherings, which included "*Christians* of all Denominations, some *Jews*, and a few, I believe, that had no Religion at all":

> Towards the last Prayer, the whole Assembly appeared more united, and all became hush'd and still; a solemn Awe and Reverence appeared in the Faces of most, a

mighty Energy attended the Word. I heard and felt something astonishing and surprizing, but, I confess; I was not at that Time fully rid of my Scruples. But as I tho't I saw a visible Presence of GOD with Mr. *Whitefield*, I kept my Doubts to my self.[19]

Indeed, with the appearance of Rev. Whitefield in the colonies, a "mighty Energy" descended on America.

Christian Pietism

George Whitefield's religious assemblies in churches, fields, town squares, and wherever he could gather a crowd epitomized a resurgence of evangelical piety that can be traced to German Lutherans in the late seventeenth century; specifically, the teachings of Philipp Jakob Spener (1635–1705) initiated a more intensely personal form of Protestant devotion known as Pietism. Beginning in 1670, Spener formed small groups of his parishioners, which he called "collegiae pietatis" ("gatherings of the pious"), to study the Bible and share their respective spiritual experiences with each other; these "pietist" gatherings began to spread across Germany and eventually encompassed much of the Lutheran world in Germany and Scandinavia. Spener stressed the practice of an active faith in contrast to the mere profession of belief. His objective was to reform the Lutheran Church, shifting its orientation from the rather dry, rational, and often polemical tone of orthodox Protestant theology to a practical emphasis on a pastoral theology that cultivated more active devotion among parishioners.[20]

Pietism came to America with the emigration of Germans to the English colonies in the eighteenth century. One community of Pietists in particular, the Moravian Church, would have an especially significant impact on English Protestants. Tracing their origins to the teachings of the proto-Protestant Czech reformer Jan Hus (1373–1415) and the *Unitas Fratrum*, or United Brethren, who formed in 1457 among followers of Hus, the Moravians, after centuries of persecution, found refuge on the estate of Count Nicholas Ludwig von Zinzendorf (1700–1760) in Upper Saxony beginning in 1722. Under Zinzendorf's leadership, the Moravians were soon defined by his Pietist theology and communal social experiments.[21]

Christian life, according to Zinzendorf's Pietist views, encompassed both a religious sense felt deep in the soul and a rational approach to the practical needs of earthly life. This melding of emotion and reason characterized much of Moravian religiosity, including their emphasis on missionary work. Zinzendorf expressed the need to spread the gospel, and he established Moravian communities in the Baltic states, England, Holland, Poland, Russia, Sweden, and Switzerland. The goal was not necessarily to attract new members to their way of thinking and living but to awaken an awareness of Christ's sufferings in relation to the lives of those in need of salvation.[22] This was especially crucial for people that Zinzendorf regarded as "heathen," including African slaves and native peoples in America. A chance meeting with a slave during his visit in 1731 to the Danish court in Copenhagen revealed the need for missionaries in the Americas; Zinzendorf soon dispatched Moravian missionaries to work in the Caribbean and England's American colonies; they built a lasting community in Pennsylvania that Zinzendorf named Bethlehem when he visited at the end of 1741. From this base, they pursued their main goal of evangelizing among Native Americans and enslaved Africans. They also attracted a number of the English colonists in America, a few of whom joined their community.[23]

The Moravians made a profound impression on one particular Englishman who would subsequently have an impact on the religious landscape of the American colonies. In late 1735 and early 1736, two brothers, John Wesley (1703–1791) and Charles Wesley (1707–1788), who would later establish an evangelical sect known as Methodism, sailed to the American colony of Georgia. On board their ship were a group of Moravians who impressed the Wesley brothers with their calm faith during a terrifying storm that tore the main mast from the ship. Once they arrived in Georgia, John and Charles Wesley learned more about the Moravian Brethren and the religious ideas of Count Zinzendorf; their acquaintance with the Moravians in America encouraged them later to associate with the Moravian community in London. In fact, John Wesley visited Count Zinzendorf and the Moravian community of Herrnhut in Germany in 1738, shortly following his own religious conversion. As his fledgling sect of Methodists grew, Wesley adapted much of what he learned from the Moravians to the Anglican circumstance. Indeed, early Methodism incorporated Wesley's adaptation of Moravian spirituality.[24]

A Great Awakening

Among those associated with John Wesley in the early days of the Methodist movement was a young Anglican by the name of George Whitefield. Whitefield met Wesley while at Oxford University, where John's brother Charles Wesley had invited Whitefield to join a small group of students called the "Holy Club," often referred to as "Method-ists," which John Wesley led. After finishing at Oxford, the Wesleys took up missionary work in America, while Whitefield began his career as an Anglican preacher in England, enjoying immediate popularity. At John Wesley's urging, Whitefield traveled to Georgia in 1738, where he took up the foreshortened work of the Wesley brothers, who had met unhappy circumstances and returned to England sooner than they had planned. Upon his arrival in Georgia, Whitefield found harsh conditions and a diverse population that was largely uninterested in his evangelistic goals. Unlike in his meteoric success in England as an electrifying sermonizer who drew large crowds, Whitefield set out to convert the Georgians one household at a time. Faced with a bewildering array of religious orientations that included German Moravians, Swiss Lutherans, French Huguenots, and Scottish Presbyterians in addition to English Anglicans, Whitefield quickly learned to adapt his approach to the inclinations of those he served. Before long he found acceptance in the colony as he threw himself into his missionary labors of preaching, teaching, organizing schools, building churches, and establishing the orphanage that he would support throughout his life. By the time he returned to England in the fall of 1738, Whitefield had devised a formula that would make him the most widely regarded celebrity in the English-speaking world of his day: an itinerant ministry for converting souls and supporting works of charity and mercy.[25]

As he traveled throughout England, Ireland, Scotland, Wales, the North American colonies, Jamaica, and Bermuda, Whitefield's electrifying preaching style thrilled crowds and stirred the faithful with its evangelical message of dedicating one's life to Christ in what he frequently called "New Birth," commonly called "regeneration," the experience of giving up one's sinful ways and committing to a more pious Christian lifestyle. An early interest in theater never left Whitefield, despite his renunciation of "reading plays" in favor of Methodist piety; he was continually drawn to the most dramatic characters and events of the Bible, and successfully incorporated techniques of the stage into his characteristically dramatic style of preaching.[26] His masterful ability to bring audiences to an emotional brink led many of his hearers into the "New Birth" experience of Christian regeneration. Moreover, he supplemented his dramatic performances in the pulpit with skillful casting of his public persona in print. His first journey to America in 1738 became an occasion for keeping a journal that would portray his evangelical adventures in heroic terms for a readership back in England.[27] As publication of his exploits increased his fame and notoriety, Whitefield realized the power of the press for promoting his message and guaranteeing large crowds to hear him preach. The "Grand Itinerant" and "Divine Dramatist" returned to England from Georgia to great acclaim and a rapidly growing notoriety that would accompany him for the rest of his life.

The sudden rise of George Whitefield's popularity coincided with a surge of pietistic spirituality throughout the Protestant world in what historians have called the Great Awakening. This loosely defined movement involved religious revivals both in England and in the English colonies in America, as well as in Scotland, Wales, and Holland.[28] In New England, a series of religious revivals that had sprung up in the early 1730s gained widespread attention through the writings of the Congregational minister and theologian Jonathan Edwards (1703–1758), a staunch Calvinist who regarded the eruption of religious excitement that he oversaw in western Massachusetts as a herald of the promised millennial age. But these were not the first revivals of religious fervor in the American colonies; in 1726 Dutch Reformed Pietists in New Jersey had joined forces with Scots-Irish Presbyterians in fervent gatherings to bring Christians into the experience of "the New Birth."[29] Even earlier, up in New England, the well-known Puritan minister Solomon Stoddard (1643–1729), grandfather of Jonathan Edwards, had conducted "harvests," as he called them, the earliest in 1690.[30] But the revivals of 1733–1734 in Northampton, Massachusetts, under Jonathan Edwards' leadership became

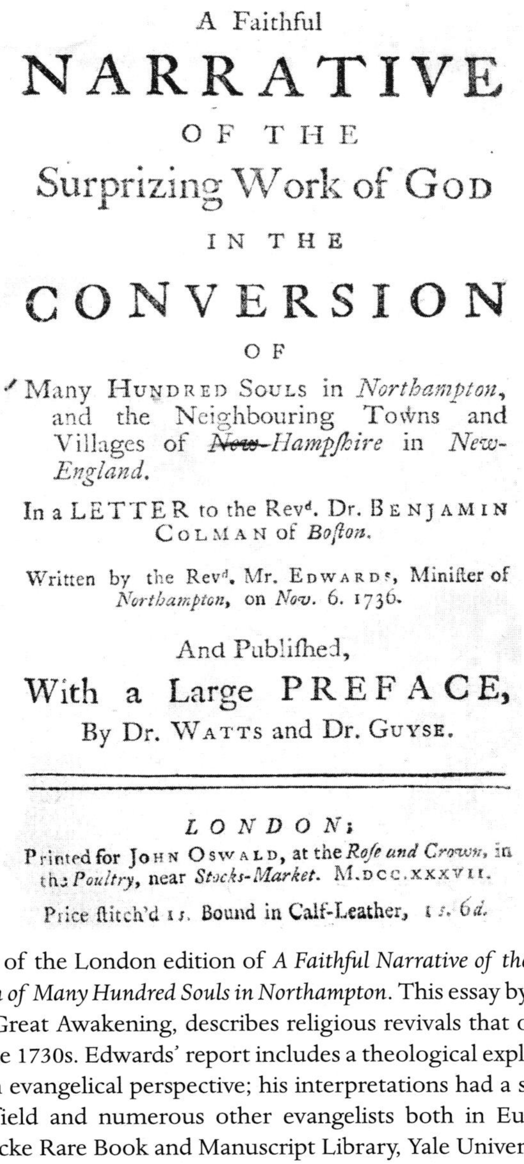

A Faithful

NARRATIVE

OF THE

Surprizing Work of GOD

IN THE

CONVERSION

OF

Many HUNDRED SOULS in *Northampton*, and the Neighbouring Towns and Villages of New-*Hampſhire* in *New-England*.

In a LETTER to the Revᵈ. Dr. BENJAMIN COLMAN of *Boſton*.

Written by the Revᵈ. Mr. EDWARDꜱ, Miniſter of *Northampton*, on *Nov.* 6. 1736.

And Publiſhed,

With a Large PREFACE,

By Dr. WATTS and Dr. GUYSE.

_____

LONDON;

Printed for JOHN OSWALD, at the *Roſe and Crown,* in the *Poultry,* near *Stocks-Market.* M.DCC.XXXVII.

Price ſtitch'd 1ſ. Bound in Calf-Leather, 1ſ. 6d.

Figure 4.3 Cover of the London edition of *A Faithful Narrative of the Surprizing Work of God in the Conversion of Many Hundred Souls in Northampton.* This essay by Jonathan Edwards, theologian of the Great Awakening, describes religious revivals that occurred in western Massachusetts in the 1730s. Edwards' report includes a theological explanation of religious conversion from an evangelical perspective; his interpretations had a significant influence on George Whitefield and numerous other evangelists both in Europe and America. (Courtesy of Beinecke Rare Book and Manuscript Library, Yale University.)

famous throughout the **Atlantic world** with the publication in 1737 of Edwards' account under the title *A Faithful Narrative of the Surprizing Work of God*, where he describes the religious zeal of the townsfolk as "a very Extraordinary dispensation of Providence."[31] His Calvinist interpretation of how the entire town submitted to the workings of God's providence in emotional experiences of regeneration that involved a visceral, bodily display of piety became a model for revivals that occurred elsewhere, not only in New England and the other American colonies but also in England and in other places where Protestants sought to revitalize their Christian faith. Among the colonists of New England, these religious revivals reached an apex in the early years of the 1740s, but they continued sporadically there and in other colonies well into the 1770s.

Turmoil in colonial society

The revivalists' embrace of a bodily Christian experience, however, was met with disdain by their rivals, who warned of too much religious "enthusiasm." Edwards' theology met opposition from the Old Lights, the more established clergy, who were opponents of the evangelical New Lights; Congregationalist minister Charles Chauncy (1705–1787) of Boston, for instance, described the revivalists' notion of a "New Birth" as a delusional fancy of imagination rather than an authentic working of religious spirit; the enthusiastic indulgences commonly witnessed at religious revivals were nothing more, according to Chauncy, than "a disease, a sort of madness."[32] Chauncy and other Old Lights distrusted the emotional outpourings of the evangelical gatherings; they insisted on a more tempered and rational approach.

Most importantly, the Old Lights feared the chaotic disorder that the revivals introduced to colonial society. Indifference to the authority of parish jurisdictions and willful disregard for social distinctions of class, religious denomination, and even race and gender all threatened the delicate order that the established churches and other colonial institutions sought to maintain. George Whitefield was particularly singled out for harsh censure. In 1744, the faculty of Harvard University declared publicly "That we look upon his going about, in an Itinerant Way, especially as he hath so much of an enthusiastic Turn, utterly inconsistent with the Peace and Order, if not the very Being of these Churches of Christ."[33] Their condemnation was followed by similar declarations from the faculty at Yale University and several New England ministerial associations.[34]

The perceived threat to colonial order posed by itinerant, evangelical preachers indicates a rapidly changing and diverse population by the middle decades of the eighteenth century. The careers of George Whitefield and the many others like him who staged religious revivals up and down the colonies challenged the spiritual laxity of established churches, including both clergy and the **lay** membership. At the same time, they opened the church doors to a more diverse mix of worshipers. Those attending the revivals were a heterogeneous mix that crossed the orderly boundaries of parish jurisdictions and encompassed differences of religion, race, gender, class, age, ethnicity, and educational level. Above all, these revivals spread religion to people not being served by the more traditional churches, especially the poor, enslaved Africans, and occasionally a few Native Americans. In doing so, they disrupted the social authority of the established churches.

For the most part, the evangelical revivals that flourished in the American colonies during the 1730s and 1740s remained local affairs, or at best had a regional impact. A key exception were the preaching tours of George Whitefield. Over the course of his seven tours in America, ending with his death while on tour in Massachusetts in 1770, Whitefield attracted large crowds, often in the thousands, to hear him preach. Everywhere he went, whether in the southern colonies, in the cities and towns of the middle colonies, or in New England, the faithful, the curious, even his critics flocked to hear the Grand Itinerant's sermons.

George Whitefield's unprecedented popularity in the colonies points to three significant developments that characterize the changing nature of American society in the eighteenth century. First, his tours thrust religious discourse into an emerging marketplace that increasingly challenged traditional structures of authority. Colonial citizens found themselves in a world of increasing complexity that relied more on impersonal relations of commerce and communication; the society of familiarity and personal trust was becoming less prominent as mobility and distant markets became more dominant in the colonies. Whitefield's itinerant approach to religion fit well with this emerging market orientation. His disregard for denominational affiliation in favor of a more personal religious message forced the established churches into the marketplace of religious discourse; they could no longer rely on their unchallenged position as the sole purveyors of religion in their locales.[35] When the "Grand Itinerant" rolled into town with his theatrical

Figure 4.4 George Whitefield's preaching tours made him the most widely known person in America. He attracted large crowds to his revivals wherever he appeared. (Image © SOTK2011 / Alamy.)

preaching that called for a personal experience of Christ, the faithful had a choice that was previously unavailable. The competing offerings served as commodities in a market of religiosity.

A second development that Whitefield's tours introduced was a heightened awareness of diversity and religious differences in colonial society. The inclusiveness of his religious gatherings opened public discourse to new audiences. Everyone was welcome, especially the irreligious and unregenerate, who were most in need of Whitefield's call to "New Birth." Thus, the poor, the young, the servant, the slave, even Jews and Indians were equally capable of hearing Whitefield's words and participating fully in his **liturgies**. In ways that had not been previously known in the colonies, Whitefield's rhetoric was radically egalitarian. Moreover, new models of communication allowed the revivalist to reach people who were not able to see him in person. Whitefield skillfully employed print journalism to promote himself and to reach those who could not be present at his revivals. His innovations in mass marketing made him available to even wider audiences.[36] In his efforts to save souls, George Whitefield widened the field of public discourse.

A third development introduced with Whitefield's tours of America derives from the first two: with America no longer a series of isolated colonies, Americans were beginning to acknowledge their common interests as a singular, unified society. Whereas most evangelical revivals in the early and middle decades of the eighteenth century were confined to local or regional interests, Whitefield's message resonated across colonial boundaries. He demonstrated that the people of New England had common cause with folks in Georgia, that Virginia's Anglicans shared interests with New Jersey Quakers. This sense of religious commonality among the colonies coincided with an emerging understanding of common interests in political and economic realms as well. As George Whitefield traversed the byways of America, he contributed to a new colonial perspective of unity that transcended the innumerable differences inherent in the diverse peoples that inhabited England's possessions along the Atlantic seaboard of North America.

The period of religious revivals beginning in the 1730s has been described as "a watershed in the history of religious differences in America," largely because it introduced notions of individual equality in matters of religion.[37] Toleration of religious differences had been official policy for some time in much of the British empire, but in America during the course of the eighteenth century the colonists moved decisively beyond tolerance toward an **ethos** of acceptance and equality in matters of religion.[38] Religious conflict and persecution did not disappear altogether, but such incidents became less likely as more colonists recognized the advantages of overcoming differences in favor of a unified society. Common interests in religion, as well as in politics and commerce, demanded that the diverse peoples of the American colonies seek prosperity through a shared sense of unity.

Box 4.1   George Whitefield's relics

The public fanaticism for George Whitefield in the American colonies did not wane with his death in 1770. Veneration of the deceased evangelist was evident at his funeral, where upwards of ten thousand mourners crowded into and around the Old South Presbyterian meetinghouse of Newburyport, Massachusetts, where he was laid to rest in a vault beneath the communion table and pulpit. For decades after his burial, faithful admirers traveled there to visit his tomb. Many of these Protestant pilgrims descended into the vault to view his final place of repose, and some took mementos of their encounter with the dead preacher. In 1775, American soldiers on their way to fight the British in Canada stopped in Newburyport to remove parts of Whitefield's collar and wristbands, which they divided among themselves before proceeding on to battle. A British visitor to the tomb in 1829 stole one of Whitefield's arm bones, and for twenty years his remains in Newburyport were incomplete; the arm bone was returned in 1849, and it was restored to the vault in a ceremony attended by two thousand celebrants.

Travelers continued arriving in Newburyport throughout the nineteenth century to visit the grave of the Grand Itinerant, but in the early decades of the twentieth century visitation declined. By the 1930s the coffin had been tiled over, and it was no longer possible to view the evangelist's remains. In the age of the automobile, guidebooks did not mention the Presbyterian meetinghouse in Newburyport as a place of interest, and the resting place of the first celebrity to capture the American popular imagination became all but forgotten. But part of George Whitefield has survived into the twenty-first century: his thumb can still be found in the Methodist archives at Drew University in New Jersey.[39]

A New Nation

The gradual shift toward more religious tolerance and unity, however, did not arrive equally in all parts of the English colonies. Baptist preachers, for instance, routinely risked official persecution in pre-revolutionary Virginia. Numerous Baptists faced the wrath of local authorities, suffering all sorts of abuses, including public whippings and odious verbal attacks; in many cases worship services were violently disrupted.[40] These harsh treatments that local officials perpetuated on Baptists and other "dissenting" sects came as a response to what members of the elite class, virtually all with close ties to the officially established Church of England, perceived as a dangerous threat to the very fabric of colonial order in Virginia; for instance, Baptists convicted of violating local laws on public worship were berated for instilling terror in the hearts of pious churchgoers, causing them "to forsake their Church and the cheerful innocent Society of their Friends and Families, and turn sour, gloomy, severe, and censorious to all about them. Wives are drawn from their Husbands, Children from their Parents, and Slaves from the Obedience of their Masters."[41] Certainly, Baptists and other religious dissenters, at least in the view of those aligned with the established church of the colony, seemed a dangerous threat to the safety and prosperity of colonial Virginia.

But this exclusivist notion that dissenters pose a threat to the social order would soon be swept away in the revolutionary tumult of the final decades of the eighteenth century. The coming of a new democratic order that brought political independence to England's American colonies also ushered in a new era of religious accommodation among the Americans. The notion that government would not interfere in matters of religion was the culmination of a historical process that had gone from enforced religious uniformity in the earliest colonies to a more tolerant acknowledgment of legitimate religious differences, and finally to the enshrinement of "religious liberty" as full acceptance of differences in the founding documents of the United States of America. At least in principle, the new nation would remain neutral in religious affairs and accepting of all sectarian modes of religious faith, practice, and community.

Box 4.2   Pluralism

The founding ideal of religious liberty at the heart of the new system of government adopted by the United States of America employs a doctrine of religious pluralism. Although "pluralism" is often used interchangeably with the term "diversity," it is helpful to distinguish between them. Diversity refers to the fact of sociological differences, while pluralism is a political principle for accommodating those differences. The idea that a multiplicity of religious orientations, beliefs, practices, and traditions constitutes a public good distinguishes pluralism as a political principle from the mere fact of diversity; simply put, pluralism involves a doctrine of inclusion that regards diversity as a strength of the political order.

This idea of pluralism as a political doctrine assumes both diversity and tolerance. A pluralistic society by definition is a diverse society – that is, one that includes differences. The very notion of religious pluralism implies a diversity of religious communities, ideas, practices, and commitments. At the same time, the doctrine of pluralism also expresses a tolerant stance toward differences within the political state. A pluralistic society, in order to thrive, must remain tolerant of all of its constituents.

By the middle of the eighteenth century, colonial America had become a religiously diverse place. The English colonies included Anglicans, Puritan Congregationalists, Baptists, Quakers, Presbyterians, a few Methodists, Catholics, some Jews, French Huguenots, Dutch Reformed, German Pietists, Swedish Lutherans, and adherents to Native American religions and indigenous African religions, plus at least a few Muslims among the slave population. But religious diversity does not imply peaceful cooperation. In fact, diversity often brings conflict and violence. Christians in general were largely insensitive to the subtleties of non-Christian religions and often regarded the eradication of others' religiosity as their religious duty. Even among the various Christian communities, differences precipitated violence, as the persecution of Baptist preachers in eighteenth-century Virginia and the execution of Quaker missionaries in seventeenth-century Massachusetts demonstrate. But, with a policy of pluralism, a degree of peaceful tolerance and even full acceptance of the differences that constitute a diverse society became possible.

A formal definition of religious pluralism offered by a political scholar acknowledges the need for tolerance and acceptance in a diverse society:

> [R]eligious pluralism refers to patterns of peaceful interaction among diverse religious actors – individuals and groups who identify with and act out of particular religious traditions. Religious pluralism, in this definition, does not posit different religions on diverse paths to the same truth, as it does in some theological contexts. And the term implies more than the social and religious diversity explored in much sociological analysis. Religious pluralism is the interaction of religious actors with one another and with the society and the state around concrete cultural, social, economic, and political agendas. It denotes a politics that joins diverse communities with overlapping but distinctive ethics and interests. Such interaction may involve sharp conflict. But religious pluralism, as defined here, ends where violence begins.[42]

As this description points out, pluralism does not necessarily mean an end to conflict between the various religious actors who constitute a diverse society. It does indicate, however, that conflict will remain peaceful. Religious people can disagree – in fact, will certainly disagree – over fundamental issues, but in a pluralistic society their disagreements will not deteriorate into violence; pluralism allows peaceful coexistence and interaction of a diverse citizenry. In colonial Virginia, for instance, Baptists and other religious "dissenters" – the term for religious groups who did not recognize the officially established church of the colony – suffered persecutions at the hands of a political order that resisted the fact of diversity. But, as the revolutionary colonists gathered to devise a new nation, they turned to religious pluralism as the doctrine of the new political order.

An enlightened people

Many of the leading citizens of England's American colonies in the eighteenth century found themselves caught up in the ideas of what has been described as the Enlightenment. In fact, the American Revolution of the 1770s and 1780s can be fairly characterized as an outcome of Enlightenment thinking, at least for important figures such as Thomas Jefferson (1743–1826) and Benjamin Franklin (1706–1790). The political logic of the colonists' break from England and the establishment of an independent nation in America relied extensively on Enlightenment principles.

The Enlightenment itself cannot be easily defined. As an era in European intellectual history, it had its origins in the humanistic studies of the late medieval and Renaissance periods, and reached its apex in the revolutionary scientific thinking of the seventeenth century; the emphasis on rationalistic thinking in the European Enlightenment is exemplified in such figures as Francis Bacon (1561–1626), Galileo Galilei (1564–1642), René Descartes (1596–1650), Isaac Newton (1642–1727), François-Marie Arouet Voltaire (1694–1778), and Denis Diderot (1713–1784). In terms of religion, however, the Enlightenment was less a period of history or a set of intellectual principles and more a shift in authority from revelation to reason. The implications of the new scientific thinking, with its greater reliance on observation and inductive reasoning, led to a reconfiguration of knowledge among Europe's philosophers and other intellectuals. The traditional Christian acceptance of revelation as the source of religious authority came under greater scrutiny

---

Box 4.3   Enlightenments

Although there are significant connections between its various instances, what has been called "the Enlightenment" was actually several different intellectual movements that took different forms in different places, sometimes producing conclusions that contradicted Enlightenment ideas from elsewhere. Distinct schools of Enlightenment thought developed in such locales as France, Germany, the Netherlands, Scotland, and England. In fact, the term "Enlightenment" was not widely associated with these movements until the nineteenth century, although the German philosopher Immanuel Kant (1724–1804), himself a leading figure of the German Enlightenment, published an influential essay in 1784 ("Answering the Question: What is Enlightenment?") that characterizes Enlightenment as "man's emergence from his self-incurred immaturity."[43] Some historians regard Kant's philosophy as the closing of the Enlightenment, although others insist that the modern world still persists in an Age of Enlightenment, evidenced by the predominance of science as the authoritative means to truth.

as Enlightenment thinkers increasingly turned toward natural religion, which considered religious precepts based strictly on the authority of experience and the application of human reason; the more extreme views of natural religion rejected all supernatural events and revelations, and accepted only what could reasonably be surmised from observation and experience in the world. Most Enlightenment views of religion, however, continued to preserve much of the accepted Christian traditions that dominated Europe, although they tended to explain traditional accounts of miraculous events in more rationalistic terms.

One of the more influential of the Enlightenment thinkers for the American colonies was the English philosopher John Locke (1632–1704). In fact, he has been described as "America's philosopher" because of his contributions to political philosophy that became embodied in the American Revolution. In matters of religion, Locke assumed a somewhat moderate position, taking a common-sense approach that was widely accepted, even in official church circles. In contrast, his political writings advocate for liberty of conscience, much like those of other liberals of his time. One's conscience, he observed, was the personal domain of the individual and could not be altered by compulsion. Moreover, he attacked the notion of innate ideas and eternal, absolute truths. In a view typical of the natural religion of the Enlightenment period, Locke was convinced that what we know of the natural and supernatural worlds comes from impressions on our senses and ideas generated by our rational minds. Consequently, error, as an inherent human characteristic, is endemic to belief systems, and disagreement is unavoidable in all human communities.[44]

Taking a far more radical position than Locke was the Scottish philosopher David Hume (1711–1776). Committed to an empiricist approach, Hume based his religious skepticism on evidence rather than beliefs. His philosophy of religion insists that, since there is never sufficient rational evidence for any religious belief, it is always unreasonable to accept a religious belief. He even suggests that religious beliefs threaten the unity and stability of human nature itself.[45] In *The Natural History of Religion* (1757), Hume argues that religion is not necessary for morality; in fact, he concludes, it perpetuates grave immoralities. He notes the tendency of religions toward dogmatic intolerance and persecution of skeptics and dissenters, as well as the preponderance of hypocrisy, fraud, and cruelty in the name of piety and devotion. For Hume, these belie any exclusive claim that religion makes on morality. He advocates instead a purely secular morality as a better option for society.[46]

Many religious skeptics found encouragement in Hume's criticisms, but not all were willing to go as far as he did in denying religion altogether. A good number of Enlightenment critics of religion adhered to a theistic notion of natural religion that became known as Deism. Deists envisioned a creator god that had established natural laws by which the universe and society operate, but they insisted that this god was not actually involved in the historical unfolding of creation. In short, they envisioned a god of nature, not one of history. The laws of nature that the creator god had established were universal, consistent, and predictable. Morality was inherent in human nature, or, at the very least, could be discovered in the natural world. The Deists emphasized human virtue, and they eschewed notions of divine revelation, claims of miraculous events, and religious dogma of all sorts; the Bible for most Deists was an error-prone human creation. They were especially distrustful of religious emotionalism, what they condemned as "enthusiasm." Religion for the Deists was a rational pursuit, an endeavor of the intellect rather than an indulgence of the emotions. Moreover, it was a private, personal affair. Deists regarded institutionalized religion as a corrupting force that had distorted the integrity of natural religion. True religion, they insisted, was to be found in the private reflections of the rational mind.[47]

Deism emerged as a rational compromise between the most critical Enlightenment attacks on traditional Christianity and the more moderate skeptics who remained unwilling to reject theistic views altogether. Deistic views flourished among English Enlightenment thinkers in the late seventeenth and early eighteenth centuries, and they became prominent among intellectual leaders in the American colonies in the middle and late decades of the eighteenth century. Deists among the colonists contemplated critiques of traditional religion that would have political implications for the future of colonial society in America and the beginnings of a new pluralist nation.

A revolution of religious liberty

By the time of the American Revolution, the colonies contained an ever-growing and widely diverse collection of religions, mostly Protestant but also including a few Catholics and Jews, some Muslims, and a range of indigenous religious groups among enslaved and free Africans as well as Native Americans. Articulating a unified religious sensibility among the colonists, even limited to those of European descent embracing a Protestant Christian orientation, was no easy task. When the colonists declared their independence from Britain in 1776, they adopted the somewhat neutral language of natural religion derived from Deistic leanings, but tempered with terms acceptable to more Calvinistic opinions. Among its many formal complaints against the British crown, the Declaration of Independence does not include any specific grievances regarding religion. But the document as a whole bases its Enlightenment formulation of the political philosophy of a democratic nation on religious grounds, claiming for the rebellious colonists "the separate and equal station to which the Laws of Nature and of Nature's God entitle them." Additionally, in declaring their independence the representatives appealed "to the Supreme Judge of the world for the rectitude of our intentions," and their final pledge to each other of their lives, fortunes, and sacred Honor came "with a firm reliance on the protection of Divine Providence." The Americans launched their new nation with religious justifications and confidence that theirs was a divinely sanctioned cause.

In the aftermath of declaring political autonomy, debates arose over the proper relationship between the political state and religious institutions. In Virginia, the first state to adopt a constitution, the General Assembly enacted a Declaration of Rights that included a guarantee that "all men are equally entitled to the free exercise of religion." Subsequent proposals to establish state-supported religion, however, met with controversy. In 1779, the Virginia General Assembly considered an alternative to designating a particular denomination as the state religion, as had been the case with the Church of England under colonial rule. A general assessment bill included a proposal to establish the "Christian Religion" more generally for state support. Although more broad than the former provision of public support for Anglicans, which caused great hardship for Baptists and others, the new proposal required profession of four articles of faith, which likely would have excluded both Quakers and Catholics, and certainly would not have included Jews. In response, Thomas Jefferson penned his "Virginia Act for Establishing Religious Freedom."[48] In it, he argues that "Almighty God hath created the mind free," and, echoing John Locke's arguments regarding liberty of conscience, contends that civic coercions in matters of faith "tend only to beget habits of hypocrisy and meanness." Jefferson goes on to insist that truth will always prevail over error if one is at liberty to freely examine one's own conscience and to openly express one's beliefs in public. Hence, his act established

> That no man shall be compelled to frequent or support any religious worship, place, or ministry whatsoever, nor shall be enforced, restrained, molested, or burthened in his body or goods, nor shall otherwise suffer on account of his religious opinions or belief; but that all men shall be free to profess, and by argument to maintain, their opinions in matters of religion, and that the same shall in nowise diminish, enlarge, or affect their civil capacities.

In short, Jefferson wished to establish religious pluralism in the Commonwealth of Virginia.

Jefferson's proposed act and the plan to make Christianity the state religion both failed in the Virginia General Assembly in 1779. Yet the issue of establishing religion did not recede, and in 1784 Patrick Henry (1736–1799) attempted a different approach with his "Bill Establishing a Provision for Teachers of the Christian Religion." Henry framed his plan as a measure supporting Christian education, but the bill was a renewed attempt to institute "multiple establishment," state support for various denominations of Christianity. It begins with the proposition that "the general diffusion of Christian knowledge hath a natural tendency to correct the morals of men, restrain their vices, and preserve the peace of society," therefore justifying financial support from tax revenue for those who provide instruction in such Christian knowledge. The bill stipulated that the leaders of the various Christian churches shall have responsibility for appropriating the funds "to a provision for a Minister or Teacher of the Gospel of their denomination, or the providing places of divine worship, and to none other use whatsoever," with a special provision for "the denominations of Quakers and Menonists, who may receive what is collected from their members, and place it in their general fund, to be disposed of in a manner which they shall think best calculated to promote their particular mode of worship." As the General Assembly considered Henry's proposal, questions soon arose about how to define "Christianity," what texts should be considered as legitimate "Gospel," and who would determine which groups properly qualified for support. James Madison (1751–1836) led the opposition to the bill, raising critical questions that highlighted the dangers of favoring one religious perspective over others. In June 1785 he issued a "Memorial and Remonstrance against Religious Assessments" that enumerated the dangers of singling out religious groups for special treatment by the state. Such policies, Madison warned, went beyond the question of equity among religious practitioners and threatened the very basis of a democratic society. Patrick Henry's proposal to give financial support to Christian teachers, in Madison's estimation, "violates that equality which ought to be the basis of every law," which then puts every law and all rights at risk. Shortly after the publication of Madison's objections to state support of religion, the Virginia General Assembly set aside Henry's proposal and once again took up Jefferson's earlier "Virginia Act for Establishing Religious Freedom." A slightly revised version of the act became law in 1786, establishing pluralistic religious freedom in Virginia.

The following year, the doctrine of religious pluralism made its way into the US Constitution. Charles Pinckney (1757–1824) of South Carolina, a delegate to the Constitutional Convention in Philadelphia, proposed that the guiding document of the new nation include the provision that "no religious test or qualification shall ever be annexed to any oath of office under the authority of the US." Remarkably, his motion was uncontroversial, a surprising development in light of the fact that eleven of the thirteen states (all except Rhode Island and Virginia) had some sort of religious test for participation in government. Pinckney's proposal, after some rewording by the Committee on Style, became Article VI, Clause 3 of the original Constitution passed by the delegates in 1787, the only mention of religion in the entire document.[49]

The near absence of religion in the Constitution, however, caused a stir in some quarters when the individual states took up the question of its ratification. Some critics objected to the lack of any reference whatsoever to God, even in the more vague and Deistic language that Jefferson had used in the Declaration of Independence. More people, though, wanted explicit guarantees of religious freedom as well as other fundamental rights. This was the case in Virginia, the home state of James Madison, chief architect of the Constitution. Madison's political rival Patrick Henry led the opposition to ratification in the state. Henry objected to a strong centralized national government that would vitiate the autonomy and prerogatives of the individual states. He suggested that Virginians stood to lose their slaves if the national government chose to end slavery and that they would be powerless to defend their rights as slaveowners. But even more alarming, Henry contended, was the absence of a Bill of Rights. He derided the notion that the new

Congress would limit itself only to powers outlined in the Constitution. Henry insisted that the rights of individuals and of states must be specified before Virginia would be willing to ratify it.

Madison rose to the defense of the document he had helped to craft. In regard to religious liberty, he argued that religious diversity remained the best guarantee of freedom, which, according to Madison, "arises from that multiplicity of sects, which pervades America, and which is the best and only security for religious liberty in any society. For where there is such a variety of sects, there cannot be a majority of any one sect to oppress and persecute the rest."[50] In his view, the "parchment barrier" of an explicit guarantee of religious freedom in the Constitution was not as effective as the actual protections afforded by religious diversity.

Eventually, though, Madison conceded the necessity for a Bill of Rights as a matter of political expediency. He faced a tight contest with the Revolutionary War hero James Monroe (1758–1831) for a seat in the First Congress, and, in danger of not winning election to the new government he had created, Madison endorsed amending the Constitution with "the most satisfactory provisions for all essential rights," including "the rights of Conscience in the fullest latitude."[51] His pledge to offer a Bill of Rights in the First Congress secured the support of Baptists in his district, giving him the necessary margin of victory. When he joined the Congress in New York that summer, Madison proposed a series of amendments to the Constitution that included the guarantee that "The civil rights of none shall be abridged on account of religious belief or worship, nor shall any national religion be established, nor shall the full and equal rights of conscience be in any manner, or on any pretext, infringed."[52] After a lengthy debate and numerous revisions, the Bill of Rights finally passed both houses of Congress on September 25, 1789. The opening clause of the First Amendment addresses the question of religious liberty: "Congress shall make no law respecting an establishment of religion, or prohibiting the free exercise thereof." With ratification of the Bill of Rights, the new nation had incorporated religious pluralism as a sacred virtue in its founding document.

The Limits of Liberty

By the end of the eighteenth century, religious pluralism was well established in the ethos of the new nation. The guarantee of religious liberty, however, was a circumscribed freedom in practice, applying almost exclusively to Protestant sects, and not even to all of those. A certain element of contradiction and paradox has been at the core of the American political experiment from its beginning, going back at least to the Declaration of Independence; this founding document exclaimed without a hint of irony that "all men are created equal" at a time when tens of thousands suffered in the bondage of slavery, when women and those without property endured political exclusion, and when the claims of native

Box 4.4   Separation of church and state

Thomas Jefferson wrote to the Danbury Baptist Association of Connecticut on January 1, 1802, thanking them for their congratulatory letter on his election as the third president of the United States. He took the occasion of his correspondence with Baptists, who had supported his campaign for the presidency, to explicate his thoughts regarding the relationship between government and religious communities and to respond to critics who claimed he lacked sympathy to religion. Jefferson wrote:

> Believing with you that religion is a matter which lies solely between Man & his God, that he owes account to none other for his faith or his worship, that the legitimate powers of government reach actions only, & not opinions, I contemplate with sovereign reverence that act of the whole American people which declared that *their* legislature should "make no law respecting an estab- lishment of religion, or prohibiting the free exercise thereof," thus building a wall of separation between Church & State.[53]

Although it appeared in several newspapers shortly after he sent it, Jefferson's letter vanished from public view for several decades, and the metaphor of a wall that separates the realms of religion and government did not become definitive of the proper church-and-state relationship for quite some time. In fact, Jefferson's interpretation first entered the arena of constitutional law in 1878, when the US Supreme Court accepted the letter to the Danbury Baptists "almost as an authoritative declaration of the scope and effect of the [first] amendment thus secured." But it was not until the middle of the twen- tieth century that the wall of separation became common legal parlance regarding church–state issues. In the landmark case of *Everson v. Board of Education* in 1947, the Supreme Court concluded, "In the words of Jefferson, the clause against establishment of religion by law was intended to erect 'a wall of separation between church and State' ... That wall must be kept high and impregnable. We could not approve the slightest breach." Since then, numerous breaches have been brought before the high court, and, although there has been no serious reconsideration of Jefferson's metaphor, the Court continues to wrestle with the contentious details of separating religion and government.[54]

peoples were routinely ignored by an expanding population. Even with the new Constitution and the guarantee of religious liberty in its Bill of Rights, significant numbers of religious people did not enjoy the benefits of equality: Catholics, Jews, Muslims, Unitarians, and others continued to suffer political restrictions and many

Figure 4.5 The Jefferson Memorial in Washington, DC, enshrines the sacred words of Thomas Jefferson, including the lines of the Declaration of Independence engraved on the wall to the rear of the statue. Surrounding the dome above Jefferson's statue is a quotation from a letter Jefferson wrote in 1800 to his friend Benjamin Rush (1746–1813), declaring, "I have sworn upon the altar of god eternal hostility against every form of tyranny over the mind of man." Jefferson's hostility, however, was aimed specifically at the tyrannical dogma of Christian ministers who opposed his political ambitions. (Image © David R. Frazier Photolibrary, Inc. / Alamy.)

times were victims of hostility and routine persecutions, while practitioners of indigenous religions of the Americas and Africa were refused even the most basic recognition of their traditions.

The implications of a pluralistic ethos and some of the more difficult issues regarding religious liberty would not be addressed until the nineteenth and twentieth centuries. At the time of the nation's founding, Americans were content to celebrate differences only within the narrow confines of Protestant Christianity as the only legitimate religion. Even so, it was a diverse Protestantism, with an ethic of inclusiveness and acceptance unmatched in the western world. Indeed, the

Puritans' "city on a hill" had become a metropolis that even the skeptical Roger Williams (ca. 1603–1683), the dissenting founder of Rhode Island, would have found satisfying.

The American metropolis, however, did not immediately have an impact on the entrenched ways of Europe and the rest of the world. As we reflect on the establishment of the American nation in the eighteenth century, it is helpful to keep in mind its modest beginnings. Geographically, the United States was a small and vulnerable country, initially consisting of only thirteen states lined up precariously along a narrow strip of eastern North America. In the immediate aftermath of the Revolutionary War, though, its citizens began to expand westward, and before long the geography of America would claim the Ohio and Mississippi Valleys west of the Appalachian Mountains. But America was more than the territories encompassed in its geography. Significantly, America was a political idea, an experiment in democracy, although with a somewhat limited scope of who was included in its political freedoms. In the struggle to free themselves from what they regarded as the tyrannical control of the English monarchy, the American colonists created a new vision of self-governance.

This new vision of America was to some extent the product of a Christian religious imagination, but Christianity was not the only religious universe in the United States and its territories at the end of the eighteenth century. A wide variety of religious orientations governed the diverse groups of indigenous Americans; African-influenced spiritual and cultural traditions flourished among enslaved peoples; and a small number of Jews and Muslims could also be found in America. And, even among the Protestant Christians who dominated the new republic, one could identify a variety of theological orientations and religious practices.

Indeed, America has never been religiously singular. Long before the first settlements of Europeans in what they regarded as the "New World," the American continents had been home to a multiverse of religious traditions, orientations, practices, and institutions, and they remained so through centuries of colonization. The history of human interactions in the western hemisphere reveals that America has always been a place of encounters, conflicts, and religious creativity that have produced novel ways of orienting the many universes found there.

Questions for Discussion

(1)   Some historians argue that the proliferation of religious revivals among colonial Christians was an important factor that encouraged colonists to declare their independence from England. Do you agree that there is a significant connection between the revivals of the Great Awakening and the American Revolution? Provide specific evidence supporting your answer.

(2)   Relatively few slaves became Christian during the colonial period in America. Explain the various factors that prevented more slaves from converting to Christianity.

(3) In what specific ways did the "natural religion" of Enlightenment thinkers differ from the evangelical Christianity of Jonathan Edwards, George Whitefield, and other figures of the Great Awakening?

(4) To what extent do the founding documents of the United States of America make religious pluralism the official policy of the nation? What limitations constrict a complete pluralistic freedom that encompasses all religious people in America?

Suggested Primary-Source Readings

Phillis Wheatley, *Poems of Phillis Wheatley: A Native African and a Slave* (Bedford, MA: Applewood Books, 1995): A collection of Wheatley's poetry.

Richard L. Bushman, ed., *The Great Awakening: Documents on the Revival of Religion, 1740–1745* (Chapel Hill: University of North Carolina Press for the Institute of Early American History and Culture, 1989): This collection of documents from the height of the Great Awakening includes journal entries from George Whitefield and essays by Jonathan Edwards among numerous other contemporaneous accounts of the revivals.

Katherine M. Faull, ed., *Moravian Women's Memoirs: Their Related Lives, 1750–1820* (Syracuse, NY: Syracuse University Press, 1997): The memoirs in this collection offer intimate glimpses into the early Moravian settlement in Pennsylvania.

John J. Patrick, ed., *Founding the Republic: A Documentary History* (Westport, CT: Greenwood Press, 1995): Besides the Declaration of Independence, the US Constitution, and its amended Bill of Rights, this collection of documents includes James Madison's "Memorial and Remonstrance against Religious Assessments" and "The Virginia Statute for Religious Freedom" by Thomas Jefferson; in addition, the collection contains a 1790 "Letter from Three Seneca Leaders to George Washington" as well as a 1791 "Sermon against Slavery."

Notes

1 Phillis Wheatley, *Poems of Phillis Wheatley: A Native African and a Slave* (Bedford, MA: Applewood Books, 1995), 16–18.

2 This brief review of Phillis Wheatley's career relies on the discussion of her life and work in Ann Allen Shockley, ed. *Afro-American Women Writers, 1746–1933: An Anthology and Critical Guide* (Boston, MA: G. K. Hall, 1988), 17–22.

3 Wheatley, *Poems of Phillis Wheatley*, 12.

4 Quoted in Arnold Arthur Dallimore, *George Whitefield: The Life and Times of the Great Evangelist of the Eighteenth-Century Revival*, 2 vols., vol. 1 (London: Banner of Truth Trust, 1970), 495–496.

5 Yvonne Patricia Chireau, *Black Magic: Religion and the African American Conjuring Tradition* (Berkeley: University of California Press, 2003), 41–42.

6 William D. Piersen, *From Africa to America: African American History from the Colonial Era to the Early Republic, 1526–1790* (New York: Twayne, Prentice Hall, 1996), 100–101.

7 David Humphreys, *An Historical Account of the Incorporated Society for the Propagation of the Gospel in Foreign Parts: Containing Their Foundation, Proceedings, and the Success of Their Missionaries in the British Colonies, to the Year 1728* (London: Printed by Joseph Downing, 1730), xxi.

8   Ibid., 232–233.

9   Shawn Comminey, "The Society for the Propagation of the Gospel in Foreign Parts and Black Education in South Carolina, 1702–1764," *Journal of Negro History* 84, no. 4 (1999), 360–361.

10   Quoted in ibid., 362.

11   Oscar Reiss, *Blacks in Colonial America* (Jefferson, NC: McFarland & Co., 1997), 220–221.

12   Comminey, "Black Education in South Carolina," 364–365.

13   Reiss, *Blacks in Colonial America*, 219.

14   Ibid., 189.

15   Ibid., 213.

16   Ibid., 204.

17   Ibid., 198.

18   Quoted in ibid., 202–203.

19   Richard L. Bushman, ed., *The Great Awakening: Documents on the Revival of Religion, 1740–1745* (Chapel Hill: University of North Carolina Press for the Institute of Early American History and Culture, 1989), 22–23.

20   Peter Heltzel, "Philipp Jakob Spener and the Rise of Pietism in Germany," in *The Boston Collaborative Encyclopedia of Modern Western Theology*, ed. Wesley Wildman (online, 1998); see also F. Ernest Stoeffler, *German Pietism during the Eighteenth Century* (Leiden: Brill, 1973).

21   Katherine M. Faull, ed., *Moravian Women's Memoirs: Their Related Lives, 1750–1820* (Syracuse, NY: Syracuse University Press, 1997), xvii–xxi.

22   Ibid., xxiv.

23   Ibid., xxv–xxvi.

24   Frederick Dreyer argues that Methodism derives from Moravianism in Frederick A. Dreyer, *The Genesis of Methodism* (Bethlehem, PA: Lehigh University Press, 1999).

25   Harry S. Stout, *The Divine Dramatist: George Whitefield and the Rise of Modern Evangelicalism* (Grand Rapids, MI: W. B. Eerdmans, 1991), 49–65.

26   Ibid., 22–24.

27   Ibid., 51–52, 64.

28   Susan O'Brien, "A Transatlantic Community of Saints: The Great Awakening and the First Evangelical Network, 1735–1755," *American Historical Review* 91, no. 4 (1986), 816.

29   Stephen A. Marini, "Cosmology," in *Religion in American History*, ed. Amanda Porterfield and John Corrigan (Malden, MA: Wiley Blackwell, 2009), 114.

30   Jon Butler, "Enthusiasm Described and Decried: The Great Awakening as Interpretive Fiction," in *Religion in American History: A Reader*, ed. Jon Butler and Harry S. Stout (New York: Oxford University Press, 1998 [1982]), 111–112.

31   Jonathan Edwards, "A Faithful Narrative of the Surprising Work of God in the Conversion of Many Hundred Souls, in Northampton, and the Neighbouring Towns and Villages of New Hampshire in New England, in a Letter to the Rev. Dr. Colman, of Boston," in *The Works of Jonathan Edwards, A.M., with an Essay on His Genius and Writings, by Henry Rogers* (New York: Daniel Appleton and Co., 1835), 349.

32   Marini, "Cosmology," 116.

33   Robert R. Mathisen, ed., *Critical Issues in American Religious History: A Reader*, 2nd rev. edn (Waco, TX: Baylor University Press, 2006), 103.

34   Marini, "Cosmology," 117.

35   Stout, *The Divine Dramatist*, xvi–xviii.

36   Ibid., xxii.

37   Chris Beneke, *Beyond Toleration: The Religious Origins of American Pluralism* (New York: Oxford University Press, 2006), 50–51.

38   Ibid., 133.

39   Information about Whitefield's funeral and the subsequent interest in his tomb and remains can be found in Robert E. Cray, Jr., "Memorialization and Enshrinement: George Whitefield and Popular Religious Culture, 1770–1850," *Journal of the Early Republic* 10, no. 3 (1990). Whitefield's thumb in the Methodist archives at Drew University is mentioned in Colleen McDannell, *Material Christianity: Religion and Popular Culture in America* (New Haven, CT: Yale University Press, 1995), 42–43.

40   Lewis Peyton Little, *Imprisoned Preachers and Religious Liberty in Virginia, a Narrative Drawn Largely from the Official Records of Virginia Counties, Unpublished Manuscripts, Letters, and Other Original Sources* (Lynchburg: J. P. Bell Co., 1938), 502.

41   Ibid., 259.

42   Thomas F. Banchoff, *Religious Pluralism, Globalization, and World Politics* (New York: Oxford University Press, 2008), 5.

43   Quoted in Lawrence E. Cahoone, ed., *From Modernism to Postmodernism: An Anthology*, expanded 2nd edn (Malden, MA: Blackwell, 2003), 48.

44   Beneke, *Beyond Toleration*, 32.

45   Keith E. Yandell, *Hume's "Inexplicable Mystery": His Views on Religion* (Philadelphia, PA: Temple University Press, 1990), 3–4.

46   Ibid., 25–30.

47   For a brief overview of Deism, see Allen W. Wood, "Deism," in *Encyclopedia of Religion*, ed. Lindsay Jones, vol. 4 (Detroit, MI: Macmillan Reference USA, 2005).

48   Beneke, *Beyond Toleration*, 162.

49   Steven Waldman, *Founding Faith: Providence, Politics, and the Birth of Religious Freedom in America* (New York: Random House, 2008), 129.

50   Madison's "Speech to Virginia Assembly Regarding Religious Freedom," June 12, 1788, quoted in ibid., 138.

51   Madison's letter to George Eve, January 2, 1789, quoted in ibid., 143.

52   Quoted in ibid., 145.

53   Jefferson's letter to a committee of the Danbury Baptist Association, Danbury, Connecticut, January 1, 1802, quoted in Daniel L. Dreisbach, "'Sowing Useful Truths and Principles': The Danbury Baptists, Thomas Jefferson, and the 'Wall of Separation'," *Journal of Church and State* 39, no. 3 (1997), 455.

54   Ibid.

Part II
The New Nation

5

An Expanding Nation

The early period of the American republic was a time of rapid territorial expansion, most notably the Louisiana Purchase in 1803, which, among other opportunities, opened new possibilities for Protestants to extend their religious reach. In this chapter we explore the religious consequences and opportunities of this volatile episode of Euro-American and European extension into new areas. As the United States moved westward, other Europeans were expanding their territorial claims eastward, specifically Russians entering Alaska. Alarmed Spanish officials attempted to secure their northern colonial borderlands with a series of new mission enterprises in Arizona, California, and Texas. Europeans also established footholds on Pacific islands, especially Hawaii, which suffered its own series of religious encounters in the late eighteenth and early nineteenth centuries. Meanwhile, an increasingly diverse citizenry in the United States found a sense of national unity in a renewed enthusiasm for Protestant Christianity. This outburst of **evangelical** activity also reached slave populations, although many of the people of African descent living in bondage maintained their traditional customs and beliefs even as they incorporated new religious influences. With so many instances of religious contact and exchange, America became in the early decades of the new nation a place of proliferating religious encounters, mutual spiritual influences, and unprecedented cultural innovations.

On a cold night in the early spring of 1805, a young Shawnee living in the Ohio Valley by the name of Lalawethika (later Tenskwatawa, 1775–1836), much maligned among his tribal compatriots, retired dejectedly to his wigwam. His efforts as an aspiring **shaman** among his people had been thwarted by an

Formed From This Soil: An Introduction to the Diverse History of Religion in America, First Edition. Thomas S. Bremer.
© 2015 Thomas S. Bremer. Published 2015 by John Wiley & Sons, Ltd.

epidemic that devastated his village; the healing ministrations of his shamanic craft had proven futile in confronting the overwhelming power of disease. Moreover, he had failed to redeem his disrepute as a boisterous and indiscreet member of the tribe whose debilitating addiction to alcohol had earned the contempt of his fellow villagers. Alone inside his wigwam that evening, Lalawethika suddenly collapsed into a deep trance. When his wife later found him, she immediately thought that her husband had died. As the tribe prepared for his funeral, however, Lalawethika awoke and told the astonished tribes-people an incredible tale of death and resurrection. He had in fact died, he exclaimed, and had been carried off to the spirit world where two escorts took him to a mountaintop overlooking a celestial paradise abounding with game and tall stalks of corn growing in fertile fields. This, he learned, was the destination of all virtuous Shawnee and other native peoples, the place where their souls would live in ease and plenty in the afterlife. Those who led lives of treachery and corruption, however, would suffer unimaginable punishments in a great wigwam where eternal fires burned. The worst of them would be reduced to ashes, while others would suffer painful torments until they had atoned for their evil; only then would they be permitted to enter the bountiful paradise, although they never would enjoy all the pleasures that their virtuous kinspeople had earned.[1]

Lalawethika's vision, he assured his listeners, was a promise from the Master of Life; this supreme power of the universe, according to Shawnee tradition, had created native peoples and provided for them with game animals and bountiful crops. The Master of Life had also established the Shawnees' sacred laws, which governed their native way of life and required from them sacred dances and ceremonies. Their traditional ways, however, had lost their effectiveness, and now, Lalawethika told his people, the Master of Life had chosen him to lead them down a new path toward redemption and prosperity. He would now be known to his people as Tenskwatawa, the "Open Door."

Over the summer of 1805, Tenskwatawa had additional visions that clarified his role as "the Prophet." His teachings lamented the loss of traditional values among native groups in the wake of Euro-American influences. In particular, Tenskwatawa condemned alcohol as "the white man's poison." He also warned against a growing propensity for sexual promiscuity among tribal people, and he forcefully denounced the accumulation of private property. He told his rapidly growing body of followers that the Master of Life regarded the selfish hoarding of food as evil and wicked, especially when their fellow kinspeople suffered from hunger. Tenskwatawa admonished them to return to the communal ways of their ancestors, to wear only traditional clothing, and to eat only the foodstuffs that sustained their forebears; he especially condemned the rivalries and violence between native groups and even between individuals within tribes. He urged all native peoples to treat each other with kindness and respect, and he emphasized special honor for tribal elders who followed the traditional ways given by the

Master of Life. Above all, he insisted that native peoples must break their reliance on trade goods received from the whites who were encroaching upon their traditional homeland. The Shawnee prophet warned his followers when meeting with white people to never touch or shake hands with them; he strictly forbade sexual relations with whites, instructing his people to bring home all Indian women living with American men but to leave behind their children born of white fathers, "so that the Nations might become genuine Indian." The Euro-Americans, as the Master of Life had revealed to Tenskwatawa, were "the children of the Evil Spirit."[2]

As word of Tenskwatawa's teachings spread among various tribal groups of the Ohio Valley and beyond, pilgrims flocked to his village to see the holy man for themselves. Many stayed, and soon a rather large gathering of devoted followers

Figure 5.1 The Shawnee prophet Tenskwatawa, the "Open Door," led a millenarian movement alongside his brother Tecumseh's diplomatic and military efforts. Together the brothers engaged their Indian allies with a religious vision opposing the incursions of Euro-Americans in the Ohio Valley in the early nineteenth century. (Courtesy of the Library of Congress, LC-USZCN4-115.)

had taken up residence with Tenskwatawa's tribe. At the same time, Tenskwatawa's brother, the famous war chief Tecumseh (1768–1813), who was an early convert to the new religion of the Prophet, spread his brother's religious teachings throughout the Ohio Valley as well as to tribes beyond the Mississippi River and even among the southern tribes. Tecumseh saw this new religious path as the foundation for building a pan-Indian coalition to oppose Euro-American advancements into traditional homelands.

The rapid success of Tenskwatawa's religious movement among a wide variety of native peoples, some of whom had formerly had been enemies, relied to a large extent on a context of growing distrust, animosity, and conflict between the Indians and Euro-Americans. His harsh condemnation of white society and his emphasis on restoring native culture resonated among people whose lives had been devastated by the intrusions of Euro-Americans moving west over the Appalachian Mountains and across the Ohio Valley toward the Mississippi River. The hope of a promised land of harmony and prosperity free from white intruders was a powerful message for people suffering displacement, disease, and loss.

Yet, despite its anti-Euro-American emphasis, Tenskwatawa's vision and the religious community that gathered around him drew significantly from the Christian religion that citizens of the United States and other people of European descent had introduced to native cultures. Indians were well aware of Christian practices and beliefs; missionaries had long operated among tribal people, including those of the Ohio Valley. In fact, a childhood friend of Tecumseh had become a Baptist minister and missionary committed to "civilizing" the Indians. French missionaries throughout the Great Lakes region and along the Mississippi River had introduced Catholicism to a number of tribes. It is not surprising, then, that native religious leaders such as Tenskwatawa incorporated Christian elements into their new syncretistic religions. The moralistic admonishments for his followers to abstain from violence and material excess, to denounce alcohol, and to live a virtuous life that would earn a heavenly reward in the afterlife and avoid the fiery punishments of hell have clear connections to the preaching of Protestant missionaries. Tenskwatawa also introduced a devotional **ritual** of "shaking hands with the Prophet" that involved a string of beans used for prayer, an obvious incorporation of Catholic rosary prayer practices. In a pattern repeated time and again in millenarian movements in the contact zones of America, the Shawnee prophecy that seized the religious imagination of native people in the Ohio Valley and beyond involved a syncretistic blending of old and new.

Tenskwatawa's religious movement did not endure very long. Caught between the ongoing conflicts between the United States and Britain, the coalition of native forces that his brother Tecumseh had organized collapsed as their British allies suffered defeat in the War of 1812. Along with most surviving Shawnee and other native peoples of the Ohio Valley, Tenskwatawa

Box 5.1   Syncretism

Historians and other scholars of religions have struggled to adequately account for the complexity of religious elements that come together in forging new religious forms, especially under conditions of intercultural contact. The most common approach to this challenge relies on the concept of "syncretism," related to transculturation (see Box 1.1) but with less emphasis on the colonial contexts of contact and exchange. In its simplest formulation, syncretism means the blending of two or more cultural (or religious) traditions to form a new tradition. An especially clear example of this appears in the teachings and rituals of Tenskwatawa, the Shawnee prophet. He appealed to the traditional Shawnee creator deity Master of Life as the ultimate source of religious authority, but much of the teachings and practices themselves, and especially the imagery of the afterlife, reflected Christian influences. The result was a blended, syncretistic religious movement.

As useful, however, as the concept of syncretism has been for scholars, it can distort historical realities. Describing a religion in terms of syncretism runs the risk of focusing too much on the new religious form while over-looking processes by which religions continue to change; in contrast, an advantage of "transculturation" as a similar concept is its focus on the processes of exchange and borrowing that occur in colonial situations. In reality, all religions are an ongoing process of syncretistic change; there are no "pure," unchanging religions entirely isolated from all other religious influences. This is as true of Christianity, with its long history of incorporating non-Christian ideas, practices, and values, as it is of Shawnee traditions and other indigenous religions. Consequently, students trying to understand religious change must rely on the concept of syncretism with caution, keeping in mind that it refers to processes of change rather than merely the outcome of such processes. This requires viewing "religion" as a dynamic, tentative, and constantly changing cultural form subject to the historical forces of ever-shifting social contexts. This view reminds us that these processes of religious innovation are not aberrant disruptions of ancient traditions that occur only under extraordinary circumstances; instead, syncretism involves the normal and regular processes of influence, interpretation, resistance, and change that happen regularly in all religious systems. As complex social and cultural arrangements that operate in dynamic and volatile social environments, religions are constantly subjected to adaptations at many levels.

moved westward to the Great Plains, where he died in obscurity in eastern Kansas in 1836.[3] By then the historical circumstances that produced his mille-narian religious movement had long passed, as former territories of the Shawnee and other tribes of the Ohio Valley became the towns, cities, and farmlands of a rapidly growing American nation spilling westward from its modest beginnings along the eastern seaboard of North America. Removed to reservations far from ancestral homelands, the previous world of the Shawnees vanished entirely.

The native worlds of the Shawnee and numerous other tribal peoples disap-peared with the rapid settlement of Kentucky, Tennessee, and the Ohio Valley following a considerable expansion of the country by Thomas Jefferson (1743–1826), the third American president, who doubled the size of the young nation with the Louisiana Purchase in 1803. This vast extension of American territory west of the Mississippi River to the Continental Divide of the Rocky Mountains encompassed a great diversity of peoples and cultures, especially the numerous indigenous tribes who resided in the region but also settlements of French and Spanish colonists. In a single purchase, the United States suddenly added a diverse collection of languages, cultures, and religions to its territory.

The purchase of the Louisiana territory, however, was not a singular transform-ation of the cultural and religious map of North America. Other European Christians continued their incursions into the western regions of North America; at the same time, the Americas became more fully incorporated into a changing global society that drew together peoples of Asia, Australia, the Pacific islands, North and South America, and Europe. In fact, as we will see, centuries of Europeans moving westward across the Atlantic Ocean to the Americas eventually met up with other Europeans as well as Asians, Pacific Islanders, and others expanding eastward onto the western portion of the North American continent. During the nineteenth century, America became home to a global array of dispar-ate cultures with an inestimable diversity of religious people pursuing their unique traditions.

America in the Pacific World

The expansion of the United States of America with the Louisiana Purchase in the first decade of the nineteenth century furthered the westward movement of European culture across the continent. But, as Jefferson dispatched explorers Meriwether Lewis (1774–1809) and William Clark (1770–1838) to survey the nation's newly acquired territories, other Europeans were extending their own cul-tures eastward into North America. In fact, an expanding Pacific world in the eighteenth century was transforming Europe into a global presence. Its westward expansion also became an eastward march, with both meeting in North America.

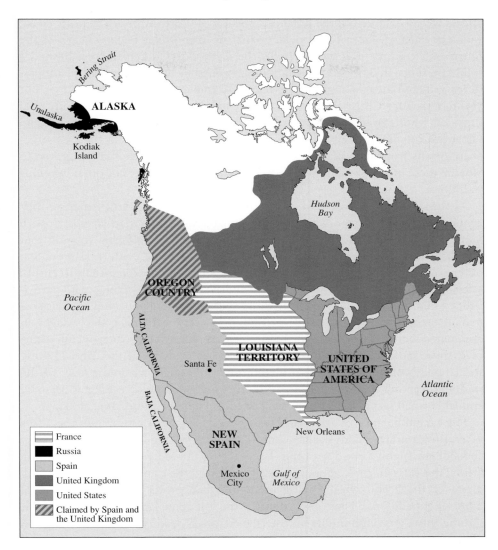

Map 5.1   North America in 1800 showing the claims of four European nations plus the United States of America. Russian eastward colonization across Siberia had entered the Alaskan region, and the Spanish had built a series of missions along the coast of Alta California. Oregon Country was claimed by both Spain and Britain, and after acquiring Louisiana from France in 1803 the United States also claimed Oregon.

Russia's eastward march

By the time English Puritans first arrived in America to establish their New England colonies, Russian Orthodox missionaries were bringing Christian icons to indigenous peoples of Siberia in northern Asia; eventually Russian colonial efforts would extend into the northern portion of North America's Pacific coast. This eastward advance of European Christians from Russia began as early as the fourteenth century, and by the 1620s the Orthodox Church had established a stable presence in Siberia. The Church proceeded to build a network of monasteries and churches throughout the region to minister to Orthodox settlers, but also to introduce Christianity to the diverse indigenous groups of northern Asia, most of whom practiced forms of shamanic animism (see Box 1.8). Russian Orthodox missionaries also ministered to other recent arrivals in the area, especially Asians from such places as China, Japan, and Korea who had migrated to Siberia; these included many Buddhists, Muslims, and followers of other religious traditions.

As Russians moved eastward across the Bering Sea into North America, they encountered the indigenous people who inhabited the Aleutian Islands. Superb hunters and fisherman, the Aleut people embraced an animistic religion that established a sacred kinship with the whales, seals, walruses, otters, salmon, and other animals that sustained their way of life, performing public rituals to ensure safe and successful hunts. These rituals included singing and dancing, with participants donning masks that represented the spirits who had appeared to their shaman leaders.[4] In addition, more private rites were held near the villages in designated sacred places, usually a natural feature, often a high rock or cliff with a cave; these sacred spaces were restricted to the adult males of the tribe. In these special places of power, the Aleut men brought offerings to gain the favor of the spirits in hunting or warfare.[5] Most Aleutian individuals also carried a personal amulet, a small sacred object to protect one from danger, misfortune, and evil.

The sacred balance of Aleutian life, however, began to crumble in the 1740s when Russians arrived in Alaskan contact zones searching for furs, especially the coats of the highly prized sea otter. Recognizing the indigenous skill in hunting otters, the Russian fur traders ruthlessly exploited the native peoples, enslaving many of them and often forcing them into dangerous and sometimes fatal hunting expeditions. They also changed the Aleutian landscape as they built trading posts and settlements on the islands, often destroying native villages in the process. By 1775, the Russians had established a permanent settlement on Unalaska Island in the Aleutian Islands, where a decade earlier native resistance to Russian incursions had been subdued in a massacre of many of the Aleuts there. This earliest settlement, however, did not include a church; the Russian fur traders who settled on the islands practiced their daily religious observances without the help of priests or monks from the Russian Orthodox Church, a common practice in colonial areas where **clergy** were in short supply. These **lay** worshipers, however, brought to Alaska the icons of the Church as well as their personal devotional icons, and they celebrated the feast days of their saints. From these lay settlers, Aleuts learned of Christianity, and many converted to Russian Orthodoxy even before the first Orthodox missionaries arrived in the region in the 1790s.

Box 5.2   Orthodox icons

Significant cultural, political, and theological differences between Greek-speaking Christians in Eastern Europe and Latin-speaking Christians in western Europe eventually led to what is known as the Great Schism of the European Christian Church in the eleventh century. What had nominally been regarded as the One Holy Orthodox Catholic Church split into two distinct Christian churches, the Eastern Orthodox Church governed by various bishops located in key Christian cities such as Constantinople, Alexandria, Antioch, and Jerusalem and the Roman Catholic Church led by a single bishop, the Pope, residing in Rome.

One significant difference between the eastern and western churches is the veneration of visual images, or "icons" (from the Greek word *eikon*, meaning "image" or "representation"). Icons play a central role in Eastern Orthodox religious practice and spirituality. The images are usually painted on wooden panels, but many are mosaics, and occasionally they are found as murals painted directly onto the walls of churches or other religious structures. They usually depict biblical scenes, angels, or especially saints of the Church, with renderings of the Virgin Mary and Jesus Christ being very common. In making the icons, Orthodox iconographers do not merely paint the images but create them through a detailed process that includes fasting, prayer, and ritualized painting. The result is not simply a visual representation but what the Orthodox faithful regard as "windows to the divine world," locating in the spatial realm of this world a sacred opening to a Christian understanding of the heavenly realm. In devotional practice, worshipers do not pray *to* the images; they pray *with* them for intercession, using the icons as a threshold to the spiritual world that lies behind and beyond the natural world. In this sense, the highly stylized and unrealistic features typical of Orthodox icons emphasize the otherworldliness of their subjects.[6]

Most Russian Orthodox believers, in contrast to other colonial Christians, were not intent on eradicating the native religions and customs of the people they encountered. Even the Orthodox missionaries at times tolerated efforts of native shamanic healers, and in some cases even accepted the traditional practice of polygamy. In fact, the animistic **worldview** of the Aleuts shared several commonalities with Orthodox Christianity, such as the symbolic importance of light, the significance of water in ritual practices, and customs of fasting and abstinence. Perhaps the relative familiarity of such traditions made Christianity more palatable to native sensibilities, explaining the willingness of so many Aleuts to readily adopt the religion of the Russian colonizers. One key feature, however, that they

Figure 5.2   St. Herman of Alaska (1756–1837), the first saint glorified (i.e., canonized) by the Orthodox Church in America, was one of the earliest Russian Orthodox missionaries in North America, arriving in the Aleutian Islands in 1793. This contemporary hand-painted icon of the saint is by a Russian iconographer based in New York. (Anna Edelman, iconographer; used by permission.)

did not share was the native peoples' sacred regard for the landscape, and especially for its fur-bearing animals, which remained outside the purview of Orthodox holiness. Even as the Russians repopulated the region with the icons of their Christian saints, they harvested from its seas the revered animals of the native world, which the Russians valued only for the riches that their furs earned in faraway markets.[7] Like other native peoples throughout the Americas, the Aleuts witnessed Christian priorities disrupt the sacred balance of their former world.

Spain's northward expansion

An expanding Russian presence in Alaska also prompted the transformation of other native worlds along the Pacific coast of North America. News of Russian settlements in America alarmed Spaniards, whose claims to the entire Pacific coast were largely undefended. In 1769 a series of Spanish expeditions set out for Alta California, or Upper California, to establish settlements as defensive barriers against the Russians. Accompanying the overland expedition from Baja California was the Franciscan missionary Fray (Friar) Junípero Serra (1713–1784). Two years earlier, the government had expelled all Jesuits from the Spanish empire; fearful of the immense wealth and power of the Society of Jesus, and convinced that their missionary enterprises had been an obstacle to generating wealth in the colonies, the King ordered that all Jesuits be forcefully removed from the entire Spanish empire. In many areas, including Baja California, Jesuit missions subsequently came under the supervision of Franciscans. Leading the contingent of Franciscan missionaries to their new posts in Baja California was the diminutive but zealous Fray Serra, who had come to the Americas in 1749 to evangelize among Indians and to obtain martyrdom. He subsequently joined the expedition to Alta California, accompanying the military commander Gaspar de Portolà (1716–1784) on his quest to establish a defensive outpost to the north. They intended to establish a capital on the previously discovered Bay of Monterey and to build a series of *presidios*, or military installations, along with religious missions and towns along the California coastal plain.[8]

Once they reached the port of San Diego, Serra remained behind to build a religious community while Portolà pushed on to find Monterey. The missionary efforts, however, proved difficult at first. The Upper California region enjoyed the highest density and greatest diversity of native peoples anywhere in North America, but the Spaniards took little interest in learning about native cultures and traditions. Soldiers were especially guilty of violating native customs, most egregiously involving sexual violations of native women. The missionary leader Serra lamented at one point, "It is as though a plague of immorality had broken out."[9] Nevertheless, a familiar combination of military force and native populations weakened by newly introduced diseases allowed the Spanish colonists to prevail in California, but not without difficulties and setbacks. A continuous regimen of harsh discipline coupled with deplorable living conditions in the missions invited resistance and rebellion. The first uprising by California Indians occurred in 1775 when Ipai people burned the mission in San Diego and killed the Franciscan priest there. But, unlike in the Pueblo Revolt of 1680 in New Mexico, the Spanish did not abandon California. In fact, the missions grew continuously, and by the time of Serra's death in 1784 the Franciscan missionaries in California were overseeing nine missions with nearly five thousand native converts in residence and producing surpluses of goods to support the colony. There would be 21,000 Christian Indians living in the twenty Franciscan missions in California by the end of the Spanish colonial era in 1821.[10]

Figure 5.3 Junípero Serra, the Franciscan missionary who founded the California missions, has been honored by the Roman Catholic Church with beatification, the penultimate step to sainthood. However, critics condemn him as an agent of genocide among the native peoples of the west coast. Shown here in an illustration holding a crucifix in one hand and a stone in the other as he preaches to a crowd of indigenous people, Serra remains a controversial figure in Californian history. (Courtesy of the Library of Congress, LC-USZ62-132753.)

Hawaii

While the Spaniards were busy building missions and Christianizing Indians along the coast of California, an English adventurer, also intent on countering Russian advances in Alaska, encountered another group of native peoples far out in the Pacific Ocean. The appearance of Captain James Cook (1728–1779) in Hawaii in January 1778 marked the first arrival of Europeans to the islands. The main objective of his expedition (his third voyage circumnavigating the globe) was to find the supposed "Northwest Passage" connecting the Atlantic and Pacific oceans across North America. During his previous two voyages Cook had explored much of the southern Pacific Ocean, but this was his first expedition into the northern Pacific. On the way to America from the south Pacific, Cook's two ships stumbled upon the Hawaiian islands, which Cook named the Sandwich Islands. The expedition stopped briefly on the island of Kauai before venturing onward to the North American continent.

Following months of exploring and mapping much of the northwest coast of America from Oregon up to Alaska and into the Bering Sea, Cook's ships returned to Hawaii in November 1778. Their arrival at this precise moment, just a week following the appearance of the Pleiades constellation on the Hawaiian horizon at sunset, as well as the captain's subsequent actions, unwittingly corresponded to key elements of the Hawaiian Makahiki, a four-month-long ritual celebration of the new year that involves the return of the deity Lono from the sea in a complex performance of the native relationship between the kingly and priestly segments of Hawaiian society. Cook and his crew were happily surprised by the enthusiastic greeting the Hawaiians extended to them; one sailor wrote of their second day in the islands, "This day our decks have been crowded with the Natives expressing the greatest joy & pleasure at the most trivial things that first represented itself to them, dancing and singing was all that could either be seen or heard."[11] The great excitement that their presence stirred among the native peoples bewildered the English sailors as they moved to the island of Hawaii and anchored in Kealakekua Bay. At one end of the harbor was the village of the ruling chiefs, and at the other end was the priestly village of Kealakekua, where the temple for the deity Lono was located; the Hawaiians ritually celebrated Lono's presence during the months corresponding to Cook's presence on the islands. The English ships remained in Kealakekua Bay for several months, and during their stay the native priests took Captain Cook into Lono's shrine, where they consecrated the English captain, perhaps as a member of their own priestly rank, perhaps as the god Lono itself. Following his initiation ritual in the temple, according to a member of Cook's crew who witnessed the ceremonies, the priests took Cook to a distant site for further rites; as they left the village, "a Herald went before them singing, and thousands of people prostrated themselves as they passed along and put their Hands before their Faces as if it was deem'd Vilation or Sacrilege to look at them."[12]

The respect afforded Cook, however, would not endure. He auspiciously departed from Kealakekua Bay precisely at the conclusion of the Makahiki celebration, when the priests once again relinquished power to the king Kalaniopu'u. But Cook's ships soon suffered damage in a violent storm and were forced to make an inauspicious return to repair a broken mast. Cook was no longer afforded the ritual protections of Makahiki, and his unexpected return threatened Hawaiian political stability at a time when Kalaniopu'u was enjoying a newly reestablished sovereignty as the Hawaiian ruler. Oblivious to native relationships and the ritual cycles of the Hawaiian people, Cook was dismayed when natives stole a supply boat during the night. In a bold move characteristic of his dismissive and often

Figure 5.4 Arriving precisely at an auspicious moment in the ritual celebrations of Makahiki, Captain James Cook elicited the respect and adoration of the Native Hawaiian people, shown here bowing down to the notorious captain. His return to the islands shortly after the conclusion of the festival, however, spelled doom as Cook reentered the contact zone without the ritual protections he had enjoyed initially. (Image © Bettmann / CORBIS.)

cruel treatment of native peoples elsewhere, Cook went ashore to take the king hostage in order to secure return of the boat. At first, Kalaniopu'u accompanied Cook willingly, but at the urging of his advisers he had a change of mind and sat down, appearing to Cook's lieutenant "dejected and frightened." As he sat contemplating his circumstance, word came to the king that another party of the British intruders had killed a chief at the other end of the bay, and with this Kalaniopu'u arose and left the scene. As Cook turned back toward the sea, the native Hawaiians gathered there on the beach killed him.[13]

The full story of Captain Cook's death will never be known. Nevertheless, the available evidence indicates that multiple religious orientations collided in the contact zone at water's edge where Cook's men watched in shocked horror as the Hawaiians killed their captain. When two sympathetic Hawaiians came surreptitiously to their ship under cover of darkness two nights later bearing a portion of Cook's upper thigh, the remaining crew learned that Cook's bones had been distributed among the Hawaiian chiefs according to native sacrificial customs. The friendly Hawaiians reportedly expressed regret, and they inquired of Cook's men when the dead captain would return.

Following Cook's demise and the final departure of his ships, no other foreigners ventured to the Sandwich Islands for seven years. But the fur trade in Alaska made the islands of the Hawaiian people a strategic port, and beginning in 1786 trade ships began to stop there. These early visitors were dismayed to learn of the esteem with which the local people still regarded the deceased Captain Cook. One observer in 1793 remarked that Cook's memory "appears on all occasions to be treated with the Greatest Veneration by all Ranks of People."[14] Even as late as the 1820s, when American missionaries from the United States began colonizing the islands, it seems that the memory of James Cook endured among some native Hawaiians.[15]

A New Awakening

The evangelical opportunities that would eventually bring American Christians to the Pacific Ocean islands rode on a wave of religious enthusiasm that swept much of the young nation of the United States at the end of the eighteenth century and into the early nineteenth century. This period of rapidly increasing church membership among Protestant Christians and a proliferation of religious activity, especially the growing popularity of evangelical revivals, has often been referred to by historians as the Second Great Awakening. Local gatherings aimed at exciting religious passions and encouraging converts to dedicate themselves to an evangelical way of life and commitment had waned somewhat since the famous tours of George Whitefield (1715–1770) in the middle decades of the eighteenth century, but they had never desisted entirely. As the young nation expanded its territory across the Appalachian Mountains into Kentucky, Tennessee, and the Ohio Valley, new opportunities for evangelical efforts followed the settlers to the west. Methodist circuit preachers, Baptist and Presbyterian missionaries, and a host of other evangelical Protestants found that revivals provided an efficient and attractive strategy for reaching larger numbers of the dispersed western populations. At the same time, earnest young Protestants attending college in the northeastern states, especially at Yale in Connecticut, also found the religious revival to be a useful tool for fulfilling their evangelical ambitions. Eventually, as young ministers graduated from these schools and followed their religious calling to the new territories across the mountains, the two lines of evangelical enthusiasm would merge into a single revivalistic movement.

The surge of revivals in the period following the American Revolution was just one indication of a momentous shift in the religious makeup of the United States that has profoundly affected the nation's history right up until the present. An emphasis on an emotional religious conversion of the individual, with the hopeful promise of eternal salvation offered to any and all who repented of their sinful ways and took up a new life of evangelical commitment, proved irresistible to many Protestants raised under the oppressive puritanical rigor of Calvinist doctrines, as well as to those seeking meaning and purpose in the hardships and uncertainties of their lives. As membership swelled the ranks of congregations and denominations that emphasized an evangelical orientation, older and more established groups that resisted the enthusiastic zeal of the revivalist tide saw their numbers plummet. Among the Protestant groups that benefited the most were Baptists, Presbyterians, and especially Methodists, who experienced a seven-fold increase in their membership during the 1780s and by the beginning of the nineteenth century were well on their way to becoming, along with the Baptists, a dominant Protestant group in America.[16]

Methodist evangelizing

John Wesley (1703–1791), who, along with his brother Charles Wesley (1707–1788), founded the Methodist movement in eighteenth-century England, had developed an inclusive doctrine of grace that emphasized the "holiness" of the individual. Wesley's theology rejected Calvinist doctrine of predestination in favor of a more populist Arminian view. Whereas Calvinists insisted that God's grace was offered only to the elect, those chosen by God and predestined to gain salvation, Wesley envisioned a more generous God accessible to all people, agreeing more with the sentiments of Arminian theology (see Box 2.3). He described three levels of grace, which he called prevenient grace, justifying grace, and sanctifying grace. The first is a general grace, offered to everyone and available to all people even before their awareness of God and his merciful presence. Christian believers receive justification, the second level of God's grace according to John Wesley, upon declaring their faith and repenting of their sinful ways. Finally, justified believers seek the perfection of sanctification with the third level of grace. According to Wesleyan tradition, this is an ongoing process of entering and maintaining a life of holiness.[17]

John Wesley's theological teachings were more suited to evangelical practice than the introspective habits of Calvinists, especially those of the Puritans. Rather than seeking signs of one's own election, the Wesleyan theological interpretation emphasized the efforts of the individual to seek sanctification. Salvation became an active process of seeking holiness in God's grace. It also involved encouraging others to engage in this active process of pursuing the holy life, which would bring everlasting joy and salvation to suffering souls. On a practical level, this meant organizing a church aimed at spreading the word, at bringing others into the community of believers who together sought God's sanctifying grace. With this in mind, Wesley developed a system of itinerant ministry in which preachers would not be tied to a single place but would carry God's word to potential converts everywhere. At the center of the Methodists' itinerant system was the imperative to share their message with new listeners, to engage anyone and everyone who would hear their story. In this way, they established new churches, often by securing members one at a time and then moving on to other uncultivated fields of potential converts, but returning periodically to support and reinforce the religious commitments of the newly formed congregations. The Methodists were formally an episcopal church organiza-tion, with a hierarchy of bishops overseeing the cadre of itinerant ministers; for the most part they eschewed the elitist tendencies of the Church of England in favor of a grassroots emphasis on starting new churches made up of new converts served by a mobile ministry dedicated to an itinerant life of evangelization.

Methodism established itself on American soil in the later decades of the eight-eenth century primarily with the efforts of John Wesley's American envoy Francis Asbury (1745–1816). A few small Methodist groups had been established in the American colonies in the 1760s, and by 1771 there was a need for additional preachers to expand the missionary field there. John Wesley chose two young vol-unteers from among his itinerant preachers to go to the colonies, including Francis Asbury. During the voyage to Philadelphia, Asbury pondered the prospects for his efforts in the colonies, writing in his journal, "I am going to live with God, and to bring others to do so." Moreover, he thought his stay in America would be brief: "I will soon return to England."[18] In fact, he would remain in America until his death forty-five years later. During that time, he would become legendary among Methodists and would change the face of American Protestantism.

When Asbury first arrived in Philadelphia in late 1771, the Methodists could claim only a handful of followers. By the middle of the next century, Methodists were the largest Protestant group in America, a distinction they held until the 1920s.[19] Even more crucial in the early nineteenth century was their influence on other Protestant groups; the Methodist emphasis on evangelizing, their system of lay leaders supported by an itinerant ministry, and their success with revivals that attracted thousands of people, including the devout, the interested, and the merely curious, were soon adopted by other religious leaders, especially among the Baptists and the Presbyterians serving the peripheral edges of the expanding nation.

The extraordinary growth of American Methodism in the late eighteenth and early nineteenth centuries owes much to the tireless efforts of Francis Asbury. During his American career, he logged over 130 000 miles on horseback as one of the most prolific American travelers of his time. He preached more than ten thou-sand sermons, and he ordained between two and three thousand Methodist minis-ters. Asbury was not a particularly **charismatic** character in the model of George Whitefield, who commanded the attention of great crowds with his oratorical skills; by most reports, Asbury was slightly awkward in front of crowds, and not particularly inspiring as a preacher. Moreover, it seems that he remained fearful of being disliked and was painfully sensitive about conflict; consequently he avoided confrontations with those who disagreed with him or opposed his leadership. Asbury's chief virtue, however, was his deep commitment to living a pious, itinerant life of voluntary poverty, which exemplified the Methodist ideal. He arose for an hour of prayer before dawn nearly every day, and he ate sparingly. He never kept a permanent home, choosing instead to live as a house guest in thousands of homes as he crisscrossed the United States. He carried very few possessions for himself, but he remained constantly generous to others in need. It seems that Francis Asbury's most remarkable talent involved connecting with people on an individual level or in small groups; by nearly all accounts, he was exceptionally likable and could endear himself even to his harshest critics.[20]

More than his exemplary character as a pious evangelical Christian and his relentless pursuit of spreading the gospel across the American nation, Asbury's greatest contribution was in his leadership of the quickly growing Methodist organization. He was, as a biographer exclaims, "a brilliant administrator and a keen judge of human motivations."[21] Asbury brought to America the system of itinerancy that John Wesley had developed in England, and in this new land during the early years of the American republic the Methodist system experienced phenomenal success. The essential element in the Methodist church-building efforts were circuit riders who served a number of congregations on a circular route that stretched usually between two hundred and five hundred miles. A typical itinerant preacher would travel a four-hundred-mile route in about four weeks, stopping to preach nearly every day before moving to the next stop, and then repeating the circuit again and again indefinitely. Instituting this vast network of peripatetic ministers throughout the overwhelmingly rural American nation and attending to all of the myriad problems it spawned proved to be Asbury's greatest challenge, but it also represents his greatest success. With thousands of congregations served by these roving preachers, and new converts entering the folds of evangelical Protestantism every day, the Methodist system not only transformed the character of American Protestantism but also contributed decisively to the civic culture of the new nation.

Nevertheless, as important as Asbury's efforts were, American Methodism relied on more than the individual accomplishments of this one man for its extraordinary growth. Behind the rapid ascension of evangelical Protestantism as a dominant religious force among citizens of the young United States was the appeal of a simplified theology that professed an inclusive doctrine of redemption for all who embraced God's grace. John Wesley's Methodism, as interpreted and propagated in America by Francis Asbury and his legions of circuit preachers, made the Christian promise of salvation available to all who would accept the gift of grace extended by a merciful God. This theological orientation was especially compatible with the early development of American democracy, which encouraged individualist values in its egalitarian rhetoric. In fact, evangelical Christianity gave diverse Americans a "common world of experience" that contributed to a common national discourse of shared values and norms.[22] Other groups, especially Baptists, also participated in this shared national discourse as they adopted the evangelizing strategies of the Methodist itinerants and established churches in new areas of settlement.

Protestant revivals

In their efforts to reach the ever-widening audience of potential converts, evangelical Protestants in the late eighteenth and early nineteenth centuries bolstered their **proselytizing** efforts with frequent religious revivals, what the Methodists called "camp meetings." These were especially popular in the newly developing frontier regions. Primarily an effective tool for enlivening their religious passions and securing a commitment to a Protestant evangelical religious orientation, revivals relied on the authority of religious experience rather than on the purely intellectual persuasions of dogma and faith. They also were important social events that in some areas served as a significant means of interaction for widely dispersed rural communities. Many of those in attendance traveled great distances to join in these evangelical gatherings, which included a good deal of socializing in addition to emotional religious exhortations.

The most famous of the revivals, and one that proved a crucial turning point for evangelical efforts in the western territories, occurred at Cane Ridge, near the town of Paris, Kentucky, in the summer of 1801. The Presbyterian minister Barton Warren Stone (1772–1844), a farmer and pastor of the frontier congregation at Cane Ridge, organized the gathering and sent word of it throughout the region. Stone's revival attracted an unprecedented number of participants, with estimates ranging between ten thousand and twenty-five thousand, from as far away as Ohio and Tennessee. Lasting six days, the meeting included a chaotic mix of preaching, praying, debating, singing, and emotional displays of religious malaise and exuberance, much of it concurrent. According to one witness,

> The noise was like the roar of Niagara. The vast sea of human beings seemed to be agitated as if by a storm. I counted seven ministers, all preaching at one time, some on stumps, others in wagons, and one … was standing on a tree which had, in falling, lodged against … another. Some of the people were singing, others praying, some crying for mercy in the most piteous accents, while others were shouting most vociferously.[23]

When the preachers served the sacrament of the Lord's Supper on Sunday, many in the crowd were overwhelmed with emotion; one preacher reported that as many as three thousand fell to the ground pleading for mercy and salvation. In all, leaders claimed somewhere between one thousand and two thousand converts submitted to the power of the evangelical stirring.

Box 5.3   Camp meetings

The Methodists and other evangelical Protestants, particularly Baptists and Presbyterians, were especially adept at inspiring new converts with outdoor, multiday religious revivals known as "camp meetings." Methodism emphasized the authority of actual religious experiences, and the potential for encounters with divine power seemed more likely at outdoor meetings, which had been part of the Methodist tradition from its earliest days; John Wesley had preached outdoors as early as 1739 and made it a regular part of his evangelical repertoire. In the western regions of the new American nation, these religious events became widely popular during the first decade of the nineteenth century. In a typical camp meeting, a particular congregation would host the revival, and a camping ground would be cleared near their meeting house. The encampment would be set up according to one of three general patterns: rectangular, in a horseshoe shape, or, the most popular arrangement, circular. In each of these, the campers' tents and wagons formed the outer perimeter, with makeshift benches occupying the central area. The most prominent feature was the pulpit, or sometimes two, usually a wooden platform raised above the crowd where preachers, exhorters, and song leaders would address those in attendance. In most camps, African Americans, both enslaved and free, occupied a separate section, often located behind the pulpit.

Most of the larger camp meetings, some of them attracting as many as twenty thousand people, were interdenominational affairs, with the joint participation of Methodists, Baptists, and Presbyterians as well as a variety of other evangelical Protestants. At the largest gatherings, as many as thirty clergy from various Protestant traditions would participate in meetings that lasted up to a week or more. The preaching, exhorting, singing of hymns, and other activities were deliberately aimed at eliciting an emotional, visceral response, often resulting in ecstatic experiences for the more spiritually prone attendees. As one Methodist preacher described the scene at a revival in 1800, "people were differently exercised all over the ground, some exhorting, some shouting, some praying, and some crying for mercy, while others lay as dead men on the ground." The various modes of being "differently exercised," according to common parlance of the time, included "falling exercise," "jerking exercise," "rolling exercise," "dancing exercise," "running exercise," and "barking exercise," the latter involving small groups "gathered about a tree, barking, yelping, 'treeing the devil.'" Actual bodily experiences gave authority to the evangelical message.

These gatherings also included significant social dimensions, not always religious in nature. Besides the powerful religious emotions aroused at the camp meetings, other less virtuous activities also were common. A good number of revivals had barrels of whiskey on hand to serve to participants, and illicit sexual liaisons were not rare in the camps.[24]

Figure 5.5 Methodist camp meetings were occasions for preaching, proselytizing, and professing religious faith, but they also served as social gatherings, especially in rural areas, where the diversions in many cases were more than merely religious in nature. (Courtesy of the Library of Congress, LC-USZC4-772.)

News of the Cane Ridge revival spread rapidly, and its success inspired a host of other evangelical Protestants to hold revivals throughout the western territories. These emotional evangelical social events spread as well to the more populated areas of the eastern states. Their proliferation in virtually every region of the United States in the early part of the nineteenth century reflected the emerging dominance of evangelical Protestantism in the new American republic. Moreover, they allowed more diverse groups of people to participate in the political and civic culture of the nation. Women, for instance, had always played a significant but subordinated role in Protestant churches, and, when religious activities moved outside the church walls to revivals, camp meetings, and household gatherings, women often constituted a majority of those who came to hear the itinerant preachers and lay leaders. A great number of devout women discovered in church life a place of refuge from the burdens of domestic life and from their strict obedience to gender-determined social roles, embracing a promise of God's mercy that superseded the male authority under which many of them suffered at home and elsewhere.

In similar fashion, a number of African Americans found some bit of cultural opportunity in the waves of religious revival that swept through America in the late eighteenth and early nineteenth centuries. A significant number of enslaved people experienced their first direct exposure to Christianity in revivals during the early part of the nineteenth century. For the most part, the racial divide between white

Euro-Americans and people of color remained strictly intact, but on occasion the lines of racial difference collapsed in the passionate tumult of religious revivals. Moreover, the revivals provided opportunities for mutual religious exchange between groups with differing cultural circumstances. Just as Euro-American Protestants introduced Christianity to African Americans, enslaved and free blacks also influenced white Christians with new practices, especially related to musical styles and forms of call-and-response preaching that heightened the passionate enthusiasm of crowds who attended the revivals.[25] Thus, the encounters between various religious orientations and various cultural, ethnic, and racial groups in the contact zones of evangelical activities produced new forms of syncretistic religious practices.

A Nation Enslaved

The religious democracy of Protestant evangelical activities of the early nineteenth century had to contend with the realities of slavery. As the nation expanded westward, slavery became an even more contentious issue. The American democratic ideal of equality that Thomas Jefferson had enshrined in the Declaration of Independence could not overcome the new American nation's reliance on the forced labor of slaves, especially in southern states where a burgeoning plantation culture thrived on the economic advantages of slave labor. Yet, despite the distance between blacks and whites socially, culturally, politically and economically, Christianity affected both slaves and slaveowners alike. Like free white Christians, enslaved people also participated in the transformation of American Christianity in the revivals of evangelical Protestantism. Their Christianity, however, differed from their Euro-American counterparts; as individuals living in bondage and other people of African descent adopted the precepts and customs of Christianity, they made it their own with a religious message and practice different from, but not entirely estranged from, the religion of white Protestants.

The history of African American religions, however, involves much more than the introduction of Christianity to enslaved populations. It also includes the persistence, sometimes in barely recognizable forms, of the many religious traditions practiced in Africa, including Islam and Christianity in addition to local tribal religions. More importantly, it highlights religious innovations that drew from syncretistic social interactions between Africans of unfamiliar traditions, Native Americans, and Euro-Americans.

Magic among the slaves

Through their exposure to English Protestantism, French and Spanish Catholicism, and Native American sacred traditions, as well as their estrangement from the distant sacred places and religious rhythms of their African homeland, enslaved

Africans in America engaged in syncretistic processes that generated new and distinctive forms of religiosity. Through this process, remnants of their African religious heritage persisted in the new lands, even under the harsh conditions of slavery. For instance, reliance on religious magic is but one indicator of how ancient African traditions found their way into American slave society. The use of protective charms against illness and injury was common among enslaved groups, even as their specific knowledge of the African spiritual practices that gave these amulets their power faded with subsequent generations of American-born slaves. Likewise, divination, the ability to read the future, persisted among many African Americans living under slavery. Moreover, their healing practices continued to assume that illness was the result of either evil spirits or human malevolence, thus preserving a logic of human health common throughout Africa. Enslaved African Americans also tended to name their children after deceased relatives, following African traditions based on beliefs in the rebirth of ancestors.[26]

Following the traditional ways of African tribal religions, however, proved difficult if not altogether impossible. Devotion to local deities and ancestors required access to specific landscape features such as auspicious hills, trees, groves, and rocks; these were made sacred as shrines and as the burial places of the dead. Without access to these African holy sites, Africans taken in slavery to America became estranged from traditional ways of life and worship. Over the course of generations, the sacred landscapes of Africa receded into collective memory as less geographically specific conceptions of the afterlife developed from the syncretistic influences of both African and Euro-American traditions as well as Native American views of the spirit world.[27]

A significant number of African Americans in the colonial and antebellum periods practiced a loosely defined folk religion widely known as "Conjure." Taking a variety of forms, Conjure in the broadest sense involves calling on powerful supernatural forces to help with practical problems in people's lives, often in healing sickness or injury but also in matters of romance, fertility, money, and conflict between rivals. Many Conjurers also practiced divination through such techniques as astrology, physiognomy, palmistry, "cutting cards," and interpreting dreams.[28]

In large part, Conjure originated in Africa, but other cultural practices influenced the tradition as it developed in the American context. For instance, Euro-Americans engaged in charm-making customs that went back to medieval Christianity, and African Americans likely borrowed elements for their own charms from the white population. In fact, Conjure in the United States became widespread among African Americans precisely in the same period when they were being exposed to Christianity in large numbers. Moreover, in addition to African and European influences, at least some black Conjurers learned their supernatural skills from Native Americans; in numerous testimonies of formerly enslaved individuals, knowledge from Indian shamans and other native practitioners of spiritual arts contributed to the development of Conjure practices among African Americans.[29]

The earliest known reports of African American Conjurers date from the seventeenth century, identifying them as "cunning men" or "witches." By the nineteenth century, they were referred to as "hoodoos" or "root workers"; the term "root doctors" was used for healers, and "Conjure doctors" referred to those who had power to either heal or bring harm. Other terms sometimes used in specific regions included "goopher-doctors," "two-head doctors," "wise men," "long-heads," and "double-sighters." In Mississippi and Louisiana, black Conjure specialists were sometimes known as "voodoos," "wangateurs," or "horses." Eventually, "Conjurer" became the most widely used term.[30] These practitioners of magical arts had the ability to do both "left-handed work" – fix a charm or curse upon an individual – and "right-handed work" – counteract a charm or curse. The charms, sometimes known as "hand," "trick," "toby," "mojo," or "gris-gris," usually included an auspicious substance, perhaps a special root or toad's head, ground into a powder. It could be given directly to the victim in food or drink, or placed in the proximity of the victim. But the power of the charm came from the spirit contained in the substance, which was ritually invoked by the Conjurer.[31]

In many places a variety of Conjurers practiced in competition with each other, and individuals often went to a competing specialist when the charms of one Conjurer failed them. In fact, belief in the magical powers of Conjure rarely waned when a particular charm proved ineffective; rather than rejecting Conjure altogether, frustrated clients usually sought another charm or a different Conjurer to address their dilemma. Even committed skeptics found occasion to rely on Conjure magic, as was the case of the formerly enslaved abolition activist Frederick Douglass (1818–1895) who, despite his profession of "a positive aversion to all pretenders to 'divination,'" accepted a root from a Conjurer who told him that it would protect him from whippings from his master or others.[32]

The practice of Conjure gave enslaved African Americans a sense of power and control over their circumstances. Like all religious traditions, Conjure helped its practitioners cope with the uncertainty, suffering, and injustice encountered in their lives. But unlike Christianity, which focused more on the hereafter with its emphasis on salvation, Conjure served more immediate pragmatic concerns. In this regard, Conjure and Christianity were not mutually exclusive religious systems but often complemented each other in the lives of individuals and communities who practiced both, often at the same time.[33]

Slave Christianity

Despite the prevalence of Conjure and other syncretic traditions, the predominant religious influence for many enslaved people in antebellum America was Christianity, in particular the Protestant Christianity of the dominant society. African Americans living under slavery transformed the Protestant tradition into their own religion according to a variety of influences and traditions. Early in the colonial period, the memory of Africa loomed in their interpretations of Christian ideas. For instance, as mentioned in the previous chapter, many African Americans in early America regarded the Christian devil as a morally ambiguous trickster figure; they also tended to put more emphasis on the direct experience of the Holy Spirit, reminiscent of African spirit possession, as an indicator of authentic religious authority. Additionally, the importance of music and dancing in African cultural traditions played a key role in bringing African Americans to Christianity. Numerous white preachers encouraged slaves' attendance at church by empha-sizing hymn singing in worship, and many adopted the practice of lining out the hymns, or reciting the words a line at a time, with the congregation answering in a call-and-response format that was common in much of African music and became dominant in African American musical styles that continue even today.[34]

A number of missionary societies operating in the southern states during the antebellum period sought to improve religious opportunities for enslaved peo-ple. In particular they invested significant effort in convincing slaveowners of the need for plantation missions, encouraging them to pay missionaries and to build a mission station or chapel on their property.[35] These missionary initiatives, how-ever, tended to present a form of Christianity aimed at appeasing the plantation owners and affirming the moral soundness of slavery. Supporters of plantation missions insisted that introducing Christianity to slaves would strengthen institu-tions of slavery, providing a morally justified basis for the relationship between slaveowner and enslaved. Masters and mistresses were instructed to play an active role in catechizing their slaves, and they were encouraged to pursue relations with their slaves built upon Christian principles, with charitable treatment of enslaved people, both physically and spiritually.[36]

Most individuals living under slavery, however, rejected the Christianity offered by their masters. From their perspective, the hypocrisy of a religious master was evident in the realities of slavery. Countless slave narratives tell of brutal masters who professed a Christian faith and even worshiped with their slaves. One for-merly enslaved person, for instance, recounted how the preacher who baptized her "had a colored woman tied up in his yard to whip when he got home, that very Sunday and her mother belonged to that same church. We had to sit and hear him preach and her mother was in church hearing him preach." Likewise, another for-merly enslaved individual in Texas recalled that "old master treated us slaves bad, and there was one thing I couldn't understand, 'cause he was 'ligious and every Sunday mornin' everybody had to git ready and go for prayer. I never could under-stand his 'ligion, 'cause sometimes he git up off his knees and befo' we git out the house he cuss us out."[37]

The rampant hypocrisy that enslaved people recognized in their masters' Christianity did not prevent them from embracing their own forms of the Christian religion. All over the antebellum south, in places where slaveowners prohibited Christian practices among their slaves as well as where enslaved people chose to pursue a Christianity at odds with that of the slaveowners, many African Americans practiced their own form of Christianity in secret, building what religious historians have described as the "invisible institution" of slave Christianity.[38] In the privacy of their living quarters and in the secret hideaways of brush arbors, sometimes known as "hush harbors," enslaved people undertook a process of syncretism that produced a uniquely African American form of Christianity.

The religion of African American Christians living under slavery took on its own distinct character as they brought their own experiences and interpretations to their religious practices. In particular, the cruel realities of bondage focused their attention more acutely on the stories and messages of deliverance and liberation found in the Christian tradition. Speaking of her own experience as a slave, one former bondswoman remarked, "I've been wanting to be free ever since I was a little child. I said to them I didn't believe God ever meant me to be a slave."[39] For many people living in captivity, their reliance on God for deliverance from bondage gained strength in the biblical story of the exodus from Egypt. The common experience of slavery they shared with the ancient Hebrew people gave meaning and purpose to enslaved African Americans as a people. God's intervention, leading the Hebrew slaves out of Egypt and eventually to their promised homeland, instilled in many enslaved African Americans a faith in a future of freedom and justice. Moreover, the many Bible tales of God's wrath shed on the enemies of Israel encouraged in some the hope of vengeance raining down on the white perpetrators of brutality toward slaves. One enslaved individual expressed her bitter desire for retribution when she proclaimed:

> Oh Lor'! hasten de day when de blows, an' de bruises, an' de aches, an' de pains, shall come to de white folks, an' de buzzards shall eat 'em as dey's dead in de streets ... Oh Lor'! gib me de pleasure ob livin' till dat day, when I shall see white folks shot down like de wolves when dey come hongry out o' de woods.[40]

As the Jewish God had delivered slaves from Egypt, as Israel's enemies time and again were swept away before God's vengeful hand, enslaved people in America sought justice and liberation through the redemptive grace of the Christian god.

Their reliance on the sacred stories of the Christian tradition was often sustained by a growing number of African American preachers living under slavery who became established wherever there were significant numbers of enslaved people. Some of these black preachers operated under the supervision of white masters, proclaiming the Christian gospel in terms acceptable to white society. White preachers and masters of the enslaved preachers insisted on a message of docility and obedience, although the black preachers sometimes slipped in a less conciliatory message. One elderly preacher was admonished for exclaiming from the pulpit, "Free indeed, free from work, free from the white folks, free from everything."[41] Another spent time in a Maryland prison "for preaching the gospel to my colored brethren."[42] Under the diligent watch of white society, black preachers operating within slavery found it necessary to craft their messages cautiously. On the other hand, many of them eluded the restraints of the dominant white society, organizing secret gatherings at night in the slave quarters or out in the woods in brush arbors.

Many of these enslaved preachers were illiterate, although their lack of education did not prevent eloquent, inspiring, and powerful preaching. As one white traveler remarked regarding black preachers he heard, "they acquire a remarkable memory of words, phrases, and forms; a curious sort of poetic talent is developed, and a habit is obtained of rhapsodizing and exciting furious emotions."[43] Central to eliciting these "furious emotions" in slave preaching was the employment of several techniques, especially the "call-and-response" pattern that engaged the congregation in the growing intensity of the sermon. This sort of African American folk style of preaching, which uses repetition, parallelisms, dramatic gestures, and intonation, became typical in evangelical worship services for both blacks and whites, and continues to characterize much of what occurs in Christian evangelical pulpits even today.[44]

Another essential element in the "furious emotions" of slave Christianity was the use of music and dance. Drawing on African traditions, but largely influenced by

Figure 5.6 A distinctive "black church" began to emerge in the antebellum period as African Americans, both enslaved and free, began forming their own Christian congregations, often in secret. Typical of these communities of African American Christians were call-and-response preaching styles that elicited "furious emotions" as well as lively traditions of music and dance. Their innovative patterns of worship eventually influenced Protestant evangelical worship practices across racial and ethnic boundaries. (Courtesy of New York Public Library, #808160.)

Box 5.4   Spirituals

The songs that typified African American Christianity under slavery and afterward are known as spirituals, or "sorrow songs," as the African American sociologist, historian, author, and civil rights activist W. E. B. Du Bois (1868–1963) famously described them in his book *The Souls of Black Folk* (1903). Du Bois regarded these slave songs "not simply as the sole American music, but as the most beautiful expression of human experience born this side the seas."[46] They often operated on various levels of meaning with implicit, coded messages that other slaves would have understood. Frederick Douglass notes this subversive aspect of the spiritual tradition:

> A keen observer might have detected in our repeated singing of
>
> > O Canaan, sweet Canaan,
> > I am bound for the land of Canaan,
>
> something more than a hope of reaching heaven. We meant to reach the *North*, and the North was our Canaan.[47]

Certainly, the otherworldly meaning of Canaan brought comfort to many of the slaves as they toiled under bondage, but *this*worldly meanings also were on their minds as well.

---

the Christian Bible, Protestant hymns, Native American ritual traditions, and responding to their own experience in bondage, enslaved African Americans developed innovative musical forms that animated their worship experiences. Often the religious gatherings of enslaved people would end with pushing aside any chairs or other furnishings and forming a large circle for the "ring shout," in which the leader would sing a verse while shouters would respond as they walked, danced, or shuffled around in a ring. These ring shouts could go on for quite a long time, building into an ecstatic dramatization of the song.[45]

Islam

Christianity and Conjure were not the only religious possibilities for enslaved African Americans. A number of Muslim captives from Africa remained faithful in their devotion to Allah under bondage. Their numbers were relatively scarce among the many non-Muslims who made up the enslaved populations of

America, but the accomplishments of the few Muslims who left a record of their slave experiences are remarkable. A significant number of enslaved Muslims had the benefits of education prior to their captivity, and at least a few of them retained their ability to read and write as bondsmen in America, a practice that likely helped ease the pain of their captivity in America as they took solace in the words of the Qur'an and in the Islamic traditions they brought from Africa. "Writing, to a Muslim," remarks one historian, "is believing and worshipping."[48]

In fact, a Muslim authored the earliest published work of African American literature, *Some Memoirs of the Life of Job Ben Solomon* (1734). Solomon (originally Ayuba Suleiman Diallo, 1701–1773) tells of his life as a Muslim slave in Maryland who ran away and came to the notice of the English nobility and intelligentsia, living for a time in England before eventually returning to his homeland in Africa.[49] While in England, he discussed the finer points of theology with Christian thinkers, he wrote down three versions of the Qur'an from memory, and he translated Arabic for leading scholars of the period. Before his triumphant return to his homeland in Africa, Job Ben Solomon also was elected to the prestigious Spalding Gentlemen's Society, where he may have met such leading citizens as Isaac Newton (1642–1727) and Alexander Pope (1688–1744).[50]

Other Muslim slaves left stories no less remarkable. One, by the name of Bilali (birth and death dates unknown), served as a plantation manager supervising between five hundred and a thousand slaves without a white overseer. More importantly, as their local imam, or religious leader, Bilali wrote in the 1840s a thirteen-page manual in Arabic for his fellow Muslims on Sapelo Island, Georgia, which was the only known community of African Muslims in the United States during the antebellum era.[51] Another literate Muslim slave, Umar ibn Said of North Carolina, left thirteen pages of translation of the Qur'an in Arabic, plus a sixteen-page "Life," written in 1831, that is one of only two known slave autobiographies written in Arabic in the Americas. In it he included Christian prayers, which was not uncommon for religious Muslims living among (and enslaved to) Christians; such prayers appeased the Christians while remaining consistent with the Qur'an, which honors Jesus as an early prophet of Allah.[52]

Many enslaved Muslims in America likely came from more socially prominent groups in Africa, and they arguably arrived on the American scene with more established religious practices and cultural traditions and a stronger sense of self than non-Muslim slaves.[53] Though greatly outnumbered, Muslims in many cases were able to retain their Islamic faith and practice their religious traditions, a remarkable feat in a predominantly hostile Christian world.[54] Their historical legacy attests to the widely diverse cultural worlds of Africa that contributed to the religious landscapes of America.

Box 5.5　Muslim slaves

The exact number of enslaved Muslims that were in America remains unknown; historians have estimated that perhaps forty thousand African Muslims were in the territory of the United States in the colonial and pre-Civil War era, but other numbers that vary widely have also been suggested.[55] All agree, however, that there was a significant number of Muslims among the slaves, and many were able to continue practicing Islam in America. The evidence for their presence comes from a variety of historical sources. These include the many Muslim names that appear in lists of slaves; indications of slaves' status as Muslims on family and church documents, including birth and death notices; descriptions of enslaved individuals as Muslim practitioners in runaway advertisements; and a few individuals who gained notice of their status as Muslims by producing written works, sometimes in Arabic.[56] But the known cases of enslaved people who were Muslim probably represents only a portion of the actual number of enslaved Africans who came to America as Muslims.

Expansion

The American religious landscape changed dramatically in the first decades of the United States. With the citizens of the new republic crossing the mountains to the west and settling new territories in Kentucky, Tennessee, and the Ohio Valley and expanding settlements in the southern region, the time was ripe for evangelical renewal among Protestants. Their efforts to bring Christian values and commitments to newly settled territories came in no small part as a response to the diversity of religious practices and orientations that inhabited the new regions. Native peoples already occupying territories that the Euro-Americans coveted for settlement displayed traditions and cultural practices altogether foreign, and for the most part entirely incomprehensible, to the newcomers. Enslaved Africans, quickly becoming a dominant economic commodity of the southern states, pursued ancient ways of their African homelands even as they incorporated the syncretistic influences of other Africans, Native Americans, and eventually a variety of Christian strains. Among Euro-American Christians, evangelical forms of Protestant sects enjoyed the greatest success in the frontier regions, led by the adaptive practices of itinerancy carried by Methodist circuit riders. Their emphasis on organizing new churches and introducing the Methodist process of holiness proved especially successful for building a frontier society with a pious citizenry who found divine meanings in the hardships, conflicts, abuses, and tragedies of their everyday pursuits. Soon Baptists and to some extent even Presbyterians adopted the Methodist example of evangelizing the far-flung territories of the new nation. Their combined efforts accomplished more than merely introducing a life in Christ to a population settling new territories of the young nation. They also instilled civic values that would characterize a unified self-understanding of a majority of citizens, at least the free white Protestant citizens that dominated American society. Among these values are an individualized sense of personal self-worth; the freedom, and its concomitant responsibility, to choose one's destiny; and a divinely bestowed entitlement to prosperity, even at the expense of others. Other traditional Christian values of charity, compassion, humility, and virtuous self-denial did not disappear entirely from the American religious landscape, but they were subordinated to an emerging dominant culture of individualism that celebrated the accomplishments of a rapidly growing nation.

Despite the remarkable growth of evangelical Protestants in the late eighteenth and early nineteenth centuries, they still constituted only one religious orientation in the vast multiverse of religiosities that comprised the Americas. Besides the diverse traditions of Africans and Native Americans, many of them exchanging mutual influences in a cauldron of cultural syncretism, other Europeans continued to vie for dominance in North America and across the Pacific Ocean with their own religious cultures. In the far western regions of North America, Europeans moving eastward across Asia and northward from New Spain converged with Euro-Americans moving westward from the United States. Eastern Orthodox Christianity arrived in the Pacific northwest with Russian colonies centered in Alaska. Roman Catholicism marched northward from Spain's colonial stronghold in Mexico with significant missionary enterprises in Texas, Arizona, and California, in addition to its long presence in New Mexico. British and later American interests laid claim to Pacific island nations, most notably in the Hawaiian islands. All of these contributed to a burgeoning religious culture marked more by its differences than by any claim of coherent consistencies in faith, practice, or tradition.

Questions for Discussion

(1) What are some of the similarities and differences between the syncretistic religious traditions of Native Americans and those of African Americans?

(2) How did Euro-American settlement in the Ohio Valley, Alaska, and the American Pacific coast affect indigenous cultures?

(3) Why did Protestant evangelical Christianity, especially the religion of the Methodists, become so popular in the early decades of the new American republic?

(4) In what ways did the Christianity of African American slaves differ from the Christian religion of white slaveholders?

Suggested Primary-Source Readings

Le Maigouis, an Ottawa warrior, his address reported in "Extract of a Letter from the Commanding Officer, at Fort Michilimakinak, to his Excellency Gov. Hull, dated May 20, 1807," which appeared in "The Indian Prophet and His Doctrine" in the *Pennsylvania Gazette* (1812): This address reported by a trader who had married into the Ottawa tribe demonstrates how Tenskwatawa's millenarian movement affected native peoples of the Great Lakes area.

George Gilbert, *The Death of Captain James Cook* (Honolulu: Paradise of the Pacific Press, 1926): Gilbert was a member of Cook's crew and witness to the captain's death at the hands of the Hawaiians, which he recounts in this selection taken from Gilbert's longer account *Narrative of Cook's Last Voyage, 1776–1780*, which he compiled after returning to England.

Junípero Serra, *Writings of Junípero Serra*, 4 vols. (Washington, DC: Academy of American Franciscan History, 1955): This is a collection of documents from the Franciscan missionary who founded the Spanish colonial missions in California. One document that offers insight into the circumstances of the missions is "Circular Letter of Fray Francisco Pangua, Guardian of San Fernando, to the Missionaries of California, Mexico, February 7, 1775," which appears in the appendix of volume 2, pages 459–463.

Frances Milton Trollope, "Camp Meeting," in *Domestic Manners of the Americans* (New York: Oxford University Press, 1984), 98–103: This controversial travel account of an Englishwoman's tour of the United States and her disparaging comments about American culture includes her observations of a frontier camp meeting in Indiana in the 1820s.

Omar ibn Sayyid, "The Autobiography of Omar Ibn Sayyid" (1831), in *The Columbia Sourcebook of Muslims in the United States*, ed. Edward E. Curtis IV (New York: Columbia University Press, 2008), 5–9: The first-person account of an educated Muslim from Africa enslaved in North Carolina; Sayyid composed this remarkable document in Arabic.

Notes

1   An account of Lalawethika's trance and the vision he experienced appears in R. David Edmunds, *The Shawnee Prophet* (Lincoln: University of Nebraska Press, 1983), 28, 32–34. See also Colin G. Calloway, *The Shawnees and the War for America* (New York: Viking, 2007), 130–131.

2   Edmunds, *The Shawnee Prophet*, 34–39.

3   Ibid., 187. For more on Tenskwatawa as well as Tecumseh, see Calloway, *The Shawnees* and R. David Edmunds, *Tecumseh and the Quest for Indian Leadership* (Glenview, IL: Scott, Foresman and Co., 1984).

4   Margaret Lantis, "Aleut," in *Handbook of North American Indians*, ed. William C. Sturtevant (Washington, DC: Smithsonian Institution, 1984), 178–179.

5   Ibid., 178.

6   Catalog to the "Windows to Heaven" exhibit at the Walsh Gallery, Seton Hall University, September–October 2009, co-curated by Sasha Makuka and Allison Stevens, available from http://academic.shu.edu/libraries/gallery/Heaven_catalog.pdf (accessed June 3, 2014).

7   Regarding the Russian colonization of Alaska, including missionary efforts there, see Gwenn A. Miller, *Kodiak Kreol: Communities of Empire in Early Russian America* (Ithaca, NY: Cornell University Press, 2010).

8   David J. Weber, *The Spanish Frontier in North America* (New Haven, CT: Yale University Press, 1992), 242–243. Regarding Spanish missions in California, see Steven W. Hackel, *Children of Coyote, Missionaries of Saint Francis: Indian–Spanish Relations in Colonial California, 1769–1850* (Chapel Hill: University of North Carolina Press for the Omohundro Institute of Early American History and Culture, 2005) and Kent G. Lightfoot, *Indians, Missionaries, and Merchants: The Legacy of Colonial Encounters on the California Frontiers* (Berkeley: University of California Press, 2005).

9   Weber, *Spanish Frontier in North America*, 247.

10 Ibid., 263.

11 Quoted in Marshall David Sahlins, *How "Natives" Think: About Captain Cook, for Example* (Chicago, IL: University of Chicago Press, 1995), 35–36.

12 Quoted in ibid., 59.

13 For a discussion of Cook's misadventures in Hawaii, see Marshall David Sahlins, *Islands of History* (Chicago, IL: University of Chicago Press, 1985), 104–135. A critical response to Sahlins' analysis appears in Gananath Obeyesekere, *The Apotheosis of Captain Cook: European Mythmaking in the Pacific* (Princeton, NJ: Princeton University Press, 1992). Sahlins answers Obeyesekere in Sahlins, *How "Natives" Think*. A supportive review of Obeyesekere's critique by a native Hawaiian scholar is in Lilikalā Kame'eleihiwa, "Review," *Pacific Studies* 17, no. 2 (1994).

14 Sahlins, *How "Natives" Think*, 87.

15 Ibid., 97–116.

16 Edwin Scott Gaustad and Philip L. Barlow, *New Historical Atlas of Religion in America* (New York: Oxford University Press, 2001), 221, 370.

17 Cristopher H. Evans, "Wesleyan Tradition," in *The Blackwell Companion to Religion in America*, ed. Philip Goff (Malden, MA: Wiley Blackwell, 2010), 686.

18 Quoted in John H. Wigger, *American Saint: Francis Asbury and the Methodists* (Oxford: Oxford University Press, 2009), 45.

19 Gaustad and Barlow, *New Historical Atlas*, 374–375.

20 Wigger, *American Saint*, 3–5.

21 Ibid., 8.

22 Donald G. Mathews, "The Second Great Awakening as an Organizing Process, 1780–1830: An Hypothesis," *American Quarterly* 21, no. 1 (1969), 42–43.

23 Quoted in Charles A. Johnson, *The Frontier Camp Meeting: Religion's Harvest Time* (Dallas, TX: Southern Methodist University Press, 1955), 64.

24 Johnson, *The Frontier Camp Meeting*, 41–62. See also Ann Taves, *Fits, Trances, and Visions: Experiencing Religion and Explaining Experience from Wesley to James* (Princeton, NJ: Princeton University Press, 1999), 104–117.

25 Regarding the interaction and mutual influence between blacks and whites in the context of religious revivals, see Ann Taves' chapter on "Shouting Methodists" in Taves, *Fits, Trances, and Visions*, 76–117.

26 William D. Piersen, *From Africa to America: African American History from the Colonial Era to the Early Republic, 1526–1790* (New York: Twayne, Prentice Hall, 1996), 91–99.

27 Ibid., 96–97.

28 Yvonne Patricia Chireau, *Black Magic: Religion and the African American Conjuring Tradition* (Berkeley: University of California Press, 2003), 32, 50.

29 Ibid., 49, 56.

30 Ibid., 20–22.

31 Albert J. Raboteau, *Slave Religion: The "Invisible Institution" in the Antebellum South,* updated edn (New York: Oxford University Press, 2004), 277–278.

32 Ibid., 281.

33 Chireau, *Black Magic*, 24–25.

34 Piersen, *From Africa to America*, 100–101.

35 Raboteau, *Slave Religion*, 152–153.

36 Ibid., 164–165.

37 Quoted in ibid., 167–168.

38 Ibid., 212.

39 Quoted in ibid., 309–310.

40 Quoted in ibid., 313.

41 Quoted in ibid., 232.

42 Quoted in ibid., 233.

43 Quoted in ibid., 235.

44 Ibid., 236–237. Regarding the influence of slave preachers on white Protestants, see Piersen, *From Africa to America*, 101.

45 Raboteau, *Slave Religion*, 245. For a description of a ring shout in an 1867 collection of slave songs, see Teresa L. Reed, *The Holy Profane: Religion in Black Popular Music* (Lexington: University Press of Kentucky, 2003), 18.

46 W. E. B. Du Bois, *The Souls of Black Folk: Essays and Sketches* (Rockville, MD: Arc Manor, 2008 [1903]), 163.

47 Frederick Douglass, *The Life and Times of Frederick Douglass: From 1817–1882* (London: Christian Age Office, 1882), 180.

48 Allan D. Austin, *African Muslims in Antebellum America: Transatlantic Stories and Spiritual Struggles*, rev. and updated edn (New York: Routledge, 1997), 24–25.

49 Ibid., 5–6.

50 Ibid., 56.

51 Ibid., 6.

52 Ibid., 7–8.

53 Ibid., 11.

54 Sylviane A. Diouf, *Servants of Allah: African Muslims Enslaved in the Americas* (New York: New York University Press, 1998), 1.

55 Ibid., 22.

56 Ibid., 5.

6

The Many Religious Voices

In this chapter we learn about various religious voices in the young democracy of the United States, where on the one hand religious freedom created opportunities for spiritual and theological innovations while on the other the pressures of deep social divisions and the dynamics of national expansion necessitated new applications of traditional religious resources. The arrival of large numbers of immigrants, most fleeing turmoil and hardships in Europe, brought new religious communities to the United States, while the shift from a primarily rural, largely subsistence economy to a more urban market economy had ramifications for religious communities, practices, and traditions. The focus in this chapter is on three interrelated religious developments that arose in these contexts of societal change. First we consider how certain marginalized groups of people used religious resources to address the challenges of oppression, aggression, and exclusion. Next we discuss the experiences of immigrants who altered the contours of the American religious landscape as they settled into a new homeland where both opportunities and hardships awaited them. Finally, we look briefly at religious innovators and reformers who creatively engaged the spirit of religious freedom but who in many cases met resistance, sometimes violent, to their unorthodox views and practices.

A young free black woman by the name of Jarena Lee (born 1783, death date unknown, sometime after 1849), while living in a small town near Philadelphia in 1811, was called to a religious life during an episode of ill health. She recalls in her autobiography that she heard a voice commanding her, "Preach the Gospel; I will put words in your mouth, and will turn your enemies to become your friends."[1] Upon recovering her health, Lee went to tell her preacher, Richard Allen (1760–1831), of her revelation. Allen had been born under slavery in Philadelphia, but he purchased his freedom at age seventeen and pursued a career of itinerant preaching. He soon had a significant following among African Americans, and when they were not afforded equal treatment in worship at St. George's Methodist Episcopal Church in Philadelphia in 1787, he and the other blacks walked out of the church in protest and established their own religious organization, the Free African Society, dedicating its first church, the Bethel African Methodist Episcopal Church, in 1794. Francis Asbury (1745–1816), the leader of American Methodists, made Richard Allen a Methodist deacon in 1799, the first African American to receive such ordination. Allen, however, eventually left Asbury's church to establish America's earliest African American religious denomination, the African Methodist Episcopal Church (commonly known as AME), in 1816.[2] Among his faithful followers was the young Jarena Lee.

When Lee told Allen of her revelation, he was sympathetic; "But as to women preaching," Lee recounts in her autobiography, "he said that our Discipline [of the Methodists] knew nothing at all about it – that it did not call for women preachers."[3] Still, despite Allen's refusal to support her, Lee did not forget her divine call to spread the Christian gospel. Some years later, with the call to preach still burning in her heart, Jarena Lee spontaneously rose to preach during a worship service at the Bethel Church when the minister preaching that morning faltered in his sermon. When done addressing the congregation, she sat down in great fear that she would now be expelled from the church for her indecorous behavior. Instead, Bishop Richard Allen arose and declared to all that he was convinced that she had been called to the work of preaching as much as any of the men.[4] With this affirmation, Lee embarked on a remarkable career, preaching to the rich and powerful as well as to the poor and destitute. Her audiences included both whites and blacks; on one occasion, an elderly slaveowner notorious for his cruelty to his slaves came to hear her preach, and afterward, according to Lee's account, "he became greatly altered in his ways for the better."[5] The thoroughness of her commitment to the Christian god and her enthusiasm for the gospel message took her far afield as an example of complete devotion and "ardour for the progress of his cause" that consumed the remainder of her life.[6]

Jarena Lee's story of religious conversion, her struggle to gain approval to speak publicly as a religious leader, and her exemplary devotion to an evangelistic piety typify the shifting religious atmosphere of early nineteenth-century America. Under the banner of their democratic experiment, the citizens of the American republic struggled with the implications of a purportedly egalitarian society. The realities of inequality abounded all around, belying the democratic rhetoric of freedom and equality for all. In Christian communities, women filled the pews every Sunday but were denied positions of leadership, and for the most part they were not permitted even to speak in any official capacity, even to express their religious fervor. African Americans, even those who had gained freedom from bondage, were confined to a second-class citizenry that excluded them from many of

From Info by A.Hoffy.   Printed by P.S.Duval.

MRS JARENA LEE.

Preacher of the A. M. E. Church.

Aged 60 years on the 11th day of the 2nd month 1844.

Philad.a 1844.

Figure 6.1 Jarena Lee's autobiography, which she first published in 1836, tells how African Methodist Episcopal founder Richard Allen authorized her as the first woman preacher in the church. The narrative goes on to detail her struggles and triumphs as an African American woman preacher in antebellum America. (Courtesy of New York Public Library, #808160.)

the benefits and privileges of a free society. Native Americans experienced the expansion of the American democracy in the wholesale loss of their homelands as they were forced to relocate to distant reservations where confinement included disease, poverty, and the systematic eradication of their traditional religious practices. Newly arrived immigrants often met with resistance from more established

Box 6.1   Voice

Scholars sometimes refer to the ability to express one's views and opinions in public, or to assert one's influence and authority over others, with the metaphor of "voice." The question of voice often has to do with the ability to gain legitimate authority, but also with the liberty to represent oneself and resist being defined, and therefore controlled, by others (this relates to the earlier discussion of "authority" as "a continuous process that engages rhetorical strategies of legitimacy and power" – see Box 2.1). These concerns in turn have to do with questions of social power, a topic that the twentieth-century French historian and philosopher Michel Foucault (1926–1984) dealt with extensively.[7] Power for Foucault was not simply something that some people or institutions possessed as a means to exert control over others. He regarded it more in terms of relations between people, often determined by social conventions and practices, that sometimes were repressive, but often productive. Moreover, Foucault noted how these relations of power are found throughout society, not merely confined to powerful individuals and institutions; conversations do not emanate only from the most powerful and prominent public figures but rather they circulate in complex webs of social interaction at the most local and personal levels. This does not mean that everyone participates equally. In particular historical circumstances, certain individuals, groups, and institutions have more influence and are more easily able to dominate and control others. Nevertheless, discourses produce what Foucault calls "counterdiscourses," views that run counter to, are highly critical of, and usually actively resist the hegemonic, or dominant, view.[8] In many cases these counterdiscourses remain concealed from the powerful and often coercive forces that dominate in a particular social context, amounting to what one scholar regards as "hidden transcripts."[9] For instance, in the early nineteenth century, enslaved people themselves participated in the counterdiscourse on slavery, usually in low-profile and often cryptic ways; secret religious gatherings of slaves where virulent condemnation of slaveowners was rampant are an example of the counterdiscourse on American slavery.

Attention to less prominent voices, such as the counterdiscourses of people living in slavery far from the public eye, reveals that "voice" is not limited to the spoken word or even to written language. Voice finds expression in many modes. Certainly, speaking and writing are important channels for expressing one's voice, especially in nineteenth-century America when much of public discourse occurred in public speeches, lectures, and sermons, as well as in newspapers, pamphlets, literary periodicals, and books. But voice also finds articulation in such forms as laws, social conventions, artistic creations, and technological developments, as well as in all sorts of human behaviors and activities, including religious **rituals** and celebrations. In fact, our understanding of any human utterance or practice can begin by asking: Whose voices are being expressed? In what manner are their voices being articulated? What interests and concerns do those voices advocate? And whose voices are not heard?[10]

groups who sought to preserve the fruits of democracy for themselves alone. New religious movements created opportunities for new voices to speak out and for innovative religious perspectives to find devoted followings, even while contending with sometimes violent persecutions. The first half of the nineteenth century in America was a time when many voices contended in the cacophony of American religious freedom.

Women's Voices

Despite the rhetoric of liberty and the celebration of freedoms guaranteed in the Bill of Rights, only a minority of the people living in the United States in the early nineteenth century enjoyed the full freedoms promised in the American embrace of democracy. Initially, only free, landholding males had full rights guaranteed under the US Constitution; not until 1870, with the Fifteenth Amendment, was voting guaranteed to all male citizens regardless of "race, color, or previous condition of servitude." The exclusion of most women from voting, however, lasted until 1920, when the Nineteenth Amendment became law. On the other hand, the historical and social conditions of marginalized populations offered opportunities for asserting some degree of influence in American society. Many of these new opportunities were found in the context of religious traditions and communities. For Protestant women in the early decades of the nineteenth century, religious revivals associated with the Second Great Awakening created new opportunities for greater involvement not only in church settings but also in society in general.

The Protestant **evangelical** revivals of the Second Great Awakening gained momentum in the early decades of the nineteenth century, pushed along by the new conditions of a democratic republic and key innovations that became conventional evangelical practices, many of which continue even today. One key religious innovator whose efforts contributed to greater religious involvement of women was Charles G. Finney (1792–1875), who rose to fame in western New York's so-called "burned-over district," a region of rapid Euro-American settlement characterized by unusually frequent revivalist activity in the 1820s. Trained as a lawyer, Finney's fiery preaching and his employment of "new measures" in his evangelical efforts brought him remarkable success in gaining new converts; it also earned him contempt from some of the more conservative ministers who opposed his methods.[11] Among his evangelical innovations, Finney's "new measures" included women's public prayers in mixed-gender settings and even public speech of women.[12] With these and other innovations, Finney opened the church door to women, African Americans, the poor, and others who were largely excluded from speaking or enjoying full participation in worship and other church activities in many places. Finney's emphasis on the unity of all Christians in God's eyes gave many of his followers new voices in the church.

Opportunities for women to be more involved in church-based initiatives, such as those advocated by people like Charles Finney, relied to a large extent on

Figure 6.2   Charles G. Finney's "new measures" introduced more diverse participation in Protestant evangelical revivals, especially allowing women's voices to be heard in ways that were not often available to them in the early nineteenth century. (Image © Universal Images Group Limited / Alamy.)

changing notions of both masculinity and femininity in Protestant American society. The emergent gender ideology in nineteenth-century America created separate spheres of action for men and women, where men engaged in economic pursuits and acted in public arenas while women concentrated on maintaining virtuous homes to raise Christian children and provide a refuge for their husbands from the tumultuous strains of public life. This conception of separate realms of masculinity and femininity resulted partially from changing labor patterns in nineteenth-century America, especially in the north, where industrialization shifted the emphasis from the home to the marketplace for providing families' needs; rather than producing the food, clothing, and necessary items themselves, families increasingly purchased manufactured goods in the marketplace, relying more on wage earnings to generate the cash needed to acquire these goods. As men went to work to earn wages in factories and other occupations related to an industry-based market economy, women took charge of maintaining the home as the center of domestic family life.[13] Thus, the ideal of "true womanhood" for many nineteenth-century Americans was in the role of wife and mother and based on virtues of purity, piety, submissiveness, and domesticity.

Box 6.2   Gender

Although differences between men and women may seem self-evident to most people, how we understand those differences and how we interpret their implications is not such a straightforward topic. One obvious approach is to consider such differences biologically. Biologists understand the differences between female sex and male sex regarding their respective roles in reproduction; these differences are most apparent in terms of female and male sex organs, but they can also be identified at the chromosomal level. Biological sex, then, is usually, but not always, an unambiguous matter of nature.[14] In contrast, gender is more a matter of the complex interplay of social and cultural contexts, at least when used by scholars to discuss the socially and culturally determined differences between women and men; in this regard, gender is not necessarily a result of or even specifically linked to biological sex, but rather is created through and by cultural actions, social performances, and a variety of societal forces (likewise, sexuality is also distinct from sex, as we will consider in Chapter 9). Thus, while sex refers to biological reproduction, gender denotes socially constructed categories of male persons and female persons. In fact, some cultures include other genders as well. Some Native American tribes, for example, include a third gender, the "two-spirit" or "man-woman," what anthropologists call "berdache," to describe members of a community who assume more than one gender role or who cross gender boundaries; these individuals of ambiguous gender are often capable of mediating not only between men and women but also between humans and the spirit world as they engage in **shamanic** practices.[15]

As useful as the distinction between sex (as biological) and gender (as social) has been for investigating the implications of differences between men and women, a facile understanding of the distinction can be misleading. More recent scholarship has emphasized the impossibility of precisely distinguishing between biological sex and social categories of gender. Critics note how these categories, whether scientific or cultural, are themselves laden with social assumptions regarding sexual differences. The insistence that humans with different biological traits (e.g., different sex organs) are distinct types of organisms (e.g., male and female) is itself a product of social discourse; consequently, critics contend, even biological sex is socially constructed. Recent studies have emphasized the importance of embodiment and bodily practices in constructing identities, including gender.[16]

Acknowledging that both sex and gender serve as socially constructed categories also raises questions about the role of religious beliefs, practices, and traditions in upholding categories of male and female. For instance, the religious authority of the Bible for Protestant Christians makes it a key source for Protestant conceptions of femininity and masculinity. Official interpretations of biblical tales and the corresponding gender models of biblical characters become the basis for perpetuating gender roles in Protestant social relations. Thus, the belief that Adam, the first male person, has precedence and authority over Eve, the first female person, serves as the template for men's authority over women's interests not only in church but also in the home and in society at large. Such interpretations of biblical authority mandating women's deference to men become naturalized in religious traditions, and individuals learn through socialization within religious communities to assume roles of masculinity and femininity without questioning their basis. At the same time, other voices have used the authority of religious narratives to instigate counterdiscourses that challenge claims of patriarchal gender assumptions in society; we will consider in Chapter 8 the example of the *Woman's Bible* by nineteenth-century women's rights advocate Elizabeth Cady Stanton (1815–1902).

The study of gender differences in American religious history has often meant paying attention to the role of women in religious traditions and communities. This approach has made great strides in helping us to better understand the essential contributions that women have made in virtually every area of American religious life, but it also has had the unfortunate effect of affirming the conventional perception that male gender is the norm and that female gender deviates from the male standard. Focusing only on women's roles neglects the ways that both femininity and masculinity, as social categories, mutually reinforce social traditions that subordinate women to the prerogatives of men. In other words, simply drawing attention to women's historical plight as subordinate figures is not always enough to show how the gender categories that make the distinction between men and women possible in the first place perpetuate such social inequities.

One corrective to overemphasizing women in discussions of gender comes from philosopher and theorist Judith Butler (born 1956); she advocates an interpretation of gender as performative rather than expressive. In other words, Butler suggests viewing gender as sets of social practices where individuals seek to conform to expectations of gender roles rather than merely expressing in their behaviors and relationships natural tendencies of their biological sex; Butler characterizes gender as "the stylized repetition of acts through time."[17] This approach requires historians to account for the various social and cultural forces that constitute both masculinity and femininity, including the role of religion in justifying the social positions of men and women.[18]

This dominant understanding of female gender roles in the nineteenth century, with its separate spheres for women and men, reinforced the patriarchal authority of men, who continued to reign in public arenas, including most areas of religious life. Yet women's domestic role, especially in the northern industrialized areas of the nation, was not merely a private affair; according to influential gender discourses of nineteenth-century America, women's so-called "cult of domesticity" was essential to the success of a democratic society. Author Catharine Beecher (1800–1878) celebrated the feminine contribution to society in her mid-century book *A Treatise on Domestic Economy for the Use of Young Ladies at Home and at School*, where she explains:

> The success of democratic institutions, as is conceded by all, depends upon the intellectual and moral character of the mass of the people. It is equally conceded, that the formation of the moral and intellectual character of the young is committed mainly to the female hand. The mother forms the character of the future man; the sister bends the fibres that are hereafter to be the forest tree; the wife sways the heart, whose energies may turn for good or for evil the destinies of a nation.[19]

Thus, according to the dominant gender ideology of nineteenth-century Protestant Americans, the future of democratic society relied on the key role of the ideal woman in raising educated, well-mannered, and morally upright children. Not only were children to learn the practical skills and knowledge for adult life as productive citizens in a democratic republic but also mothers were expected to foster their children's moral character. Religion, nearly all nineteenth-century American Christians agreed, was the foundation of morality, making church and pious spiritual devotion indispensable for raising children. Consequently, the sphere of the ideal wife and mother extended to the public life of churches.

Women's greater involvement in the public life of churches, however, did not extend to church leadership. They remained for the most part barred from serving in positions of public leadership as pastors and priests; with only rare exceptions of a handful of women preachers, men occupied the pulpits. The enduring patriarchal prerogatives of Christian tradition continued to dominate Protestant institutions. Nevertheless, female authority was felt in virtually all Protestant sects, as women filled the pews, comprising a clear majority of members in churches and other religious organizations throughout North America.[20] Moreover, much of the social activism of religious groups in America came at the initiative of women members. Especially important to the growth of churches were women's associations; Bible societies; charities for widows, orphans, and the poor; Sunday schools; and groups supporting missionary activities both at home and abroad. These enterprises contributed to the rapid expansion of evangelical Protestant denominations in American society, and none would have been possible without the dedicated efforts of thousands of church women. Moreover, many key political issues of the nineteenth century originated in churches with women at the forefront. Among the controversies that came to national attention with the help of women's voices were policies regarding more humane treatment of Native American peoples, specifically a movement to "civilize" the "savages" (itself a highly problematic solution to the "Indian problem" but regarded as preferable to outright extermination of indigenous tribes); the movement seeking the full abolition of slavery in all parts of the United States; calls for temperance laws restricting the manufacture, sale, and consumption of alcoholic beverages; and the insistence on women's suffrage, granting women equal political rights as men, especially the fundamental right to vote. Even when the origins of such issues cannot be traced with certainty to American church women, they nevertheless found impassioned support among the female members of many Christian churches.

On the other hand, although the rhetoric of nineteenth-century gender ideology suggested all women were equal in occupying a sphere separate from men, they did not all share a common experience in American society. Dominant voices such as Catharine Beecher's portrayed American women as "descendants of English progenitors," Protestant, white, and middle class or upper-middle class. This view disregards the differences between women, which undermine any notion of a universal feminine experience. In particular, differences in ethnicity, race, and class each contributed to the diverse experiences of American women in the nineteenth century.

The efforts of those who dedicated themselves fully to the elevation of women in all areas – including social, political, economic, and religious – tended to focus on a specific segment of the female population. This is apparent in the proceedings of the landmark Seneca Falls convention of 1848, which formally initiated the women's rights movement in the United States with a "Declaration of Rights and Sentiments." Introducing the Declaration to the gathering of supporters, reformer Elizabeth Cady Stanton exclaimed, "all men and women are created equal." Yet, despite this assumption of equality, the Declaration and other resolutions adopted at the convention reflect the social and political context of the time as they elevated white, middle-class women to a position above others. These privileged women demanded precedence over male immigrants, free blacks, and the destitute. They also reflected exclusively Protestant Christian representation; of the one hundred signatories to the Declaration of Rights and Sentiments, roughly a quarter were Quakers, and the rest were of various other Protestant denominations, mostly Congregational, Episcopalian, and Methodist, with only one Presbyterian; no Catholics or Jews signed the Declaration.[21]

Yet, despite the somewhat exclusive tenor of the Declaration of Rights and Sentiments, the call for women's rights coincided with agitations to end slavery, as indicated by the prominent appearance of Frederick Douglass (1818–1895) at the first women's rights convention. At the time, Douglass was the most famous and highly respected African American voice in America. An ex-slave, his 1845 autobiography *Narrative of the Life of Frederick Douglass* had brought him international acclaim, and his newspaper, the *North Star*, published in Rochester, New York, not far from the site of the women's rights convention in Seneca Falls, was a leading antislavery

Figure 6.3 A monument dedicated to three of the most prominent nineteenth-century women's rights leaders, Susan B. Anthony, Lucretia Mott, and Elizabeth Cady Stanton, was unveiled in Washington, DC, in 1921. The monument celebrates their contribution to women's suffrage, which would eventually culminate with the passage in 1920 of the Nineteenth Amendment to the US Constitution, guaranteeing women the right to vote. (Courtesy of the Library of Congress, LC-DIG-hec-35259.)

publication. He took the podium at the convention to advocate women's suffrage, a more radical proposition than many in attendance were ready to support. "In this denial of the right to participate in government," Douglass declared, "not merely the degradation of woman and the perpetuation of a great injustice happens, but the maiming and repudiation of one-half of the moral and intellectual power of the government of the world." His words convinced most in attendance, and the suffrage resolution became part of the seminal document of the American movement for women's rights; the voices of women and men who supported full rights and privileges for citizens of female gender entered the national debate.[22]

Displaced Voices

Two years after the Seneca Falls convention on women's rights, another meeting for women's rights took place in Massachusetts with a more diverse platform of speakers. Included in the 1850 national convention were the radical socialist

Ernestine (Potowski) Rose (1810–1892), a Polish Jew; also featured was the **charismatic** African American female preacher and lecturer Sojourner Truth (ca. 1797–1883). In a discussion of biblical authority regarding women, Sojourner Truth stated that in Christian scripture "the Spirit of Truth spoke" but "the recorders of those truths had intermingled with them ideas and suppositions of their own" inimical to women. She also delivered a speech to the convention regarding women and slavery that greatly moved those in attendance. Women's rights leader Lucretia Mott (1793–1880) closed the Convention by urging the delegates to embrace "the simple and truthful words of Sojourner Truth."[23] This appearance at the 1850 convention anticipated Sojourner Truth's most famous speech ("Ain't I a Woman?") delivered the next year at the Ohio Women's Rights Convention in Akron. Her talk was not published until more than a decade later, and there were differing accounts

Figure 6.4   Sojourner Truth's voice resounded powerfully when she demanded a place for African Americans in the women's movement by declaring "I am a woman" in 1851 at the Ohio Women's Rights Convention. (Courtesy of the Library of Congress, LC-USZ62-119343.)

of what she actually said at the convention, but contemporary reports indicate she did not begin her lecture with the question "Ain't I a Woman?"; instead, she asserted "I *am* a woman," and went on to describe in detail the backbreaking labor she had endured as a slave, equal to or exceeding any hardship that a man had suffered.[24] Her assertion to the Akron gathering claimed a place for women of color in the women's movement.

African Americans

Sojourner Truth's assertion of her rightful place alongside the white women campaigning for the rights of women joined a growing number of African American voices holding forth against racial exclusion, most often aimed at the continuing practice of slavery in the American south. Their criticism of endemic racism and the atrocities of institutionalized bondage frequently appealed to Christian morality, often depicting Christian supporters of slavery as blatant hypocrites. Most prominent among these African American voices was Frederick Douglass, whose critiques of slavery and the pervasive racism of American society included his condemnation of Christianity as practiced by slaveholding southerners. He wrote in his 1845 autobiography:

> I assert most unhesitatingly, that the religion of the south is a mere covering for the most horrid crimes, – a justifier of the most appalling barbarity, – a sanctifier of the most hateful frauds, – and a dark shelter, under which the darkest, foulest, grossest, and most infernal deeds of slaveholders find the strongest protection … For, of all slaveholders with whom I have ever met, religious slaveholders are the worst. I have ever found them the meanest and basest, the most cruel and cowardly of all others.[25]

In the appendix to his narrative, Douglass emphasizes that his criticism of Christianity applies only to "the *slaveholding religion* of this land," and not to all of Christianity. He distinguishes between "the pure, peaceable, and impartial Christianity of Christ" and "the corrupt, slaveholding, women-whipping, cradle-plundering, partial and hypocritical Christianity of this land."[26] It is clear, though, that Douglass thought all Christians who in any way condoned slavery and did not support its immediate eradication fell into the latter version of the religion, which he roundly condemned.

Sojourner Truth and Frederick Douglass were just two of the many African American voices agitating for an end to slavery in the United States. In the early post-Revolution era, a class of relatively prosperous free African Americans in the northern states took up the cause of ending human bondage in the country.[27] Many of these leading antislavery voices were religious leaders, such as the African American Baptist minister Nathaniel Paul (ca. 1793–1839) of Albany, New York, who not only battled against southern slavery but also condemned the implicit hypocrisy of sympathetic white northerners. In his address to the 1838 Albany

Anti-Slavery Convention, Paul confronted the mostly white delegates about their own racism. He rebuked abolitionists who, in his estimation, "as bad as they hate slavery, they hate a man who wears a colored skin, worse." Paul continued, however, by praising another kind of abolitionist, "those whose principles are based on the word of God and the Declaration of Independence. It is self-evident that God has created all men equal."[28] The northern antislavery movement, emerging from the wellspring of Christian doctrine married to the civil virtues of democracy, came first and most passionately from African American voices.

But few African Americans were in a position to confront the racial prejudices of the dominant white society in America; most expressed their abhorrence and disgust in ways hidden from public view. At least some African American voices, however, found fewer restrictions in distant lands. Africa in particular offered opportunities for a few pious African American Protestants to contribute to American religious discourses by participating in foreign missionary efforts. Uneasy with the prospect of integrating a large population of free African Americans into the mainstream of white American culture, many white Americans thought that black Americans would fare better in Africa, returning to an imagined aboriginal life; thus, white Protestant missionaries advocated colonizing Africa with freed slaves from America. Although most African Americans rejected the idea as a ploy to strengthen the institution of slavery in America, at least a few supported the idea of an African colony for freed slaves, but for different reasons from their white missionary counterparts. For some African Americans, a new home in Africa seemed a more attractive option than the pervasive culture of racism in America.

Paul Cuffee (1759–1817), a Quaker of both African and Native American descent who had gained prosperity as a ship owner, in 1816 took a small group of African Americans to the British colony of Sierra Leone on the African continent to establish the beginnings of a colony. Cuffee died before his colonial enterprise came to fruition, but his venture inspired others to establish a new colony of Liberia on the coast north of Sierra Leone, with a capital of Monrovia (named after the American president James Monroe). Few African Americans emigrated to the African colony on their own initiative; nearly all African Americans rejected a return to Africa as a solution to racial strife in the United States, and most of the new arrivals were recently freed slaves whose manumission was contingent on emigration to Liberia, usually paid for by their former masters.[29] This does not mean that the Liberians did not value their new lives in Africa. For instance, Robert E. Lee (1807–1870), later famous as a Confederate military leader, freed his slaves in the 1850s and paid their passage to Liberia. One of Lee's former slaves, William Burke (birth and death dates unknown), received an education in Monrovia and became a Presbyterian minister; in comparison to his early life in bondage, he enjoyed relative prosperity and happiness in the Liberian colony. He wrote after five years there, "so far from being dissatisfied with the country, I bless the Lord that ever my lot was cast in this part of the earth. The Lord has blessed me abundantly since my residence in Africa, for which I feel that I can never be sufficiently thankful."[30] At least for Burke, Liberia was a more hospitable place than his American homeland for exercising his voice.

Muskogees

While William Burke and other African American missionaries resettled in Liberia and elsewhere on the African continent, Native Americans were also experiencing displacement and resettlement. American expansion into southern and western territories of the United States brought new pressures and challenges to native societies; in many cases, Native Americans used their traditional cultural and religious resources in response to these displacements. One salient example occurred among the native Muskogee peoples living in what is now Alabama and western Georgia, where Euro-American trade and settlement contributed to internal conflicts within Muskogee society between those benefiting from contact with outsiders and traditionalists who sought to preserve long-established structures of Muskogee society and the sacred bonds of their culture.[31]

Traditional Muskogee society was organized in relation to what one historian describes as a "culture of the sacred."[32] The cosmos, according to the traditional Muskogee **worldview**, involves three primordial spheres: the Upper World, This World, and the Lower World. Only the creator god, what the Muskogees call Hesákádum Eseé, literally "the Holder of Breath" or "the Maker of Breath," can maintain the equilibrium between the three spheres that makes the reality of This World possible. According to this traditional Muskogee understanding of the cosmos, all good comes from the Maker of Breath, who made the waters pure and who brought success to the hunt and abundant harvests of the corn crop.[33]

The Muskogee people in the early nineteenth century had recourse to sacred powers in the performance of their rituals.[34] The most important of Muskogee communal rituals was the *póskita*, or "Busk," an annual harvest ritual usually performed in July or August with the ripening of the second crop of corn for the year. The Busk celebrated the origins of corn, the Muskogee's main staple crop, and marked the transition from summer, the season of growing and harvesting crops, to winter, the season of hunting and gathering the harvests of the land.[35] The Busk activities also involved the ceremonial lighting of a new communal fire that marked the beginning of a new year and renewed the Muskogee bond to sacred power. It also renewed the bonds between individuals and social groups through acts of forgiveness and reconciliation. Indeed, the summer Busk ceremonies were an occasion for strengthening the ties between people by setting aside personal grievances and animosity.

At the same time, however, the Busk ritual reinforced gender differences, with men and women strictly segregated and performing different duties. For the most part, Muskogee people lived in what anthropologists describe as a matrilineal, matrilocal society. Social power and control of property were vested in women and passed from mothers to daughters; women remained close to their clans when they married, and husbands went to live with their wives' clans. But, during the Busk, men were closely associated with the ritual space of the sacred fire, aligning themselves with its sacred powers and relegating women to the peripheral sphere of mundane responsibilities. The Busk ceremony thus was a powerful enactment of patriarchal authority in predominantly matriarchal Muskogee society.[36]

The reinforcement of social distinctions evident in the Busk ceremony, bolstered by their alignment with the sacred purity of the new fire, provided a powerful template for resisting the intrusions of foreigners into the Muskogee territory. Alarmed by American invasions and encroachments that brought chaotic disorder to the Muskogee cosmos, a group of traditional shamanic leaders turned to the Maker of Breath for help. With support from the sacred powers of their deity, these Muskogee leaders instigated a revolution in 1813 against those who cooperated with American schemes to gain more Muskogee land. Using ritual models practiced in the Busk and other ceremonies, Muskogee shamans prompted a rebellion that would restore order and balance in their universe. Much like the Busk ceremony, they were convinced that purifying their universe of the polluting influences of the Americans would herald a new era of sacred power.[37]

The millenarian "Redstick Rebellion," as it was called by the Muskogees' American foes because of the ceremonial sticks painted red that the militants carried, afforded the Muskogees a collective voice of resistance patterned on the Busk ritual.[38] Their assertion of a native voice, though, provoked the US government into action, and the Redstick warriors were soon engaged in a military struggle with US forces. In March 1814, after months of fighting the Americans and their allies, one thousand Muskogee warriors faced a much larger American army joined by Cherokee warriors and even a few fellow Muskogees who remained friendly to the Americans. The Redstick rebels awaited the final assault of the American militiamen with the belief that their sacred powers made them invincible. But their confidence was quickly shattered once the enemy force attacked, delivering a final crushing blow to the native Redstick Rebellion.[39] The religious powers and ritual models that the shamans had relied on were no match for the onslaught of western civilization streaming into their traditional homelands.

The flood of outsiders only increased following the defeat of the Redstick Rebellion as Euro-Americans perceived an end to the Indian threat in the region, exacerbating pressures to rid American lands of all native peoples. The Indian Removal Act of 1830 made the displacement of native peoples national policy, allowing the US government to forcibly evict most of the Indians still living east of the Mississippi River in what has become known as the "Trail of Tears," a rough translation of what the Cherokee people would remember as Nunna daul Isunyi, the "Trail Where We Cried."[40] Although this is most commonly associated with the forced march of Cherokee people in 1838–1839, they comprised only part of the total number of people who suffered on the Trail of Tears in the 1830s. This ill-conceived and largely disastrous episode involved tens of thousands of native

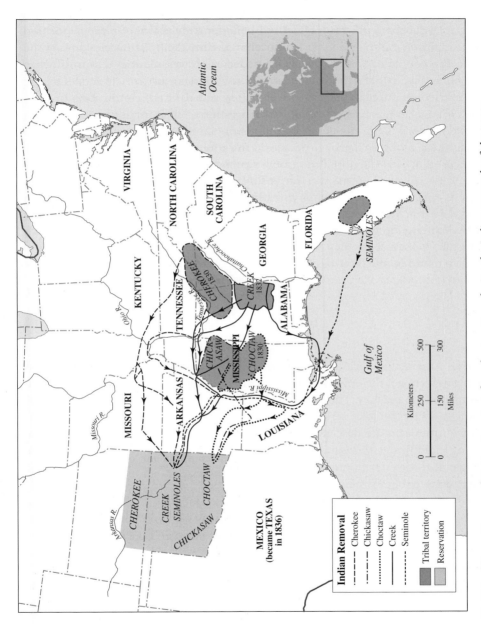

Map 6.1 Trail(s) of Tears. Routes of Native American forced migrations during the Indian removals of the 1830s.

peoples from numerous tribes, including the Chickasaw, Choctaw, Muskogee, Seminole, and Shawnee peoples in addition to the Cherokee, all of whom had their own tragic experiences of the Trail of Tears.

The Cherokee are most often associated with the Trail of Tears mainly because the public debate in the 1830s about implementing the policy of removal focused almost entirely on their plight. The success of Christian missionaries among the Cherokee people had produced native leaders who were educated in missionary schools and who understood the intricacies of American justice. Consequently, the Cherokees were able to voice their objections and fight the confiscation of their lands in American courts, even gaining recognition of their tribal sovereignty from the US Supreme Court in a landmark case in 1832. But the effort turned out to be futile, at least for the Cherokee people, as the administration of President Andrew Jackson (1767–1845) ignored the Court's ruling and continued removing Indians from lands coveted by American settlers.[41] When most Cherokees refused to leave their homelands, federal troops forcibly rounded them up and marched them west. Like the Muskogees before them, the Cherokee people could not resist the overwhelming force of American conquest. Despite help from their alliance with Christian missionaries, they too suffered displacement as their voices were routinely ignored in official circles.

Immigrant Voices

Native Americans, African Americans, and other non-Euro-Americans in US territory were not the only ones who experienced displacements and migrations in the nineteenth century. The United States, in fact all of the Americas, is a land of immigrants; if we take seriously the preponderance of scientific evidence that Native Americans are descendants of ancient peoples from Asia who crossed the Bering Land Bridge thousands of years ago, we could state unequivocally that all people in the western hemisphere, including indigenous populations, arrived by migrations, either by themselves or their ancestors.[42] As new arrivals seek out their place among others who came before them, they face the challenge of adapting their familiar traditions and ways of living to new environments and social settings. For all immigrants, there remains a tension between the old and the new.

A significant surge in the numbers of immigrants entering the United States occurred in the 1840s and 1850s, changing the religious character of the nation. Most of these newcomers arriving in the first half of the nineteenth century came from Europe. Very few Asians, Pacific Islanders, or other non-Europeans found their way to the American continent during this period, although the discovery of gold on the American west coast brought significant numbers of Chinese across the Pacific beginning late in the 1840s. Nevertheless, Asians remained a nearly insignificant minority in American society until later in the century.[43]

Catholics

The impact of immigration on the religious makeup of America can be seen most clearly with Catholics. At the beginning of the nineteenth century, Christians affiliated with the Roman Catholic Church made up one of the smallest Christian denominational groups in the United States, but by mid-century they ranked as the largest single religious group in the country, and they have remained so ever since. The unprecedented growth in the numbers of American Catholics during this period was almost entirely the result of immigration. Large numbers of Irish Catholics crossed the Atlantic to America when potato blight in Ireland, exacerbated by political and social upheavals, brought famine and widespread starvation throughout the island nation; an estimated one million Irish died between 1845 and 1852, and another million left their homeland to settle elsewhere, many in America. Likewise, political unrest in the German states beginning in 1848 brought large numbers of German-speaking Catholic immigrants to America.

Although they shared a common religious orientation and were connected to the same ecclesiastical structures emanating from Rome, Catholic immigrants displayed a surprising diversity of religious traditions and practices, and most spoke languages other than English. Many of them had to contend with cultural differences within the Church itself, including priests who did not share a common cultural heritage with their parishioners and in some cases did not even speak the same language as the majority of those in their care. This diversity of American Catholics was apparent to the archbishop in Baltimore, Maryland, as early as 1818, when among his fifty-two priests he counted fourteen French, twelve Americans, eleven Irish, seven Belgians, four English, three Germans, and one Italian.[44]

French Catholics had significant influence on American Catholicism in the early part of the nineteenth century, especially in regard to the education of priests. The French Revolution at the end of the eighteenth century and the violent anti-Catholic backlash that followed in France sent many French priests and members of religious orders into exile, with a good number arriving in America. One group, Sulpicians from Paris, who were dedicated to the education of Catholic **clergy**, fled to Baltimore, where they established St. Mary's Seminary, the first Catholic institution in the United States dedicated solely to the training of priests. Attending this seminary were not only American candidates for the priesthood but also Europeans, many of them French, who remained in the United States to serve American parishes. As the Catholic Church established itself more broadly in American society, a significant number of St. Mary's graduates, trained by French Catholics and many of them French themselves, served as bishops throughout the nation.[45]

French Catholicism also was a formative force in introducing parochial education in America; the earliest Catholic schools in North America were established in French regions. In New Orleans, the Sisters of the Order of Saint Ursula, commonly known as the Ursulines, opened a school for girls in 1727 that still operates today as the oldest Catholic school in the United States. The Ursulines offered literacy and education to women and people of color throughout the colonial period, but, when Louisiana became part of the United States in the early nineteenth century, these Catholic women were targets of persecution. Their vows to a celibate religious life as well as their efforts to educate other women put them in conflict with the gender ideologies of most Americans, for which they suffered much hostility and outright persecution. Nevertheless, they continued to provide educational and relief services to Catholic women in America.[46]

Under the guidance of French clergy, another Catholic women's religious order began addressing the educational needs of free blacks in Baltimore, Maryland, in the late 1820s. A French Sulpician priest, Friar Jacques Joubert (1777–1843), helped to organize the Oblate Sisters of Providence, made up of free black women in Baltimore, many of them Haitian refugees, dedicated, according to their Rule, to "the Christian education of young girls of colour." The Oblates initially were led by Mary Elizabeth Clovis Lange (1784–1882), whose family had come to Baltimore as refugees from the French colony of Haiti. By the time Friar Joubert arrived in Baltimore, Lange and another Haitian refugee, Marie Balas (birth and death dates unknown), had been running a private school among the French-speaking blacks in the city. With the help of Friar Joubert, in 1828 these women of color founded the Oblates, the first African American Catholic religious order in the United States, and they subsequently expanded their efforts to educate Baltimore's African American children, eventually establishing schools in other cities as well.[47]

Despite the important influence of the French, much of the rapid expansion of American Catholic education in the nineteenth century resulted from the leadership of an American-born Catholic convert responsible for founding another order of Catholic women in Baltimore nearly two decades before the Oblates began their work. The Sisters of Charity of St. Joseph were first established by a former Protestant woman who had converted to Catholicism following her husband's death. Elizabeth Ann Seton (1774–1821) had enjoyed a comfortably upper-middle-class upbringing in a family with strong connections to the Anglican/Episcopalian Church. Following her husband's early death while they were in Italy, she returned to the United States, where, as a young widow with five children struggling in poverty, she converted to Catholicism. Eventually Seton moved to Maryland to open a school for girls; there she established St. Joseph Academy (now St. Joseph College) and also took holy vows as a Sister of Charity of St. Joseph, effectively founding the first American Catholic order for women. Mother Seton, as she was known thereafter, was joined by other women as she expanded her school; she sent Sisters of Charity to establish schools in Philadelphia and New York and had plans for others at the time of her death in 1821.[48]

Elizabeth Seton often came into conflict with powerful men as she struggled to live under the authoritarian rule of the Catholic hierarchy. But she eventually succeeded in leading the newly formed Sisters of Charity and expanding their educational mission through a delicate balance of assertion and compliance in dealing with the male hierarchy of the Catholic Church. Her efforts, brief as they were (she died after only a little more than twelve years leading the Sisters of Charity) had an incalculable impact on the future of American Catholicism, as she is largely credited with the system of Catholic parochial schools that the Sisters of Charity operated throughout the nineteenth and twentieth centuries and up to the present.[49]

Struggles over public education for all children spurred the rapid growth of Catholic parochial education in nineteenth-century America. As Protestants began to establish public schools in American cities, resistance grew from Catholics. Especially contentious were Bible readings in the classrooms of public schools; many Catholics regarded the Protestants' King James version of the Bible as a heretical recitation of anti-Catholic dogma. A number of violent confrontations between Catholics and Protestants erupted over the schools issue. An early incident involved the burning of an Ursuline convent and school for girls in Charlestown, Massachusetts, in 1834; a decade later a "Bible riot" broke out in Philadelphia over Protestant rumors that Catholics were attempting to remove Bibles from school classrooms.[50] In response, many Catholics refused to send their children to public schools and instead enrolled them in schools operated under the authority of the Catholic Church.

Jews

As Catholics swelled American cities in the middle decades of the nineteenth century, Jewish immigrants also began arriving in significant numbers, especially from Germany. Suffering from many of the same forces that brought Christian immigrants to America, Jews additionally faced anti-Semitic backlashes to liberal reforms in Europe; fleeing oppression and violent persecutions, a number of Jews sought greater freedoms in America. These new arrivals settled throughout the United States and its territories, not only in the more established states of the eastern seaboard. In contrast to the predominantly laborer and farming populations of Christian immigrants, a good number of Jews who immigrated before the Civil War were entrepreneurs from lower-middle-class backgrounds who engaged in mercantile and other small business activities in America.[51]

One of the early concentrations of Jews in America was in Charleston, South Carolina. By the middle of the eighteenth century, the local Jewish community in Charleston had organized a congregation, the fifth such Jewish community in America, and by the beginning of the nineteenth century they had built an impressive synagogue that served the largest group of Jews in the United States; roughly six hundred Jewish people resided in Charleston, a cosmopolitan city that prospered as a major port in transatlantic trade and welcomed a diverse religious population.[52]

Meanwhile, many European Jews were experiencing new freedoms after centuries of isolation from majority Christian populations. As they gained greater

Box 6.3   Nativism

America's **providential** claim to be a Protestant nation chosen by God, a widely shared attitude across Protestant denominations in nineteenth-century America, was challenged by religious, racial, cultural, and national differences of Americans who did not conform to the majority perception of a homogeneous nation. As those differences became more apparent with the influx of immigrant populations, at least a few of the white, English-speaking, Protestant Americans who were born in the United States (sometimes only second-generation arrivals, but often with longer family histories in America) became anxious that the "foreign" element represented a threat to their understanding of an authentic American nation.[53] This antipathy toward difference is often referred to as "**nativism**."

American "nativists" (so called because of their native birth in America and because they perceived themselves as defending the country's native traditions and values from foreign influence) sometimes organized into groups intent on ridding American society of what they believed was the subversive presence of people whose differences they thought were inimical to American ideals. The most widespread nativist movement in the period before the Civil War was a national political party formed in the 1850s commonly known as the Know-Nothing Party, a secretive organization that brought together disparate anti-immigrant and anti-Catholic groups. They were dubbed the "Know-Nothings" because of their standard reply of "I know nothing" whenever questioned about the organization. Their secretive organization and rituals, in addition to their vehement anti-foreigner and usually anti-Catholic stance (Know-Nothings in the American south and on the Pacific coast were less anti-Catholic than elsewhere in the country) gave the Know-Nothings an advantage in recruiting new members, and in the state and local elections of 1854 they achieved surprising success.[54] Their success, however, turned out to be their undoing as the rising tide of anti-Catholic nativism in the 1850s contributed to a decline in immigration; the hostile atmosphere generated by nativist activities discouraged European Catholics, especially Irish, from migrating to the United States. This decrease in immigration eventually brought an end to the Know-Nothing movement; along with internal conflicts among its members, fewer immigrants coming into the country deprived nativist partisans of their strongest political argument. Following their disappointing results in the 1856 elections, the Know-Nothings were soon displaced by the newly rising antislavery party of Republicans.[55]

access to the benefits of secular education and commerce, as well as the ability to freely pursue professional careers, a movement emerged to reform traditional Jewish practices; in the early decades of the nineteenth century, German Jews influenced by Enlightenment thinking introduced a series of innovations aimed at modernizing Judaism. These included new roles for local rabbis, especially the presentation of sermons in vernacular languages; **liturgical** innovations, which introduced more musical elements into worship; and other reforms, such as the nonobservance of Jewish dietary laws. As news of these changes reached the American Jewish community in Charleston, an initiative to implement "the holy work of reformation" attracted a sufficient following to establish a separate group in 1825; they called themselves the Reformed Society of Israelites, preferring "Society" over "Congregation" to indicate the broad changes to Jewish life they hoped to instigate.[56]

The movement to reform traditional Jewish practices in America grew slowly following its establishment in Charleston. But Jewish immigration in the 1840s, especially from Germany, brought prominent voices for reform. These advocates for change found able leadership in Isaac Mayer Wise (1819–1900), a young former schoolmaster who emigrated from Eastern Europe in 1846. Soon after his arrival in America, Wise was elected rabbi of a synagogue in Albany, New York, where he

Figure 6.5 This 1812 sketch shows the Kahal Kadosh Beth Elohim synagogue in Charleston, South Carolina, where Reform Judaism was first introduced in the United States. (Courtesy of the Library of Congress, LC-DIG-ppmsca-05439.)

instituted a number of liturgical reforms. His leadership there, however, quickly stirred controversy, even erupting in a melee between his supporters and opposition within the congregation. Wise and those loyal to him subsequently formed their own congregation of Reform Judaism. Among the innovations introduced at the new Anshe Emeth synagogue in Albany was the use of a family pew, introducing mixed-gender seating in synagogues, a momentous change that became widespread among American Reform Jewish congregations and later spread to Europe.[57]

Wise left Albany in 1854 to become rabbi at a more traditional synagogue in the western city of Cincinnati, Ohio, which was undergoing a shift toward Reform Judaism. Soon after arriving in Cincinnati, Wise began publishing a national Jewish newspaper that aspired to be the official voice of American Judaism. In an attempt to unite the rivaling voices of Judaism, split between Orthodox traditionalists and Reform progressives, Wise organized a conference in 1855 that brought together leaders on both sides in an attempt to unite American Jews. Although they agreed to affirm the Hebrew Bible as "of immediate divine origin" and the Talmud, the authoritative text of traditional Rabbinic Judaism, as the source for "the traditional, legal, and logical exposition of the biblical laws," uniting Orthodox and Reform Jews remained an elusive aspiration.[58]

Restorationist Voices

Another sort of voice, one with millennial urgency of impending **apocalypse**, captured the American Protestant imagination in the 1840s. William Miller (1782–1849) was a relatively prosperous farmer and **lay** Baptist preacher in the so-called burned-over district of western New York. His careful studies of the Christian Bible convinced him that the exact time of Christ's return could be deciphered in the text. Miller's calculations in 1818 revealed that the current age would end in twenty-five years with the Second Coming of Christ occurring in 1843. At first Miller kept these findings to himself for the most part as he continued his close examination of the sacred texts, but in the 1830s he began to publicize the coming end of the world. A series of newspaper articles on the topic piqued public interest, and soon Miller's predictions became a sensation among Christians throughout New England and much of the northern United States, even gaining some international attention. The advent of Christ's return, between March 21, 1843, and March 21, 1844, as Miller proclaimed, prompted his followers to prepare for the end; as the appointed time drew nearer, hospitals and other facilities for the "insane" experienced a considerable increase in admissions of patients suffering from "the Miller excitement."[59] When the time passed with no sign of Christ's arrival, and when subsequent recalculations that placed the expected return in April of 1844 also did not prove accurate, skeptical voices became more prominent and disappointed believers began abandoning Miller's following. Nevertheless,

Miller held on to his belief in an imminent return of Christ; in a lengthy exhortation to his followers, he wrote, "I *confess my error*, and acknowledge *my disappointment*; yet I still believe that the day of the Lord is near, even at the door."[60] Another calculation projecting fulfillment of Miller's prediction later in 1844 also passed, leaving most of the Millerite faithful disheartened in what became known as the Great Disappointment. A handful never lost hope that the return of the Christian Messiah was near, and they eventually reconfigured Miller's teachings in a movement known as Adventism, forming the Seventh-Day Adventist and other related denominations. The vast majority, though, suffered deep disillusionment and abandoned all faith in Miller's predictions.[61]

The widespread attention that American Protestants gave to William Miller's predictions in the 1840s reflects the attraction of millennialist ideas in antebellum America; the fervent hope and the subsequent disillusionment of the Millerites serve as an apt metaphor for an age of opportunity also beset with disappointments for many Americans of the time. The first half of the nineteenth century in America was a period of growth and seemingly endless prospects that encouraged optimistic visions for the nation; these hopeful outlooks reached cosmic proportions in the millennialist logic of Protestant thinkers such as William Miller. Yet underneath this exuberant national optimism lay pervasive uncertainties and fears that manifested themselves in the Great Panic of 1837, the worst economic downturn the nation had experienced to that time; also, the increasingly divisive question of slavery generated constant uncertainty in political life. In these unsettled times a diverse set of voices contended for the essential meaning of America and its ultimate destiny.

Most American Protestants in the first half of the nineteenth century framed national purpose and destiny in the logic of a millennialist perspective. Consequently, William Miller's pronouncement of a premillennial return of Christ made immediate sense in the context of American uncertainty; his prediction offered a solution to the interpretive chaos many American Protestants were experiencing at the time. Meanwhile, many of the revivalist Protestants of the Second Great Awakening pursued a postmillennialist vision through religious conversions of individuals; when all people had accepted Christ, they contended, the conditions would be achieved for the millennial perfection required for the Messiah's return. Other postmillennialists, however, realized that individual conversions were not enough; righteous people needed proper social conditions, and the current structures of American society would not do for the sort of perfectionism needed to realize the millennial promise. An altogether new social arrangement was needed, and a number of American Christians looked to biblical sources for the model of a perfect society. In particular, they sought to restore the society of the first-century apostles. These "restorationists" convinced themselves that living as Christ's first followers did would create the conditions for the Second Coming of Christ.

Modeling society on the scant and ambiguous evidence of first-century society found in nineteenth-century versions of the Protestant Bible poses numerous

Box 6.4   Millennialism

Protestant Americans in the nineteenth century often interpreted America in a millennialist theological frame. This specifically Christian view is distinct from "millenarianism," a term used for any religio-social movement that attempts to transform current social conditions by predicting an ideal society to come once the sources of oppression and suffering are removed, usually by violent resistance or overthrow (see Box 3.1). Protestant millennialism is specifically a Christian notion of eschatology (i.e., a view of the eventual outcome and purpose of history; in other words, eschatology is the theological concern for "last things") that predicts a thousand-year period (or sometimes less specifically a long period) of peace and prosperity on earth. This "millennium" involves the thousand-year reign of Christ while Satan is bound, as described in the twentieth chapter of the Christian sacred Book of Revelation. Many Christian advocates of millennialism insist that this millennium will begin with the promised return of Jesus Christ to earth; these so-called "premillennialists" believe that, once the Second Coming of Christ arrives, the millennial age of peace, harmony, and prosperity will commence. In contrast, other Christians known as "postmillennialists" insist that the millennial period will serve as preparation for Christ's return to earth; they maintain that Christ's Second Coming cannot occur until humans have established a perfect, righteous society.

In the early part of the nineteenth century, American Christians promoted both premillennialist and postmillennialist views. Many revivalist preachers of the Second Great Awakening created urgency with a premillennial message suggesting the imminent advent of the millennium. A good number of other Christian leaders in antebellum America argued for social reforms, especially the abolition of slavery, in reference to a postmillennial view that insisted on perfecting society in anticipation of the return of Christ. These assumptions about a millennial age that is related to the return of Christ have continued in American religious culture up to the present, but urgent attention to premillennial and postmillennial distinctions has waned considerably among Christians. Although many conservative Christians still advocate a premillennial eschatology, the use of "postmillennial" to describe Christians who urge social reforms and justice has nearly disappeared; such views are not often thought of in purely eschatological terms, and instead they are more often regarded now as "socially progressive."[62]

challenges, and the many Christian restorationist communities that took form in the nineteenth century, most of them to quickly disappear, demonstrated the wide variety of possible interpretations. Various assumptions about how the apostles lived in fact had less to do with accurate elucidation of first-century realities and more to do with the pressing problems and tensions of nineteenth-century American society. Virtually all of the Christian restorationist movements used their purported retrieval of the first-century world as an applied critique of their own nineteenth-century society. This can be plainly seen in the very different ways that three particular restorationist groups – the Shakers, the Mormons, and the Oneida Perfectionists – applied interpretations of the same Bible verse in addressing a thorny domestic issue for many of their contemporaries: the proper relations between husbands and wives, in particular regarding sexuality. These three communities pursued radically different understandings of proper marital relations, all of them seemingly bizarre, even dangerous, to conventional nineteenth-century American Protestant sensibilities, but they each sought to restore marital relations based on a teaching attributed to Jesus in the biblical book of Luke: "The children of this world marry, and are given in marriage: But they which shall be accounted worthy to obtain that world, and the resurrection from the dead, neither marry, nor are given in marriage: Neither can they die any more: for they are equal unto the angels; and are the children of God, being the children of the resurrection."[63] The divergent marital practices of these three communities indicate not only the creative interpretations that American Protestants could attach to their sacred texts but also how the tensions of American society in the first half of the nineteenth century urged new critical approaches to social relations, even in the intimacy of marriage.

Shakers

One interpretation of Jesus' pronouncement on marital relations insists that sexual intimacy between married couples has no place in the world of restored perfection envisioned in the Bible. Such was the view of the English religious leader Mother Ann Lee (1736–1784), the charismatic founder of a small community of Christians who adopted the name United Society of Believers in Christ's Second Appearing, more commonly known as Shakers (an originally derogatory term shortened from "Shaking Quakers," because of their roots in Quakerism and the unique bodily motions practiced in their worship). While in jail in England for taking part in raucous religious services that had "disturbed the peace," Ann Lee had a vision of the first couple in Judeo-Christian heritage, Adam and Eve, engaged in sexual intercourse. Following four very difficult and painful experiences of childbirth, with all four of her children subsequently dying in early childhood, Ann Lee herself had become terrified by the prospect of sexual relations, and her religious vision affirmed for her that the great sinful transgression of humanity was sex. In a second vision, Jesus Christ himself appeared to comfort Ann Lee and to encourage her mission to spread her newfound knowledge of human depravity to the world. She began by ridding her small group of Shaking Quakers of their lustful temptations, but continuing persecutions and failure to attract new members forced the tiny community to leave England and relocate in America, with just eight of Lee's followers arriving with her in New York in 1774. The early years in America continued to be difficult as Revolution broke out; the community established a settlement near Albany, New York, but it was several years before they had any new members. Ann Lee's outspoken views condemning lustful ways earned continuing persecution from the community's American neighbors. By the time of her death in 1784, the Shakers remained an insignificant community struggling for their survival. It was only in the closing years of the eighteenth century that the Shakers became a viable community under the leadership of Joseph Meacham (1742–1796), a former Baptist preacher from Connecticut who had converted to Ann Lee's religion and joined her community in 1779.[64]

Mother Ann Lee was by all accounts a vibrant and skillful leader; in fact, her followers regarded her as the incarnation of God's spirit in female form, just as Jesus had been the male incarnation of God. This is not to say that Shakers thought that Mother Ann Lee represented the Second Coming of Christ in the way that evangelical Protestants anticipated it. More in line with the radically egalitarian view of Quakers, her followers believed that Lee simply displayed in an exemplary manner in her life the spirit of God that is present in all lives.

As the Shaker community grew, it developed a more intricate and thorough communal life to support the faithful in their every activity. Most important was avoiding contact and interaction between women and men in order to quell any lustful inclinations. Housing, meals, worship, and nearly all activities of the community were segregated by gender. Members did not live in family units, and all sexual intimacy was strictly forbidden. Conjugal relations were prohibited even for married couples who joined the Shakers; when such couples entered the community, they immediately separated to live with other members of their own sex. Children also were separated from parents and raised communally so as to avoid unwarranted loyalties that would disrupt harmony in the community.

Communal harmony also involved commonly held property and joint govern-ance of the community by females and males. When Joseph Meacham assumed leadership following the death of Ann Lee's immediate successor, he appointed Lucy Wright (1760–1821) as his co-equal, a controversial arrangement even among many of the Shakers; only a revelation from God satisfied members of the community to allow a woman to share in leadership. Together Meacham and Wright formulated a system of government that gave full and equal authority to men and women in all spheres. Strict celibacy and communal rearing of the chil-dren who entered the community with their parents or as orphans adopted by the community freed women to share equally in all aspects of authority over the Shakers. By restoring a divine community, free from sexual debauchery and with their full loyalty only to God, Shakers could disregard the patriarchal elements of the Bible and live according to the Christian apostle Paul's admonition that there is "neither male nor female in the Lord."

Their insistence on shared leadership and authority between women and men disturbed many of the Shakers' critics. Likewise, their ecstatic spiritual practices

Figure 6.6 Shaker worship practices kept women and men separate from each other even as they engaged in their distinctive ritual dances. (Courtesy of the Library of Congress, LC-USZ62-13659.)

also brought reproach from their foes. Not only did many of the believers lapse into bodily convulsions and spontaneous leaping and dancing during their worship but they also spoke in tongues, sang, and shouted out invectives against sin and especially against carnal pleasures. All of this seemed strange and deeply disturbing to many of the outsiders who witnessed it or heard reports of such behaviors. Consequently, Shakers experienced constant persecution; in fact, Ann Lee's premature death came in part from the many beatings and other incidents of physical abuse she suffered from mobs opposed to her religion.[65]

Yet, despite widespread opposition, the Shakers grew. From the arrival of Ann Lee and her eight followers in New York in 1774, Shaker communities in the United States grew in fits and starts over the first half of the nineteenth century, approaching a peak of nearly five thousand members by the middle of the century. Separate communities were established throughout the northeastern United States and in the western regions of Ohio, Indiana, and Kentucky; Shakers were gathered in nearly twenty separate settlements by the 1820s.[66] Their success benefited greatly from the evangelical revivals of the Second Great Awakening, as a number of newly converted Christians sought a home where they could sustain their newfound religious commitment; the simple life of piety among the Shakers, without the complications of family ties or sexual temptations, proved an attractive arrangement for some of the newly reborn Christians. With the waning of revival activity in the middle decades of the nineteenth century, however, the Shakers lost an important source of new members. Since celibacy precluded natural growth of the community, they relied solely on converts entering the community; by the time revivals came to a near standstill with the Civil War, the Shakers were already in decline. Although a bare remnant survives in the twenty-first century, and their cultural influence in the "simple gifts" of Shaker music, furniture, and other arts has been significant in American culture, Shaker religion and their radically celibate attempts to restore a divine community have had little impact outside the pious lives of their few remaining community members.

Mormons

Another marginal religious group with equally controversial sexual precepts, the Mormons, first emerged in western New York in the early 1830s. According to Mormon tradition, Joseph Smith, Jr. (1805–1844) made a remarkable discovery near his family's farm when still an adolescent in the early 1820s. While praying alone in the woods, young Smith encountered an angel by the name of Moroni, who revealed to him the location of "plates of gold" with ancient texts inscribed upon them. Eventually he retrieved the golden plates and over the subsequent years, according to traditional accounts, the young, illiterate Joseph Smith sat behind a curtain with the tablets and a "seer stone," a special glass through which he was able to decipher the texts written on the tablets, which he recited to others who wrote it down. The resulting text is *The Book of Mormon* (1830), the sacred scripture (along with the Christian Bible) of the Church of Jesus Christ of Latter-Day Saints and numerous other denominational descendants of Joseph Smith's religious movement.[67]

The Book of Mormon reconfigures Christian narratives of the Bible by telling of a band of ancient Israelites whose exodus from Egypt took them to the Americas. The Mormon scripture then recounts rivalries, wars, and the fate of these wayward descendants of the original tribes of Israel. The climactic episode is a visit from Christ to these ancient Americans; great catastrophes befell the Americas following Christ's crucifixion but before his resurrection, killing all evil people and leaving only the righteous to witness the appearance of the resurrected Christ, who taught them for a number of days, repeated his Sermon on the Mount for their benefit, and administered to them the Lord's supper before ascending into heaven.[68]

Besides the Mormon retelling of the Christian narrative, the new religion that grew up around Joseph Smith and his book allowed for an "open canon." Unlike most other Christian traditions, which believe the accepted scriptures contain all of the authoritative revelations from God and thus adhere to a "closed canon," Mormon doctrine holds that God's revelations are continuous and that God communicates new revelations through prophets. Moroni's first revelation to Joseph Smith, according to Mormon tradition, initiated a modern era of continuous revelations to church prophets that continues through the present, collected in another sacred text, *The Doctrine and Covenants*. Thus, Mormons engage in an ongoing dialogue with God, whose revelations guide followers on a range of issues.

Among the earliest of the revelations that Joseph Smith experienced were visitations from John the Baptist and the New Testament disciples Peter, James, and John. They instructed Smith to restore the original Christian Church of the first century CE through the authority of "the Priesthood of Aaron," referring to the Old Testament priesthood first conferred upon Aaron, the brother of Moses. In these revelations, the holy emissaries ordained Smith and his associate Oliver Cowdery (1806–1850) as priests, authorizing them to conduct "divine ordinances," or sacraments of the Church. Smith subsequently ordained the authority of priesthood on all male members of the Church.[69]

Figure 6.7 This stylized nineteenth-century illustration shows the Christian biblical character John the Baptist conferring the Aaronic priesthood on Mormon leaders Joseph Smith, Jr., and Oliver Cowdery. (Courtesy of the Library of Congress, LC-DIG-pga-03080.)

Shortly after publishing his *Book of Mormon* and founding his new Church, Joseph Smith sent out missionaries to spread the gospel of his new revelations. A group of converts in Kirtland, Ohio, northeast of Cleveland, convinced Smith to move his community from western New York state to the Ohio town near Lake Erie. From there, Smith led a small group of followers west in the summer of 1831, and a revelation in Independence, Missouri, disclosed to him that this town on the western edge of Euro-American settlement would become the New Jerusalem, the center of the new religion and a gathering place for devout Mormons to build their holy empire and find refuge from the calamities that would precede the return of Christ. Thousands of Mormon converts from all over the world began arriving in Missouri to dedicate their lives to God, and also to contribute their wealth and skills to the socialistic community that Smith had ordained. Joseph Smith himself, however, did not remain in Missouri but instead returned to Ohio, where the small Mormon community erected their first temple in Kirtland.

Beset by violent attacks on the Mormons in Missouri, including an order from the governor to either expel them from the state or exterminate them, plus an economic collapse in Kirtland that precipitated persecution there from non-Mormon residents, Smith and his followers were forced to find a new location for their rapidly growing community. A large bend in the Mississippi River provided an attractive location in Illinois for their refuge, and Smith settled there to build a thriving Mormon community that they named Nauvoo, a Hebrew word meaning "the city beautiful." As ambitious plans unfolded there, Smith announced a number of divine revelations that would have consequences for subsequent Mormon history. The temple, he instructed, would be a place for rituals limited only to Mormons; no longer a meeting place open to the public, Mormon temples in the future would be reserved for sacramental exercises with only Mormons in good standing allowed entry. Among the rituals to be performed in the temple was vicarious baptism, or baptism of the dead; Smith revealed that baptizing people posthumously would allow all of humanity to receive the sacrament.

Perhaps most controversial of Smith's revelations in Nauvoo were his pronouncements on marriage. He stated that husband and wife were to be "sealed" for eternity in the temple ritual; their marriage would not end with death, and their children would remain with them through eternity. More shocking was Smith's allowance for a man to be sealed to more than one wife. Introducing the practice of plural marriage among the Mormons represented a return to the Old Testament practice of polygamy.

The practice of plural marriage among Mormons was especially controversial, even among portions of the Mormon faithful. As the community in Nauvoo grew and prospered, opposition from anti-Mormon groups as well as dissension within the community meant constant threat to Smith's leadership. In 1844 a warrant for his arrest forced him to surrender, and he was placed in the jail at nearby Carthage, Illinois, in part for his own protection. An angry mob, stirred up by inflammatory accounts in the local papers, overran the jail and killed the Mormon prophet and his brother.

Following the death of Joseph Smith, the Mormon community broke up into several factions competing for control of the Church. The largest segment of the

Mormon community followed Brigham Young (1801–1877), the charismatic leader of Smith's appointed Twelve Apostles, to the Great Salt Lake basin in the intermountain west, where they could settle relatively free of persecution. Under Young's leadership, they set out to build a Mormon empire throughout the intermountain west. As we will see in Chapter 7, the Latter-Day Saints Church was not free from challenges and persecutions, but establishing a new base in the American west allowed the community to flourish and continue growing even without its charismatic prophet who founded the sect.[70]

Oneida Perfectionists

A third group that formed in the intense millennialist atmosphere among American Protestants in the early 1840s instilled a far different practice of marital relations than either the celibacy of the Shakers or the plurality of the Mormons. John Humphrey Noyes (1811–1886) brought together a community of believers around what he called the "positive heresy" of preparing for what he calculated to be the second resurrection, a final judgment of humanity that was soon approaching; the goal of his "perfectionist" community was "to meet the approaching kingdom in the heavens, and to become its duplicate and representative on earth."[71] By restoring divine relationships that souls would experience in heaven, unhindered by such social conventions as monogamous marriage, Noyes sought to create a perfect community on earth.

His small band of followers began their community in Putney, Vermont, in 1841, where they instituted Noyes' understanding of Christian perfection. His interpretation of the Christian apostle Paul's writings led Noyes to conclude that perfection involved the inner life rather than legalistic adherence to proper living in one's outer life; if a believer had the proper attitude and motives, then the commitments, actions, and events of that person's life would be acceptable to God. Applying these ideas to relations between men and women, Noyes considered carefully whether Perfectionist life meant celibacy, but he concluded that prohibiting sex would improperly exclude the full range of human experience. Instead, he sought a view of sexuality based on proper attitudes and motives that would lead to sexual relations pleasing to God. This naturally involved a critical attitude to marriage practices of the day, which he aimed to replace with a divine form of marriage that would do away with what he regarded as the limitations and inadequacies of conventional monogamy; as he wrote to his intended wife in 1838 in a letter proposing an unorthodox marriage, "I know that the immortal union of hearts, the everlasting honeymoon, which alone is worthy to be called marriage, can never be *made* by a ceremony, and I know equally well that such a marriage, can never be *marred* by a ceremony."[72] The binding of two souls in marriage for Noyes had little to do with the legal and ceremonial formalities commonly practiced in nineteenth-century America.

The early years of the Perfectionist community in Putney, Vermont, saw little growth as they gradually instilled a communistic system of joint ownership of all property. It was not until 1846 that Noyes would introduce a system of "complex marriage" in the community. His unusual system of marriage aimed to rid the community of the emotional and moral complications arising from "the exclusive possession of one woman to one man" that characterized monogamous marriage, with women treated as property and all the problems of selfishness, greed, jealousy, and envy attendant upon property ownership. In place of conventional marriage between individuals, Noyes instituted a more complex system of marriage attachment (or, more accurately, unattachment) with all men in the community married to all women in the community. This included sexual intimacy with various partners; freed from the possessiveness of monogamous marriages, individuals married to all other members of the community were at liberty to enjoy sexual pleasures with any partner of the opposite sex in the community (whether homosexual encounters occurred is unclear; there is no mention of them in the surviving records of the community). Key to sexual freedom in the community was avoiding pregnancy, which was achieved by what Noyes called "male continence," involving sexual intercourse and other sexual activities without male ejaculation. This allowed, in Noyes' view, "the natural instinct of our nature" to engage in sexual pleasures "not for propagative, but for social and spiritual purposes."[73] The practice of complex marriage, however, did not mean random promiscuity according to lustful impulses. "Free love with us does not mean freedom to love to-day and leave tomorrow," states the *Handbooks* of the Oneida Community.

> Our Communities are families, as distinctly bounded and separated from promiscuous society as ordinary households. The tie that binds us together is as permanent and sacred, to say the least, as that of marriage, for it is our religion … The honor and faithfulness that constitutes an ideal marriage, may exist between two hundred as well as two; while the guarantees for women and children are much greater in the Community than they can be in any private family.[74]

In practice, loving encounters between individuals were communally regulated through several means, most prominently by regular group discussions known as "mutual criticism" or "free criticism." At first these collective conversations about individuals' strengths and weaknesses involved everyone in the community of complex marriage, but later the community was broken into smaller groups for their "criticism" discussions. These involved frank expositions of how others saw the individual; faults and irritating traits were aired openly and dealt with, rather than allowing problems between individuals to worsen without the knowledge of others. One particular problem that threatened the entire system of complex marriage were special attractions and attachments between two individuals; as one Community leader explained, "No matter what his other qualifications may be, if a man cannot love a woman and be happy in seeing her loved by others, he is a selfish man, and his place is with the potsherds of the earth. There is no place for such in the 'Kingdom of Heaven.'"[75] When "mutual criticism" was unable to break such romantic attachments, stronger measures were implemented; in many cases, community leaders suspended or severely limited sexual privileges of the offending individuals, and in some instances one or the other were sent away to a sister community until their ardor subsided. In at least one case, two romantically attached individuals were told to find other partners and have children by them, which they obediently did.

As expected, the radically innovative social, economic, and sexual notions that Noyes and his followers implemented caused tensions within their community and unrelenting criticism from outsiders. Eventually, the State of Vermont indicted Noyes and others on criminal adultery charges, and the community was forced to relocate elsewhere. They found a more hospitable reception in New York state, at a place called Oneida, where they set up a permanent community beginning in 1848. Membership in the community rose to around 250, with another 50 at an allied community of Perfectionists in Connecticut. Not a particularly significant population, the community however remained remarkably stable until its final break-up more than three decades later. In the early years at Oneida, the community experienced substantial internal tension and disharmony; Noyes himself left with a few followers to live separately in Brooklyn for nearly five years. He continued to direct the community from afar; he also publicized his rather unorthodox communal ideas in a newspaper he published, which incited outside critics. Meanwhile, the difficulties of adjusting to their communistic economic system, especially during the years of poverty after their move to Oneida, as well as the social challenges inherent in complex marriage, created internal pressures for the Perfectionists. Nevertheless, the community grew and eventually achieved economic prosperity, social stability, and relative tranquility once Noyes returned to assume leadership.

As Noyes and other original members of the community aged, a new generation showed less commitment to the community values of complex marriage. With growing dissatisfaction among community members, Noyes fled to Canada in 1879 under threat of an external campaign to have him arrested. Never denying the divine sanction of their communal arrangement, Noyes and his loyalist followers finally submitted to the inevitable; shortly after his exile, Noyes conceded it was time for the community to give up their practice of complex marriage. Little more than a year later, the Oneida Community converted to a business enterprise, which eventually grew into a major producer of flatware. John Humphrey Noyes never returned to Oneida as the radical social innovations he had attempted in his restorationist experiment finally sank beneath the pressures of more forceful voices. Only after his death was his body returned for burial on the ground where his Perfectionist community had once flourished.

The Diversity of Religious Voices in America

The free love involved in the complex marriage that Noyes instituted among his Oneida Perfectionists represents a drastic contrast to the radical celibacy of Shaker communities and the practice of plural marriage among the Mormons. For all three groups, however, sexual relations and concerns over the marital bond had profound theological significance as they attempted to instigate a restored Christian society. Each in their own way voiced concerns about conventional understandings of marital relationships and sexual intimacy between spouses that dominated Christian culture; all three groups suffered intense persecution because of their novel views of marriage and sex. None, however, strayed from strictly heterosexual assumptions about sexuality; they all developed their views of sex based on mutual desire between men and women. None suggested that loving physical intimacy between partners of the same sex would have a place in the perfect society of a restored Christianity.

Also excluded from these various visions of a perfect society were other groups of people who did not conform to the Restorationists' embrace of homogeneous Christian culture. Racial difference, linguistic difference, religious difference, and ethnic difference were not seriously contemplated by any of the religious groups attempting to build new communities separate from the dominant American society. In this, they resembled the dominant voices of the society they attempted to escape from. Most American Christians in the nineteenth century had limited tolerance for diversity.

Nevertheless, the religious voices in nineteenth-century America certainly did not speak a single language. Evangelical Protestants gained dominance in public venues, with the male pastors of prominent churches becoming the apparent public voice of religion not only in spiritual matters but also in politics and social affairs. At the same time, though, other voices articulated contrary views in ways not always heard in public. Within Protestant churches, women's newly emerging gender roles allowed them some autonomy to assert themselves in ecclesiastical concerns, often spearheading initiatives in religious education, missionary endeavors, and social welfare. For many women, more authority and influence in church mirrored greater autonomy at home, although for most this did not mean parity with the patriarchal authority of husbands, fathers, pastors, or priests. But a few prominent women demanded that their voices be heard more fully in secular society, insisting on equality in the spirit of a free democratic society.

Besides women, other significant groups of people remained excluded from full participation, and in many cases *any* participation, in the benefits of democratic society. Native Americans, African Americans both free and enslaved, immigrants – all faced formidable obstacles to claiming membership in the American republic. Virtually all of these groups relied on religious traditions and resources in dealing with their excluded status. Muskogee shamans used their spiritual powers and ritual traditions to lead the resistance to Euro-American encroachments on tribal territories and ancient ways of life. African American Conjure practices mixed with newly acquired Christianity to resist apartheid conditions in the new republic, and particularly to endure slavery; an emerging African American preaching tradition associated with the evangelical revivals of the Second Great Awakening allowed suppressed voices to be heard by ever-expanding audiences. Immigrants on the other hand built new communities in America centered around church traditions as they settled into a new homeland. Facing hostile receptions from nativists and **proselytization** from zealous Protestants, the newly arrived Catholics from Ireland, Germany, and other European nations turned to the church not only for material help and spiritual solace but also for education and a degree of protection from the dangers they faced as newcomers in a less-than-welcoming land. In contrast, Jewish immigrants introduced religious reforms that made integration into the dominant Christian culture less contentious.

There is no doubt that, throughout the nineteenth century, the solid majority of Americans were Protestant, and the evangelical strains of Protestant Christianity became the dominant religious voices in America. Nevertheless, diverse voices within Protestantism, the growing presence of other Christians (namely Roman Catholics), greater numbers of Jews, and the continued presence of racial and cultural others (most prominently among enslaved African Americans and the diverse communities of Native Americans) undermined any claim to a singular religious voice in the growing nation.

Questions for Discussion

(1) In what ways did racial, ethnic, and gender differences constrain one's "voice" in nineteenth-century America, and how did religious traditions and communities create opportunities for these constrained voices to assert themselves?

(2) How were gender roles for nineteenth-century Euro-American Protestants different from the gender roles in traditional Muskogee society?

(3) Why did some Americans react with nativist attitudes toward immigrants?

(4) How did millennialist attitudes determine the views of Shakers, Mormons, and Oneida Perfectionists regarding marriage and sexuality?

Suggested Primary-Source Readings

Jarena Lee, "The Life and Religious Experience of Jarena Lee," in *Sisters of the Spirit: Three Black Women's Autobiographies of the Nineteenth Century*, ed. William L. Andrews (Bloomington: Indiana University Press, 1986), 25–48: Lee recounts her spiritual and material struggles as an African American woman preacher in the early decades of the nineteenth century.

Charles G. Finney, *The Original Memoirs of Charles G. Finney* (Grand Rapids, MI: Zondervan, 2002): This is Finney's account of his career and theological views. In addition, many of Finney's sermons can be found online.

Lucretia Mott, "Discourse on Women" (1849), available online and in Ellen Skinner, ed., *Women and the National Experience: Primary Sources in American History* (Harlow: Longman, 2003): A leader of the women's movement and co-organizer of the initial convention at Seneca Falls expounds on "the true and proper position of woman."

The Doctrine and Covenants of the Church of Jesus Christ of Latter-Day Saints: The Pearl of Great Price (Salt Lake City, UT: Church of Jesus Christ of Latter-Day Saints, 1982), Section 132: Joseph Smith's revelation from God, received July 12, 1843, in Nauvoo, Illinois, establishes the eternity of marriage and authorizes plural marriage when commanded by the Lord.

"Bible Argument Defining the Relations of the Sexes in the Kingdom of Heaven," in *Bible Communism: A Compilation from the Annual Reports and Other Publications of the Oneida Association and Its Branches* (Brooklyn, NY: Office of the Circular, 1853), 24–64: This tract written by John Humphrey Noyes explains the Oneida Community's views on sexuality and marital relations.

Notes

1   Jarena Lee, "The Life and Religious Experience of Jarena Lee," in *Sisters of the Spirit: Three Black Women's Autobiographies of the Nineteenth Century*, ed. William L. Andrews (Bloomington: Indiana University Press, 1986), 35.

2   For details on Allen's life and career, see Richard S. Newman, *Freedom's Prophet: Bishop Richard Allen, the AME Church, and the Black Founding Fathers* (New York: New York University Press, 2008).

3   Lee, "The Life and Religious Experience of Jarena Lee," 36.

4   Ibid., 44–45.

5   Ibid., 47.

6   Ibid., 48.

7   For a good introduction and overview of Foucault's concepts and philosophy, see Clare O'Farrell, *Michel Foucault* (Thousand Oaks, CA: Sage, 2005).

8   For a discussion of Foucault's theory of discourse, see Chris Weedon, *Feminist Practice and Poststructuralist Theory* (Oxford: Blackwell, 1987), 104–131. According to Weedon, Foucault regards discourses as "ways of constituting knowledge, together with the social practices, forms of subjectivity and power relations which inhere in such knowledges and relations between them." Moreover, Weedon continues, "discourses are more than ways of thinking and producing meaning. They constitute the 'nature' of the body, unconscious and conscious mind and emotional life of the subjects they seek to govern. Neither the body nor thoughts and feelings have meaning outside of their discursive articulation, but the ways in which discourses constitute the minds and bodies of individuals is always part of a wider network of power relations, often with institutional bases" (p. 105).

9   James C. Scott, *Domination and the Arts of Resistance: Hidden Transcripts* (New Haven, CT: Yale University Press, 1990).

10 The question of voice has been foundational to postcolonial studies, especially in reference to the impact of Gayatri Spivak's seminal essay "Can the Subaltern Speak?" in *Marxism and the Interpretation of Culture*, ed. Cary Nelson and Lawrence Grossberg (Urbana: University of Illinois Press, 1988), 271–313. See Rosalind C. Morris, ed. *Can the Subaltern Speak? Reflections on the History of an Idea* (New York: Columbia University Press, 2010).

11 Keith Hardman, *Charles Grandison Finney, 1792–1875: Revivalist and Reformer* (Syracuse, NY: Syracuse University Press, 1987), 84.

12   Susan Hill Lindley, *You Have Stept out of Your Place: A History of Women and Religion in America* (Louisville, KY: Westminster John Knox Press, 1996), 62.

13   Sarah E. Johnson, "Gender," in *The Blackwell Companion to Religion in America*, ed. Philip Goff (Malden, MA: Wiley Blackwell, 2010), 149–150.

14   Actually, biological sex is not so unambiguous in many species; even among humans, investigators have estimated that approximately 1.7 percent of the population is not clearly male or female from a biological perspective. See Anne Fausto-Sterling, "The Five Sexes, Revisited," *Sciences* 40, no. 4 (2000), 20.

15   For discussions of Native American two-spirit or berdache traditions, see Brian Joseph Gilley, *Becoming Two-Spirit: Gay Identity and Social Acceptance in Indian Country* (Lincoln: University of Nebraska Press, 2006); Sue-Ellen Jacobs, Wesley Thomas, and Sabine Lang, eds., *Two-Spirit People: Native American Gender Identity, Sexuality, and Spirituality* (Urbana: University of Illinois Press, 1997); Will Roscoe, *Changing Ones: Third and Fourth Genders in Native North America* (New York: St. Martin's Press, 1998); and Walter L. Williams, *The Spirit and the Flesh: Sexual Diversity in American Indian Culture* (Boston, MA: Beacon Press, 1986). For a study cautioning against simplistic interpretations of complex cultural understandings of gender roles in Native American societies, see Jean-Guy A. Goulet, "The 'Berdache'/'Two-Spirit': A Comparison of Anthropological and Native Constructions of Gendered Identities among the Northern Athapaskans," *Journal of the Royal Anthropological Institute* 2, no. 4 (1996), 683–701.

16   Regarding the social construction of biological sex, see Fausto-Sterling, "The Five Sexes, Revisited." For the importance of bodily practices in constructing gender, see Saba Mahmood, "Politics of Piety: The Islamic Revival and the Feminist Subject," *Cultural Anthropology* 16 (2001).

17   Judith Butler, "Performative Acts and Gender Constitution: An Essay in Phenomenology and Feminist Theory," in *Feminist Theory Reader: Local and Global Perspectives*, ed. Carole R. McCann and Seung-Kyung Kim (New York: Routledge, 2013), 462–474.

18   For a good overview of the study of gender in American religious history, see Johnson, "Gender."

19   Quoted in ibid., 150.

20   Ann Braude, "Women's History *Is* American Religious History," in *Retelling US Religious History*, ed. Thomas A. Tweed (Berkeley: University of California Press, 1997), 88.

21   Sally Gregory McMillen, *Seneca Falls and the Origins of the Women's Rights Movement* (New York: Oxford University Press, 2008), 84–95.

22   Ibid., 93–94.

23   Margaret Washington, *Sojourner Truth's America* (Urbana: University of Illinois Press, 2011), 201–205.

24   Ibid., 229.

25   Frederick Douglass, *Narrative of the Life of Frederick Douglass* (New York: Oxford University Press, 1999), 72.

26   Ibid., 101.

27   Ira Berlin, *Generations of Captivity: A History of African-American Slaves* (Cambridge, MA: Belknap Press of Harvard University Press, 2003), 109–110.

28   The Rev. Nathaniel Paul's address to the Albany Anti-Slavery Convention appears in *The Friend of Man*, a weekly newspaper of the New York State Anti-Slavery Society,

volume 2, number 39, March 14, 1838, available online from Cornell University at http://fom.library.cornell.edu/cgi-bin/cornell-fom (accessed February 18, 2013).

29 Regarding African American colonization in Africa during the nineteenth century, see Laurie F. Maffly-Kipp, *Setting Down the Sacred Past: African-American Race Histories* (Cambridge, MA: Belknap Press of Harvard University Press, 2010), 154–200.

30 Letter from William Burke to ACS president Ralph R. Gurley, July 26, 1858, American Colonization Society Papers, Manuscript Division, Library of Congress, excerpt available online at www.loc.gov/exhibits/african/afam004.html (accessed February 18, 2013). On Liberia, see G. E. Saigbe Boley, *Liberia: The Rise and Fall of the First Republic* (New York: St. Martin's Press, 1984) and Tom W. Shick, *Behold the Promised Land: A History of Afro-American Settler Society in Nineteenth-Century Liberia* (Baltimore, MD: Johns Hopkins University Press, 1980).

31 Joel W. Martin, *Sacred Revolt: The Muskogees' Struggle for a New World* (Boston, MA: Beacon Press, 1991), 79–81.

32 Ibid., 17.

33 Ibid., 24.

34 Ibid., 23–24.

35 Ibid., 35–36.

36 Ibid., 30, 37–39.

37 Ibid., 114–128.

38 Ibid., 134.

39 Ibid., 1–2.

40 David S. Reynolds, *Waking Giant: America in the Age of Jackson* (New York: Harper, 2008), 316.

41 Theda Perdue and Michael D. Green, *The Cherokee Nation and the Trail of Tears* (New York: Viking, 2007), 94.

42 Dale R. Steiner, *Of Thee We Sing: Immigrants and American History* (San Diego, CA: Harcourt Brace Jovanovich, 1987), 2.

43 Thomas A. Tweed and Stephen R. Prothero, eds., *Asian Religions in America: A Documentary History* (New York: Oxford University Press, 1999), 2.

44 Edwin Scott Gaustad and Philip L. Barlow, *New Historical Atlas of Religion in America* (New York: Oxford University Press, 2001), 155.

45 Patrick W. Carey, *Catholics in America: A History* (Westport, CT: Praeger, 2004), 21–22.

46 Emily Clark, *Masterless Mistresses: The New Orleans Ursulines and the Development of a New World Society, 1727–1834* (Chapel Hill: University of North Carolina Press, 2007), 1–5. See also Marie Madeleine Hachard, *Voices from an Early American Convent: Marie Madeleine Hachard and the New Orleans Ursulines, 1727–1760* (Baton Rouge: Louisiana State University Press, 2007). I thank my student Stephanie Veech for drawing my attention to the story of the Ursulines in New Orleans.

47 Thadeus J. Posey, "Praying in the Shadows: The Oblate Sisters of Providence, a Look at Nineteenth-Century Black Catholic Spirituality," in *This Far by Faith: Readings in African-American Women's Religious Biography*, ed. Judith Weisenfeld and Richard Newman (New York: Routledge, 1996), 73–93.

48 Ellin Kelly and Annabelle Melville, eds., *Elizabeth Seton: Selected Writings* (New York: Paulist Press, 1987).

49 Ibid.

50 Carey, *Catholics in America: A History*, 31.

51 Max I. Dimont, *The Jews in America: The Roots, History, and Destiny of American Jews* (New York: Simon and Schuster, 1978), 125–126.

52 Michael A. Meyer, *Response to Modernity: A History of the Reform Movement in Judaism* (New York: Oxford University Press, 1988), 228.

53 Ira M. Leonard and Robert D. Parmet, *American Nativism, 1830–1860* (New York: Van Nostrand Reinhold, 1971), 6–7.

54 Ibid., 85–97.

55 Raymond L. Cohn, "Nativism and the End of the Mass Migration of the 1840s and 1850s," *Journal of Economic History* 60, no. 2 (2000).

56 Meyer, *Response to Modernity*, 229.

57 Ibid., 235–242.

58 Ibid., 242–243.

59 Ronald L. Numbers and Janet S. Numbers, "Millerism and Madness: A Study of 'Religious Insanity' in Nineteenth-Century America," in *The Disappointed: Millerism and Millenarianism in the Nineteenth Century*, ed. Ronald L. Numbers and Jonathan M. Butler (Bloomington: Indiana University Press, 1987), 92–117.

60 Sylvester Bliss and Apollos Hale, *Memoirs of William Miller, Generally Known as a Lecturer on the Prophecies, and the Second Coming of Christ* (Boston, MA: J. V. Himes, 1853), 256 (emphasis in the original).

61 Sources on Millerism include Ruth Alden Doan, *The Miller Heresy, Millennialism, and American Culture* (Philadelphia, PA: Temple University Press, 1987); Edwin S. Gaustad, ed., *The Rise of Adventism: Religion and Society in Mid-Nineteenth-Century America* (New York: Harper & Row, 1974); and Ronald L. Numbers and Jonathan M. Butler, eds., *The Disappointed: Millerism and Millenarianism in the Nineteenth Century* (Bloomington: Indiana University Press, 1987).

62 For a concise summary of millennialism in American history, see Stephen J. Stein, "Millennialism," in *The Blackwell Companion to Religion in America*, ed. Philip Goff (Malden, MA: Wiley Blackwell, 2010), 215–227.

63 Luke 20:34–36 in C. I. Scofield, ed., *The New Scofield Reference Bible; Holy Bible, Authorized King James Version, with Introductions, Annotations, Subject Chain References, and Such Word Changes in the Text as Will Help the Reader* (New York: Oxford University Press, 1967).

64 An excellent source for the Shakers is Stephen J. Stein, *The Shaker Experience in America: A History of the United Society of Believers* (New Haven, CT: Yale University Press, 1992).

65 Lawrence Foster, *Religion and Sexuality: The Shakers, the Mormons, and the Oneida Community* (Urbana: University of Illinois Press, 1984), 33, 36.

66 Gaustad and Barlow, *New Historical Atlas*, 243–244. Much later, in the 1890s, when Shaker membership was in steep decline, two additional communities were established in southern states, one in Florida and the other in Georgia, to help attract new members.

67 For a concise account of Joseph Smith's discovery and translation of *The Book of Mormon* by Mormon scholars, see Claudia L. Bushman and Richard L. Bushman, *Building the Kingdom: A History of Mormons in America* (New York: Oxford University Press, 2001), 1–13. A more detailed account and analysis by a non-Mormon scholar appears in the first two chapters of Jan Shipps, *Mormonism: The Story of a New Religious Tradition* (Urbana: University of Illinois Press, 1985).

68   Bushman, *Building the Kingdom*, 10.

69   Ibid., 18–19.

70   The early history of the Mormons can be found in ibid., 14–36.

71   Quoted in Foster, *Religion and Sexuality*, 77. Other sources for the Noyes' Oneida community include Louis J. Kern, *An Ordered Love: Sex Roles and Sexuality in Victorian Utopias: The Shakers, the Mormons, and the Oneida Community* (Chapel Hill: University of North Carolina Press, 1981), 207–279 and Spencer Klaw, *Without Sin: The Life and Death of the Oneida Community* (New York: Allen Lane, 1993).

72   Quoted in Foster, *Religion and Sexuality*, 83.

73   Noyes discusses complex marriage in his essay "Bible Argument Defining the Relations of the Sexes in the Kingdom of Heaven" (1848), quoted in ibid., 94.

74   Quoted in ibid., 72.

75   Abel Easton quoted in ibid., 107.

7

One Nation

Considering the role of religion during the tumultuous middle decades of nineteenth-century America, this chapter begins by contemplating the religious nature of Texas' independence with the symbolic importance of the Alamo in relation to American nationalistic spirit, especially in terms of Manifest Destiny. We will then consider the significance of Transcendentalism for American culture before turning to the divisive struggle over slavery, which eventually tore the nation apart in civil war. We learn about the religious aspects of racial attitudes for many nineteenth-century Americans as they considered the theological and moral arguments on both sides of the slavery issue. Following the war, Protestant enthusiasm for rebuilding a unified nation was tempered by continuing conflicts as white southerners attempted to reassert racial preferences in the south and a surge of settlement in the west exacerbated religious tensions with Native Americans, Chinese immigrants, Mormons, and others.

In March 1836, a small band of Texan rebels, mostly Euro-Americans from the southern region of the United States who had come to Mexican territory in search of economic opportunities, huddled together in the derelict compound of an unfinished Spanish Catholic mission church in San Antonio commonly known as the Alamo. For ten days this ragtag band of rebels, which included a number of Tejanos (Hispanic Texans of Mexican nationality) sympathetic to their cause as well as a few women and children and at least one enslaved African American, had been under siege by the overwhelming force of the Mexican army. Yet, despite their extreme disadvantage in numbers, provisions, and weaponry, they refused to

Formed From This Soil: An Introduction to the Diverse History of Religion in America, First Edition. Thomas S. Bremer.
© 2015 Thomas S. Bremer. Published 2015 by John Wiley & Sons, Ltd.

surrender. Their leader, the youthful William Barret Travis (1809–1836) probably did not draw a line in the sand, as legend has it, but clearly the rebels remained obstinate in not giving in to the superior forces of General Antonio López de Santa Anna (1794–1876), military leader and president of the Mexican nation. Finally losing his patience with the rebels, General Santa Anna ordered an assault on the Alamo; within hours the battle was over with all of the rebels dead except the women, children, and an enslaved African American named Joe.

Remembering the Alamo soon became a maxim of religious proportions in American culture, a patriotic adage of courage and principle in the face of indomitable odds. In particular, the story of the Texas patriots who died rather than surrender accorded well with Protestant notions of a chosen nation standing up like the biblical hero David to face down the evil Goliath who would stymy the **providence** of the American nation. The fact that, unlike the traditional tale of David and Goliath, these heroes were defeated and met ignoble deaths only served to enhance the drama and the value of the Alamo story, creating Protestant martyrs who gave their lives for the national cause that God had ordained.

Figure 7.1   As early as the 1840s, the unfinished chapel of the Alamo in San Antonio, Texas, became a sacred site commemorating the famous battle and the martyrs of the Texas Revolution. The Alamo, shown here in an 1844 engraving, and the Texas rebels who died there subsequently became icons of American providentialism as the nation asserted Manifest Destiny across the continent. (Courtesy of the Library of Congress, LC-USZ61-292.)

Remembering the Alamo, however, also involved significant forgetfulness. In particular, the story of heroic martyrdom has overshadowed the diversity of the combatants who died in San Antonio on that fateful day in 1836. Certainly, Euro-American Protestants led the force, but among their ranks were Catholics, Jews, and practitioners of other traditions. In addition, although they agreed on independence from Mexico, participants came to the fight with different motives. Economic issues ranked high, and slavery was no small concern; among the rebels were Euro-American slaveowners who resented Mexico's prohibition of slavery, an issue of less concern to Mexican nationals who joined the cause. Religious freedom remained largely in the background; with Roman Catholicism as the state religion in Mexico, Protestantism was officially banned in Texas. Although the ban was not effectively enforced, Protestant missionary activity was nearly nonexistent prior to Texas' independence. In the aftermath of the Texas Revolution, though, following Santa Anna's ultimate defeat less than two months after his victory in San Antonio, the newly independent Republic of Texas began to host Protestant missionaries, initiated by Methodist itinerant preachers, and eventually Protestant churches were established in nearly every settlement.

The arrival of Protestants in Texas contributed to the larger story of Christian destiny for the American nation. When the United States annexed Texas in 1845, exacerbating territorial disputes with Mexico that led to the outbreak of the Mexican–American War in 1846, the newly coined term "Manifest Destiny" became justification for partisans of expansion. The American victory in 1848, which transferred nearly one-half of the Mexican nation's territory to the United States, only bolstered Protestant confidence in providential purpose for the expansion of the nation. On the other hand, northern abolitionists balked at the idea of God's blessing in the Manifest Destiny of the American nation when it meant the extension of slavery into new territories. The Protestant fulfillment promised in American westward expansion could not be wholly manifest without settling the divisive issue of legalized human bondage. As some abolitionists surmised, the nation must suffer for its great sin against the divine will for human freedom. Prominent Unitarian preacher William Ellery Channing (1780–1842) observed that, before spreading American virtues of liberty and democracy to new territories, "we must first cherish them in our own borders."[1]

Eventually, the moral argument against slavery in the industrial north would prevail over the economic necessity of slave labor for the southern agrarian states, but only after great national calamity in the violent upheavals of civil war. On both sides, Christians insisted on divine will in support of their respective causes; theological arguments condemning enslavement on the part of abolitionists were matched with equally passionate theological justifications of slavery by southern theologians. Neither side harbored much doubt that the Christian god blessed their views, that providence would vindicate their position in the unfolding of the nation's divinely ordained purpose.

Box 7.1   Providentialism

In its simplest formulation, providentialism is a primarily Protestant belief "that God controls everything on earth."[2] This belief understood in terms of a providentially sanctioned purpose for the American nation has been part of the culture ever since British Puritans established their colony in New England in the seventeenth century. The early Puritan colonists regarded their new American homeland as sacred, the New Canaan to be conquered and reworked at God's direction; as a natural outgrowth of their Calvinistic acceptance of God's predestination, the Puritans and their various Protestant successors interpreted their own American story in biblical terms, confident of God's purpose for them to plant the ideal Christian society in the American wilderness. This notion of providential purpose for America became a powerful image guiding the course of British colonial efforts in America and later national identity for the new nation.[3] In the nineteenth century, the assumption of a providential purpose for the American nation took the form of "Manifest Destiny," a term coined in 1845 when journalist John O'Sullivan (1813–1895) proclaimed "the right of our manifest destiny to overspread and to possess the whole continent which providence has given us for the development of the great experiment of liberty and federated self government."[4]

The appeal of the idea that providence was guiding the course of the nation gained popular support in antebellum America, in part due to assumptions about race, gender, and religion. Proponents of Manifest Destiny implied that God wanted American democracy specifically for white, male, Protestant citizens of the United States. This became clear at the conclusion of the Mexican–American War in 1848, when the United States had defeated the Mexicans and taken control of Mexico City. Rather than adhere to the logic of American Manifest Destiny by annexing the whole of the Mexican nation, American racial attitudes balked at the prospect of such a large population of people of Native American descent suddenly entering the United States, possibly adding twenty additional states with forty new senators, most of them non-white, and consequently eroding Anglo-Saxon privilege. Instead, the US government opted to purchase from Mexico the less populous territories of Texas, California, and other areas that have become the southwestern United States.[5] In the words of John Calhoun (1782–1850), a prominent US senator from South Carolina and a vocal critic of annexing Mexico, the "high mission of heaven" providentially prescribed for America was to benefit the "Caucasian race – the free white race."[6] For some of the more prominent voices subscribing to the providential understanding of the nation's destiny, America was a place of white privilege.

Spiritual Purposes

The battles over American destiny were fought ideologically in debates over Christian theology; there were also constant political engagements in the halls of Congress and in the national print media that proliferated during the nineteenth century; and the struggle over American destiny was also waged on actual battle-fields in the war with Mexico, the Civil War, the US government's ongoing conflicts with Mormons in the intermountain west, and the Indian wars later in the closing decades of the nineteenth century. This national concern mirrored the personal struggles of many American Christians. The Arminian theological slant of most Protestant **evangelical** Christians in the nineteenth century put considerable emphasis on individual choice and the piety of proper behaviors, habits, and religious practices. At the same time, another influential strain of Protestant Christianity emerged from a more skeptical and liberal theological orientation. Although it never matched the evangelicals' numbers in terms of followers, the religious and aesthetic movement known as Transcendentalism likewise had a profound impact on subsequent American culture and society.

Transcendentalism

The origins of the Transcendentalist movement go back to religious skeptics in New England who had found a sympathetic doctrine in Unitarianism. The early Unitarians opposed key doctrines of Calvinism, especially regarding original sin and God's predestinated election for chosen individuals; instead they emphasized the individual's moral responsibility, and they regarded God as an inherently benevolent force. Unitarian theology, which developed in the late eighteenth and early nineteenth centuries, included a critique of the traditional Christian theology of the Trinity, which regarded God as three distinct but unified beings – transcendent Creator God, human Savior God (i.e., Jesus Christ), and immanent Spiritual God (i.e., the Holy Spirit). Unitarians viewed this understanding of God as a later theological corruption, and they embraced a view of God as a singular, unified entity; in most Unitarian theological interpretations, Jesus Christ retains highest respect as a spiritual and moral teacher of unparalleled insight and sensitivity, but he is not regarded as divine, or at least his divine nature is not on the same level as the singular and unique Creator God. As a liberal alternative to the harsh demands of the Puritans' Trinitarian God, religious skeptics in New England welcomed the largely benevolent deity of the Unitarians, and by the end of the eighteenth century they had formed congregations throughout the region. The largest and most influential of these groups were located in Boston; Harvard College in nearby Cambridge, Massachusetts, became the center of Unitarian intellectual activity, and many of Harvard's graduates in the late eighteenth century and early nineteenth century went on to serve as **clergy** for Unitarian congregations.[7]

One such Harvard graduate was Ralph Waldo Emerson (1803–1882), whose ordination in 1829 landed him a junior pastor position in a prominent Boston Unitarian congregation. But his religious skepticism left him dissatisfied with Christianity, even the liberal theological orientation of the Unitarians, and Emerson eventually abandoned his church appointment to pursue a career of writing and lecturing. Along with other leading intellectuals, writers, and artists in Massachusetts, Emerson promoted Transcendentalism, a religious, philosophical, and aesthetic movement that emphasizes the transcendent nature of the human soul.[8] Never amounting to a formal, institutionalized religious movement, Transcendentalism originated with a gathering of like-minded skeptics in Boston who called themselves the "Transcendental Club." They began in 1836, the same year that Emerson's essay "Nature" was published; it served as an inspirational text for their association. Dominated by Unitarians (or, like Emerson, ex-Unitarians), the small but exceptionally influential group included women among its active participants, notably Margaret Fuller (1810–1850), who co-edited with Emerson the Transcendentalist literary journal *The Dial*.

Although often characterized as the liberal opposition to the Protestant evangelicalism of the Second Great Awakening, the Transcendentalists shared with the evangelical Protestants a highly individualistic view of religion. Rather than focusing on religion in terms of community or institutionalized structures, what mattered most to the Transcendentalists of the nineteenth century, much like their evangelical counterparts, was the individual's religious or spiritual well-being. Unlike for evangelicals, however, one's spiritual connection is never purely personal for followers of a Transcendentalist perspective. As Emerson explained in an 1842 lecture, Transcendentalism derives from the thinking of the German Idealist philosopher Immanuel Kant (1724–1804), who emphasized "intuitions of the mind itself," which Kant called "Transcendental forms." The Transcendentalist, according to Emerson, "wishes that the spiritual principle should be suffered to demonstrate itself to the end, in all possible applications to the state of man, without the admission of anything unspiritual; that is, anything positive, dogmatic, personal."[9] This spiritual principle that suffuses human experience, as Emerson explains in his early essay on "Nature," is an "ineffable essence" that speaks through Nature as "the present expositor of the divine mind."[10] Unlike the evangelical Christianity of the Protestant revivalists, whose dichotomous **worldview** separated people according to categories of good and evil, the Transcendentalists' understanding of personal religious experience connected them to all things and all people, a unified singularity of goodness and beauty.

The Transcendentalist aesthetic

The Transcendentalists' emphasis on divine unity served as the basis of a pervasive religious aesthetic. Their recognition of goodness and beauty in all things revived an appreciation of mystical experience in American culture. Taking up "the question of Mysticism," as Emerson explained it, the Transcendental Club adapted the ancient Christian mystical tradition to fit contemporary American cultural values, in particular the Transcendentalist values they favored.[11] The mystical experiences these spiritual seekers advocated required the deliberate practice of solitude, a virtue famously exemplified by the Transcendentalist writer Henry David Thoreau (1817–1862), whose reflections on his sojourn to Walden Pond near Concord, Massachusetts, have become a classic of American literature and a seminal work of American nature writing and environmentalism. Lamenting the "lives of quiet desperation" that most people are resigned to in the modern world, Thoreau's celebration of life "rapt in a revery, amidst the pine and hickories and sumachs, in undisturbed solitude and stillness" extolled a contemplative life in Nature; a certain wholesomeness comes from being alone, Thoreau insisted, far from the turmoil of petty human concerns: "I never found the companion as companionable as solitude," he wryly concludes.[12]

Another writer heavily influenced by the Transcendentalists gave lasting poetic praise to both the individual spirit and a unified vision of the American nation. Walt Whitman (1819–1892) wrote exuberant verse of a universal self in consort with all people; the opening poem of the initial 1855 edition of his book *Leaves of Grass*, which he described as "the new Bible" in his desire to "inaugurate a religion,"[13] is among his most famous poems, later titled "Song of Myself." It begins,

> I celebrate myself, and sing myself,
> And what I assume you shall assume,
> For every atom belonging to me as good belongs to you.

The poem continues, giving voice to all sorts of folks not usually represented in the literature of the period:

> Through me may long dumb voices,
> Voices of the interminable generations of prisoners and slaves,
> Voices of the diseased and despairing and of thieves and dwarfs,
> Voices of cycles of preparation and accretion …
> Through me forbidden voices,
> Voices of sexes and lusts, voices veiled and I remove the veil,
> Voices indecent by me clarified and transfigured.[14]

This Transcendentalist recognition of oneself in all others suggests a unifying vision of American society during the divisive years leading up to the Civil War, a vision that Whitman would make more explicit in subsequent editions of *Leaves of Grass*.[15] His poetry presents an interpretation of the republic that is less about a chosen nation progressing westward in providential leaps and bounds and more about a radically inclusive democracy in the cities and settled countrysides of America.

The Transcendentalists' propensity for an inclusive sense of America made important contributions to equality for women and for the abolition of slavery in the United States. The most notable advocate for the rights of women among the inner circle of Transcendentalism was Margaret Fuller, whose essay "The Great Lawsuit: Man *versus* Men, Woman *versus* Women" (appearing in book form in 1845 as *Woman in the Nineteenth Century*) sounded a Transcendentalist call for women's equality. Not only did she insist on an inherent parity between genders but she also related the plight of women to that of slaves, remarking, "As the friend of the Negro assumes that one man cannot by right hold another in bondage, so should the Friend of Woman assume that Man cannot by right lay even well-meant restrictions on Woman."[16] This confluence of women's equality and slaves' liberty found a sympathetic reception among other Transcendentalists who advocated both issues, notably Emerson, Thoreau, and the ardent abolitionist Theodore Parker (1810–1860), a Unitarian minister and founding member of the Transcendental Club.

Figure 7.2 Unitarian minister Theodore Parker was a founding member of the Transcendentalist Club, and he later emerged as a leading advocate of the abolitionist cause. This 1856 illustration shows him lecturing on the evils of slavery. (Courtesy of the Library of Congress, LC-USZ62-52144.)

The Transcendentalists also cultivated religious interests beyond the conventional Protestant Christianity of their received heritage – they were among the first to take a sustained interest in religions arriving from Asia. European colonization and increased trade with Asian nations, along with the entrance of Christian missionaries among the Hindus, Buddhists, and other religious people of Asia, had introduced the rudiments of these religious orientations to western thinkers, who in turn were applying philological studies of ancient Asian texts in the beginnings of the field of comparative religion.[17] The Transcendentalists took an early interest in the lessons of eastern thought. The religious concepts of Asian traditions especially intrigued Emerson, and the influence of such notions as *maya* (commonly translated as "illusion"), *karma* (the law of cause and effect), and the Asian understanding of reincarnation is evident in several of his essays; he even claimed in one that "The Buddhist ... is a Transcendentalist."[18] Thoreau also found treasures in Asian sacred texts; in his book *A Week on the Concord and Merrimack Rivers* (1849) he lavishes praise on the Hindu text of the *Bhagavad Gita*, which he insists "deserves to be read with reverence even by Yankees, as a part of the sacred writings of a devout people."[19] Not satisfied with what they regarded as the restrictive dogmas of the Judeo-Christian traditions, Transcendentalist seekers welcomed a widening range of sacred teachings in their inclusive view of humanity.

Despite the impact of Transcendentalist perspectives on art and literature in the nineteenth century, its religious impact was markedly less than that of the Christian evangelical revivals of the Second Great Awakening or the movement of European religions, especially Roman Catholicism and Reform Judaism, to American shores in the communities of immigrants settling throughout the republic. Besides the meetings of the Transcendental Club in the 1830s, Transcendentalists never developed formal religious institutions or clearly bounded religious communities, although Unitarians incorporated much of Transcendentalist philosophy and religious interpretations into their own institutional forms. Nevertheless, the universal self of Transcendentalist philosophy stood alongside the individualistic propensity of evangelical Christianity with a liberal contribution to American ideals of individualism, self-reliance, and personal responsibility that suited American democracy and the enterprising markets of the American economic system; the spirit of freedom was quickly becoming the defining feature of the American self. Yet this nation of individuals still faced formidable challenges over the exclusionary exceptions to its most cherished political and economic ideals. The most divisive issue by the middle of the nineteenth century was the continued enslavement of nearly four million Americans.[20]

A Nation Divided

In the decades prior to the American Civil War, a time commonly known as the antebellum period, slavery had an impact on nearly every aspect of American public life. Political battles raged over the question of slavery with every addition of new territory and the admittance of each new state. Economic consequences rode on the fate of slave labor. Grave moral debates issued from the pulpits and print media of American churches; the largest Protestant denominations split apart in acrimonious fights over the moral implications of human bondage. Compromise became more difficult and less likely; the nation could no longer avoid the paradox of owning slaves in a democratic society where the majority of citizens endorsed Christian values of love and benevolence to others.

The apparent hypocrisy of Christians owning other Christians as slaves was painfully evident to the enslaved people themselves. By the middle of the nineteenth century, large segments of the African American population had adopted Christianity. In fact, African American enthusiasm for the Christian message sometimes brought whites to a new (or renewed) Christian life, with numerous accounts of Euro-Americans accepting a vigorous Christian faith at the urging of black evangelical preachers and exhorters. Even white slaveholders, in at least a few instances, found Christ through African American evangelists.[21] But, more often, an unfathomable gulf lay between master and slave, between whites and blacks. In most cases their respective adherence to Christianity relied on far different understandings of the religion's tenets; in fact some observers concluded that they followed different religions. Slaveowners, and the larger slaveholding society in general, demanded a Christianity of docility and obedience, one that justified the institutions of slavery with the promise of a glorious afterlife for compliant Christian slaves. But many people living in captivity were well aware of white hypocrisy in professing a religious worldview that perpetrated the brutalities of a life in bondage. For many of them, the afterlife meant the absence of slaveowners, as succinctly stated by one escaped slave who refused to believe "that a slaveholder can get to heaven";[22] the Christianity of enslaved people provided a powerful moral voice in speaking out against the nation's continued endorsement of human bondage.

On a few occasions the enslaved individuals' more revolutionary interpretation of the Christian message led to slave rebellions. In 1800, for instance, a group of slaves planned an insurrection in Richmond, Virginia, that became known as "Gabriel's rebellion," in which religion played a key role. One of the organizers was a preacher who invoked biblical interpretations; he likened their plot to the cause of the Israelites, who also faced an adversary of far greater numbers. Once this planned attack on white society was discovered and put down, laws were passed in Virginia and South Carolina that prohibited blacks from assembling "for the purpose of mental instruction or religious worship."[23]

Another slave rebellion in Virginia was led by Nat Turner (1800–1831) in 1831; fifty-five whites and roughly two hundred blacks were killed in the uprising, including the execution of fifty-six blacks in the aftermath of the rebellion. It seems that Turner understood his insurrection as an act of religious duty; he had received religious visions much of his life, and he was known locally as "the Prophet." According to testimony compiled by his white lawyer, who took it upon himself to publish *The Confessions of Nat Turner: The Leader of the Late Insurrection in Southampton, Virginia* (1831), Turner experienced a vision in 1828:

> I heard a loud noise in the heavens, and the Spirit instantly appeared to me and said the Serpent was loosened, and Christ had laid down the yoke he had borne for the sins of men, and that I should take it on and fight against the Serpent, for the time was fast approaching when the first should be last and the last should be first.

This vision convinced Turner of his need to take up arms against his white enemy, and he soon began plotting his insurrection. As he and his followers shed the blood of white slaveowners and their families, terror spread throughout southern slaveholding regions. The purported religious justifications of Turner's vengeance only heightened white fears about the dangers of religious instruction and devotional practices of enslaved people; South Carolina responded to the Turner rebellion by strengthening prohibitions against religious gatherings of African Americans.[24]

NAT TURNER & HIS CONFEDERATES IN CONFERENCE.

Figure 7.3 This engraving of the infamous slave insurgent Nat Turner appeared in a Civil War-era book titled *History of American Conspiracies*; the caption reads, "Nat Turner & his confederates in conference." Motivated by a religious vision, Turner's rebellion registered terror among slaveowners everywhere. (Courtesy of New York Public Library, #1229308.)

The fear inspired among white Americans by slave rebellions, not only in the south but throughout the nation, affirmed their assumptions about the African race. Dominant racial attitudes among Euro-Americans in nineteenth-century America widened a moral gulf between blacks and whites among Christians in America; for most of white society, perceived racial differences sharply delineated social boundaries between themselves and other cultural groups, especially African Americans, Native Americans, Mexicans, and later in the century Chinese and other Asians. With only rare exceptions of the most zealous abolitionists, racist assumptions for the most part went unchallenged among the majority white citizenship of the United States, even in the north; for many supporters of abolition, the issue focused solely on the moral question of enslaving others and usually did not seriously challenge racist assumptions about the inherent differences between racial groups. Most white northerners assumed that slavery had made the black race incapable of full participation in a free society, and some argued that physical differences or, for a few, God's providence, had made black people inferior to the white race.[25]

Box 7.2   Race

In the modern world, racial differences have played significant roles in social organization and have often contributed to conflicts between people. These differences, much like gender, rely more on social and cultural categories rather than on biological features or characteristics. The presumption of natural, biological differences between races derives from classifications of people based on shared physical features, most notably skin pigmentation; these categories originated during the Enlightenment as part of the early scientific studies of natural history.[26] Biological and anthropological studies in the twentieth century, however, have concluded that the degree of variation within each racial category far exceeds variation between purported races, with uncertain boundaries between their respective characteristics; this lack of clarity regarding racial differences makes identifying specific racial categories problematic if not impossible.[27] Nevertheless, claims of racial difference have had wide acceptance in the modern world, mainly in justifying social, cultural, and economic disparities by naturalizing presumed hierarchies associated with constructed racial categories. These racist assumptions can appear explicitly in interpersonal relations between individuals or groups; more commonly, they remain implicit in "common-sense" attitudes based on unexamined prejudices; and they can take the form of "institutionalized racism" at the social level with disparities in housing, education, job opportunities, healthcare, and other social benefits aligned with and explained by purported racial categories.[28]

Religious justifications have often supported the presumption of racial differences for the benefit of Euro-American Christians, especially regarding attitudes toward Africans and people of African descent. The biblical "**myth of Ham**" in the Book of Genesis, for example, validated the enslavement of Africans; in this story, the patriarch Noah curses Canaan (the son of Ham, Noah's youngest son) and his descendants by stating, "the lowest of slaves shall he be to his brothers."[29] When medieval Arabs began importing slaves from East Africa, they regarded Ham as the progenitor of all Africans and attributed the darker skin of Africans to the curse on Ham's descendants.[30] This legend of the Hamitic curse subsequently became a popular justification of divinely ordained slavery among religiously minded proslavery defenders in the American south.[31]

The perception of racial differences has also affected Euro-American attitudes toward Native Americans. Throughout history, Euro-Americans have demonstrated a confusing ambivalence about native peoples, with perceived racial differences justifying a presumed natural basis for cultural and religious differences. One clear instance of this ambivalence in nineteenth-century America can be seen in *The Book of Mormon*, which explains racial differences according to its epic tale of Israelites in ancient America. The Mormon story separates the native inhabitants of the continent into two warring factions, the Nephites and the Lamanites; the latter, ancestors of the native peoples still living in the Americas when Joseph Smith, Jr. (1805–1844) first published his holy book in 1830, lose their whiteness in a divine curse: "wherefore, as they were white, and exceedingly fair and delightsome, that they might not be enticing unto my people the Lord God did cause a skin of blackness to come upon them."[32] As a cursed people of darkened skin, Native Americans stood outside the holy community that the Mormons sought to establish in the American west; at the same time, however, they were capable of restoration to the piety of their original ancestors. In fact, the title page of *The Book of Mormon* itself states that it is written specifically for the Lamanites of the contemporary world, "to show [them] what great things the Lord hath done for their fathers … that they are not cast off forever."

Abolitionism

Despite a society deeply divided along perceived lines of racial differences, a small but vocal group of Americans opposed to slavery began to be heard in the 1830s and grew in size and influence over the following decades. Picking up the call from African American voices, most white abolitionists relied on Christian moral teachings to oppose what they regarded as the abomination of slavery. The earliest religious opponents to slavery in America were the Society of Friends (i.e., Quakers), whose Germantown Quaker Petition against Slavery in 1688 represents the first formal call to end slavery in Britain's American colonies.[33] Quakers were among the very few religious groups in America that refused a general toleration of slavery, and they became the dominant group promoting abolition prior to 1830.[34] By the 1830s, however, the Society of Friends began finding a growing number of allies in its opposition to slavery.

One of the more forceful allies calling for radical abolition was William Lloyd Garrison (1805–1879), whose periodical *The Liberator* served as a leading mouthpiece of the movement in the antebellum period. Garrison and other like-minded antislavery advocates convened in Philadelphia in 1833 to establish the American Anti-Slavery Society (AAS). The group's constitution, authored by Garrison, references the Christian Bible but also alludes to the revolutionary language of the Declaration of Independence; it begins by noting that "the Most High God 'hath made of one blood all nations of men to dwell on all the face of the earth,' and hath commanded them to love their neighbors as themselves"; it goes on to declare that "Slavery is contrary to the principles of natural justice, of our republican form of government, and of the Christian religion," concluding that "we believe we owe it to the oppressed, to our fellow-citizens who hold slaves, to our whole country, to posterity, and to God, to do all that is lawfully in our power to bring about the extinction of Slavery." Their radical demand for ending slavery and immediately emancipating all slaves was controversial, but it struck a chord with a significant following in the north; within five years, the AAS had over one thousand chapters with roughly a quarter million members, many of them veterans of religious revivals of the Second Great Awakening.[35] The tide began to turn against the quiet acceptance of slavery in America.

The abolition movement from the beginning had an interracial component, especially in the integrationist philosophy of the AAS leadership.[36] Frederick Douglass (1818–1895) and other prominent African Americans were among the early leaders of the Society and spoke at AAS meetings and other gatherings of antislavery advocates. A rival organization that formed in 1840, the American and Foreign Anti-Slavery Society (AFASS), also included African Americans among its leadership; in fact, blacks were far more visible among AFASS officers than they were in the AAS. The AFASS had closer ties to Protestant churches, especially those of an evangelical orientation; nearly half of the leaders were ordained clergy, and a significant number of these were African Americans.[37]

Southern Christians, however, did not stand idly by while the northern abolitionists campaigned for the end of slavery. As the abolitionists gained momentum, southern religious leaders responded with theological arguments justifying the south's "peculiar institution" of slavery. An essay by a Baptist minister from

---

Box 7.3   Lucretia Mott (1793–1880)

Among the most influential female abolitionists was the outspoken Quaker activist Lucretia Coffin Mott. Despite her matronly appearance and disposition, she gained notoriety for her zealous activism as both an abolitionist and a women's rights crusader. Mott relished the role of self-proclaimed heretic when it came to what she regarded as the abomination of slavery; disputing the criticisms of fellow Quakers who preferred a quietist view of their religion, Mott declared that it was the duty of reformers to "stand out in our heresy," not conforming to the norms of a society and religious traditions that condoned injustices. She characterized the early adherents of the Society of Friends as "agitators; disturbers of the peace," and she perpetuated that strain of Quaker tradition in her abolitionist campaigns.[38]

Mott's career exemplifies the confluence of religious sentiment and social activism in nineteenth-century America that produced both the abolitionist and the women's rights movements. One of the few women present at the founding of the American Anti-Slavery Society in 1833, Mott was also an organizer and "the moving spirit" of the first women's rights convention, at Seneca Falls, New York, in 1848. For her, however, her Quaker faith insisted on a vision that went beyond the immediate goals of the women's rights movement. Unlike other delegates at the Seneca Falls convention, most notably Elizabeth Cady Stanton (1815–1902), Mott's Quaker commitments convinced her of the need to link the rights of women to other social justice issues, particularly antislavery, prison reform, temperance, and pacifism.[39]

The pacifist commitments of her Quakerism also made the elderly Mott an opponent of the Civil War. Her radical abolitionist sentiments gave her a low opinion of Abraham Lincoln (1809–1865), especially early in his presidency; she regarded him as a "miserable compromiser." Rather than armed conflict, Mott supported moral means as "more effectual," insisting that "moral protest & demand of the people" were "likely to do more, than any of the armies have yet accomplished,"[40] anticipating to some extent the nonviolent protests of the Civil Rights Movement in the twentieth century. A pacifist to the end, Mott never compromised her radical Quaker views.

Virginia, Thornton Stringfellow (1788–1869), circulated widely throughout the south in 1856; using arguments and references familiar in southern religious circles, Stringfellow's treatise "A Scriptural View of Slavery" explicates biblical support condoning enslavement. It sets out to demonstrate

Figure 7.4   Activist Lucretia Mott exemplified the Quaker virtues of social protest as an "agitator" who advocated the duty to "stand out in our heresy" in her public efforts as a women's rights leader and abolitionist. (Courtesy of the Library of Congress, LC-USZ62-42559.)

that the institution of slavery has received, in the first place,

1st. The sanction of the Almighty in the Patriarchal age.

2d. That it was incorporated into the only National Constitution which ever emanated from God.

3d. That its legality was recognized, and its relative duties regulated, by Jesus Christ in his kingdom.[41]

Stringfellow begins by identifying what would serve many of the theological defenders of slavery as the fundamental justification for enslaving Africans and their descendants: "The first recorded language which was ever uttered in relation to slavery, is the inspired language of Noah."[42] Noah's infamous curse condemning Canaan, the son of his youngest son Ham, to a life of servitude became *prima facie* evidence of divine blessing on southern practices of racial slavery.

Box 7.4   Archaeological evidence justifying slavery

Christian theological arguments in nineteenth-century America over moral justifications for slavery extended to the nascent scientific field of archaeology. At stake were two fundamentally opposing theories about the origins of humans. On the one hand there were "monogenesis" claims that all humans have a common origin. Religious support for this view comes from the biblical account that all humans descend from the original couple, Adam and Eve. Northern opponents of slavery favored this interpretation, which reasoned that, since all people belonged to a single human family, there could not be moral justification for enslaving each other. Proponents of slavery, on the other hand, relied on archaeological evidence of different groups of people roaming the earth long before Moses, Abraham, and even Adam; they espoused the theory of "polygenesis," which recognizes distinct races with different origins. Southern physician Josiah Nott (1804–1873) advocated this latter position to great acclaim among those defending the right to own slaves; his 1854 book, *Types of Mankind*, includes two chapters presenting scientific refutations of the biblical account of common human origins in Genesis.[43] For polygenesists, interpretations of the Bible positing a single race are mistaken and not supported by scientific archaeological evidence. Moreover, the enslavement of wholly different and unrelated species did not pose a moral dilemma, and in fact was amply justified in both God's law and natural law.

These different assumptions about human origins came to national attention in the 1860s with archaeological discoveries at the Newark Earthworks, ancient monumental structures laid out in massive geometric forms in central Ohio. In 1860, a local surveyor and antiquarian David Wyrick (1804–1864) unearthed a small carved and polished stone with an inscription in ancient Hebrew buried in the Newark Earthworks. For Wyrick and others, this artifact confirmed the so-called "Jewish theory," that the Earthworks had been built by the Lost Tribes of Israel, a widespread nineteenth-century explanation of ancient America that survives today as a central component of *The Book of Mormon*. Although many thought the discovery was a hoax, a second artifact, the "Decalogue Stone," so-called because of its Hebrew inscription of the Ten Commandments, was found nearby five months later, further confirming that ancient Israelites had built the Earthworks. This material evidence that ancient Israelites had constructed the Earthworks bolstered the monogenesis theory of the biblical account, thus demonstrating the moral transgression of slavery. Ironically, this notion that a tribe of wayward Jews built these ancient structures relied on racist assumptions that Native American people were incapable of the mathematical preciseness and engineering sophistication needed to construct the Newark

Earthworks. In contrast, proponents of the polygenetic theory of human races insisted on evidence of a Native American origin for the Earthworks, which in turn contradicted the biblical account of a single race descended from the original human couple of Adam and Eve, thus morally justifying the enslavement of other racially distinct people.

Once the nation had settled the question of slavery with the Civil War, the controversy over the "holy stones" of Newark, Ohio, faded from public memory; today experts who have examined the two stones that Wyrick found nearly all agree that they were nineteenth-century artifacts planted in the Earthworks for Wyrick to find, although it remains unclear whether Wyrick himself was in on the hoax.[44]

Catholics in the Civil War

Reverend Stringfellow was not alone in pointing out biblical sanction in favor of slavery. Numerous Protestant preachers, theologians, and **lay** members filled books, pamphlets, and newspapers with religious evidence condoning human bondage. But, although Protestant thinkers were most prominent among the defenders of slavery on religious grounds, they were not the only people who owned slaves. Going back to colonial times, a number of Catholics in Spanish, French, and English settlements had slaves. Like others in the American south, Catholics relied on enslaved laborers to work plantations and build churches and to enable the financial prosperity that allowed them to contribute money and other resources to missionary and **proselytization** efforts. Their acceptance of slavery found support in the teachings of the Catholic Church. Catholic justifications of slavery were articulated, for instance, in a defense of the institutions of bondage in 1840 by the South Carolina bishop John England (1786–1842), originally from Ireland, who became a vocal apologist for the compatibility of Catholicism and American democracy. Personally, Bishop England regarded slavery as repugnant and devoted much attention to the education and pastoral care of African Americans, but he nevertheless defended slaveholding as consistent with Christian scriptures and tradition; consequently, his defense of slavery made him widely respected and accepted even by its non-Catholic advocates.[45]

Catholic support of slavery, even among northern Catholics, derived in part from their distrust of the abolitionist movement, which most Catholics recognized as **nativist** and anti-Catholic. The rhetoric of such groups as the Know-Nothing Party had to some extent equated Catholicism with slavery, characterizing Catholics as the natural enemies of abolition. Consequently, most Catholics remained wary of supporting a cause that in their understanding was essentially hostile to their religion.[46] As a result, Catholics as a whole tended to avoid the moral debate. For the most part, American bishops regarded the question of slavery as a sensitive and divisive political issue that they preferred to stay away from; and, since it was a civil institution, the bishops tended to believe that resolution of the slavery question would have to come from civil and legislative means, not religious involvement. But, when war broke out between north and south, the Southern Catholic bishops immediately supported the Confederacy. Northern Catholics, in contrast, were slower to acknowledge the Union cause; eventually, the northern bishops showed reluctant support of the Union, but they remained unenthusiastic about ending slavery. The Civil War, they argued, was justifiable only on constitutional grounds, not on moral opposition to holding people in bondage.[47]

Like Americans of virtually all religious persuasions, Roman Catholics were deeply involved in the war effort, and Church leaders on both sides of the Civil War served as diplomats for their respective governments. Catholic clergy served both armies as chaplains, and by one estimate roughly twenty percent of Civil War nurses were Catholic nuns. Their involvement in the Civil War transformed American Catholicism, which afterward enjoyed greater acceptance in American society; non-Catholic Americans were more willing to accept Catholics, who had fought, nursed, consoled, and sacrificed on both sides of the conflict. Nativist resentment of Catholics subsided considerably during and after the war, to the point where at least one observer in 1868 could make the claim, somewhat exaggerated, that the "despised minority" of Catholics in America was now "well on its way to complete acceptance in Protestant American society." It would still be nearly a century before Catholics could be confident in complete acceptance, but the Civil War marked an important turning point in American attitudes toward Catholicism.[48]

Jews in the Civil War

Similarly to Catholics, American Jews suffered divided loyalties during the Civil War. The great influx of Jewish immigrants in the antebellum period brought Jewish communities to every region of the United States. Consequently, Jews were among the supporters on both sides of the slavery debate, with at least a few Jewish voices among the northern abolitionists and a number of Jewish slaveholders disbursed throughout the south. For the most part, however, Jews were wary of getting involved in controversial, highly visible issues of the day. This was particularly frustrating and puzzling to some northern abolitionists, who remarked in 1853, "The objects of so much mean prejudice and unrighteous oppression as the Jews have been for ages, surely they, it would seem, more than any other denomination, ought to be the enemies of caste, and the friends of universal freedom."[49] A few northern Jews, in fact, did embrace the abolitionist cause; most were Reform Jews, with the important exception of Orthodox Rabbi Sabato Morais (1823–1897) of Philadelphia. The preponderance of the Reform tradition among Jewish abolitionists was in large part a result of the success of the Reform movement in the United States, which had claimed a majority of the Jewish congregations by the beginning of the Civil War. But it also stemmed from the theological orientation of the Reform tradition, concisely summarized by Reform leader and abolitionist David Einhorn (1809–1879), who characterized the Reform creed as "one humanity, all of whose members, being of the same heavenly and earthly origin, possess a like nobility of birth and a claim to equal rights, equal laws, and in an equal share of happiness."[50] At least from the perspective of one leading Jewish abolitionist, Reform Judaism and abolition shared a common set of concerns and commitments to a liberated humanity.

On the other hand, a good number of other Jews felt no common cause with the abolitionists. Rabbi Morris Jacob Raphall (1798–1868), an Orthodox leader in New York City, preached a highly controversial sermon in January 1861 depicting abolitionists as "impulsive declaimers, gifted with great zeal, but little knowledge; more eloquent than learned; better able to excite our passions than to satisfy our reason." He then proceeded to explicate the biblical justifications of slavery so often rehearsed by southern proslavery apologists, concluding that "slaveholding is no sin" precisely because "slave property is expressly placed under the protection of the Ten Commandments."[51] This defense of southern slaveholders by a prominent northern Jew was immediately embraced in the south as evidence of Jewish support for southern secession. But, beyond its political implications, the controversy surrounding Rabbi Raphall's sermon also indicated a theological divide between the more conservative Orthodox Jews, who tended toward literal interpretations of the Torah, and the more liberal-minded Reform Jews, who were more willing to interpret the sacred texts historically and more critically.[52]

In contrast, nearly all Jews in the south supported slavery. The relatively small number of southern Jews and their thin distribution throughout the south made their opinions on social issues hardly distinctive from those of their non-Jewish neighbors. Moreover, the race-based social hierarchy in the south gave Jews, as whites, a social advantage that was less pronounced in the north.[53]

The most prominent southern Jew in the Civil War era was Judah Benjamin (1811–1884), whose father was among the founders of the first Reform congregation in Charleston, South Carolina. Benjamin never drew attention to his ancestral religion; in fact, he harbored ambivalence about his Jewish heritage, evident in his willingness to be married in a Catholic church: early in his career, Benjamin practiced law in New Orleans, where he married a Catholic French Creole woman. Elected to the United States Senate in 1853, Benjamin was the first Jew offered a seat on the US Supreme Court, a position he declined to accept, preferring instead to remain a Senator. Once war broke out, Benjamin found himself within the inner circle of the southern elite as a close confidante of Confederate President Jefferson Davis (1808–1889) and a member of his cabinet. Benjamin initially served as Attorney General of the Confederacy. He soon took over as Secretary of War, but his lack of military experience proved disastrous for the Confederates, and so President Davis subsequently made him the Confederacy's Secretary of State; in this role he also assumed the position of Confederate spymaster, overseeing covert operations in the north. When the war ended, Benjamin successfully fled to England to avoid treason charges. There he enjoyed a successful career in commercial law.[54]

Although Benjamin routinely downplayed and largely disregarded his Jewishness, his critics both north and south constantly brought it up; he suffered anti-Semitic attacks throughout his life. This may explain his unwillingness to draw attention to his status as a southern Jew, but it also reveals something about religious diversity in the Confederacy. The south was by no means entirely Protestant in the nineteenth century. Southern religious diversity included Jews, Catholics, Native American indigenous practitioners, the persistence of indigenous African traditions and even some remnants of Muslim practitioners among the African American populations, both slave and free. On the other hand, Benjamin's reluctance to draw attention to himself as a Jew may indicate a dominant social view of southerners, especially those supporting the Confederacy, as a single people without differences. Similarly to many Confederate loyalists, Benjamin presented himself above all as a southerner rather than a Jew.

During the war, Jews fought on both sides, but anti-Semitism sometimes superseded gratitude for Jewish contributions. This was the case with General Order Number 11 issued by General Ulysses S. Grant (1822–1885) in December 1862, what his wife called "That obnoxious order." It expelled from the Tennessee Territory held by Grant "The Jews, as a class," because of their perceived violations of trade regulations. Relying on current stereotypes of "Jew pedlars," Grant sought to banish all Jewish people from the region, ignoring the fact that a number of loyal Jews were among his own soldiers. When word of the order reached Washington, DC, it was quickly revoked. The official explanation sent to Grant stated, "The President has no objection to your expelling traders & Jew pedlars, which I suppose was the object of your order, but as it in terms prescribed an entire religious class, some of whom are fighting in our ranks, the President deemed necessary to revoke it." General Grant rescinded his order and avoided in later years explaining his reasons for targeting an "entire religious class" for expulsion.[55]

Other religious slaveholders

Even among groups less willing to identify as southerner Confederates, slavery abounded. Numerous Native American groups, for instance, had their own ancestral traditions of servitude, although virtually all were markedly different from the race-based plantation slavery that became dominant in the southern United States. Some of these groups, however, began to adopt Euro-American versions of slave-ownership, especially those who had close contact with white society. The so-called "Five Civilized Tribes" – the Cherokee, Chickasaw, Choctaw, Creek (or Muskogee), and Seminole nations – held a relatively large number of African American slaves. When these groups were forced out of their homelands along the Trail of Tears in the 1830s, many of them took their slaves with them.[56]

Surprisingly, even a few African Americans could be counted among the slave-holders. In nearly all cases, however, black ownership of slaves involved family members, either a free husband purchasing his enslaved wife or vice versa. In many cases enslaved children were also purchased. In at least a few instances, spouses hesitated to emancipate their purchased mate until it was certain that the marriage would last, reserving the right to sell their spouse if the marital relationship did not go well.[57]

In all, one's stance on slavery, it seems, did not align with any particular religious orientation. The moral debate that engrossed American consciences in the antebellum period crossed religious lines and inserted indomitable wedges within religious bodies. Among the largest of the Protestant groups, the Presbyterians were the first to suffer a denominational split when they divided into separate northern and southern denominations in 1837; the Methodists split into separate bodies in 1844, and the Baptists followed with the formation of the separate Southern Baptist Convention in 1845. Pious people on both sides found ways to reconcile their religious commitments with their political allegiances on the slave question, even when it meant irreconcilable differences with their coreligionists.

The Nation at War

As the controversy over slavery raged among American Christians, the nation moved ever closer to armed conflict. The raid led by John Brown (1800–1859) in 1859 on the United States Armory and Arsenal at Harpers Ferry, Virginia, galvanized the resolve on both sides and deepened the divisions between the proslavery and antislavery factions. Brown was a zealous abolitionist with close ties to Frederick Douglass and other antislavery leaders. Opposed to the pacifist inclinations of many abolitionists, including William Lloyd Garrison, Brown sought to rid the nation of slavery through armed insurrection, relying on the uprising of slaves to initiate a forceful overthrow of southern slaveholders. With a small band of armed supporters, including five African Americans, Brown quickly captured the Virginia arsenal in October 1859, but the government response was rapid and overwhelming, and soon the whole affair ended with the capture of a wounded Brown. Nearly half of his company was killed in the raid, and Brown himself, still wounded and carried on a stretcher, was put on trial. The immediate sensation of the court proceedings gave Brown a stage for depicting himself as a martyr for the antislavery cause, an image played up in the northern press, while in the south the papers demonized him as "an irresponsible madman." Drawing on his Calvinist heritage, Brown presented himself as God's instrument in the tradition of Christian biblical heroes, including Old Testament figures such as Moses and Samson and New Testament disciples Peter and Paul, even Jesus himself; a millennialist logic justified his raid, as he explained in a prison letter: "our seeming disaster will ultimately result in the most glorious success." Brown's success in exploiting the publicity surrounding his trial to present himself as a national martyr, a sacrificial lamb in the Christian tradition to bring an end to the abomination of slavery in the United States, was evident in the response of many northerners; as Ralph Waldo Emerson remarked, Brown stood as "the Saint ... whose martyrdom ... will make the gallows as glorious as the Cross."[58]

The religious zeal of John Brown and other leading abolitionists translated to the political realm as the divisions between north and south became insurmountable. When war broke out in early 1861 following the election of Abraham Lincoln as president and the consequent secession of southern states from the Union, it was clear that the passionate influences of evangelical Protestantism on both sides could not be contained by the American democratic system; the most prominent political issues, above all slavery, were at their core moral issues that could not be solved by political compromises.[59] The resultant moral crises thrust the United States into the most devastating military conflict in its history.

For many Americans at the time, the Civil War itself had millennialist meaning; as the war drew to a close in early 1865 and Americans both north and south began

Figure 7.5   The abolitionist John Brown encounters a slave mother and her child as he is being led to his execution in this 1867 painting by artist Thomas S. Noble (1835–1907), himself a Confederate Army veteran who professed a hatred of slavery. (Courtesy of New York Public Library, #1162899.)

looking beyond the conflict, Protestant millennialism became the frame for a hopeful future of reconciliation and rebuilding. The nation turned its attention to the gaunt figure of its president, Abraham Lincoln, as he delivered his Second Inaugural Address in March 1865, little more than a month before losing his own life to an assassin's bullet. In what amounts to a theological rendering of the conflict, Lincoln characterized the immensity of suffering, destruction, and loss in the war as divine retribution for the nation's sinful perpetuation of human slavery: "Fondly do we hope," he exclaimed,

> fervently do we pray – that this mighty scourge of war may speedily pass away. Yet, if God wills that it continue, until all the wealth piled by the bondman's two hundred and fifty years of unrequited toil shall be sunk, and until every drop of blood drawn with the lash, shall be paid by another drawn with the sword, as was said three thousand years ago, so still it must be said, "the judgments of the Lord, are true and righteous altogether."

But the searing judgments of God were not the final word in Lincoln's message to the nation; his address ends with a hopeful image of reconciliation between foes that would herald a lasting peace:

> With malice toward none; with charity for all; with firmness in the right, as God gives us to see the right, let us strive on to finish the work we are in; to bind up the nation's wounds; to care for him who shall have borne the battle, and for his widow, and his orphan – to do all which may achieve and cherish a just, and a lasting peace, among ourselves, and with all nations.[60]

Reconstructing the Nation

At the end of the Civil War, both northerners and southerners attempted to interpret the meaning of the war in millennialist terms. For those embroiled in the conflict, their various religious views provided languages and structures of meaning to make sense of such senseless mayhem, destruction, and loss. Abraham Lincoln, most notably in his Second Inaugural Address, was especially adept at applying religious language to frame the great struggle in more cosmic nationalistic terms. His murder at the very end of the war sealed the cosmic meanings as he became, at least in the minds of many northern Christians, the ultimate martyr for the good of the country. America was a nation reunited and baptized in holy blood, and thus the millennialist view of the nation seemed assuredly fulfilled; now that it had eliminated the sinful institution of slavery, many thought, America was prepared to fulfill its millennial potential.

This resurgence of millennialist hope among Protestants turned American attentions optimistically toward a prosperous future, with significant resolve to build a stronger industrial economy and to extend civilization westward across the continent; together these twin developments involved the necessity of conquest, often with the religious justification of conquering non-Christian peoples for Christ. The optimism of renewed Manifest Destiny inspired missionary efforts among newly freed slaves in the southern states, as well as aggressive military actions against what many Euro-Americans regarded as "heathen" and "savage" Native Americans in western territories.

Rebuilding the American south

During the period following the Civil War, known as Reconstruction, African Americans established new Christian congregations and built many churches, especially in the south. The African Methodist Episcopal Church (commonly known as AME), the African Methodist Episcopal Zion Church, and the Colored (later renamed Christian) Methodist Episcopal Church all experienced spectacular growth in membership during the decades following the Civil War, as did African American Baptist congregations, which proliferated throughout the southern region of the country. A significant number of the independent African American Baptist congregations eventually came together in 1895 to form the National Baptist Convention, with headquarters in Nashville, Tennessee.[61]

In many cases, Christian congregations became the central social institution for African American communities, centers for social interaction, political solidarity, and economic opportunity. Moreover, churches often provided political leadership for African Americans; in South Carolina, as one example, AME missionary Richard Harvey Cain (1825–1887) came south in 1865 to help organize congregations among the newly freed blacks. He not only became an important religious leader in the south but also entered the political arena during Reconstruction and eventually was elected to the US Congress as a representative from South Carolina.[62]

Another key contribution of Christians in the aftermath of emancipation was the establishment of educational institutions for African Americans. The predominantly Congregationalist organization the American Missionary Association, with the help of a Methodist philanthropist from Pittsburgh, Pennsylvania, opened the Avery Institute in Charleston, South Carolina, a free secondary school for African American students. Numerous other schools and seminaries for African Americans were established by Freedmen's Aid Societies and a host of Protestant denominational organizations. Among the colleges and universities opened during Reconstruction to serve African American students were Clark Atlanta University (originally two separate institutions) in Atlanta, Georgia; Fisk University in Nashville, Tennessee; Howard University in Washington, DC; Morehouse College; and Wilberforce University in Ohio (originally started in 1856 by Methodists and the AME Church but reopened after the Civil War by the latter).

As African Americans during the Reconstruction years realized opportunities in education, in political life, and in forming religious communities, some Euro-Americans in the south attempted to reassert white supremacy, often appealing to religious means in renouncing the advancement of blacks. One group that saw rapid growth after its founding in 1866 in Tennessee was the Ku Klux Klan, formed in defense of "a white man's government in this country" and "opposed to negro equality, both social and political," according to the professed views of new members as stipulated in the Klan's "Prescript." Their creed states clearly the evangelical, providential commitments of the organization, linking their reverence for God to nationalist sentiment: "We, the Order of the [Ku Klux Klan], reverentially acknowledge the majesty and supremacy of the Divine Being, and recognize the goodness and providence of the same. And we recognize our relation to the United States Government, the supremacy of the Constitution, the Constitutional Laws thereof, and the Union of the States thereunder."[63] The terror that the Klansmen perpetrated on African Americans as well as the Klan's resistance to the occupying forces of the federal government during Reconstruction relied to a large extent on Protestant religious orientations linked to claims of divine entitlement for white people.

Like most social movements, the Ku Klux Klan **ritualized** much of their formal activities. Relying to a large extent on popular forms of theater in the nineteenth century, Klansmen donned costumes and were sometimes mistaken for circus performers.[64] Their elaborate performances were aimed at intimidating, humiliating, and sometimes harming, even killing, their enemies. Actual attacks on their victims often took the form of ritualized performances involving the torture and killing of accused lawbreakers in a wave of lynching rituals meant to enforce racial and gender roles that emphasized white male supremacy. The reign of terror brought by the Ku Klux Klan and other southern vigilante groups haunted southern states in the aftermath of the Civil War, drawing on both religious ritual and theatrical performance in gruesome acts of intense cruelty.[65]

Christianizing the American west

While the southern states created a new postbellum reality that reasserted racial divides, a different kind of reality was taking form in the western states and territories. There, a postbellum resurgence of Manifest Destiny asserted a Christian identity. Euro-American Protestants resolved to purge the nation of "heathen" influences, especially those of Native American religions, either through conversions to Christianity via the work of missionaries sent to "civilize the savages" or through outright warfare to subdue and confine non-Christian peoples. The end of the Civil War allowed more resources to be allocated for building railroads and other infrastructure in western territories, encouraging a surge of settlers wanting to rebuild their war-torn lives in new lands. At the same time, military resources were redirected to assist in the conquest and settlement of the American west. Alongside and sometimes ahead of the soldiers and the settlers were Christian missionaries determined to bring the religion of "civilized" people to what they regarded as untutored and irreligious "savages." Intent on fulfilling the promise of Manifest Destiny with Christian civilization stretching across the whole of the North American continent, Euro-Americans set out to systematically disassemble the vestiges of native cultures.

Numerous Native American groups continued to inhabit much of the territory in the west, and virtually all of them continued their indigenous sacred traditions, even as they embraced the introduction of foreign religions. As early as the 1830s, a few tribal people in the northwestern intermountain region had sent delegations east to the American city of St. Louis asking for Christian missionaries to bring the "white religion" to their people. It remains unclear exactly what the native peoples expected from these expeditions, but word spread throughout Christian America that western Indians were in desperate need of Christianity, and within a decade both Catholic and Protestant missionaries were establishing themselves in the Pacific northwest. Among the first to respond to these requests were the Catholic Jesuits, who already had established missionary ventures out of the St. Louis area. In 1840 the Flemish Jesuit Father Pierre-Jean De Smet (1801–1873) went to establish a mission among the Salish (often referred to as Flathead), the Coeur d'Alene, and the Pend d'Oreilles peoples in what is now northern Idaho and western Montana.[66] Other Jesuits followed, and by the 1850s Catholic missions were serving native peoples throughout the Pacific northwest.[67] Protestant groups also sent missionaries to the American northwest; Methodists established a mission in Oregon's Willamette Valley in 1834, and Presbyterian missionaries followed with mission stations built among several native tribes in what is now Washington state.[68]

As Christian missionaries labored to introduce their religion to native tribes in the Pacific northwest, other religious orientations and practices were entering North America from Asia. Initially, a flood of Chinese immigrants in search of Gam Saan, or Gold Mountain, landed on the Pacific coast and spread inland to mining towns in California, and later to Idaho, Montana, Nevada, Oregon, and elsewhere in the west. Predominately younger males, these Chinese immigrants to America came primarily for economic opportunities, planning to make their fortunes and then return to their Chinese homeland. Consequently, they established very little in the way of a permanent religious presence in America; nevertheless, Asian sojourners in the American west brought with them their native religious orientations and practices, including Buddhism, Confucianism, Taoism, and a variety of Chinese folk religious traditions.[69] Without temples, shrines, or religious leaders, however, their practices remained for the most part personal and private.

Mormons in the American west

Besides the religious orientations of Asians and Native Americans, another group in the intermountain region of Utah and the surrounding territories posed a different sort of challenge to the dominant Protestant view of Christian America. The

Figure 7.6 Fascination and repulsion, especially regarding plural marriage, defined popular attitudes toward Mormons by non-Mormon Americans in the nineteenth century. Their rightful place in the American nation became a political issue and even involved a military occupation. This nineteenth-century illustration depicts some of Brigham Young's wives in the Salt Lake City Tabernacle with the American flag draped over the railing beside them. (Image © CORBIS.)

Church of Jesus Christ of Latter-Day Saints, the Mormons, flourished under the leadership of Brigham Young (1801–1877) after settling in the Great Salt Lake basin. At first the relative isolation of their settlement removed them from direct conflict with non-Mormon Christians, but, with mining booms in California and Nevada, traffic through their territory increased significantly in the 1850s. Old animosities resurfaced, especially around the issue of plural marriage, which Brigham Young had encouraged, himself taking fifty-five wives;[70] ridding the country of the Mormons' polygamous practices became a key issue in the 1856 presidential race, as did their tenacious political independence, which aligned them with "states' rights" arguments regarding popular sovereignty that southerners proclaimed in defense of slavery. After his election the following year, President James Buchanan (1791–1868) sent federal troops to assist the newly appointed territorial governor of Utah to take over local government from the Mormon leader Brigham Young. The ensuing standoff, known as the "Utah War," was eventually settled without armed engagement, but the federal troops remained in the territory.[71]

Tensions over the military occupation as well as the increased number of non-Mormons passing through the Mormons' territory resulted in a brutal massacre of hapless travelers on their way to new lives in California, bringing national outrage toward the Utah Mormons. While passing through southwestern Utah, more than one hundred members of the Baker-Fancher party were killed by a local Mormon militia with help from a few Native American allies at a place known as Mountain Meadows; only a handful of small children were spared. It was initially blamed on Indians, but a subsequent investigation revealed that Mormons had conducted the raid and massacre and then orchestrated a cover-up to avoid jeopardizing Utah's bid for statehood.[72] It took nearly two decades to bring the leaders of the massacre to justice; even then, the militia leader John D. Lee (1812–1877), who was brought to trial and eventually executed for the crime, insisted that he was being made a scapegoat; Lee, who was subsequently excommunicated from the Church of Jesus Christ of Latter-Day Saints, blamed the Church leaders for drawing attention away from themselves by condemning him, and in his final words before facing a firing squad at the site of the Mountain Meadows massacre he exclaimed, "I have been sacrificed in a cowardly, dastardly manner."[73] His 1877 execution marked an official end to the investigation of the massacre, although national media coverage of his trial and execution only heightened anti-Mormon sentiments.

The repulsion over plural marriage and the perceived threat it represented to nineteenth-century Christian ideals of gender, family, and moral propriety kept the Mormons in the American popular imagination and made them a topic of political debate. In 1862, the US Congress passed the Morrill Anti-Bigamy Act, intended to dismantle plural marriage among the Mormons by prohibiting bigamy and adultery. President Abraham Lincoln signed the law, but, in an effort to appease the Mormons and keep them out of the Civil War, he made no effort to enforce the legislation. The Mormons, however, resented the criminalization of what they regarded as a sacred practice, and they challenged the law in the courts, arguing that it violated the constitutional guarantee of freedom of religion. In its first ever ruling on the First Amendment, the US Supreme Court in 1879 stated unanimously that the Bill of Rights protects religious beliefs and opinions but not practices, citing human sacrifice as a religious practice that would also justify government prohibitions; according to the court's opinion, polygamy represented an "odious" practice that the government was justified in outlawing.[74] The ruling did not bring an end to polygamy among Mormons, but it did indicate that conflict with the federal government would not abate as long as polygamy remained an official doctrine of the Church. Eventually, the Church reversed its policy on plural marriage. In 1890, under increasing pressure from the US government, Wilford Woodruff (1807–1898), president of the Church of Jesus Christ of Latter-Day Saints in Salt Lake City, the largest of the Mormon denominations, issued a "Manifesto" that declared "we are not teaching polygamy or plural marriage, nor permitting any person to enter into its practice." The document explained the Church's commitment to civic laws banning polygamous marriage arrangements, and it asserted the Church's intent to abide by such laws and to advise its member-ship "to refrain from contracting any marriage forbidden by the law of the land." Although it did not reverse existing plural marriages, the 1890 Manifesto ended all new polygamous relationships for the vast majority of Mormons, and, with the exception of a few small dissenting groups that broke off from the main Church over the issue, polygamy had disappeared from the Church of Jesus Christ of Latter-Day Saints by the early twentieth century.[75]

Diverse Voices of the Unified Nation

In the decade following the Civil War, the federal government reasserted its authority in rebuilding a unified nation. This included not only recovery from the physical destruction of war but also defining the ideals of a democratic nation newly freed from the scourge of slavery. Providing opportunities for African Americans to partici-pate fully in political processes included new constitutional guarantees abolishing slavery (the Thirteenth Amendment, 1865); affirming full citizenship for anyone "born or naturalized in the United States," including providing all citizens with "equal protection under the laws" (the Fourteenth Amendment, 1868); and granting voting rights without regard for "race, color, or previous condition of servitude" (the Fifteenth Amendment, 1870). At the same time, religious organizations assumed leadership in assimilating former slaves to a post-slavery society by forming new African American congregations and establishing schools, colleges, and universities serving African American students. Their efforts, however, also provoked resistance to the newfound freedoms and opportunities for African Americans in the southern states; using the religious resources of ritual performances, groups such as the Ku Klux Klan brought intimidation, violence, and terror to individuals perceived as upsetting traditional racial hierarchies.

Meanwhile, a resurgence of national expansion brought religious conflicts west-ward. Christian missionaries were at the forefront of efforts to contain Native American peoples by "civilizing" them, largely through religious instruction that sought to displace their native religious orientations with the stories, beliefs, and practices of Christianity. Likewise, Euro-Americans who deviated from the cultural norms of nineteenth-century American religious values, in particular Mormon settlers in the intermountain west who challenged marital standards with their polygamous arrangements, found themselves persecuted at the hands of the US government. Even the Supreme Court would not recognize the Mormons' consti-tutional rights to practice their religion freely according to their own interpreta-tions and commitments. The federal government colluded with dominant Protestant groups in nineteenth-century America to enforce narrowly defined boundaries of acceptable religious belief and practice.

The confluence of American civil culture and dominant Protestant attitudes tended to occlude the multiplicity of national origins and the diverse cultures, including the many religious orientations, that made up the American nation in the late nineteenth century. Dominant voices generated a discourse of national identity with clear racial, gender, and religious foundations; the prevalent view of Americanness in the final decades of the nineteenth century was a white, manly, Protestant citizen. All others, according to this discourse articulated in countless ways throughout nineteenth-century American culture, were subordinate to or, in the case of the Chinese, excluded altogether from the prerogatives of the manly white Christian of the American ideal; the providence of the Christian god had bestowed favor on white Protestant males, and they assumed their responsibilities with alacrity. But this confluence of racial, gender, and religious ideals could not erase the reality of a diverse American population, and marginalized groups did not always acquiesce to the dominant ideology. With good reason, the ideal of the white Protestant male American asserted itself with a degree of uncertainty, while other voices challenged its supremacy in the closing decades of the nineteenth century.

The diverse voices challenging the hegemony of white, male Protestant ideals included Hispanic Catholics in the American southwest, Mormons in the inter-mountain west, newly freed ex-slaves throughout the former Confederate states, and indigenous American peoples across the plains and throughout the American west. Moreover, Russian settlements in Alaska (which became a territory of the United States in 1867), native Hawaiians and other Polynesian peoples, Chinese and sundry other Asian immigrants, and the growing tide of newcomers arriving each year from various parts of Europe tended to view Americans as alien to their own cultural understandings, social traditions, and religious orientations. Protestant Christians, particularly those of evangelical tendencies, may have been a majority in the United States and have easily dominated public life and national discourse, but they were still a rather small and relatively insignificant voice even among Christians around the world, and certainly in a global context of religious people in general. The Civil War may have resolved some fundamental inner tensions in American national life, but it did not yet thrust the American people onto a global stage. In most places of the global community during the middle decades of the nineteenth century, the American millennialist light of the city on the hill remained a dim glow faintly noticed.

Questions for Discussion

(1) What role did providentialism play, specifically Manifest Destiny, in creating Protestant understandings of the American nation?

(2) Is Transcendentalism a religion? Explain why or why not.

(3) In what ways did religious beliefs and orientations contribute to the Civil War?

(4) Compare the experiences of African Americans in the American south and Native Americans in the American west in regard to their respective engagement with Protestant Christianity during the Reconstruction period. In particular, what factors made their experiences different?

(5)   How did religious differences affect relations between the US government and the Church of Jesus Christ of Latter-Day Saints in Utah?

Suggested Primary-Source Readings

Ralph Waldo Emerson, "Nature," in *Nature, Addresses and Lectures* (Boston, MA: Phillips, Sampson, 1850), 5–74: Emerson's seminal essay that inspired the Transcendentalist movement is available in many collections; the 1850 version is available online from Google Books.

Margaret Fuller, *Woman in the Nineteenth Century* (New York: Greeley & McElrath, 1845): Fuller's essay, originally titled "The Great Lawsuit: Man *versus* Men, Woman *versus* Women," uses a Transcendentalist theological perspective to argue for equal rights for women.

Frederick Douglass, *Narrative of the Life of Frederick Douglass* (New York: Oxford University Press, 1999): Douglass' autobiographical narrative includes much criticism of Christian hypocrisy among slaveholders, especially in the appendix, where Douglass specifies that he condemns "the *slaveholding religion* of this land" (emphasis in the original).

Abraham Lincoln, Second Inaugural Address: The text of Lincoln's last great speech, which frames the meaning of the Civil War in religious terms, is readily available online.

Pierre-Jean De Smet, "Religious Opinions of the Assiniboins" (1854) in *Life, Letters and Travels of Father Pierre-Jean De Smet, S. J., 1801–1873; Missionary Labors and Adventures among the Wild Tribes of the North American Indians*, 4 vols. (New York: F. P. Harper, 1905), volume 3, 933–45: The pioneering Jesuit missionary De Smet, who introduced Roman Catholicism to native peoples of the northern Rocky Mountain regions of western Montana and Idaho, relates his impressions of Native American religiosity.

Notes

1   Nicholas Guyatt, *Providence and the Invention of the United States, 1607–1876* (New York: Cambridge University Press, 2007), 221.
2   Ibid., 5.
3   Anders Stephanson, *Manifest Destiny: American Expansionism and the Empire of Right* (New York: Hill and Wang, 1995), 6.
4   Quoted in ibid., 42.
5   Guyatt, *Providence*, 227–230.
6   Ibid., 229.
7   Regarding Unitarianism, see David Robinson, *The Unitarians and the Universalists* (Westport, CT: Greenwood Press, 1985).
8   Regarding Emerson's views on religion and his understanding of human spirituality, see the introduction to Ralph Waldo Emerson, *The Spiritual Emerson: Essential Writings* (Boston, MA: Beacon Press, 2003). For the "Transcendentalist Controversy" in Unitarianism, see Robinson, *The Unitarians and the Universalists*, 75–86.
9   The lecture "The Transcendentalist" is available in Ralph Waldo Emerson, *Nature, Addresses and Lectures* (Boston, MA: Phillips, Sampson, 1850), 316–347.
10   Ibid., 59, 63.

11   Leigh Eric Schmidt, *Restless Souls: The Making of American Spirituality* (San Francisco, CA: HarperSanFrancisco, 2005), 29–35.

12   Henry David Thoreau, *Walden: A Fully Annotated Edition* (New Haven, CT: Yale University Press, 2004), 7, 108, 31. Regarding Thoreau's praise of solitude, see Schmidt, *Restless Souls*, 63–67.

13   David S. Reynolds, *Walt Whitman's America: A Cultural Biography* (New York: Knopf, 1995), 236.

14   Walt Whitman, *Leaves of Grass* (Brooklyn, NY: Printed by Andrew and James Rome, 1855), 13, 29.

15   Regarding Whitman's poetic response to the nation's turmoil in the 1850s, see Reynolds, *Walt Whitman's America*, 306–309.

16   Margaret Fuller, *Woman in the Nineteenth Century* (New York: Greeley & McElrath, 1845), 26.

17   Thomas A. Tweed and Stephen R. Prothero, eds., *Asian Religions in America: A Documentary History* (New York: Oxford University Press, 1999), 62.

18   Emerson, *Nature, Addresses and Lectures*, 327; see also Tweed and Prothero, *Asian Religions in America*, 92–93.

19   Quoted in Tweed and Prothero, *Asian Religions in America*, 96.

20   For helpful tables on enslaved and free black populations in American history up to the Civil War, see Ira Berlin, *Generations of Captivity: A History of African-American Slaves* (Cambridge, MA: Belknap Press of Harvard University Press, 2003), 272–279.

21   For example, Jarena Lee documents her success in altering the ways of a cruel slave-holder in Jarena Lee, "The Life and Religious Experience of Jarena Lee," in *Sisters of the Spirit: Three Black Women's Autobiographies of the Nineteenth Century*, ed. William L. Andrews (Bloomington: Indiana University Press, 1986), 46–47.

22   Quoted in Albert J. Raboteau, *Slave Religion: The "Invisible Institution" in the Antebellum South*, updated edn (New York: Oxford University Press, 2004), 291–292.

23   Ibid., 147.

24   As compiled by his attorney Thomas Ruffin Gray, Nat Turner's "confession" emphasizes, perhaps exaggerates, the fanatical religious motivations behind his murderous plot; it appears that Gray wished to quell fears in the south of a general malaise among enslaved people by portraying Turner as an aberrant religious fanatic. Nevertheless, Turner's reputation for religious visions and his profound interest in studying the Christian Bible indicate some degree of religious motivation in his plan. His "confession" appears in Milton C. Sernett, ed., *Afro-American Religious History: A Documentary Witness* (Durham, NC: Duke University Press, 1985), 88–99.

25   Berlin, *Generations of Captivity*, 232.

26   For a history of the modern notion of race, see George M. Fredrickson, *Racism: A Short History* (Princeton, NJ: Princeton University Press, 2002), 52–68.

27   See for instance the "American Anthropological Association Statement on 'Race'" (May 17, 1998), available at www.aaanet.org/stmts/racepp.htm (accessed February 20, 2013).

28   Peter Brooker, *A Glossary of Cultural Theory*, 2nd edn (London: Arnold, 2003), 213–214.

29   Genesis 9:25 in Michael D. Coogan, ed., *The New Oxford Annotated Bible with the Apocryphal/Deuterocanonical Books*, 3rd edn (New York: Oxford University Press, 2001), Hebrew Bible 23.

30   Fredrickson, *Racism*, 43.

31   Ibid., 45. Regarding southern theological reliance on the "myth of Ham" to justify slavery, see Stephen R. Haynes, *Noah's Curse: The Biblical Justification of American Slavery* (Oxford: New York, 2002).

32   2 Nephi 5:21 in *The Book of Mormon: An Account Written by the Hand of Mormon, Upon Plates Taken from the Plates of Nephi*, trans. Joseph Smith (Salt Lake City, UT: Church of Jesus Christ of Latter-Day Saints, 1987), 66.

33   A digital image with transcript of the 1688 Germantown Quaker Petition Against Slavery can be viewed at http://triptych.brynmawr.edu/cdm/ref/collection/HC_QuakSlav/id/5837 (accessed September 22, 2013).

34   Frederick J. Blue, *No Taint of Compromise: Crusaders in Antislavery Politics* (Baton Rouge: Louisiana State University Press, 2005), 16–17 and John R. McKivigan, *The War against Proslavery Religion: Abolitionism and the Northern Churches, 1830–1865* (Ithaca, NY: Cornell University Press, 1984), 14.

35   McKivigan, *The War against Proslavery Religion*, 36–38. Regarding the founding convention of the AAS, see Henry Mayer, *All on Fire: William Lloyd Garrison and the Abolition of Slavery* (New York: St. Martin's Press, 1998), 173–177. Text of the AAS constitution appears in William MacDonald, ed., *Documentary Source Book of American History, 1606–1926*, 3rd edn (New York: Macmillan, 1926), 354–355, available online at http://archive.org/details/documentarysourc00mac (accessed September 22, 2013).

36   Regarding the integrationist policies of the AAS, see Mayer, *All on Fire*, 351–352.

37   McKivigan, *The War against Proslavery Religion*, 76–78.

38   Carol Faulkner, *Lucretia Mott's Heresy: Abolition and Women's Rights in Nineteenth-Century America* (Philadelphia, PA: University of Pennsylvania Press, 2011), 2.

39   Ibid., 5, 138–143.

40   Ibid., 178–179.

41   Thornton Stringfellow, "A Scriptural View of Slavery," in *Slavery Defended: The Views of the Old South*, ed. Eric L. McKitrick (Englewood Cliffs, NJ: Prentice Hall, 1963), 86.

42   Ibid., 86.

43   Josiah Clark Nott and George R. Gliddon, *Types of Mankind: Or, Ethnological Researches: Based Upon the Ancient Monuments, Paintings, Sculptures, and Crania of Races, and Upon Their Natural, Geographical, Philological and Biblical History, Illustrated by Selections from the Inedited Papers of Samuel George Morton and by Additional Contributions from L. Agassiz, W. Usher, and H. S. Patterson* (Philadelphia, PA: J. B. Lippincott, 1854), 466–574.

44   For an account of the Newark Earthworks "holy stones" controversy, see Robert W. Alrutz, *The Newark Holy Stones: The History of an Archaeological Tragedy* (Granville, OH: Denison University, 1980).

45   Patrick W. Carey, *Catholics in America: A History* (Westport, CT: Praeger, 2004), 41, 90–91.

46   Ibid., 42–43.

47   Ibid., 41–44.

48   Ibid., 44–46.

49   Report of the American and Foreign Anti-Slavery Society, quoted in Jayme A. Sokolow, "Revolution and Reform: The Antebellum Jewish Abolitionists," in *Jews and*

the Civil War: A Reader, ed. Jonathan D. Sarna and Adam D. Mendelsohn (New York: New York University Press, 2010), 125.

50 Quoted in ibid., 132.

51 Quoted in ibid., 134.

52 Ibid., 136.

53 Bertram W. Korn, "Jews and Negro Slavery in the Old South, 1789–1865," in *Jews and the Civil War: A Reader*, ed. Jonathan D. Sarna and Adam Mendelsohn (New York: New York University Press, 2010), 116–117.

54 For details on Benjamin's life, see Eli N. Evans, *Judah P. Benjamin, the Jewish Confederate* (New York: Free Press, 1988).

55 John Simon, "That Obnoxious Order," in *Jews and the Civil War: A Reader*, ed. Jonathan D. Sarna and Adam Mendelsohn (New York: New York University Press, 2010), 353, 361. I thank my student Bailey Romano for pointing out Grant's order as an instance of anti-Semitism during the Civil War.

56 Michael F. Doran, "Negro Slaves of the Five Civilized Tribes," *Annals of the Association of American Geographers* 68, no. 3 (1978).

57 Research Department of the Association for the Study of Negro Life and History, "Free Negro Owners of Slaves in the United States in 1830," *Journal of Negro History* 9, no. 1 (1924).

58 Quoted in Zoe Trodd, "Social Reform," in *The Blackwell Companion to Religion in America*, ed. Philip Goff (Malden, MA: Wiley Blackwell, 2010), 341–343.

59 This argument appears in David R. Goldfield, *America Aflame: How the Civil War Created a Nation* (New York: Bloomsbury, 2011), 1.

60 Ronald C. White, *Lincoln's Greatest Speech: The Second Inaugural* (New York: Simon & Schuster, 2002), 18–19.

61 Edwin Scott Gaustad and Philip L. Barlow, *New Historical Atlas of Religion in America* (New York: Oxford University Press, 2001), 69–73.

62 Ibid., 71.

63 The Prescript of the Ku Klux Klan is available online at www.sewanee.edu/reconstruction/html/docs/kkkprescript.htm (accessed September 22, 2013).

64 Elaine Frantz Parsons, "Midnight Rangers: Costume and Performance in the Reconstruction-Era Ku Klux Klan," *Journal of American History* 92, no. 3 (2005), 817.

65 For the ritual aspects of lynching practices in nineteenth- and twentieth-century America, see W. Fitzhugh Brundage, *Lynching in the New South: Georgia and Virginia, 1880–1930* (Urbana: University of Illinois Press, 1993), 1–85 and Trudier Harris, *Exorcising Blackness: Historical and Literary Lynching and Burning Rituals* (Bloomington: Indiana University Press, 1984), 1–28.

66 Ferenc M. Szasz and Margaret Connell Szasz, "Religion and Spirituality," in *The Oxford History of the American West*, ed. Clyde A. Milner II, Carol A. O'Connor, and Martha A. Sandweiss (New York: Oxford University Press, 1994), 364–365.

67 See Figure 2.53 in Gaustad and Barlow, *New Historical Atlas*, 116–117.

68 Szasz and Szasz, "Religion and Spirituality," 365–366.

69 Tweed and Prothero, *Asian Religions in America*, 62.

70 Regarding the confusion over the number of Brigham Young's wives, see Jeffrey Ogden Johnson, "Determining and Defining 'Wife': The Brigham Young Households," *Dialogue* 20, no. 3 (1987).

71   Matthew Burton Bowman, *The Mormon People: The Making of an American Faith* (New York: Random House, 2012), 117–119.

72   Ibid., 120–122.

73   Lee's final statement appears in Juanita Brooks, *The Mountain Meadows Massacre* (Stanford, CA: Stanford University Press, 1950), 151–152; other historical studies of the Mountain Meadows massacre include Will Bagley, *Blood of the Prophets: Brigham Young and the Massacre at Mountain Meadows* (Norman: University of Oklahoma Press, 2002); Sally Denton, *American Massacre: The Tragedy at Mountain Meadows, September 1857* (New York: Alfred A. Knopf, 2003); and Ronald W. Walker, Richard E. Turley Jr., and Glen M. Leonard, *Massacre at Mountain Meadows* (New York: Oxford University Press, 2008).

74   Bowman, *The Mormon People*, 143–144 and Richard N. Ostling and Joan K. Ostling, *Mormon America: The Power and the Promise* (San Francisco, CA: HarperSanFrancisco, 1999), 70.

75   Claudia L. Bushman and Richard L. Bushman, *Building the Kingdom: A History of Mormons in America* (New York: Oxford University Press, 2001), 71–72.

8

Changing Society

In the closing decades of the nineteenth century, the American nation experienced rapid changes in demographics, economic opportunities, and continued expansion and settlement of new territories. These developments brought pressures, tensions, and opportunities for religious peoples of all sorts. This chapter explores how changes in American society affected various religious groups, and how new religious communities and movements emerged in these times of change. We also will learn how newly arriving immigrants from Europe, Asia, the Caribbean, and elsewhere introduced new religious orientations and practices to American society. Protestants remained dominant, but the proliferation of religions, both Christian and non-Christian, made Protestant dominance less coherent. Our studies will reveal that America's religious landscape changed drastically between the start of the nineteenth century and the opening decades of the twentieth century.

On the shores of Lake Pontchartrain, the enormous estuary adjacent to New Orleans in Louisiana, crowds consisting mostly of immigrants from Haiti turned out each year in the 1870s on St. John's eve, the night before the feast day of John the Baptist on June 24 in the Roman Catholic calendar, to celebrate with wild reveries, according to reports in the local papers. In 1875 the *New Orleans Times* described a ceremony in which adherents

> moved to and fro in a monotonous swaying dance ... accompanying themselves
> [with] unintelligible chant, as dreary as their motions. ... [Then] the chant changed
> to a discord more rapid and grotesque. ... The group seemed suddenly to become
> excited, their contortions increased, they clung to each other in a state of semi-frenzy,
> and one woman, reeling over apparently in an epileptic fit, fell to the floor.

Formed From This Soil: An Introduction to the Diverse History of Religion in America, First Edition. Thomas S. Bremer.
© 2015 Thomas S. Bremer. Published 2015 by John Wiley & Sons, Ltd.

According to the *Times* reporter, the "work was still in enthusiastic progress" when he departed at 3:30 a.m.[1] These sorts of energetic religious celebrations attracted much interest among the general public in New Orleans throughout the 1870s. The papers regularly published sensationalist "orgy stories" of huge bonfires, bloody sacrifices of live animals, drumming, chanting, dancing, drunkenness, nudity, and sex in frenzied gatherings of people of color, many of them originating from Haiti and other Caribbean locales.

Newspaper reporters attended these wild scenes in hopes of seeing Marie Laveau (1801–1881),[2] the purported "Queen of Voodoo," presiding over the celebrations. It seems, however, that her infamy as the spiritual leader of New

Figure 8.1   Even today the enigmatic Marie Laveau, legendary "Queen of Voodoo," attracts visitors to her gravesite in St. Louis Cemetery No. 1, New Orleans, Louisiana; shown here are recent offerings left by devotees at her tomb. In the nineteenth century Laveau reigned as an icon of exotic culture for Euro-Americans in the Crescent City. (Image © Irene Abdou / Alamy.)

Orleans' Vodou practitioners has been more a matter of legend than fact; no contemporary accounts mention her presence at the St. John's eve festivities. Little is known of Marie Laveau's personal life, and even during her lifetime contrasting images formed an enigmatic public persona. In subsequent decades her legend only grew, so that today her home on St. Ann Street in New Orleans and her tomb in St. Louis Cemetery No. 1 remain tourist attractions that demonstrate the exotic element of New Orleans' history.

Box 8.1   Afro-Caribbean religions

A variety of syncretistic religious systems grew out of the colonial legacy of the Caribbean region, invariably in contexts of slavery, melding various indigenous religious traditions of Africa with European folk magic, the formal practices of Roman Catholicism, and the conjuring traditions of enslaved African Americans. Among these traditions is Vodou (sometimes referred to as Vodoun or Voodoo), which has been a prominent cultural tradition in New Orleans since Haitian refugees fleeing the Haitian Revolution of 1791–1804 brought it to the city in the early part of the nineteenth century. The complexity of Vodou escapes any simple explanation; it revolves around a pantheon of *loa* or *lwa*, supernatural beings consisting of a syncretic fusion of African gods, ancestor spirits, and Catholic saints; devotees serve the *lwa* with both individual and communal **rituals**. Followers of particular *lwa* demonstrate their allegiance by wearing the *lwa*'s colors, feeding the spirits, and offering sacrifices. Group rituals involve energetic music and dance, prayer, food preparation, and animal sacrifices; the *lwa* communicate through spirit possession where devotees are "mounted" by the spirit in a trancelike state and become the vehicles of the *lwa*, who communicate through words and stylized dances. These ritual visitations by the Vodou deities often involve receiving advice on urgent matters or experiencing healing of various sorts.

A similar tradition developed in Cuba, where Santería (or Regla de Ocha) grew out of the colonial slave culture, with indigenous African practices and traditions preserved under the façade of a purported Catholicism. Although many adherents clearly distinguished between Christian and indigenous African worship, the combination of the two was pervasive, with the Christian saints, Jesus, and the Virgin Mary all identified with African gods or ancestors who would protect followers in exchange for sacrifices.

Other syncretistic religious traditions developed throughout the Caribbean region; all of them share similar historical circumstances in developing their own unique practices and beliefs. Among these are Rastafari in Jamaica; the Orisha traditions of Trinidad and Tobago; and Obeah, found in the British islands of the Caribbean (Antigua, the Bahamas, Barbados, Jamaica, and Surinam).[3]

The story of Marie Laveau reveals the changing nature of American society in the final decades of the nineteenth century. The sudden presence of substantial numbers of immigrants in American cities introduced unfamiliar religious practices and traditions to the Protestant majority. Specifically, the cultural imagination that made Marie Laveau an icon of New Orleans' exotic past on the one hand shows how religious differences became appealing objects of curiosity in the contact zones of nineteenth-century American society; but, on the other, it also demonstrates how the burgeoning economy of America during the "Gilded Age" (a period of intense industrial growth and relative prosperity between the Civil War and the end of the nineteenth century) in the later decades of the nineteenth century capitalized on religious developments for monetary gain. According to one observer, "Those who sought out [Laveau's] purported magical powers were predominately white people who were mostly ignorant about Vodou as a religion."[4] Her example and its enduring legacy in New Orleans reminds us how much religious developments of the nineteenth century are still with us today. They also show that religious people are more than merely religious, that their religious orientations, moral commitments, and ritual practices connect to and sometimes define other aspects of their lives, including economic concerns.

In the final decades of nineteenth-century America, even the dominant Protestant culture needed to adapt itself to the rapid changes taking place in American society. The most prominent of these changes was the explosive economic growth that the nation experienced with industrialization; new factories and mills were built, with railroad lines installing tracks from town to town, linking America's great cities with distant corners of the nation. The completion in 1869 of the first transcontinental railroad established an intimate connection between the Pacific and **Atlantic worlds**, introducing new religious orientations and transforming those already in America. By the beginning of the twentieth century, the American religious landscape had exploded into a chaotic jumble of differences that heightened religious conflict even as they encouraged religious exchanges and innovations. The changing society of America in some ways itself became an "orgy story" of religious encounters.

New Lands

Changes in American society had a remarkable impact in the west, where the rapid expansion of Euro-American settlements reignited the long history of conflicts with indigenous people. The newcomers battled with Native American groups on numerous fronts, both through forced cultural assimilation and through military engagement. A coordinated strategy of treaties, confinement to reservations, and enforcement of government mandates through military actions effectively eliminated nearly all Native American resistance to Euro-American incursions by the end of the nineteenth century. At the core of these strategies were devastating attacks on indigenous religious practices and traditions; a pervasive expectation on the part of Euro-Americans for Indians to assimilate to the Christian culture of "civilization" meant foremost eradicating longstanding religious orientations that supported native lifestyles. The alternative, in the view of the federal government, was genocide. President Ulysses S. Grant (1822–1885) made this clear in his State of the Union Address on December 4, 1871, when he remarked:

> Through the exertions of the various societies of Christians to whom has been intrusted the execution of [federal policy regarding Native Americans] ..., many tribes of Indians have been induced to settle upon reservations, to cultivate the soil, to perform produc- tive labor of various kinds, and to partially accept civilization. They are being cared for in such a way, it is hoped, as to induce those still pursuing their old habits of life to embrace the only opportunity which is left them to avoid extermination.[5]

Thus, according to the president of the United States of America, the choice for native peoples was either to give up their "old habits of life," including their reli- gious traditions, or face extermination. The opportunity to accept "civilization" came through efforts of Christian missionaries, an official policy that benefited both the religious societies entrusted with care of the Indians and the federal government, which enjoyed a reduced responsibility for the well-being of native peoples confined to reservations. Making good Christians of the Indians, officials believed, would make them good citizens; as a result, large numbers of Native Americans adopted a Christian religious orientation as they became more dependent on the colonizer's culture.

One of the most effective but controversial strategies for "civilizing" Indians was through Christian boarding schools. Often frustrated by their efforts to con- vince adult Native Americans of the benefits of Christianity and modern civiliza- tion, missionaries turned their attention to children; they surmised, following a well-established missionary tradition, that educating young children was the best way to change native cultures. This involved removing the children from their native contexts and placing them in boarding schools where they were prohibited from retaining their native languages, customs, clothing, hairstyles, and other fac- ets of native culture; immersed in the culture of Euro-American missionaries, the native children were forcibly transformed into "civilized" people. Of course, separ- ation from their children was devastating to native families; as one Navajo parent testified, "The parents of those children who were taken away are crying for them. I had a boy who was taken from this school [the local school] to Grand Junction [an off-reservation boarding school]. The tears come to our eyes whenever we think of them. I do not know whether my boy is alive or not."[6] As we might expect, many Native American families resisted sending their children to boarding schools, and missionaries and their agents sometimes resorted to trickery and even kidnapping to compel native peoples to place their children in the missionary schools.[7]

To assist missionaries' efforts to eradicate native religious traditions and replace them with Christianity, the federal government implemented a policy of actively suppressing what they termed the "evil practices" of tribal religions. The US Interior Department issued in 1883 a "Code of Indian Offenses," which established a special court on most Indian reservations to prosecute Native Americans who participated in tribal religious dances and feasts, those who engaged in polygamy, and those who practiced the arts "of so-called 'medicine-men'." Although enforcement varied from place to place, the official policy of the federal government specifically forbade the practice of Native American religions for the half-century that the Code was operative.[8]

Native American resistance

The conversion of Indians to Christianity, however, did not eliminate a pervasive native attachment to sacred ground and the ancestral **myths** that animated traditional lands; even as they became Christians, many Native Americans preserved oral traditions that related the histories of their peoples to the sacred lands and the mythological characters who inhabited those lands. In the American southwest virtually all native groups continued to relate important geographical features, especially mountains, to sacred stories; for example, the San Francisco Peaks in what is now northern Arizona remain sacred even today to such groups as the Havasupai, Hopi, Navajo, and Zuni peoples. Likewise, most Indians of the Great Plains refused to relinquish traditional ties to sacred geographies that had sustained them for generations, even when they were forced to accept reservations far from their former homelands; the geographical centers of the Black Hills, for instance, remained holy to the Lakota and numerous other native peoples. Religious orientations that tied sacred stories to particular landscapes and geographical features persisted, even when overlaid with Christian narratives and commitments introduced by Euro-American missionaries.[9]

As we have seen throughout the history of encounters between Native Americans and Euro-Americans, native tribes turned once again to religious powers in the contact zones of western North America during the late decades of the nineteenth century. In the early 1870s a Paiute prophet by the name of Wodziwob (birth date unknown, died ca. 1872) in Nevada led his people in what became known as "ghost dances"; these involved ritual dancing that communicated with ancestor spirits in a native millenarian movement. Under pressure from white settlers encroaching on their ancestral lands, Wodziwob promised his followers that the world would come to an end with the demise of the whites and that the Paiutes would be joined by their ancestors in a renewed land of prosperity and happiness. Other native prophets led similar movements in examples of transculturation that drew on indigenous traditions while incorporating Christian influences.[10] The largest and most widely known of these millenarian movements was the Ghost Dance religion, which spread rapidly throughout the Rocky Mountains and the Great Plains beginning in the late 1880s. Wovoka (ca. 1856–1932), also known by his

Box 8.2 The Black Hills

An unnamed Hopi man explained in 1951, "Our land, our religion, and our life are one,"[11] a view shared in many Native American traditions. For most indigenous groups, cultural identity is religiously tied to specific sacred geographies, a topocentric religious orientation that distinguishes native spiritual understandings from the bibliocentric monotheisms of Europeans and Euro-Americans.

One prominent example of the acute difference between Native American religious regard for land and the more pragmatic economic orientation of the American judicial system involves the Black Hills region of western South Dakota and eastern Wyoming. This mountainous area on the northern Great Plains has had spiritual significance to numerous Native American groups for centuries. A cycle of myths among the Lakota relates one example of the intricate web of mythical narratives and ceremonial practices related to astronomical observations and topographic features connected to the region. In these sacred narratives, the hero Falling Star (or Star Comes Out) moves through identifiable sites in the Black Hills in his various adventures, but his travels also take him to seven "star villages," which one Lakota informant associates with the seven stars of the Pleiades constellation and those of the Big Dipper constellation. Falling Star himself is both human and star-person, thus serving as an intermediary between the terrestrial world and the heavens. Consequently, for the Lakota, their communal identity and the connection of their people to the cosmos rely on the recitation and ceremonial commemoration of these myths in the sacred lands of the Black Hills. Additional groups with similar connections to these mountains include the Arapaho, Cheyenne, Kiowa, Kiowa-Apache, and others.[12]

Although the Lakota people were latecomers to the northern plains, they inhabited the Black Hills region at the time of Euro-American settlement in the nineteenth century, making them the most recent group to claim the mountains as sacred. The US government seized the land from them in 1877, a move that federal courts in 1980 ruled had been illegal. But, although the Lakota people have successfully proven their claim on the Black Hills, they have refused to accept the substantial monetary settlement awarded them by the courts, maintaining that the money is unacceptable to them and other native groups who regard the Black Hills as sacred: in their view, sacred ground cannot be sold, and they continue to insist on a return of the Black Hills to native ownership.[13]

Euro-American name Jack Wilson, was the son of a follower of Wodziwob. Orphaned as an adolescent, Wovoka had been taken in by Euro-American settlers and worked for them for a number of years; during this time he learned of Christianity and became familiar with the Christian Bible. He eventually returned

Figure 8.2 This fanciful illustration of a Lakota Ghost Dance appeared in a London newspaper just weeks after the Wounded Knee massacre in 1890 that ended the millenarian Ghost Dance movement for most of its practitioners. (Courtesy of the Library of Congress, LC-USZ62-52423.)

to his native people, and during a solar eclipse on New Year's Day 1889 Wovoka experienced a vision of renewal for Indians. In the tradition of his father's religion, he promised an imminent future when whites would be destroyed and native ancestors would return. This new age could be initiated, Wovoka told his followers, by regular dancing of the Ghost Dance, by regarding all native peoples as brothers and sisters, and by adhering to the traditional customs of the ancestors. He had up to twenty thousand followers, many of them among native groups of the Plains who had heard of this new religion in the intermountain west and had sent emissaries to learn the Ghost Dance and bring it back to their own tribes. The movement came to a tragic end, however, when the US Cavalry slaughtered a group of Lakota people, including many women and children, who were involved in the Ghost Dance movement at Wounded Knee Creek, South Dakota, in December 1890.[14]

Religious changes in Alaska and Hawaii

Alaska became a territory of the United States in 1867 when the Russians sold it to the Americans and withdrew from North America. Many of the Russian settlers, traders, and missionaries in Alaska returned to Russia, but some stayed on to serve native peoples there. In the 1860s, nine Russian Orthodox churches and thirty-five chapels were served by more than thirty **clergy**, who remained and competed with Protestant and other Christian missionaries for the souls of native peoples in the subsequent decades.[15] In addition, many of these native peoples of Alaska perpetuated the Russian Orthodox traditions they had adopted under the missionaries without help from Church officials after most of the Russians left in 1867.[16] Meanwhile, American Christians were slow to set up operations in their newly purchased territory, but within a decade Protestant missionaries were making progress in Alaska. Presbyterians took the lead in this effort, with Sheldon Jackson (1834–1909), the Presbyterian minister who served as superintendent of the Home Mission of the Territories, initiating Protestant efforts in the territory in 1877. Jackson had worked as a missionary in the American west as part of the federal efforts to civilize Native Americans, and he brought to Alaska the logic of missionaries as the harbingers of modern civilization; he concentrated on establishing schools for Alaskan natives, and encouraged other Protestant denominations to do the same in the territory. In contrast to the more culturally sensitive efforts of Russian Orthodox missionaries, who sought to accommodate native languages and traditions in their adaptation of Orthodox Christianity to native Alaskan cultures, American Protestants came to Alaska immersed in policies that sought to eradicate native languages, customs, and religious orientations while instilling Christian beliefs and American values. Jackson, however, differed from other missionary educators of his time by allowing some accommodation of local indigenous cultures. As the territory's first General Agent of Education, his curriculum goals included "moral training," which meant teaching Indians "that both the law of God and the law of the land forbid more than one man and one woman living together as husband and wife; that each family should have a separate home, however small; that lying, stealing, and impurity of speech and behavior are alike offenses to God and man."[17] But Jackson preferred locating schools in villages with students remaining at home in their native cultures and remaining there upon graduation, allowing their communities to remain economically self-sufficient.[18] In a departure from the logic of boarding schools that removed Indian children from their homes and severed all ties to native culture, Jackson encouraged Christianization within native cultural contexts.

Meanwhile, Christianization in Hawaii set the pace for American colonization of the Pacific island kingdom. The changing socioeconomic circumstances brought by European and Euro-American trading and whaling ships weakened the traditional customs related to local deities. In 1819 the newly ascended Hawaiian monarch, Liholiho (Kamehameha II, ca. 1797–1824), declared an end to the indigenous *kapu* system, the complex sociocultural arrangement of laws and customs related to sacred prohibitions and obligations regulating rituals and ceremonies, dietary restrictions, gender relations, proper behavior toward chiefs, and numerous other facets of native life. Liholiho ordered that native religious images were to be destroyed; consequently, traditional Hawaiian religion disappeared from public life, although many of the customs and traditions continued to be practiced in private. Shortly after the king ended *kapu*, American Christian missionaries began to arrive in Hawaii. Although Hawaiians had traveled to America since the 1790s, and a number of them had received educations in New England missionary schools, it was not until 1820 that the first contingent of American missionaries traveled to Hawaii. Like the Protestant missionary efforts elsewhere, these first religious emissaries to the islands had no intention of acculturating to local traditions; they sought to instill their American values among native Hawaiians, although, in an effort to reach greater numbers of converts, they did learn the indigenous language for use in their preaching.[19]

Protestant missionaries from New England were especially adept at maneuvering themselves into places of power in the island kingdom. Two missionary advisers to King Kamehameha III (1813–1854) convinced him in 1840 to dispense with his feudal monarchy and instead adopt a constitutional monarchy modeled on European governments. One of the missionaries, Gerrit P. Judd (1803–1873), served as the first prime minister under the new government, allowing him to institute numerous changes that gave more power to non-native whites, known locally as *haoles*. One effect of this American influence in Hawaii was increasing economic dominance; sugar plantations supplanted whaling in the middle decades of the nineteenth century as Hawaii's leading export industry, helped by land reforms that favored foreign acquisition of native Hawaiians' lands. Many of the plantation owners were missionaries or the children or grandchildren of missionaries, most with close ties to the New England region of the United States.

The rapid growth of the plantations under *haoles'* control also brought a diversity of other people to the islands. Sugar cultivation required more labor than native Hawaiians could supply, and plantation owners turned to foreign labor to work the fields; Chinese, Japanese, Galicians, Germans, Portuguese, and Scandinavians were all well represented in Hawaii by the end of the nineteenth century.[20] With these immigrants to the Hawaiian islands came a variety of cultural traditions and religious orientations; nevertheless, the *haoles*, white American Protestants for the most part, dominated public life in the islands, and, when the United States needed a strategic base for military operations in the Pacific during the Spanish–American War in 1898, Congress agreed to annex Hawaii. Along with native peoples of North America, the Hawaiians found themselves, despite their great distance from the continental mainland, under the jurisdiction of the United States.

Sacred landscapes

As ever more territory fell under the dominion of the United States, at least a few Euro-Americans became more attentive to the desecration of lands transformed by modern development. Inspired by the Transcendentalists' reverence for wildness, articulated most directly in the admonition by Henry David Thoreau (1817–1862) that "In Wildness is the preservation of the world,"[21] a religious aesthetic of nature emerged late in the nineteenth century that capitalized on newly discovered scenic wonders of the American west. As industrialization estranged modern people from the natural rhythms of the earth, a wistful longing for simpler lives in close connection to nature took shape in such nostalgic tales as the legend of Johnny

---

Box 8.3 The legend of Johnny Appleseed

In the late 1790s, John Chapman (1774–1845) crossed the Allegheny Mountains to settle in Ohio, where he earned a reputation as a somewhat eccentric itinerant backwoodsman but where he also was able to secure significant landholdings. It was not until the 1870s, however, that he became canonized in American lore as the renowned "Johnny Appleseed," the ascetic wandering saint of the wilderness spreading a mystical nature religion and planting apple orchards throughout Ohio and Indiana in the early nineteenth century. His legend was first introduced in a feature that appeared in the November 1871 issue of the popular periodical *Harper's New Monthly Magazine*.[22] The exploits of Johnny Appleseed highlighted concerns in the late nineteenth century over development in the American west; the *Harper's* article begins, "The 'far West' is rapidly becoming only a traditional designation: railroads have destroyed the romance of frontier life, or have surrounded it with so many appliances of civilization that the pioneer character is rapidly becoming mythical." In contrast to the waning romance of the American west, the article goes on to present "Jonathan Chapman" as obsessively consumed by a "monomania" of "planting apple seeds in remote places." He also displayed a mystical bent in his ascetic wanderings, claiming "to have frequent conversations with angels and spirits." Chapman became somewhat of a mystical evangelist, bringing to the lonely inhabitants of western woods "news right fresh from heaven"; he would tell folks he met, according to the *Harper's* article, "that God has appointed him a mission in the wilderness to preach the Gospel of love, and plant apple seeds that shall produce orchards for the benefit of men and women and little children whom he has never seen."

This image of the wandering hermit-saint evangelizing a strange mystical Christianity to pioneers in the Ohio Valley took on legendary proportions in subsequent decades, albeit largely stripped of the mystical encounters with otherworldly beings that included claims of angelic matrimony. In the twentieth century, poet Vachel Lindsay (1879–1931) described the fabled Johnny Appleseed as "much like a Hindu saint, akin to Thoreau and Emerson," and he often was compared to the medieval mystic St. Francis of Assisi (ca. 1181–1226), patron saint of animals and nature; his legend grew as America's "modern hermit of the wilderness."[23]

Appleseed and in a growing desire for sublime experiences of grand landscapes and the wondrous features of spectacular mountains, unfathomable canyons, towering heights of giant trees, and breathtaking waterfalls. In 1872 Congress approved America's first national park, Yellowstone in Wyoming, and by the end of the century another three parks had earned the designation, a trend that would only accelerate in the following century.

At the helm of this movement to sacralize special landscapes was the naturalist John Muir (1838–1914), who wrote in 1890, "In God's wildness lies the hope of the world – the great fresh unblighted, unredeemed wilderness."[24] Best known as a naturalist and vocal advocate of wilderness preservation, Muir was also the leading theologian of an American wilderness religion in the nineteenth century. Born in Scotland and having emigrated to the United States as a child, the youthful John Muir suffered under the strict discipline of his father, with only the Christian Bible as reading material in his childhood home. This imbued him with an earnest piety but it also instilled an appreciation for nature as the holy manifestation of God's majesty.[25] By the time he arrived in California in 1868, he had given up his father's narrow biblical fundamentalism and replaced it with a natural theology that found the immediacy of God's revelation in nature.[26] His first summer in the majestic mountains of California's Sierra Nevada range, he would recall some years later, allowed him to wander "these love-monument mountains, glad to be a servant of servants in so holy a wilderness." He found in alpine landscapes a spiritual awakening, where "Everything turns into religion, all the world seems a church and the mountains altars."[27] In later years Muir would don the mantel of a latter-day John the Baptist of Christian tradition transposed to a "Sequoical" (in reference to California's giant Sequoia redwood trees) evangelism, wishing "to preach the green brown woods to all the juiceless world, descending from this divine wilderness like a John Baptist eating Douglass Squirrels & wild honey or wild anything, crying, Repent for the kingdom of Sequoia is at hand."[28] Following an inspiring visit in Yosemite in 1871 by the aging Ralph Waldo Emerson (1803–1882), Muir took up the pen and began putting his wilderness experiences and theological renderings of nature into books and articles. By the end of the nineteenth century, Muir enjoyed a national and even international reputation as the prophet of wilderness preservation; as a founding member and unanimous choice as the first president of the Sierra Club conservation organization, intent on protecting the mountains, Muir solidified his legacy as the inspiration for an American reverence of wild lands.

The religious regard for stunning American landscapes as sacred manifestations of God's will cannot be disentangled from Euro-American expansion into western territories and the consequent havoc suffered by native peoples. Euro-Americans came west for economic opportunity, but they also brought **evangelical** intentions based on millennial assumptions about the Christian triumph of uncivilized lands. The awe that many Euro-Americans experienced in American landscapes often served to affirm their Christian interpretations of God's will for America. But, as we have seen time and again, other religious orientations

Figure 8.3 California's Yosemite Valley, shown here in a nineteenth-century engraving, inspired John Muir's reverence for nature. In 1871 Muir hosted the aging Transcendentalist Ralph Waldo Emerson in Yosemite; Emerson convinced Muir to pursue a career of writing about his beloved mountains. (*America Illustrated*, 1883.)

provided alternative interpretations about the meaning of land, of history, and of the encounter with unfamiliar peoples.

New People

While new settlements drew Christian missionaries westward, evangelical opportunities also awaited Protestant efforts in the quickly growing cities of the United States. The shift from a rural to an urban economy and the sudden influx of millions of foreign immigrants fleeing hardship and oppression in their homelands for opportunities afforded by the burgeoning American economy nearly overwhelmed American cities across the continent, but especially in the east. Similarly to what we saw in the case of the first major surge of immigration in the 1840s and 1850s (see Chapter 6), a good number of the new arrivals were Roman Catholics from western Europe, but the immigrants also included people with a wide range of religious traditions, including various Eastern Orthodox Christians as well as non-Christian groups led by Jewish immigrants from Eastern Europe and a variety of Asian and Pacific religions. Very quickly, American cities grew into worldly, cosmopolitan conglomerates of the world's cultures, languages, and religions.

The experience of migration itself often had a spiritual dimension for many immigrants. For many devout migrants the journey to a new home involved a spiritual journey of transformation, supported by devotions and religious celebrations upon departure from the hometown and accompanying prayers and pious acts throughout the voyage to the new land.[29] But, as new immigrants entered America's cities, towns, and countrysides, they faced an alien world of unfamiliar customs, languages, and expectations; adapting to their new environments was essential for immigrants' success in settling into their new lives. American cities particularly were inhospitable places for most new arrivals. Squalor proliferated in sections where immigrants tended to first settle, and city services were lacking for the most part. Periodic epidemics of such deadly diseases as cholera, tuberculosis (commonly called "consumption" in the nineteenth century), diphtheria, and in southern states malaria and yellow fever swept through many cities, hitting impoverished residents especially hard. As they faced these hardships and adjusted to new lives as Americans, many of these immigrants relied on religious traditions for strength, solace, and building communities.

Christian immigrants

The total number of Catholics in the United States grew by 1300 percent between 1830 and 1870, so that, as America recovered from the Civil War, roughly thirteen percent of the population were Roman Catholics; by then, the Church had established its institutional presence throughout the nation. Most of the growth in the number of American Catholics during this period came from immigration, with large numbers of Irish and German Catholics arriving in the 1840s and later; in addition, territorial expansion in the American southwest added significant numbers of Hispanic Catholics to the United States.[30]

As the number of Catholics in America surged, their diversity also grew. At the beginning of the nineteenth century, most Catholics were Anglo-Americans concentrated in Maryland, with a significant number later settling in Bardstown, Kentucky. In Louisiana, stretching up the Mississippi River from New Orleans to St. Louis and into the Great Lakes region, French and Spanish Catholics dominated, along with significant numbers of creoles of African, Native American, and European descent. In addition, a sizable population of African American Catholics could be found throughout the southern region of the United States. Irish and German Catholic immigrants settled mostly in the northeastern and midwestern parts of the country, and a sizable community of German Catholics established communities in Texas. A few French Canadian Catholics wound up in the northeastern United States, and Hispanic Catholics were the predominant religious group in much of the American southwest and California. By the end of the nineteenth century the Roman Catholic Church in the United States was a decidedly immigrant religion, dominated by Irish and Germans but with a wide range of other ethnicities, languages, and national origins among American Catholics.[31]

Another Christian strand finding a new home in America during the nineteenth century was the Orthodox churches of Eastern Europe and the Middle East. Besides the Russians in Alaska, other Orthodox Christians established congregations elsewhere in the United States; Greek Orthodox Christians settled in Florida as early as the 1760s, but they had no formal places of worship for another century; the first Greek Orthodox Church opened in 1864 in New Orleans, Louisiana. Like other early Orthodox communities, the parish in New Orleans encompassed diverse ethnicities, including Russians, Serbs, and Syrians in addition to Greeks, but the **liturgy** initially was conducted in English. With the rising tide of Orthodox immigrants arriving in the closing decades of the nineteenth century, new Orthodox congregations were established in communities across North America. Many of these churches were led by bishops and priests from the homelands of the ethnic groups that established the churches, and, like many immigrant groups, they retained close connections to their ethnic heritage as well as to the episcopal authority of their homeland churches, identifying themselves respectively as Antiochian Orthodox, Greek Orthodox, Russian Orthodox, Serbian Orthodox, and other ethnically distinctive Orthodox communities.[32]

Jewish immigrants

The final decades of the nineteenth century also witnessed a significant surge of Jewish immigration to the United States. By the 1880s more than a quarter million Jews resided in the nation, many of them originating from Germany and embracing Reform Judaism in America; even some Orthodox congregations had felt the impact of the Reform movement.[33] Yet, despite their influence among American Jews, Reform congregations still struggled to clearly define their distinctive variety of Jewish belief and practice. Consequently, they convened a meeting in Pittsburgh, Pennsylvania, in 1885 under the leadership of Kaufmann Kohler (1843–1926) and presided over by Isaac Mayer Wise (1819–1900) to produce a unified statement of Reform Judaism; together this gathering of influential leaders of the Reform movement declared eight principles that subsequently became known as the

"Pittsburgh Platform," the guiding document of the Reform movement during a period known as "Classic Reform" that lasted well into the twentieth century. The principles affirm "the God-idea as taught in our Holy Scriptures and developed and spiritualized by the Jewish teachers, in accordance with the moral and philosophical progress of their respective ages." In terms of community, the Pittsburgh Platform declares Jews are "no longer a nation, but a religious community" and it explicitly rejects Zionist calls for a return to the Jewish homeland in Palestine, regarding America as their new home.[34]

Even as the Reform movement continued to mature, mass persecution of Jews in Russia and elsewhere in Eastern Europe in the 1880s caused large numbers of Orthodox Jews to emigrate to America. Like many of their German counterparts, most of these eastern European Jews spoke Yiddish, the vernacular German-Hebrew language that had widespread usage among European Jews, but many had been educated in Russia; strands of Russian-influenced socialism and anarchism among a few of these immigrants eventually gave rise to a Jewish labor movement.[35]

As subsequent generations of Orthodox Jews achieved some degree of middle-class status in America, they were less apt to adhere to the demands of traditional religious laws. Realizing that Reform Judaism had little appeal for them in its radically modernizing impulse, a competing mode of liberalized Judaism known as "Conservative" emerged around the beginning of the twentieth century centered at the Jewish Theological Seminary in New York City. Prominent Jews in New York brought the noted Jewish scholar and religious leader Solomon Schechter (1847–1915) from England to direct the seminary; they built a new large building for the school, provided an impressive Jewish library, and hired an outstanding faculty of Schechter's choosing. Although he sought to build a leading institution of Jewish learning, his sponsors had more practical goals; they wanted to educate rabbis who could serve as an "Americanizing" influence on eastern European Jewish immigrants.[36] The resulting Conservative Judaism that emanated from Schechter's seminary offered a middle way between Orthodox and Reform approaches to Jewish tradition and its relationship to modern culture; Conservative Jews adhere to many traditions that Reform Judaism rejects while at the same time accommodating the Jewish heritage to the realities of modern American culture. Theologically they affirm the reality of a god whose will has been revealed to humans, and they consider the scriptures of the Torah and Talmud to be sacred texts of divine origin; at the same time, however, they affirm biblical scholarship that reveals ancient cultural influences, exposing the human element in the texts. A Committee on Jewish Law and Standards sets out a range of acceptable positions on such issues as the participation of women in worship services and adherence to traditional dietary laws, which local rabbis may decide to either adopt or reject for their congregations. Some standards, though, are not open to local choice, especially regarding intermarriage and conversion to Judaism.

Asian immigrants

Besides the preponderance of western monotheistic religions, especially the over-whelming dominance of Christians, a modest number of Asian religious traditions began to appear in America as well. As immigration from Asia picked up through the final decades of the nineteenth century, a variety of religious orientations, including Hindu and Buddhist traditions but also other religious systems origi-nating in Asia, established a foothold on American soil. Their numbers were quite small at first, but by the turn of the twentieth century adherents of Asian religions had become a recognizable presence in the United States, and today they represent a significant portion of the population in some areas of the nation.

The most prominent of these Asian religions is Hinduism, which ranks as the third-largest religious tradition in the world in terms of the number of adherents, behind only Christianity and Islam. Derived from ancient sacred texts known as the *Vedas*, Hinduism originated on the Indian subcontinent and encompasses numerous supernatural characters related in various mythological epics such as the *Ramayana*, the story of the cosmic battle between the great Hindu god Vishnu and the forces of evil, and the *Mahabhatra*, which addresses questions of meaning, purpose, and truth and includes the famous *Bhagavad Gita*, or "Song of the Beloved One." Hindu religious practices include disciplining the mind and body through meditation and yoga as well as devotions to specific gods through offerings, prayers, and pilgrim-ages. They also include social practices in a caste system that maintains strict distinctions between socioeconomic classes based on spiritual presumptions. The Hindu **worldview** presumes a cosmology involving the soul's reincarnation through multiple lives and the cosmic reality of *karma*, a concept of cause and effect that carries on from life to life in what is referred to as *samsara*, the endless cycle of birth and death, rebirth and death again, over and over through eternity.

Within the context of early Hinduism, another religious orientation that would become the fourth largest religion in the world originated in northern India with the teachings of Siddhartha Gautama (ca. 563–483 BCE), referred to by his followers as the Buddha ("the Enlightened One"). From its start in India, Buddhism spread southward to Sri Lanka and southeast Asia over several centuries, and later Buddhists introduced the tradition to China and eventually to Korea and Japan. Retaining the Hindu understandings of reincarnation, *samsara*, and *karma*, Buddhist teachings focus on the attainment of Enlightenment, the ultimate wisdom that signifies buddhahood. As followers of Buddhism took the tradition beyond India, two main branches developed: Theravada (the Path of the Elders), a monastic-oriented practice that claims to adhere more closely to the original teachings of the Buddha, and Mahayana (the Greater Vehicle), which is more open to introducing new ideas and practices; the former became dominant in South and Southeast Asia while the latter prevailed in East Asia. A third tradition, Vajrayana (the Diamond Vehicle, or Tantric Buddhism), which combines elements of both Theravada and Mahayana and includes elaborate rituals and colorful imagery that reflect a greatly expanded pantheon of sacred characters and entities, developed first in India and later became dominant in Tibet. Among these various branches are many forms of Buddhist practice and belief, some of which involve devotion to supernatural bodhisattvas (buddhas in the making), some of which emphasize the necessity of monastic life, and many of which have elaborate texts, or *sutras*, commenting on and expanding Buddhist teachings.

Other significant religious systems of the Indian subcontinent include Jainism and Sikhism. Jainism, like early Buddhism, is largely atheistic; rather than believing in a creator deity, Jains regard the cosmos as a series of processes involving evolution and degeneration; the human soul travels through reincarnated states until it reaches a permanent and pure state of blissful omniscience that liberates it from the continuous cycles of *samsara*. Jains follow an ascetic life of renunciation and restraints that govern behavior, especially in regard to nonviolence, not lying, not stealing, refraining from illicit sex, and nonattachment to worldly possessions. The origins of Jainism were roughly contemporary with the beginnings of Buddhism, around 500 BCE, and its long history in Indian culture has involved the integration of Hindu elements.

Sikhism came along much later, originating in the sixteenth century CE in the context of interactions between Hinduism and Islam, the latter of which had a significant following in Asia at the time. Among Sikhs, the Hindu cycles of reincarnation in *samsara* lead to the soul's union with the one God through love that experiences divine dwelling within the soul. Sikhs worship the deity in the *gurdwara*, the place of Sikh worship, with prayerful submission to God and in practicing the pious study of and meditation on the *Adi Granth*, their sacred text. Worship is egalitarian, with no priests, monks, or others to lead the worship community; anyone with proficiency in Punjabi, the language of the *Adi Granth*, can lead services, including women.

In East Asia the spread of Buddhism brought it into contact with indigenous traditions, such as Confucianism and Taoism in China and the state religion of Shintoism in Japan. Sometimes characterized as more of a philosophy and ethical system rather than a religion, Confucianism is based on texts known as the *Analects*, attributed to the ancient teacher Confucius (551–479 BCE) and his followers. Confucian philosophy emphasizes humane goodness in social harmony learned primarily through careful study of ancient Chinese philosophical teachings, collected as the "Five Classics," which make up the core of Confucian sacred texts. Confucius also taught that the "Way of Heaven" is the supreme moral authority of the universe, believing that his philosophy and ethical teachings were aligned with a so-called "Mandate of Heaven."

More ancient than Confucian teachings in China are traditions of the Tao, or "the Way." Whereas Confucius emphasized the Way in harmonious and humane social relations, other Chinese thinkers regarded social life as antithetical to the Tao. These Taoists sought true harmony in withdrawing from society in favor of more authentic experience of the universe. As a religious system, Taoist tradition attributes its beginnings to an older contemporary of Confucius, the sage Lao Tzu (birth and death dates unknown), who, according to Chinese legend, wrote down his accumulated wisdom in a collection known as the *Tao Te Ching*, the revered text of Chinese Taoism, which characterizes the Tao as the sacred principle immanent in the natural world, the source of all things and that to which all returns.

A different sort of native religion, Shintoism, which focuses on reverence for the imperial rulers, emerged in the island nation of Japan. Shinto has its roots in ancient oral traditions of devotion to various local *kami* (gods or sacred entities), amounting to a sort of animistic regard for nature and ancestors. Mythologies of the *kami* tell of the origins of the imperial family as well as the beginnings of all Japanese people; they also explain the many shrines, festivals, and rituals in Japanese culture. When Buddhism arrived in Japan, syncretistic innovations incorporated Buddhist texts and practices at Shinto shrines, and similarly *kami* regarded as "protectors of the Buddha's Law" were installed in Japanese Buddhist temples. The introduction of Zen Buddhism during the medieval period of Japan attracted the attention of the *samurai*, the Japanese warrior class; this more contemplative form of Buddhism seeks enlightenment through the practice of *zazen*, sitting in meditation, to awaken the Buddha-nature within each person. The samurai combined Zen with Confucian teachings brought from China to form *bushido*, the way of the warrior. As a result, the religious synthesis of Shinto worship, Buddhism, and Confucian teachings together form the foundation of distinctly Japanese aesthetics and cultural forms.[37]

Beginning in the nineteenth century and accelerating dramatically in the late twentieth century, virtually all of these Asian religious orientations have found their way into American society. Most came with immigrants, but, as we will see in this and later chapters, Asian immigrants were not the only ones who took an interest in the various religions coming east from Asia; by the final decades of the twentieth century, a significant number of Euro-American, African American, and even some Native American converts in numbers that rival the immigrants had adapted Asian spiritual orientations and practices to their own circumstances.

In the first decade of the twentieth century, the US census noted 62 Chinese temples and 141 Chinese shrines located in twelve states. At the same time, Japanese Buddhists counted more than three thousand official members in the United States, with likely many more loosely affiliated with Buddhist and Shinto traditions; a good number of Koreans working sugar plantations in Hawaii also followed Buddhist precepts and practices. In addition, some three thousand Asian Indian immigrants entered the United States during the first decade of the twentieth century, most of them Hindus but also many Sikhs. Concentrated in the cities and towns of the American west as well as in the Hawaiian islands, Asian immigrant communities had established a foothold for their various religious orientations by the beginning of the twentieth century.[38]

Nativism

With so many newcomers of diverse origins and ethnicities crowding the poorest sectors of America's cities, a crisis simmered in the imaginations of Americans who felt threatened by the rapid transformations occurring all around them. The sudden influx of foreigners into American society revived **nativist**, anti-immigrant sentiments based on the millennialist notion of an American "Manifest Destiny" (see Box 6.3 and Box 7.1). As before, much of the animosity directed at immigrants in the final decades of the nineteenth century carried strong anti-Catholic and anti-Semitic assumptions as well as racist sentiments; the hostility directed toward immigrants arriving from Europe revived age-old religious enmity.[39]

Among the many books and articles invoking the specter of the foreign threat posed by European immigrants was *Our Country* (1885) by Josiah Strong (1847–1916), a prominent Congregational minister in Cincinnati, Ohio. Strong's book combined warnings about the dangers of ignoring social ills in American cities with an insistence on Protestant and Anglo-Saxon (meaning white, English-speaking) supremacy in a triumphant American imperialism; he envisioned the world entering

> a new stage of its history – *the final competition of races, for which the Anglo-Saxon is being schooled*. Long before the thousand millions are here, the mighty *centrifugal* tendency, inherent in this stock and strengthened in the United States, will assert itself. Then this race of unequaled energy, with all the majesty of numbers and the might of wealth behind it – the representative, let us hope, of the largest liberty, the purest Christianity, the highest civilization – having developed peculiarly aggressive traits calculated to impress its institutions upon mankind, will spread itself over the earth.[40]

Strong's confidence in the triumph of white Protestants, however, signaled a more benevolent and conciliatory tone than other more harshly vindictive instances of nativist agitation experienced in earlier decades. The way forward for him involved helping immigrants to become fully American Protestants; Strong implored his fellow white Christians to take up the cause of missionary work among the "foreign element" in American society, anticipating the subsequent reform movement known as the "social gospel."[41]

European immigrants were not the only ones experiencing an inhospitable welcome to America; Asians also felt the harsh backlash of American nativist attitudes. For some Euro-American Protestants, the strangely unfamiliar languages, cultures, and religions of Asian immigrants, in addition to the threat that their low-wage labor posed to established vocations, incited strongly racist emotions that resulted in vicious attacks, especially on Chinese immigrants in the American west.[42] In fact, the "Chinese problem" in California superseded rancor between Christians as it brought together Protestants and Catholics in a united effort to oppose, in the words of San Francisco's Catholic newspaper in 1873, "the presence of a common danger."[43] In 1882, the US Congress enacted legislation excluding Chinese immigration, based largely on economic claims of unfair labor competition but undergirded by fears of religious and racial differences; in debating the bill, one Senator expressed the fear that allowing unlimited Chinese immigration would threaten American racial and religious purity by creating "a mongrel race, half Chinese and half Caucasian [producing] a civilization half pagan, half Christian, semi-Oriental, altogether mixed and very bad."[44] Indeed, nativist logic found its strongest support in opposing "the pagan Oriental."

On the other hand, not all Americans supported nativist exclusionary policies; in fact, vocal critics of anti-immigrant forces expressed hopes for a nation of diverse peoples of many traditions. Frederick Douglass (1818–1895), for example, recognized the advantages of a diverse culture as he extended his abolitionist vision of a global humanity into the postbellum period. He predicted in 1869 that Chinese immigration would soon become "our irrepressible fact," establishing a significant Asian element in the American nation, which he welcomed. Douglass envisioned America as a "composite nationality," what he called "the most perfect illustration of the unity and dignity of the human family that the world has ever seen." Besides their contributions to American economic growth, Chinese and other Asians would strengthen American religious life by broadening religious liberty; Douglass argued, "We should welcome all men of every shade of religious opinion, as among the best means of checking the ignorance and intolerance which are the almost inevitable concomitants of general conformity. Religious liberty always flourishes best amid the clash and competition of rival religious creeds."[45] For Douglass, the Chinese, Filipinos, Japanese, Koreans, and other Asians brought to America a religious diversity that could only strengthen the nation.

Social gospel

Frederick Douglass' prescient vision of a society strengthened by its diversity was not shared by most Americans in the nineteenth century. Most of the concerned citizens of the day, and especially those working with Christian benevolent societies and other religious groups addressing the plight of immigrants, aimed to "Americanize" the foreign newcomers by facilitating their assimilation to American society. These benevolent Christians presumed that the best way for immigrants to prosper in their new communities was for them to adopt the language and customs of American civil society and to convert to Protestant Christianity. At the same time, most newly arrived immigrants faced deplorable conditions in the neighborhoods where they settled, with poverty, disease, inadequate housing, and unsanitary housing awaiting the new arrivals. These circumstances stirred the sympathies of Christian workers dedicated to the social betterment of immigrants; their efforts, collectively regarded as the "social gospel" movement, included campaigns for child-labor laws and better regulation of factory safety, stricter housing codes, and public health regulations.[46] One of the leading proponents of this effort at social betterment famously defined the social gospel as "the application of the teaching of Jesus and the total message of the Christian salvation to society, the economic life, and social institutions such as the state [and] the family, as well as to individuals"; this late-nineteenth-century movement sought the total conversion of society in addition to personal religious conversions of individuals. Indebted to American Protestant millennialist traditions, the social gospel movement envisioned the fulfillment of God's will in the creation of a just social order.[47]

Among the earliest advocates of the social gospel was the Congregational pastor Washington Gladden (1836–1918) of Columbus, Ohio. Labor unrest in Ohio motivated Gladden to publish in 1876 *Working People and Their Employers*, in which he articulated a social gospel theology that rejects both a social Darwinist survival-of-the-fittest view that leaves the poor and vulnerable to their own devices as well as a socialist approach that invites excessive government involvement; instead, Gladden advocates a socially conscious Christianity, seeking to persuade Christian capitalists to abide by the moral precepts of their faith in treating workers fairly. For Gladden and many other social gospel advocates, evangelism involved doing battle with social inequities that robbed workers of their human dignity.[48]

The most influential theologian of the social gospel movement was the Baptist minister and seminary professor Walter Rauschenbusch (1861–1918), who laid out a theological basis for Christian social justice in the early twentieth century. Rauschenbusch made a historical argument regarding God's will for social progress; he wrote, "All history becomes the unfolding of the purpose of the

Figure 8.4 Hull House in Chicago, founded by Jane Addams and Ellen Gates Starr, exemplified the social gospel movement in offering support, companionship, and various types of assistance for immigrants. (Courtesy of New York Public Library, #1263883.)

immanent God who is working in the race toward the commonwealth of spiritual liberty and righteousness. History is the sacred workshop of God."[49] In particular, God's involvement in human history required economic reforms; Rauschenbusch proposed "that the overgrowth of private interests has institutionalized an unchristian principle, and that we must reverse the line of movement if we want to establish the law of Christ."[50] Even among the most liberal Protestants, instituting Christian law guided efforts for social reforms.

The social reforms called for by Christian activists such as Gladden and Rauschenbusch often involved efforts to Americanize immigrants. A well-known example of such assimilation initiatives is the famous settlement house in Chicago, Illinois, the Hull House, founded in 1889 by Jane Addams (1860–1935) and Ellen Gates Starr (1859–1940). They began by offering opportunities for their poorer neighbors to enjoy art and literature, but soon they concentrated on practical skills for immigrants adjusting to American society, with lessons in such areas as language, cooking, and sewing plus provision of services such as child care, a public kitchen and baths, and a playground. Residents and neighbors alike gathered at Hull House for support, companionship, and assistance in adapting to urban life in America.[51]

The reformers of the social gospel movement aimed some of their most vehement criticism toward the powerful industrialists of the Gilded Age. The ruthless policies of such magnates as John D. Rockefeller (1839–1937), whose Standard Oil Company made him America's first billionaire, and Andrew Carnegie (1835–1919), a Scottish-born immigrant whose success in the steel industry allowed him to reign as America's greatest philanthropist at the turn of the twentieth century, were common targets of social reform activists. Rockefeller was a lifelong Baptist, remaining active in his local congregation even after he became the world's richest person. He attributed his financial success to his evangelical commitments, believing that God had rewarded his piety with wealth.[52] At the same time, though, he embraced social Darwinist ideas to explain his business success as "survival of the fittest." Andrew Carnegie, in contrast, preferred to stay aloof from his Presbyterian heritage through much of his life; in his autobiography he explains, "Not only had I got rid of the theology and the supernatural, but I had found the truth of evolution."[53] Yet later in his life he was active in the Madison Avenue Presbyterian Church in New York City, led by the renowned social gospel preacher Henry Sloane Coffin (1877–1954), although his religious views remained distinctively unorthodox for Protestants of his day.

Rockefeller and Carnegie are just two of the most well-known philanthropists of their day whose infamy as industrialists was softened by their charitable generosity. The constant criticisms from social gospel activists of their business practices, especially in regard to their treatment of workers, had an impact on their public image, if not them directly. Their personal beliefs resonated with the Christian social gospel, and they took seriously their own moral obligations with regard to the vast resources at their disposal. In his 1889 essay "Wealth"

Box 8.4   Gospel hymns

Advocates of the social gospel were not the only Protestants evangelizing in America's cities; a spate of urban revivals erupted in the 1870s, led most prominently by the evangelist Dwight L. Moody (1837–1899). One feature of this new awakening of Protestant evangelism was the introduction of music as a key ingredient in the revivalist repertoire. Singing had been part of earlier revivals, but in the 1870s Christian hymns became an indispensable element in revival events. Moody teamed up with musician and composer of Christian hymns Ira D. Sankey (1840–1908), and the overwhelming acclaim they enjoyed made clear that Sankey's music was as much of an attraction as Moody's preaching; specifically, his new style of "gospel hymns" immediately became widely popular among evangelical Protestant Christians. Described by one historian as "sentimental spiritual lyrics … set to various styles of Victorian music," the gospel hymn as a new style of Christian sacred song combined emotional first-person lyrics with the strong melodies and close harmonies of operettas, glees, and barbershop choral styles popular in the late nineteenth century.[54]

Alongside the sudden growth of gospel hymns in the 1870s and 1880s was a revival of Negro spirituals among African American Christians. Many of the formerly enslaved African Americans initially avoided the old spirituals as too closely associated with their bitter memories of bondage. But the unprecedented popularity of the Fisk Jubilee Singers among white and black audiences alike, not only in America but also in their extensive tours of Europe, gave the traditional spirituals legitimacy in African American churches.[55] Initially begun as a fund-raising effort to save the faltering Fisk University in Nashville, a school founded in 1866 to serve African Americans in the Reconstruction era, the Fisk Jubilee Singers embarked on their first singing tour in 1871. Included in their repertoire were formal arrangements of traditional spirituals, and they electrified audiences with their startling performances. By 1875 they were internationally famous, and they raised enough money not only to keep Fisk University operating but also to build Jubilee Hall, the first permanent building in the American south dedicated to the education of African American students; the building is now a National Historic Landmark, but the greatest legacy of the Fisk Jubilee Singers are the many spirituals they introduced that are still sung in churches and other performance venues throughout America and around the world, including such classics as "Steal Away" and "Swing Low, Sweet Chariot."

Figure 8.5 The Fisk Jubilee Singers, shown here in a group portrait from the 1870s, introduced traditional spirituals to audiences throughout America and Europe, giving legitimacy to a musical style that became a standard feature in many African American churches. (Courtesy of the Library of Congress, LC-DIG-ppmsca-11008.)

(commonly known as "The Gospel of Wealth"), Andrew Carnegie presents a defense and justification for his prosperity; but the wealth one accumulates, Carnegie goes on to argue, must be put to good use in charitable causes that benefit all of society. His plan envisions

> an ideal state, in which the surplus wealth of the few will become, in the best sense the property of the many, because administered for the common good, and this wealth, passing through the hands of the few, can be made a much more potent force for the elevation of our race than if it had been distributed in small sums to the people themselves.[56]

In a view of capitalist prosperity still embraced in the twenty-first century by such wealthy figures as Warren Buffet (born 1930) and Bill Gates (born 1955), Carnegie insisted on the philanthropic distribution of wealth during one's lifetime; he exemplified his philosophy by donating to numerous causes, most famously the many local libraries he funded throughout the nation. Likewise, Rockefeller also set out to share at least part of his fortune through socially beneficial charities, especially colleges and universities, founding such institutions as the University of Chicago and Rockefeller University in New York City.

Crises of gender

While the industrial and political matters of the day remained largely a male concern, women of the Gilded Age period pursued their own interests. The dominant gender ideology of middle- and upper-class Americans continued to separate male and female spheres, with men active in public affairs while women remained out of the limelight in the home and in churches. But challenges to this state of affairs grew as the movement for women's rights regained some of its momentum after the Civil War. Two organizations established in 1869, the National Woman Suffrage Association and the American Woman Suffrage Association, brought national attention to the exclusion of women from the political process; they worked at both state and federal levels to change voting laws, and by the end of the century three states and one American territory, all in the American west, allowed voting rights for women.

Women's concerns about social reform extended well beyond the right to vote. The largest reform organization for women in the late nineteenth century was the Woman's Christian Temperance Union, begun in 1873 in Ohio and quickly becoming a national political force. Aimed at protecting homes and families from the scourge of alcoholism, the Union sought to ban alcohol while spreading the evangelical Protestant gospel. The organization's rhetoric relied heavily on the gender ideology of women's domesticity even as it expanded the public role of women. Initially, Union activists confined themselves to "womanly" means of moral persuasion, but later they became more politically active with such slogans as "Organized Mother Love" and "Home Protection." They also extended their temperance initiative to include other reforms, including women's suffrage, which they insisted would strengthen domesticity with legislation supporting the womanly responsibility for protecting the home and nurturing the family.[57]

The political activism of women in national campaigns for temperance, voting rights, and other causes spurred a reaction on the part of some Protestant Americans. By the end of the nineteenth century, the accepted gender ideology had begun to crumble; the need for religious virtues such as restraint, thrift, and humility to serve as the moral underpinning of democracy began to erode in favor of consumerism and speculative risk-taking in Gilded Age America. The consolidation of corporate culture and its **ethos** of growth and progress in an industrialized, post-Civil War nation encouraged criticisms of religion specifically as the source of a perceived "crisis in masculinity." Pointing to the fact that the majority of members in the nation's Protestant churches were female (ignoring that this had always been the case), influential voices advocated regendering religious institutions with a "muscular Christianity" that would remove religion from its effeminate state and align it with the manly world of commerce and politics. Conservative evangelists such as Billy Sunday (1862–1935), a former baseball player who delighted in criticizing effeminate liberalism, regarded Christianity as a man's religion. But conservatives were not alone in asserting

Box 8.5 The *Woman's Bible*

As an elderly veteran of the women's rights movement, Elizabeth Cady Stanton (1815–1902) resented the exclusion of women on religious grounds. She wrote in 1886, "We can make no impression on men who accept the theological view of woman as the author of sin, cursed of God, and all that nonsense. The debris of the centuries must be cleared away before our arguments for equality can have the least significance to any of them." Consequently, she set about the task of clearing Christian misogynist debris by recruiting a committee of like-minded women to revise the Christian Bible. Published in two volumes in 1895 and 1898, the *Woman's Bible* presents biblical passages referring to women or women's concerns and includes commentaries on them, written by Stanton and her committee members. Stanton regarded this final project in her very long and prolific career as her "crowning achievement."

Stanton expected that her *Woman's Bible* would mark a pivotal moment in American attitudes about the rights of women; reactions to the book, however, were nearly the opposite. Partisans on both sides of the suffragist debate roundly condemned her work; the opposition cited it as proof of the suffragists' motives to undo Christian society in America, whereas her feminist allies thought that she had gone too far in criticizing Christianity as the moral basis of American society. The National American Woman Suffrage Association denounced the book in 1896, even with Stanton herself as their honorary president. With condemnation coming from all sides, the beleaguered Stanton soon found herself nearly alone in her prescient criticism of Christian patriarchy. Abandoned by a younger generation of women's rights activists and largely dismissed by subsequent historians of the movement, Stanton and her *Woman's Bible* nearly disappeared from public view. It would not be until the feminist movements of the 1970s that her insightful criticisms of Christian gender ideology would be revived in several new editions of the *Woman's Bible*.[58]

gender ideologies in religious life; liberal Christians also chimed in with their own masculinizing views. Indeed, many Protestants in the late nineteenth century, both conservative and liberal, emulated a brawny, fearless Jesus in an attempt to reassert the male prerogative in Christian culture.[59] One result of this turn toward a more masculine Christianity was the increasing popularity of the Young Men's Christian Association (YMCA) in American cities; founded in the 1840s in England, this ecumenical Protestant organization established branches in most American cities by the end of the nineteenth century with its blending of a manly concern for physical fitness with its evangelical religious efforts.[60]

New Religious Ways

The conservative reassertion of male prerogative in a muscular Christianity was as much a reaction to the emergence of new Christian forms and other religious movements led by women as it was an adaptation to social and economic developments in Gilded Age America. In particular, a number of new religious movements in the final decades of the nineteenth century included women in positions of leadership. Although the success of the women's rights movement in the nineteenth century was limited, the call for equal rights allowed some women to assert themselves in new ways at the forefront of various religious movements. At the same time, a number of liberal Christians were reevaluating the relationship between the human soul and the physical body as new innovations entered American Christian culture.

Apocalyptic Christianity

In the aftermath of the unrealized **apocalyptic** expectations of the Millerites in the 1840s (see Chapter 6), a handful of the faithful still believed that the promised millennium was not far off. A young girl by the name of Ellen G. Harmon (1827–1915, widely known by her married name of White), who had converted to Methodism but subsequently became a devout follower of the Millerite movement along with her family, experienced a powerful prophetic vision of the advent people (Millerites convinced of the advent of Christ's return) on their way to the city of God. Subsequent visionary experiences led her to share her revelations with other Adventists, initiating a ministry involving visions, interpretations of her revelations, and teachings based upon them. She married James Springer White (1821–1881) in 1846, and the couple soon met Joseph Bates (1792–1872), another former Millerite, who introduced the Whites to seventh-day Sabbatarianism; Bates was convinced that the great apostasy of Christianity was celebration of a first-day Sabbath, or worship on Sundays. According to Bates' interpretation, the Sabbath celebrates creation and therefore should be celebrated on the seventh day of the week, or Saturday, as is the custom of Jews. Christians who observe the Sabbath on Sunday, according to Bates and the Whites, will not experience salvation. Other distinctive features of these early Seventh-Day Adventists included a pacifist ideology, which kept most of their followers out of combat duty in the Civil War, and dietary rules that urged abstinence from meat, coffee, and tea and warned against consuming excessive amounts of food.[61]

Together the Whites and Joseph Bates pursued an aggressive evangelical campaign in the 1850s, with constant revivals and publication of their journal, *The Advent Review and Sabbath Herald*. The Whites settled in Battle Creek, Michigan, which became the headquarters of the Adventist movement and later the location of a cereal food industry based on Adventist dietary beliefs. Indispensable to their theology was the notion of a pure body, and the Adventists emphasized health and hygiene in their publications and preaching. Supporters of temperance, they

Figure 8.6 The Western Health Reform Institute, more commonly known as the Battle Creek Sanatorium, introduced healthy nutrition and exercise and treated patients with hydrotherapy, in line with Seventh-Day Adventist doctrines. John Harvey Kellogg directed the Institute for many years, and his commitment to Adventist dietary principles led to the invention of corn flakes, which his brother developed into a major breakfast-cereal company based in Battle Creek, Michigan. (Courtesy of the Library of Congress, LC-DIG-ggbain-15053.)

advocated abstention from all alcohol, and a prophecy from Ellen G. White in the 1850s initiated a campaign against tobacco use. The Adventists established in Battle Creek the Western Health Reform Institute, based on their theories of sickness and health, with an emphasis on hydropathic therapy, or water cures, for treating ailments without drugs; a young physician, John Harvey Kellogg (1852–1943), headed the new institute, which eventually grew into a large and famous sanatorium that treated numerous well-known and influential Americans in the nineteenth and early twentieth centuries. In line with Adventist dietary needs, Kellogg developed a method of turning cooked grains into dry flakes, which later became the basis of the Kellogg cereal empire built by his brother, Will Keith Kellogg (1860–1951). A competing cereal company also was established in Battle Creek by a former patient at the Adventist sanatorium, C. W. Post (1854–1914). In the subsequent decades more Adventist hospitals were built based on their health principles, especially water cures, but over time these methods were blended with more modern medical procedures. Still, a commitment to vegetarianism and abstinence from alcohol and tobacco continue to characterize Adventist lifestyles.[62]

In later years Ellen G. White took a more active role in the leadership of Adventism. Her prophetic visions, though, had long been a source of controversy. Early Adventist leaders stressed that Church doctrine rested solely on the authority of biblical scriptures, not prophetic proclamations. Nevertheless, White settled key doctrinal disputes with revelations that favored one side or the other. She announced and interpreted her visions in her prodigious writings, which established her place as the authoritative visionary voice of the Church; her writings also became the basis for charges of blasphemy by other Christian groups. In later years, a falling out with John Harvey Kellogg led to a bitter dispute that only enhanced the reception of White's prophetic teachings among the faithful. It also moved the Church toward a more doctrinally conservative position that characterizes its subsequent history.

Another movement among Christians concerned about an imminent apocalypse was the Jehovah's Witnesses (originally called simply the Bible Students; their name changed to Jehovah's Witnesses in 1931). Charles Taze Russell (1852–1916) encountered Adventism in his teens, and in 1870 he began an intensive Bible-study group in Pittsburgh, Pennsylvania, which would eventually grow into a worldwide denomination. In 1886 Russell began publishing his six-volume work *Studies in the Scriptures*, which lays out his interpretation of world history and the doctrines of the new movement he had founded. The Adventist influence appears in the emphasis on Christ's imminent return to establish a millennial age on earth. Russell denied the existence of hell, and regarded death, rather than the eternal torment popular among many American Protestants, as the punishment for sin. The most radical of his ideas was the rejection of the Christian Trinity; Russell regarded Jesus as a fully human person, not a deity, and the Holy Spirit as the power and energy of God, not a person. His theology insisted on a singular and unitary God. The Christian Church in Russell's estimation consisted of two classes of people: the 144 000 saints promised in scripture who are assured of eternal life with the angels and the vast majority of devout followers who would live in the heavenly kingdom as natural humans, still at risk of losing their salvation through disobedience or collusion with Satan's forces. Also essential to Russell's religious views was continuity with the Jewish religion; the earthly millennial kingdom that he envisioned would be a new Israel, with the saved saints and others all becoming Jews.[63]

The Church that Russell established consisted initially of little more than a collection of Bible-study groups. He directed their studies, however, through publications issued through his publishing enterprise, the Zion's Watch Tower Bible and Tract Society, especially the periodical *Zion's Watch Tower and Herald of Christ's Presence*, still published today as *The Watchtower*. In fact, the only ecclesial structure of Russell's Bible Students movement was the publishing society; without a clergy and with completely autonomous local congregations, their only common connection was the evangelical distribution of their literature. Their worship in the nineteenth and early twentieth centuries consisted primarily of intensive Bible study and a commitment to spread the truth in the sale and distribution of *The Watchtower* and other Society publications.[64]

New Thought for healthful bodies

While the Adventists and Bible Students emphasized pure and healthful living in anticipation of an imminent apocalypse, a related movement known as New Thought advocated mind-cure techniques for attaining health and happiness. Nineteenth-century American mind healing developed into a fully organized religious movement around the leadership and writings of Mary Baker Eddy (1821–1910), whose Church of Christ, Scientist became the leading proponent of curing illness with faith and a disciplined mind. Mary Baker's childhood was riddled with sickness, and ill health would remain throughout her lifetime. She tried various therapeutic approaches popular in her day, including the water-cure techniques advocated by the Adventists, all to no avail, until she met Phineas P. Quimby (1802–1866), a successful mind-cure healer in Portland, Maine. He had begun his practice using hypnotism, or mesmerism as it was called then, but later gave up hypnotic techniques for a verbal therapy supplemented with massage. He explained the seemingly miraculous recovery of his patients by maintaining that one's false beliefs cause physical maladies; he demonstrated that, by repudiating erroneous thinking and substituting new, healthful beliefs, the body would return to its naturally healthful state. Mary Baker Eddy's recovery under his care seemed miraculous to her, and she began studying and lecturing about Quimby's methods. Although her illness eventually returned, and later she would downplay his influence on her own ideas about health and illness, Quimby certainly played a large role in Eddy's emerging reputation as a mind healer.[65]

After years of practicing and teaching her mind-cure techniques, Eddy published the first edition of her book, *Science and Health*, in 1875. She would continue to revise the text that her followers regard as scripture, with a final version published in 1907, although the central tenets changed little in its various editions. Its key insight asserts that reality consists of a singular, unified, and perfect whole, which Eddy names variously as God, Mind, Spirit, Soul, Principle, Life, Truth, and Love, among other terms. This singular reality, according to Eddy, transcends human description but is manifest in each person as a reflection of divine essence; in other words, each person or spirit is unified with God, and therefore is perfect. Humans, according to her interpretations, are immortal spiritual beings, without error, absent of suffering or death. Unfortunately most people do not know this, Eddy contends; they think of themselves as material beings. Their illusions of material reality cause suffering, illness, and mortality. But, by realizing the illusory character of the material world, individuals could overcome their own illness and suffering; healing, according to Eddy, involves changing one's erroneous beliefs and overcoming one's sins.[66]

Mary Baker Eddy's book did not enjoy much circulation at first; most purchasers were students who had paid for formal mind-cure training with her. Over the years, however, a growing group of disciples formed a recognizable Christian Science movement in several US cities. Eddy asserted control of the movement despite numerous conflicts with rebellious members. In the 1890s she was able to centralize administration of the Church of Christ, Scientist and to stipulate a form of worship that involved weekly readings from the Christian Bible and *Science and Health*. Even today, the mother church in Boston stipulates the readings for all congregations each week, and these constitute the central component of weekly worship. Rather than clergy, two **lay** readers, usually one male and one female, lead local meetings. They begin with the Bible reading, then read the assigned passage from *Science and Health*; no sermon nor even commentary, questions, or discussion of the readings occur; adult leaders of Sunday school for children and youth interpret the weekly passages for young members. All official theological and doctrinal determinations emanate only from the mother church in Boston.[67]

Beyond churches

Religious influences in nineteenth-century American popular culture were evident well beyond the churches, synagogues, temples, and shrines of the American cultural landscape; in fact, disenchantment with the dominant Christian churches of the era motivated many of the prolific religious innovations. During the middle decades of the nineteenth century, a popular religious movement known as Spiritualism became ubiquitous in American culture, operating outside formal religious organizations and crossing boundaries between religion and secular entertainments. Communication with spirits of the dead had exceptional religious appeal to some nineteenth-century Americans, but entrepreneurs quickly learned that it had profitable entertainment value as well. The solace it provided to those who had lost loved ones afforded a livelihood to mediums and promoters who profited from the sincere faith of believers; they also benefited from the entertainment pleasure that Spiritualism offered to the incredulous and the merely curious.[68]

The Spiritualist phenomenon began in 1848 in the same region of New York state where both Mormonism and Millerism originated. It started when two young sisters, Margaret Fox (1833–1893) and Kate Fox (1837–1892), living with their family in a home long reputed to be haunted, established communication with spirits; the spirit haunting the house would answer their inquiries by rapping on walls and furniture. Soon a crowd of townspeople gathered to witness the young girls' coded exchanges with the spirit. When the girls moved to Rochester, New York, to live with their much older sister, Ann Leah Fox (later Fish, 1814–1890), their powers to communicate with the spirits of the dead quickly gained the attention of local reformers, who established weekly meetings to ascertain truths revealed by spirits mediated by the young sisters, along with their older sister Leah, who also discovered a clairvoyant talent. Eventually their fame took them to New York City, where renowned newspaper publisher Horace Greeley (1811–1872) brought national attention to their public performances and private séances. Soon thousands of Americans took to communicating with dead spirits in public demonstrations and private consultations with clairvoyant practitioners in cities and towns throughout the nation.[69]

The phenomenal interest in clairvoyant communications never developed into a formal religious organization; Spiritualist conventions became common, but the movement remained a strictly individualistic practice of mediumship. Although it captured the imagination of a broad swath of the American population and attracted a fair share of opportunistic charlatans as well as a host of critics and detractors, the most fervent adherents to the Spiritualist path were liberal reformers. As an alternative to the dominant Protestant Christianity of American society, regarded as excessively oppressive by many reformers, Spiritualist practice affirmed an optimism of a new era based on unprecedented achievements at both the individual and social levels under the guidance of the spirits of the departed. This was especially true in the area of women's rights; as movement leaders Elizabeth Cady Stanton and Susan B. Anthony (1820–1906) exclaim in their *History of Woman Suffrage* (1881–1922), "The only religious sect in the world … that has recognized the equality of woman is the Spiritualists."[70] In all areas of Spiritualist practice and ideology, women enjoyed equal status, and sometimes superior status, to men.

Spiritualism flourished into the postbellum era, but its popularity contributed to its demise, although the Spiritualist strain in American religiosity has never disappeared completely and would periodically enjoy revived popularity in American culture. The radically nonconformist nature of Spiritualism became less appealing in the 1870s and 1880s as social reformers tended to take more moderate stances; moreover, a growing liberal movement among Protestants and increased opportunities for women both in churches and in society at large eroded some of the distinctive contrast that Spiritualism offered to those alienated from conventional Christian communities. A series of scandals and revelations among Spiritualist practitioners contributed to its decline, and in time other interests, especially Mary Baker Eddy's Christian Science movement, would claim many of the former followers of Spiritualism.

Another movement that gained attention beginning in the 1870s, Theosophy, also had its roots in the popular attractions of Spiritualism. The main personalities who established Theosophy in nineteenth-century America came together through a shared interest in Spiritualism. In time, though, they turned from the individual concerns of the Spiritualists toward a more universalistic understanding that incorporated Asian religious and philosophical traditions. Helena Petrovna Blavatsky (1831–1891), daughter of a well-to-do Russian family who as a young woman displayed a gift of psychic powers, had been exposed to various religious traditions and movements as she traveled widely in Europe, Asia, and the Americas before settling in New York City in 1873. There she joined with Henry Steel Olcott (1832–1907), a Civil War veteran and lawyer, to inaugurate the Theosophical Society in 1875. They initially met through their common interest in Spiritualism, and they formed a close friendship as they added increasingly esoteric elements to their spiritualist practices, including ancient traditions of alchemy and magic. The Theosophical Society itself became an outlet for the dissemination of esoteric wisdom, but it also aimed to reveal the universal wisdom underlying all religions. Consequently, its publications and activities helped to introduce key Asian concepts into the American spiritual lexicon. Such ideas as *karma*, the cosmic law of

Box 8.6   Orientalism

Scholars studying the aftermath of European colonial empires have adopted the term "orientalism" to indicate the colonial representation of "Orientals" in European politics, literature, art, and culture. Literary theorist Edward Said (1935–2003), a Palestinian Arab educated in the United States, brought attention to the colonial assumptions and consequences of European representations of Arabs, Asians, and other so-called "Orientals" in his 1978 book *Orientalism*. In this seminal work of postcolonial criticism, Said describes orientalism in terms of several interdependent meanings. Most generally, it refers to what he calls "a style of thought based upon an ontological and epistemological distinction between 'the Orient' and (most of the time) 'the Occident.'" In other words, Orientalist perspectives generally assume a fundamental difference between people of the east, most often regarded as static and simplistic, although in many cases as aesthetically appealing, and the west, depicted as progressive and complex; the Oriental, then, serves as the "other" to Europeans, who rely on their supposed superiority, in Said's analysis, "for dominating, restructuring, and having authority over the Orient."[71]

The colonial contexts giving rise to these patronizing attitudes and representations also have privileged European and Euro-American interpretations of religions. As we have seen over and over throughout this book, the dynamics of encounter in colonial contact zones often rely on religious resources and perspectives for interpreting differences between cultures. As the work of Edward Said and other twentieth-century postcolonial scholars has demonstrated, this certainly has been true of non-Asian encounters with the people and cultures of Asia. As a result, most non-Asian Americans have had a simplistic and often idealized view of Asian religions filtered through strongly orientalist interpretations. These sorts of distorted views became commonplace as Christian Euro-Americans first became aware of Asians in American society in the nineteenth century; moreover, orientalist perspectives were perpetuated with sympathetic and admiring attitudes when people such as Helena Petrovna Blavatsky and Henry Steel Olcott settled in Asia and sent back to western audiences their Theosophist interpretations of Asian cultures and religions. Perhaps the most obvious orientalist occasion in nineteenth-century America occurred with the inclusion of Asian spiritual leaders at the 1893 World's Parliament of Religions in Chicago. By the turn of the twentieth century, orientalist perspectives reigned as the dominant view of Asian cultures, including religion, in American public life.

cause and effect, as well as reincarnation as a spiritual path through multiple lives toward ultimate wisdom, received public attention in America through the efforts of the Theosophical Society.[72]

Another Theosophist, Annie Besant (1847–1933), contributed to the American interpretive transformation of Asian religions with her own importation of New Thought ideas into Theosophical universalism. Endorsing meditation, her 1908 book *Thought Power: Its Control and Culture* advocated the systematic cultivation of concentration, especially in devotional discipline according to whatever religious orientation the practitioner preferred. Besant published another book the same year that recommended meditation along with Hindu practices of yoga; *An Introduction to Yoga* depicts the bodily exercises of yogic practice as an effective means to quiet the "restless, storm-tossed mind."[73]

Quieting the mind and disciplining the body through the borrowing and reinterpretation of Asian religious practices added another dimension to the American religious landscape that would come to full blossom later in the twentieth century. Theosophists and others intrigued by Buddhism, Hinduism, and various orientations of Asian provenance remained a small minority, but they gained enough attention by the end of the nineteenth century to warrant consideration by mainstream Americans. Although not completely divorced from the dominant Christian culture that defined much of American society, the proliferation of new religious movements began to change the texture of religion in America.

America's Double Consciousness

A growing interest in unfamiliar religious traditions from places such as Asia and the Caribbean region, as well as the resistance and even hostility sometimes voiced in condemnation of such "pagan" religions, indicate a gradual transition in American religious culture. The pressures of industrialization and a rapidly expanding nation plunged America into an era of religious changes; pious Americans of all sorts found creative means of adapting their moral and religious commitments to the dynamic circumstances of the late nineteenth century. Indicative of these changing circumstances, a grand spectacle of religious diversity, the World's Parliament of Religions, staged as part of the 1893 World's Columbian Exposition in Chicago, reveals the paradoxical religious tensions within American society at a moment of transition between the nineteenth and twentieth centuries. This ambitious gathering of religious leaders and scholars from around the world hoped on the one hand to demonstrate religious differences and the unique qualities of the world's great religions in an extravaganza of interfaith presentations and discussions. On the other hand, the organizers also harbored a liberal agenda of universalism that sought "to unite all religion against all irreligion" and "to indicate the impregnable foundations of theism."[74] As the parliamentarians gathered in the

Figure 8.7   Delegates to the World's Parliament of Religions pose on stage while members of the press look on. Participants gathered in Chicago's Memorial Art Palace during the 1893 World's Columbian Exposition to celebrate "the sun of a new era of religious peace and progress." (Frontispiece to Barrows, ed., *The World's Parliament of Religions*, 1893; photo courtesy of Newberry Library.)

Memorial Art Palace (today the site of the Chicago Art Institute) to celebrate this great in-gathering of religions, Charles Carroll Bonney (1831–1903) welcomed the assemblage by declaring, "This day the sun of a new era of religious peace and progress rises over the world, dispelling the dark clouds of sectarian strife … This day a new fraternity is born into the world of religious progress, to aid the upbuilding of the kingdom of God in the hearts of men."[75] Over the seventeen days of the Parliament, delegates heard from Buddhists, Christians, Confucians, Hindus, Jains, Jews, Muslims, Shintoists, Taoists, and Zoroastrians in a dizzying array of philosophies, theologies, creeds, and cultural expressions presented in 216 lectures.

With such a diverse gathering of religious views, it seems in retrospect somewhat audacious and naïve for the organizers to expect a common goal of unity among those present. In fact, the World's Parliament of Religions became an occasion for some of the delegates to criticize the underlying Protestant and imperialistic logic of world religious unity. In a condemnation of Christian missionary efforts in India, Virchand Gandhi (1864–1901), a Jain representative, declared, "Abuses are not arguments against any religion, nor self-adulation the proof of the truth of one's own." In his remarks at the closing of the Parliament, Hindu delegate Swami Vivekananda (1863–1902) characterized the desire for religious unity achieved "by the triumph of any one of these religions and the destruction of others" as "an impossible hope."[76] Instead of unity, the World's Parliament of Religions offered a global stage for diverse voices to air their grievances but also to explain the integrity and insights of their own cultural perspectives.

The World's Parliament of Religions represents a useful historical marker in the transition from the national concerns of nineteenth-century America to the global concerns of America's twentieth-century experience. It reveals for American religiosity something akin to what the African American scholar and civil rights activist W. E. B. Du Bois (1868–1963) identified as "double consciousness" for African American identity in his classic collection of essays *The Souls of Black Folk*, first published in 1903. Du Bois asserted that "the problem of the Twentieth Century is the problem of the color line" and that for African Americans this produces

> a peculiar sensation, this double-consciousness, always looking at one's self through the eyes of others, of measuring one's soul by the tape of a world that looks on in amused contempt and pity. One ever feels his two-ness, – an American, a Negro; two souls, two thoughts, two unreconciled strivings; two warring ideals in one dark body, whose dogged strength alone keeps it from being torn asunder.[77]

In the multiverse of American religious consciousness at the beginning of the twentieth century, a duplicity existed for many people between on the one hand one's religious commitments and concerns and on the other hand one's Americanness, one's connection to, and for some people a resistance to, national identity and its associated civil and economic concerns. These two aspects of American cultural identity were behind many of the tensions, conflicts, even outright violence between religious groups and individuals, but they also created opportunities for innovation and mutual appreciation between people. But, unlike the double consciousness of black Americans that DuBois emphasizes, most religious Americans were incapable of seeing themselves as others saw them; especially for the white Protestant majority, the view that non-Protestants and people of color had of them remained entirely beyond their consciousness.

The underlying tensions of American religious double consciousness became more pronounced over the long nineteenth century, stretching from the end of the American Revolution to the beginning of World War I, an era of incredible growth and transformation in American society. Our studies of this complicated period in history show us that "religion" took many forms. For nearly all Americans, what they regarded as their religion provided them with purpose and meaning. This is especially true when we think of religion as a system of beliefs. Belief in God, or multiple gods, imbues human existence with cosmic significances. Humans often define their purpose in terms of serving the gods, obeying holy commandments and laws, and living their lives according to the exemplary models of divine beings. We have seen this with the evangelical Protestants of the nineteenth century's Second Great Awakening as they exercised the divine imperative to spread the gospel. A good number of these evangelical Protestants took their desire to emulate the early Christians to extremes in restorationist communities organized according to their interpretations of first-century Christianity; this desire to live in faithful obedience to their beliefs inspired new religious movements among Christians such as the Mormons and the Shakers.

Beyond belief and modes of worship, religion also can be seen in its indispensable social role as the central institution of community. As enslaved African Americans adopted Christianity during the Second Great Awakening, worship became an occasion of social interaction and organization where an emerging sense of communal identity gestated. Likewise with Catholic and Jewish immigrants to the United States throughout the nineteenth century; assimilation to American society relied largely on communal associations through religious institutions. The various religious orientations of Americans also served as moral foundations for every facet of their lives, including their political stances in the nineteenth century on such issues as abolition, women's rights, and aid for the poor. As we have noted, most of the great controversies of the period that were fought in legislatures, in newspapers and magazines, and even on battlefields were informed by the moral imperatives inculcated in religious settings. Religious orientations provided ethical guidance on both sides of nearly every issue Americans debated and fought over.

The increasing diversity of the American scene in the nineteenth century, however, reminds us how limiting a Judeo-Christian view of religion can be to our scholarly inquiries. Unlike the nativist and other xenophobic reactions to cultural and social systems different from our own, religious scholars cannot easily dismiss the unfamiliar as evil or dangerous; nor can we simply disregard it as irreligious or beyond the purview of our intellectual concern. The challenge for historians and other scholars of religions remains to describe and to explain the many ways that humans make their lives meaningful, organize their communities, adhere to the imperatives of moral precepts, and garner help in bettering their lives, all in reference to perceived realities that transcend the apparent and obvious empirical circumstances of their lives. Whether conjuring African ancestors to intervene in social conflicts, performing ritual offerings in sacred locations for the benefit of the community, or calling on the dead to gain reassurance about the afterlife, religious means underlie virtually every aspect of human life. In the contact zones of nineteenth-century America, a diversity of religious orientations was apparent in every facet of national life, from the intensely personal and private ruminations of pious worshipers to the very public cataclysmic conflicts that erupted between groups of differing interests; by the end of the century, America had become a simmering pot of cosmopolitan religiosity.

Questions for Discussion

(1)   How did religious people in America respond to the rapid economic and technological changes occurring in the final decades of the nineteenth century?

(2)   In what ways did Euro-American interpretations of important landscape features differ from Native American regard for sacred lands?

(3)   Why was religion important to immigrants' experiences as they settled in America during the nineteenth century?

(4)   How did new religious movements of the late nineteenth century alter conventional views of the relationship between the human body and the spirit world?

(5)   What was the historical significance of the World's Parliament of Religions?

Suggested Primary-Source Readings

John G. Neihardt, *Black Elk Speaks: Being the Life Story of a Holy Man of the Oglala Sioux* (Lincoln: University of Nebraska Press, 2004): This first-person account of Native American religion and conflicts with Euro-Americans in the final decades of the nineteenth century was related by the famous Oglala holy man Black Elk (1863–1950) to poet and historian John Neihardt (1881–1973) in the 1930s.

Josiah Strong, *Our Country: Its Possible Future and Its Present Crisis* (New York: Baker & Taylor for the American Home Missionary Society, 1885): Strong's response to what he regarded as a crisis in Christian civilization includes warnings about non-Protestant forms of Christianity; see for instance chapters five and seven, which warn about Catholicism and Mormonism respectively.

Union of American Hebrew Congregations, "Pittsburgh Platform," adopted November 1885: In an effort to consolidate the various strands of Reform Judaism, the Union of American Hebrew Congregations convened in Pittsburg in 1885 and adopted these principles, which became the basis of "Classical Reform" Judaism.

Ralph Waldo Trine, *In Tune with the Infinite* (Mineola, NY: Dover, 2014): This bestselling book, first published in 1897, is an influential explanation of New Thought principles.

John Henry Barrows, ed., "The Assembling of the Parliament: Words of Welcome and Fellowship," in *The World's Parliament of Religions: An Illustrated and Popular Story of the World's First Parliament of Religions, Held in Chicago in Connection with the Columbian Exposition of 1893* (Chicago, IL: Parliament Publishing Co., 1893): Barrows' two-volume account of the World's Parliament of Religions includes detailed records of the speakers and activities of this 1893 spectacle of inter-religious dialogue. The welcoming addresses in chapter three ("The Assembling of the Parliament") reveal the tone and objectives of the conference.

Notes

1   Quoted in Carolyn Morrow Long, "Marie Laveau: A Nineteenth-Century Voudou Priestess," *Louisiana History: The Journal of the Louisiana Historical Association* 46, no. 3 (2005), 282–283.

2   Regarding confusion over Marie Laveau's date of birth, see ibid., 270.

3   See Margarite Fernández Olmos and Lizabeth Paravisini-Gebert, *Creole Religions of the Caribbean: An Introduction from Vodou and Santería to Obeah and Espiritismo* (New York: New York University Press, 2003).

4   Brenda Marie Osbey, "Why We Can't Talk to You about Voodoo," *Southern Literary Journal* 43, no. 2 (2011), 5.

5   Grant's address is available online at http://en.wikisource.org/wiki/Ulysses_S._Grant%27s_Third_State_of_the_Union_Address (accessed December 20, 2013).

6   Quoted in David Wallace Adams, *Education for Extinction: American Indians and the Boarding School Experience, 1875–1928* (Lawrence: University Press of Kansas, 1995), 215.

7   Regarding Indian boarding schools, besides ibid., see K.Tsianina Lomawaima and Teresa L. McCarty, *"To Remain an Indian": Lessons in Democracy from a Century of Native American Education* (New York: Teachers College Press, 2006) and Clifford E. Trafzer,

Jean A. Keller, and Lorene Sisquoc, eds., *Boarding School Blues: Revisiting American Indian Educational Experiences* (Lincoln: University of Nebraska Press, 2006).

8   A transcript of the Code of Indian Offenses is available online at http://en.wikisource.org/wiki/Code_of_Indian_Offenses (accessed December 20, 2013).

9   As Native American scholar and theologian Vine Deloria, Jr. has pointed out, "Tribal histories, for the most part, are land-centered. That is to say, every feature of a landscape has stories attached to it." See Vine Deloria, Jr., *For This Land: Writings on Religion in America* (New York: Routledge, 1998), 252.

10   Ferenc M. Szasz and Margaret Connell Szasz, "Religion and Spirituality," in *The Oxford History of the American West*, ed. Clyde A. Milner II, Carol A. O'Connor, and Martha A. Sandweiss (New York: Oxford University Press, 1994), 375 and Robert H. Ruby and John A. Brown, *John Slocum and the Indian Shaker Church* (Norman: University of Oklahoma Press, 1996).

11   Quoted in Joel W. Martin, *The Land Looks after Us: A History of Native American Religion* (New York: Oxford University Press, 2001), ix.

12   Linea Sundstrom, "Mirror of Heaven: Cross-Cultural Transference of the Sacred Geography of the Black Hills," *World Archaeology* 28, no. 2 (1996), 177–180.

13   Ibid., 177.

14   Michael Hittman, *Wovoka and the Ghost Dance* (Lincoln: University of Nebraska Press, 1997); James Mooney, *The Ghost-Dance Religion and the Sioux Outbreak of 1890* (Lincoln: University of Nebraska Press, 1991); and Szasz and Szasz, "Religion and Spirituality," 375–376.

15   Victoria Wyatt, "Alaska and Hawai'i," in *The Oxford History of the American West*, ed. Clyde A. Milner II, Carol A. O'Connor, and Martha A. Sandweiss (New York: Oxford University Press, 1994), 577.

16   Amy A. Slagle, "Eastern Orthodoxy Christianity," in *The Blackwell Companion to Religion in America*, ed. Philip Goff (Malden, MA: Wiley Blackwell, 2010), 530.

17   Quoted in Stephen W. Haycox, "Sheldon Jackson in Historical Perspective: Alaska Native Schools and Mission Contracts, 1885–1894," *Pacific Historian* 28, no. 1 (1984).

18   Ibid.

19   Wyatt, "Alaska and Hawai'i," 578–580.

20   Ibid., 580, 582–583.

21   This appears in his essay "Walking," which can be found in Henry David Thoreau, *The Essays of Henry D. Thoreau* (New York: North Point Press, 2002), 162.

22   W. D. Haley, "Johnny Appleseed: A Pioneer Hero," *Harper's New Monthly Magazine* 43, no. 258 (1871), 830–837. The original article is available online at http://memory.loc.gov/ammem/ndlpcoop/moahtml/title/lists/harp_V43I258.html (accessed June 16, 2014).

23   Leigh Eric Schmidt, *Restless Souls: The Making of American Spirituality* (San Francisco, CA: HarperSanFrancisco, 2005), 91–93.

24   Quoted in Catherine L. Albanese, *Nature Religion in America: From the Algonkian Indians to the New Age* (Chicago, IL: University of Chicago Press, 1990), 93.

25   Donald Worster, *A Passion for Nature: The Life of John Muir* (New York: Oxford University Press, 2008), 36–66.

26   Ibid., 141–145.

27   These quotes are from Muir's book *My First Summer in the Sierra*, quoted in ibid., 161.

28   Quoted in Albanese, *Nature Religion*, 100.

29   Robert A. Orsi, *The Madonna of 115th Street: Faith and Community in Italian Harlem,*

1880–1950 (New Haven, CT: Yale University Press, 1985), 150.

30 Patrick W. Carey, *Catholics in America: A History* (Westport, CT: Praeger, 2004), 30.

31 Ibid.

32 John H. Erickson, *Orthodox Christians in America: A Short History* (New York: Oxford University Press, 2008) and Slagle, "Eastern Orthodoxy Christianity."

33 Lloyd P. Gartner, "American Judaism, 1880–1945," in *The Cambridge Companion to American Judaism*, ed. Dana Evan Kaplan (New York: Cambridge University Press, 2005), 43.

34 Ibid., 44–45. The principles of the Pittsburgh Platform are available online at www.jewishvirtuallibrary.org/jsource/Judaism/pittsburgh_program.html (accessed December 20, 2013).

35 Gartner, "American Judaism," 46–47.

36 Ibid., 50–52.

37 There is abundant literature detailing all of the traditions summarized here as well as those of other Asian religions; concise summaries can be found in any of the many "world religions" or "comparative religions" textbooks available. For the discussion here I have referred to Theodore M. Ludwig, *The Sacred Paths: Understanding the Religions of the World* (New York: Macmillan, 1989).

38 Thomas A. Tweed and Stephen R. Prothero, eds., *Asian Religions in America: A Documentary History* (New York: Oxford University Press, 1999), 8.

39 John Higham discusses anti-Catholicism and anti-Semitism in John Higham, *Strangers in the Land: Patterns of American Nativism, 1860–1925* (New York: Atheneum, 1963), 23–34.

40 Josiah Strong, *Our Country: Its Possible Future and Its Present Crisis* (New York: Baker & Taylor for the American Home Missionary Society, 1885), 222 (emphasis in the original).

41 Anders Stephanson, *Manifest Destiny: American Expansionism and the Empire of Right* (New York: Hill and Wang, 1995), 79.

42 Higham, *Strangers in the Land*, 25.

43 See Joshua Paddison, *American Heathens: Religion, Race, and Reconstruction in California* (Berkeley: Huntington-USC Institute on California and the West by University of California Press, 2012).

44 Gabriel J. Chin, Victor C. Romero, and Michael A. Scaperlanda, *Immigration and the Constitution: The Origins of Constitutional Immigration Law*, 3 vols. (New York: Garland, 2001), 150, footnote 61.

45 An abridged version of Douglass' 1869 essay "Our Composite Nationality" appears in Tweed and Prothero, *Asian Religions in America*, 67–70.

46 Paul Boyer, "An Ohio Leader of the Social Gospel Movement: Reassessing Washington Gladden," *Ohio History* 116 (2009), 91.

47 Wendy J. Deichmann Edwards and Carolyn De Swarte Gifford, *Gender and the Social Gospel* (Urbana: University of Illinois Press, 2003), 2. Shailer Mathews' definition of social gospel appears on page 2.

48 Regarding Washington Gladden, see Boyer, "Reassessing Washington Gladden" and Susan Curtis, *A Consuming Faith: The Social Gospel and Modern American Culture* (Baltimore, MD: Johns Hopkins University Press, 1991), 35–48.

49 Walter Rauschenbusch, *Christianizing the Social Order* (New York: Macmillan, 1912), 121.

50 Ibid., 290.

51   Among the many works about Jane Addams and Hull House are Robin K. Berson, *Jane Addams: A Biography* (Westport, CT: Greenwood Press, 2004) and Victoria Brown, *The Education of Jane Addams* (Philadelphia: University of Pennsylvania Press, 2004).

52   Ron Chernow, *Titan: The Life of John D. Rockefeller, Sr* (New York: Random House, 1998), 52–55.

53   Andrew Carnegie, *Autobiography of Andrew Carnegie* (Boston, MA: Houghton Mifflin, 1920), 339.

54   Stephen A. Marini, *Sacred Song in America: Religion, Music, and Public Culture* (Urbana: University of Illinois Press, 2003), 81, 111.

55   Ibid., 111.

56   Andrew Carnegie, "Wealth," *North American Review* 148, no. 391 (1889), 653–665 (reprinted as "The Gospel of Wealth"; the essay is available online at http://carnegie. org/fileadmin/Media/Publications/PDF/THE_GOSPEL_OF_WEALTH_01.pdf, accessed June 3, 2014).

57   Sarah E. Johnson, "Gender," in *The Blackwell Companion to Religion in America*, ed. Philip Goff (Malden, MA: Wiley Blackwell, 2010), 150. See also Ian R. Tyrrell, *Woman's World / Woman's Empire: The Woman's Christian Temperance Union in International Perspective, 1880–1930* (Chapel Hill: University of North Carolina Press, 1991).

58   Kathi Kern, *Mrs. Stanton's Bible* (Ithaca, NY: Cornell University Press, 2001), 1–4.

59   Johnson, "Gender," 155–156.

60   For a brief summary of the YMCA's early history, see Clifford Putney, *Muscular Christianity: Manhood and Sports in Protestant America, 1880–1920* (Cambridge, MA: Harvard University Press, 2001), 64–72.

61   Paul Keith Conkin, *American Originals: Homemade Varieties of Christianity* (Chapel Hill: University of North Carolina Press, 1997), 125–133.

62   Ibid., 134–137.

63   Ibid., 145–151.

64   Ibid., 147–151.

65   Ibid., 231–234.

66   Ibid., 237–242.

67   Ibid., 249–261.

68   Ann Braude, *Radical Spirits: Spiritualism and Women's Rights in Nineteenth-Century America* (Boston, MA: Beacon Press, 1989), 2.

69   Ibid., 10–25.

70   Quoted in ibid., 2.

71   Edward W. Said, *Orientalism* (New York: Vintage, 1994), 2–3.

72   Schmidt, *Restless Souls*, 158–160.

73   Ibid., 161–162.

74   Quoted in Richard Hughes Seager, *The World's Parliament of Religions: The East/West Encounter, Chicago, 1893* (Bloomington: Indiana University Press, 1995), xvi–xvii.

75   Quoted in ibid., 43.

76   Quoted in ibid., 82, 83.

77   W. E. B. Du Bois, *The Souls of Black Folk: Essays and Sketches* (Rockville, MD: Arc Manor, 2008 [1903]), 12.

Part III
The Modern World

9

Modern Worlds

Advances in science and technology introduced fundamental changes to American society and culture in the modern worlds of the twentieth century. This chapter considers the implications of modern developments for religious life in America and how some religious groups responded to these changes. Special attention is given to how the Darwinian theory of evolution conflicted with religious creation **myths**, highlighting the controversy between modernist and fundamentalist views among American Protestants. We also will consider how the new fields of psychology and anthropology had an impact on popular views of religion, with particular focus on issues of sexuality. Finally, the changing opportunities made available by scientific and technological advancements in the modern world propelled increased migrations, both within the United States and of foreign immigrants who continued to bring new religious communities onto American soil.

By the 1920s, William Jennings Bryan (1860–1925) was the most prominent populist leader in America. Having run three times for president, all unsuccessfully, Bryan had earned the title of the Great Commoner for his moral stands against the powerful interests of banks and railroads, and for opposing American reliance on the gold standard (which fixed the monetary system according to the value of gold). As a pacifist, he objected to entering World War I and even resigned as Secretary of State over the issue. He also advocated prohibition and supported the Eighteenth Amendment to the US Constitution outlawing alcoholic beverages. Alarmed by what he regarded as an erosion of Christian values, Bryan joined forces in the 1920s with Christian fundamentalists to oppose the teaching of evolution in American

Formed From This Soil: An Introduction to the Diverse History of Religion in America, First Edition. Thomas S. Bremer.
© 2015 Thomas S. Bremer. Published 2015 by John Wiley & Sons, Ltd.

public schools. When the state of Tennessee put a local school teacher on trial in 1925 for violating the state's newly enacted law prohibiting the inclusion of evolutionary theory in science curricula, Bryan brought national attention to the case by joining the prosecution team as an assistant prosecutor.

Bryan's participation in the criminal prosecution of John T. Scopes (1900–1970) in Dayton, Tennessee, in the summer of 1925 motivated America's most famous defense lawyer of the time to get involved. Clarence Darrow (1857–1938) had recently retired from the legal profession, but news of Bryan's involvement in the Tennessee case provoked him to offer his services to Scopes. Darrow's fame had been built on nationally prominent criminal cases, but he had also earned a reputation as an agnostic who delighted in ridiculing the beliefs of Protestant Christianity; in particular he regarded the notion of universal original sin and salvation for a select few through divine grace as "a very dangerous doctrine."[1] He relished the opportunity to refute Bryan's attempt to impose Christian values in public schools.

During the trial, Darrow successfully maneuvered Bryan to testify as an expert witness on the Christian Bible. As Darrow's questions became an assault on the veracity of biblical truths, the chief prosecutor attempted to intervene and end the interrogation; Bryan, however, shouted that the defense was not there to try the case at hand, but instead, "They came to try revealed religion. I am here to defend it, and they can ask me any question they wish." When he indicated how Darrow insulted the believing Christians who applauded Bryan's stance against Darrow's questioning, Darrow shot back, "You insult every man of science and learning in the world because he does not believe in your fool religion." He then continued by questioning Bryan on the biblical tale of Noah and the worldwide flood, on ancient civilizations, comparative religions, and the age of the earth; Bryan struggled to offer plausible answers, and, as the questioning veered further from the topic of teaching evolution in Tennessee schools, the chief prosecutor once again objected, asking, "What is the purpose of this examination?" Darrow answered, "We have the purpose of preventing bigots and ignoramuses from controlling the education of the United States, and that is all."[2]

The 1925 trial pitting two of the era's great public figures against each other over the issue of evolution highlights religious disruptions in the newly emerging modern world of early twentieth-century America. Scientific discoveries and the development of new technologies introduced new tensions in American culture and exacerbated older conflicts. In particular, new social sciences of sociology, psychology, and anthropology, along with new paradigms in the natural sciences, especially physics and biology, brought difficult challenges to traditional understandings of revealed truth; among Christians, modern perspectives directly challenged the authority of ancient texts and the miraculous tales of the Bible. Many Protestant thinkers attempted to accommodate the authority of scientific truths by reinterpreting biblical truths, but others asserted the literal truth of the Bible as the moral basis of American society. For the latter group, modern sciences, or at least particular hypotheses that contradicted biblical representations, exemplified the moral degradation of a society turned away from God.

Figure 9.1 William Jennings Bryan faces Clarence Darrow during an outdoor session of the Scopes Trial in July 1925 in Dayton, Tennessee. The trial pitted the claims of religion against the evidence of science as fundamentalist Christians, led by Bryan, challenged Darwin's theory of evolution in a trial that caught the attention of the nation. (Smithsonian Institution Archives, image number SIA2007-0124.)

The battle between Christians who welcomed new scientific views of the world and those who resisted the challenges that science brought to traditional religious authority has a long history in Christian thought. A tension between faith and reason has been an enduring theme in Christian theological debates at least since the early medieval period, and it gained even greater prominence in the Enlightenment era. The exact terms of contention, however, always reflect current social and cultural concerns that go beyond simple theological issues of divine authority. In the early decades of twentieth-century America, national attention to the issue of schoolchildren learning about evolution took on epic proportions; the future salvation of the nation was at stake in the minds of many partisans on both sides of the debate. For many faithful Protestants, at least, America wavered between the authority of God on the one hand and the authority of scientific thought and methods on the other.

Science

Beginning in the nineteenth century and accelerating through the twentieth century, modern science introduced new views of nature, society, and individuals. Earlier geological studies had revealed that the Earth is far older than characterized in many religious traditions. Assuming immense geological time spans, new scientific ideas began revolutionizing modern understandings. In the area of biology, two pivotal books by the British naturalist Charles Darwin (1809–1882), *On the Origin of Species* (1859) and *The Descent of Man, and Selection in Relation to Sex* (1871), proposed a theory of life's origins and evolutionary development over many millennia that disputes the creation stories of most religious mythologies, including the Genesis accounts of the Hebrew Bible. Other monumental shifts in scientific understanding followed. The German physicist Albert Einstein (1879–1955) laid out a fundamental rethinking of physics in the early decades of the twentieth century; about the same time, the Austrian psychologist Sigmund Freud (1856–1939) was writing about the human psyche, demonstrating how much of human behavior, attitudes, fears, and desires are determined by psychological forces that lie below the surface of consciousness. Meanwhile, French sociologist Émile Durkheim (1858–1917) drew attention to social forces that govern human life; in the area of religion, he proposed that religious beliefs and practices originate in particular social functions that make religious systems indispensable to human society. For many modern people in the twentieth century, their understanding of themselves, their communities, and the world in general underwent a wholesale transformation in light of new scientific ideas and discoveries.

Evolution

The appearance of Charles Darwin's book *On the Origin of Species* in 1859 marked a fundamental departure in western Christian society from the ancient **cosmogony** of the earth's creation by an omnipotent, beneficial god, as told in the biblical Book of Genesis. Darwin's observations of the natural world led him to posit a process by which organisms adapted to particular environmental conditions over many millennia, evolving into the immense variety of species extant throughout the world. The theological implications of his theory were immediately apparent for the predominantly Christian society of Europe and America where his book had its greatest influence. When the American botanist Asa Gray (1810–1888), who arranged for publication of Darwin's book in America, suggested to Darwin that the hand of God operated in evolutionary processes, Darwin replied that he could not see "as plainly as others do, and as I should wish to do, evidence of design and beneficence on all sides of us. There seems to me too much misery in the world."[3] To an astute and sensitive observer of nature such as Darwin, the reality of the natural world undermined any claim of a benevolent and intelligent god who had purposively designed creation. On the other hand, people such as Gray, who remained a committed Protestant Christian even as he also enjoyed an eminent scientific reputation, allowed for both a creator god and Darwinian processes of evolution. From the beginning, Christians struggled to reconcile evolutionary theory with their religious faith.

The sudden popularity of Darwin's ideas in European and American intellectual circles gave wider legitimacy to evolutionary ideas that had been developing in nineteenth-century England. The English philosopher, sociologist, and political theorist Herbert Spencer (1820–1903) had coined the term "survival of the fittest" in reference to the growth of biological populations well before Darwin published his theory. Spencer had postulated in an 1852 article that the success of a particular population depended on the species' fertility, with the fittest species surviving while unfit species languished. After Darwin's book gained a wide and somewhat contentious audience for biological evolution, Spencer's phrase became a useful shortcut for describing evolution in a number of areas beyond biology; it also became a common explanation for hierarchal divisions not only in the natural world but also in human society. Some theorists in the newly emerging field of sociology used Spencer's "survival-of-the-fittest" notion in what would later be pejoratively called "Social Darwinism," and it especially resonated with the individualist emphasis of capitalist society: such captains of industry as John D. Rockefeller (1839–1937) and Andrew Carnegie (1835–1919) routinely explained their personal success in terms of "survival of the fittest." It easily linked biological explanations to social evolution, giving an organic justification to such things as class divisions, poverty, racial differences, and colonial domination of some nations over others.[4]

Psychology

While Darwin's and Spencer's evolutionary theories resonated among biologists, sociologists, and other intellectual communities throughout Europe and America, other scientists considered the nature of the human mind and the underlying causes of human behavior. By the end of the nineteenth century, the Austrian neurologist Sigmund Freud had begun work on a theory of the human psyche that would dramatically affect how people in Europe and America would understand the human individual. His first book, *The Interpretation of Dreams* (1899), included the profoundly revolutionary notion that one's dreams had meanings that could be deciphered, and that they could reveal explanations for behaviors, attitudes, and relationships in one's waking life. Freud's attention to dreams, his explanations of the unconscious as a key to understanding human personality, and his assessment of human sexuality all initially met with intense resistance and even condemnation from a largely uncomprehending scientific community.[5]

Much of the public reaction to Freud's psychological theories focused on the central role of sexuality in his understanding of human personality and behavior. His *Three Essays on the Theory of Sexuality* (1905) proposes that even the behavior of infants is governed by sexual urges, and that repressed sexuality operates powerfully among adults, most often in unconscious ways. Neuroses (mental or emotional disorders) according to Freud originate in sexual fantasies; adult sexuality has roots in one's childhood sexuality; and children are predisposed to what he called "polymorphous perversion." Moreover, he maintained that homosexuality did not constitute unnatural, sinful, degenerate, psychotic, or criminal behavior.[6] Rather than demonizing homosexuality or any sort of sexual orientation or behavior, Freud proposed that one's sexuality could be understood by deciphering the human unconscious and the history of an individual's sexual urges and traumas extending back to early childhood.

Freud's rather shocking psychological theories of the human personality, including his ideas about childhood sexuality, also related to his understanding of religion. He developed a model of human history that presumed humans would outgrow religion and would enter a modern era free from the constraints of religious dogma, **rituals**, and tradition. Raised in a nominally Jewish family in the predominantly Catholic city of Vienna, Freud regarded himself as a lifelong atheist; in the preface to one of his influential books on religion, he revealed that he was a man "completely estranged from the religion of his fathers – as well as from every other religion."[7] He related religious ceremony to the behaviors of the mentally ill, arguing in an early essay that the repetitive actions of rituals resembled the obsessive habits of neurotic patients; in a later book he concluded that religion represents "the universal obsessional neurosis of humanity."[8] In Freud's view, the doctrines, behaviors, and traditions of religion keep humans from full, healthy, and mature lives as modern people.

Meanwhile a more sympathetic psychological understanding of religion was being developed in the United States. The philosopher and psychologist William James (1842–1910) exemplifies the early science of psychology in America; his widely influential book *The Varieties of Religious Experience* (1902) portrays religion as the sum total of ideas, feelings, actions, and experiences of whatever people regard as "divine." In particular, he regards religion as a psychological state that orients one's feelings, experiences, beliefs, and actions. For James, religion in its essence becomes an entirely subjective phenomenon.[9]

The emphasis on subjectivity in the work of William James focuses on universal dimensions of religious experience recognized in comparative studies of various traditions from around the world. James' efforts to study religion scientifically involved comparative studies of religious trances and other subconscious states that took seriously both the insights of religious mystics and the theorizing of social scientists.[10] His work emphasizes an empirical approach to understanding religious experiences, which he privileges over religious doctrines, ritual practices, and institutional structures. Consequently, James' studies have exerted wide influence, especially among twentieth-century American scholars of religion, in defining religion in terms of individualistic, solitary encounters of powerful forces beyond ordinary human experiences, encouraging later scholars to emphasize the human experience of the sacred found universally in the world's religions.[11] In popular parlance, James' tendency to abstract private, subjective experiences from their historical context within particular systems of belief and practice gave rise to the modern distinction between religion and spirituality that became common in late twentieth century American culture.

New technologies

Along with the new developments in modern science came new technologies that changed how Americans lived, how they moved around, and how they communicated with each other. These developments had significant impacts on religious life. The introduction of radio broadcasts in the 1920s and television in the 1930s created new opportunities for religious leaders to reach ever wider audiences. Automobiles offered mobility to religious adherents, allowing them a greater choice of religious communities to join. Improved train and ship transportation made long-distance travel more convenient, and later airplanes dramatically reduced the time needed to reach distant destinations. Technological advances in modern warfare created unprecedented levels of death, morbidity, and destruction that had unsettling moral consequences. Indeed, technology generated new ethical quandaries for religious people even as it created new religious opportunities for them.

Technological advancements produced religion as a mass commodity for some followers, enabling numerous religious figures to become nationally known personalities in the first half of the twentieth century. As one Chicago radio preacher recalled, "I realized a long time ago that if I was to spread the Word, radio would reach more people and get the message across to more people. Religion can be sold as well as other products."[12] Among the earliest and most controversial of the radio preachers was Aimee Semple McPherson (1890–1944), a Canadian-born Pentecostal evangelist whose shrewd use of new technologies made her one of the most widely known personalities in the United States during the 1920s and 1930s.[13] Sister Aimee, as she was known, appeared on radio and later on television; one of the first to broadcast her sermons over the airwaves, she acquired a broadcast license in 1924 and opened her own radio station in Los Angeles that sent her voice out to a sizable radio audience throughout the American west.[14] Critical of show-business values and what she regarded as the abhorrent lifestyles of the entertainment industry in California, McPherson was nevertheless willing to use show-business techniques in her ministry; she often had theatrical sets built to dramatize the messages of her religious revivals. As one historian has noted, "She would not hesitate to use the devil's tools to tear down the devil's house."[15] Her sensational theatricality and her savvy use of new technologies made Aimee Semple McPherson an early media celebrity, which set the stage for subsequent religious luminaries among the revivalists and televangelists of later decades.

Figure 9.2　Ever the dramatist, even in casual settings like the one shown in this 1927 photograph, Pentecostal preacher Sister Aimee Semple McPherson used radio technology and later television to broadcast her religious performances to broad audiences, making her a national celebrity. (Courtesy of the Library of Congress, LC-DIG-npcc-16474.)

Religious Responses to Modern Sciences

The theories and discoveries of modern science in the early decades of the twentieth century challenged the beliefs, doctrines, and basic assumptions of Christians and other religious people. Among early twentieth-century American Protestants a group of "modernists" embraced a willingness to adapt their Christian faith to the insights of modern natural and social sciences as well as to the modern historical studies of the ancient texts that constitute the Christian Bible. One such modernist was the influential Protestant theologian Shailer Mathews (1863–1941), who defined modernism in the 1920s as "the use of the methods of modern science to find, state and use the permanent and central values of inherited orthodoxy."[16] Modernists like Mathews, himself a lifelong Baptist, did not disavow their religious faith; but they looked to science as the authority by which Christians should decide matters of religion, and they rejected some key aspects of traditional Christian doctrines. For instance, modernist theologians relied on the scientifically informed critical studies of sacred texts known broadly as "higher criticism" (which questioned divine authorship of the Bible) to conclude that, although the Christian Bible may have been inspired by religious faith, it nevertheless remains a human creation, not the divine edicts of the Christian god. Certainly, it contained valid human perceptions of God and the human relationship to the divine, and its ethical teachings were based on vital human truths that went beyond historical accuracy; but biblical truths, according to the modernists, display the fallibility of human authors.

Fundamentalists

The growing acceptance of modernist interpretations of Christianity and the Bible among liberal Christian scholars and **clergy** prompted a conservative backlash in the early decades of the twentieth century. Alarmed by what they perceived as the "irreligion of the modern world,"[17] conservative **evangelical** Christians fought the modernist "heresy" by asserting what they regarded as the fundamentals of their Christian faith. In the first years of the twentieth century, a religious coalition developed, represented most clearly by the formation in 1903 of the Bible League of North America, whose antimodernist purpose consisted of a single goal: "to maintain the historic faith of the Church in the divine inspiration and authority of the Bible as the Word of God."[18] This conservative Protestant interdenominational alliance had grown into a religious movement by 1920, by then called "fundamentalists," a term coined to reflect a set of volumes titled *The Fundamentals*, published between 1910 and 1915 and distributed to evangelical pastors, missionaries, teachers, students, and other conservative Protestant leaders. The books themselves were somewhat moderate in their stance, but their overriding concern was the authority of the Christian god in relation to the authority of modern science, especially the science of higher criticism of the Bible. While lauding the legitimacy of the "Scientific and Historical method" as a necessary approach to understanding the scriptures, the early fundamentalist writers decried what they regarded as its "illegitimate, unscientific and unhistorical use," which they accused the modernist advocates of higher criticism of perpetuating.[19]

Protestant fundamentalists in the early part of the twentieth century drew on evangelical strains of American culture going back to the eighteenth century, but their distinctive concern was with the question of biblical inerrancy, the notion that the Christian Bible represents the unequivocal word of God. Conservative Protestant theologians and leaders had been insisting on the literal truth of the Bible for decades in response to the interpretations offered by proponents of higher criticism. Among American Presbyterians, the conservative faction prevailed in the 1890s to declare scriptural inerrancy as a fundamental teaching of the Church. In 1910, the Presbyterian General Assembly declared five "essential" doctrines that would later become the defining "five points of fundamentalism" for the interdenominational conservative movement; they are, "(1) the inerrancy of Scripture, (2) the Virgin Birth of Christ, (3) his substitutionary atonement, (4) his bodily resurrection, and (5) the authenticity of the miracles."[20] These were shared points that most conservative Protestants could agree on across interdenominational boundaries in the 1920s.

Box 9.1   Fundamentalism

In 1920 a Baptist newspaper editor coined the term "fundamentalist" to describe advocates of a conservative faction among American Baptists who were intent "to do battle royal for the Fundamentals," referring specifically to battles within Baptist ranks over doctrinal issues.[21] The term quickly became accepted to describe conservative Protestants in general who were alarmed by the advancement of liberal theological accommodations of new scientific theories; fundamentalists insisted on preserving the integrity of literal interpretations of biblical truths.

In its origins, then, fundamentalism refers to the very specific doctrinal debates within American Protestantism in the early twentieth century. But over the course of the twentieth century the term was extended to refer to any conservative religious group regarded as extremist, specifically those who rely on literal interpretations of sacred texts. Various forms of fundamentalism have been identified among Buddhist, Hindu, Jewish, Muslim, Sikh, and other groups, all sharing "family resemblances" with each other in their usually militant resistance to changes that they regard as violating the fundamental beliefs and practices of their respective religious traditions. The term has even been applied to contexts clearly beyond religion; political movements, economic policies, and social programs have been called "fundamentalist" in popular media. One scholar, however, has objected to applying the label of fundamentalism too far beyond its origins; secular "fundamentalisms," Malise Ruthven (born 1942) argues, are more analogies than family resemblances. For him, fundamentalism describes "a 'religious way of being' that manifests itself in a strategy by which beleaguered believers attempt to preserve their distinctive identity as a people or group in the face of modernity and secularization."[22] In the modern world, according to Ruthven, fundamentalism marks a religious response to the problem of diversity, which he notes "is an inescapable feature of modernity. It implies choice, inviting the suspicion that there may be more than one path to salvation."[23] Inevitably, when multiple voices, both religious and non-religious, all propose various paths for human destiny, a fundamentalist reaction will enter the fray to reassert more traditional paths.

Protestant fundamentalism flourished as a viable movement between 1920 and 1925, but quite suddenly it broke up into small, isolated factions thereafter. One area of initial success was in disputing the teaching of Darwinian evolution in public schools. When the inveterate political crusader William Jennings Bryan adopted the antievolution cause for a national campaign in 1920, the fundamentalist movement lurched onto the American political scene as a formidable conservative voice. Bryan famously quipped, "It is better to trust in the Rock of Ages, than to know the age of the rocks; it is better for one to know that he is close to the Heavenly Father, than to know how far the stars in the heavens are apart."[24] But his criticism was not aimed specifically at science. Darwinism, he contended, was not true science; it amounted to nothing more than "guesses strung together" in "a mere hypothesis." This pseudo-science, in Bryan's estimation, had an insidious effect on civilized society; its atheistic materialism undermined Christian values and morality, which he regarded as the foundations of civilization, and he led the charge to outlaw its appearance in public schools.[25] Bryan even blamed the atrocities of World War I on Darwinism, and he found a willing audience well beyond the denominational confines of Protestant fundamentalists; the Great Commoner galvanized a generation of American conservatives seeking an explanation for perceived crises gripping America. Many Americans, especially in rural areas, joined the antievolutionary campaign, even though they had little interest in the specific theological concerns of the fundamentalists.[26]

Several states entertained legislation barring the teaching of evolution in schools, but Bryan and his supporters had little success in getting such laws passed. In 1925 they targeted Tennessee, a stronghold of conservative Protestant belief but also a southern center of modernism, in Bryan's estimation. He declined an invitation to address Tennessee legislators, who were debating a proposal to outlaw evolutionary teaching, but other conservative leaders raced to Tennessee to drum up support. The famous revivalist Billy Sunday (1862–1935) held an eighteen-day crusade in the state's largest city, Memphis, that attracted over two hundred thousand people; Sunday repeatedly denounced Darwin and his "old bastard theory of evolution." In the wake of such public enthusiasm, the state legislature passed the bill against teaching evolution, and Tennessee became the first state to attach penalties to exposing schoolchildren to Darwin's ideas.[27]

The new law created an opportunity for modernists and advocates of evolutionary theory to refute the claims of Bryan and the fundamentalists. When the American Civil Liberties Union advertised for Tennessee teachers to challenge the law against teaching evolution, local civic leaders in Dayton, Tennessee, schemed to stage a test case in their town; they convinced the young science teacher John T. Scopes to stand trial for violating the law. Soon the small Tennessee town attracted the attention of the national and even international media as local officials prosecuted the so-called "monkey trial." The theatrical air of the trial riveted the nation as two of the most widely known attorneys of the day battled over the validity of evolution and the role of religious dogma in education. Representing the Christian fundamentalists, William Jennings Bryan joined the prosecution team and made the trial less about individual freedoms and more about evolution itself. On the other side, Clarence Darrow joined Scopes' defense team, bringing his professed agnostic views to the public debate. Darrow had long held Christianity in contempt, and he regarded the opinions of Bryan and his Christian fundamentalist allies as an affront to free thought and a threat to "enlightenment." He exclaimed to the press, "Had Mr. Bryan's ideas of what a man may do towards free thinking existed throughout history, we would still be hanging and burning witches and punishing people who thought the earth was round."[28] The monkey trial quickly became a publicity circus pitting the Christian orthodoxy of the fundamentalists against the scientific consensus of the modernists, with two of the most notorious defenders of the respective sides leading the charge.

In the end, Darrow and those who supported the authority of scientific knowledge lost the battle but won the war, at least as far as public opinion is concerned. Scopes was convicted of a misdemeanor violation of the Tennessee statute; the Tennessee State Supreme Court later overturned his conviction on a legal technicality, but they allowed the law to remain in force. It would not be until the 1960s that the United States Supreme Court would declare as unconstitutional statutes such as the Tennessee law that have religion as their main purpose. But Darrow's grilling of Bryan on the witness stand shook confidence in the priorities of religious claims for many people. Whereas the prosecutors could claim victory in gaining a conviction, the defense claimed a moral victory in public opinion.[29] The optimism of the modernists, however, who hoped that the trial had dealt a fatal blow to fundamentalist opposition to scientific authority, was premature. Bryan immediately rallied his supporters to pursue similar antievolution laws in other states, and many American Christians took offense at Darrow's unceasing attacks on the Bible. But Bryan's sudden death only five days after the trial hindered the momentum of the fundamentalist crusade, and fundamentalism soon lost its prominence as a national voice of conservative Christian morality. Although they were no longer a formidable national coalition after 1925, the fundamentalists remained a significant subculture within American Protestantism and would emerge in new political battles later in the century.[30]

Rethinking religion

As scientific developments threw religious Americans, specifically members of the major Protestant denominations, into crisis over the authority of divine revelation in light of scientific knowledge, the social sciences created opportunities for non-Christian peoples to reassert the influence of their own cultural traditions. In particular, scholars such as William James in psychology and Émile Durkheim in sociology were expanding the category of religion beyond the institutions of the Abrahamic religions (Judaism, Christianity, and Islam). Interest in indigenous religions, including those of Native Americans but also those of the Aboriginal tribes of Australia and the various tribal religions of Africa, had introduced comparative studies of religious traditions that involved more than merely cataloging followers' beliefs and ritual practices. Attention to religious experiences across cultures and insights into the social functions of religious systems generated greater appreciation for unfamiliar traditions.

Certainly, Christianity continued to dominate in most Americans' assumptions about religion, but other religious orientations were making inroads that influenced attitudes about religion. The presence of greater numbers of Buddhists in America, for instance, added a nontheistic element to how people thought about religions. In fact, at least one advocate of Asian traditions, author and publisher Paul Carus (1852–1919), regarded Buddhism as superior to theistic religions on rational grounds. He defended Buddhism in the 1890s as a "religion of science," characterizing it as a sophisticated philosophical and ethical system based on reason rather than revelation.[31] Buddhism, in the estimation of Carus, was fully amenable to modern science in ways that Christianity could never be.

One area of science that had considerable impact on defining religion for many people was cultural anthropology. In the United States the German Jewish immigrant Franz Boas (1858–1942) made significant contributions in bringing unfamiliar cultural traditions into popular understanding and acceptance; his influence was both direct in his own scholarly investigations and indirect through the influential generation of anthropologists he trained at Columbia University in New York City in the first decades of the twentieth century. Boas and his students disputed claims of cultural superiority between racial groups by developing anthropological theories of cultural relativism, judging the customs and behaviors of a society according to that society's own cultural norms rather than imposing the moral standards of an outsider's (i.e., the anthropologist's) culture onto the society and its members. Specifically, these university-trained secular scientists of human cultures objected to assuming that the Protestant Christian values of the dominant society in the United States were universally applicable to all cultures.[32]

This more culturally sensitive approach of Boasian anthropology created opportunities for non-Christian Americans to challenge the assumptions of the Protestant majority regarding issues of religious liberty. In the case of indigenous traditions of Pueblo peoples in the American southwest, a controversy arose in the 1920s that pitted anthropologists, artists, and other cultural progressives against the conservative forces of Christian missionaries and their allies in the federal government; factions within the Pueblo tribes themselves gravitated toward one side or the other. The discord revolved around traditional dance ceremonies performed within the Pueblo communities, many of them closed to outsiders. The assumptions of the dominant, non-Native American society, informed largely by Protestant missionaries intent on Christianizing the Indians, were that unfamiliar and inaccessible cultural practices of indigenous people had morally corrupt, evil objectives. This view of native culture as "savagery" informed government policies toward Native American tribes until well into the twentieth century, and the furor in the 1920s over the purported licentious nature of the Pueblo dance ceremonies elicited official directives for Bureau of Indian Affairs agents to end what was regarded as "degraded" dances among the Indians.[33]

The Christian missionaries who complained about the immorality of Pueblo dance ceremonies, however, encountered stiff opposition from anthropologists,

Figure 9.3 This photograph from the 1920s shows a ceremonial dance in Zuni Pueblo, New Mexico. The Pueblo dance controversy involved a defense of Native American rituals as legitimate religious practices protected under the First Amendment of the US Constitution. Christian missionaries working among native tribes regarded their indigenous dances and other practices as "pagan rites" that should be outlawed. (Courtesy of New York Public Library, #92309.)

artists, and other sympathetic Euro-American reformers who objected to the government's restrictions on Native American cultural traditions; they claimed that the Bureau of Indian Affairs directives violated the Pueblo peoples' constitutionally guaranteed freedom of religion. In response to these charges, the Christian establishment retorted that such allegations about Indians' religious liberty only obfuscated the real issues regarding the perpetuation of "pagan rites." They saw such claims merely as an attempt to protect the illicit activities of Indian pagans.[34]

At stake in the dispute was the concept of religion itself. The Christian partisans based their understanding of religion on their own religious orientation, a monotheistic, textually oriented tradition; as Protestants, they especially detested ritualistic practices, which they associated with their old nemesis, Roman Catholicism. On the other side, the progressive anthropologists, artists, and others who advocated for religious freedom on the part of the Pueblo peoples were influenced by ethnographic sciences, especially the concept of cultural relativism; for them, Indian traditions had their own integrity as religious systems, not subject to the standards of Christianity or any other outside cultural configuration.

As for the Indians caught between the two sides, they were not unanimous in their desire to perpetuate the ceremonial dances. Certainly, nearly all Native Americans involved in the controversy insisted that restricting their dances amounted to an unlawful infringement on their religious freedom, but a few saw it differently. One particular Native American voice, a Hopi Christian by the name of Otto Lomavitu (1896–1963), objected in 1923 to "endless religious ceremonies" of the Hopi traditionalists, and he praised the Protestant missionaries for replacing native practices with what he regarded as "better learning and religious instruction." He claimed that as many as forty-five percent of the Hopi people objected to the "degrading" influence of the dance ceremonies, and he suggested that the real purpose of continuing them was "only for the benefit of the tourist." Lomavitu's claims made him a useful example of a "progressive" Indian for the missionaries and other Christians who sought to extirpate all native religious and ceremonial practices.[35]

Public opinion in American society began to shift as the argument over Pueblo dances became viewed as an assault on Indian religions. Eventually, the government adopted a compromise solution: the Bureau of Indian Affairs would not interfere with native ceremonies as long as the tribes did not force any individuals to participate – Native American groups and individuals both were granted religious freedoms.[36] Thus, in an age of science and growing uncertainty about the absolute authority of Christian claims, the public definition of religion expanded beyond the confines of a textually oriented monotheism; the Christian god and the Holy Word of the Christian Bible were no longer the only authoritative indicators of authentic religion.

Sexual concerns

Much of the public uproar over the Pueblo ceremonial dances had to do with American cultural anxieties regarding sexuality; reported displays of sexual promiscuity in the dances incited conservative Christians to demand their censure. At the same time, a growing public conversation about sexual freedoms and individuals' rights for sexual expression justified the defense of Native American traditions in the minds of some of their most liberal advocates. To a large extent, the Pueblo dance controversy of the 1920s simply brought national focus to a public discourse already underway regarding sexuality.

A particularly contentious element in the public debate about sexuality was the question of homosexuality. Same-sex attraction and erotic behaviors have clearly been present throughout human history. In medieval Europe, the Christian Church regarded same-sex relations as mortally sinful, resulting in eternal damnation if not forgiven; those engaging in what the Church regarded as such unnatural and

Box 9.2   Sexuality

Distinct from both sex and gender, sexuality refers specifically to identities and practices related to erotic desires, or, more precisely, "aspects of personal and social life which have erotic significance."[37] As one scholar has described it, sexuality in its broadest application simply refers to the "never-ending constellation of factors that inform how people understand their sexual desires and actions."[38] Similarly to debates about the distinction between sex and gender that we reviewed earlier (see Box 6.2), discussions of sexuality often revolve around the tension between an "essentialist" view that assumes sexuality is an inherent, naturally endowed, and therefore fixed characteristic of the individual and a "constructionist" perspective that regards sexuality as socially and culturally constructed, a product of the individual's socialization. The essentialist perspective regards one's sexual orientation as a result of genetics and biology; it insists that the range of sexual proclivities, from asexual to homosexual to bisexual to heterosexual, occur naturally in human populations as well as in other species, and that sexual orientation's genetic basis makes it unalterable. This sort of essentialist view, however, has been criticized for its tendency to universalize sexuality across all cultures and social circumstances; moreover, it relies on a decisively heterosexual bias in its assumptions. In contrast, the French philosopher Michel Foucault (1926–1984) took a more constructionist approach by highlighting particular mechanisms in modern societies that organize and regulate sexual behaviors according to a binary between "normal" and "deviant." He famously argued that sexuality "is a name that can be given to a historical construct."[39] Moreover, Foucault documented what he regarded as "techniques of the self," which individuals engage in to produce their sexuality; it is the historian's obligation, he suggested, to investigate the history of such techniques and the particular social constructs of sexuality that they produce.

Both the essentialist and constructivist views assume that one's sexuality is determined by something outside the self, either by nature for the essentialists or by culture for the constructivists. In contrast, postmodern perspectives have introduced a "performative" theory that allows for self-determination according to the individual's preferences. Many recent theorists have been influenced by the work of American philosopher Judith Butler (born 1956), who in turn relies on the insights of Foucault. Contemporary scholarship has placed more emphasis on the variety and fluidity of sexual desires, identities, and behaviors that go beyond the binaries of heterosexual and homosexual; in fact, some of these theorists consider bisexuality a "third kind" of sexual identity that disrupts the simple binary of heterosexual versus homosexual, and many scholars of sexuality prefer the term "queer" to indicate a wide range of sexualities and sexual preferences.[40] Yet, despite broader recognition of identities and behaviors that undermine sexual binaries, heteronormativity (i.e., the notion that opposite-sex attraction and relationships are the normal and natural way for humans to interact sexually) remains the dominant perspective of sexuality in most sectors of American society, where the diversity and fluidity of sexual orientations as well as the variety of alternative sexual practices and desires are largely overlooked, remain hidden, or in some cases among more conservative religious voices are vehemently condemned.[41]

unmentionable acts between same-sex partners were referred to as "sodomites." It was not until 1869 that the term "homosexual" was first used to describe a person with same-sex erotic desires or who engaged in sexual relations with someone of the same sex. Women who loved other women were referred to as "sapphists" in nineteenth-century parlance, the word derived from the ancient Greek poet Sappho; she was from the Isle of Lesbos, and in the final years of the nineteenth century the term "lesbian" was adopted as a technical term signifying women involved in same-sex relations. In the 1920s "queer" became a common word of disparagement for homosexuals, joined later by the terms "faggot," "dyke," and "gay," which became popular during the 1930s in the United States.[42]

Same-sex relations were not universally condemned in nineteenth-century America. In fact, many friendships between adults of the same sex had what appears to later scrutiny an ambiguous sexual undertone. Throughout most of the nineteenth century, same-sex friends of all ages, both male and female, occasionally held hands, kissed each other on their lips, and often shared beds, even while committed to heterosexual relationships and marriages. In a culture more comfortable with physical intimacy as a common expression of friendship, such behaviors, although somewhat marginal, were not regarded as unusual or in any way aberrant.[43] The bonds of same-sex friendship found erotic expression in the poetry of Walt Whitman, whose book *Leaves of Grass* included clearly homoerotic imagery. Whitman's intent, however, was not salacious; his poetry articulated an ethic of comradeship, a vaguely religious sentiment of manly love that forms the ideological core of his poetic project.[44]

Certainly, Whitman's poetry attracted criticism for its "obscene" subject matter, but he suffered minimal condemnation compared to others.[45] His poetic expressions and the distinctively American democratic ideal that depicted sexual freedom alongside inclusive views of racial, gender, and class differences made the homoerotic allusions less threatening to many readers. In contrast, a new scientific field of "sexology" emerged toward the end of the nineteenth century that introduced a more straightforward technical language that attracted the wrath of critics. In contrast to the moralizing tendencies of most discussions about sexuality, sexologists attempted to approach sexual desires and activities from a scientific, nonjudgmental perspective. The taxonomies of the various forms of sexuality that sexological researchers developed placed homosexuals in a larger context of sexual desires and practices rather than considering them as aberrant and devious transgressors of social norms. This view of homosexuality based on scientific authority gave sexual reformers ammunition for demanding equal treatment for persons desiring same-sex relationships.[46] It also created opportunities for homosexual individuals to tell their personal stories in "scientific" autobiographies that contributed to the beginnings of a public homosexual identity.[47]

The public discussion of same-sex relationships initiated in sexology studies around the turn of the twentieth century increased anxiety in many sectors of American society. Leading the resistance to accepting homosexuality as normal human behavior were Christian church groups that published moral guides for youths living in American cities. These guides combined religious teachings with advice about sex, in effect turning sex education into a regulatory enterprise. By the 1920s, the moral guides for youth were supplemented by marriage manuals that explained proper sexual relations between married couples. Even the guides written by professional sexologists and physicians did not always escape broader social attitudes toward homosexuality, such as a 1926 bestseller that, despite its relatively tolerant stance on same-sex relations, concludes, "we should rid ourselves of the notion that we are the keepers of the natural homosexual, but we should hearten ourselves to prevent and cure those who accidently or deliberately acquire vicious sexual habits."[48] Yet, despite religious moralizing about human sexual desires and behaviors, a new modern attitude had taken hold by the 1920s, that sexual expression was a normal and necessary component of human activity and a key component of personal happiness.[49]

New attitudes about sexuality were evident in popular entertainments in the early part of the twentieth century. Burlesque theater of the nineteenth century entertained through social satire, and sexuality proved an attractive topic for American audiences. As motion pictures replaced burlesque as popular entertainment, religious groups sought to suppress the sexual content of cinema, especially the progressive acceptance of homosexuality that appeared in early films. Following on from the success of the New York Society for the Suppression of Vice, powerfully backed by both Catholic and Protestant religious groups, a coalition of Protestants and Catholics in the 1920s devised a code of self-censorship for the Hollywood film industry that specifically stated "pictures shall not imply that low forms of sex relationship are the accepted or common thing." The filmmakers accepted the code, fearing government intervention if they failed to address "immorality" in popular entertainment; in doing so, they effectively agreed to never depict adultery or non-marital sex in neutral or positive terms, and they banned references to homosexuality for the nearly two decades that the code governed American cinema.[50]

Migrations

Newly emerging sciences and technologies of the modern world, with improvements in transportation and communications, only encouraged the flood of immigration that began in the closing decades of the nineteenth century and continued through the early decades of the twentieth century. Catholics, Jews, and Protestants were most prominent among the new arrivals from Europe to America. This heyday of immigration also witnessed large numbers of Asians as well as a much smaller number of immigrants from Africa and the Arab nations of the Middle East and a significant number of migrants from the western hemisphere, especially Central America and islands of the Caribbean region. By the 1920s, America had become a nation of immigrants.

The overwhelming numbers of new arrivals forced changes in established religious groups as they adapted to the realities of accommodating new members of their local communities while they also sought accommodation with the modern world. Judaism serves as a useful example: as large numbers of Jews arrived in America each year in the early decades of the twentieth century, Jewish leaders grappled with the tension generated by the demands of traditional Judaism and the social, political, cultural, and economic conditions of living in the American system of democracy. Orthodox rabbis who resisted the pressures of modernization suffered an erosion of authority among their followers; in one prominent example, the rabbis' orders of *herem*, or excommunication, against Mordecai Kaplan (1881–1983) went unheeded, having virtually no effect on him or his followers. Kaplan, the progressive co-founder of the short-lived Reconstructionist movement in American Judaism, had raised the ire of some Orthodox traditionalists, who resented his willingness to accommodate modern science and the norms of American society.[51] Yet in the democratic American context, without traditional means of controlling the Jewish community, the rabbis' decrees were to no avail in halting Jewish participation in the changing modern world. Meanwhile, Kaplan successfully introduced modern innovations into American Judaism; for example, in 1922 he created the Bat Mitzvah ceremony, the initiation ritual that introduces young females into the Jewish community as full adult members. Kaplan introduced this modern innovation of gender parity in the wake of ratification of the Nineteenth Amendment to the US Constitution, which gave women the right to vote. Later he issued a *Sabbath Prayer Book* (1945) that purged references to gender differences.[52] Though his religious movement did not endure, many of his innovations were adopted by Reform and Conservative Jews.[53] Like other immigrants, Jews underwent processes of assimilation and adjustment that remade their religious and ethnic traditions, producing uniquely American forms of Jewish life.

Japanese immigrants

Around the turn of the twentieth century, people of Japanese descent eclipsed people of Chinese origin as the most numerous Asian group in America. Immigrants from Japan, most with a Buddhist religious orientation, began arriving on the west coast of the United States in the 1890s. In response to the missionary activities of the Japanese Gospel Society, a Protestant evangelical organization formed in 1877 to **proselytize** among Japanese Buddhists in San Francisco. The Hompa Hongwanji, a Japanese sect of Pure Land Buddhism (a Buddhist tradition focused on devotion to one of the many forms of the Buddha in order to gain help in attaining rebirth in a salvific "pure land" prior to achieving enlightenment), sent representatives to investigate the religious needs of Japanese immigrants in the United States. Shortly after the arrival of the Pure Land Buddhist emissaries in 1898, the Young Men's Buddhist Association was established (in an obvious response to the Christian evangelical Young Men's Christian Association), and later that year a Buddhist temple was built in San Francisco, the first in the United States. The following year the Hompa Hongwanji sent actual missionaries, Shuye Sonoda and Kakuryo Nishijima (birth and death dates unknown for both) to serve the American immigrants and to proselytize among non-Buddhists.[54] Sonoda explained their mission in an interview with the *San Francisco Chronicle*: "Our plan here is first to establish a church, then an evening school for our own people, and as we become more proficient in English, to communicate with those among Americans who wish to investigate Buddhism."[55] Other Buddhist priests followed from Japan, and within a decade they were publishing two Buddhist magazines, one in Japanese and one in English. They also organized a formal study group, the Dharma Sangha of Buddha, for non-Asian converts to Buddhism.

The Pure Land Buddhists from Japan directly challenged the precepts of Christianity. Dr. Sonoda explained to the reporter from the *San Francisco Chronicle* that, in the Buddhist understanding, humans are governed by the cosmic law of the universe and "not by any personified God." In particular, the Buddhist law of *karma* serves as the best guide for human behavior. Moreover, in a direct disparagement of theistic religious orientations, Sonoda declared, "We ourselves create God. He is not a real existence, but a figment of the human imagination." He went on to emphasize the need to engage in constant self-improvement: "We should seek the highest development of our inner nature, and we must remove our own imperfections, relying on no other power." Sonoda concluded by emphatically stating the superiority of Buddhist teachings: "I firmly believe that Buddhism is a better moral guide than Christianity."[56] In fact, Sonoda declared in a private letter shortly after his arrival in the United States that Buddhism "is destined to be the universal religion."[57] In the context of American evangelizing culture, these missionaries drew on their experiences defending their religion from Christian missionaries working in Japan; they brought religious competition to Protestant evangelicals' home turf in America.

Yet, despite the Buddhists' efforts to serve the immigrants' religious needs, not all Asians in America shunned Christianity. In fact, the success of Protestant missionaries in Asia meant that at least some Asian immigrants came to America as Christians, and others were familiar enough with the religion to join Christian churches once they were in America. In Seattle, Washington, as an example, a

Japanese Presbyterian congregation was established in 1907 under the leadership of Orio Inouye (1863–1937), who had arrived the previous year on a pledge drive to raise funds for his Christian church in Japan. He met the pastor of Seattle's First Presbyterian Church, who convinced Reverend Inouye to minister among the Japanese immigrants in the city. They began offering Bible-study classes that also served as English-language lessons for immigrants, and soon the Japanese Presbyterian Church was formed as a mission branch of the First Presbyterian Church. It welcomed all Japanese residents of the city, even non-Christians, and by the 1920s it had separated from its parent congregation to become an autonomous ethnic Japanese church with its own leadership and building, attracting numerous converts from the immigrant population.[58]

The Japanese immigrant population in America experienced a drastic demographic shift in the first decades of the twentieth century. A so-called "Gentlemen's Agreement" between the United States and Japan in 1907 effectively ended the migration of Japanese laborers to America, allowing only non-laborers with existing ties in the United States to migrate. Consequently, as more family members joined immigrants already in America, the Japanese immigrant community became more oriented around kin, with greater emphasis on religious traditions aimed at sustaining domestic harmony.[59] The unofficial agreement with Japan limiting immigration became official when the United States enacted new legislation in 1924 restricting immigration from all Asian nations.[60] For nearly four decades from the 1920s until the 1960s, almost no new Asian immigrants entered the country; nevertheless, Asian ethnic communities and their religious traditions and institutions became well established in the American multiverse of religions and cultures.

The Great Migration

Just as significant as the vast numbers of foreign immigrants settling in the United States each year was a significant internal migration that affected virtually the entire country in the first half of the twentieth century. Known as "the Great Migration," the substantial movement of African Americans out of the rural American south into the industrialized cities of the northern, midwestern, and western states precipitated significant cultural innovations that had an impact well beyond African American communities. Some four hundred thousand African Americans made their way out of the racially repressive conditions of the southern states between 1900 and 1930, and the number would soar to over six million by the 1970s. This unprecedented movement within the nation changed America's cities racially, politically, economically, and religiously.[61]

The cosmopolitan milieu that African American migrants encountered in urban settings created innovative opportunities for religious practice. New musical traditions entered black churches; composers set pious and uplifting Christian lyrics to southern blues and jazz musical styles to create a distinctive tradition of gospel

Figure 9.4 Membership at the Olivet Baptist Church in Chicago, shown here in the 1920s, grew dramatically as African Americans moved north in the Great Migration during the years between World War I and World War II, making it America's largest Protestant congregation by 1940. (Courtesy of the New York Public Library, #1217232.)

music. Unable to afford elaborate church buildings, numerous storefront churches sprang up in African American neighborhoods. Meanwhile, joining a more established African American church, with more refined styles of worship, often signaled respectability among a growing African American middle class. The Olivet Baptist Church, an African American congregation in Chicago, became the largest Protestant church in the nation.[62]

Among the many religious practitioners vying for their attention, African Americans living in New York City in the 1930s could hear the exhilarating claims of Father Divine, the adopted title of George Baker (1879–1965), whom many of his followers regarded as the incarnate God. Besides the thousands of African American followers who came to New York City to see Father Divine or who read the widely circulated newspaper *New Day* expounding his unique theological viewpoints, he also attracted a significant number of white adherents to his religious movement. Influenced by the ideas of Mary Baker Eddy (1821–1910) and other New Thought advocates (see Chapter 8 for a discussion of the New Thought movement) but rejecting their antimaterialist emphasis, Father Divine proffered a unique theology of holy bodies, pleasure, and plenitude in elaborate Holy Communion banquets that were the main practice of his religious ministry. He would greet those gathered for the feasts with the invocation, "Peace everyone! Good Health, Good Will and a Good Appetite." Not satisfied with the merely symbolic promises of Christianity, Father Divine insisted that the meal of which they were to partake was the material fulfillment of scripture, with food as the tangible symbol of heavenly love; eating at the banquet involved a union of body and soul, with food given by Father Divine himself, the embodiment of God. Both African American and Euro-American followers adored the short, squat, balding body of Father Divine, and many tried to emulate his image.[63]

Pentecostalism

By the time that Father Divine's feasts were attracting a considerable following, another religious development made possible by the movements of the Great Migration was having a profound impact on Christianity in America and around the world. Pentecostalism originated on the plains of Kansas, but it experienced its most conspicuous beginnings in Los Angeles, California, where, like Father Divine's ministry several decades later, it also involved both white and black adherents, at least in the beginning. Its most direct religious influences came from Holiness churches, a distinctive tradition developed in the nineteenth century by radical Methodists. Dissatisfied with the tendency of many Methodists to conform to the conventions and comforts of mainstream American culture, some Methodist followers began emphasizing the Wesleyan notion of sanctifying grace (see Chapter 5 for a discussion of Wesleyan views of grace). Once having attained the perfection of sanctification, the Wesleyans contended, the believer naturally adhered to a strict Christian piety. Over time, these Holiness Christians identified their experience of sanctification as "baptism in the Holy Spirit," in accordance with descriptions of conversion in the Christian biblical book Acts of the Apostles. As it grew, this widespread but fragmented religious movement crossed denominational and racial lines among Protestant Christians; moreover, it allowed opportunities for female leadership, with many Holiness followers believing that restrictions based on gender had no bearing under the power of the Holy Spirit. By the 1870s, several Holiness groups were practicing the "faith cure," divine healing that regarded the curing of illness as God's will for those who accepted it through their faith.[64]

In the first decade of the twentieth century, an African American Holiness evangelist by the name of William Seymour (1870–1922) joined the earliest migrants of the Great Migration as he relocated from Houston, Texas, to Los Angeles, California. While in Houston, Seymour had been allowed in 1905 to listen to a Bible-study class led by Charles F. Parham (1873–1929); as a Ku Klux Klan sympathizer, Parham would not permit the African American student to enter the class, but allowed him to listen through an open window or sit in the hallway on rainy days.[65] Formerly a Methodist minister in Kansas, Parham had struck out on his own as an independent evangelist in the Holiness tradition. A trip to northeastern states had exposed Parham to glossolalia, or speaking in tongues, which became for him the evidence of genuine baptism with the Holy Spirit. He and his students subsequently experienced speaking in tongues for themselves, and Parham began preaching about the experience of "tongues," relating it to the experience of the Christian disciples on the day of Pentecost, according to the scripture found in the Acts of the Apostles. Parham eventually moved his headquarters from Kansas to Houston, where he opened a school. It was here that William Seymour learned about Parham's doctrine of tongues.[66]

Seymour soon left Houston for California to help minister a small African American Holiness congregation in Los Angeles. His emphasis on speaking in tongues, however, was not well received by the Holiness followers, and soon Seymour rented a dilapidated former African Methodist Episcopal Church building on Azusa Street in Los Angeles, where he began holding revival meetings. Very quickly he was attracting large crowds of diverse followers, including blacks, whites, Hispanics, and others from all socioeconomic backgrounds. The Pentecostal movement that Charles Parham originated became an international sensation with Seymour's so-called Azusa Street Revival, which began in Los Angeles in 1906 and flourished through 1909.[67]

Figure 9.5 Pentecostalism traces its roots to a series of revivals organized by William Seymour beginning in 1906 held in this building at 312 Azusa Street in Los Angeles. From its humble beginnings on Azusa Street, the various branches of the Pentecostal movement have grown into one of the largest and most influential Christian sects in the world. (By permission of Apostolic Faith International Headquarters, Portland, Oregon.)

Among those participating in the Azusa Street Revival was a Holiness minister from Memphis, Tennessee, by the name of Charles H. Mason (1866–1961); his congregation had sent him to Los Angeles in 1907 to investigate the news of miraculous occurrences there. Formerly a Baptist minister who had embraced the Holiness tradition, Mason had joined with another disaffected Baptist minister, Charles Price Jones, Sr. (1865–1949), to form a Holiness church called the Church of God in Christ (COGIC). Following his experience of "the baptism of the Holy Ghost" at the Azusa Street Revival, Mason returned home determined to transform his Holiness church into a Pentecostal organization. His partner Jones resisted the imposition of Pentecostalism, and the two parted over their theological differences. Each went on to lead separate denominations, the COGIC denomination led by Mason developing into the largest African American religious denomination in the world.[68]

Initially the Pentecostal movement emanating from Los Angeles was racially and ethnically diverse. With an emphasis on spontaneity and freedom in the Holy Spirit, early Pentecostals resisted structural forms that tended to divide communities according to distinctions of race and class. Some, such as Charles H. Mason, actively sought racial integration of Pentecostal communities; Mason welcomed white members in COGIC congregations and ordained a number of white COGIC ministers.[69] With time, however, organizational structures took form; besides COGIC, which dominates among African American Pentecostals, the predominantly white Assemblies of God organized in the mid-1910s from several Pentecostal strands to become the largest Pentecostal denomination.[70] As in other Protestant Christian denominations, various theological differences have produced numerous distinct Pentecostal groups, such as those associated with Oneness Pentecostalism, who deny the Christian Trinity in favor of a single godhead.[71]

Much of the attraction of Pentecostalism's rapid rise in the early twentieth century involved divine healing. The immediate presence of the Christian god in the form of the Holy Spirit often manifested itself in the healing of ill and injured bodies. By the 1920s a number of Pentecostal healing ministries commanded broad appeal in American society. The most famous of these was the International Church of the Foursquare Gospel in Los Angeles, led by Aimee Semple McPherson, who regularly performed elaborate healing services in front of large audiences. In Chicago, the African American Pentecostal healer Lucy Smith (1875–1952) built a radio ministry from her All Nations Pentecostal Church aimed at reaching the migrants recently arrived in Chicago's neighborhoods as part of the Great Migration.[72]

The Azusa Street Revival also instigated a worldwide Pentecostal missionary effort. Thomas Ball Barratt (1862–1940), a British-born Methodist minister working in Norway, visited Los Angeles in 1906 where he was baptized in the Pentecostal spirit; he carried its message back with him to Scandinavia, stopping first in England, where he planted the seeds of Pentecostalism there. The Pentecostal movement spread rapidly in Norway from Barratt's efforts, and by 1910 Norwegian Pentecostal missionaries could be found in Africa, Asia, and South America. Likewise, American missionaries carried the Pentecostal message abroad in the

Box 9.3   Sister Rosetta Tharpe and the electric guitar

In the late 1930s and through the 1940s, the lifelong Pentecostal adherent Sister Rosetta Tharpe (1915–1973) ranked as one of the most widely known musical celebrities in America. Her popularity rose on a tension between the gospel music of her Pentecostal heritage as a devout member of the Church of God in Christ (COGIC) and her willingness to sing and play for secular audiences. As a guitar virtuoso, she helped to introduce the electric guitar to both church audiences and American popular music; she was, according to her biographer, "gospel's original crossover artist, its first nationally known star, and the most thrilling and celebrated guitarist of its Golden Age."[73]

Sister Rosetta's childhood exposure to many different cultural settings as she traveled with her mother, a COGIC evangelist, allowed her to incorporate elements of gospel music, blues, jazz, popular ballads, and country music in her musical talents. She pioneered a style of music that used the intersections and overlaps of popular music and the church music sung in Pentecostal congregations. Above all, she capitalized on the new technologies of amplification emerging in the 1930s to highlight her virtuosity as a guitarist. She energized audiences by pushing the volume on her guitar to its limits. Always mindful of her religious roots, Sister Rosetta regarded loud music as conforming to her Pentecostal belief "that the Lord smiled on those who made a joyful noise."[74]

Sister Rosetta Tharpe's negotiation between religious and secular music earned a measure of enmity from conservative elements among Pentecostals, but she remained convinced that she was doing God's work, even in her popular tunes. This did not stop her, however, from occasionally taking critical aim at the Church. Her 1945 hit record "Strange Things Happening Every Day" includes a humorous commentary on religious hypocrisy; it also has been suggested to be the earliest rock-and-roll record. In fact, Tharpe's influence has been enormous, with such artists as Ruth Brown, Johnny Cash, Red Foley, Isaac Hayes, Etta James, Jerry Lee Lewis, Elvis Presley, Bonnie Raitt, and Little Richard acknowledging their debt to the pioneering musical talent of Sister Rosetta Tharpe and her popularizing of the electric guitar.[75]

early years of the movement.[76] From humble beginnings in Los Angeles, Pentecostalism quickly became a worldwide Christian movement and continues to have a significant impact in numerous locations worldwide.

As Pentecostal organizations developed in subsequent decades, the early spontaneity and diversity subsided somewhat. Racial harmony retreated as distinctly white and black denominations gained institutional structure and power. Leadership positions for women, including female-led ministries, became less

Figure 9.6 Pentecostal singer Sister Rosetta Tharpe popularized amplified guitar music in the church as well as for secular audiences. (Image © JazzSign / Lebrecht Music & Arts / Corbis.)

common; prominent women Pentecostals such as Aimee Semple McPherson resorted to establishing their own separate church organizations rather than work within the confines of larger denominational structures controlled by male leaders. At the same time, the distinctions between Pentecostals and other evangelical Protestants diminished, with a number of fundamentalists incorporating Pentecostal elements into their religious practices.[77] Slowly, Pentecostalism edged toward the mainstream of American Protestantism.

Black Muslims

Islam has been in America from the earliest colonial days, although it nearly disappeared from American religious culture in the nineteenth century. Early American slave populations included a number of African Muslims, but the contexts of slavery and the total absence of Islamic religious institutions and resources made it impossible to sustain Muslim religious life in America. The religion of the Prophet Muhammad, though, would return in the twentieth century as an alternative for African Americans critical of the dominant Christianity. As greater numbers of blacks moved with the Great Migration into northern and western cities, many readily embraced a religious system critical of the stark inequalities and rude treatment they encountered in predominantly Christian America.

The contrast between Christianity and Islam as a means to criticize the culture of white supremacy had begun by the turn of the twentieth century. The notable educator and statesman Edward Wilmot Blyden (1832–1912) wrote devastating critiques of white Christian missionaries in Africa in the final decades of the nineteenth century and the first decade of the twentieth century. Blyden, who was originally from the Dutch West Indies, came to the United States as a young man, where his attempt to enroll in a seminary was refused due to his race. Subsequently he went to Africa, where he became a Presbyterian missionary in Liberia. Eventually Blyden became a college president and prominent government leader in Liberia. At the same time, his exposure to indigenous Muslim cultures in West Africa convinced him of the superior nature of Islam. He concluded that white people were naturally prone to imperialist goals, and especially that white Christian missionaries were more intent on enslaving blacks than on saving their souls. In contrast to the racist and exclusionary practices of Christians that he encountered in Africa, Blyden characterized Islam as a religion of human equality that embraces people of all backgrounds and races: "all unite under its banner and speak its language," he wrote.[78] Blyden promoted his own vision of African unity as he traveled widely in Europe and the United States in his position as the Liberian ambassador to Britain and France. His "Pan-African" view, though, relied on an elitist commitment to "civilizing" Africa through the unification of all blacks throughout the world. Blyden's view of racial separatism and black superiority would serve as a powerful paradigm for African Americans in the twentieth century with Islam as the counter to racist Christianity, but his regard for Islam ignored the repressive history of Muslims in Africa; he tended to downplay the sometimes violent suppression of local cultures that Muslim conquerors had inflicted on Africans. In short, Blyden created what one historian has described as "the myth of a race-blind Islam," a view of Islam without its history of racial prejudice and discrimination.[79]

The Pan-Africanism that Blyden first articulated became central to the Garveyite movement, which captured the imagination of urban African Americans in the early twentieth century. On August 2, 1920, Marcus Garvey (1887–1940), a Jamaican who led an international Pan-Africanist movement with his Universal Negro Improvement Association (UNIA), was greeted by thousands of African Americans lining the streets of Harlem in New York City as he proceeded to Madison Square Garden to address the second International Convention of the Negro Peoples of the World. In the crowd of twenty-five thousand delegates assembled to hear him speak were representatives from twenty-five nations on four continents; they were a religiously and politically diverse group, including Catholics, Hindus, Jews, Muslims, Protestants, socialists, and Marxists. Garvey's message of racial pride and self-help under the Pan-Africanist banner was the foundation of the convention's "Declaration of Rights for the Negro Peoples of the World," which included demands for "social and political separatism and the recognition of UNIA as sovereign representative of the race." The delegates ended by declaring Garvey "President General" and the "Provisional President" of Africa.[80]

Figure 9.7   Parades sponsored by the Universal Negro Improvement Association (UNIA), the Pan-African organization led by Marcus Garvey, attracted sizable crowds in the Harlem section of New York City in the 1920s. Although its founding document includes the promotion of Christian worship in Africa as a goal, UNIA declined to declare Christianity its "state religion," acknowledging the diversity of religious orientations among its members. (Courtesy of the New York Public Library, #1228871.)

As the public symbol of African American political power in America, Marcus Garvey became the focal point of the first African American mass movement in the United States, connecting struggles experienced in American cities and towns to the plight of Africans and other people of African descent throughout the world. The founding manifesto of UNIA called on "all people of Negro or African parentage" to participate in the effort to "establish a Universal Confraternity among the race." Besides its political and social goals, the UNIA manifesto included a religious objective "to promote a conscientious Christian worship among the native tribes of Africa."[81] Garvey's movement, however, was not exclusively Christian, even though he himself was a convert to Roman Catholicism and many of his followers were committed Christians of various sorts. Delegates to the movement's Fourth International Convention of the Negro Peoples of the World in 1924 proclaimed, "as there are Moslems and other non-Christians who are Garveyites, it was not wise to declare Christianity the state religion of the organization."[82] In particular, the writings of Blyden and other Pan-Africanists in the early twentieth century stressed the importance of Islam in African history, especially characterizing its racial attitudes as superior to those of Christianity. Moreover, an interpretation of Islam as a world religion that unifies diverse peoples fit well with the global Pan-Africanist movement that Garvey led. At one point, Muslim delegates proposed a plan to make Islam the official religion of UNIA; although Garvey preferred to maintain a strictly non-sectarian status for his organization, the rhetoric and symbols of Islam were widely appropriated in his movement.[83] Officially, UNIA emphasized a black theology that focused on a non-sectarian "God of Ethiopia," encouraging followers to regard the divine as a black god that supported their efforts for advancing the rights and social power of blacks everywhere.[84]

Another Pan-Africanist, Timothy Drew (1886–1929), identified Marcus Garvey as the precursor to an American Muslim movement among African Americans of the Great Migration. Drew adopted the title Noble Drew Ali and produced a sacred text for his movement, the *Holy Koran of the Moorish Science Temple*, which explains, "In these modern days there came a forerunner, who was divinely prepared by the great God-Allah and his name is Marcus Garvey, who did teach and warn the nations of the earth to prepare to meet the coming Prophet, who was to bring the true and divine Creed of Islam, and his name is Noble Drew Ali."[85] As the first of the self-designated prophets of American Islam, Drew incorporated diverse traditions in an eclectic religious mix that included Islam, Garveyism, and even Theosophy.[86]

Drew's movement began in 1913 when he opened the Canaanite Temple in Newark, New Jersey; within a decade his followers numbered thirty thousand with temples in most of the major cities in the northern states. Their headquarters moved in 1923 to the Moorish Holy Temple of Science in Chicago, and Drew renamed his organization the Moorish Science Temple of America. In 1927 he published the *Holy Koran of the Moorish Science Temple* (sometimes known as *Circle Seven Koran*), which bore little resemblance to the Qur'an revealed to the Prophet Muhammad in Arabia. Drew's text emphasizes industriousness and proper moral behavior of adherents; it also glorifies Jesus as a direct ancestor of Moorish Americans. Yet, despite his emphasis on Jesus, Drew portrayed Christianity as a religion of Europeans, and he argued that the future of civilization was the responsibility of descendants of Asiatic nations, which according to his teachings included the people of South and Central America, Arabia, China, Egypt, India, Japan, and Turkey as well as African Americans. Noble Drew Ali's appropriation of Islamic symbols and practices subverted the racist and ethnocentric assumptions of white American Christians. By revealing a lost identity as Muslims, Drew connected his African American followers to what he claimed was their "true religion" in an attempt to transform their marginal status in American society.[87]

Following Drew's death in 1929, his Moorish Science Temple struggled to continue as multiple successors vied for leadership. Within a few years, another group emerged to become the dominant African American Muslim organization in the nation. In 1930 a peddler in the neighborhoods of Detroit, Michigan, began espousing a black nationalist message that condemned white Christianity and depicted him as a black messiah sent "to displace the old Christ that Christianity gave black people." W. D. Fard (known variously as Wallace D. Fard, W. F. Muhammad, and Wallace Fard Muhammad; birth and death dates unknown) foretold a final War of Armageddon in the United States between black people and white people; if African Americans were to prevail in this ultimate battle of humanity, he claimed, they must adopt their "natural religion," which he identified as Islam, and "reclaim their original identity as Muslims." Soon a following of local African Americans were coming to meetings to hear the mysterious prophet, who revealed the true origins of African Americans as the "members of the lost tribe of Shabazz, stolen by traders from the Holy City of Mecca 379 years ago." He established the Lost-Found Nation of Islam in the Wilderness of North America and promised his followers that if "they obeyed Allah, he would take them back to the Paradise from which they had been stolen – the Holy City of Mecca."[88]

Fard's sudden disappearance in 1934 remains as much a mystery as his puzzling arrival four years earlier. One of his closest associates, Elijah Muhammad (1897–1975; originally Elijah Poole, and given the name Elijah Karriem by Fard, who later gave him the name Muhammad), had recognized Fard as "God himself," and took over leadership of the group following Fard's departure. Born in Georgia, Elijah Muhammad had joined the thousands of other African Americans moving north in the Great Migration when in 1923 he relocated his young family from rural Georgia to the urban environs of Detroit. As an African American factory worker trying to support a large and growing family in the 1930s, Elijah Muhammad was immediately convinced by Fard's religious proclamations, and he quickly became Fard's chief minister.

Elijah Muhammad had been a follower of Marcus Garvey and even had served as a local officer in Garvey's UNIA, but later he became disenchanted with the movement. Like thousands of other African Americans who had followed the Great Migration to northern cities, he suffered the debilitating consequences of economic failure that plunged the nation into the Great Depression; besides losing factory jobs, African Americans in places like Detroit had to compete with immigrants for menial jobs. In addition, they faced the constant threat of terror from the Ku Klux Klan, whose membership had grown dramatically in the 1920s, as they viciously targeted blacks and other minorities. In the context of such dire circumstances in Detroit's African American neighborhoods in 1930, Fard's preaching of black superiority and redemption through the true religion of Islam was a welcome message.[89]

Following Fard's disappearance, Elijah Muhammad became the Prophet of the Nation of Islam; he emphasized the "hidden truth" that Fard had brought to African Americans in Detroit: that black people did not come from the same God as white people. Characterizing blacks as "righteous and divine" in contrast to the wickedness of white people, Elijah Muhammad taught that "America is under Divine Judgement to destroy her for the evils done to Allah's people in slavery." In order to correct the debasement experienced in bondage, he required converts to change their surnames to X as an erasure of their names given in slavery.[90] Under Elijah Muhammad's leadership, Nation of Islam members were prohibited from such "slave behaviors" as eating pork or drinking liquor, and they were exhorted to live in a most morally upright fashion.[91]

Elijah Muhammad's leadership of the Nation of Islam did not go unchallenged among the followers of Fard's teachings. The greatest threat, however, came from federal law enforcement authorities, who were monitoring African American Muslims in the 1930s and 1940s on suspicions of sedition and Selective Service violations. The FBI finally arrested Elijah Muhammad in 1942 for failing to register for the military draft and for encouraging his members not to register. He served four years in federal prison, but he maintained his leadership of the Nation of Islam through his wife, Clara Muhammad (1899–1972), who served as the supreme secretary of the Nation of Islam and relayed her husband's orders to ministers and captains of the movement while he was imprisoned. A respected leader of the movement, Clara Muhammad kept the Nation of Islam functioning through trying times, and she served as an exemplary role model for the ideal black Muslim woman. Meanwhile, Elijah Muhammad conducted weekly religious services in prison and converted many of the prisoners to his faith. By the time he was released in 1946, Elijah Muhammad was the undisputed leader and revered Prophet of the Nation of Islam.[92]

The Nation of Islam, however, was not the sole representative of African American Muslims in the middle decades of the twentieth century. A good number of African Americans converted to Sunni Islam, the predominant form of the religion, which had come to America with Arabian immigrants; the First Cleveland Mosque, for instance, was led by an African American convert, Wali Akram (1904–1994), and followed Sunni doctrine emphasizing the Qur'an as revealed to the Prophet Muhammad. In the 1940s an immigrant from the Caribbean island of Grenada, Sheikh Daoud Ahmed Faisal (1891–1980), established the most successful early African American mosque, the Islamic Mission of America, in Brooklyn, New York. Other such groups appeared elsewhere in American cities, adding to the diversity of African American Muslims.[93]

Islam in America, of course, was not only an African American religious movement. As alluded to above, Muslim immigrants from Arabian nations, from Africa and elsewhere, also began establishing themselves in the early decades of the twentieth century. The number of foreign-born Muslims increased decisively following World War II as the United States became a world power with economic and political interests in the Middle East; many came as students who subsequently settled in the United States following their education.[94] Although their numbers would not approach the numbers of African American Muslims in the twentieth century, Muslim immigrants were certainly present in America throughout the century and occasionally engaged with converts who had come to the religion of Muhammad through the various black Muslim groups.

Global America

Immigration once again changed the religious landscape in America during the early part of the twentieth century. European immigrants brought varieties of Christianity and Judaism to the United States; new arrivals from Asia built temples, mosques, gurdwaras, and other sites of community gathering and devotion for Buddhists, Hindus, Jains, Sikhs, and others. At the same time, Christian missionaries spread out across the globe as they ministered to non-Christian populations; in one particularly ambitious effort, an interdenominational conference of Protestant missionary representatives met in Cairo, Egypt, in 1906 to plot a coordinated strategy for evangelizing the world's Muslims.[95] With Americans taking their religious messages to nearly every nation and people from all over the world coming to settle in the United States, America had become a thoroughly global nation.

Alongside the globalizing tendencies of the early twentieth century were developments in science and technology that both abetted the spread of religious views and produced new challenges for religious communities. We have highlighted in this chapter how new developments in biology, psychology, sociology, and anthropology, along with technological advances in communications and transportation, fundamentally changed the modern outlook, at least for most Americans living in the twentieth century. Among the many implications for religious people devoted to traditional interpretations and doctrines, the very idea of religion itself came under scrutiny in several arenas. As Darwin's notions of evolutionary history posed direct challenges to literal views of divine creation, instigating doctrinal battles between Christian modernists and fundamentalists in the 1920s, a variety of minority religious groups claimed their own interpretations of what should be regarded as legitimate religion in pluralistic America. We have considered how Native Americans, for instance, asserted their rights to practice centuries-old religious traditions in the Pueblo dance controversy as just one example of how Americans confronted new perspectives introduced by developments in the sciences of anthropology and sociology.

The dynamic transformations of American society accelerated in the twentieth century, with religion at the center of many large-scale changes. No longer a provincial nation on the world stage, the United States was becoming a leading world power. At the same time, America's religious character was also changing. The millennial hopes of nineteenth-century Christians to establish a divine kingdom in North America had less impact in unifying the dizzying array of religious orientations and commitments of the American people. In the first half of the twentieth century, America was becoming a fully modern nation.

Questions for Discussion

(1) How did advancements in science and technology affect religions in twentieth-century America?

(2) In what ways did ethnographic research by anthropologists such as Franz Boas and his students introduce new perspectives on "religion" as a category of culture?

(3) What were some of the religious responses to scientific perspectives regarding variations in sexual orientation?

(4) Increased immigration during the early decades of the twentieth century brought new religious voices to America. How were some of the religious traditions of immigrants altered by their adherents' experiences of assimilation and acculturation in America?

(5) The Great Migration of the twentieth century moved millions of African Americans into American cities. What religious developments occurred in the urban environments that resulted from burgeoning African American populations in the first half of the twentieth century?

Suggested Primary-Source Readings

William James, *The Varieties of Religious Experience: A Study in Human Nature* (New York: Oxford University Press, 2012): This book, which originally appeared in 1902, argues against the philosophical and scientific dismissal of religion; it is by a renowned American pragmatist philosopher and psychologist who proposed a more personal, individualist approach to studying religions that would become dominant in twentieth-century academic studies of world religions.

J. Gresham Machen, *Christianity and Liberalism* (Grand Rapids, MI: William B. Eerdmans, 2009): The Introduction to this book, first published in 1923, provides a conservative Protestant defense against the perceived threat of liberalism; Machen was a prominent Protestant theologian who resisted identifying himself as a fundamentalist but who nevertheless defended the fundamentalist view.

Don C. Talayesva, "The Making of a Man," in *Sun Chief: The Autobiography of a Hopi Indian*, 2nd edn (New Haven, CT: Yale University Press, 2013), 157–178: Chapter eight of this autobiography of a Hopi Indian born in 1890 and educated in Christian boarding schools before returning to Hopi culture includes a description of the initiation ceremonies into his Hopi clan.

Frank Bartleman, *Azusa Street* (Plainfield, NJ: Logos International, 1980): This eyewitness account comes from one of the leaders of the revival in Los Angeles that initiated the worldwide Pentecostal movement.

Noble Drew Ali, excerpt from the Holy Koran of the Moorish Science Temple, in Edward E. Curtis IV, ed., *The Columbia Sourcebook of Muslims in the United States* (New York: Columbia University Press, 2008), 59–64: The chapters reprinted from the Moorish Science Temple sacred text characterize Marcus Garvey as the forerunner of Noble Drew Ali, God's chosen prophet to lead the Moorish nation in America.

Notes

1 Edward J. Larson, *Summer for the Gods: The Scopes Trial and America's Continuing Debate over Science and Religion* (Cambridge, MA: Harvard University Press, 1997), 71.

2 The exchange between Bryan and Darrow is detailed in ibid., 3–8.

3 Quoted in ibid., 17.

4 Gregory Claeys, "The 'Survival of the Fittest' and the Origins of Social Darwinism," *Journal of the History of Ideas* 61, no. 2 (2000), 223–228.

5 Peter Gay, ed., *The Freud Reader* (New York: W. W. Norton, 1989), xvii.

6   Ibid., xvi.
7   Freud's statement is in the Preface to *Totem and Taboo* (1913) and is quoted in ibid.
8   Sigmund Freud, *The Future of an Illusion*, ed. and trans. James Strachey (New York: W. W. Norton, 1961), 55.
9   Robert E. Brown, "Theology and Belief," in *The Blackwell Companion to Religion in America*, ed. Philip Goff (Malden, MA: Wiley Blackwell, 2010), 358–359.
10 Ann Taves, *Fits, Trances, and Visions: Experiencing Religion and Explaining Experience from Wesley to James* (Princeton, NJ: Princeton University Press, 1999), 249.
11 Ann Taves, *Religious Experience Reconsidered: A Building Block Approach to the Study of Religion and Other Special Things* (Princeton, NJ: Princeton University Press, 2009), 4–5.
12 Quoted in Wallace D. Best, *Passionately Human, No Less Divine: Religion and Culture in Black Chicago, 1915–1952* (Princeton, NJ: Princeton University Press, 2005), 5.
13 Daniel Mark Epstein, *Sister Aimee: The Life of Aimee Semple McPherson* (New York: Harcourt Brace Jovanovich, 1993), 156.
14 Ibid., 264.
15 Matthew Avery Sutton, *Aimee Semple McPherson and the Resurrection of Christian America* (Cambridge, MA: Harvard University Press, 2007), 70.
16 Shailer Mathews, *The Faith of Modernism* (New York: Macmillan, 1925), 23.
17 In the words of journalist Walter Lippman, quoted in George M. Marsden, *Fundamentalism and American Culture: The Shaping of Twentieth Century Evangelicalism, 1870–1925*, 2nd edn (New York: Oxford University Press, 2006), 3.
18 Quoted in ibid., 118.
19 Ibid., 120.
20 Ibid., 117.
21 Ibid., 159.
22 Malise Ruthven, *Fundamentalism: The Search for Meaning* (New York: Oxford University Press, 2004), 8.
23 Ibid., 33–34.
24 William Jennings Bryan, *In His Image* (New York: Fleming H. Revell, 1922), 93. Bryan often repeated this point in his lectures and speeches in the 1920s.
25 Marsden, *Fundamentalism and American Culture*, 169.
26 Ibid., 170.
27 Larson, *Summer for the Gods*, 47–59.
28 Quoted in ibid., 103.
29 Ibid., 201.
30 Marsden, *Fundamentalism and American Culture*, 6.
31 Thomas A. Tweed and Stephen R. Prothero, eds., *Asian Religions in America: A Documentary History* (New York: Oxford University Press, 1999), 148–149.
32 Tisa Wenger, *We Have a Religion: The 1920s Pueblo Indian Dance Controversy and American Religious Freedom* (Chapel Hill: University of North Carolina Press, 2009), 73–81.
33 Ibid., 1–7.
34 Ibid., 7.
35 Ibid., 164–165.

36   Ibid., 6.

37   Stevi Jackson and Sue Scott, eds., *Feminism and Sexuality: A Reader* (Edinburgh: Edinburgh University Press, 1996), 2.

38   Michael Bronski, *A Queer History of the United States* (Boston, MA: Beacon Press, 2011), xviii.

39   Michel Foucault, *The History of Sexuality: An Introduction* (New York: Vintage, 1990), 105.

40   The term "queer" is often replaced by or used in conjunction with the abbreviation LGBTQQIA (lesbian, gay, bisexual, transgender, queer, questioning, intersex, asexual), many times shortened to LGBTQ, which attempts to encompass the range of possible sexual identities and preferences.

41   Peter Brooker, *A Glossary of Cultural Theory*, 2nd edn (London: Arnold, 2003), 231–232; for an example of scholarship on theological views of sexuality, see Mark D. Jordan, *The Invention of Sodomy in Christian Theology* (Chicago, IL: University of Chicago Press, 1997).

42   Bronski, *A Queer History of the United States*, xvi–xvii.

43   Juan A. Herrero Brasas, *Walt Whitman's Mystical Ethics of Comradeship: Homosexuality and the Marginality of Friendship at the Crossroads of Modernity* (Albany: State University of New York Press, 2010), 99 and D. Michael Quinn, *Same-Sex Dynamics among Nineteenth-Century Americans: A Mormon Example* (Urbana: University of Illinois Press, 1996), 1.

44   For a thorough study of Whitman's religious project built on his ideology of comradeship, see Herrero Brasas, *Walt Whitman's Mystical Ethics of Comradeship*.

45   Bronski, *A Queer History of the United States*, 80.

46   Ibid., 78.

47   Ibid., 96–97.

48   This quotation is from *The Doctor Looks at Love and Life* (1926) by Joseph Collins, MD, quoted in ibid., 102.

49   Ibid.

50   Ibid., 119.

51   Hasia Diner, "From Convenant to Constitution: The Americanization of Judaism," in *Transforming Faith: The Sacred and Secular in Modern American History*, ed. M. L. Bradbury and James B. Gilbert (New York: Greenwood Press, 1989), 17.

52   Ibid., 21.

53   Max I. Dimont, *The Jews in America: The Roots, History, and Destiny of American Jews* (New York: Simon and Schuster, 1978), 178–180.

54   Thomas A. Tweed, *The American Encounter with Buddhism, 1844–1912: Victorian Culture & the Limits of Dissent* (Chapel Hill: University of North Carolina Press, 2000), 36.

55   The interview appeared in the *San Francisco Chronicle* on September 12, 1899; the text was reprinted in an article "Missionaries of the Buddhist Faith" in the Summer 1996 issue of *Tricycle* magazine, available online at www.tricycle.com/ancestors/missionaries-buddhist-faith (accessed August 21, 2013).

56   Ibid.

57   "Letter of Shuye Sonoda to Paul Carus, September 14, 1899," reprinted in Tweed and Prothero, *Asian Religions in America*, 80.

58 Madeline Duntley, "Heritage, Ritual, and Translation: Seattle's Japanese Presbyterian Church," in *Gods of the City: Religion and the American Urban Landscape*, ed. Robert A. Orsi (Bloomington: Indiana University Press, 1999), 290–291.

59 Ibid.

60 Tweed and Prothero, *Asian Religions in America*, 159–160.

61 Sylvester Johnson, "The Black Church," in *The Blackwell Companion to Religion in America*, ed. Philip Goff (Malden, MA: Wiley Blackwell, 2010), 454 and Isabel Wilkerson, *The Warmth of Other Suns: The Epic Story of America's Great Migration* (New York: Random House, 2010), 8–11. For a thorough study of the religious effects of the Great Migration in Chicago, see Best, *Passionately Human, No Less Divine*.

62 Johnson, "The Black Church," 457.

63 R. Marie Griffith, *Born Again Bodies: Flesh and Spirit in American Christianity* (Berkeley: University of California Press, 2004), 140–145.

64 Jonathan R. Baer, "Holiness and Pentecostalism," in *The Blackwell Companion to Religion in America*, ed. Philip Goff (Malden, MA: Wiley Blackwell, 2010), 571–573.

65 Harvey Cox, *Fire from Heaven: The Rise of Pentecostal Spirituality and the Reshaping of Religion in the Twenty-First Century* (Reading, MA: Addison-Wesley, 1995), 49.

66 Vinson Synan, *The Holiness-Pentecostal Tradition: Charismatic Movements in the Twentieth Century*, 2nd edn (Grand Rapids, MI: Eerdmans, 1997), 90–94.

67 Ibid., 94–106.

68 Estrelda Alexander, *Black Fire: One Hundred Years of African American Pentecostalism* (Downers Grove, IL: IVP Academic, 2011), 173–177.

69 Ibid., 177–180.

70 Edith L. Blumhofer, *Restoring the Faith: The Assemblies of God, Pentecostalism, and American Culture* (Urbana: University of Illinois Press, 1993), 2.

71 Baer, "Holiness and Pentecostalism," 577–578.

72 Regarding McPherson, see Epstein, *Sister Aimee* and Sutton, *Aimee Semple McPherson*. For healing traditions in African American Pentecostalism, with mention of Lucy Smith, see Yvonne Patricia Chireau, *Black Magic: Religion and the African American Conjuring Tradition* (Berkeley: University of California Press, 2003), 109–111.

73 Gayle Wald, *Shout, Sister, Shout! The Untold Story of Rock-and-Roll Trailblazer Sister Rosetta Tharpe* (Boston, MA: Beacon Press, 2007), viii.

74 Ibid., 216.

75 Ibid., ix.

76 Baer, "Holiness and Pentecostalism," 578–579.

77 Ibid., 579.

78 Quoted in Edward E. Curtis, *The Columbia Sourcebook of Muslims in the United States* (New York: Columbia University Press, 2008), 19.

79 Richard Brent Turner, *Islam in the African-American Experience* (Bloomington: Indiana University Press, 1997), 55–56.

80 Ibid., 87.

81 Quoted in ibid., 81.

82 Quoted in ibid., 83.

83 Ibid., 87–90.

84 Johnson, "The Black Church," 456.

85 Quoted in Turner, *Islam in the African-American Experience*, 90.

86   Ibid.

87   Ibid., 90–97.

88   Ibid., 148–51; Edward E. Curtis IV, *Black Muslim Religion in the Nation of Islam, 1960–1975* (Chapel Hill: University of North Carolina Press, 2006), 2.

89   Turner, *Islam in the African-American Experience*, 151–156.

90   Ibid., 157–159.

91   Curtis, *Columbia Sourcebook*, 43.

92   Turner, *Islam in the African-American Experience*, 168–169.

93   Curtis, *Columbia Sourcebook*, 43–44.

94   Yvonne Yazbeck Haddad, "The Shaping of Arab and Muslim Identity in the United States," in *Immigration and Religion in America: Comparative and Historical Perspectives*, ed. Richard D. Alba, Albert J. Raboteau, and Josh DeWind (New York: New York University Press, 2009), 149–150.

95   Thomas S. Kidd, *American Christians and Islam: Evangelical Culture and Muslims from the Colonial Period to the Age of Terrorism* (Princeton, NJ: Princeton University Press, 2009), 58.

10

Cold War and Civil Rights

In this chapter we consider how religious understandings of the American nation contributed to conflicts over patriotic loyalty on the one hand and the ill treatment of marginalized populations on the other. Controversies surrounding the Pledge of Allegiance and the emphasis on the religious nature of American society in the aftermath of World War II contrast with religious movements that addressed economic and racial injustices. The long global rivalry between the United States and the Soviet Union known as the Cold War made the religious elements of American society a national cause. At the same time, religious leaders brought attention to social ills of the nation. In particular, the Civil Rights Movement and other related efforts relied on multiple religious perspectives to bring social reforms in areas of race, gender, labor practices, and other areas of injustice. As the United States emerged as a leading global power in the middle of the twentieth century, Americans often turned to religion as they defined the character and purposes of the nation.

Pilgrims gathered outside the storage room of an automobile service station converted into a "monastic cell," awaiting an opportunity to see, to touch, to kiss, to make offerings to a frail man lying in the repose of a holy fast beneath a crucifix hung on the wall above him. Some twenty thousand faithful followers of César Chávez (1927–1993) descended on this California scene over the twenty-five days of his fast in early 1968, many of them crawling on their knees from the highway up to the small room where he fasted, prayed, and received the Eucharist from

Formed From This Soil: An Introduction to the Diverse History of Religion in America, First Edition. Thomas S. Bremer.
© 2015 Thomas S. Bremer. Published 2015 by John Wiley & Sons, Ltd.

Catholic priests. Throughout the entire fasting period, devotees kept vigil at one of several makeshift shrines to the Virgin of Guadalupe erected on the grounds.[1]

Chávez had retreated into the small room on a personal spiritual quest for strength and discernment, not to draw attention to his campaign of social justice for migrant farm workers. By the time he broke his fast, though, much attention had come his way. Senator Robert F. Kennedy (1925–1968), candidate for the presidency, was on hand to lend his support, bringing with him the national and international press, who depicted Chávez as a courageous political activist. His followers, on the other hand, especially the impoverished farm workers and their families, regarded him as a holy man, a person of exceptional spiritual powers sent as an emissary of God to deliver the downtrodden from their misery; to many of them, Chávez courted sainthood in the tradition of Roman Catholic mystics.[2]

Figure 10.1　US senator and presidential candidate Robert F. Kennedy kneels in prayer at the conclusion of the 1968 fast of United Farm Workers leader César Chávez, shown seated in prayer behind Kennedy, in Delano, California. Chávez's fast attracted national attention, and thousands of pilgrims visited him during his religious retreat. (Image © Everett Collection Historical / Alamy.)

The achievements of César Chávez as the leader of the United Farm Workers of America made him one of the most recognizable and widely celebrated civil rights leaders of twentieth-century America. But, like many other social activists of his era, Chávez's political efforts sprang from his personal religiosity. Profoundly influenced by the examples of the medieval Catholic saint Francis of Assisi (ca. 1181–1226) and by the Hindu independence leader Mohandas Gandhi (1869–1948), but especially by the Christian model of Jesus Christ as a champion of the poor, Chávez was a lifelong Roman Catholic who experienced a religious awakening in early adulthood that initiated religious practices that guided the rest of his life.[3] Regular religious fasts of "about eight to twelve days every forty-five to sixty days … [and] every day between midnight and noon the following day" comprised his most conspicuous spiritual exercise. These fasts were not strategies for inciting social change; they were not hunger strikes in protest of farm workers' conditions, although they informed his social activism. Instead, Chávez fasted for personal transformation; as he once explained, "It is not intended as a pressure on anyone but only as an expression of my own deep feelings and my own need to do penance and to be in prayer."[4] Fasting involved a highly personal devotion to the Christian god.

Chávez, however, did not confine his religious discipline and devotion to purely personal matters. He revealed that any major decisions regarding the union or the activities of his followers were made in times of fasting; he also incorporated the imagery and practices of his religious devotion into public efforts on behalf of migrant farm workers. His speeches and pronouncements were filled with biblical references, and he spoke with the **charismatic** authority of a religious prophet. One of his earliest protests involved a march to the state capitol in Sacramento, California, during the Catholic season of Lent that drew on the model of traditional Lenten pilgrimages. The protestors' march "was penance more than anything else," Chávez later recalled, "and it was quite a penance, because there was an awful lot of suffering involved in this pilgrimage, a great deal of pain." Priests performed mass for the marchers every day, and they walked behind a banner bearing an image of the Virgin of Guadalupe. The pilgrims arrived on the capitol steps on Easter Sunday in 1966, with ten thousand of them celebrating victory in announcing a settlement in their strike.[5]

César Chávez's activities in support of migrant farm workers were part of a larger movement among Mexican Americans and Mexican immigrants commonly known as the Chicano movement; this political, social, and cultural movement among Hispanics followed on a series of social upheavals in twentieth-century America. The experiences of global war and international rivalry with an avowedly anti-religious foe in the Cold War heightened the religious elements of American society. The national effort to characterize America as a nation of religious freedom and faith, though, urged a conformity that overlooked diversity among America's religious communities. At the same time, the unprecedented national prosperity in the decades following World War II brought more attention to those excluded from the opportunities and freedoms promised in American democracy. As we will see in this chapter, both conformity and resistance to the Cold War views of the American nation had roots in the spiritual orientations of America's most prominent leaders and its diverse citizenry.

Religion of the Nation

From the time of its founding until the present, the United States of America has been bound up with religiosity. The provisions regarding religion in the First Amendment of the US Constitution guarantee in principle that religious people can freely exercise their freedom of conscience in religious matters and engage in religious activities without undue interference or coercion from the government. Thomas Jefferson's (1743–1826) interpretation of religious disestablishment, subsequently affirmed in Supreme Court opinions, built a "wall of separation" between church and state that serves as the normative understanding of religious freedom for most Americans. In the context of the early American republic, when nearly everyone thought of religion in terms of formal Christian institutions, keeping separate the institutional structures of religion (church) and government (state) afforded necessary protections for both sides of the wall. Yet, as we have repeatedly shown, religion can be far more than merely "church." Even among the dominant Christians, religion has involved activities and moral commitments that go beyond involvement with a church, as exemplified in the nineteenth-century social movements for the abolition of slavery and for the rights of women. Moreover, the religions of non-Christian groups often entail communal arrangements, spiritual orientations, and **ritual** practices that do not easily fit into categories of church and state; the Pueblo dance controversy of the 1920s discussed in Chapter 9 demonstrated the difficulty of imposing Christian religious categories on other cultural circumstances.

Despite the historical American perception of separate and distinct realms for religion and government, the idea of the American nation has been closely bound to Christian interpretations of religious purpose from the earliest times. In fact, there has never been a time since the arrival of the first British colonists that America has not been conceived of in Christian millennialist terms; the history of Christians in America abounds with interpretations of God's will for the meaning and purpose of nationhood. Since the founding of the United States in the late eighteenth century, elements of what has been called a "civil religion" have lent authority and solemnity to the machinations of governing the nation.

In the twentieth century, the rising prominence of the United States as a world power drew attention to nationalist loyalties that were sometimes couched in terms of religious commitments. Using the millennialist assumptions of America as God's promised land, a good number of citizens regarded one's love of nation as a clear indication of religious devotion. Following World War II, the Cold War

Box 10.1 Civil religion

Scholars have designated the nationalistic practices and traditions related to legitimizing state authority with reference to transcendent powers as "civil religion." This term gained much attention in modern scholarship beginning in the 1960s when sociologist Robert Bellah (1927–2013) claimed that there exists in the United States an "American civil religion" that persists alongside other religious traditions; this religiosity of nationalism, derived from the ideas of civil religion first proposed by the Enlightenment philosopher Jean-Jacques Rousseau (1712–1778), involves, according to Bellah's definition, "a collection of beliefs, symbols, and rituals with respect to sacred things and institutionalized in a collectivity [i.e., the United States of America]." Bellah emphasized the non-sectarian character of American civil religion, although he highlighted the Christian millennialist belief in America as a promised land.[6]

Bellah argued "that the civil religion at its best is a genuine apprehension of universal and transcendent religious reality as seen in or ... revealed through the experience of the American people." As evidence, he discussed references to God in presidential addresses; he characterized the Declaration of Independence and the US Constitution as "sacred scriptures" of the nation; and he highlighted the religious aspects of the American Revolution and the Civil War.[7] Other scholars have used Bellah's concept in numerous studies regarding the relationship between religion and nationalism; some examples include interpretations of national symbols such as the flag of the United States of America and rituals of flag devotion such as the Pledge of Allegiance; analyses of religious aspects in judicial decisions; and studies of nationally significant places, such as monuments in Washington, DC, and elsewhere in the nation that celebrate national history and heritage, as well as traditions of pilgrimage to these sites.[8]

Its broad application across many aspects of American culture demonstrates the usefulness of Bellah's concept of civil religion, but its usefulness also has been its shortcoming. In fact, the idea of a distinct civil religion existing alongside other religious traditions throughout American history has been widely criticized from a variety of viewpoints, largely because its many uses detract from a coherent understanding of what exactly is meant by civil religion. One religious historian, for instance, takes issue with designating "an incredibly rich and internally complex culture" in simple terms of "religion."[9] Another critic argues that Bellah's concept itself must be understood as a response to a particular social context in the middle decades of the twentieth century; specifically, the cultural and religious circumstances in the decades following World War II created a sense of shared identity for the predominant Protestant denominations that allowed scholars such as Bellah to imagine, in the critic's estimation, "a mythic past sustaining an American civil religion that gave coherence and cohesion to the common life of the American people." Much of the American population, though, remained excluded from this **mythic** past, "making the civil religion really the prerogative of white males of economic privilege."[10]

Despite its drawbacks as an interpretive category, studies regarding the purported American civil religion have yielded useful insights in American religious history more broadly. These include better understandings of how Americans and others attribute meanings and values to the idea of "America"; cultural studies of how religious concerns have contributed to American nationalist identity; analyses of the impact of religious orientations, especially versions of Protestantism, on the political and other secular affairs of the American nation; and the apparent religious elements in political and governmental culture. Regardless of whether we term these aspects of American public life as "civil religion," they certainly constitute a key aspect of American religious history.[11]

context reemphasized the religious nature of the American nation in stark contrast to the godless communist regime of the Soviet Union. For many Americans, loyalty to America was loyalty to God and sympathy for communism amounted to sympathy for the devil.

The Pledge of Allegiance

The most popular and widely recognized national ritual of American loyalty has been the recitation of the Pledge of Allegiance. Throughout the twentieth century and up to the present time, millions of schoolchildren have dutifully recited the Pledge at the beginning of every school day; it concludes the naturalization ceremony that new citizens undergo; and it ritually opens every legislative session of the United States Senate, as well as countless other government, public, and private gatherings. Although requiring children to recite it in public schools is unlawful, and even its voluntary recitation at schools and other state-sponsored meetings remains of dubious constitutionality, banning the Pledge of Allegiance has proven politically impossible.[12] The oath functions as a ritual of belonging for American citizens.

The Pledge of Allegiance was first introduced in the 1890s as part of a patriotic upsurge to remember the sacrifices of the Civil War; the American flag had become the hallowed symbol of national suffering in the aftermath of the war, and a flag movement in the 1880s sought to ensure that the sacred banner would "wave over every schoolhouse." A popular magazine of the day, *Youth's Companion,* joined the effort to promote reverence for the flag in the nation's schools, and the magazine designated the quadricentennial of Columbus' discovery of America in October 1892 as the date for a national flag ceremony that would involve raising an American flag over every school in the nation. The magazine published a program for local flag ceremonies to be performed on that day, and it included a Pledge of Allegiance composed by Francis Bellamy (1855–1931), a former Baptist minister who had left the ministry over his increasingly socialist political views. The original oath read, "I pledge allegiance to my Flag and to the Republic for which it stands – one Nation indivisible – with Liberty and Justice for all." The instructions for the flag ceremony stipulated that students, teachers, and others present were to give a military-style salute, "right hand lifted, palm downward, to a line with the forehead, and close to it," as they recited the Pledge in unison, "gracefully" extending their right arm, palm upward, toward the banner as they said the words "to my Flag." Afterward, they were to sing, "America – 'My Country 'Tis of Thee'" and then offer an "Acknowledgment of God," either by prayer or the reading of scripture. The program also encouraged local leaders to include additional addresses, songs, and "historical exercises."[13] In October 1892, schoolchildren across America recited the Pledge of Allegiance for the first time.

Flag salute activists turned to legislatures to perpetuate ritual recitations of the Pledge of Allegiance; the patriotic fervor that accompanied the outbreak of the Spanish–American War in 1898 spurred lawmakers in New York to enact the first state law requiring a daily flag salute in all state schools.[14] But few states followed suit before World War I. As devotion to the flag grew in the early twentieth century, so did the variety of flag salutes and pledges that accompanied them. Following World War I, a movement to standardize respect for the American flag resulted in two National Flag Conferences that produced an official Flag Code. Among its provisions was adoption of Francis Bellamy's Pledge of Allegiance as the official **liturgy** of the flag salute, but with a revision that reflected the delegates' strongly anti-immigrant anxieties; Bellamy's original "my flag" was altered to say "the flag of the United States of America." The new code also stipulated that one should stand with "the right hand over the heart" and then extend the hand, "palm upward, toward the Flag" upon saying the words "to the Flag."[15]

Not all Americans were enthusiastic about what one critic called "idiotic flag-fetishism."[16] In the early decades of the twentieth century, a scattering of students objected to mandatory recitation of the Pledge of Allegiance. One eleven-year-old African American student in Chicago refused to salute what he regarded as the "dirty" flag that represented a nation intent on oppressing and lynching blacks. More common were religious objections to the Pledge. In Ohio in 1918, a Mennonite father went to jail for preventing his nine-year-old daughter from pledging to the flag. As an Anabaptist sect with strong pacifist commitments, Mennonites objected to the implication in the Pledge of Allegiance that the flag would be defended "against all of its enemies, which would mean to resort to arms and to take human life," in violation of their religious beliefs. On these premises, thirty-eight Mennonite children were expelled from a school in Greenwood, Delaware, in 1928 for refusing the flag salute. Another group, the Jehovites (not related to the Jehovah's Witnesses), a small Christian sect in Colorado, regarded the Pledge of Allegiance as a form of "idol worship" and prohibited their children from reciting it, resulting in the expulsion of fifty Jehovite children from Denver schools in 1926. In Bellingham, Washington, a nine-year-old boy was removed from his family and placed in the state children's home when his parents disallowed him to salute the flag based on the beliefs of their religion, another local sect of Christians called the Elijah Voice Society that objected to the flag salute because, they maintained, "national patriotism tends toward militarism and war." After a separation of two years, the boy was allowed to return to his family only when a new judge rescinded the initial ruling on the agreement that the parents would enroll their son in a private school that did not require flag salutes.[17]

These and other confrontations between religious sects and school boards appeared sporadically through the 1920s and into the 1930s. A coordinated national campaign began in 1935 when the Jehovah's Witnesses challenged the requirement for schoolchildren to recite the Pledge of Allegiance. Their leader, Joseph Rutherford (1869–1942), denounced Hitler's Germany for persecuting Jehovah's Witnesses who refused to give the "Heil Hitler" salute; Rutherford then likened the German salute to the American flag salute, which used nearly identical hand motions, condemning both as "unfaithfulness to God." Rutherford's denouncement inspired Jehovah's Witnesses across the country to refuse to salute the American flag, resulting in numerous school expulsions and even the firing of three teachers. In many cases children were also whipped and sometimes beaten for their refusal to say the Pledge of Allegiance. As a result, the Jehovah's Witnesses used their considerable legal clout to challenge laws requiring children to recite the Pledge of Allegiance, claiming that such laws amounted to an unconstitutional violation of their religious rights. After losing in state after state, one of their cases finally reached the US Supreme Court in 1940; with German threats in Europe looming in the national consciousness, the justices overwhelming rejected the religious argument in favor of "national unity." A dissenting opinion, however, warned against the state's coercion to violate students' religious convictions, arguing that national unity was insufficient reason to override religious freedom. The dissent received favorable reaction in many newspapers across the country, but violent persecutions against Jehovah's Witnesses increased after the ruling.

American opinions about the Pledge of Allegiance began to shift as the nation entered World War II; the comparison to the Nazi salute made more Americans uncomfortable with their own flag salute. When the Jehovah's Witnesses brought another case to the Supreme Court, an altered panel of justices overturned the Court's previous ruling; announcing their decision on Flag Day in 1943, the majority opinion explained that no government official at any level "can prescribe what shall be orthodox in politics, nationalism, religion, or other matters of opinion or force citizens to confess by word or act their faith therein." The ruling was widely applauded in the national press; *Time* magazine regarded it as a "Blot Removed." Unlike the Nazis, Americans now saluted their flag voluntarily without government coercion.[18]

The Cold War context of the post-World War II period brought new concerns and further changes to the Pledge of Allegiance. In their protracted rivalry with the Soviet Union, Americans sought to emphasize a religious grounding for their nation. Presidents Harry S. Truman (1884–1972) and Dwight D. Eisenhower (1890–1969) both used the term "under God" often to characterize the United States in contrast to the "godless" Soviets. Although veterans groups and other specifically patriotic organizations had taken the lead in requiring recitation of the Pledge in schools and at official meetings, it was a religious group, the Roman Catholic fraternal organization called the Knights of Columbus, who initiated the campaign to amend it with a direct reference to God. Originally concerned with celebrating Catholic contributions to American society and fighting anti-Catholic **nativism**, the aims of the Knights of Columbus had shifted by the middle of the twentieth century as Catholics enjoyed a more mainstream status among America's religious communities. Their leadership took special interest in defending America against the communist threat, especially following the communist suppression of the Catholic Church in Poland and elsewhere in Eastern Europe. In 1951, their national board required local chapters to add the phrase "under God" when reciting the Pledge of Allegiance at the opening of all meetings. A resolution the following year called on the US Congress to amend the Pledge of Allegiance with the words "under God." With the support of other fraternal organizations, the Knights of Columbus undertook a lobbying campaign that resulted in the introduction of legislation in the Congress; yet, even with polls showing support from nearly seventy percent of all Americans, the proposed law languished. But the political climate changed in 1954 when President Eisenhower took an interest in the issue following an impassioned sermon he heard by Reverend George Macpherson Docherty (1911–2008) at the New York Avenue Presbyterian Church in Washington, DC. The sermon noted that, other than the reference to "the United States of America," the Pledge of Allegiance could refer to any country, even communist nations. Adding the phrase "under God," taken from Lincoln's Gettysburg Address, Docherty insisted, would make it specifically American: "An atheistic American," he declared, is "a contradiction in terms." Eisenhower agreed with Docherty's proposal, and the sermon received favorable attention in newspapers across the country. Soon several bills were moving through Congress, and on Flag Day, June 14, 1954, President Eisenhower signed a Joint Resolution of the US Congress to officially amend the Pledge of Allegiance with the words "under God."[19]

The evolution of the American pledge to the flag and the republic it symbolizes reflects changing anxieties within the nation's civic culture. This brief review of its history makes clear that concerns about the meaning of the American nation are often tied to assumptions about its religious character. In fact, we might say, a religious regard of nation potentially takes precedence over sectarian religious commitments, a point that motivated the Jehovah's Witnesses' objections to reciting the Pledge. When communism became a sinister force in the minds of most Americans, religion became the defining contrast that set America apart from the irreverent communists; proclaiming America as "one nation under God" became the official litany of loyal, freedom-loving Cold Warriors.

Zionism

On the other hand, loyalty to the nation had different meanings for various Americans. In contrast to the Jehovah's Witnesses, who rejected any sort of allegiance above their devotion to Jehovah, most American Jews remained timid about asserting religious priorities over nationalist loyalties. Unlike European Jews, whose experience under repressive regimes had convinced them that anti-Semitism was a pervasive, unrelenting, and ineradicable force in modern society, many American Jews put their faith in a democracy that allowed them full participation in American society. Most Jewish leaders in nineteenth-century America remained skeptical of European Zionism, which called for a separate Jewish state; they already had a nation and saw the Zionist movement as a threat to their status as American citizens.[20]

As a nationalist movement among certain European Jewish intellectuals and activists, Zionism was a response to changing conceptions of nationality and the increase of anti-Semitism. Dignity and freedom from oppression for the Jewish people could come, the Zionists proclaimed, only by establishing their own nation in the Palestinian homeland where they could live authentically Jewish lives without encumbrance of political or cultural compromises.[21] Initially, most American Jews, especially nineteenth-century followers of Reform Judaism, resisted Zionist ideology. Specifically, they disputed the notion that Jews needed a separate nation; the 1885 Pittsburgh Platform (discussed in Chapter 8) clearly asserted that Judaism is "no longer a nation."[22]

Over the ensuing decades, Reform Jews in America split over the Zionist movement. As increasing numbers of eastern European Jewish immigrants joined Reform congregations, many Reform leaders took a more sympathetic view of Zionism. Their main concern, though, had to do with the persecution of east European Jews; most American Zionists in the early part of the twentieth century were more interested in alleviating the suffering of Jews than in establishing a new nation as a Jewish refuge. A turning point in American Jewish acceptance of Zionism came in the example of Supreme Court Justice Louis Brandeis (1856–1941), who advocated a "practical Zionism" that stressed economic and agricultural development in Palestine. This emphasis on development and relief efforts allowed American Jews to embrace Zionism without fully subscribing to its nationalist ideals.[23]

The horrifying realities of Jewish loss during World War II transformed American Jews' relationship to Zionism. At the end of the war, more than 2.5 million Jews in the United States belonged to organizations endorsing a Jewish state in Palestine, and, in the years leading up to the United Nations' establishment of the nation of Israel, American Jews contributed four hundred million dollars for relief efforts, development, and defense of the new nation. They lobbied the US Congress relentlessly, and their lobbying efforts convinced President Harry Truman to go against the advice of the US State Department and endorse the creation of the Jewish state. Although an anti-Zionist faction remained within American Judaism, the vast majority of American Jews advocated for a Jewish state in Palestine. After its establishment in 1948, Israel galvanized American Jewish identity as a powerful symbol of Judaism. Even the main anti-Zionist group, the American Council for Judaism, acknowledges that "[t]he State of Israel has significance for the Jewish experience," and they "share the hope for the security and wellbeing of the State of Israel, living in peace and justice with its neighbors."[24]

The overwhelming support of Israel by American Jews complicates perspectives on national loyalty. The notion of an American civil religion that unites the people of the United States seems plausible when one considers such ubiquitous rituals as the Pledge of Allegiance. Even religious objections to the Pledge highlight its religious nature in connecting citizens to a civic identity. But, as we contemplate the usefulness of the notion of civil religion for thinking about America as a religious idea, we also need to consider its limits when thinking about groups who have a more complicated relationship to the nation. Jews are just one instance of such complications; people of Japanese descent during World War II, African Americans in a racially segregated society, women excluded from many of the opportunities and benefits afforded men, and other diverse groups often have ambivalent feelings regarding their allegiance to an America that promises liberty and justice for all and yet does not always fulfill the promise.

Clash of Classes

One constant issue of difference that restricts some groups from full participation in American democracy is socioeconomic class status. Concern for impoverished people is a moral feature of nearly every religious orientation. With the onset of the Great Depression, which lasted throughout the 1930s, poverty became a dominant concern in America as social and economic inequities came to the forefront of national debates. Helping to implement many of the New Deal programs that President Franklin D. Roosevelt (1882–1945) initiated to address the economic calamity of the Depression was Secretary of Labor Frances Perkins (1882–1965), the first woman to serve as a presidential cabinet secretary; she was an Episcopalian who famously recalled, "I came to Washington to work for God, FDR, and the millions of forgotten, plain, common workingmen." Ever mindful of the religious grounding of her work, Perkins often took retreats from her governmental duties into the silence of the All Saints Convent in Catonsville, Maryland.[25]

Roosevelt characterized his New Deal as "an instrument of unimagined power for the establishment of a morally better world."[26] His vision of a more ethical economic order gained the support of many religious leaders, especially Protestants, Catholics, and Jews who had been influenced by the social gospel movement in the early decades of the twentieth century. But political opposition to the New Deal reforms also included religious objections. A report regarding the president's political outlook in 1935 estimated that the strongest opposition to his reelection bid "would come, not from the economic reactionaries, but from the religious reactionaries (if you can separate the two). ... The opposition of what one can call the evangelical churches is growing steadily more bitter and open." Fundamentalists and other conservative Christians regarded the New Deal according to millennialist views that framed the rise of totalitarian governments in **apocalyptic** terms; they feared that totalitarian states would make way for a world-wide antichrist dictator controlled by Satan.[27] This opposition did not end with the coming of World War II; American business leaders kept up the attack on New Deal reforms into the 1980s, when they finally turned the political tide with the election of Ronald Reagan (1911–2004) to the presidency.

Catholic workers

The most obvious inequalities in Depression-era America had to do with socioeconomic class. When the prosperity of the American economy collapsed with the fall of stock prices in 1929, the traditional disparities between rich and poor took on epic proportions. Critiques of capitalist industrialism came from many quarters but often most loudly from religious voices. Millions of the nation's workers lost jobs and had no economic safety net to ensure their well-being, and religious groups attempted to provide some relief; the magnitude of the problem, though, overwhelmed the resources of both local and national church organizations. More and more calls came for government intervention to provide relief and security for workers.

Catholics were among the strongest supporters of New Deal reforms. Many adherents of the Roman Catholic Church were among the working classes who suffered most during the Great Depression, and the Church leadership supported governmental initiatives to bring relief, equity, and security to parishioners. Pope Leo XIII's (1810–1903) **encyclical** *Rerum Novaum* (1891) had addressed economic disparities in a critique of both socialism and laissez-faire capitalism, carving out what Catholic theologian and social thinker John A. Ryan (1869–1945) described as "a middle ground between capitalism and communism, between individualism and socialism." Building on the Catholic Church's "middle ground," the American bishops published in 1919 the Bishops' Program of Social Reconstruction, a plan to advocate a range of legislative initiatives dealing with labor issues that would

Box 10.2   Class

Social scientists often refer to the fact of social stratification according to relative socioeconomic status as "class" or "socioeconomic class." Although they do not always agree on what exactly constitutes the differences between lower, middle, and upper classes, many scholars assume some level of class structure in society. Much of social and economic theory has been developed around issues of class differences and conflicts between people of different socioeconomic status; these theories have implications for understanding the social role of religion among the various socioeconomic classes.

The nineteenth-century German social philosopher Karl Marx (1818–1883) proposed a materialist philosophy that regarded class struggle as the central problem of human society and history. From observing class relations in industrial Europe, Marx understood society to be divided between the interests of an upper-class "bourgeoisie" who owned property, factories, and other "modes of production" and the interests of a working-class "proletariat" who supplied labor for the benefit of the bourgeoisie. Religion, according to Marx, facilitated class exploitation by making workers compliant with the interests of the elite classes; he regarded religious ideas as ideological illusions that served as "the opium of the people," comforting workers in their suffering and promising their reward in the afterlife, allowing the bourgeoisie to perpetuate abuses in this life.[28]

Another German social philosopher, Max Weber (1864–1920) had a more nuanced and sympathetic perspective on religion's social role. Whereas Marx argued for a one-dimensional view that focused on class conflict over material resources, Weber argued that religious ideas and commitments were equally important in determining behavior, not just the result of previous behaviors; this includes economic concerns. In his first and most famous work, *The Protestant Ethic and the Spirit of Capitalism* (1905), Weber demonstrates a close connection between the Protestant religion, the rise of capitalism, and the beginnings of modern society. The practice of what he calls "inner-worldly asceticism," the fulfilling of one's religious calling through hard work, efficiency, and rational business practices informed by Calvinistic Protestantism, resulted in economic profits; in short, the Protestant work ethic, according to Weber, contributed to efficient and profitable behaviors that made possible the capitalist economy. Moreover, distinct social groups are formed not only by economic differences, as they are for Marx, but also by such things as location (e.g., rural versus urban), vocation (e.g., craftsman versus farmer), and especially by social respect (status group). Weber also noted that different social groups tended to adopt different religious orientations and practices most suited to their circumstances; for instance, peasants and others close to nature tend to rely more on magical practices, whereas those of more desperate economic circumstances tend to adopt "salvation religions" that offer redemption from the suffering of life's hardships.[29]

A later theorist, the French cultural philosopher and sociologist Pierre Bourdieu (1930–2002), takes account of later scholarship about race, gender, ethnicity, and other elements of identity to depict socioeconomic status in more dynamic terms as a cultural construct that is constantly contested in terms of social, cultural, and economic power and authority. Bourdieu's view of religion remains rather one dimensional, although his insights in other aspects of culture can be fruitfully applied to religion. As he notes, "The sociology of culture is the sociology of the religion of our day"; consequently, Bourdieu's concept of "cultural capital," in reference to non-economic assets and advantages such as education, intellectual ability, language skills, aesthetic tastes, even physical appearance, can also be applied in analyses of religious practices and communities. Unlike Marx, who distinguished between the material and the ideal, Bourdieu regards both as aspects of a more comprehensive economy of power.[30]

later be incorporated into the New Deal reforms of the Franklin presidency. The bishops' proposal addressed issues of a living wage, public housing for workers, social insurance, vocational training, and the prohibition of child labor. Catholic leadership in America took the lead in arguing for ethical treatment of and conditions for American workers as they pursued their middle way of what Ryan termed "true economic liberalism."[31]

Other elements in the Roman Catholic Church proposed more extreme measures. Among the most radical and widely influential initiatives by American Catholics to help the poor was a **lay** movement instituted by Peter Maurin (1877–1949) and Dorothy Day (1897–1980), who together founded the Catholic Workers' movement in the 1930s. Advocating for a more radical economic transformation than the American Catholic bishops, Maurin and Day subscribed to an anarchist theology that distrusted government and rejected social programs granting welfare assistance to the destitute. Maurin was a French immigrant who had come to the United States after a stay in Canada. In 1933 Maurin met Dorothy Day, a journalist of radical political views who had converted to Catholicism; together they began publishing a newspaper in New York City that they called *The Catholic Worker* based on Maurin's revolutionary interpretation of Christianity, which emphasized personalism and anarchism. Maurin espoused the views of French philosopher Emmanuel

Mounier (1905–1950), who championed a communitarian philosophy of Christian personalism. Mounier's ideas were especially apparent in the Catholic Workers' emphasis on human dignity over economic concerns; the capitalist obsession with profits, he contended, had taken precedence over the needs of individuals and communities, and especially over the priority of faith and values. An ethical view of economics requires the priority of human dignity over capitalist profits.[32]

Day and Maurin implemented the communitarian revolution that they advocated with a series of hospitality houses and rural agricultural communes, what Maurin called "agronomic universities," that operated on a core principle of the Catholic Worker movement, voluntary poverty. Maurin and Day committed themselves to lives of poverty in order to better understand and respond to the personal experience and indelible dignity of the poor. "One must live with them," Day wrote in her famous memoir, *The Long Loneliness* (1952), "share with them their suffering too. Give up one's privacy, and mental and spiritual comforts as well as physical." Along with a moral commitment to social justice, Day recognized the psychological and social benefits of communal living. Convinced that loneliness was part of the human condition, she wrote, "The only answer in this life, to the loneliness we are all bound to feel, is community. The living together, working together, sharing together, loving God and loving our brother, and living close to him in community so we can show our love for Him."[33]

Figure 10.2 Dorothy Day (far right) is shown at work with the editorial staff of the *Catholic Worker* in 1934. Teaming up with French immigrant philosopher, poet, and street theologian Peter Maurin, Day led a Roman Catholic lay movement emphasizing voluntary poverty, pacifism, and communitarian values that included urban hospitality houses, rural communes, and a radical newspaper still published today and sold for a penny a copy as it was in 1933. (Courtesy of the Department of Special Collections and University Archives, Marquette University Libraries.)

Showing their love also involved a rigorous commitment to pacifism, which made the Catholic Worker movement suspect to many patriotic Americans, especially during World War II, when nationalist sentiments made patriotism a matter of national security. Even the official "peace organization" of the Catholic Church in America, the Catholic Association for International Peace, criticized pacifist sentiments, stating unambiguously that it "supported the war effort and did not help any individual who objected to World War II, whether they registered their dissent within the law or were resisters."[34] Dorothy Day, though, kept up her relentless editorializing against the war, and especially against the military draft, even when members of the Catholic Worker movement disagreed with her inflexible stance. Her outspoken opposition cost the Catholic Worker movement during the war; circulation of its paper dropped considerably and a number of its hospitality houses across the nation were forced to close.[35]

For Day and Maurin, military conscription violated the individual's freedom to choose a vocation and to act according to one's calling. Their opposition comported with the holistic vision of the Catholic Worker movement, to create a classless society of mercy and peace grounded in communitarian and personalist values. It is a vision that has inspired generations of progressive Catholics and has influenced even non-Catholics who do not share their religious devotion.

Mobilizing business

As the nation moved beyond the experience of economic turmoil during the Great Depression and through massive industrial mobilization during World War II, businesses regained their eminent position in American society. Following the war, leaders of industry and commerce again sought to undo what they regarded as interference from government regulations and social programs implemented during the Roosevelt years. The business community sometimes enlisted the help of religious leaders in its quest to repeal the Depression-era reforms, as was the case with a group called Spiritual Mobilization that had begun in the 1930s and was revived at the end of World War II with the help of oil company executive and devout Presbyterian J. Howard Pew (1882–1971). Pew described the purpose of the group as fostering "the development among the clergymen of this country, of a proper conception of just what constitutes our American way of life and how this ties in with sound religious principles." Active through much of the 1950s, Spiritual Mobilization attempted to link conservative economic reforms to mainline Protestant Christianity. Not interested in the fundamentalists' literal interpretations of Christian scripture, the **evangelical** efforts of groups such as Spiritual Mobilization, according to one historian, were not "to save souls but rather to save American capitalism."[36]

This goal of saving American capitalism in the Cold War years of the 1950s relied to a large degree on a revival of religious commitments. In particular, it involved a campaign aimed at mobilizing religious faith as a defense against the irreligion and perceived immorality of the communist menace; it construed religion as the foundation of freedom and American ideals. Rather than an organized or centralized movement, the emergence of a so-called "spiritual–industrial complex" in the 1940s and 1950s pervaded every facet of American society in a religious revival reminiscent of the evangelical revivals of the eighteenth and nineteenth centuries. But, unlike those earlier revivals marked by fervent outpourings of Protestant sentiment, neither grassroots devotion nor theological innovation instigated the Cold War version of religious upsurge. It came instead from the boardrooms of Wall Street, the advertising efforts of Madison Avenue, the studios of Hollywood, and even the military concerns of the Pentagon.[37] Moreover, the religious revival of the early Cold War era was not narrowly sectarian; President Dwight D. Eisenhower put it in terms of a broadly Christian–Judaic civil religion when he famously quipped that "our form of government has no sense unless it is founded in a deeply-felt religious faith, and I don't care what it is."[38] In squaring off with the godless communists, Americans needed to be religious, without heed to the particularities of sect or theological disposition.

At the forefront of the renewed emphasis on religious faith in America was the neofundamentalist evangelical revivalist Billy Graham (born 1918), who was easily the most recognizable religious leader in 1950s America. Besides leading religious revivals that drew record-breaking crowds to some of the largest venues in the nation, Graham served as the personal spiritual adviser to President Eisenhower; he undertook evangelical diplomatic tours of India and China under the sponsorship of the US State Department; and he maintained a prominent media presence with a

Figure 10.3 Reverend Billy Graham preaches to the largest crowd he had addressed at the time, fifty thousand people gathered outdoors on Boston Common in the spring of 1950. The evangelical preacher's sermon called for a presidential declaration of a "National Repentance Day" to "seek God's forgiveness." (Image © Bettmann / CORBIS.)

syndicated newspaper column, radio and television shows, and his own film company. Billy Graham had first come to national attention in 1949 when he staged an evangelical revival in circus tents set up in a Los Angeles parking lot; the event attracted the attention of the conservative anticommunist newspaper mogul William Randolph Hearst (1863–1951), whose papers gave national coverage to Graham's religious antics. His continuing revivals, what he called "crusades," drew ever larger crowds. In 1954 he was featured on the cover of the popular news magazine *Time*. By then Graham had become the public face of Protestant evangelical Christianity.[39]

Graham's religious leadership included his involvement in the 1950s with the Foundation for Religious Action in Social and Civil Order, organized by some of the most powerful Protestants in the nation to resist the communist threat: besides Graham, its board included industrialist Henry Ford II (1917–1987); former president of the United States Herbert Hoover (1874–1964); publisher Henry R. Luce (1898–1967), whose magazines included the widely influential *Fortune*, *Life*, and *Time*; and labor leader George Meany (1894–1980), among others. The Foundation's purpose, as its mission statement put it, was "To unite all believers in God in the struggle between the free world and atheistic communism which aims to destroy both religion and liberty." It used the vast resources of its board members in 1954 to stage the highly publicized First National Conference on the Spiritual Foundations of American Democracy, followed by three more such conferences in the 1950s; it also supported educational initiatives with its Committee on American Education and Communism, and promoted spiritual concerns in the Armed Forces, even funding covert operations in southeast Asia to stem the advance of communism in the region.[40]

As we reflect on the diversity of religious communities active in the middle decades of the twentieth century, it is easy to see that saving capitalism was not the main concern of most Americans. Economic prosperity certainly ranked high during the postwar years as American business and industry expanded to serve a rapidly growing consumer culture, but other concerns also loomed in American religious imaginations. The Cold War threat of communism brought the patriotic values of American civil religion to the fore. At the same time, the persistent realities of poverty, racial inequality, and the exclusion of women from many of the opportunities afforded by the burgeoning economy all ranked high for many citizens. A good number of these people turned to religion as a powerful resource to assert their dignity and rights.

Box 10.3   The Judeo-Christian tradition

In the middle decades of the twentieth century, a discourse around what was called "the Judeo-Christian tradition" linked a common religious heritage of Jews and Christians to American democracy and identity. Initially, this purported tradition was a product of an antifascist discourse contrasting American respect for liberty and individual dignity to the despotic regime of the Nazis in Europe. Moreover, it sought to encourage interfaith acceptance of a "tri-faith" view of America involving Protestants, Catholics, and Jews in the wake of the surge of the latter two groups through immigration in the later part of the nineteenth century and the early decades of the twentieth century. Following World War II, the Judeo-Christian tradition became a stalwart of Cold War anticommunist rhetoric, depicting America as essentially religious with its tri-faith demographic.[41]

Scholarly support for the idea of a Judeo-Christian tradition came from sociologist Will Herberg (1901–1977), whose book *Protestant, Catholic, Jew* (1955) identified religion as the common American identity for immigrants; his book notes how later immigrant generations replaced their ethnic identity with a religious consciousness in a process that he calls the "triple melting pot." Specifically, Herberg's book argues that "the American Way of Life," as he calls it, involves a "common religion" that "constitutes a faith common to Americans and genuinely operative in their lives."[42] Americans for the most part, he contends, have only a superficial understanding of the religious traditions they subscribe to, but they are fully committed to and engaged with the shared religion of the American Way of Life. Moreover, this religion distinguished America from communist nations, as Americans had converted their "immense and undeniable moral superiority over Communist tyranny into pretensions to unqualified wisdom and virtue." But Herberg warns, "inordinate national pride and self-righteousness" were bound to lead the nation into "moral confusion, political irresponsibility, and the darkening of counsel."[43]

Herberg's assessment of American society draws attention to the rhetorical uses of the so-called Judeo-Christian tradition. In fact, as it has been characterized in American discourses, the Judeo-Christian tradition has little in common with the various institutional forms and established traditions of Judaism or Christianity. It is more like the idea of a "civil religion" (see Box 10.1) in that it lacks a distinct religious community and has no official leadership, and most people who subscribe to it simultaneously identify with a more traditional religious community. In other words, the notion of an American Judeo-Christian tradition has more to do with debates about whether or not America is fundamentally a religious nation or a secular people. This has been a perennial question in American political life; during the Cold War, a purported Judeo-Christian tradition served as one part of the answer to the question of religion's proper place in a common American identity.[44]

Confronting Racial Apartheid

Racial divisions have been part of American society from the earliest days, as we have seen throughout our studies of American religious history. Since their first arrival in the western hemisphere Euro-Americans have used racial justifications for the abusive treatment of Native Americans, for centuries of enslavement of Africans and their descendants, and for the intense persecution and exclusion of Asians in the American west during the nineteenth and early twentieth centuries. In the latter half of the twentieth century, however, race relations began to change. World War II marks a significant turning point in American racial history. National unity in the fight against Nazism and Japanese imperialism only exacerbated racial tensions already present in the nation. At the same time, the collapse of European colonial empires in Asia and Africa allowed for some people to envision a post-European world, an appealing prospect to persecuted people everywhere, including African Americans suffering under racial apartheid in the United States.

Internment camps

The immediate racial consequences of World War II had a direct impact on Asian Americans, especially those of Japanese descent. Just months after the Japanese bombing of Pearl Harbor in December 1941, President Franklin Roosevelt authorized the Secretary of War to designate "military areas ... from which any or all persons may be excluded." Entire communities of Japanese Americans on the west coast of the United States were subsequently removed from their homes and "relocated" to camps where they remained confined for most of the war. Suddenly uprooted from homes, farms, and businesses, these American citizens of Japanese heritage found themselves living in one of ten makeshift internment camps with few belongings and nearly no comforts; in some cases family members were separated from each other. A 1982 federal report on the camps concluded that such drastic measures "were motivated largely by racial prejudice, wartime hysteria, and a failure of political leadership." The same report noted the harsh treatment of the detainees: "In the detention centers, families lived in substandard housing, had inadequate nutrition and health care, and had their livelihoods destroyed: many continued to suffer psychologically long after their release."[45]

Asian religions were officially discouraged in the camps as the government attempted to "Americanize" the detainees. Buddhist priests, along with Shinto religious leaders and Japanese-language school teachers, had been arrested in the first days following the attack on Pearl Harbor and incarcerated separate from other detainees. Officials denigrated the Asian religious traditions as "pagan" and discouraged their practice. Many practitioners of Buddhist and Shinto traditions either destroyed or kept hidden the shrines, scrolls, and other paraphernalia of their religious faith, and a few actually attended Christian religious services, some

Figure 10.4 This winter scene captured by photographer Ansel Adams (1902–1984) in 1943 shows Japanese detainees at the Manzanar Relocation Center in California as they leave the camp's Buddhist church following devotions. Despite official attempts to Christianize the internees held in the camps during World War II, Buddhism, Shinto, and other non-Christian religious practices continued and even flourished. (Courtesy of the Library of Congress, LC-DIG-ppprs-00179.)

even converting to Christianity, to avoid being suspected of disloyalty to the United States. Japanese American detainees during World War II felt much pressure to conform to American Christian expectations. Nevertheless, official efforts to "Americanize" the prisoners were largely unsuccessful. In open defiance of such initiatives, many of the internees affirmed their Buddhist commitments, and Buddhism even gained new followers in the camps.[46]

In fact, not even all of the Christian detainees conformed to the expectations of camp officials and their efforts to Americanize the prisoners. A number of Japanese American Christian ministers in the camps objected to the assimilationist orientation of their parent churches and advocated instead an emphasis on ethnic identities for Japanese American congregations.[47] Others drew upon their religious moral understanding to resist the camps through civil disobedience, as in the case of Gordon Hirabayashi (1918–2012). Raised by immigrant parents who had converted to Christianity in Japan, Hirabayashi had joined the Quakers in 1940 and registered with the Selective Services as a conscientious objector. With the imposition of restrictions on the activities of Japanese Americans and their forced relocation following the attack on Pearl Harbor, Hirabayashi refused to obey what he

considered to be unconstitutional laws that were racially motivated, and he surren-
dered himself to the FBI as a test case. Although his case was heard by the US
Supreme Court, the justices refused to rule on the constitutionality of confining
Japanese American citizens during World War II. After serving a short term in
federal prison for curfew violations, Hirabayashi returned to work for a Quaker
relief organization in Spokane, Washington. He subsequently refused to complete
what is known as the "loyalty" questionnaire from the Selective Service, a form
titled "The Statement of United States Citizens of Japanese Ancestry," because in
his opinion it unconstitutionally singled out a particular race. His further refusal to
fulfill requirements of his conscientious objector status landed him another prison
sentence. In later years, his wartime commitment to Quaker pacifist views and his
challenges of the racially motivated treatment of Japanese Americans earned
Gordon Hirabayashi recognition as an early advocate of civil rights.[48]

The Civil Rights Movement

The Civil Rights Movement has often been characterized as a defining political
event of twentieth-century America that radically altered race relations in the
country, especially in southern states. More than just a political movement, however, this momentous social upheaval involved the deployment of significant religious resources; the Civil Rights Movement was in large part a religious effort
that used the ethical underpinnings of various faith traditions in an appeal to
national moral conscience. Many of the most recognizable leaders of civil rights
activism in the 1950s and 1960s were pastors of Protestant congregations or at
least devout members of Christian churches. But Christians were not the only
religious people involved at the forefront of the Civil Rights Movement; Muslims
and Jewish leaders also played key roles, and one of the most effective strategies
was nonviolent direct action inspired by a Hindu, Mohandas Gandhi. The
movement to challenge institutionalized racial segregation and prejudice and to
end the regime of white supremacist privilege in the United States was indeed an
ecumenical, interfaith effort.[49]

   In the southern parts of the nation, resistance to the ideology of white
supremacy went back to long before the Civil War, although in the late nineteenth
and early twentieth centuries it remained mostly invisible as legally enforced apartheid policies known as "Jim Crow" became prevalent. In the 1930s, labor organizers sometimes addressed racial divisions, as was the case with the interracial
Southern Tenant Farmers' Union, which advocated and organized on behalf of
sharecroppers. Among the activists were Owen Whitfield (1892–1965), a black
Baptist preacher and sharecropper from Mississippi influenced by the ideas of Pan-
Africanist leader Marcus Garvey (1887–1940), and Claude Williams (1895–1979), a
white Presbyterian minister from eastern Tennessee. Frustrated with atheist and
agnostic tendencies among their fellow activists, Whitfield and Williams established

the People's Institute for Applied Religion to emphasize the religious justifications of their labor activism. With the support of a number of prominent liberal Protestant organizations, the People's Institute was able to reach tenant farmers and industrial workers through an appeal to their religious beliefs.[50]

Racial inequality in the south gained national attention with the 1954 US Supreme Court ruling in the case of *Brown v. Board of Education*, which overturned decades of the "separate but equal" doctrine by declaring that "separate educational facilities are inherently unequal." In the aftermath of this momentous ruling, other areas of unequal treatment based on racial identities came under attack. In December 1955, an African American woman by the name of Rosa Parks (1913–2005) intentionally challenged segregated seating on public buses in Montgomery, Alabama. Her act of civil disobedience resulted in arrest; the Montgomery African American community rallied around her defiance by initiating a boycott of city buses that lasted a year and brought national and even international notice to the segregationist laws and the ill treatment of African Americans in southern states. Montgomery's African American community gathered in churches to organize their boycott, using worship spaces for their mass meetings. These churches functioned as social centers, as was the case with religious institutions in most African American communities in the 1950s. More than places of worship, they were clearinghouses of communications and news within the community; many served as credit unions that financed African American commerce and personal needs, and in many cases the churches played a judicial role in adjudicating conflicts among members of the community. Moreover, the importance of churches in most African American communities gave special authority and privilege to ministers, especially among the Baptists.[51] Consequently, when the people of Montgomery came together to fight the oppressive conditions of segregation in 1955, they chose the young pastor of the Dexter Street Baptist Church, the Rev. Dr. Martin Luther King, Jr. (1929–1968), as their leader.

King's successful leadership of the bus boycott in Montgomery brought him national and international fame as the quest for civil rights and the end of segregation spread throughout the American south. His position as a Baptist minister, though, did not limit religious involvement in the Civil Rights Movement to Baptists or even Christians. Americans of all religious persuasions participated in overturning the laws and traditions of racial apartheid in southern states and fought for racial equality in all areas of American society everywhere. Protestant Christians, though, were the most visible leaders in the movement. Among the most prominent of these leaders were the African American **clergy** who made up the Southern Christian Leadership Conference, formed in 1957 to coordinate nonviolent protests of segregated busing across the southern states. The delegates to the first assembly of the Conference elected Martin Luther King, Jr., to lead the organization, which consisted of local affiliates, most of which were Protestant churches.

The Conference's strategy for bringing an end to racial segregation in the south focused on nonviolent direct action, a technique patterned on the Hindu independence leader Mohandas Gandhi. This approach to protesting social conditions involves bringing attention to inequalities and oppressive conditions without resorting to violent measures. King appealed to the example of Gandhi to encourage participants in the Montgomery bus boycott to resist violent means; he told them early in the strike, "Our weapons are protest and love." The boycotters' first public statement of their position explained, "We, the oppressed, have no hate in our hearts for the oppressors, but we are, nevertheless, determined to resist until the cause of justice triumphs."[52] Later, King traveled to India to learn firsthand of Gandhi's philosophy and use of nonviolence for the cause of justice. He met with India's leaders and with activists who had worked beside the revered leader of the Indian nationalist movement that had ousted their British colonizers through nonviolent means. When King returned from his sojourn to the south Asian subcontinent, he reported to his congregation in Montgomery on Gandhi's impressive "absolute self-discipline" and his "amazing capacity for internal criticism," traits that would serve King and others in the fight for civil rights.

Besides Hindu influence in patterning their approach on Gandhi's philosophy of nonviolence, civil rights leaders also welcomed Jewish involvement in their

Figure 10.5 Abraham Joshua Heschel (center) described his participation with Martin Luther King, Jr. (right) during the 1965 civil rights march from Selma to Montgomery in Alabama by recalling, "I felt my feet were praying." (Courtesy of the Jacob Rader Marcus Center of the American Jewish Archives, Cincinnati, Ohio; www.americanjewisharchives.org.)

struggle. As the protests over segregation grew and turned violent, Jews were among the many activists who responded by joining the ranks of protesters and civil rights workers in the south. Some suffered violence, even death, at the hands of southern segregationists; Andrew Goodman (1943–1964), a twenty-year-old Jewish activist from New York was among the three Freedom Summer volunteers killed in Mississippi in 1964. Another Jewish ally, Rabbi Abraham Joshua Heschel (1907–1972), an eminent Polish theologian and philosopher who had come to the United States to escape the Nazis, walked beside Martin Luther King, Jr. in the famous march from Selma, Alabama, to Montgomery in 1965; Heschel later remarked, "When I marched in Selma, I felt my feet were praying."[53] He kept up a long friendship with King; in March 1968, less than two weeks before King's death, the civil rights leader appeared before the Rabbinical Assembly in New York, in part to celebrate Heschel's sixtieth birthday. As King entered the assembly hall, the rabbis sang "We Shall Overcome" in Hebrew; in his keynote address that evening, King acknowledged the importance of Jewish support in the Civil Rights Movement: "Probably more than any other ethnic group, the Jewish community has been sympathetic and has stood as an ally to the Negro in his struggle for justice."[54] Certainly, Jews were among the strongest supporters of the movement for civil rights.

Not everyone, of course, supported the Civil Rights Movement. Especially frustrating to King were moderate Christian pastors who criticized his activities and confrontational strategies. While he was jailed in Birmingham, Alabama, in 1963, a group of local white Protestant pastors issued an open letter that decried "a series of demonstrations by some of our Negro citizens, directed and led in part by outsiders." They urged patience and appealed "to both our white and Negro citizenry to observe the principles of law and order and common sense." Incensed, King penned a response from his jail cell, which was smuggled out piece by piece and later published. In his "Letter from Birmingham Jail," King assails the call for patience, citing the principle that "Justice delayed is justice denied." In regard to the accusation of outsiders causing trouble in Birmingham, King wrote, "Injustice anywhere is a threat to justice everywhere. We are caught in an inescapable network of mutuality, tied in a single garment of destiny. Whatever affects one directly, affects all indirectly. ... Anyone who lives inside the United States can never be considered an outsider." He goes on to relish the accusation that his approach is extremist, relating the long tradition of extremism within Christianity: "Was not Jesus an extremist for love," he asks. "Was not Amos an extremist for justice. ... Was not Paul an extremist for the Christian gospel. ... Was not Martin Luther an extremist." He concludes, "Perhaps the South, the nation and the world are in dire need of creative extremists."[55]

The extremism that Martin Luther King, Jr. advocated brought monumental changes to the American south, the nation, and to the global community. National legislative efforts resulted in the passage of the Civil Rights Act of 1964, prohibiting discrimination based on "race, color, religion, or national origin" in employment

Box 10.4   The apotheosis of Martin Luther King, Jr.

From the time of his death, Martin Luther King, Jr., has been characterized as a national martyr. In fact, thinking of him as religiously significant, beyond the obvious connection in his vocation as a Baptist minister, began during his lifetime. King himself used religious imagery to interpret his role in the Civil Rights Movement. His final speech at the Mason Temple in Memphis, Tennessee, the headquarters of the largest African American Pentecostal denomination, the Church of God in Christ, ranks as the most famous example, coming on the eve of his martyrdom. It includes clear reference to the imagery of the biblical character Moses standing on Mount Nebo, where he would perish before entering the land of Israel (in the Hebrew book of Deuteronomy, Chapter 34); King declared, "I just want to do God's will. And He's allowed me to go up to the mountain. And I've looked over. And I've seen the Promised Land. I may not get there with you. But I want you to know tonight, that we, as a people, will get to the promised land!" He then ended, "And so I'm happy, tonight. I'm not worried about anything. I'm not fearing any man! Mine eyes have seen the glory of the coming of the Lord!" The next afternoon an assassin's bullet ended his life, making Martin Luther King, Jr., a martyr in the quest for equal rights in America.

Since his death, the apotheosis of King has involved commemorating his legacy with a national holiday and designating his tomb and the Atlanta church where he pastored as a National Historic Site. The Lorraine Motel in Memphis where he was murdered immediately became a shrine where reverent visitors could pay respects; today it is the site of the National Civil Rights Museum, preserving the solemn atmosphere of a pilgrimage destination. Numerous schools, community centers, and other local buildings bear his name, and more than nine hundred US cities have a street or highway named after the civil rights leader. In 2011 King joined the pantheon of American heroes with a memorial dedicated to him on the national mall in Washington, DC. The religious nature of the American nation is not complete without Martin Luther King, Jr. among its deities.

and public accommodations; the Voting Rights Act of 1965 protects citizens' rights in elections; and the Fair Housing Act of 1968 forbids discrimination in the sale or rental of housing. As legalized racial segregation came to an end in the 1960s, King turned his attention to other problems; specifically, he organized a campaign against economic injustice, engaging in the fight against poverty. King also spoke out against American involvement in Vietnam. These issues did not receive the same overwhelming acceptance among his followers, and the rise of a Black Power movement that eschewed King's Christian commitments to a nonviolent approach to social change challenged his leadership. He struggled to gain support for the Southern Christian Leadership Conference's most recent effort, the Poor People's Campaign, highlighted by a planned march on Washington, DC. In the end King did not live to lead the march; while supporting a sanitation workers' strike in Memphis, Tennessee, in April 1968, he was killed by an assassin.

The Nation of Islam

Another martyr in the racial conflicts of the twentieth century had a very different message from King's integrationist vision. By the 1960s, the most visible representative of the Nation of Islam was Malcolm X (originally Malcolm Little and later El-Hajj Malik El-Shabazz, 1925–1965). Heir to both the Great Migration and the Pan-African nationalism of Marcus Garvey, Malcolm's childhood suffered the traumas of American racist attitudes. Both of his parents were involved in Garvey's Universal Negro Improvement Association (UNIA), which brought them to the attention of white racists. Malcolm was born in Omaha, Nebraska, where his parents were publicly active in UNIA; the Ku Klux Klan forced them to leave Omaha, and they went to Milwaukee, Wisconsin, where white supremacists again forced them out of the city. They settled in East Lansing, Michigan, but Malcolm's father died there shortly afterward in a mysterious accident rumored to be orchestrated by another white supremacist group because of his continued political activism. His mother struggled to keep her large family together while enduring the hardships of the Great Depression compounded by continual harassment by authorities; eventually her children were sent to foster homes, and officials subsequently declared her insane and sent her to a state mental hospital.

Eventually Malcolm moved to the northeast as a young adult, first Boston and later New York City, where he assumed the identity of a hustler by the name of "Red," for his red hair, and became involved in the nefarious activities of urban criminal subculture, including the sale of drugs, prostitution, gambling, and eventually armed robbery, the latter earning him a prison term. Malcolm began his incarceration in the same year, 1946, that Elijah Muhammad (1897–1975), leader of the Nation of Islam, was finishing his federal sentence for resisting the military draft. While serving his prison term for robbery, Malcolm engaged in study, debate, and contemplation that gave him a political awareness for understanding his circumstances as an African American suffering under white supremacy in America. At the same time, his brother wrote to him about the Nation of Islam, suggesting that belief in Allah would release him from prison. At the urging of his siblings, who had embraced the religion of Elijah Muhammad, Malcolm corresponded with the venerable leader of the Nation of Islam. When he left prison in 1952, Elijah Muhammad bestowed him with a new name, Malcolm X, the X signifying an original African name lost to his ancestors in slavery. He went to live with his brother in Detroit, where he worked in a factory by day and recruited new members to the Nation of Islam by night. His success in recruiting efforts came to the attention of Elijah Muhammad, who offered him the position of minister at the Nation's temple in Boston. A charismatic style and immense talent as a public speaker facilitated Malcolm X's rapid rise in the ranks of the Nation of Islam; in 1957 Elijah Muhammad appointed him chief minister, making him the most recognizable figure in the movement.[56]

As the Nation of Islam grew dramatically during the 1950s, Elijah Muhammad maintained a strictly racial-separatist orientation, despite his awareness of Islamic orthodoxy in other parts of the world and his relations with other Muslim leaders who regarded the American "Black Muslims" as "improperly informed." Both Elijah Muhammad and Malcolm X regarded the Nation of Islam as part of worldwide Islam; their religious interpretations, practices, and messages, however, were uniquely adapted to the historical and social contexts of African Americans who suffered under the legacies of slavery and continued racial persecution. Black separatism and self-determination were crucial to the success of Islam spreading through the African American communities.[57]

As national spokesperson for the Nation of Islam, Malcolm X delivered a blistering critique of white Americans in his relentless "jihad of words." Nation of Islam doctrine during this period claimed that black people are the original people of the world, and it regarded the white race as devils who eventually would be destroyed. Justifying this view of whites, Malcolm X explained, "Anybody who rapes, and plunders, and enslaves, and steals, and drops hell bombs on people … anybody who does these things is nothing but a devil."[58] Moreover, Malcolm X had little patience for what the Nation of Islam regarded as the conciliatory politics of the Civil Rights Movement; he insisted that

> The white man supports Reverend Martin Luther King, subsidizes Reverend Martin Luther King, so that Reverend Martin Luther King can continue to teach the Negroes to be defenseless – that's what you mean by nonviolent – be defenseless in the face of one of the most cruel beasts that has ever taken people into captivity – that's this American white man, and they have proved it throughout the country by the police dogs and the police clubs. … Martin Luther King is just a twentieth-century or modern Uncle Tom or religious Uncle Tom, who is doing the same thing today to keep Negroes defenseless in the face of attack that Uncle Tom did on the plantation to keep *those* Negroes defenseless in the face of the attack of the Klan in that day.[59]

Unwilling to accommodate the evil of white society in any way, the only solution, according to the teachings of Elijah Muhammad, was a separate nation of their own, apart from white America.

By 1964 differences had developed between the leader Elijah Muhammad and his protégé Malcolm X. Despite his constant condemnation of white society and his predictions of an imminent Battle of Armageddon that would end white domination, Elijah Muhammad maintained a relatively conservative plan for black liberation, relying on the development of black capitalism and racial uplift. In

Figure 10.6 Malcolm X (right) with Martin Luther King, Jr., in their only meeting, a brief encounter when both attended the US Senate hearings on civil rights legislation in March 1964, the same month that Malcolm X ended his affiliation with Elijah Muhammad's Nation of Islam. Their meeting was amicable, despite Malcolm X's past condemnations of King's approach to racial reconciliation. (Courtesy of the Library of Congress, LC-USZ6-1847.)

contrast, Malcolm X's exposure to the radical politics of postcolonial nations in Africa, Asia, and Latin America as well as his experience of the Hajj, the Muslim annual pilgrimage to the holy city of Mecca, had made him more willing to break from the more conservative views of Elijah Muhammad. Impatient with a static racial separatism that emphasized self-reliance and political isolation, Malcolm X became more willing to entertain political alliances that would unite the Nation of Islam with Black Power advocates and leaders of the Civil Rights Movement as well as with other oppressed peoples in the world, forming a coalition to confront the powers of racial oppression and imperialism. He began to emphasize political concerns rather than merely religious solutions to black suffering.[60]

Following a period of acrimony between the two most public figures among American Muslims, Malcolm X left the Nation of Islam in 1964 and opened his own religious establishment, the Muslim Mosque, Inc. Shortly thereafter he left for an extended trip to participate in the Hajj and then visit a number of African nations. This sojourn to the Arab and African worlds precipitated even more radical changes for the African American Muslim leader. His acceptance on the Hajj allowed him to adopt a new name, El-Hajj Malik El-Shabazz, emphasizing his Muslim identity over his African American identity. He also developed a new understanding of racism. No longer regarding it as an inherent characteristic of white people, Malik realized that racist attitudes, policies, and institutions were a result of the political and economic realities of capitalism. White people were not demonic, but their political, economic, and social system in America most certainly was.[61]

Malcolm X, now El-Hajj Malik El-Shabazz, had little opportunity to deploy his newly realized understanding of race, politics, and Islam. Nine months after his return to the United States, assassins killed him at a speaking engagement in New York City. His vision of a world community of Muslims battling the oppressive regimes of colonial and capitalist imperialism never developed into lasting institutions. The hail of bullets that brought him down also silenced one of the most articulate critics of American racial politics; African Americans lost a radical voice that had brought cogent religious arguments for resisting racism in American society.

Liberated People

Social tensions around racial issues have been a defining characteristic of America since long before the establishment of the United States, and they remain a fundamental aspect of American society even today. Similarly, questions of religious difference have also been a source of contention throughout American history. As the nation became a leading global power, Americans had to define themselves in broader contexts, bringing up old questions about the nature of America, what it means to be an American, and who to include as legitimate Americans.

With America having become a world leader in a protracted rivalry with communist nations, the complexities and moral compromises of American society became sources of criticism, not only from outside rivals but also from those within America who had been marginalized socially, politically, and economically by social arrangements and dominant views that excluded equal freedoms for all. The Jehovah's Witnesses provide an apt example of a group that took the lead to challenge the dominance of Protestant orthodoxy in determining acceptable religious beliefs and behaviors in the United States, not only in regard to the Pledge of Allegiance but also concerning a range of issues regarding religious freedom. Between 1929 and 1960, the Witnesses repeatedly defended themselves in opposition to the opinions and standards of mainstream American culture; more than fifty times in this period their members had cases reach the US Supreme Court, with more than thirty separate decisions being made on issues involving their constitutional rights to freely practice their religion. Most of these decisions went in favor of the Jehovah's Witnesses and established important new precedents in free speech and the freedom of religion for all Americans.[62]

The tensions of Cold War America among oppressed groups spurred many of them to fight back in the courts, in political discourse, and on the streets. In some cases, the authority of religious teachings justified oppression; these teachings consequently hence became the object of criticism and attack. In other instances, oppressed peoples found sources of resistance and critique within the moral structures of their religious orientations, and they used religion as a weapon to challenge oppressive powers and bring social change. This was most evident in the Civil Rights Movement, where the moral voice of activists relied on a variety of religious orientations that compelled the nation to account for the systematic exclusion of African Americans from the normal dignities of American citizenship and freedom. Uniting these various religious views was a quasi-religious regard for the nation, including the ritualized recitation of the Pledge of Allegiance; its declaration of "liberty and justice for all" inculcated a vision of American inclusiveness for generations of citizens, a vision that civil rights activists would hold the nation accountable to in their struggles to end racial apartheid in the southern states and bring equal opportunities to people of all races throughout the nation.

The struggle for civil rights in the 1950s and 1960s, culminating with a series of court decisions and federal legislation ending legal segregation based on racial difference, also inspired a variety of liberation movements among other oppressed groups. The Chicano movement recounted at the beginning of this chapter took its inspiration and many of its tactics from the example of African Americans in the Civil Rights Movement. At the same time, Chicano activists, African American civil rights workers, and others involved in liberation movements lent their support to the American Indian Movement, an organization begun in the 1960s as an umbrella political organization for native peoples in America. This pan-Indian coalition brought attention to Native American concerns through protests, confrontations, and a series of highly publicized occupations of symbolic sites, including the takeover of Alcatraz Island in San Francisco Bay in California in 1969 and of the Wounded Knee site in South Dakota in 1973. Part of uniting the disparate native cultures represented in the movement was identifying shared spiritual values and religious practices.[63]

A renewed effort to address the unequal treatment of women in American society also gained momentum in the aftermath of the Civil Rights Movement. Often regarded as "second-wave feminism" in contrast to the initial wave of women's activism in the nineteenth and early twentieth centuries, the feminist movement of the 1960s and 1970s included a denouncement of religion in its more general critiques of patriarchal social structures and cultural traditions. Feminist theologians attacked patriarchal images of "God the Father" in Christian and Jewish traditions, while at the same time they demanded more access for women in leadership positions within religious communities. Some communities responded positively to the criticisms, with women gaining ordination in Reform Judaism and several major Protestant denominations in the 1970s. On the other hand, more conservative Christians condemned the attacks on patriarchal traditions and argued that gender roles were divinely created and sacrosanct; Roman Catholics, Southern Baptists, and many other Christian groups continue to refuse ordination for women on theological grounds.

Another issue that gained national attention in the wake of the Civil Rights Movement involves discrimination and persecution of people with nonheterosexual orientations. The gay rights movement entered the national scene with the so-called "Stonewall riots" in 1969 in New York City, which erupted in response to continuing police harassment and abuse of homosexuals. The subsequent decades of struggle for recognition of homosexual orientations and the legitimacy of same-sex relationships has incurred a vehement response on the part of religious groups who regard heterosexuality as divinely ordained and any deviations from heteronormative standards as morally repugnant.

All of the various liberation movements that sprang up in the second half of the twentieth century made reference in one way or another to various visions of the American nation, and many of these diverse views of America appealed to religious understandings of nation, either implicitly or in some cases through explicit assumptions of divine intention for national destiny. In fact, we have seen throughout history a tension in America between on the one hand a democratic openness to diverse opinions and various ways of living and on the other an insistence on conformation to normative beliefs about transcendent purposes and meanings of the nation. The nativist attacks on immigrants in the nineteenth century, alongside the appeal to Manifest Destiny in the conquest of Native Americans, were met by other voices who envisioned a more inclusive America. The religious and moral grounding of abolitionists fighting against slavery was answered by the theological interpretations of proslavery Christians. At the end of World War II, these tensions that have always been part of American society continued in a global context of Cold War politics; condemning communism in the early years of the Cold War meant in part asserting the religious nature of America. But the exclusion of marginalized groups elicited protests, resistance, and social turmoil grounded in the moral teachings of diverse religious orientations; at the same time, such disturbances also provoked those who objected to the changes as contrary to their religious traditions. Religious arguments proliferated as partisans on both sides of these struggles turned to their most cherished religious traditions in response to a changing society.

Questions for Discussion

(1) In what ways does the American Pledge of Allegiance serve as an example of American civil religion, and how does it demonstrate the limitations of the concept of civil religion when applied to American civic culture?

(2) Why did some American Jews oppose the Zionist movement, and what developments convinced many of them to subsequently support the establishment of Israel in Palestine?

(3) To what extent can an understanding of class differences explain the contrasts between the Catholic Workers and Rev. Billy Graham?

(4)   Compare and contrast Martin Luther King, Jr. and Malcolm X as leaders who used their religious commitments as a basis for criticizing American racial policies and race relations in twentieth-century America.

Suggested Primary-Source Readings

A selection of poems by Nyogen Senzaki, a Japanese American Zen Buddhist, written during his incarceration in the internment camp at Heart Mountain, Wyoming, during World War II, reprinted in Thomas A. Tweed and Stephen R. Prothero, eds., *Asian Religions in America: A Documentary History* (New York: Oxford University Press, 1999), 166–168.

Rev. George Macpherson Docherty, "Under God" sermon, preached February 7, 1954, New York Avenue Presbyterian Church, Washington, DC: Docherty's influential sermon urging the insertion of the phrase "under God" into the Pledge of Allegiance was delivered on "Lincoln Sunday" with Dwight D. Eisenhower, President of the United States, sitting in Lincoln's pew. Eisenhower subsequently urged Congress to change the Pledge of Allegiance to include the divine reference, and he signed the bill adding the phrase on Flag Day in June 1954.

Dorothy Day, *The Long Loneliness: The Autobiography of Dorothy Day* (San Francisco, CA: HarperSanFrancisco, 1997): Day's autobiography includes details of the beginnings of the Catholic Worker movement intertwined with her spiritual growth as a Catholic convert.

Will Herberg, *Protestant, Catholic, Jew: An Essay in American Religious Sociology* (Chicago, IL: University of Chicago Press, 1983): Herberg's influential study of American society during the early Cold War era draws attention to the distinct cultures of Protestants, Catholics, and Jews.

Martin Luther King Jr., "Letter from Birmingham Jail," in *Why We Can't Wait* (New York: Signet Classic, 2000), 85–109: In this letter written while in jail in 1963, King succinctly argues for the moral justification of nonviolent direct action in resisting racial segregation in America.

Malcolm X and Alex Haley, *The Autobiography of Malcolm X* (New York: Ballantine Books, 1992): This dramatic autobiography of the Nation of Islam leader, written in collaboration with Alex Haley and published after Malcolm X's death, details the racism suffered by many African Americans of the Great Migration era and offers an insider's view of the Nation of Islam in its formative years and during the civil rights era.

Notes

1   Stephen R. Lloyd-Moffett, "Holy Activist, Secular Saint: Religion and the Social Activism of César Chávez," in *Mexican American Religions: Spirituality, Activism, and Culture*, ed. Gastón Espinosa and Mario T. García (Durham, NC: Duke University Press, 2008), 106.

2   Ibid.

3   Ibid., 113–114.

4   Ibid., 108–109.

5   Ibid., 115–116.

6   Bellah's original essay on the topic was presented at a conference in May 1966 and subsequently published in *Dædalus, Journal of the American Academy of Arts and Sciences* 96, no. 1 (1967); a reprint appears in Robert N. Bellah, *Beyond Belief: Essays on Religion in a Post-traditional World* (Berkeley: University of California Press, 1991), 168–189.

7   Ibid., 179.

8   Derek Davis, "Civil Religion as a Judicial Doctrine," *Journal of Church and State* 40 (1998); Jeffrey F. Meyer, *Myths in Stone: Religious Dimensions of Washington, DC* (Berkeley: University of California Press, 2001); Richard Ellis, *To the Flag: The Unlikely History of the Pledge of Allegiance* (Lawrence: University Press of Kansas, 2005); and Grace Y. Kao and Jerome E. Copulsky, "The Pledge of Allegiance and the Meanings and Limits of Civil Religion," *Journal of the American Academy of Religion* 75, no. 1 (2007).

9   John F. Wilson, *Public Religion in American Culture* (Philadelphia, PA: Temple University Press, 1979), 148, 175.

10   Charles H. Lippy, "American Civil Religion: Myth, Reality, and Challenges," in *Faith in America, Vol. 2: Religious Issues Today*, ed. Charles H. Lippy (Westport, CT: Praeger, 2006), 24, 34.

11   Ira Chernus, "Civil Religion," in *The Blackwell Companion to Religion in America*, ed. Philip Goff (Malden, MA: Wiley Blackwell, 2010), 68–69.

12   For a summary of the 2002 judicial challenge to the Pledge of Allegiance and the public reaction, see Ellis, *To the Flag*, ix–xi and Kao and Copulsky, "Pledge of Allegiance," 122–123.

13   Ellis, *To the Flag*, 19–20.

14   Ibid., 52.

15   Ibid., 50–67.

16   Ibid., 52.

17   Ibid., 85–88.

18   Ibid., 91–113.

19   Ibid., 124–137.

20   Steven T. Rosenthal, "Long Distance Nationalism: American Jews, Zionism, and Israel," in *The Cambridge Companion to American Judaism*, ed. Dana Evan Kaplan (New York: Cambridge University Press, 2005), 209.

21   Ibid.

22   Lawrence Grossman, "Jewish Religious Denominations," in *The Cambridge Companion to American Judaism*, ed. Dana Evan Kaplan (New York: Cambridge University Press, 2005), 83.

23   Rosenthal, "Long Distance Nationalism," 210–211.

24   From the American Council of Judaism's statement of "Principles" on its website, www.acjna.org/acjna/about_principles.aspx (accessed June 24, 2013).

25   G. Scott Cady and Christopher L. Webber, *A Year with American Saints* (New York: Church Publishing, 2006), 361.

26   Roosevelt made this statement in his Second Inaugural Address, in 1937; a transcript of the address is available at http://avalon.law.yale.edu/20th_century/froos2.asp (accessed September 7, 2013).

27   Mattew Avery Sutton, "Was FDR the Antichrist? The Birth of Fundamentalist Antiliberalism in a Global Age," *Journal of American History* 98, no. 4 (2012), 1052.

28   For an overview of Marx's regard for religion, see Daniel L. Pals, *Eight Theories of Religion*, 2nd edn (New York: Oxford University Press, 2006), 118–148.

29   Ibid., 149–192; Richard J. Callahan Jr., "Class and Labor," in *The Blackwell Companion to Religion in America*, ed. Philip Goff (Malden, MA: Wiley Blackwell, 2010), 73–74.

30   Callahan, "Class and Labor," 83; Bradford Verter, "Spiritual Capital: Theorizing Religion with Bourdieu against Bourdieu," *Sociological Theory* 21, no. 2 (2003).

31   Quoted in Zachary R. Calo, "'True Economic Liberalism' and the Development of American Catholic Social Thought, 1920–1940," *Journal of Catholic Social Thought* 5, no. 2 (2008).

32   Mark Zwick and Louise Zwick, *The Catholic Worker Movement: Intellectual and Spiritual Origins* (Mahwah, NJ: Paulist Press, 2005), 107.

33   Dorothy Day, *The Long Loneliness: The Autobiography of Dorothy Day* (San Francisco, CA: HarperSanFrancisco, 1997), 214, 243.

34   Quoted in Zwick and Zwick, *Catholic Worker Movement*, 253.

35   Ibid., 260.

36   Kim Phillips-Fein, *Invisible Hands: The Making of the Conservative Movement from the New Deal to Reagan* (New York: W. W. Norton, 2009), 70–75.

37   Jonathan P. Herzog, *The Spiritual-Industrial Complex: America's Religious Battle against Communism in the Early Cold War* (New York: Oxford University Press, 2011), 3–7.

38   Quoted in Patrick Henry, "'And I Don't Care What It Is': The Tradition-History of a Civil Religion Proof-Text," *Journal of the American Academy of Religion* 49, no. 1 (1981).

39   Jason W. Stevens, *God-Fearing and Free: A Spiritual History of America's Cold War* (Cambridge, MA: Harvard University Press, 2010), 44–45.

40   Herzog, *The Spiritual-Industrial Complex*, 162–163.

41   K. Healan Gaston, "Interpreting Judeo-Christianity in America," *Relegere: Studies in Religion and Reception* 2, no. 2 (2012), 291–292.

42   Will Herberg, *Protestant, Catholic, Jew: An Essay in American Religious Sociology* (Chicago, IL: University of Chicago Press, 1983), 75–77.

43   Ibid., 264.

44   Gaston, "Interpreting Judeo-Christianity in America," 302–303.

45   The report, *Personal Justice Denied: Report of the Commission on Wartime Relocation and Internment of Civilians*, is available online at www.nps.gov/history/history/online_ books/personal_justice_denied/index.htm (accessed September 7, 2013).

46   Gary Y. Okihiro, "Religion and Resistance in America's Concentration Camps," *Phylon* 45, no. 3 (1984), 222–223.

47   Ibid., 224.

48   Cherstin M. Lyon, "Gordon Hirabayashi," in *Densho Encyclopedia*, http://encyclo-pedia.densho.org/Gordon%20Hirabayashi (accessed July 7, 2013).

49   This is not to insist that civil rights was strictly or even essentially a religious under-taking. For a challenge to the tendency to interpret the movement in narrowly reli-gious terms, see Glenda Elizabeth Gilmore, *Defying Dixie: The Radical Roots of Civil Rights, 1919–1950* (New York: W. W. Norton, 2008).

50   For the story of Whitfield and Williams, see Erik S. Gellman and Jarod Roll, *The Gospel of the Working Class: Labor's Southern Prophets in New Deal America* (Urbana: University of Illinois Press, 2011).

51 Taylor Branch, *Parting the Waters: America in the King Years, 1954–1963* (New York: Simon and Schuster, 1988), 3.

52 David J. Garrow, *Bearing the Cross: Martin Luther King, Jr., and the Southern Christian Leadership Conference* (New York: W. Morrow, 1986), 32.

53 This widely quoted remark from Heschel is variously attributed to a diary entry, a letter to Martin Luther King, Jr., and a later conversation with King.

54 "Conversation with Martin Luther King," *Conservative Judaism* 22, no. 3 (1968), 10. I am grateful to my student Morgan D. Grigsby for alerting me of King's appearance at the Rabbinical Assembly in 1968.

55 The "Letter from Birmingham Jail" appears in Martin Luther King, Jr., *Why We Can't Wait* (New York: Signet Classic, 2000), 85–109.

56 Richard Brent Turner, *Islam in the African-American Experience* (Bloomington: Indiana University Press, 1997), 176–190.

57 Ibid., 191–193. For a detailed study of the devotional practices and religious views of members of the Nation of Islam in the 1960s and 1970s, see Edward E. Curtis IV, *Black Muslim Religion in the Nation of Islam, 1960–1975* (Chapel Hill: University of North Carolina Press, 2006).

58 1963 interview with Louis Lomax; transcript available at http://teachingamericanhistory.org/library/document/a-summing-up-louis-lomax-interviews-malcolm-x (accessed July 14, 2013).

59 Ibid.

60 Turner, *Islam in the African-American Experience*, 203–214.

61 Ibid., 214–219.

62 Eric Michael Mazur, *The Americanization of Religious Minorities: Confronting the Constitutional Order* (Baltimore: Johns Hopkins University Press, 1999), 30.

63 As an example, see Vine Deloria, Jr., *God Is Red: A Native View of Religion*, 2nd edn (Golden, CO: Fulcrum, 1994 [1973]).

11

A Spiritual Nation

This chapter considers the distinction between religion and spirituality by focusing on new religious developments of the late twentieth century in America and how some of those developments have translated into profitable moneymaking opportunities for religious entrepreneurs. In particular, it explores the consequences of new immigration policies that brought considerable numbers of adherents of Asian religious traditions to America; these new arrivals altered the religious landscapes in many American cities and towns while also gaining converts from other religions who sought spiritual fulfillment in a variety of eastern traditions. Likewise, immigrants from Latin America established Latino/a spirituality as a religious staple across the nation. At the same time, the revival of feminism in American culture inspired spiritual traditions with liberalized assumptions about gender and sexuality. On the other hand, the growing acceptance of feminist perspectives elicited a countermovement among conservative Christians, especially following the legalization of abortion in the 1970s. By the end of the century, America had become a more religiously diverse place, but it remained a place where differences created both new spiritual opportunities and new religious conflicts.

Oprah Winfrey (born 1954), arguably the most recognizable woman in the world by the end of the twentieth century, converted her immensely popular television talk show in the 1990s from what she described as "guilty of doing trash TV and not thinking it was trash" to a mission of uplift and enlightenment in what she called "Change Your Life TV." The new format aimed "to use television to

Formed From This Soil: An Introduction to the Diverse History of Religion in America, First Edition. Thomas S. Bremer.
© 2015 Thomas S. Bremer. Published 2015 by John Wiley & Sons, Ltd.

transform people's lives, to make viewers see themselves differently, and to bring happiness and a sense of fulfillment into every home." Winfrey went on to explain:

> I am talking about each individual having her or his own inner revolution. I am talking about each individual coming to the awareness that, "I am Creation's son. I am Creation's daughter. I am more than my physical self. I am more than this job that I do. I am more than the external definitions I have given myself. ... [U]ltimately I am Spirit come from the greatest Spirit. I am Spirit.'[1]

Thereafter her television program became a sort of religious mission; as she herself acknowledged, "My show is really a ministry, a ministry that doesn't ask for money. I can't tell you how many lives we've changed – or inspired to change."[2] Oprah remade herself as the icon of a "Live Your Best Life" spirituality.

Oprah's concern for others extended beyond the guests and viewers of her television broadcasts. She also undertook charitable projects on a global scale with her Angel Network, with special interest in Africa. Most famously, the Oprah Winfrey Leadership Academy for Girls in South Africa provides education to some three hundred girls in a facility sporting a yoga studio, original African tribal art, and colorful tiled sidewalks. Oprah explained the mission of the school as a place "for powerful girls who will use their power in service to their nation and to our world." Achieving those goals, it seems, required a designer's caring touch. The Oprah web site declared, "Every tile, every doorknob, has been Oprah's specific choice." A report on the school tells how "Oprah made decisions that ranged from the buildings' softly curving contours to the school's classy yet kicky uniforms and included the fine-art and crafts pieces ... as well as the lighting fixtures, bathroom tiles, linens, rugs, chairs, and hardware." Oprah herself revealed that "I am creating everything in this school that I would have wanted for myself – so the girls will have the absolute best that my imagination can offer."[3] Indeed, through the generous temperament of her spiritual endeavors, Oprah seeks to spread abundance to those most in need, a bounty that reflects the middle-class values of American society.

Although Oprah's personal concern for the well-being of others appears altruistic, her turn toward the good of Spirit also marks the domineering rise of her corporate empire. As one scholar has noted, "Her spiritualization programmed her incorporation. This is how Oprah Winfrey became Oprah, how she became a product." Besides the daily television program, her corporate enterprises included her own magazine, the largest book club in the world, a philanthropic organization that encouraged others to become involved in charitable work, a web site with nearly seven million visitors each month, satellite radio, sold-out speaking tours, and eventually her own multimedia network. Oprah seemed ubiquitous in American popular culture at the turn of the millennium. And, at every turn, she sold products, including books, clothing, accessories for a better life, and especially herself. As she remarked, "When you get me, you are not getting an image, you

Box 11.1   Spirituality

Oprah Winfrey's religious importance at the end of the twentieth century cap-italized on cultural perceptions that distinguish between "religion" and "spiritu-ality." A noted sociologist of religion defines spirituality as "the ways people express their personal relationships to the sacred," which usually is a private matter mostly hidden from public view; spirituality from this sociological view-point consists of "all the beliefs and activities by which individuals attempt to relate their lives to God or to a divine being or some other conception of a tran-scendent reality."[4] But, as another scholar suggests, we have more to learn from observing the different ways that practitioners actually use the term "spiritu-ality" than from academic attempts to define it.[5] In doing so we begin to pay attention to the various interests and debates involved in claims of spirituality.

The popular uses of spirituality in contemporary society often invoke a distinction between religion and spirituality that in most cases has to do with the level of social organization; in contrast to "religion," which is associated with formal social structures such as congregations and denominations, usually identifiable with particular traditions involving sacred texts and communal practices, "spirituality" has a more individual, personal character, unorganized and not associated with recognizable institutions and structures. Moreover, the actual practices that many people regard as "spiritual" often occur in institutional settings beyond typical religious organizations, appearing in more secular contexts such as in medical practices and in artistic pursuits.[6]

Escaping the boundaries of typically religious settings indicates another distinctive characteristic of spirituality that separates it from religion; spirituality occupies an ambiguous place within the distinction between reli-gious and secular. On the one hand, spirituality, with its close connection to claims of authentic religious experience, can seem more genuine and ful-filling than what some people regard as the religious. On the other hand, spiritual pursuits often remain unabashedly entangled in the secular world of commerce and exchange; much of what passes for spirituality relies on market forces and tends to be prone to commodification. One may not be able to purchase spiritual fulfillment itself, but teachers, guides, workshops, retreats, and an endless line of spiritual accessories and paraphernalia stand ready to lead practitioners to greater spiritual awareness and fulfillment.

are not getting a figurehead. You're not getting a theme song. You're getting all of me. And I bring my stuff with me." Oprah has become the very product that con-sumers desire; she sells herself by creating a Best Self that others want to become.[7]

Oprah Winfrey epitomizes the commodification of religion as spirituality for late twentieth-century Americans. Although she eludes typical assumptions about religion, without a church or an organized congregation, her corporate success taps into religious patterns and resources that have long histories in American culture. She has drawn attention to her own early influences in African American Protestant churches, and her image as an authoritative black woman has precedent in Baptist and Methodist traditions and especially in Holiness and Pentecostal churches.[8] Moreover, her message resonates with religious lessons of uplift and betterment that have been staples in twentieth-century African American Protestant churches as well as a common theme among many mainline Christians more broadly. Oprah more than anyone has taken the "Live Your Best Life" desires of American religious people and transformed them into a profitable corporate conglomerate.

In this chapter we consider how the burgeoning religious diversity in America in the second half of the twentieth century contributed to spiritual pursuits that often have profitable impacts in consumer markets. As we continue to reconsider our presuppositions about what constitutes religion in the modern world, figures such as Oprah Winfrey provide occasions for thinking about how religious traditions contribute to and actually participate in profitable economic pursuits. Oprah may have been the dominant religious entrepreneur at the end of the twentieth century as she linked spiritual abundance to the consumer **ethos** of American culture, but other religious traditions also capitalized on consumer desires for personal betterment and uplift as well as on the salvific concerns more often associated with American religiosity, especially in Protestant **evangelical** circles. By the end of the millennium, spiritual pursuits offered a profitable range of products in the consumer marketplace.

Spiritual Immigrants

America has become the most religiously diverse nation on earth, explains a leading scholar, largely due to the rapid increase in the numbers of Hindus, Buddhists, Sikhs, Muslims, and adherents of other religious traditions since passage of the Immigration and Nationality Act of 1965. This legislation replaced the previous system of quotas that favored immigrants from Europe; the new law opened a virtual floodgate of new arrivals from all over the world. The resulting shift in the cultural demographics of the United States has significantly altered the American religious landscape; religious communities with roots in Africa, Asia, Latin America, and the Middle East are now common in nearly every American city.[9]

Newly arrived citizens in the late twentieth century faced many of the same challenges that earlier immigrants had faced regarding the perpetuation of communities and traditions in new surroundings. A shortage of religious specialists to lead their communities, absence of sacred sites or necessary implements for performing devotional exercises, tension between preserving old traditions on the one hand and pressures to assimilate to the dominant American culture on the other, and the loss of languages and other cultural resources in subsequent generations have been constant problems for most immigrant communities. New challenges and novel opportunities also faced the post-1965 immigrants to the United States. Many of the newer arrivals were better educated with more economically stable means than immigrants in earlier eras, allowing for more rapid assimilation and greater acceptance in American society. Relatively higher incomes paired with developments in transportation and communication technologies created opportunities to stay more connected to original homelands, generating "transnational" identities among immigrants who regularly call family and friends back home and often travel between their new homes in the United States and old communities in their native countries. Proximity also plays a role in the continuity of relationships between the old and the new. Many immigrants from the Caribbean region and Latin America routinely circulate between their new homes in the United States and their native homelands in places like Haiti, the Dominican Republic, Guatemala, and Mexico. In many cases religious holidays, festivals, or lifetime events such as baptisms, weddings, or burials precipitate a return to native lands. Consequently, immigration no longer entails a complete separation from one's former life and relationships.[10]

Asian immigrant places of worship

The influx of so many religious communities from around the world has left its imprint on the American landscape. Hindu temples, Sikh gurdwaras, Buddhist monasteries, Muslim mosques, *botánicas* (retail stores selling supplies needed in Latin American and Afro-Caribbean folk religious practices), and storefront churches catering to immigrant communities have become regular sights in American cities, suburbs, and even rural areas. Some of the new religious centers for immigrant communities are small, modest structures that are hardly recognizable, but many are lavish and imposing buildings that serve as community centers for large groups of immigrant worshipers and practitioners. Among the more striking buildings are religious architectures of Asian influence, which have become common in many American cities and towns. In fact, the United States by the end of the twentieth century had more Hindu temples than anywhere in the world outside India.[11] Los Angeles at the same time had more different kinds of Buddhists than any city in the world, with a wide range of temples, from devotional spaces in residential homes to elaborate temple complexes built in traditional styles imported from Asia.[12] Likewise, Sikh gurdwaras have appeared in cities across the United States, some occupying formerly Christian buildings, others built according to traditional Sikh architectural styles, and a few adopting innovative designs to blend in with local communities.[13]

As immigrants establish their religious communities and build new places of devotion, they sometimes must innovate on ancient traditions. The ornate Sri Siva

Vishnu Temple, for example, stands in a residential neighborhood outside Washington, DC; it began with the purchase in 1984 of a split-level house in suburban Maryland. The local Hindu community brought a renowned temple architect from India to oversee the construction of the permanent temple structure, and in 1991 priests from Hindu communities across America assisted in the elaborate **rituals** to install the first of the sacred images in the temple, followed in subsequent years with ceremonies to consecrate additional stone images. Both Siva and Vishnu, the two main manifestations of the Hindu deity, have separate shrines in the same building, thus uniting the two main devotional traditions of the Hindu community under a single roof. To ensure authenticity, the architect accommodated the split-level temple design with an innovation that allowed the sacred images, installed on the upper level, to remain in direct contact with the earth, as required in ancient texts: beneath each image is a hollow pillar filled with dirt; from the basement level, these appear as support pillars for the building, but in reality their only function is to allow the images to sit directly on the ground. Thus, this Hindu temple in America adheres to orthodox requirements in an unorthodox setting.[14]

The two levels of the Sri Siva Vishnu Temple not only accommodate the diversity of devotional traditions among the Hindu immigrants but also serve generational differences between the adult immigrants and their children, as well as reflecting the gendered social roles of men and women. Ritual performances serving the gods occur upstairs; cultural and educational activities happen downstairs. Assimilating the middle-class values of suburban America, domestic life has entered the sacred realms of the temple and occupied the lower floor. This domestic area hosts activities aimed more at younger generations, with summer camps, yoga and dance classes, and language instruction. Second- and third-generation Hindu immigrants are often confused by the solemn devotional rituals held in the shrines upstairs, and are more at home with the cultural and educational activities held on the lower level. The upstairs–downstairs division also marks gender differences. The downstairs kitchen is for women, whereas the priestly duties upstairs are for men only. Ironically, the segregation and subordination of confining women to the kitchen actually has a feminist spin to it; in India, women are not permitted to prepare *prashad*, the sanctified meal that devotees eat as a sacrament; only men with requisite purity can handle the holy food in the Indian temples. In America, the domestic role of middle-class women allows them to claim the temple kitchen, in effect assuming a priestly role closed off to them in the homeland.[15]

The Sri Siva Vishnu Temple in Maryland typifies the accommodations of recent Hindu immigrants, who negotiate between the traditions of Indian temple worship and the middle-class values of America. Elaborate buildings with the ornate architecture of India now house Hindu deities across the American continent. But tradition meets innovation in the lives of devotees who live in the transnational spaces between continents; generational differences, changing gender roles, and assimilation to broader cultural realities make American Hinduism a distinct tradition of its own.

Besides the rapid increase in Hindus and other immigrants from South Asia, Buddhism has also experienced a larger presence in American communities. Among the many Buddhist groups to have arrived since the loosening of immigration restrictions in 1965 have been Vietnamese immigrants who have come to America as refugees. With the collapse of the South Vietnam government in 1975, the United States set up four refugee camps on US military bases to help Vietnamese fleeing their homeland to settle in America. The government used a dispersion plan to settle the refugees throughout the nation rather than in centralized communities, hoping to facilitate their assimilation to American society and to avoid the establishment of ethnic ghettos. After initial resettlement, many of the Vietnamese immigrants relocated elsewhere in the United States, mostly to live closer to family or other Vietnamese people, and often because of job opportunities or the desire to live in a more familiar climate. The consolidation of sizable Vietnamese immigrant communities made possible the establishment of their own religious communities, both Buddhist and Roman Catholic, the two predominant religious groups in Vietnam. At the same time, most Vietnamese, regardless of their religious affiliations, acknowledge the *Tam Giao* (Three Religions), Buddhism, Confucianism, and Taoism, as a significant cultural influence. Its ubiquity in popular folk culture has made the influence of the three religious systems of *Tam Giao* an element of Vietnamese identity.[16]

Typical of Vietnamese Buddhist communities settling in the United States is the establishment of Chua Duc Vien, the "Perfect Harmony Temple," in San Jose, California. The temple originated in the efforts of the Venerable Thich Dam Luu (1932–1999), a Buddhist nun who had fled from Vietnam in the 1970s. In the 1940s at the age of sixteen, Dam Luu had been one of the first women in Vietnam to be ordained as a Buddhist nun. She became involved in political activism and was jailed in 1963 for protesting the Vietnamese government. Later she traveled to Germany, where she earned a master's degree in social work; upon her return to Vietnam she operated an orphanage in Saigon (now Ho Chi Minh City), but it closed following the communist victory in 1975. Dam Luu escaped from Vietnam on a boat crowded with refugees; after two years in a refugee camp in Malaysia she arrived in California in 1980 at age forty-eight with just twenty dollars. Undeterred, she soon founded the Perfect Harmony Temple as a home temple in a rented house in San Jose. Between donations from the Buddhist community and her own efforts to collect aluminum and newspapers to redeem for cash, Dam Luu began a fund to build a permanent temple. By 1993, she had collected enough funds to build an elaborate temple in the traditional Vietnamese style, which has become an active center of immigrant life in the Bay Area region of northern California. Daily devotional sessions, language classes, and regular festival celebrations bring substantial numbers of Buddhist devotees to the temple; it also houses the first Buddhist nunnery in the United States. By the time of Dam Luu's death in 1999, Buddhists throughout America and even in Europe and Asia recognized the importance of her temple and the community that it supports; more than four thousand people from around the world attended her funeral.[17]

War refugees such as Dam Luu have made up only a portion of Asian immigrants bringing Buddhism to America since the immigration reforms of the 1960s. Although Chinese immigrants established the earliest significant Buddhist presence in North America, their influence was largely eclipsed in the twentieth century by Japanese Buddhist traditions. In the final decades of the twentieth century, however, the Chinese have established notable Buddhist sites on American soil. The Sino-American Buddhist Association began in 1959 and built an impressive monastery in California known as City of Ten Thousand Buddhists, which serves as the headquarters of the renamed organization, the Dharma Realm Buddhist Association. Since then, other Chinese groups have established Buddhist communities in the United States; by the end of the twentieth century some 125 Chinese Buddhist organizations could be found in America, more than half in California.[18]

Like other immigrants from earlier centuries, people from Asia have made their own sacred places in their new American homeland. Indeed, places of religious devotion that Asians and their descendants have established on American soil are now common sights throughout America. The added presence of Buddhist

Figure 11.1   Among the many temples and shrines in California, the Hsi Lai Temple, located in Hacienda Heights near Los Angeles, is one of the largest Buddhist temples in North America. (Photograph by the author.)

monasteries, Hindu temples, Sikh gurdwaras, and other sites where religious communities of Asian origin gather have added new dimensions to the diversity of the American spiritual marketplace.

Converts to Asian religious orientations

Besides establishing sacred places to preserve their religious orientations within their ethnically bound communities, Asian immigrants have also introduced their religions to non-Asian converts. Transcendental Meditation, for instance, was one of the first of the many spiritual practices originating in India that captured public imagination among non-Asian Americans in the 1960s and 1970s. Many of its followers have denied that Transcendental Meditation is a religion at all, regarding it instead as "a scientific discovery" that "does not involve any religious belief or practice." Proponents describe it as "a simple, natural, effortless process that allows the mind to experience subtler and subtler levels of the thinking process until thinking is transcended and the mind comes into direct contact with the source of thought."[19] The process itself involves repeated chanting of a **mantra**, which brings benefits both to the individual and to the community; in fact a political party, the Natural Law Party, seeks to heal American social problems through the practice of Transcendental Meditation.[20]

Much more successful in attracting American converts were the Hare Krishnas, or members of the International Society for Krishna Consciousness (ISKON), brought to America during the 1960s by A. C. Bhaktivedanta Swami Prabhupada (1896–1977), a devotee of the Hindu deity Krishna. Followers join communities to pursue an ascetic lifestyle that includes vegetarianism and refraining from sexual activities other than for the purpose of creating devoted children; they also observe prohibitions against intoxicants (alcohol, drugs, coffee, tea, cigarettes) and gambling. Central to the ISKON lifestyle is devotion to Krishna through the chanting of the Hare Krishna mantra: "Hare Krishna Hare Krishna, Krishna Krishna, Hare Hare, Hare Rama Hare Rama, Rama Rama, Hare Hare"; members of the community begin with early morning chants and repeat the mantra throughout the day.[21]

Prabhupada first established ISKON in New York City but after a year relocated to the Haight Ashbury district of San Francisco in California, the center of American hippie culture in the 1960s; many of the young people attracted to the hippies found a welcoming home in the ISKON community. But a number of these new members who joined the Hare Krishnas found themselves socially isolated, their only contacts with the outside world involving the sale of religious literature and their **proselytizing** efforts; their relative seclusion created tensions, dissension, and accusations of abuse within the ISKON community.[22]

Since Prabhupada's death in 1977, struggles over leadership and dealing with several scandals, including lawsuits over child abuse allegations, have altered the

Figure 11.2 After relocating to San Francisco, members of the International Society for Krishna Consciousness, commonly known as the Hare Krishnas, were a common sight on the local cultural scene. Here they are shown in a parade during their annual gathering in Golden Gate Park in 1977. (Photograph by Dave Glass, San Francisco, USA.)

communal emphasis of ISKON; in the early years they actively discouraged marriage and childrearing as distractions from communal devotion to Krishna in an atmosphere that overtly denigrated female members, but since the 1970s they have come to value the nuclear family and have become more accepting of women and children. They also have moved from a near-exclusive interest in proselytizing among non-Asians to more efforts to attract members of the India-born immigrant community.[23]

Like other religions originating in Asia, Buddhism has attracted significant non-Asian converts. Among the most popular Buddhist traditions among non-Asians has been Rinzai Zen, a Japanese Buddhist tradition emphasizing meditation practices promoted most prominently in the United States by D. T. Suzuki (1870–1966) through lectures and books, especially his two collections of *Essays in Zen Buddhism* (1927 and 1933), which were widely influential in the period before World War II. Suzuki's return to the United States in the 1950s reinforced the popularity of Zen Buddhism among a generation of countercultural

Box 11.2   Yoga

Other than cuisine, yoga has been the most widely assimilated Asian import in American culture.[24] By the end of the twentieth century, this ancient spiritual practice had caught the imagination of Americans far beyond the Hindu traditions of its origin; today, some twenty million Americans attend yoga classes, go on yoga retreats, or simply engage in yoga exercises on their own, spending over ten billion dollars each year in pursuit of their yoga practice.[25] It even received presidential approval when the Obama administration added yoga to the annual Easter Egg Roll on the White House lawn.[26]

In India, yoga refers to a variety of meditation practices, usually involving bodily movements and postures with controlled breathing; there has never been a singular, coherent yoga tradition there, but separate traditions with hundreds of different lineages perpetuated by thousands of different gurus, or spiritual guides.[27] The tradition came to America in the nineteenth century, but it did not enjoy widespread popularity there until the twentieth century. Its initial ambassador was Swami Vivekananda (originally Narendranath Datta, 1863–1902), who first arrived in the United States to participate in the 1893 World's Parliament of Religions, where he gained much attention as a Hindu representative. Following the meetings in Chicago, Vivekananda taught a variety of spiritual topics, including yoga, at the "spiritual summer camp" at Green Acre in New England.[28]

Following Vivekananda's initial introduction, American interest in yoga caught on slowly. In the first half of the twentieth century, the Self-Realization Fellowship, led by Swami Paramahansa Yogananda (1893–1952), was the most influential Hindu movement in America, with headquarters in Los Angeles, California; by the middle of the century the group claimed 150 000 followers with 150 centers in the United States, based on the practice of kriya yoga, which Yogananda described as "the scientific technique of God-realization." The movement's stated objectives included, "To advocate cultural and spiritual understanding between East and West, and the exchange of their finest distinctive features."[29] Much of its success relied on Yogananda's flair for self-promotion, and his organization issued a richly illustrated magazine, offered a correspondence course, and sold cards, calendars, and other products, usually emblazoned with the Swami's face.[30]

By the end of the twentieth century, yoga had become a favored fitness pursuit for millions of Americans. But the version found in most American yoga studios is largely stripped of its specifically Hindu religious roots and transformed into a more general practice of health and fitness that is less threatening to American religious sensibilities. Certainly, some practitioners still concentrate on the transcendent and ecstatic elements of yogic traditions, such as the Kundalini traditions celebrated at the annual Rainbow Gathering of the Tribes, a countercultural festival held every summer.[31] But most of the yoga practiced in the United States aligns more with American puritanical principles underlying fitness movements that value exertion and pain in efforts of self-improvement. For instance, the wildly successful yoga franchise empire of Bikram Choudhury (born 1946) relies on followers' unwavering devotion to lengthy sessions in heated studios, demanding daily workouts of ninety minutes in what Choudhury himself describes as "Bikram's torture chamber!" The abuse, the strenuous exertion, and the pain that devotees experience also bring pleasure, with promises of vitality, mental acuity, and improved energy.[32] Moreover, the franchise has made Choudhury a remarkably wealthy man as he dominates one strand of the multi-billion-dollar yoga industry.

proponents.[33] Another influential popularizer of Buddhism, Alan Watts (1915–1973), did not come from Asia but was a British subject who had left the Episcopal Church in a quest for spiritual truths that led him to an eclectic religious orientation that he described as "between Mahayana Buddhism and Taoism, with a certain leaning toward Vedanta and Catholicism, or rather the Orthodox Church of Eastern Europe."[34] Watts wrote more than twenty-six books and lectured widely across North America. In the Preface of his influential volume *The Way of Zen* (1957), which introduced a whole countercultural generation to Buddhist teachings and practices, he describes his first book, *Spirit of Zen* (1936), as "a popularization of Suzuki's earlier works,"[35] acknowledging his own and many converts' debt to the Japanese scholar's efforts to make the peculiar practices of Zen Buddhism dominant in America. The popularity of Suzuki, Watts, and others helped to secure a place for Buddhist views in countercultural aesthetics, appearing centrally in the work of such artists as novelist Jack Kerouac and poet Gary Snyder.

Besides the meditative, aesthetic orientation of Zen Buddhism as adopted by non-Asian converts in America, a very different Buddhist orientation has also had an impact since its arrival in the 1960s. An organization known as Nichiren Shōshū of America, headquartered in Santa Monica, California, has introduced the Japanese Sōka Gakkai movement to large numbers of American converts. This non-meditative form of Buddhism focuses on the doctrines and practices derived from the ancient *Lotus Sutra* text. In particular, spiritual benefits derive from daily chanting of the phrase "nam(u)-myoho-renge-kyo," a mantra revealed by the Japanese Buddhist teacher Nichiren (1222–1282) that expresses reverence for the *Lotus Sutra* and, according to the Sōka Gakkai, will bring spiritual awakening to devotees. The Sōka Gakkai are very active in proselytizing and have had much success winning converts among Euro-Americans and African Americans; as early as the 1970s they claimed to have over two hundred thousand American followers.[36]

The increasing popularity of Buddhism among American converts has forced Buddhist practitioners to face some of the same questions about gender and race that other religious groups have contended with. Sandy Boucher (born 1936), a feminist convert to Buddhism, characterizes both feminism and Buddhism as liberatory pursuits: "the goal of both," she writes, "is liberation from limiting ideas and conditions." The emphasis on personal insight and freedom through meditation practices complements the authority of women's experiences; Boucher explains, "Many women see this [Buddhist] practice as a way to augment or continue their own process of self-discovery and activism, for it offers techniques designed to awaken us and bring us fully present to life."[37] But she also calls attention to the misogynist tendencies in much of Buddhist tradition, especially among American Buddhist leaders. The near absence of female leadership in American Buddhist communities well past the middle of the twentieth century, and a number of incidents of sexual impropriety among male leaders, stood in stark contrast to the egalitarian teachings that attracted feminist practitioners such as Boucher. As more women took up Buddhist practices in the 1970s and 1980s, some groups attached greater emphasis to the universality of the teachings for all people without special privilege for males, altering the understanding of Buddhist teachings in America, according to Boucher, "by filling in the dimension of women's participation, women's insights and visions."[38]

Buddhist converts in America have confronted racial divisions as well. Not only has racism affected immigrant Buddhist communities in ways that exacerbate divisions between native Buddhists of Asian descent and non-Asian Buddhist converts,[39] but also racial considerations divide convert communities. Although significant numbers of African Americans and other people of color pursue Buddhist practices and teachings, they often remain marginalized in many convert communities. "When people of color are reluctant to enter predominantly white Buddhist settings," explains feminist theorist and cultural critic bell hooks (born 1952), "it is not out of fear of some overt racist exclusion, it is usually in response to more subtle manifestations of white supremacy." She calls for people of color to speak up about their spiritual practices, for only in "profound spiritual practice," hooks insists, will Buddhists be able to challenge the inherent white supremacy that has dominated Buddhist convert communities in America.[40]

The racial and gender differences within convert communities reflect what we have seen throughout our studies of American religious history: conflicts arise constantly along the fault lines of difference. At the same time, however, changing circumstances create new opportunities for religious exchanges and sharing across the boundaries of differences regarding race, ethnicity, gender, sexual orientation, socioeconomic class, and other aspects of social identity. New immigration policies in the second half of the twentieth century significantly increased the presence of Asian immigrant communities, bringing new spiritual perspectives and practices into the mainstream of American cultural life. In communities throughout the United States, new places of Asian religious practice and worship have joined the churches, mosques, and temples of the Abrahamic traditions in the American sacred landscape; Buddhist temples, Hindu community centers, Sikh gurdwaras, and a variety of other locations where Asian immigrants practice their traditional forms of spirituality are now common in America. Their presence has also encouraged increased interactions with non-Asian converts who have adopted religious orientations of Asian origin; in at least a few cases, the introduction of Asian religions to non-Asian converts has produced new spiritual traditions in contexts of adaptation and innovation. Within the contact zones of modern America, new religious opportunities continue to arise.

Religious Bodies

The hopeful prospects of new religious opportunities, however, were not accomplished in all communities of faith. Regarding opportunities for women in the Christian Church, the Roman Catholic pontiff declared in 1963, "Women are becoming ever more conscious of their human dignity. They will not tolerate being treated as mere material instruments, but demand rights befitting a human person both in domestic and public life." The Catholic Church responded to these and other pressures of the modern world by convening a series of extended discussions aimed at reforming the Church. The outcome of the Second Vatican Council, or Vatican II, as the series of conferences in the years 1963–1965 are commonly known, altered Church policy and practice in significant ways. The bishops participating in the Council stated clearly their intentions regarding discriminatory attitudes: "Every type of discrimination," they declared, "whether social or cultural, whether based on sex, race, color, social condition, language, or religion, is to be overcome and eradicated as contrary to God's intent." Yet, despite intentions for more parity between men and women in the Church, the all-male assembly fell far short in granting equal status to women. One witness to the proceedings, feminist theologian Mary Daly (1928–2010), criticized the Church for its institutionalized discrimination against women in her book *The Church and the Second Sex* (1968), where she proposes allowing girls to be altar servers in church services; giving female religious orders more autonomy from the oversight of priests and bishops; rejecting theological traditions that regard women as inferior to men; and especially ending Church prohibitions on the use of birth control. Her emphasis on the disparity between the Church's pronouncements about human dignity and its shameful disregard for the dignity of women brought hostility from Church officials; they moved to dismiss her from Boston College, the Catholic institution where she worked. But Daly's book earned support from many in American society, where a renewed women's movement was gaining widespread attention; student protests at the all-male college and a public outcry led to her reinstatement.[41]

Mary Daly's confrontation of what she regarded as hypocrisy in the Roman Catholic Church typifies a growing awareness of internal inequalities among religious groups in the late decades of twentieth-century America. The patriarchal orientations of Buddhism, Christianity, Hinduism, Islam, Judaism, and most other religions with a significant presence in America came under scrutiny and criticism as feminist theologians and scholars pointed out discrepancies within religious organizations between claims of equality on the one hand and actual social practice on the other. In a related development, although heteronormative assumptions have been promoted by many religious leaders, alternative sexual orientations have gained wider acceptance as moral debates among religious people have shifted from patriarchal concerns for authority to compassionate concerns for the well-being of others.

Gender, sexuality, and the pursuit of spirituality

Political gains for women in the 1960s and 1970s translated as well into new opportunities for spiritual pursuits. Sharing Mary Daly's frustration with the patriarchal traditions of Christianity and other established religious communities, many women turned to Neopagan and New Age traditions to seek spiritual fulfillment without onerous restrictions on women's involvement and leadership.[42] Neopagan communities include groups who follow ancient Celtic Druidism, consisting of sun worshipers who convene in sacred groves of trees; the practice of Wicca, or witchcraft; and those who focus on ceremonial magic or neo-**shamanism**, reviving ancient practices of ecstatic journeys to the spirit world. All of these various Neopagan traditions seek to revive ancient pre-Christian nature religions.[43] Similarly, New Age religious groups draw from an eclectic assortment of traditions; practitioners of New Age seek transformation of the self and of society through such strategies as channeling of spiritual entities, spiritual visualization, astrology, meditation, and alternative healing techniques. They often combine their interests in psychic phenomena, miracles, angels, and other paranormal occurrences with elements of Asian religions, Native American traditions, and holistic healing movements. Whereas Neopagans usually associate in groups that meet periodically for communal rituals, New Age adherents tend toward more individualized practice in specialist–client relationships that concentrate on self-growth and physical or psychic healing.[44]

Among the assortment of Neopagan groups, the most popular have been the covens of witches known as Wicca, or "eclectic Witches." Most of these borrow from traditional witchcraft groups originating in Britain, whose beliefs include worship of both a male god and a female goddess; Wiccans also tend to incorporate a broad range of traditions such as African indigenous practices, ancient Egyptian influences, and occasionally Native American elements. Most adherents share a few common beliefs, in particular "The Wiccan Rede: An it harm

Figure 11.3   New Age seekers gather in the inner circle of a labyrinth at the Angel Valley Sedona retreat center in Arizona. Long regarded as a "vortex" of powerful spiritual energies, Sedona attracts many practitioners of New Age and Neopagan traditions who patronize the numerous spiritual entrepreneurs and facilities in the area. (Photograph by Amayra Hamilton, Angel Valley.)

none, do what you will" as well as "The Law of Threefold Effect," which states that all actions return threefold; many non-Wiccan Neopagans adhere to these creeds as well, with their common origins in early twentieth-century British occultism.[45]

Liberated attitudes regarding gender made New Age and Neopagan spiritual traditions attractive to Americans called to the emancipatory messages of 1970s feminism. Women in roles of priestess and healers assumed positions of leadership not available to them in their former religious communities, especially for those raised in Christian and Jewish traditions, where many of the New Age and Neopagan faithful had come from. Some Neopagan and New Age feminist writers reinterpreted archaeological evidence to reconstruct what they regarded as women-centered societies of the ancient world; a widely read book, *The Chalice and the Blade* (1987) by Riane Eisler (born ca. 1937), summarizes the story of these ancient matriarchies, what Eisler terms "partnership societies," which were subsequently destroyed by male-controlled "dominator societies." Such works not only posed a feminist critique of patriarchal histories but also provided new models for ritual practices and social relations for Neopagan and New Age communities.[46] In particular, Goddess worship served as an authentic alternative to the patriarchal regimes that religious people had suffered under for millennia. As one influential Neopagan writer explained in the early 1970s:

> In the olden times, The Goddess had many groves and wimmin served her freely and in dignity. The Goddess' presence was everywhere, and her wimmin knew her as the eternal sister. The patriarchal powers burned down her sacred groves, raped and killed her priestesses, and enslaved wimmin. Her name was stricken from history books, and great darkness and ignorance descended upon womankind.[47]

Retrieving ancient devotion to the Goddess became an act of defiance in the face of oppressive conditions in modern America.

A similar movement that came later among men paralleled the interest in Goddess worship and the liberated views of women among Neopagan and New Age practitioners. Though not as widespread as the emphasis on women, the men's movement in the 1990s encouraged male followers to celebrate masculinity through explorations of male gods as role models as well as a reconfiguration of the warrior archetype that does not stress aggression and violence. Like feminist writers, leaders of the men's movement insisted that the patriarchal patterns of modern society were oppressive and limiting to everyone, both male and female.[48]

The critique of patriarchal society that proved appealing to women and men in Neopagan and New Age circles extended to sexuality as well. Adherents' tendency to celebrate the human body and a concern with healing often involve explorations of the connection between spirituality and human sexuality. In general, both Neopagans and New Age adherents tend to be more accepting and supportive of sexual diversity; one New Age leader explains, "Sex is energy. From this point of view there are no value judgments and there are no morals and no ethics about sex. What we're working towards here is unconditional acceptance of your own sexuality and, of course, unconditional acceptance of everyone else's sexuality."[49] This acceptance of sexuality, especially for Neopagans, sometimes includes participation in rituals of sacred sexual expression where cosmic forces are manifest in sexual unions. Borrowing freely and often loosely from certain Asian religious traditions, these ritual practices usually seek a mystical connection not only with one's sexual partner but also with the entire cosmos; as the Neopagan activist Starhawk (born 1951) explains, "Sexuality is sacred because it is a sharing of energy, in passionate surrender to the power of the Goddess, immanent in our desire. In orgasm, we share in the force that moves the stars."[50] The union of self, other, and the cosmos occurs, at least for some Neopagan and New Age enthusiasts, in the orgasmic union of sexual rituals that celebrate the sacredness of bodies.

The spiritual family

The feminist celebration of sacred bodies among Neopagan, New Age, and other religious groups did not translate immediately into a general shift in American attitudes regarding gender and sexuality. Despite increased public acceptance of feminist critics, not all women embraced the liberating claims of late twentieth-century feminism. Women across a variety of religious orientations, from fundamentalist Christians to Sunni Muslims to mainline Mormons and many others, continued to define their female identity in religious terms as wives and mothers. This does not necessarily mean that they simply defer to the authority of men in the absolute terms of patriarchal arrangements. As studies of female groups among evangelical Protestants and African American Sunni Muslims at the end of the twentieth century have shown, many conservative women do not regard submission to the patriarchal authority of husbands, fathers, and religious leaders as merely subordination but often seek within their religious traditions an affirmation of their specific roles of caring for family and teaching the values of their faith traditions to their children.[51]

A momentous development for both sides of the cultural debates over gender and sexuality in American society was the legalization of abortion in the *Roe v. Wade* court case. In 1973 the US Supreme Court ruled that the Fourteenth Amendment of the Constitution guarantees a woman's right to decide for herself whether or not to have an abortion.[52] The decision sparked widespread resistance among conservative women and provoked the political involvement of evangelical Christians, which influenced national politics for a generation. The divisive issue involving a woman's right to make her own reproductive choices on the one hand and the sanctity of a fetus' life on the other certainly motivated the political voices of many Americans not usually inclined to political involvement. At the same time, it resonated far beyond the legislative battles, court cases, and abortion clinic protests of the public debate. Attention to the decision of whether or not to terminate a pregnancy and the contentious arguments over who should make the decision and when turned a public eye to a very personal and private matter that included, among the myriad concerns at stake in the decision, the deepest levels of religious commitments and moral orientations.

Evangelical Protestants were not the first Americans to oppose the legalization of abortion in the late twentieth century; in fact, religious conservatives were among the early supporters of making abortions legal under certain circumstances. Early on it was the Roman Catholic Church that opposed the liberalization of state abortion laws; it argued against abortions in any circumstances in accord with the Church's official stance of "reverence for life," which also opposed capital punishment and unjust wars; for Catholic leaders, abortion was a human rights issue. Prior to the *Roe v. Wade* decision in 1973, Catholics were the main voice condemning abortion in America, with most conservative Americans, including the Republican political party and most Protestant groups, calling for more liberal policies toward abortion. Catholics had more sway with Democratic politicians, so liberalization of abortion first came in states with Republican leadership, with Governor Ronald Reagan

(1911–2004) endorsing a 1967 California law allowing abortions for women whose physical or mental health was in danger and Republican governors in Colorado and New York following suit. But, in a deliberate political strategy to win more Catholics to their party, Republicans reversed course on the abortion issue in the early 1970s. At the same time, a conservative backlash against feminism and more liberal social attitudes toward sexuality made the opposition to abortion appealing to groups beyond the Catholic Church. Once the Supreme Court loosened restrictions on abortions throughout the United States, conservatives across the religious spectrum made abortion a national issue, convincing Ronald Reagan to reverse his earlier support of abortion and ride the wave of "Christian right" activism to the White House.[53]

For evangelical Christians, the legalization of abortion struck at the heart of their understanding of gender roles, their attitudes about sexuality, and the prominence of family in evangelical culture. For them, the nineteenth-century valorization of woman as mother and wife survived as a central value. As a Southern Baptist official proclaimed in 1989, "The highest form of God's creation is womankind," and celebrations of women's identity tied to motherhood and to "the oft-maligned delights of homemaking" appear throughout evangelical literature and media representations of the late twentieth century. One evangelical woman wrote, "In many ways God measures a woman's success by her relationship with her husband and children. Many women ache to learn how to be truly successful in marriage and motherhood."[54] Such success, according to the preponderance of twentieth-century evangelical opinions, means adhering to traditional gender roles, reserving sexuality for procreative purposes, and valuing family above all other social institutions.

Concern over gender and sexuality among evangelical Christians in the late decades of the twentieth century also revived apprehensions about masculinity and the male role in the family. In the 1990s, football coach Bill McCartney (born 1940) initiated a movement of evangelical men known as Promise Keepers. By 1993 this movement had attracted fifty thousand men to fill the University of Colorado's football stadium in a Christian celebration that included heartfelt pledges to fulfill their roles as husbands, fathers, and church members. By the peak of the movement in 1996, more than a million men had attended twenty-two Promise Keepers rallies in stadiums across the United States. With a champion college football coach at its helm, the multi-million-dollar Promise Keepers organization reasserted men's prerogatives with athletic rhetoric in the all-male gatherings in major sports facilities; women were prohibited from attending but played supportive roles "praying and working behind the scenes." The primary message of the Promise Keepers was for husbands to reclaim their households; one leader urged men to sit down with their wives and tell them, "Honey, I've made a terrible mistake. I've given you my role. I gave up leading this family and I forced you to take my place. Now I must reclaim that role."[55] In retaking American households, the Promise Keepers movement sought to counter the gains of feminism and the shifting gender roles it initiated.

The Promise Keepers was a predominantly white male evangelical movement. African American leaders also expressed concerns about the status of men in

Figure 11.4   Protestant men gathered at Promise Keepers rallies across the United States in the 1990s to proclaim their faith in Jesus Christ and to reclaim their gendered roles as husbands, fathers, and church members. (Image © Brooks Kraft / Sygma / CORBIS.)

local communities, but their concern extended to negative racial stereotypes in addition to gender roles. Louis Farrakhan (born 1933), the controversial leader of the Nation of Islam, called for a Million Man March to Washington, DC, in October 1995. Although it brought something less than the million participants organizers hoped for, the rally successfully challenged negative stereotypes of violent and troubled black men while urging African American men to become politically involved and to revitalize their spiritual commitments. In a moving address that quoted both the Bible and the Qur'an, Farrakhan concluded with a prayer:

> That America may see that the slave has come up with power. The slave is been [*sic*] restored, delivered, and redeemed. And now call this nation to repentance. To acknowledge her wrongs. To confess … her faults before the world because her sins have affected the whole world. And perhaps, she may do some act of atonement, that you may forgive and those ill-affected may forgive, that reconciliation and restoration may lead us to the perfect union with thee and with each other.[56]

Tying the troubles of late twentieth-century America to the long history of racial strife, Farrakhan took an ecumenical stance to reclaim more than the lost gender roles that Christian Promise Keepers lamented; he urged participants in the Million Man March to overcome the differences in gender, race, class, and religion in repairing the history of divisions in American society that still plagued the nation at the end of the millennium.

As we consider the divisions between Americans that remained at the end of the century, we see that immigration introduced new ethnic and religious elements into the demographics of the nation while shifting attitudes about race, gender, and sexual orientation brought new conflicts for religious communities. Conservative religious organizations such as the Roman Catholic Church balked at granting greater authority for women; at the same time, new religious groups such as the Neopagans and New Age practitioners attracted members seeking greater spiritual autonomy unencumbered by constraints of gender or sexual norms imposed by traditional Church authorities. But greater freedoms in gender expectations and sexual orientations also engendered a reaction from conservative elements in American religious communities. This can be seen plainly in the debate over abortion; advocates for women's rights insist on the autonomy of a woman to decide whether or not to undergo an abortion, but conservative religious leaders and politicians have used a theological concern for the dignity of fetuses to resist greater autonomy for women. Related to the divide between religious Americans over abortion, the integrity of American families served as a unifying concern for conservative religious adherents by the end of the twentieth century. Groups such as the Promise Keepers and events such as the Million Man March reasserted the patriarchal role of men in reestablishing the family as the bedrock of American society and as the venue for spiritual fulfillment. These sorts of reactions to liberalized attitudes regarding gender attempted to revive traditional roles for men and women in society, and especially in families.

Spiritual Borderlands

In addition to conservative Protestants and black Muslims, a surge of immigrants from Mexico, Central and South America, the Caribbean, and elsewhere in the Spanish-speaking western hemisphere has brought other spiritual views of family values in America. By the end of the twentieth century, people identified as "Spanish/ Hispanic/Latino" by the US Census Bureau accounted for about 12.5 percent of the total US population, well on their way to overcoming African Americans as the largest minority group in the country.[57] Many of them had family roots in North America going back to colonial times, but their numbers have been greatly increased by new arrivals since the 1960s, with the largest group coming from Mexico. As this rapidly growing Hispanic population took up residence in cities, towns, and rural regions throughout the nation, the iconic Virgin Mary, the Mother of God in the particular form of the widely venerated Virgin de Guadalupe (Nuestra Señora de Guadalupe, or Our Lady of Guadalupe) became ubiquitous in the American religious landscape. Her presence encompasses both the historical and the contemporary relationships in the borderlands between the United States and Mexico.

Box 11.3   *Mestizaje*

For many observers, the Virgin of Guadalupe symbolizes the *mestizo*, or hybrid, nature of American societies. *Mestizo*, a Spanish adjective derived from the verb *mezclar*, which means "to mix" or "to blend," provides a useful description of Mexican American experience that can be extrapolated to other societies of the Americas in what the Roman Catholic theologian Virgilio Elizondo (born 1935) identifies as *mestizaje*, which he defines as "the process through which two totally different peoples mix biologically and culturally so that a new people begins to emerge."[58] It is precisely this process of mixing and blending that characterizes the cultural, and to a large extent the religious, history of America (for more about cultural and religious "blending," see Box 5.1).

Published in the last decade of the Cold War, Elizondo's theological work on *mestizaje* parallels the contemplations of Chicana poet and cultural theorist Gloria Anzaldúa (1942–2004), who describes "borderlands" as "physically present wherever two or more cultures edge each other, where people of different races occupy the same territory, where under, lower, middle, and upper classes touch, where the space between two individuals shrinks with intimacy."[59] Both the feminist poet and the Catholic theologian explore the displacements and the creative potentials of cultural hybridity. Elizondo's book includes an autobiographical element of his experience growing up in San Antonio, Texas, where culturally he realized that, although his family lived outside of Mexico, "Mexico was not outside of us." As a child, he had a growing awareness of the experience typical of Chicanos in the twentieth century, who were "always the distant and different 'other'"; Elizondo came to realize that he was neither a "regular U.S.-American" nor *"puro Mexicano,"* but instead, "I was a rich mixture but I was not mixed up!"[60]

Elizondo's theological account regards racial and cultural diversity as a strength of American society; he expresses optimism about the emergence of "a great common unity" that is not about homogeneity but about what he calls "a new mosaic of the human race." In Elizondo's estimation, the reforms of Vatican II that modernized the Roman Catholic Church in the 1960s were positive developments for generating a cultural *mestizaje*, which in turn will produce a religious *mestizaje*. He envisions a universal Christianity in the model of the Virgin of Guadalupe, who achieved a synthesis of Spanish Catholicism and indigenous religions of ancient Mesoamerican cultures.[61]

Virgilio Elizondo's theology has reinvigorated Mexican American Catholicism in the United States; his emphasis on *mestizaje* depicts the marginal experience of immigrants and Latino/a citizens as a cultural model for American society. On the other hand, as a Catholic priest and theologian,

Elizondo presents a story of Christian triumphalism in his celebration of diverse cultures in America; for him, the indigenous image of Guadalupe beckons the Native American Juan Diego and his indigenous cohorts to the ultimate truth of the Christian tradition rather than asserting the theological legitimacy of native understandings. Nevertheless, Elizondo's insights from his own experience as a Mexican American offered a decidedly hopeful outlook for the *mestizaje* of American society in the final decades of the twentieth century.

A spiritual patroness

The familiar image of Guadalupe, the Christian "Mother of God" recognized in her specifically Latina manifestation, stands serenely with her hands in a prayerful gesture, wearing a blue-green shawl adorned with stars, surrounded by a radiant halo and perched upon an upturned crescent above an angel grasping the hem of her cloak. She appears wherever devout Mexican and Mexican American Catholics gather; her likeness has become a staple of Catholic parishes throughout the United States that serve Latino/a parishioners.

Historically, the Virgin of Guadalupe emerged as a potent symbol of Mexican independence in the nineteenth-century nationalist struggle against Spanish colonial domination. Her spiritual power, however, exceeds Mexican and even Hispanic boundaries in her role as "Patroness of the Americas," a designation bestowed by the Catholic Pope in 1946; even non-Catholics recognize her significance as a cultural and political symbol. The symbolic value of Guadalupe, though, remains contestable, with various groups asserting contentious interpretations of her meaning. On the one hand, she represents a hopeful figure that celebrates the *mestizo*, hybrid nature of society; on the other hand, the Virgin of Guadalupe reflects the oppressive and patriarchal colonial legacy; she serves as a symbol of both domination and resistance. For her most devout followers, she bestows hope for deliverance from the hardships and perils of everyday life.

The story of the Virgin of Guadalupe situates her miraculous appearance to a Native American peasant in the early colonial period of New Spain in what is now central Mexico. Barely a decade after the Spanish conquest of Mexico, amid the oppressive brutality that the Spanish conquistadors brought to native populations as they took control of the region, an Indian who had converted to Christianity and adopted the Christian name of Juan Diego was walking to religious training classes on a Sunday morning in December 1531. As he crested the hill of Tepeyac, the traditional site of devotion to the Aztec goddess Tonantzin, he heard a voice beckoning him. A woman with skin dark like his own appeared in a halo of sunbeams radiating outward from her figure; she spoke to him in his native language, commanding him to go to the bishop and tell him that she wished for a hermitage

Figure 11.5 Devotional images of Nuestra Señora de Guadalupe, the Virgin of Guadalupe, can be found wherever Latino/a Catholics worship, as well as in homes, in businesses, and even in tattoos on the bodies of the faithful. This tiled version of the Guadalupe image appears in a niche at Mission San Gabriel near Los Angeles, California. (Photograph by the author.)

to be built on Tepeyac in her honor. Reluctantly Juan Diego visited the bishop, who at first rejected his appeal to honor the miraculous figure who had appeared to the lowly peasant; but, after two more encounters, the bishop was convinced when roses miraculously poured out of Juan Diego's cloak, revealing the colorful image of the Virgin imprinted on the inside of his tunic. The bishop ordered that a hermitage was to be built atop Tepeyac, and Juan Diego's cloak with the famous image of the Virgin of Guadalupe became an object of veneration there.[62] Although much developed over the centuries, the site at Tepeyac on the outskirts of Mexico City still houses the original image in a modern basilica that attracts millions of pilgrims each year.

Scholars, theologians, and others have debated the historical veracity of the tale of Juan Diego's encounter with the Virgin Mary atop the hill of Tepeyac in 1531. But, regardless of whether or not an actual supernatural occurrence took place there in the sixteenth century, the social, political, and cultural reality of the Virgin of Guadalupe cannot be denied; her image has served both colonial and revolutionary causes, as well as both patriarchal and feminist views of womanhood. The Virgin of Guadalupe has been a powerful political symbol and an intimate source of personal consolation, as both religious icon and commodified brand. In the borderland territories of the modern world, Nuestra Señora de Guadalupe reigns as the ubiquitous patroness of Chicana/o identity.

In fact, the image of the Virgin of Guadalupe appears nearly everywhere in Hispanic America, especially in relation to people of Mexican descent. In one example, devotion takes on highly personal dimensions in the tradition of *altaristas*, Mexican American women who maintain elaborate home altars. These configurations of devotional images and personal items express the *altarista's* personal relationships with deities, saints, ancestors, and other characters important in the curator's life. Special attention to the Virgin of Guadalupe often entails an assertion of maternal power; as one longtime keeper of a home altar in Texas explained, "I have my Virgin of Guadalupe [on my altar] because She is the protectoress of all us Mexicans. ... She is a mother of the best kind for us."[63] Operating outside Church institutional structures, the *altaristas* reinterpret the religious imagery with meanings that emphasize their personal needs and experiences. In particular, as one scholar has noted, maintaining these domestic shrines integrates spiritual practices with maternal practices; in short, their altars represent "a sacred validation of mothering."[64]

The maternal aspect of the Virgin of Guadalupe elicits a different set of interpretations from feminist critics, who object to the heavily patriarchal renderings of Guadalupe as an ideal woman whose motherly role confines women to the home. As a Catholic saint, the Virgin of Guadalupe has faithfully served the patriarchal structures of the Church. But Chicana feminists have claimed Guadalupe as their own in challenging these patriarchal structures. For many of these later interpreters of the Virgin's significance, she reigns as the Aztec goddess Tonantzin rather than Mary of Nazareth, the mother of Jesus Christ. In opposition to traditional Catholic interpretations of Guadalupe, Chicana scholars, authors, artists, and other intellectuals have depicted her as a potent symbol of feminine empowerment. In particular, she signifies female sexuality; writer Sandra Cisneros (born 1954) argues that Latina women have been confined by a "double chastity belt of ignorance and *vergüenza*, shame," but she regards the Virgin as "Guadalupe the sex goddess, a goddess who makes me feel good about my sexual power, my sexual energy," empowering Cisneros to write from her specific experience as a woman, to "write from my *panocha* [vulva]."[65] This image of the Virgin of Guadalupe as an icon of empowering sexuality extends as well to sexual orientation; writer Carla Trujillo (birth date unknown) imagines her as a lesbian partner; in Trujillo's reimagining of the holy mother, Guadalupe becomes accepting of all people, including those of a non-heterosexual orientation. These sorts of interpretations attempt to realign the spiritual and the sexual, which patriarchal traditions have separated.[66]

Like many religious symbols in the contested arenas of gender and sexuality, the Virgin of Guadalupe has been used both for progressive attitudes of greater freedom and as a stalwart of conservative commitments to more traditional roles and practices. As a potent icon of spiritual power, the Virgin empowers multiple sides in the contentious struggles of American religions at both the personal and public levels.

Spiritual healing

For both the more conventional interpretations of Guadalupe in the domestic contexts of the *altaristas* and the more critical renderings of feminists, healing remains a key dimension of Latino/a popular spirituality. An ancient tradition of *curanderismo*, or curing practices, continues with local *curanderas* (folk healing specialists), who can be found in many predominantly Hispanic areas in *botánicas*, stores that sell a variety of spiritual items and supplies for practitioners of folk healing. Although usually displaying characteristic signs of Catholicism, such as images of the Virgin of Guadalupe and other saints, the *curanderismo* tradition combines Catholicism with indigenous healing practices that go back to ancient Mexico. Many practitioners demonstrate a sophisticated knowledge of anatomy and physiology, and most value modern medicine, often referring their clients to medical doctors. But some maladies have supernatural causes that modern medicine cannot treat; for these, one can find help with a *curandera*. The Catholic Church discourages their practices, although most who seek their services are Catholics; most know the Church's attitude, regarding *curanderismo* as contrary to Church doctrine, but they see their choice to seek the services of a *curandera* as a matter of personal conscience and not sinful.[67]

Of course, not all Latinos/as belong to the Catholic Church; the variety of religious orientations among Hispanic Americans parallels religious diversity among other Americans. And, though Catholicism remains by far the most dominant religion of Latinos/as, the rise of Pentecostalism in the twentieth century has made a significant impact among Spanish-speaking Americans. Much like the folk Catholicism of *curanderismo*, Pentecostal churches have a long tradition of religious healing, which accounts in large part for Pentecostalism's success among Latino/a followers. In the early part of the twentieth century, Latino/a Pentecostal evangelists such as Francisco Olazábal (1886–1937) led revivals in *barrios* (predominantly Hispanic urban neighborhoods) and rural *colonias* (encampments of migrant workers) that resulted in significant numbers of converts and the establishment of Latino/a Pentecostal churches in Los Angeles, El Paso, Houston, San Antonio, Chicago, the Spanish Harlem sector of New York City, and Nogales,

Arizona. Their success came largely from the Pentecostal strategy of combining instances of faith healing with evangelizing. Olazábal's efforts included the formation of the Interdenominational Mexican Council of Christian Churches (Pentecostal) in 1923 after he left the Assemblies of God because of racist attitudes that limited his leadership there; later, his ecumenical endeavors led to the founding of the Latin American Council of Christian Churches. Olazábal's **charismatic** leadership and his miraculous feats of divine healing gave Pentecostalism a solid foundation among Latinos/as, making it the largest Protestant orientation among Latinos/as in the United States.[68]

Even as the promises of healing coupled with aggressive evangelism allowed Pentecostals to make significant inroads among Hispanics, a resurgence of devotion and a revival of folk traditions in many Latino/a Catholic communities during the closing decades of the twentieth century brought more visibility to the religious lives of Spanish-speaking immigrants in the United States. Images of the Virgin of Guadalupe can be seen in Catholic parishes across the nation, and many churches, both Catholic and Protestant, have weekly Spanish-language religious services. But, beyond the official confines of church, spiritual concerns resonate in bilingual, hybrid forms that reflect the *mestizo* reality of religions in America.

Religious America

As numerous studies have repeatedly shown, new immigrants since 1965 have significantly altered the religious landscape of the United States. People living according to religious orientations stemming from Latin America, Asia, and Africa now reside across the land alongside those professing faith in the various Abrahamic religions, dominated by Christianity, as well as the many traditions of Native Americans, which have roots older than the earliest colonial settlements in the Americas. Indeed, by the end of the twentieth century, assumptions about religion and America, especially regarding what constitutes "American," had become excessively complicated. As a place of intense contact, borrowing, mixing, and selective experimentation in the many spiritual practices and beliefs found in the country, America had become a *mestizo* nation of religious eclecticism.

This eclectic tendency in the spirituality of late twentieth-century America contributed to a profitable industry of religious pursuits and paraphernalia. Religions of all kinds everywhere have significant economic entanglements, and the consumer culture of twentieth-century America has been no exception. The acknowledged queen of religious marketing has been Oprah Winfrey, whose "Live Your Best Life" TV enterprise never hesitated to sell accessories for spiritual fulfillment. At the same time, with an occasional promotional nudge from Oprah and other entrepreneurial spirits, South Asian spiritual practices have translated into a multi-billion-dollar yoga industry. Not to be left behind, conservative Christians have capitalized as well on marketing to the faithful, with best-selling books, movies, television programs, and innumerable items for devotional practice. By the end of the millennium, religion had become a profitable enterprise.

Finding profit in religion, of course, can have a dark side when it comes to the appropriation, exploitation, and outright thievery of other peoples' sacred objects, places, and traditions. The history of colonial domination, which included attempts to eradicate Native American religions, has also involved the collection of indigenous cultural objects, especially religious items; much of the cultural bounty seized by non-native peoples has been taken from holy sites, often from graves, and a good amount of this has ended up in museums and a variety of anthropological collections, both public and private. In an attempt to rectify the legacy of colonial defilement of Native American cultures, in 1990 the United States enacted the Native American Graves Protection and Repatriation Act to protect graves located on federal lands and to facilitate the return of human remains and certain cultural items that have been held in federally funded institutions. The law has instigated the return of thousands of objects, and it has guided the handling of newly found graves. On the other hand, competing claims by multiple Native American groups compounded by the inability to conclusively identify the cultural affiliation of many of the remains has made enforcement of the law contentious.[69] Nevertheless, the act affords some protections to the sacred legacy of native peoples throughout the United States.

Native Americans have not been the only people attempting to rectify religious wrongs. As might be expected from the long history of **nativist** attitudes in America, many of the new immigrants have faced some degree of inhospitality, and even outright persecution in some cases, for their religious traditions. One example of this reached the US Supreme Court in 1993; it involved a Santería community called the Church of Lukumi Babalu Aye in Hialeah, Florida. An Afro-Caribbean religion originating in Cuba, Santería's rituals involve the sacrifice of a live chicken. Other citizens of the Florida community not familiar with such practices expressed fears of what many of them regarded as a "regress into paganism"; to appease the residents who were fearful of their new neighbors, the city council passed an ordinance banning all animal sacrifices. The Santeríans realized that the new law was aimed at criminalizing their religious traditions, and they challenged it in the federal courts; as one astute observer noted, "An animal can be killed for any reason in Hialeah, except for religious and ceremonial ones. You can boil lobsters alive; feed live rats to pet snakes; kill for food or for sport; slaughter unwanted pets in your front yard – as long as you do not perform a ritual while doing so." Singling out a particular religious group without any justification other than to prevent the free exercise of their religion seemed an affront to the First Amendment of the US Constitution. The Supreme Court justices agreed when they ruled unanimously to nullify Hialeah's animal sacrifice ordinance.[70]

Not only Santeríans but also members of more widely familiar religious groups have encountered difficulties when they have taken controversial stances. Religious people who affirm non-heterosexual orientations, for instance, have often encountered resistance and sometimes outright hostility from their coreligionists. For example, in 1993 when Congregation Beth Simchat Torah of New York City, the largest Jewish synagogue in the United States welcoming gay and lesbian members, sought to participate in New York City's annual Salute to Israel parade, organizers denied their request, allowing homophobic voices within the Jewish community to prevail. Supporters of Congregation Beth Simchat Torah subsequently organized an alternative event at Central Synagogue near the parade route, and many of the city's politicians acknowledged the legitimacy of the gay synagogue by appearing at both celebrations.[71] Despite the backlash of those committed to heteronormativity, people of all sexual orientations have asserted the legitimacy of their religious commitments and passions.

The controversies and difficulties that religious people encountered in the closing years of the twentieth century remind us again of the limitations of pluralism. Changing demographics resulting from more liberal immigration policies have undoubtedly complicated the religious scene in America. Likewise, the proliferation of spiritual practices operating outside traditional religious structures and institutions has introduced new approaches to religion in America; a distinction between "spiritual" and "religious" became more common among Americans critical of institutional forms of religion who nevertheless wished to pursue a meaningful spirituality in their personal lives. Yet, despite the increasing diversity of spiritual perspectives and religious affiliations at the turn of the twenty-first century, still more than eighty percent of Americans professed a Christian faith.[72] A good number of these faithful followers of Jesus Christ regarded the United States as a Christian nation, and at least a few of them actively resisted any developments that would suggest otherwise. America had become a more welcoming place for people of differing religious orientations, but dangers still lurked for those who followed many of the diverse traditions that had come to flourish on American soil.

Questions for Discussion

(1)   How is spirituality different from religion?
(2)   In what ways has immigration since 1965 changed the religious makeup of the United States?
(3)   Feminists in the closing decades of the twentieth century have criticized many religious traditions for their disregard of women. What are some of the ways that women have responded to feminist critiques of religions?
(4)   Using the examples of men's religious movements among Neopagan and New Age practitioners, as well as the Promise Keepers and the Million Man March, discuss how feminist views have also influenced attention to masculinity.

(5)   To what extent have religious traditions become profitable economically? Include examples of how religions have entered the commercial marketplace.

(6)   Some Americans still regarded America as a Christian nation at the end of the twentieth century. Were they justified in thinking of America in this way? Explain why or why not.

Suggested Primary-Source Readings

Buntwal N. Somayaji, "Sri Ganesha Temple, Nashville, Recounting History and Nurturing Youth (1985–95)," in *Asian Religions in America: A Documentary History*, ed. Thomas A. Tweed and Stephen R. Prothero (New York: Oxford University Press, 1999), 299–303: A leader of the Hindu temple in Nashville recounts the early history of this cultural center for Indian immigrants, which is typical of similar temples built in many American communities in the final decades of the twentieth century.

Mary Daly, *The Church and the Second Sex* (Boston, MA: Beacon Press, 1985): This feminist theologian's first book, originally published in 1968, criticizes the Catholic Church's pervasive sexism.

Starhawk, *The Spiral Dance: A Rebirth of the Ancient Religion of the Great Goddess*, 20th anniversary edn (San Francisco, CA: HarperSanFrancisco, 1999): This influential book of Neopagan belief and practice, first published in 1979, emphasizes Goddess worship and has become a canonical text among many Neopagans.

Louis Farrakhan, transcript of remarks at the Million Man March, October 16, 1995, available online from CNN at www.cnn.com/US/9510/megamarch/10-16/transcript/index.html: The leader of the Nation of Islam addressed the crowd of African American men who had gathered in Washington, DC, for a massive show of solidarity to bring issues of justice, economic disparities, and racial prejudice to public attention.

Virgilio P. Elizondo, *The Future Is Mestizo: Life Where Cultures Meet*, rev. edn (Boulder: University Press of Colorado, 2000): A leading Mexican American theologian reflects on his experience in his native San Antonio, Texas, to propose a theology of *mestizaje*.

Notes

1   Quoted in Kathryn Lofton, *Oprah: The Gospel of an Icon* (Berkeley: University of California Press, 2011), 4.
2   Quoted in ibid., 8.
3   Ibid., 194–195.
4   Robert Wuthnow, *After Heaven: Spirituality in America since the 1950s* (Berkeley: University of California Press, 1998), vii–viii.
5   Courtney Bender, *The New Metaphysicals: Spirituality and the American Religious Imagination* (Chicago, IL: University of Chicago Press, 2010), 5–6.
6   Ibid., 23.
7   Lofton, *Oprah*, 5–7.
8   Ibid., 134.

9   Diana L. Eck, *A New Religious America: How a "Christian Country" Has Now Become the World's Most Religiously Diverse Nation* (San Francisco, CA: HarperSanFrancisco, 2001), 1–5.

10   Ibid., 5; Karen McCarthy Brown, "Staying Grounded in a High-Rise Building: Ecological Dissonance and Ritual Accommodation in Haitian Vodou," in *Gods of the City: Religion and the American Urban Landscape*, ed. Robert A. Orsi (Bloomington: Indiana University Press, 1999), 79–80.

11   Vasudha Narayanan, "Sacred Land, Sacred Service: Hindu Adaptations to the American Landscape," in *A Nation of Religions: The Politics of Pluralism in Multireligious America*, ed. Stephen R. Prothero (Chapel Hill: University of North Carolina Press, 2006), 140.

12   Eck, *A New Religious America*, 3.

13   Gurinder Singh Mann, "Making Home Abroad: Sikhs in the United States," in *A Nation of Religions: The Politics of Pluralism in Multireligious America*, ed. Stephen R. Prothero (Chapel Hill: University of North Carolina Press, 2006), 166–168.

14   Joanne Punzo Waghorne, "The Hindu Gods in a Split-Level World: The Sri Siva-Vishnu Temple in Suburban Washington, DC," in *Gods of the City: Religion and the American Urban Landscape*, ed. Robert A. Orsi (Bloomington: Indiana University Press, 1999), 111–116.

15   Ibid., 121–124.

16   Hien Duc Do, "Reproducing Vietnam in America: San Jose's Perfect Harmony Temple," in *A Nation of Religions: The Politics of Pluralism in Multireligious America*, ed. Stephen R. Prothero (Chapel Hill: University of North Carolina Press, 2006), 82–84.

17   Ibid., 79–90.

18   Charles S. Prebish and Kenneth Kenichi Tanaka, eds., *The Faces of Buddhism in America* (Berkeley: University of California Press, 1998), 5–6.

19   From *A TM Catechism* (1975), quoted in Thomas A. Tweed and Stephen R. Prothero, eds., *Asian Religions in America: A Documentary History* (New York: Oxford University Press, 1999), 242.

20   Ibid., 241.

21   E. Burke Rochford, *Hare Krishna Transformed* (New York: New York University Press, 2007), 9–12.

22   Ibid., 12–14.

23   Ibid., 1–15.

24   Stefanie Syman, *The Subtle Body: The Story of Yoga in America* (New York: Farrar, Straus and Giroux, 2010), 9.

25   These numbers were reported in a 2012 study by Sports Marketing Surveys USA on behalf of *Yoga Journal*, available from the *Yoga Journal* blog at http://blogs.yogajournal. com/yogabuzz/2012/12/new-study-find-more-than-20-million-yogis-in-u-s.html (accessed August 12, 2013).

26   Syman, *The Subtle Body*, 3–4.

27   Ibid., 4; Tweed and Prothero, *Asian Religions in America*, 15.

28   Syman, *The Subtle Body*, 37–61.

29   Quoted in Tweed and Prothero, *Asian Religions in America*, 182–185.

30   Syman, *The Subtle Body*, 172.

31   Ibid., 5–6.

32 Ibid., 274–278.

33 Prebish and Tanaka, *Faces of Buddhism*, 4 and Tweed and Prothero, *Asian Religions in America*, 161.

34 Quoted in Tweed and Prothero, *Asian Religions in America*, 229.

35 Alan Watts, *The Way of Zen* (New York: Vintage, 1999), ix.

36 Prebish and Tanaka, *Faces of Buddhism*, 5.

37 Sandy Boucher, *Turning the Wheel: American Women Creating the New Buddhism*, updated and expanded edn (Boston, MA: Beacon Press, 1993), 2–3.

38 Ibid., 22.

39 Rick Fields, "Divided Dharma: White Buddhists, Ethnic Buddhists, and Racism," in *The Faces of Buddhism in America*, ed. Charles S. Prebish and Kenneth Kenichi Tanaka (Berkeley: University of California Press, 1998), 199.

40 The essay "Waking Up to Racism" by bell hooks appeared in the Buddhist magazine *Tricycle* in 1994; it is reprinted in Tweed and Prothero, *Asian Religions in America*, 277–281.

41 Ann Braude, *Sisters and Saints: Women and American Religion* (New York: Oxford University Press, 2008), 95–97.

42 Sarah M. Pike, *New Age and Neopagan Religions in America* (New York: Columbia University Press, 2006), 118.

43 Ibid., 19.

44 Ibid., 22–23.

45 Ibid., 20.

46 Ibid., 119.

47 This quotation from writer Zsuzsanna Budapest appears in ibid., 120.

48 Ibid., 134–135.

49 Quoted in ibid., 137.

50 Quoted in ibid., 140.

51 Rebecca L. Davis, "Family," in *The Blackwell Companion to Religion in America*, ed. Philip Goff (Malden, MA: Wiley Blackwell, 2010), 125.

52 For the history of abortion in America and the aftermath of the Supreme Court decision, see N. E. H. Hull and Peter Charles Hoffer, *Roe v. Wade: The Abortion Rights Controversy in American History* (Lawrence: University Press of Kansas, 2001).

53 Daniel K. Williams, "The GOP's Abortion Strategy: Why Pro-Choice Republicans Became Pro-Life in the 1970s," *Journal of Policy History* 23, no. 4 (2011).

54 Randall Herbert Balmer, *Blessed Assurance: A History of Evangelicalism in America* (Boston, MA: Beacon Press, 1999), 72–73.

55 Ibid., 84–91.

56 The transcript of Louis Farrakhan's speech at the Million Man March is available online at www.cnn.com/US/9510/megamarch/10-16/transcript/index.html (accessed January 17, 2014).

57 See Betsy Guzmán, "The Hispanic Population: Census 2000 Brief" from the US Census Bureau (May, 2001), available online at www.census.gov/prod/2001pubs/c2kbr01-3.pdf (accessed March 7, 2014).

58 Virgilio P. Elizondo, *The Future Is Mestizo: Life Where Cultures Meet*, rev. edn (Boulder: University Press of Colorado, 2000), 17, footnote.

59   Gloria Anzaldúa, *Borderlands/La Frontera: The New Mestiza* (San Francisco, CA: Aunt Lute Book Co., 1987), vii.

60   Elizondo, *The Future Is Mestizo*, 12–26.

61   Ibid., 102–107.

62   Socorro Castañeda-Liles, "Our Lady of Guadalupe and the Politics of Cultural Interpretation," in *Mexican American Religions: Spirituality, Activism, and Culture*, ed. Gastón Espinosa and Mario T. García (Durham, NC: Duke University Press, 2008), 155–157.

63   Quoted in Kay Turner, "*Voces De Fe*: Mexican American *Altaristas* in Texas," in *Mexican American Religions: Spirituality, Activism, and Culture*, ed. Gastón Espinosa and Mario T. García (Durham, NC: Duke University Press, 2008), 185.

64   Ibid., 182.

65   Cisneros' essay appears in Ana Castillo, ed., *Goddess of the Americas: Writings on the Virgin of Guadalupe* (New York: Riverhead Books, 1997).

66   Castañeda-Liles, "Our Lady of Guadalupe," 169–170.

67   Luis D. León, "Borderlands Bodies and Souls: Mexican Religious Healing Practices in East Los Angeles," in *Mexican American Religions: Spirituality, Activism, and Culture*, ed. Gastón Espinosa and Mario T. García (Durham, NC: Duke University Press, 2008).

68   Gastón Espinosa, "Brown Moses: Francisco Olazábal and Mexican American Pentecostal Healing in the Borderlands," in *Mexican American Religions: Spirituality, Activism, and Culture*, ed. Gastón Espinosa and Mario T. García (Durham, NC: Duke University Press, 2008).

69   For an in-depth study of disputes regarding the act in Hawaii, see Greg Johnson, *Sacred Claims: Repatriation and Living Tradition* (Charlottesville: University of Virginia Press, 2007).

70   Eric Michael Mazur, *The Americanization of Religious Minorities: Confronting the Constitutional Order* (Baltimore, MD: Johns Hopkins University Press, 1999), 1–3.

71   Moshe Shokeid, *A Gay Synagogue in New York* (Philadelphia: University of Pennsylvania Press, 2003), 3–4.

72   Source: Gallup Poll historical trends data available online at www.gallup.com/poll/1690/religion.aspx (accessed September 19, 2013).

12

Crossing Borders

A short final chapter reflects on our studies of American religious history from the perspective of the twenty-first century. As we look forward from the perspective of a post-9/11 world, we can consider how the various critical terms and interpretive concepts introduced in previous chapters might help us not only to understand the past of American religious history but also to make sense of the present and to think about the future.

The nation awoke to unimaginable horror coming from the crystal-clear skies over the eastern part of the country on the morning of September 11, 2001. On television screens everywhere people watched in shock as first one and then another jetliner slammed into the twin towers of the World Trade Center in New York City. News cameras recorded the burning of the two buildings and their subsequent collapse in the financial district of the nation's largest city, while reports came in of a third plane that crashed into the Pentagon building in Washington, DC, and still another that came down in a rural area of Pennsylvania. America was under attack.

Very quickly, the terrorist aggression of 9/11 was characterized as a religious act. Media reports identified the perpetrators as Muslim terrorists, igniting public debates regarding Islam and the presence of Muslims in America. At least a few Americans came to believe that Muslims were the enemies of Christendom, as numerous leaders among **evangelical** Christians condemned the religion of Muhammad as a fundamentally violent faith.[1] Others sounded a cautionary note; many leaders warned against identifying all of Islam with the actions of a few extremists who claimed to be acting as Muslims. Even George W. Bush (born 1946), president of the United States and a self-proclaimed Christian evangelical, reassured Muslims of the world, "We respect your faith. ... Its teachings are good

Formed From This Soil: An Introduction to the Diverse History of Religion in America, First Edition. Thomas S. Bremer.
© 2015 Thomas S. Bremer. Published 2015 by John Wiley & Sons, Ltd.

and peaceful, and those who commit evil in the name of Allah blaspheme the name of Allah."[2] Islam was not to blame, the president insisted; this was the work of terrorists.

The emotional impact of the 9/11 attacks seemed to unify the disparate peoples of the nation in a collective moment of grieving. A particularly memorable occasion of unity involved the prayer service at Yankee Stadium in New York City, which brought together national leaders, celebrities, and representatives of diverse religious groups, all led by Oprah Winfrey (born 1954) serving as master of ceremonies. In a service interspersed with prayers and music, both sacred and patriotic, religious leaders representing Greek Orthodox, Hindus, Jews, Muslims, Protestant Christians, Roman Catholics, and Sikhs remembered the victims of terrorism on 9/11. At the beginning of the service, actor James Earl Jones (born 1931) proclaimed:

> We are united not only in our grief, but also in our resolve to build a better world. At this service we seek to summon what Abraham Lincoln called "the better angels of our nature" in recognition that this was not just an attack on the city of New York or the United States of America, but on the very idea of a free, inclusive, and civil society. To people around the world, our nation is a symbol of liberty, equal opportunity, democracy, and diversity.

Imam Izak-El M. Pasha (birth date unknown), the Muslim chaplain for the New York City Police Department, reminded the crowd that the many Muslims who call America their home love their nation and have felt the losses of 9/11 as profoundly as anyone; "We are Muslims," he declared, "but we are Americans." Oprah Winfrey, as America's "Live Your Best Life" priestess, used the occasion to urge everyone "to turn up the volume in our own lives, to create deeper meanings, to know what really matters: what really matters is who you love and how you love."[3]

The appearance of America's diverse religious people together on the podium in Yankee Stadium; the heartfelt messages of unity, pride, and love; the occasion of collective grieving did not inspire benevolence in everyone. Critical voices of religious leaders with less capacious views of the American nation spoke in condemnation of allowing the participation of "pagan religions." The Missouri Synod of the Lutheran Church, the conservative evangelical faction of Lutherans in America, suspended their New York bishop following his appearance in the prayer service. An official for the Church explained, "To participate with pagans in an interfaith service and, additionally, to give the impression that there might be more than one God, is an extremely serious offense." Although the bishop was later reinstated, anger over his participation serves as a reminder of the limits of religious pluralism in the American nation.[4]

The limits of pluralism also took a violent turn. In particular, Muslims and others mistaken for Muslims suffered numerous attacks, some of them deadly; according to the Federal Bureau of Investigation, there was a 1700 percent increase

Figure 12.1   Religious leaders and political luminaries along with Master of Ceremonies Oprah Winfrey (front row, left) join hands on the stage at New York's Yankee Stadium while the Harlem Boys and Girls Choir sing "We Shall Overcome" during the memorial service "A Prayer for America" on September 23, 2001. (Courtesy of NY Daily News via Getty Images.)

in hate crimes against Muslim Americans between 2000 and 2001.[5] Sikhs were also targeted, as their familiar turbans fed mistaken stereotypes about Muslims; the Sikh Coalition, a national organization advocating civil and human rights, documented over three hundred instances of violence and discrimination against Sikh people in the first month following the 9/11 attacks.[6] Just four days after the terrorism in New York City, an attack in Arizona killed a forty-nine-year-old Sikh; the attacker had assumed his victim was Muslim, and told police when he was arrested, "I'm a patriot and an American."[7]

The contrary reactions in the wake of the 9/11 terrorist attacks, with violence on the one hand and the celebration of religious diversity and freedom on the other, remind us of the complexities of religion in America. In an uncanny reversal of history, America in the twenty-first century is revisiting the circumstances that brought Europeans to the Americas in the fifteenth century. Recalling the colonial **Atlantic world** that we encountered in Chapter 1, rivalry between Christians and Muslims inspired explorers such as Christopher Columbus (1451–1506) to seek alternative routes to Asia; among the many motivating factors involved in his voyages, Columbus himself revealed his desire to recapture Jerusalem from the Muslims. At the turn of the twenty-first century, one group of extremist Muslims sought to recapture Jerusalem from non-Muslims. Associated with the al-Qaeda militant organization, the 9/11 terrorists operated under the religious rhetoric of a *fatwa*, a religious edict, which the al-Qaeda leader Osama bin Laden (1957–2011) had issued in 1998 to justify attacks on what he regarded as a degenerate society that perpetuated persecutions and suffering among Muslims worldwide. In particular, his pronouncement stated:

> the ruling to kill the Americans and their allies – civilians and military – is an individual duty for every Muslim who can do it in any country in which it is possible to do it, in order to liberate the al-Aqsa Mosque [in Jerusalem] and the holy mosque [in Mecca] from their grip, and in order for their armies to move out of the lands of Islam.[8]

Certainly, the terrorists provoked responses from Christian extremists in America. But many more Americans realized that the political views of hate groups who perpetuate violence did not represent the opinions of the vast majority of Muslims. Most Americans, from the president on down, affirmed that Muslims had an irrefutable place in America, a view confirmed in the historical record; indeed, the very first Europeans in North America brought Muslims with them, and there has been a Muslim presence ever since, albeit nearly invisible until the twentieth century. Muslims belong in America as much as anyone.

In fact, most Americans affirm that nearly every religion in the world today has a rightful claim to America. The diversity of religions in the United States has been "formed from this soil," in the poetic words of Walt Whitman (1819–1892); there are traditions in the nation today from virtually all areas of the world, and most have been refashioned in the contact zones of America. They include the spiritual traditions and religious institutions of Native Americans, Europeans, Africans, Asians, Arabs, the people of Oceania, and elsewhere. Through the continuing contacts and interactions on American soil, in the tensions experienced in efforts to preserve traditions while adapting to new conditions, these religions have become distinctly American. At the same time, the trajectory of American religious history is taking these dynamic forces of religious contact, conflict, and exchange into a world of global proportions. American religions are everywhere, even as all of the world's religions have made America what it has become.

Rethinking America and Religion

The American nation has become more difficult to define in the twenty-first century. Recalling the discussion at the beginning of this book, America is more than its geographical boundaries, its political and legal structures of democracy, or

Box 12.1   Globalization

Religion in America is no longer confined to the United States. Certainly, religious people in the Americas have always crossed borders, not only geographical boundaries but also cultural, linguistic, social, political, and economic borders. At the beginning of the twenty-first century, however, these processes of religious encounter and exchange have reached global proportions; people of the Americas have carried their religious orientations and practices throughout the settled world, while religious traditions from virtually all of the world's societies and cultures have in one manner or another found their way into America. This so-called "globalization" of religions parallels trends in economics and politics that researchers in the social sciences have identified. Indeed, recent studies demonstrate that the world's cultures, economies, and political systems are intimately linked in a worldwide process of globalization.

One influential definition regards globalization as the "intensification of worldwide social relations which link distant localities in such a way that local happenings are shaped by events occurring many miles away and vice versa."[9] This view emphasizes social relationships, especially economic and political, that cross national borders and have consequences for local people. Other scholars go even further to suggest that globalization represents the wholesale erasure of borders and relationships of power; this more radical interpretation regards globalization "as utter fragmentation, fluidity, and ephemerality." The impacts of these processes and tendencies have a variety of consequences. Those who benefit the most from globalization tend to see it in positive terms, as the triumph of free-enterprise capitalism, while critics regard globalization as an insidious process of imperialism that results in the homogenization of cultures and the exploitation of local communities.[10]

Regardless of whether scholars assess the consequences of globalization in positive, negative, or neutral terms, most agree that in the twenty-first century the world's people have become more interconnected with each other at multiple levels. Moreover, these connections include what some scholars have called a "time–space compression," involving ever-increasing immediacy of contacts, interactions, and exchanges between peoples far removed from each other.[11] In short, over the course of several decades, especially with the ubiquity of electronic media, the world has become a much smaller place with instantaneous communications.

Globalization has had implications for the study of religions. Not least has been an emphasis on religious mobility and the transnational identities of religious individuals and communities. With religions no longer confined only to local conditions with identifiable communities who interact face to face, studies of religions in globalized contexts must account for displacements and long-distance connections of religious communities. Scholars also have begun to rethink ideas of sacred space and religious geographies in a world consisting of global networks. In this regard, the concept of "glocalization," or "global localization," has been used to better understand the link between global movements and local communities, as well as that between the universal claims of a religious tradition and the particular experiences of local individuals and groups. Specifically, glocalization refers to the ways that the global becomes the local as people on the ground use and reinterpret universal claims to fit their actual circumstances; this in turn contributes new dimensions to the more abstract universal claims. In a dialectic process between the global and local, the universal becomes relevant in terms of the particular.[12]

its ideological values. American culture of all sorts can now be found virtually everywhere in the world; American films, literature, art, sports, technological innovations, foods, clothing, and countless consumer items have found their way to every continent. At the same time, much of what people regard as "American" originated elsewhere and came to America through immigration, through trade, and by other means in a world now subject to the forces of globalization. The borders between America and the rest of the world become less clear with every passing decade.

The view of America in the twenty-first century as a part of a globalized world economy has implications for religion. On the one hand, religion can justify and facilitate the expansion of global networks. As it has in many of the historical contexts we have studied, religion in the twenty-first-century world can serve as justification for dominating other peoples. On the other hand, similarly to the transculturation strategies that colonized groups adopted in early colonial settings, religion can also serve to resist and subvert processes of globalization; over and over again local people appeal to religious resources to challenge the imposition of global needs and the displacements that globalization often entails.

The various uses of religion in both facilitating and resisting globalization raise again the question of what we mean by "religion." We have explored throughout this book various ways of viewing things deemed religious without resorting to the futile undertaking of defining the term "religion." Thus, we have used conventional, uncritical understandings of religion to introduce particular religious traditions such as the Abrahamic religions of Judaism, Christianity, and Islam as well as religions of Asian origin such as Hinduism, Buddhism, and Sikhism. We also have paid attention to indigenous "tribal" religions of the Americas and Africa, plus syncretistic religions such as the Afro-Caribbean traditions that come from the colonial circumstances of the Atlantic world. But alongside these conventional views of religion we have considered a number of critical terms and interpretive concepts for expanding how we might regard religions and interpret their role and significance in the Americas. From contact zones and transculturation to syncretism and spirituality, we have employed critical tools to look at religions in less conventional ways. Moreover, attention to questions of religious authority, of racial and gender differences, of sexual orientation and socioeconomic class status, have all added to our historical interpretations of religions in America.

All of these various perspectives on what we might call religion, including an acknowledgment of the globalized contexts of religion in the twenty-first century, can contribute to critical interpretations of the 9/11 events. Not only can we consider them as yet another moment in the long historical narrative of religions in America but also our studies have given us critical tools for exploring the particular significance and implications of the terrorist attacks themselves as well as the subsequent responses to the assault on the American nation. Some of the critical concepts are directly relevant to the terrorists' actions. For instance, we can consider 9/11 as an instance of violent encounter in modern contact zones; we might pay attention to the authority of the fundamentalist religious rhetoric of the perpetrators and their supporters; other analyses could ask about the role of **providential** assumptions on the part of the terrorists or how millenarianist logic might be operative in the terrorists' plot to rid the world of perceived evil forces. In regard to the memorial service at Yankee Stadium, concepts of civil religion, pluralism, and even spirituality seem useful approaches for interpreting the event. Similarly, the patriotic force of civil religion might prove helpful in understanding the proliferation of hate crimes against Muslims, Sikhs, and others, as well as how **nativist** sentiments and racial attitudes contributed to the odious nature of such crimes. Indeed, there are numerous ways of discussing religion in relation to 9/11 and its aftermath.

Among the various learning goals of this book is for readers to gain an appreciation of the complexity of phenomena we or others might regard as religious or spiritual. Resisting the temptation to define religion in simple, straightforward terms allows us to bring a number of perspectives and interpretations to our appreciation of American religious history. In this way we can concentrate on particular details without diminishing the richness, complexity, or contested claims about religion in America.

The richly diverse, complicated, sometimes detestable, sometimes inspiring history of religious life in America has no clear ending in sight. Certainly, more than a few readers of this book will themselves be active participants in the tales that future historians will add to this story. New religious movements are just now in their infancy, and others have not yet been imagined, while older established traditions continue to change, some adjusting to new circumstances and continuing to grow while others fade slowly into irrelevance and memory. Other ways of thinking about religion will certainly add new interpretations of the past, and the globalizing forces of politics and economic relations will undoubtedly introduce new ways of regarding the American nation. Religion in America will surely become something very different in the coming decades and centuries.

Questions for Discussion

(1) In what ways were the terrorist attacks of September 11, 2001 and the subsequent reactions to them religious in nature?
(2) How are contexts of globalization relevant to religion?
(3) What is the future of religion in America?

Suggested Primary-Source Reading

George W. Bush, "Address to the Joint Session of the 107th Congress," September 20, 2001, in *Selected Speeches of President George W. Bush, 2001–2008*, available online at http://georgewbush-whitehouse.archives.gov/infocus/bushrecord/documents/Selected_Speeches_George_W_Bush.pdf, 65–73 (PDF pages 73–81): The address of the President of the United States to Congress following the terrorist attacks of September 11, 2001 stresses the unity of American civil religion even as it calls for war against the Muslim extremists who perpetrated the attacks and warns those who harbor them.

Notes

1   Richard Cimino, "'No God in Common': American Evangelical Discourse on Islam after 9/11," *Review of Religious Research* 47, no. 2 (2005).
2   President Bush's remarks were in his address to Congress on September 20, 2001; a transcript of the speech is available online in *Selected Speeches of President George W. Bush, 2001–2008* at http://georgewbush-whitehouse.archives.gov/infocus/bushrecord (accessed September 19, 2013).
3   A video of the entire New York City prayer service of September 23, 2001 is available online at www.c-spanvideo.org/program/166250-1 (accessed September 19, 2013).
4   A report on the Lutheran Church-Missouri Synod's actions appeared in the *New York Times* on May 13, 2003, available online at www.nytimes.com/2003/05/13/nyregion/lutheran-panel-reinstates-pastor-after-post-9-11-interfaith-service.html   (accessed September 19, 2013).
5   This statistic is noted in Mussarat Khan and Kathryn Ecklund, "Attitudes toward Muslim Americans Post-9/11," *Journal of Muslim Mental Health* 7, no. 1 (2012).
6   Their report is available at www.sikhcoalition.org/images/documents/fact%20sheet%20on%20hate%20against%20sikhs%20in%20america%20post%209-11%201.pdf (accessed September 19, 2013).

7   This case is reported at www.huffingtonpost.com/simran-jeet-singh/a-unique-perspective-on-hate-crimes-the-story-of-a-convicted-killer_b_1685020.html (accessed September 19, 2013).

8   For a discussion of the 1998 bin Laden *fatwa* and the Muslim concept of *jihad* on which it relies, see James Turner Johnson, "Jihad and Just War," in the June/July 2002 issue of *First Things*, available online at www.firstthings.com/issue/2002/06/junejuly (accessed September 19, 2013).

9   Anthony Giddens, *The Consequences of Modernity* (Palo Alto, CA: Stanford University Press, 1990), 64.

10 Manuel A. Vásquez and Marie F. Marquardt, *Globalizing the Sacred: Religion across the Americas* (New Brunswick: Rutgers University Press, 2003), 2–3.

11 Ibid., 37.

12 Roland Robertson, "Glocalization: Time-Space and Homogeneity-Heterogeneity," in *Global Modernities*, ed. Mike Featherstone, Scott Lash, and Roland Robertson (Thousand Oaks, CA: Sage, 1995), 25–44.

Glossary

The following list includes common terms that may be unfamiliar to you. This is not intended to be a comprehensive listing but is meant to be a quick reference for terms that you will encounter more regularly; many of the concepts discussed in more detail in individual chapters have been excluded from this glossary. The first occurrences in each chapter of these terms are noted in bold.

apocalypse In both Jewish and Christian messianic traditions, a prophesied end of the world in a cosmic cataclysm that destroys the powers of evil, prophesied in Jewish scripture in the Book of Daniel and in Christian scripture in the Book of Revelation, involving God's judgment of humanity and the establishment of a new kingdom of righteousness; most Christians relate the destructive violence of the apocalypse to the return of Jesus Christ, whom they regard as the Messiah.

Atlantic world The colonial world of interdependent social, economic, political, and cultural connections between peoples of Africa, the Americas, and Europe.

charisma Derived from Christian usages, meaning "gift of grace," charisma refers to the divinely given powers or talents that certain people or groups possess; those with charisma demonstrate exceptional powers, insights, or talents of a divine source.

clergy Officially recognized religious leaders, usually installed through a specified ritual process. Most often the term is associated with the various forms of Christianity to describe priests and ministerial leaders of congregations who have been formally ordained by an institutional authority; more broadly, it is often used to describe formal religious leaders of other traditions.

Formed From This Soil: An Introduction to the Diverse History of Religion in America, First Edition. Thomas S. Bremer.
© 2015 Thomas S. Bremer. Published 2015 by John Wiley & Sons, Ltd.

Common Era (CE) The designation for the current historical period of the Gregorian calendar, indicating the era of Christianity, in contrast to Before Common Era (BCE), which designates the historical period prior to the beginning of Christianity. This widely accepted terminology replaces the former Christian-specific designations of Anno Domini (AD) and Before Christ (BC).

cosmogony Often described as a "creation story," this is a community's explanation of the origins of the world as they know it. It involves a mythical description of the beginning of all things, and especially the origins of the community as a people. Many religious communities place great importance on the periodic ritual enactment of their cosmogonical myth.

encyclical In the Roman Catholic Church, a letter from the Pope usually addressed to patriarchs, primates, archbishops, and bishops of the entire Church, although sometimes it is addressed to a more restricted group, such as the bishops of a particular nation. These letters deal with important matters confronting the Church, often condemning what the Church regards as some prevalent form of error, encouraging Catholics to be constant in their religious faith and habits, highlighting apparent dangers that threaten Catholic faith or accepted morals, or prescribing specific approaches regarding evils. Such pronouncements carry the weight of the Pope's authority, although the degree of authority of a particular encyclical among Catholics varies with the context, intent, and language of the document.

ethos The distinctive values, both moral and aesthetic, by which an individual, group, or society structures their lives and finds meaning and purpose in reality; a person's or a group's ethos makes up their most fundamental commitments and underlies their particular beliefs, practices, and traditions, producing the distinctive character of their lives and how they interpret reality, including how they interpret relations between people or between humans and the natural world.

evangelicalism A Protestant Christian movement that arose initially in the religious revivals of eighteenth- and nineteenth-century America. This movement derives from the Christian imperative to evangelize, specifically to spread the Christian gospel, or good news, to non-Christian peoples (see **proselytization**). Evangelical Protestants in general tend to regard the Christian Bible as the authoritative and reliable word of God; they insist that eternal salvation is possible only by what they call "regeneration," or being "born again" in a religious revival of one's personal faith and trust in Jesus Christ. Following regeneration, evangelical Protestants seek to live a spiritually transformed life of strict moral conduct, personal piety, and a zeal for evangelizing others.

laity, or lay members Unordained religious adherents who make up the membership of a religious community. The laity contrast with the ordained **clergy**, who serve as leaders of religious communities. Most often, the term "laity" is associated with the membership of Christian churches, but it can apply to non-leaders of any religious group.

liturgy The formal order of a Christian worship service; initially "liturgy" referred to the performance of the Christian Eucharist, the central rite of the worship service in Roman Catholic, Eastern Orthodox, and other branches of the Christian Church, involving the ingestion of bread and wine as the body and blood of Christ. As other Christian denominations put less emphasis on the Eucharistic rite, "liturgy" has taken on a more broad meaning in reference to worship service in general, sometimes being applied to the devotional rituals of non-Christians as well.

mantra An auspicious sound used as an aid to meditation in various contemplative traditions. Mantras are usually chanted in an effort to reach a different level of consciousness. Many traditions regard the sound of the mantra itself as possessing sacred powers.

myth A narrative of what a particular community understands as the real and true beings, events, and forces underlying the community's perception of reality. Mythic tales represent the community's articulation of reality as its members understand it; they serve to explain natural phenomena, justify social arrangements and relations, and reinforce the community's moral code.

nativism Sociopolitical and cultural movements resisting changes introduced by newcomers, usually characterized by a return to perceived native traditions and values. It is usually associated with anti-immigration sentiments, and often appeals to religious beliefs and practices.

proselytization (verb: proselytize) Efforts by religious adherents to convert people of other religious orientations to their own religious beliefs, practices, values, and traditions.

providence The religious belief, common among certain sects of Christianity, that all things occur according to God's will and design, that God controls all that happens.

reformation Processes of institutional change in Christianity, often resulting in new sects. Most commonly associated with Martin Luther's criticisms of the Roman Catholic Church in sixteenth-century Europe, "The Reformation" usually refers to the beginnings of Protestantism as a Christian movement in opposition to Catholicism. Sixteenth-century reformations among European Catholics, however, encompassed the entirety of western Christianity, including significant reforms within the Catholic Church.

ritual Formal actions and behaviors performed for specific purposes that usually convey symbolic meanings. Various subcategories of ritual include such religious activities as devotional worship, passage rites marking transitions in stages of life, public ceremonies, and private contemplative practices. Rituals often enact and reinforce mythical narratives such as **cosmogonical** tales.

shaman A religious specialist in animistic traditions who mediates between the human world and the world of spirits, usually through ritual practices that induce ecstatic trances involving travel to the spiritual realm.

worldview Sometimes referred to as "cosmology," worldview represents an individual's, a society's, or a culture's understanding and assumptions about the nature and structure of reality – that is, the perspective through which an individual or group interprets reality. Worldview is how people understand the way things are in their sheer actuality, how the universe operates, and what forces and powers underlie the events and patterns of reality, including social relations. A community's worldview or cosmological understanding is most clearly articulated in mythical narratives and ritual practices.

Index

Page numbers relating to figures, figure captions, or maps are given in *italic* type.

Formed From This Soil: An Introduction to the Diverse History of Religion in America, First Edition. Thomas S. Bremer.
© 2015 Thomas S. Bremer. Published 2015 by John Wiley & Sons, Ltd.